INSIDERS' GUIDE® TO
WASHINGTON, D.C.

Help Us Keep This Guide Up to Date

Every effort has been made by the authors and editors to make this guide as accurate and useful as possible. However, many things can change after a guide is published—establishments close, phone numbers change, hiking trails are rerouted, facilities come under new management, etc.

We would love to hear from you concerning your experiences with this guide and how you feel it could be improved and be kept up to date. While we may not be able to respond to all comments and suggestions, we'll take them to heart, and we'll also make certain to share them with the authors. Please send your comments and suggestions to the following address:

The Globe Pequot Press
Reader Response/Editorial Department
P.O. Box 480
Guilford, CT 06437

Or you may e-mail us at:

editorial@globe-pequot.com

Thanks for your input, and happy travels!

Insiders' Guide®
to Washington, D.C.

FIFTH EDITION

Mary Jane Solomon
and
Barbara Ruben

Guilford, Connecticut
An imprint of The Globe Pequot Press

The prices and rates listed in this guidebook were confirmed at press time. We recommend, however, that you call establishments before traveling to obtain current information.

Cover photo: Henryk Uniser, Index Stock.

Maps: Brandon Ray
Metrorail System map courtesy of the Washington Metropolitan Area Transit Authority

ISSN: 1538-8174
ISBN: 0-7627-2261-4

Manufactured in the United States of America
Fifth Edition/First Printing

Contents

Directory of Maps

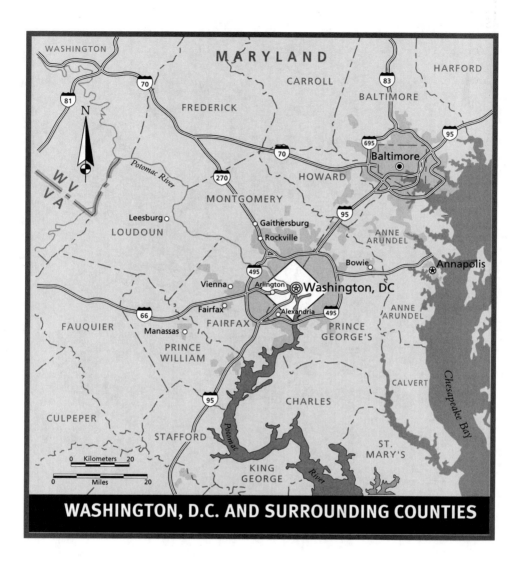

WASHINGTON, D.C. AND SURROUNDING COUNTIES

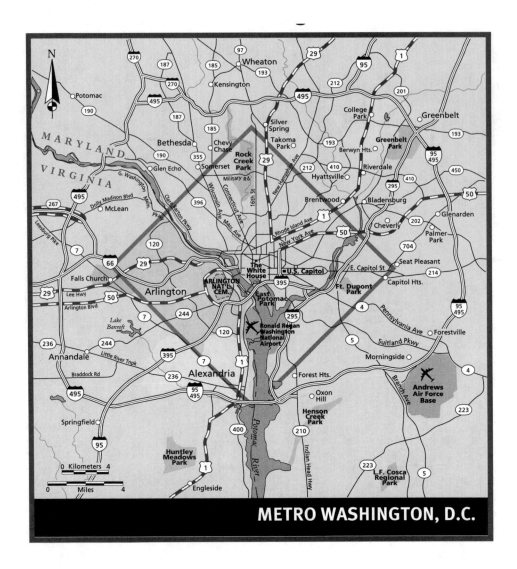

METRO WASHINGTON, D.C.

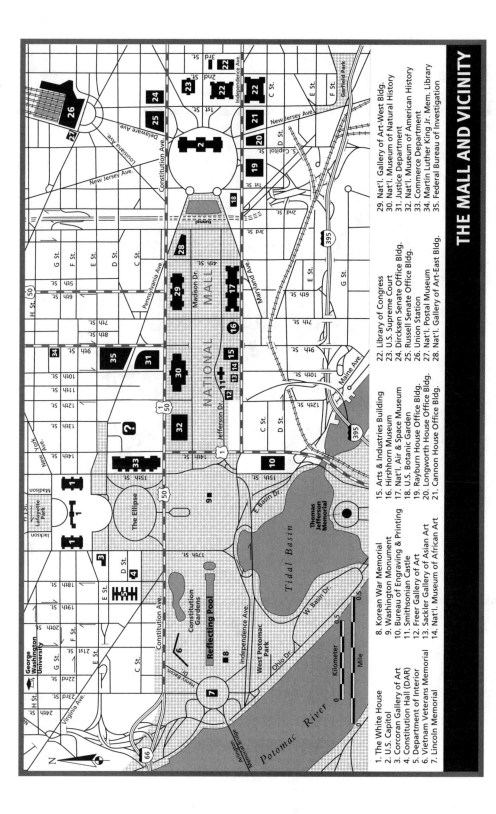

THE MALL AND VICINITY

1. The White House
2. U.S. Capitol
3. Corcoran Gallery of Art
4. Constitution Hall (DAR)
5. Department of Interior
6. Vietnam Veterans Memorial
7. Lincoln Memorial
8. Korean War Memorial
9. Washington Monument
10. Bureau of Engraving & Printing
11. Smithsonian Castle
12. Freer Gallery of Art
13. Sackler Gallery of Asian Art
14. Nat'l. Museum of African Art
15. Arts & Industries Building
16. Hirshhorn Museum
17. Nat'l. Air & Space Museum
18. U.S. Botanic Garden
19. Rayburn House Office Bldg.
20. Longworth House Office Bldg.
21. Cannon House Office Bldg.
22. Library of Congress
23. U.S. Supreme Court
24. Dircksen Senate Office Bldg.
25. Russell Senate Office Bldg.
26. Union Station
27. Nat'l. Postal Museum
28. Nat'l. Gallery of Art-East Bldg.
29. Nat'l. Gallery of Art-West Bldg.
30. Nat'l. Museum of Natural History
31. Justice Department
32. Nat'l. Museum of American History
33. Commerce Department
34. Martin Luther King Jr. Mem. Library
35. Federal Bureau of Investigation

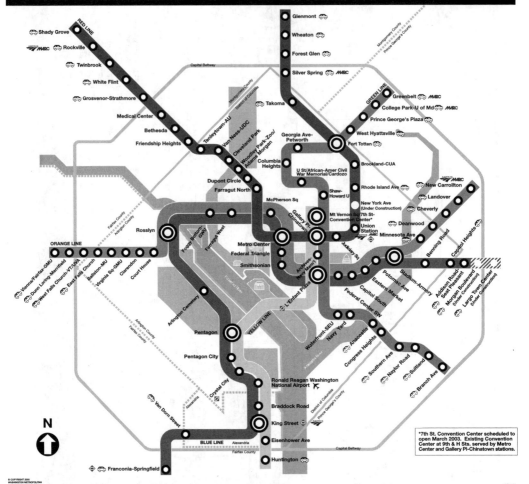

Preface

Setting about the task of writing *The Insiders' Guide® to Washington, D.C.* is every bit as daunting as it is exciting. Perhaps no other region in the country is as diverse, dynamic, intriguing and, for that matter, misunderstood as the Nation's Capital.

All of us, no doubt, have strong perceptions of Washington. It is, after all, a city that lives and breathes under an international microscope. The idealist in us views Washington as a great shrine to the American heritage, a beacon reinforcing the beliefs in freedom and democracy for all nations. We are awed by the inspiring landmarks, monuments, and memorials; the broad avenues; sprawling parks; world-class museums and galleries; and stately embassies. The cynic in us, however, takes another view, one that frames the Nation's Capital as a maze of longstanding problems, and new ones brought in the wake of the September 11, 2001 terrorist attacks. Today, it's not just the political problems of swollen bureaucracies and the District's own colonial status but staying safe in a world where microscopic anthrax spores closed down Capitol Hill and were responsible for the death of two U.S. postal workers. Beyond terrorism's impact, we are dismayed by inner-city poverty and the sight of homeless people sleeping on steam grates and park benches within earshot of the White House. Horrific traffic on the Beltway and elsewhere is the second worst in the nation, just after Los Angeles.

In fact Washington must claim both these realities, but those of us who are troubled by all of this will be heartened to know that problems are being addressed. Perhaps this is why a new optimism has taken hold in Washington. Mayor Anthony Williams believes in concrete achievement and is determined to bring dramatic improvement to the city. His no-nonsense approach, stimulating new commercial investment, has already won high marks from the business community. Crime is on the decline. Furthermore, in the last decade or so, we all have come to view Washington in a dramatically new light. This once largely one-dimensional government town has blossomed into a premier national and global business center; it is in Washington where the rules are made for the complex game of international trade and commerce. The decision-makers are here. The information is here. The communication channels are here. It might surprise you to learn that only about 13 percent of the area's residents are employed by the federal government. The rest have jobs in Washington's burgeoning service industries, including tourism, and in law, banking, medical research, telecommunications, publishing, and higher education. Indeed, these factors might be why you are, or are soon to be, headed here.

And you're not alone.

Metro Washington's population now stands at some 4.64 million, an increase of more than half a million since 1990, and its annual visitor count tops 20 million.

Despite the area's growth, Washington doesn't have the sprawling metropolitan feel of other large cities. There are no skyscrapers, the streets are clean, and flowers and trees abound. The city is alive with outdoor cafes, colorful neighborhoods, and inviting parks. Visitors are more likely to compare it to Paris than New York.

The neighborhood feeling isn't limited to just the 63-square-mile stretch of federal land bounded by the Potomac River, Virginia, and Maryland. "Washington" has come to mean much of Northern Virginia, including Fairfax, Arlington, Loudoun, and Prince William Counties as well as the city of Alexandria. "Washington" also is the fast-growing Suburban Maryland counties of Prince George's, Montgomery, and Anne Arundel. Residents of each area can be fervent advocates of their own stomping grounds, but what holds the vast array together is the District of Columbia.

For practical purposes, this book concentrates primarily on the District and the aforementioned core counties of Northern Virginia and Suburban Maryland. They encompass what we view as Metro Washington, D.C., or the Nation's Capital.

In the pages that follow, you will find what we hope is a fresh, insightful, and comprehensive guide to our region. It is our goal that *The Insiders' Guide to Washington, D.C.,* proves to be an invaluable source for newcomers, as it sketches the nuts and bolts of touring the area or even relocating here.

Acknowledgments

Mary Jane Solomon

I'm delighted to collaborate on this edition with long-time friend Barbara Ruben, whose skills, dedication, and good humor proved invaluable during last fall's turbulent times. Gratitude also goes to our patient and understanding Insiders' Guide editorial staff.

Thanks to all the folks who promptly and cheerfully provided facts and photographs for this update. Laura Bergheim's *The Washington Historical Atlas: Who Did What When and Where in the Nation's Capital* and Suzanne Hilton's *A Capital Capital City, 1790–1814* served as helpful and entertaining references regarding Washington history.

As always, special thanks to my English teachers and professors, without whom I wouldn't have a career; and to the many editors—especially those at *Weekend, KidsPost,* and *Virginia Parent News*—whose great assignments contribute to my "Insider's" knowledge.

I'm blessed with wonderful friends who provide unlimited encouragement and support, not to mention lots of wonderful ideas. You know who you are. Thank you, all!

Finally, I'm eternally grateful to my loving, understanding family for putting up with wacky hours, overlapping deadlines, and unwashed dishes and laundry. My heartfelt thanks especially go to Donald and Johanna Hoak; Sheldon and Sharon Solomon; Susan Hoak and Terry Layne; Jeff, Rachael, and Julianna Solomon; and, most of all, my treasures, Steve, Rachel, Anna, and Macaroon.

Barbara Ruben

My thanks go to my co-author, friend, and long-ago college roommate Mary Jane Solomon for recruiting me to help write this book and her invaluable assistance in navigating the editing process. I'm also indebted to the many helpful organizations that offered information and photos, including the Washington, D.C. Convention and Tourism Corporation, the Metropolitan Washington Council of Governments, Metropolitan Regional Information Systems, and the U.S. Census Bureau. The tireless efforts of Google were also indispensable in researching this book.

Thanks also to my five-year-old daughter Sarah, adventuress extraordinaire, for her unbridled enthusiasm for visiting sites in this book and her patience during my umpteen phone calls.

How to Use This Book

Whether you're visiting the Nation's Capital for a business trip or family vacation, relocating to the Washington Metro area or just looking for new ways to spend your leisure time, you'll find something of interest in this book. As longtime local residents, the authors are well acquainted with the area, from its awe-inspiring landmarks to its diverse educational and cultural opportunities. We know firsthand the joy of hearing the National Symphony perform at the Kennedy Center, and the frustration of almost being late for the concert because of a Beltway traffic tie-up! We relish dining at Bethesda's intriguing restaurants—when we're not gazing at Van Goghs at the National Gallery of Art or bagging bargains at Potomac Mills.

We've designed this book as a portable, accessible guide to Washington, D.C. and its surrounding suburbs: Northern Virginia and Suburban Maryland. The paperback is small enough to stuff in a suitcase or backpack, yet detailed enough to give you an overview of this vast region's best cultural, historical, and recreational attractions, as well as tips on how to get around and where to dine and sleep. If you're planning to stay awhile, check out the chapters on real estate, education, retirement, child care, and healthcare. We also describe a variety of weekend getaways, ideal for travelers extending their vacations or residents in need of quick escapes.

In most chapters you'll find information organized in a listing format under the three regional headers. Northern Virginia listings encompass the cities of Alexandria and

The 12-foot bronze Albert Einstein Memorial *by sculptor Robert Berks beckons tourists to the grounds of the National Academy of Sciences.*

1

Fairfax and the counties of Arlington, Fairfax, Loudoun, and Prince William. Suburban Maryland includes Montgomery and Prince George's Counties, as well as occasional notable attractions in nearby Anne Arundel and Howard Counties.

Wherever possible, we include an address, phone number, and Web address followed by a description of the attraction, event, or organization, often including admission costs and hours of operation. We also list Web sites for many popular attractions. For Restaurants, Accommodations, and Bed-and-Breakfasts and Country Inns, we include a price code with each listing. Check the price-code keys for explanations. Please be aware that prices and hours are subject to change. You'll find some attractions mentioned in more than one chapter, and cross-referenced accordingly. For instance, we describe Smithsonian Institution museums in Attractions, but detail their family programs in Kidstuff and highlight their collections of paintings and sculpture in The Arts.

One special note: As this book went to press, tours at many federal sites in and around the city had been shut down indefinitely due to heightened security measures. You'll find each of these entries—such as the Pentagon and U.S. Capitol—labeled with an asterisk preceding the attraction's name. Before visiting these locations, call ahead for up-to-date information about the current schedule.

Throughout the book, you'll also find Insiders' Tips, helpful or entertaining tidbits of information appearing at the bottom of some pages. We've also included occasional Close-ups, informative profiles, and accompanying photos of special events and attractions.

We hope you'll find this guide to be a handy reference book. We also appreciate hearing from our readers. Tell us what you find helpful and let us know if something is missing. We update the book regularly and find your comments invaluable.

Metro Washington Overview

Like the elected officials that come and go, Washington is in perpetual transition. It's a markedly different creature today than it was just 10 years ago—let alone in 1800, the year it became the Nation's Capital. It is fitting that Washington's growing pains reflect America's. It was almost destroyed in the War of 1812, and in the Civil War it reflected the nation's hotly divided sentiments. It celebrated the arrival of the Second Industrial Revolution and the success of the great barons who transformed the nation's economic landscape. It teemed with energy and a sense of sacrifice during World Wars I and II. It grew wary and then outright divided over the Korean and Vietnam Wars. It became cynical in the wake of Watergate; hopeful, then pessimistic during the Carter years; and a bit overconfident during the Reagan/Bush tenure. And after eight years of the Clinton era, the changing of the guard that came with the George W. Bush administration brought yet another crop of newcomers to town.

The downtown area and many of the surrounding suburbs are in the midst of a building boom, even a cultural renaissance. Trend-setting restaurants and retailers, which in past years eschewed Washington as too stodgy, now compete for hot metro locations. High-ticket designer boutiques are represented here, as are star conglomerates like Hard Rock Cafe.

To really understand where the District and its surrounding suburbs are today and where they're headed in the twenty-first century, it's helpful to go back a few decades, to at least the beginning of the post–World War II years. As the 1940s gave way to the '50s, Washington's population soared. In the nearby countryside of Maryland and Virginia, forests of oak and pastures of blue grass yielded to subdivisions and shopping centers. Business was booming. The future looked bright. As the federal government continued to grow dramatically during the '60s, so did the physical size (and, some may say, the ego) of the region.

Then came a bombshell, a watershed event that changed the face of Washington and impacted the entire country: the 1968 assassination of the Rev. Martin Luther King Jr. Parts of Washington erupted into a riot zone. Many residents who could afford to fled to suburban enclaves. The city became a ghost town by night. The suburbs ballooned farther out, and the resulting polarization was both psychological and physical. On the one hand were the commuters, a daily influx who increased traffic problems exponentially but paid no taxes that might have helped the D.C. infrastructure meet new demands placed on it. Remaining in Washington were the riot survivors, who lived in burned-out neighborhoods a few blocks from the White House. Amidst the downtown chaos were pockets of extreme affluence: Georgetown, Foxhall Road, Embassy Row. The lines of demarcation were clear and rarely crossed.

The Vietnam War and the Watergate era, culminating in President Richard Nixon's resignation in 1973, only added to the divisiveness in Washington. But those events also indirectly revitalized D.C. because they brought about a new era of grassroots activism. The activism resulted in closer interaction between government and industry as consumer advocates and environmental groups demanded that Washington investigate and regulate U.S. business. No large company or industry in America could afford to be without a presence in the Nation's Capital. Some opened government relations offices, some funded industry coalitions, and some even moved their companies' headquarters to the area. Big government started to get strong competition from big business for the Metro D.C. labor force. In reality, each was fueling the growth of the other as business realized that it would have to answer to government. At the same time government experts on industry were a labor pool in high demand by the very companies they oversaw. Many were and are wooed by the private sector, thus the infamous Washington "revolving door."

Today, about 700 foreign-owned firms or affiliates have a foothold here, and a third, or nearly 2,500, of the nation's trade and professional associations are headquartered in Metro D.C.

The Washington area claims more than 200 telecommunications and information giants, including America Online, MCI WorldCom, Discovery Communications, and COMSAT. Journalism is big business here as there are some 4,300 correspondents, newspapers, wire services, news agencies, and radio and television networks (the highest concentration of journalists in the world is here). Fortune 500 companies as diverse as Mobil, Gannett, General Dynamics, USAir, Marriott, and Lockheed Martin also call the Metro area home.

But Washington's growth hasn't all been a facile, downhill coast. In the mid- to late 1980s, local business development officials used to talk of Washington's "recession-proof" economy. They touted the fact that the federal government's employment and spending base had a stabilizing effect on the economy and that the diversity of business here was too great to allow for any major slowdowns.

Well, things didn't quite turn out that way. Washington, like everywhere else, was hit hard by the last recession. Commercial real estate, already dangerously overbuilt, took a

The Lincoln Memorial, the Washington Monument, and the U.S. Capitol mark the beginning, middle, and end, respectively, of the National Mall. PHOTO: COURTESY OF WASHINGTON, DC CONVENTION AND TOURISM CORPORATION

beating in the early 1990s, primarily due to unleased existing space and a dramatic slowdown in new development. Defense contractors awoke to a post–Cold War New World Order and an anticipation of scarcer federal outlays. Banks failed. Engineers, architects, technicians, and journalists, among others, were handed pink slips faster than Congress writes checks. Local governments wrestled with fiscal problems. Those accustomed to the prosperity of the '80s were thinking the world was coming to an end.

But in just a few years, the Washington economy grew faster than anyone imagined. Unemployment dropped to a record low of 2.6 percent in some suburban areas. With booming job growth, especially in the technology sector, record home construction, and a thriving, even frantic, home sales market, no one imagined Washington's economic bubble would burst.

But with job loss already on the rise since late 2000 as technology jobs disappeared, the terrorist attacks in September 2001 fueled the unemployment rate. In Washington, D.C. the jobless rate rose from 6 percent in October 2000 to 6.3 percent a year later. Although job losses were high in the hospitality and entertainment sectors due to the drop in tourism, these sectors began to rebound in early 2002. The suburbs fared better but still lost jobs: Virginia's jobless rate rose from 2.2 percent to 3.6 percent and Maryland's from 3.9 percent to 4.4 percent. The national unemployment rate at the time was 5.7 percent.

One factor keeping the unemployment rate from worsening is the enormous amount of money the government has pumped into the region to fight the war on terrorism.

Although the business development people may have blown their recession-proof theory, they were on target as far as the diversity of the economy is concerned. The region's broad mix of industry is one of the great untold economic stories of the past two decades.

Today, private-sector jobs outnumber government jobs practically four to one, with much of the job growth in high-tech and service industries. To be sure, federal employment has remained steady but now it is only 12.8 percent of the total work force compared with 25 percent at the beginning of the Reagan/Bush era. On top of that, even when you factor in the thousands of jobs supplied by local and state governments, the private sector still comes out way ahead of the game. All told, businesses employ 78 percent of Metro Washingtonians, while big government employs 22 percent.

So what does this tell us? First, we'd be kidding ourselves to dismiss the economic importance of the government's presence. Nobody spends money like federal Washington, and no one feels the effects of those shopping sprees more than our local economy. The feds spent $74.7 billion in the region in 2000, up from $62.3 billion in 1997.

At the same time, Washington's growing stature as a high-tech and international business center has brought the benefit of a more robust and flexible economy.

A culture of entrepreneurship is growing in our region, fueled by the strong presence of new telecommunications and Internet-related businesses, especially in the suburbs of Northern Virginia and Maryland. Some 340,000 people work in the high-tech computer industry, almost as many as in the federal work force.

> **Insiders' Tip**
>
> The area climate is temperate. The average maximum summer temperature is 88; the minimum is 70. The average maximum winter temperature is 43 degrees; the minimum is 32. The average annual rainfall is 39 inches, while average snowfall is 16 inches. An average 202 days per year are sunny, while 111 days bring precipitation.

All this economic growth has had a revitalizing effect on the region's psyche, even as it strains our roads and school systems—especially in the outer western suburbs. The region grew by more than 15 percent between 1990 and 2000, with most of the growth happening in the western half of the region.

Although the District lost 5.2 percent of its population between 1990 and 2000, out-lying counties gained huge numbers of people: Loudoun County's population nearly doubled, while Prince William's grew by 30 percent.

Unfortunately, this recent growth has deepened the divisions between the "haves" and have-nots" in the metro area. Increasingly, better-off communities lie west of Interstate 95 in the suburbs and 16th Street in the city (with some exceptions in Prince George's County). So although one half of the area enjoys robust growth, there's not enough growth in large parts of the eastern half, according to a study released by the Brookings Institution.

Racial and ethnic living patterns further divide the area. Seventy percent of African Americans live in the District and Prince George's County, leaving the most prosperous western region largely white.

Parallel with the growth in the most affluent parts of the area is the ongoing renewal of downtown D.C.—particularly in the districts bearing our leading attractions and activities.

Practically every block of the District's major, historic artery, Pennsylvania Avenue, has been renovated with new plazas, office space, retail areas, theaters, restaurants, and more. The "Avenue of the Presidents," once deserted by night, has again become a thriving thoroughfare, and its renewal has sparked development throughout the rest of downtown. On Capitol Hill, Washington's historic Union Station was painstakingly restored over several years and is now the "grande dame" of all train stations. It houses Amtrak corporate headquarters and serves as their flagship station, with trains arriving and departing from beneath the magnificent, statue-lined roof.

In the District of Columbia, information and power spring not only from business and government but also from global financial institutions such as the World Bank and the International Monetary Fund. Equally vital are the city's 150-plus embassies that provide instant access to commercial and government representatives from nearly every nation.

Washington's transformation from a government- to a private-sector information-driven economy mirrors one of the most pervasive trends in our global society. The international marketplace at the turn of this century is fueled first and foremost by information. Information is power, and Washington is a wellspring of both commodities.

Chances are, if you're a newcomer to the Nation's Capital, you're part of this new dynamic.

The Washington Work Force

If you're looking for a job in Metro D.C., or even if you've already landed one, it's good to know a few vital statistics about the Washington work force. Besides, a few provocative figures here and there will go a long way on the Washington cocktail party circuit.

Let's start with the big picture: Some 2.7 million people are employed in the Washington area, with roughly three-quarters working in white-collar jobs. Sounds impressive enough, but wait—it gets even more striking. The region has claimed the largest percentage of executive, administrative, managerial, professional, and technical workers among the nation's largest metropolitan areas. The proportion of scientists, technicians, and Ph.D.s working in Metro D.C. is among the highest in the nation, and nearly one in seven employees works in computer- and telecommunications-related industries. The service industry overall has doubled since 1980, to a total of 1.02 million positions.

The USA Today *towers provide an outstanding view of the Lincoln Memorial.* PHOTO: MARK DOWNEY, COURTESY OF VIRGINIA TOURISM CORPORATION

If you're a woman, you're in good company here. A full 68.8 percent of working-age women in greater Washington are employed, with 25 percent of them in professional and managerial positions. Again, on both accounts, these are far ahead of the national average.

With three out of five of its residents African American, the District of Columbia has long been the nation's most influential and affluent predominantly black city. Today, the entire region boasts the leading percentage of black executives, administrators, and managers. Little surprise then that the fast-growing cable network, Black Entertainment Television, is headquartered in the District. In recent years Washington also has experienced a surge in entrepreneurship among its growing Asian, Hispanic, Middle Eastern, and Indian communities.

Of course, at the root of Washington's white collars is education. The metro area inarguably has the best-educated work force in the United States. More than 17 percent of the adult population living inside the District holds graduate degrees,

ranking Washington first among the states and more than double the national metro average of 8 percent.

Beyond all the grand statistics, however, are some very down-to-earth implications. More and more young people are launching their careers in Metro Washington despite the intensely competitive nature of the labor force, especially for entry-level positions.

Maybe more important, fewer are packing their bags after a couple of years. A full 37 percent of the region's population is between the ages of 25 and 44, making the Washington work force the youngest in the nation.

Where the Jobs Will Be

Despite recent economic turmoil, experts say Metro Washington is well positioned for long, sustained growth over the next two decades. As the shift from federal to private-sector employment continues unabated, it's estimated there will be 1.3 million more workers out there by the year

2010, the vast majority in highly skilled occupations (including business, healthcare, law, and education). In 2000, *Fortune* chose Washington, D.C. as one of the four best cities for business in the country. That same year, *Inc.* rated D.C. as the ninth-best city to start and grow a business, and *Black Enterprise* called Washington the nation's second-best city for work.

We'll likely see a climb in the numbers of high-tech, biotech, and telecommunications workers, as well as in manufacturing, retail, and clerical positions. Loudoun, Frederick, Prince William, and Stafford Counties are projected to experience the greatest job growth, with employment in the entire outer suburbs expected to expand by 138 percent in the next 20 years.

Crime in D.C.

Drug trafficking, primarily in crack cocaine, began paralyzing neighborhoods throughout the inner city in the mid '80s, and by 1988, the District of Columbia was known as the "Murder Capital of the World."

Happily, the crime rate has dropped dramatically since those dark days, and in fact was lower in 1998 than it had been in 25 years. It's crept up slightly since then, but not by too much. Here are a few statistics that should comfort visitors to Metro D.C. The area's violent crime rate is actually 14 percent *lower* than the average U.S. metropolitan area, according to FBI crime figures. The Washington area's total crime, violent crime, and property crime rates are below the national average, and well below the U.S. metropolitan average.

The best advice for visitors to Washington, as in any big city in the world, is to use caution and common sense. Random acts of violence in usually quiet areas are of course a reality, yet by simply using everyday street smarts, locals and tourists alike should feel perfectly comfortable in Washington's tourism and business sectors.

One of the city's most well-known bad boys—now apparently reformed—is the former mayor himself, Marion Barry, who in 1990 was arrested for possessing and using the same crack cocaine that was devastating so much of his city. His actions, which were captured on film by police using a hidden camera, severely scarred Washington's national and international image. Who would have imagined that in 1994, after serving time in a federal prison, Barry would be reelected to the same office he left in disgrace? Barry remains somewhat of a fixture in D.C. affairs, but Mayor Anthony Williams has stolen the show, restoring confidence among business and civic leaders and steadily improving the quality of life in the District.

Washington in the Twenty-first Century

In the twenty-first century, for better or for worse, Washington remains the single most important political center in the world. In Berlin and Moscow communism has been dismantled and the countries' entrepreneurs have embraced U.S.-style capitalism with gusto. In South Africa the U.S.-initiated embargo led to the abandonment of apartheid. In recent years the U.S. has taken center stage in places like the Middle East, the Balkans, and Haiti. So as Moscow fumbles over social and economic woes, and Tokyo reels from the effects of an overheated economy, no real challenge to Washington's power appears on the horizon.

Illustrative of Washington's power is the aforementioned revival of the city itself. A 20,000-seat sport/entertainment complex called the MCI Center opened in midtown in 1997. The arena generates more than $150 million a year in economic benefits and $10 million a year in taxes. Ronald Reagan Washington National Airport's dazzling new terminal opened in 1997 after $400 million of construction to provide new air-traffic-control facilities, a moving sidewalk system, expanded parking, shops, restaurants, and a network of convenient walkways (see the Transportation chapter). If you arrive at Dulles International Airport, you'll see that an expansion of equal proportions is ongoing there.

It's not only the residents of the area that recognize we live in a special place. An increasing number of influential publications do, as well. In 2001, *Forbes* magazine rated Washington as the number one place for singles in the county, while that year *Bridal Guide* magazine selected it as the top destination for honeymooners. At the same time, *Family Fun* magazine called Washington the nation's number one destination for family travel.

Northern Virginia

The Monolith That Is Fairfax County

Since 1980, the suburbs have claimed 80 percent of Metro Washington's employment growth, and two-thirds of these new jobs are in Northern Virginia, principally Fairfax County. In 2000 there were an estimated 1.06 million jobs in Northern Virginia, compared with the District's 646,600 and suburban Maryland's 873,000.

Fairfax County, which encircles the self-governed municipalities of Falls Church, Fairfax City, Vienna, and Herndon, is the dominant economic force in the metro area, housing some of the biggest employers, including Inova Health Systems, Mobil, Columbia Energy Group, AT&T, Gannett Corporation, and First Virginia Bank. Each has offices with more than 3,000 employees in the county. Defense giant, General Dynamics, moved

its national headquarters here from St. Louis. With a population of 969,749, it has more residents than several states and almost twice the number of the District of Columbia. Moreover, nearly one in seven Virginians lives in the county.

Its 23,500 businesses currently employ more than 527,000 people and pay out more than $16 billion in gross wages. But it's more than jobs that attract people to Fairfax County. Steeped in history—this is, after all, the home of George Washington and George Mason, father of the American Bill of Rights—the county is defined by a sense of civic orderliness and a commitment to a high standard of living. When English explorer John Smith, the first European to set eyes on the area that is present-day Washington, D.C., ventured into the county in 1608, he was taken aback by the amount of wildlife and natural resources that graced the area—bounty he would later help claim for England.

If Smith were in Fairfax County today, he would also want to claim some of the finest public schools in the nation, a work force that is among the nation's most educated and affluent, and a public safety

> ### Insiders' Tip
> A little-known spot in Fairfax County is the historic village of Clifton at its southwestern tip. Great for a Sunday drive, the village is a patchwork of quaint houses, shops, and restaurants surrounded by winding country roads, meadows, and horses. It looks like Virginia hunt country, but it's only 35 minutes from downtown Washington, D.C.

record that is the envy of most suburban jurisdictions.

Equally alluring to newcomers—especially families—are the county's extensive parklands, myriad shopping malls—including one of the nation's largest in Tysons Corner Center—upscale neighborhoods, and abundant historical and recreational attractions.

The flip side to the county's fortunes are home costs, which are among the highest in the nation (as are housing costs in most of the metro area), with affordable housing in seriously short supply. In addition, the infrastructure lags behind the pressures of a booming population. No matter what time of day, you can find a traffic jam somewhere in Fairfax County, though matters have improved with the construction of the Fairfax County Parkway, which winds its way from the northernmost limits of the county to the southern tip.

Although the local government is largely responsive to these and other problems, Fairfax, especially to the uninitiated, must seem like a congested and hectic place. That aside, the county continues to be one of the region's most popular relocation sites. So much so that by 2000, the county's population was just 30,000 shy of 1 million residents.

Urban Cousins: Arlington County and the City of Alexandria

Arlington County and the city of Alexandria are the alter egos to suburban Fairfax. Much more in tune with the urban pace of Washington (they were in fact part of the District of Columbia at one time), Arlington and Alexandria command a great influence on the Nation's Capital.

In Arlington, the self-proclaimed "Virginia Side of the Nation's Capital," you can find such Washington icons as the Pentagon, Arlington National Cemetery, the Iwo Jima Memorial, and Reagan National Airport. As in Alexandria, economic activity in Arlington historically has been tied to the federal government. In addition, both jurisdictions house hundreds of national and international associations, lobbyists, and special-interest groups, as well as a fair number of federal government offices. Nevertheless, Arlington and Alexandria contain their share of private industry. Arlington County serves as headquarters for US Airways, the Pentagon, and the U.S. Patent and Trademark Office. Other large employers include MCI WorldCom and Bell Atlantic. Next door in Alexandria—one of the nation's oldest port cities and business centers—are the headquarters for the Public Broadcasting System, Crown Life Insurance USA, Time-Life Books, Inc., and the Independent Insurance Agents of America.

Over the years, Arlington has assumed somewhat of a multiple personality. Self-contained communities such as Ballston, Crystal City, Pentagon City, and Rosslyn, each with its own central business district, bloom with shopping centers, towering offices and condos, and an inexhaustible supply of restaurants. The northern edge of the county contains upscale single-family homes, many on large lots with views of the Potomac and the District beyond, while the extreme southern end borders on seedy, with crime being a major concern. All told, some 189,000 people now call Arlington home. But unlike Fairfax County, which is the refuge of families with children, 73 percent of Arlington County's households are comprised of singles or two-adult families—perhaps the most persuasive indication of Arlington's urban atmosphere.

Mention the word *Alexandria* and most people immediately think of Old Town, the city's charming and affluent historic district that hugs the banks of the Potomac. And for sure, history is a way of life in Old Town. Settled in 1749 by Scottish merchants, the city blossomed into one of the leading ports of Colonial America, driven in good measure by a lucrative trade in Virginia-grown tobacco. George Washington conducted a lot of business here, and Robert E. Lee grew up here, later moving to Arlington House, now part of Arlington National Cemetery. Alexandria's venerable Christ Church has been visited by almost every president. The Revolutionary and Civil Wars played out on

Alexandria's streets, some of which look much the same today as they did in the early nineteenth century.

Walk around and you'll find block after block of painstakingly restored Federal-style homes interspersed between curio shops, inns, bars, restaurants, parks, churches, and museums. So picturesque is Old Town that it draws 1.5 million visitors a year. Old Town wasn't always so gentrified, though. From the 1940s through the early '70s, hard times set in and much of the area was blighted with boarded-up shops and dilapidated homes. When the revitalization bug kicked in some 20 years ago, entire blocks of houses could have been purchased for a fraction of the present-day cost of a single home here. As you can imagine, many a fortune was made in Old Town. Among the upscale renovations, there still exist several housing projects, and most of the crime in Old Town occurs here in the form of drug-related wrongdoing. Residents of nearby homes, no matter how affluent and well protected, are also subject to burglaries and muggings from time to time. For the most part, you can avoid trouble by sticking to the crowded commercial areas and steering clear of the shadowy residential streets, whose many trees and alleys provide strategic hiding places for mischief makers.

Alexandria is more than Old Town, though many visitors think the two are synonymous. Most of its 120,000 residents live in diverse, outlying neighborhoods, like the West End, with its many high-rise apartments, and Beverly Hills, an established community of shaded streets and gracious homes. Further confusion arises from the fact that the city of Alexandria is surrounded by Alexandria, Fairfax County. Perhaps the most famous landmark in the expanded area is the community of Mount Vernon (mailing address Alexandria), with homes ranging from modest to baronial. As the name implies, George Washington's estate—also Mount Vernon—sits smack in the middle of the area. Leading to it is a bicycle path offering Potomac River vistas, a route popular with both tourists and residents. In fact, the George Washington Memorial Parkway, and the national parkland adjoining it,

The Washington Monument as seen across the reflecting pool is a favorite photo subject for visitors and professional photographers alike.

PHOTO: COURTESY OF WASHINGTON, DC CONVENTION AND TOURISM CORPORATION

make this one of the most scenic and bucolic corners of the metro area.

Prince William County

With more than 40 percent of its working-age residents commuting out of the county to their jobs, Prince William County is pretty much a vintage bedroom community. Since 1990, the county's population jumped from 245,667 to 280,813, a rise of 30 percent, making it one of the nation's biggest gainers.

Newcomers arrive in masses here to live in nice, relatively affordable neighborhoods with improving schools and a surprisingly large amount of cultural and recreational diversions. It's a good place for families just starting out, and that's reflected by the median age of residents: 29 years. The county also has the highest percentage of

Washington's Brave New Postterrorism World

In mid-September 2001, a hand-lettered sign appeared on a tree in the verdant Chevy Chase traffic circle at the border of Washington, D.C. and Montgomery County, Maryland. Be Brave, it read in big block letters.

Just a few weeks before, residents could have taken it as a light-hearted piece of advice to drivers daunted by merging with three lanes of spiraling traffic in one of the area's abundant—and dizzying—traffic circles. But for most living in the Washington region, the admonition took on a far graver meaning in the wake of the September 11 terrorist attacks that left 189 dead at the Pentagon. The nearby Reagan National Airport was shut down for more than three weeks as fears abounded of more planes becoming guided missiles aimed at the U.S. Capitol and White House just across the Potomac River. By the end of the year, just half of the number of postattack flights were taking off, all with armed sky marshals aboard.

A month after the September attack, two D.C. postal workers were dead after contracting the inhaled form of anthrax while sorting mail at the District's largest postal facility. Congress all but shut down for several days, and months later the Hart Senate Office Building, where the anthrax-laden envelope addressed to South Dakota Senator Tom Daschle was opened, remained closed. By the end of the year, the Department of Health and Human Services was recommending a still-experimental anthrax vaccine for thousands of workers on Capitol Hill.

Washington's much-vaunted Metro system removed trash cans and newspaper vending machines so they couldn't be used to camouflage bombs. The transit system also ordered sensors to detect a chemical attack.

Day after day, headlines in the venerable *Washington Post* sounded the alarm: "Terrorism Casts a Long Shadow Over Daily Life," one read. "Anthrax Scare Comes to Capitol Hill," blared a banner headline across the front of the paper in October.

Much of the appeal for tourists and residents alike in Washington is its proximity to power and prestige, from the White House and the Capitol to the world-renowned Smithsonian museums. But many fear that same cache has made Washington a bull's-eye for terrorists.

Some suburbanites feared venturing downtown. Legions of tourists canceled trips. In September and October 2001 alone, the Washington-area tourism industry lost more than $1 billion in revenue. By November more than half of the District's 26,000 hospitality workers had been laid off, and job losses regionwide topped 50,000 by the end of the year.

Tourist meccas across the city became virtual ghost towns. The number of visitors to the Smithsonian was 44 percent lower in October 2001 than the previous October. Monuments registered a 25 percent drop in visitors.

Tours at the Capitol were suspended for three months. And tours of the White House, attracting nearly 1.5 million visitors a year, were suspended even longer. Officials made the long-standing tradition of touring the White House while it's all decked out for the holidays off-limits, but visitors could take a virtual tour via the White House's Web site. To help lure tourists back to Washington, stars of the NBC-TV White House drama *The West Wing* have taped a commercial touting D.C.'s charms.

And for the intrepid tourists who keep Washington on their itinerary, there may never have been a better time to visit: Hotel rates have been slashed, with even the Four Seasons offering some rooms for just over $200 a night. Reservations at red-hot restaurants like Kinkead's and Restaurant Nora are now a snap to get. And you may have been able to get up close and personal with paintings in art museum exhibits that previously had been elbowroom only.

Although a few denizens of the Washington region have headed for the hills and one prominent *Washington Post* reporter wrote about trying to find a gas mask for her dog, most residents have adjusted to life in a new era of security. Concrete jersey walls abound, blocking many former entrances to everything from the National Institutes of Health to Fort Belvoir. Lines at security checkpoints at Baltimore-Washington International (BWI) Airport sometimes snake throughout the terminal, and the airport generated more complaints in the month after the terrorist attacks than any airport in the country, according to the Air Travelers Association. In addition, buses and trucks have been banned from some streets around the Capitol.

For most, life goes on. According to a December 2001 survey by the Greater Washington Bureau of Trade measuring the quality of life for Washington residents, only a small percentage of people have made big changes to their lives after September 11. About 15 percent report they are going into downtown Washington less often. Eleven percent said they have stopped opening some or all of their mail, and 8 percent said they have thought about moving out of the area because of terrorism.

And so as they go to Congressional hearings, attend Redskins games, and take their children to Saturday soccer games, many Washingtonians are trying to keep in mind the words of one resident of the White House almost three-quarters of a century ago, "We have nothing to fear but fear itself."

children, 30 percent, in the region. A home that would cost $300,000 in Fairfax County might range in cost from $200,000 to $250,000 in Prince William, depending on its proximity to the county border, Interstate 66, or Interstate 95.

Prince William still contains huge tracts of undeveloped land and is home to sprawling national and state parks, including the Manassas National Battlefield, one of the most important sites of the Civil War. Other attractions include a minor-league baseball team, several community theater groups and museums, and the Nissan Pavilion at Stone Ridge, a state-of-the-art concert amphitheater. Here you'll also find the FBI Academy, Quantico Marine Base, and Quantico National Cemetery, which is actually larger than Arlington National Cemetery.

Prince William has been extremely proactive in efforts to lure more employers to the county. However, not every corporate entity is welcome. The Walt Disney Company was sent packing in 1994 after encountering fierce—and largely unexpected—opposition to an American history theme park it had proposed for the rolling countryside near the history-rich town of Haymarket. Easily the biggest attraction in Prince William, though, is Potomac Mills, one of the biggest outlet shopping centers in the world and—sad, but true—the single most popular tourist attraction in the entire commonwealth.

The Virginia Exurbs: Loudoun, Fauquier, and Stafford Counties

The outlying Virginia counties of Loudoun, Fauquier, and Stafford are at a crossroads as Metro Washington continues to expand in its radial fashion. Not quite totally suburban but neither completely rural anymore, the counties are what may be termed *exurban*.

In a way, we're hesitant to lump Loudoun County into this category, since it is easily the fastest-developing outer jurisdiction in either Virginia or Maryland. Since 1990 its population has nearly doubled, surging to 169,000. Nevertheless, with only about one-seventh the number of residents of Fairfax County, Loudoun is still mostly wide-open spaces. Just under 200,000 acres are devoted to agriculture, compared with just more than 78,000 for housing and 19,141 for commercial enterprises. A vocal group of natives and newcomers would like to keep it that way. That's why you'll see the heaviest concentration of commercial and residential activity kept to the eastern stretches of the county, from Leesburg to the Fairfax County line. Here is where you'll also find Washington Dulles International Airport (although a small piece sits in Fairfax), a major catalyst behind the county's growth, and a major source of employment.

Other heavy hitters headquartered in Loudoun include United Airlines, America Online, and Atlantic Coast Airlines (United Express). High-tech industries continue to relocate and expand in the area. UUNet recently opened a new facility on 530 acres north of Dulles Airport. They now have a total of around 6,500 employees, with 3000 at the Loudon County location. Tellabs, a global leader in voice technology, opened its headquarters in Loudoun in late 1998.

To the south and west of Leesburg, the county seat, is a sprawling patchwork of farms, orchards, and horse pastures. It is here where Virginia's famed Hunt Country begins. South of Loudoun is Fauquier County, with its equally beautiful horse farms and country estates. New housing developments in and around Warrenton, the county's largest community, are attracting more and more Metro D.C. commuters and even a growing number of retirees. Fauquier contains some of the most scenic land in the Old Dominion and consequently, like Loudoun, there is a considerable antigrowth sentiment here. People move out here to get away from traffic congestion, crime, and overcrowding so they want to preserve the county's rural character. Stafford County is a bit of

a different story, however. Located just south of Prince William, it is actively wooing new residents and businesses with affordable land prices, the promise of relaxed living, and easy access to I-95. Folks are responding to the offer. During the '90s, the county's population recorded one of the highest percentage gains in Virginia. Stafford enjoys a close proximity to both Washington and Richmond and is bordered immediately to the south by the city of Fredericksburg, one of the most charming and historic communities in the commonwealth. However, the access to I-95 is a mixed blessing, because the road is almost always snarled with traffic. Rush hour begins at noon on Fridays, because this is also the most widely used interstate route for tractor-trailers and others traveling along the East Coast. At peak hours the drive from Stafford County to Washington, D.C. can take up to two hours, so investigate carefully before you believe claims by realtors of an "easy commute."

Suburban Maryland

The "State" of Montgomery County

Although diehards on both sides of the Potomac would probably never admit it, Montgomery County is to Maryland what Fairfax County is to Virginia. In terms of population, jobs, median household income, and size, the two counties are strikingly similar. In other words, Montgomery County is an aberration of sorts. As Maryland's largest and most affluent county, one could argue—as do many lawmakers in Annapolis—that Montgomery is its own separate state. That might be overdoing it a bit, but this mega-county of about 873,341 residents is far more aligned, socially and economically, with the District and Northern Virginia than with Baltimore or any other part of the Free State.

At the same time, Montgomery in many ways is Metro D.C.'s most diverse jurisdiction. The southern half of the county is overwhelmingly white collar and decidedly urban. Here, you'll find the posh

Magnificent old buildings make Washington one of the most beautiful cities to explore on foot.

PHOTO: COURTESY OF ORGANIZATION OF AMERICAN STATES

homes and estates of Potomac and Chevy Chase, the retail meccas of White Flint and Montgomery malls, and the lost-in-time Victoriana of Kensington and tiny Garrett Park (which has declared itself a nuclear-free zone). Here, you'll also find an interesting mix of both highly successful and struggling immigrants hailing from Central America, Vietnam, India, Iran, and China. Many come to work at the impressive campus of Bethesda's world-renowned National Institutes of Health or at the high-tech companies that flank Interstate 270. Others clean the buildings, work the landscapes, and wash the dishes.

Major employers in lower Montgomery County include Marriott International, Lockheed Martin, the country's largest defense contractor, the National Naval Medical Center and Discovery Communications, which is building a new headquarters in downtown Silver Spring. In all, there were 444,500 jobs in the county in 2000.

The northern portion of Montgomery, or the "Upcounty" as locals emphatically refer to it, moves to a gentler, less urban beat. Here, it's not unusual to see large dairy farms abutting business parks, or commuters coming to a halt at cattle crossings and creeping slowly behind tractors in the spring. A few years ago, a black bear cub emerged from the woods of Seneca Creek State Park and onto a heavily trafficked road. The cub returned to the wilds unscathed, but not before setting off one of the region's more memorable traffic jams. Although the Upcounty is proud of its efforts to preserve open space—Montgomery reportedly set aside more farmland than any other suburban county in the nation—the tenor of the place is rapidly changing. Subdivisions now extend north of Gaithersburg, transforming once-sleepy areas like Germantown and Damascus into bustling bedroom communities favored by young professionals seeking affordable housing. Onetime apple orchards and wheat fields increasingly are sprouting single-family homes and shopping centers.

The Melting Pot of Prince George's County

In 1988, one of the largest commercial developers in Metro Washington broke ground on an ambitious project that came with the promise of virtually reinventing the image of Prince George's County. The huge development was to be called Port America, a stately, multipurpose business and residential community that would grace the banks of the Potomac River, within earshot of the busy Woodrow Wilson Bridge. But the national recession set in, legal hassles ensued, and Port America fell apart. Now a major development called National Harbor is planned for the same site and will feature hotels, entertainment, upscale shops, and a marina modeled after the Inner Harbor in Baltimore.

It's safe to say that Prince George's has still not yet totally arrived, at least not to the same degree as its more prosperous neighbors to the north and west. A chronic crime problem in the urban areas closest to Washington, coupled with some highly publicized criminal cases involving local government officials, have taken their toll on the county's image. Don't count "P.G."—as it's commonly called—and its 801,515 residents out of the picture, however.

> ## Insiders' Tip
> Before you mail a letter to an address in Chevy Chase, be sure you know whether the person lives in D.C. or Maryland. The two communities border each other.

The positives far outweigh the negatives. The county is undergoing an economic upswing, with several major federal facilities constructed here in recent years. These include the recently built 1.2 million-square-foot IRS headquarters in New Carrolton, USDA building in College Park, and National Archives II facility.

More than 14,000 businesses employ 300,000 workers. P.G. is home to the University of Maryland, the state's flagship university with more than 33,000 students and a tradition-rich athletic program. Andrews Air Force Base, which is used by the president and many other government officials, the National Agricultural Research Center, NASA's Goddard Space Flight Center, and the U.S. Census Bureau also call P.G. home.

P.G., among other things, has always been the region's—if not one of the nation's—most established multiracial communities. Black, Caucasian, Hispanic, and Asian Americans live side by side and largely in harmony in Prince George's. Affordable housing isn't a catchy buzzword; it's a reality. The county's public school system has made tremendous inroads in recent years, but with the recent dismissal of the school board is still on shaky ground.

If you're into spectator events, chances are you'll be spending some time in Prince George's USAir Arena (concerts, ice skating, gymnastics) in Landover, Rosecroft and Laurel Raceways (horse racing), the new Jack Kent Cooke football stadium less than a mile away, and the Prince George's Equestrian Center in Upper Marlboro. These venues entertain many thousands of Washingtonians throughout the year (see the Spectator Sports chapter).

A Sense of Place in Anne Arundel County

There's a certain feeling that pervades Anne Arundel County. Maybe it's due to Annapolis, the splendid Maryland capital city, with its colonial waterfront homes, the oldest State House in continuous use in the United States (since the 1770s), and imposing campuses of St. John's College and the United States Naval Academy. Maybe it's the quiet coves and inlets of the Magothy, Severn, and South Rivers. Or maybe it's the broad, sweeping views of the Chesapeake Bay afforded from atop hilly pastures dotted with wooden tobacco barns and thoroughbred horses. From whatever it springs, it's hard not to feel an acute sense of place in Anne Arundel, a county as beautiful as its name suggests.

Not too many decades ago, Washingtonians built summer homes here, and the county's economy was associated largely with the state government and the fishing and sailing trades of the Chesapeake Bay.

Today, Anne Arundel is grappling with a new identity. The past decade ushered in a surge in population, fueled in large part by the well-documented economic fortunes of nearby Baltimore and Washington. Many of the county's 489,656 residents now make the 25-plus-mile commute into the District and other parts of Metro Washington—a feat virtually unheard of 20 years ago. Rapid suburbanization has had its share of nasty side effects like increased crime and housing costs, but all told, Anne Arundel retains a remarkably high quality of life. Indeed, this is its main selling point. And although longtime residents vehemently resist the notion of being part of Metro D.C. or Baltimore, there is an accommodating attitude toward newcomers that are drawn to this enchanting, history-filled corner of Maryland.

Maryland's Exurbs: Frederick, Howard, and Charles Counties

As suburban Maryland continues to creep farther out into the countryside, it's markedly changing the face of at least three outlying communities: Frederick, Howard, and Charles Counties.

Bounded by Pennsylvania to the north and Montgomery County to the south, Frederick County offers the perks of a relaxed country setting—this is the land of covered bridges, inns, vineyards, and roadside produce stands—but with an undeni-

Insiders' Tip

Instead of driving into D.C., park in the bargain-priced lot at The Fashion Centre at Pentagon City shopping center, then take the Metro.

able air of big-city sophistication. In downtown Frederick, the county's principal city, one can munch on blue-corn tortillas and other trendy fare before taking in a gallery opening or browsing through dozens of antique shops. From here, you're about equal distance from Gettysburg, Pennsylvania, and downtown Washington, although the commute north is much easier. In winter the ski slopes of White Tail and Liberty in Pennsylvania are only a bit more than 30 minutes away. Still, Frederick is less than an hour's drive from much of Metro D.C., and housing prices won't send your heart rate through the roof.

Howard County, lodged between Montgomery and Baltimore Counties, is easily the most established Maryland exurb. Columbia, its largest community, is a planned city developed by the same folks responsible for revitalizing the inner harbors of Baltimore and Norfolk, Virginia. In Columbia one can find the comforts of suburbia and the home investment security that goes with intense zoning regulations. Like its Northern Virginia counterpart, Reston, Columbia may be a tad sterile for some, but its numerous tree-lined parkways and quiet residential areas give the impression of country living just 25 miles from either Washington or Baltimore. Merriweather Post Pavilion, one of the nation's first outdoor concert venues, brings top-name entertainment to the county throughout the warm-weather months.

South of Prince George's County, and just 20 miles from the District line, lies Charles County, a place where not too long ago tobacco and truck farming reigned supreme. An influx of new housing developments, especially along the

U.S. Highway 301 corridor between Waldorf and La Plata, and the opening of the county's first shopping mall are helping to create a bona fide suburban atmosphere. The challenge of the future for Charles County inevitably will be forging a balance between development and preservation of its long-cherished rural lifestyle.

(For information about independent cities within the above mentioned counties, consult our Neighborhoods and Real Estate chapter.)

Suggested Readings and Resources

A good number of books deal with finding a job in Metro Washington. Some of the most helpful are:

• *The Metropolitan Washington, D.C., Job Bank* edited by Michelle Ray Kelley, Adams Media Group—A popular job hunters' guide to the D.C. area, with comprehensive listings of companies and contacts selected by trade.

• *Federal Career Opportunities* by Federal Research Service Inc.—A regularly updated booklet, found in virtually every bookstore in Washington, that lists all current job openings in the federal government, plus qualifications, contacts, salary structure, and responsibilities.

• *The Book of U.S. Government Jobs: Where They Are, What's Available, and How to Get One,* by Dennis V. Damp, Brookhaven Press—Now in its sixth edition, this book on federal employment offers a practical guide for finding government work.

• *Government Job Applications and Federal Resumes,* by Anne McKinney, Prep Publishing—This guide walks federal job seekers through the labyrinth of applying for a job with the government, including what to include on your resume and how to untangle an alphabet soup of federal forms and requirements, from KSAs to forms 171 and 612.

Contacts

If you'd like to receive more specific information about the Metro Washington economy and/or labor market, we encourage you to contact the following agencies:

• District of Columbia Department of Employment Services, Labor Market Information Research Staff, 77 P Street NE, Room 3302, Washington, D.C. 20002, (202) 671-1633, does.ci.washington.dc.us

• The Greater Washington Board of Trade, Office of Research, Policy, and Transportation, 1129 20th Street NW, Suite 200, Washington, D.C. 20036, (202) 857-5900, www.bot.org. Or at the same address, the Greater Washington Initiative, a regional economic development marketing organization, (800) 555-6783, www.greaterwashington.org

• Maryland Department of Economic and Employment Development, Office of Labor Market Analysis and Information, 1100 North Eutaw Street, Baltimore, Maryland 21201, (410) 767-2250

• Metropolitan Washington Council of Governments, 777 North Capitol Street, NE, Suite 300, Washington, D.C. 20002-4239, (202) 962-3200, www.mwcog.org

• Virginia Employment Commission, 703 East Main Street, Richmond, Virginia 23219, (804) 786-1485, www.vec.state.va. us

Selected Economic Development Authorities

If you're interested in starting or expanding a business in Metro Washington or simply want to know more about companies in specific jurisdictions, we recommend that you contact the following economic-development groups:

• D.C. Office of Business and Economic Development, 717 14th Street NW, Washington, D.C. 20004, (202) 727-6365, www.dcworks.gov

• Montgomery County Office of Economic Development, 101 Monroe Street, Suite 1500, Rockville, Maryland 20850, (240) 777-2000, www.co.md.us

• Prince George's County Economic Development Corporation, 4640 Forbes Boulevard, Suite 200, Lanham, Maryland 20706, (301) 429-3044, www.pgcedc.com

• Anne Arundel County Office of Economic Development, 2660 Riva Road, Annapolis, Maryland 21401, (410) 222-7410, www.aaedc.org

•Fairfax County Economic Development Authority, 8300 Boone Boulevard, Suite 450, Vienna, Virginia 22182, (703) 790-0600, www.fairfaxcountyeda.org

•Alexandria Economic Development Partnership Inc., 1729 King Street, Suite 410, Alexandria, Virginia 22314, (703) 739-3820, www.alexecon.org

•Arlington County Economic Development Division, One Courthouse Plaza, 2100 Clarendon Boulevard, Suite 608, Arlington, Virginia 22201, (703) 228-0808, www.smartplace.org

•Prince William County Office of Economic Development, 10530 Linden Lake Plaza, Suite 105, Manassas, Virginia 20109, (703) 392-0330, www.pwecondev.org

Convention and Tourist Bureaus/Tourist Information

Contact the following agencies to receive free, comprehensive travel and tourism information packets.

Washington, D.C.
• Visitor Information Center, 1300 Pennsylvania Avenue NW, Washington, D.C. 20004, (202) 328-4748, www.dcvisit.com
• Washington, D.C. Convention and Tourism Corporation, 1212 New York Avenue NW, Washington, D.C. 20005, (202) 789-7000, www.washington.org

Northern Virginia
• Virginia Tourism Corporation, 901 East Byrd Street, 19th Floor, Richmond, Virginia 23219, www.virginia.org; Local office: 1629 K Street NW, Washington, D.C. 20006, (202) 872-0523, (800) 934-9184
• Alexandria Convention & Visitors Bureau, 221 King Street, Alexandria, Virginia 22314, (703) 838-4200, www.funside.com
• Arlington Convention and Visitors Service, 735 South 18th Street, Arlington, Virginia 22202, (703) 228-5720, www.co.arlington.va.us
• Fairfax County Tourism and Convention Bureau, 8300 Boone Boulevard, Suite 450, Vienna, Virginia 22182, (703) 790-3329, www.visitfairfax.org
• Loudoun Tourism Bureau, 108-D South Street SE, Leesburg, Virginia 22075, (703) 771-4682, www.visitloudoun.org
• Prince William County/Manassas Conference and Visitors Bureau, 200 Mill Street, Occoquan, Virginia 22125, (703) 491-4045, www.visitpwc.com

Suburban Maryland
• Maryland Office of Tourist Development, 217 East Redwood Street, Baltimore, Maryland 21202, (800) 543-1036, www.mdisfun.org
• Annapolis and Anne Arundel County Conference and Visitors Bureau, 26 West Street, Annapolis, Maryland 21401, (410) 280-0445, www.visit-annapolis.org
• Montgomery County Conference and Visitors Bureau, 12900 Middlebrook Road, Suite 1400, Germantown, Maryland 20874, (301) 428-9702, www.cvbmontco.com
• Prince George's County Conference and Visitors Bureau, 9200 Basil Court, Suite 101, Largo, Maryland 20774, (301) 925-8300, www.co.pg.md.us

Getting Around the Metro Area

Natives of Los Angeles or New York may chuckle at this notion, but getting around Metro Washington can be an intimidating experience for newcomers. Even longtime residents will concede that negotiating the network of often-congested highways, byways, and bridges that serves more than 4.5 million people often isn't the most pleasant of tasks.

In fact, recent research studies confirm that Washington, D.C. drivers suffer from headaches with good reason. According to the Texas Transportation Institute, Washington tops the list for the amount of time—roughly 59 hours annually per person—wasted during traffic tie-ups. Traffic jams also waste fuel, at the number 1 rate of one quart per person for each workday. According to the institute's report, only Los Angeles has worse traffic congestion. Meanwhile, a detailed transportation study by the Greater Washington Board of Trade cites the need for new roads and Potomac bridges to keep up with the D.C. area's steady population increase.

While the region has grown dramatically over the past 30 years or so in both population and the rate of commercial and residential development, the transportation infrastructure—due to a combination of political and bureaucratic stagnation, fiscal belt-tightening, and an acute case of shortsightedness—unfortunately has not kept pace. As shopping malls, housing tracts, and office parks sprouted on the landscape, roads, mass transit, and other transportation improvements all too often became an afterthought. Subsequent changes in commuting patterns further challenged planners, as more and more suburban residents began driving to neighboring suburbs to go to work instead of into the District. Although this shift took some of the strain off downtown, it resulted in rush-hour problems never envisioned in the 1960s.

On an average day, the sheer volume of traffic can make an ordinary nonrush hour journey aggravating. Toss in an accident (even a fender bender that's been moved to the road shoulder), a few snowflakes, some rain, a holiday weekend, or a Friday afternoon during the summer, and you've got the makings of a potentially harrowing ordeal.

That's the bad news.

Now for the good news:

With few exceptions, Metro Washington's roads are generally clean, well maintained, and even downright scenic in places (we offer the George Washington Memorial Parkway, Dulles Greenway, and even the unusually verdant Capital Beltway in spring as prime examples). Drivers can take comfort in knowing that many of the primary roads, notably the Beltway, are patrolled by motorist-assistance units—a courtesy service provided by the Virginia State Police. The assorted trucks and vans prove a welcome sight for countless folks confronting a flat tire, spewing radiator, empty gas tank, or other vehicular challenge.

Some notable progress also has been made in improving Metro Washington's transportation network. Major stretches of roadway have been widened; once nightmarish intersections have been transformed into the safer and far more efficient under/over configuration; and the designation of HOV (high-occupancy vehicle) lanes, requiring two or three persons to a vehicle during rush hour, has encouraged carpooling. New roads like the Dulles Greenway, Fairfax County Parkway, and Franconia-Springfield Parkway have helped ease traffic burdens in Northern Virginia.

The area's biggest road construction project, the Virginia Department of Transportation's rebuilding of the notorious Springfield Interchange, started in March of 1999 and may take as long as eight years to complete. The nonrush-hour work no doubt will cause stress for motorists dealing with lane changes and closures, but the end result should be worth any inconvenience. Known as the "Mixing Bowl," this area where Interstates 95, 395, and 495 converge is considered the Capital Beltway's most dangerous stretch. VDOT reports that 179 accidents took place here during a two-year period. To keep motorists on their toes and help lower the risk of serious accidents, state and county police patrol the interchange. The department provides daily construction updates so that drivers will know when to avoid the area. Call (877) 959–5222 for the latest information or log onto www.springfieldinterchange.com.

Another huge project in the works will replace the much-despised Woodrow Wilson Bridge, where Interstates 95 and 495 cross the Potomac between Alexandria and Prince George's County. The only federally owned drawbridge in the interstate highway system, the 1961 structure is living on borrowed time. It proves a frequent source of gridlock and accidents for commuters. Construction on the $1.6 billion project may continue until at least 2004. In the meantime, obtain updated information by visiting or contacting the Woodrow Wilson Bridge Center, 1800 Duke Street, Suite 200, Alexandria, Virginia, (703) 519–9800. It's open from 10:00 A.M. to 4:00 P.M. Fridays and by appointment other days. Check out the Web site at www.wilsonbridge.com.

VDOT also helps maintain smooth traffic flow through use of the high-tech Smart Traffic management system, a computerized highway monitoring and control program that oversees approximately 70 miles of Interstates 66, 95, and 395 and helps detect and clear accidents and disabled vehicles. In this case, it's nice to know Big Brother is watching. Smart Traffic uses closed-circuit cameras to keep an eye on traffic conditions, traffic counters embedded in the pavement to convey important information, ramp meters to regulate the number of vehicles entering the roadway, and variable message signs that alert motorists to accidents and other traffic-related events ahead. VDOT personnel monitor the system at a control center in Arlington, where they communicate not only with the public but with service patrols, state police, and traffic reporters.

In Maryland a similar traffic-management system called CHART, short for Chesapeake Highways Advisories Routing Traffic, also uses state-of-the-art technology (message signs, cameras, and detection devices, as well as patrol vehicles) to provide quick response to accidents and other road emergencies and help reduce congestion. The statewide program covers some 400 miles of highway and another 400 miles of major arterial roadways in Maryland's eight heavily traveled traffic corridors. The system covers roadways primarily in the Metro Washington and Baltimore areas, including such locations as Interstates 95 and 395 at the Woodrow Wilson Bridge, I-495 north of the American Legion Bridge, and Interstates 95 and 495 south of U.S. 50.

Future major transportation improvement proposals include constructing bypasses to the Capital Beltway, adding bridges, and expanding rail systems and other means of getting people out of their single-passenger vehicles. Although these plans have been hotly debated at times, they are nevertheless cause for optimism.

In the meantime, you've got to deal with the situation at hand, and that's where we hope this chapter proves helpful. There's no substitute for experience, and that's particularly true when it comes to trying to find your way around unfamiliar territory. We hope that the following information will give you a feel for the region's overall transportation system and perhaps make those initial journeys somewhat less intimidating.

First, here are a couple of suggestions. Before tackling Metro Washington from behind the wheel or from any other perspective, we suggest that you get a good map and keep it nearby. We recommend the book-style variety produced locally by Alexandria Drafting Company (ADC), "The Map People," as they proudly bill themselves. ADC's detailed and easy-to-use maps of cities, counties, and the region are invaluable resources, as well as great providers of peace of mind. Updated frequently, they're widely available at convenience stores, drugstores, supermarkets, and bookstores. For more information, call ADC at (703) 750–0510.

You'll also be wise to keep an ear tuned to the radio for the latest traffic information, both before you leave home or office and while in the car. All it takes is one nightmarish backup that could have been easily avoided and you'll soon become a devout listener. Most local stations broadcast traffic reports frequently during the morning and evening rush hours, and a few offer updates throughout the day. Some of the most comprehensive coverage is on WMZQ (98.7 FM), WMAL (630 AM) and WTOP (1500 AM).

Roadways

The Capital Beltway and Connecting Interstates

No matter how much you may wish to avoid it, as a driver in Metro Washington you're bound to travel the Capital Beltway (I-495), that 66-mile, 55-interchange ring of asphalt so many people love to hate. Envisioned as a bypass to Metro Washington when construction began in the early 1950s, it became instead the area's Main Street—at once a transportation lifeline and the bane of our existence. We curse it for legendary traffic jams, ill-conceived interchanges and entrance/exit ramps (though many of these have been dramatically improved), and that confusing Inner and Outer Loop business (we'll clear this up shortly)—but we also can't imagine living here without the Beltway.

History and Statistics

The road opened in stages beginning in 1957, with the federal government picking up 90 percent of the $189 million construction tab; the four- and six-lane version that was completed in 1964 was subsequently widened to eight lanes. No matter the number of lanes, at times it never seems to be enough. One workday soon after opening, the Beltway carried about 48,000 automobiles; today, the daily figure tops 600,000, with vehicles logging some 8 million miles in an average 24-hour period.

Virginia and Maryland state police have jurisdiction over the Beltway and maintain a high profile in both marked and unmarked cruisers, ready to nab drivers exceeding the 55-MPH speed limit, although off-peak traffic often zooms along at 60 MPH or higher speeds. Flashing lights less likely to send your blood pressure skyward are yellow and found atop specially equipped vehicles that come to the aid of stranded motorists, helping prevent ordinary breakdowns from becoming extraordinary backups.

Tractor-trailers constitute only about 6 percent of Beltway traffic, yet studies have shown that they're involved in nearly 20 percent of the accidents. Truckers, of course, are not always at fault; in fact, they're usually considered among the best drivers on the road, although police are adamant about spot safety inspections to ensure the vehicles themselves don't pose unusual risks. As a further precaution, the big rigs are prohibited from traveling in the far-left fast lanes of the Beltway. Vehicles that transport hazardous materials—gasoline, chemicals, etc.—are encouraged, whenever possible, to travel in the wee hours of the night and early morning when traffic is light and the risks of a mishap are greatly reduced. When tractor-trailer accidents happen, they can paralyze the roadways for hours on end: A truck filled with 20 tons of explosives overturned recently at the "Mixing Bowl," stopping traffic for 20 miles and causing commuter nightmares during both morning and evening rush hours!

Which Loop Is Which?

Sooner or later you'll hear about or see the Inner and Outer Loops, the two portions of road that comprise the Beltway. Discerning which is which is actually pretty simple. Using Washington, D.C. as a reference point (better yet, refer to your handy ADC map), with the 12 o'clock position at the top, the Inner Loop is physically closer to the city, and traffic travels in a clockwise motion. The Outer Loop, naturally, sits a bit farther out and traffic moves counterclockwise. This is easy, right? Well, you don't have to think about it as much as you used to. To alleviate some of the confusion, the Virginia and Maryland state highway departments several years ago posted signs that tell you which loop you're traveling.

Major Roads That Intersect the Capital Beltway

You could almost say that all roads in Metro Washington lead to the Beltway. Circumnavigating Washington, D.C. like a giant lasso with numerous appendages, it slices through Fairfax County and Alexandria in Northern Virginia, and Prince George's and Montgomery Counties in Maryland. It crosses the Potomac River twice, via the American Legion (also called Cabin John) Bridge at the northern border of Fairfax County and southern border of Montgomery County, and the aforementioned Woodrow Wilson Bridge, where eastern Fairfax County and western Prince George's County meet.

The Beltway offers access to these major thoroughfares:

I-66 intersects near Tysons Corner in Fairfax County, heading east into Arlington and the District and west toward Prince William County.

I-95 overlaps the Beltway's eastern side, veering south at Springfield for drivers headed toward Richmond, and north in Prince George's County for those traveling toward Baltimore.

I-270 connects to I-495 in Montgomery County and leads north to Frederick, where it becomes I-70.

I-295, also known as the Baltimore-Washington Parkway, heads through southern sections of the District and up through Prince George's County toward Baltimore-Washington International Airport (BWI).

I-395, also known as Henry Shirley Memorial Highway, heads north into Arlington and the District, where it becomes I-295.

The Beltway also provides access to the Dulles Toll Road and the parallel Airport Access Road; the scenic George Washington Memorial Parkway; well-traveled U.S. 1, 29, and 50; Virginia Routes 7, 123, 236 and Maryland Routes 355; and numerous secondary roads.

Insiders' Tip

The I-95 Corridor Coalition provides a quarterly "Northeast Travelers Alert" map with accompanying descriptions of construction projects and probable bottlenecks on the major roadways from Virginia to Maine. Look for it at travelers information centers or contact I-95 Consultants, 1900 North Beauregard Street, Suite 300, Alexandria, VA 22311.

Bridges and Traffic

No other highway in the area carries as much clout or can get us to so many places in so short a time, barring those horrendous traffic jams. While we're mentioning traffic, we'd better point out that the two bridges across the Potomac are the sites of some of the worst Beltway backups. Maryland and Virginia finally got wise and began stationing tow trucks at either end of each span during the morning and evening rush hours to remove disabled vehicles quickly. We already mentioned the dreaded Woodrow Wilson. Motorists on the American Legion Bridge, which has seen great improvement through widening, often still find themselves in rush-hour gridlock.

Keep this in mind: Coming from Virginia, you must cross a bridge to get into the District. (If you manage to accomplish this otherwise, let us know and we'll put together an amazing magic act.) Your five choices, starting north and working south, are Chain Bridge, linking the McLean/Arlington areas with Canal Road and upper northwest; Key Bridge, named for "Star-Spangled Banner" author Francis Scott Key, joining Rosslyn and Georgetown; Roosevelt Bridge, in the shadows of Rosslyn, where I-66 runs into Constitution Avenue NW; stately Memorial Bridge, perhaps the most picturesque of all, stretching from Arlington National Cemetery to the Lincoln Memorial at Rock Creek Parkway; and the 14th Street Bridge, where I-395 winds past the Pentagon and crosses the Potomac near the Tidal Basin and the Jefferson Memorial.

If you drive to work, remember that the morning rush hour in Metro Washington can begin as early as 5:00 A.M. along some stretches of the Beltway and other heavily traveled routes, such as Interstates 66, 95, 270, and 395, and as early as 3:30 P.M. for the drive home. Factor in extended crunch times during inclement weather, Fridays, and holiday weekends.

Beltway Safety Tips

Now that you know a little bit about the major thoroughfares, keep in mind some pointers to lessen aggravation and enhance safety:

- Leave earlier and know where you're going.
- Gas up before you go—remember that traffic jams can eat up a lot of fuel.
- Drive courteously and be alert.
- Learn alternate routes to avoid traffic jams.
- Don't rubberneck!

To avoid confusion on roads that intersect the Beltway, remember that the same highway can have several different names. Here are a few prime examples: Virginia Route 7 is called Leesburg Pike in the Tysons Corner area, Broad Street in the City of Falls Church, and King Street in Alexandria. Virginia Route 236 is known as Duke Street in the Alexandria area, Little River Turnpike in Annandale, and Main Street in Fairfax City. Virginia Route 123 is Ox Road in southern Fairfax County, Chain Bridge Road in the Fairfax City area and again in Tysons Corner, Maple Avenue in the Vienna town limits, and Dolly Madison Boulevard in McLean. Maryland Route 355 also is known as Wisconsin Avenue inside the Beltway, and, in Rockville and beyond, Rockville Pike and Frederick Road. Nothing like a little variety to enhance your driving pleasure, eh?

Toll Roads

Dulles Toll Road
P.O. Box 9430
McLean, VA 22102
(703) 383–2700
www.smart.tag.com

The Dulles Toll Road (Route 267), the region's only toll road except for the connecting Dulles Greenway, exceeded popularity expectations almost immediately after opening in 1984. Despite today's heavy traffic burden, commuters in the corridor, primarily from western Loudoun County and the Fairfax County communities of Herndon, Reston, Tysons Corner, Vienna, and McLean, are much better off with the road than they were before it was built.

The 13-mile highway, with eight exits, runs parallel to the airport-only Dulles Access Road and feeds into I-66. The toll road consists of four lanes in each direction, with the far left lanes designated HOV-2.

Attendants staff the main toll plaza, between Spring Hill Road and Route 7, 24 hours a day. Booths at other entrances and exits are attended 16 hours a day (5:30 A.M. to 9:30 P.M. daily); outside of these hours, motorists need exact change for automatic toll machines. The toll is 50 cents at the main plaza except for single-axle, Spring Hill Road commuters, who ride through a designated lane and pay 25 cents. The fee is 25 cents at all other gates except Route 28, where it costs 35 cents.

Drivers who frequent the toll road may want to buy a high-tech Smart Tag, a tiny electronic transponder that attaches to the rearview mirror and enables cars to pass through any toll lane without stopping. An initial Smart Tag account costs $35 if paid by credit card; a check payment requires an additional $15 deposit. For information on signing up for the program, call (703) 736–9300 or (877) 762–7824, ask for an application at the tollbooth, or visit the Web site at www.smart-tag.com.

Dulles Greenway
45240 Business Ct., Ste. 100
Sterling, VA
(703) 707–8870
www.dullesgreenway.com
Privately operated by Toll Road Investors Partnership II (TRIP II), this 14-mile extension of the Dulles Toll Road opened in September 1995. The four-lane highway has eight interchanges. With a 65-MPH speed limit, the scenic road offers a quick

Insiders' Tip
Even a dusting of snow can send local motorists into a panic. Drive defensively and be extra careful on shady spots and bridges, which ice up fast.

route to Leesburg, and an increasing number of motorists are willing to fork over the tolls, the highest ranging from $1.50 on weekends to $2.00 on weekdays for cars. The road is a welcome addition for folks who commute into the city from bucolic Loudoun County: You can get from Leesburg to Herndon in about half the time required for the same commute relying on Routes 7 and 28. As an added bonus, commuters can receive cash-back bonuses by enrolling in the VIP Miles Frequent Rider Program. Drivers also can enroll in the Smart Tag program, described in the Dulles Toll Road listing.

Major Parkways

Fairfax County Parkway
Rte. 7100
Fairfax County, VA
(703) 324–1100
This 35-mile, cross-county road has opened gradually in connecting sections since September 1987. It's especially handy for folks commuting between communities in different parts of the county. The road starts in western Fairfax County and crosses over U.S. 50, I-66, and Route 123 before turning into the Franconia/Springfield Parkway (Route 7900) at Rolling Road in Springfield. Travelers can follow Route 7900 to I-95. Total estimated cost of the entire, nearly completed project, which is funded through the county and Virginia Department of Transportation (VDOT), is $620 million.

George Washington Memorial Parkway
Turkey Run Park, McLean, VA
(703) 285–2598
www.nps.gov/gwmp
This parkway along the Potomac is one of the prettiest routes to travel into the District, but it can also be one of the most dangerous. Watch out for aggressive drivers and treacherous curves, but don't allow our words of caution to steer you away from this road, which runs from George Washington's home, Mount Vernon, to Great Falls, Maryland. (For more about the parkway's abundant natural,

recreational and historic sites, see our Parks and Recreation and Attractions chapters.)

HOV Restrictions

If you can get people to ride with you, the HOV lanes often get you home or to work faster, although a shorter trip is never guaranteed, given the unpredictable nature of our roads. Still, when you consider the chances of having a shorter ride plus the certainty of reduced auto and fuel expenses, air pollution, and traffic congestion, you can see why the HOV program is so popular with many commuters.

If you're a newcomer and wonder how you'll be able to distinguish the HOV lanes, fear not; they're well marked with signs and either physical barriers (gates, concrete dividers) or diamond-shaped lane markings. Members of the law-enforcement community will be more than happy to remind you as well. Don't take HOV restrictions lightly. Scofflaws face healthy fines plus several points on their licenses for moving violations. You'll pay $50 for a first offense, $100 for a second, $250 for a third within two years of the second, and $500 for a fourth violation within three years of the second! Forget about putting a mannequin or some other human substitute in your car to get around the passenger requirements. The police have seen it all and don't take kindly to motorists trying to put one over on them.

Here's a summary of the regional HOV scene (restrictions apply Monday through Friday only, excluding holidays).

•I–395/I–95: HOV-3 (three or more people)

Where: A 30-mile stretch of road runs from the 14th Street Bridge in the District to Route 234 in Prince William County.

When: Two lanes, separated by barriers, operate northbound from 6:00 A.M. to 9:00 A.M., and southbound from 3:30 P.M. to 6:00 P.M.

•I–66, inside the Capital Beltway: HOV-2 (two or more people)

Where: A 10-mile length of road stretches from Theodore Roosevelt Bridge to the Capital Beltway eastbound.

When: Two eastbound lanes are designated HOV-2 from 6:30 A.M. to 9:00 A.M. Two westbound lanes are designated HOV-2 from 4:00 P.M. to 6:30 P.M.

•I–66 outside the Beltway: HOV-2

Where: An 18-mile stretch runs from the Capital Beltway to Route 234 in Manassas.

When: Outside the Beltway, the far-left lane in each direction is painted with diamonds to designate HOV travel from 5:30 to 9:30 A.M. eastbound and from 3:00 to 7:00 P.M. westbound.

•Dulles Toll Road: HOV-2

Where: The road runs from Route 28 to the main toll plaza.

When: The far-left lane is reserved for HOV-2 travel from 6:30 to 9:00 A.M. eastbound, 4:00 to 6:00 P.M. westbound.

During these times, the far right "lanes" (note the electronic green and red control signals overhead) that run for about 7 miles are open to traffic; otherwise, these stretches of dark pavement (to distinguish them from the regular lanes) are used as shoulders only, and traffic is strictly prohibited, so please heed the signs. It can make for a dangerous situation if drivers aren't paying attention or choose to ignore the restrictions. To alleviate the nasty bottleneck conditions that have long plagued I-66, the road is being gradually widened to the west, but the project is far from complete. Expect to see construction work and experience some related traffic tie-ups during off-peak hours along this heavily traveled corridor for quite some time.

For More Info

For answers to questions about highway travel in the region, we suggest you contact the following offices:

•Virginia Department of Transportation, 1401 East Broad Street, Richmond, Virginia, (804) 786–5731, www.virginia dot.org

•Maryland Transportation Authority, 303 Authority Drive, Baltimore, Maryland, (410) 288–8400, www.mdta.state. md.us

•District of Columbia's Department of Public Works, Sixth Floor, 2000 14th Street NW, Washington, D.C., (202)

727-1000, www.publicworks.ci.washing
ton.dc.us

A Washington Driving Primer

Washington is indeed one of the most beautiful and well-planned cities any-where—with its broad avenues, abundant parks, and open space—but that doesn't mean it's a pleasure to drive in, especially for newcomers.

Confusing one-way streets, traffic circles, a critical shortage of on-street parking spaces, outrageous prices for parking garages (expect to pay $10 or more a day), and other factors can frustrate the uninitiated. Finding a place to park can be both costly and aggravating, and police don't hesitate for a moment to hand out tickets. Ignore those and you may find your car towed or perhaps wearing a boot, a heavy steel clamp attached to a front wheel, preventing the car from being driven and ensuring the car owner a bit of embarrassment. All of this underscores the beauty of walking and using public transportation such as Metrorail, Metrobus, or one of the area's 9,000 or so taxicabs. Fortunately, the city's relatively small size and its grid system street layout are helpful to newcomers. With a good map, some patience, and a bit of practice, Washington is actually not a difficult place to get around.

When pondering Washington's street system, remember that the U.S. Capitol is the geographic center. The city is arranged in four sections—Northwest, Northeast, Southwest, and Southeast—with the dividing lines being North Capitol Street, South Capitol Street, East Capitol Street, and the National Mall, radiating like spokes of a wheel from the Capitol building. The Northwest, Northeast, Southwest, and Southeast used in addresses are very important. An address on M Street NW could also be found on M Street SE, so keep this in mind when mailing something, and especially when trying to get somewhere.

Streets that run north-south (14th, 15th, 18th, etc.) are numbered in sequence, while those going east-west are lettered (H, M, R, and so forth) in alphabetical order. There are no J, X, Y, or Z Streets. Streets with state names (Pennsylvania, Connecticut) are all diagonals. Circles and squares occur at the intersections of diagonal avenues and numbered and lettered streets.

The Metro System and Other Ground Transportation Networks

The Metro

Washington Metropolitan Area Transit Authority (Metro)
600 5th St. NW
Washington, DC
(202) 637-7000, (202) 638-3780 TTY
www.wmata.com

Metro Washington is blessed with a first-rate rail and bus system, Metro, short for the Washington Metropolitan Area Transit Authority (WMATA). The acclaimed Metrorail is clean, efficient, inexpensive, and, yes, even attractive. Good luck finding any graffiti, but you will see some spectacular concrete work, dramatic arched ceilings, graceful lines, and towering escalators, giving the primarily underground system a futuristic appearance.

Metro is generally safe, but deadly accidents have happened on rare occasions. Be careful not to ensnare loose clothing in the moving steps of the escalators. Keep a cautious distance from the platform edge, and make sure to enter and exit quickly. When you hear a loud electronic bell-like tone, watch for the doors to snap open or shut.

"America's Subway" first opened in 1976, and has grown to link a large portion of the National Capital Area. It's especially loved by commuters and tourists, as it offers superb access to the major business districts as well as such popular destinations as the Smithsonian, the Pentagon, the National Zoo, Ronald Reagan Washington National Airport, and Arlington National Cemetery.

Metro's general manager reports to the Metro Board, whose members include representatives from the District, Maryland, and Virginia. Area jurisdictions served by Metro pay a subsidy to the system, and residents pay a few cents extra per gallon of gasoline to help fund Metro's operation, maintenance, and expansion.

Each of Metrorail's five lines—Orange, Red, Green, Blue, and Yellow—passes through the District at some point. The recently expanded Green Line now extends from Branch Avenue in Prince George's County to Greenbelt, on the other side of P.G. County. The Orange Line stretches from Vienna, Virginia, to New Carrollton, Maryland; the Red, from Shady Grove, Maryland, to Glenmont, Maryland. The Blue Line runs from Addison Road in the District to Franconia-Springfield, which opened in June of 1997 at Frontier Drive, right off the convenient Franconia/Springfield Parkway; two additional stops are planned in P.G. County. The Yellow Line goes from the Huntington area of Fairfax County to Mt. Vernon Square in the District. Metrorail boasts 83 stations along 103 miles of track.

The system operates from 5:30 A.M. to midnight, Monday through Thursday, 5:30 A.M. to 2:00 A.M. Fridays, 8:00 A.M. to 2:00 A.M. Saturdays, and 8:00 A.M. to midnight Sundays. The last trains leave some stations prior to midnight; refer to signs in stations for details. Trains as well as buses run on a reduced schedule on certain holidays.

Large brown pylons topped with Metro's distinctive "M" logo mark all station entrances. There's also good signage along roads for those stations accessible by auto.

Instead of cash or tokens, Metro operates on a farecard system. Every passenger must have a farecard to enter and exit, except children younger than age five, two of whom may travel free with a paying rider. Fares start at $1.10 and vary depending on the time of day and distance traveled. To determine your fare, look at a hard-to-miss map to determine your destination, and then check the posted fee schedule for the peak and off-peak fares to

Clean, efficient, and inexpensive, Washington's Metrorail offers easy access to major business districts and popular attractions. PHOTO: LARRY LEVINE, COURTESY OF WASHINGTON METROPOLITAN AREA TRANSIT AUTHORITY

that station. Peak (rush) hours of operation are 5:30 A.M. to 9:30 A.M. and 3:00 P.M. to 7:00 P.M., Monday through Friday. Off-peak occurs all other times and on federal holidays. Although the system is far busier during the peak periods, the trains also run more often—the wait any time of day is rarely longer than 15 minutes.

Purchasing a farecard may seem confusing at first, but it's easily mastered. Farecard machines in every station accept nickels, dimes, quarters and $1.00 and $5.00 bills; some machines also accept $10 and $20 bills. Be aware, however, that change comes in coins only, and machines provide no more than $4.95 in change. Put your money in the machine, and when you've pushed the "+" and "-" buttons to reach your desired fare amount, press another button to receive your card. To avoid having to run to an Addfare machine to get in or out of a station, you should consider purchasing a little more fare than you think you might need for a roundtrip. Better still, just keep a farecard with $10 or $20 worth of travel stashed in your wallet or purse at all times. You never know when it might come in handy.

When you buy a farecard for $20 or more, you receive a 10 percent bonus. You also can purchase special passes, such as a $5.00 one-day pass geared toward tourists, who can ride after 9:30 A.M. on weekdays and all day on weekends and holidays. Metro also offers various large-denomination passes that save time and expense for commuters. Purchase special passes at Metro Headquarters, 600 Fifth Street NW, Washington, D.C. It's open from 8:00 A.M. to 1:00 P.M. on weekdays and from 2:00 to 4:00 P.M. on weekends. You also can purchase special farecards at the Metro Center Sales Office, 12th and F Streets NW, Washington, D.C., open from 7:30 A.M. to 6:30 P.M. on weekdays, or at the Pentagon Sales Office at the Pentagon Concourse, open from 7:30 A.M. to 1:00 P.M. and 2:00 to 3:00 P.M. on weekdays. You can purchase special passes at Giant, Safeway, or Superfresh supermarkets; at TicketMaster (202-637-7000); at the Commuter Stores at the Ballston, Crystal City, and Rosslyn stops; and at the White Flint Transit Store.

Metrobus goes everywhere the rail system does, and then some, reaching far into suburban areas as well as the inner city. More than 70 percent of the buses in Metro's 1,300-plus fleet come equipped with wheelchair lifts. Bus routes and schedules are coordinated with rail routes and schedules to provide a comprehensive transportation system. Individual bus routes are detailed on brochures available at Metrorail stations and in various town, city, and county transportation offices. Metrobus fares are $1.10 for regular routes, $2.00 for express routes. Senior citizens and disabled passengers ride for 50 cents with valid IDs and transfers.

Parking is available at many Metrorail stations, but be forewarned that it often fills up quickly on weekdays. It costs $1.00 to $2.25 on weekdays and is free on weekends and holidays. Some stations also feature a limited number of metered spaces, as well as short-term parking for driver-attended vehicles picking up passengers. If you're dropping off someone, follow signs for the kiss and ride lane.

If you have questions while at a Metrorail station, don't hesitate to ask an employee in the information booth near the entrance gates. Otherwise, for general Metrorail and Metrobus details and timetables, call the ridership information line listed above. Operators are on duty daily from 6:00 A.M. to 10:30 P.M. weekdays, and 8:00 A.M. to 10:30 P.M. weekends. Transit Police can be reached in emergencies at (202) 962-2121. Did you leave something behind? Call Lost and Found at (202) 962-1195.

Insiders' Tip

Elderly and disabled passengers receive fare discounts by showing their WMATA ID Cards. Obtain one by calling (202) 962-1245.

Bus Systems

Greyhound Bus Lines
1005 1st St. NE, Washington, D.C.
(202) 289–5154, (800) 231–2222
www.greyhound.com

Greyhound offers a less expensive, albeit more time-consuming, alternative to air and rail travel. The automated phone line lists departure times and fares for Atlanta, Boston, New York, Newark, Norfolk, Philadelphia, Pittsburgh, and Richmond. Greyhound offers package express and charter services, and the buses also travel to and from a few suburban stations.

Northern Virginia

Alexandria Transit Company's DASH
116 S. Quaker La.
Alexandria, VA
(703) 370–3274
www.dashbus.com

DASH buses offer daily service in Alexandria and provide links to Metrobus, Metrorail, Virginia Railway Express, and the Fairfax Connector bus system. DASH takes rush-hour passengers to all Alexandria Metrorail stations, as well as the nearby Pentagon station. Base fares are $1.00, with a 25 cents supplemental charge for Pentagon service. Kids younger than age five ride for free, with up to two per paying customer. A $25 Dash Pass,

available at Alexandria City Hall and other locations, is good for unlimited rides for a month. To arrange for pickup by a bus equipped with a wheelchair lift, call by 3:00 P.M. the day before your trip. Call the city at (703) 370-3274 for information about door-to-door service for mobility-impaired passengers.

City of Fairfax CUE Bus Service
10455 Armstrong St.
Fairfax, VA
(703) 385–7859
www.ci.fairfax.va.us/services/cuebus/cuebus.htm

This daily service offers rides in the city and to the Vienna Metrorail Station and George Mason University. Regular fares are 50 cents. You can purchase convenient 10-ticket booklets through the City Treasurer's Office (703-385-7900). High school students with school IDs, elementary and intermediate students, and ID-carrying seniors age 60 and older ride for free, and George Mason students, faculty, and staff with university IDs ride for free. Children ages three and younger ride for free when accompanied by an adult. On weekdays, passengers can ride for 25 cents from the Vienna station by presenting to the driver a Metro rail-to-bus transfer, available at the station. Disabled persons should call the service to arrange City Wheels or Metro Access transportation.

Fairfax Connector
12055 Government Center Pkwy.,
Ste. 1034
Fairfax, VA
(703) 339–7200, (703) 339–1608 TDD
www.fairfaxconnector.com

One of the largest community bus systems, with around 50 routes, the daily Fairfax Connector serves much of Fairfax County, supplementing Metrobus routes. Riders need exact cash or Metrobus flash passes, tokens, or commuter tickets, and rides cost 25 cents to $2.50. All buses in the Reston/Herndon area are wheelchair lift-equipped. To schedule a wheelchair-accessible ride elsewhere, call a day in advance. Pick up timetables at food stores, post offices, libraries, drugstores, government centers, and various Metro stations.

> ## Insiders' Tip
> The U.S. Transportation Department, 400 7th Street SW, Washington, D.C., (202-366-4000), offers toll-free consumer hotlines on such topics as air travel, truck and bus complaints, and auto, aviation, and boating safety.

Loudoun Transit
48A Sycolin Rd.
Leesburg, VA
(703) 777–2708
www.transitservices.org

This bus service, operated by the non-profit Loudoun County Transit, offers a fixed route in Leesburg and door-to-door service throughout the county on weekdays and Saturdays. Fixed-route service includes travel from Leesburg to the new county hospital east of town and from the hospital to Reston in western Fairfax County. Fares range from 50 cents to $6.00, depending on the type of trip.

OmniRide
14700 Potomac Mills Rd.
Woodbridge, VA
(703) 490–4811
www.omniride.com

This Prince William County–based commuter bus service is managed by the Potomac and Rappahanock Transportation Commission. The service goes to Franconia-Springfield, West Falls Church, the Pentagon, Crystal City, Vienna, and the District. Fares are $5.00, free for children younger than six. A 10-ride pass costs $35. The commission also manages OmniLink, a local weekday bus service serving eastern Prince William County and Manassas, and OmniMatch, a car pool coordinating service.

Suburban Maryland

The Bus
Prince George's County Department of Public Works and Transportation
9400 Peppercorn Pl., Ste. 320
Landover, MD
(301) 883–5656, (800) 486–9797 in Maryland
www.co.pg.md.us/Government/dpwt/transit/thebus

The county's newest bus service covers 12 routes from Upper Marlboro to the New Carrollton and Addison Road Metrorail stations. Fares are 75 cents for adults, 35 cents for senior citizens age 55 and older and disabled persons, and free for children younger than 5, one child per paying adult.

Call-A-Bus
Prince George's County Department of Public Works and Transportation,
9400 Peppercorn Pl., Ste. 320,
Landover, MD
(301) 499–8603, (800) 899–2287 in Maryland

This curb-to-curb bus service is available to all Prince George's County residents who are unable to use existing bus or rail service. Seniors and the disabled receive priority. The service runs weekdays, 8:30 A.M. to 3:30 P.M., with fares of $1.00; seniors and disabled persons pay 50 cents. You can make a reservation up to 14 days in advance; same-day requests are subject to availability.

Ride-On
110 N. Washington St.
Rockville, MD
(240) 777–7433, (800) 732–3327
www.dpwt.com/TransSvcDiv/TransSvcDiv.html

This Montgomery County bus service runs daily, supplementing Metrobus service. Fares are $1.10 during the peak weekday hours of 6:00 A.M. to 9:30 A.M. and 3:00 P.M. to 6:30 P.M.; all other times, fares are 90 cents. Children age four and younger ride for free, up to two per fare-paying passenger. High school and elementary students with IDs also ride free. Fares for seniors and persons with disabilities are 50 cents at all times with valid IDs. You can obtain special passes, such as the Regional One Day Bus Pass for $2.50, and a 20-trip ticket for $10, at local Giant supermarkets, government service centers, and libraries. Riders ages 18 and younger can obtain Monthly Cruiser Passes for $10 each.

Train Service

Amtrak
Union Station, 50 Massachusetts Ave. NE
Washington, DC
(202) 484–7540, (800) 872–RAIL,
(800) 523–6590 TDD
www.amtrak.com

The 125-MPH Metroliner service runs between Washington's grandly restored

Besides serving as a working railroad station, D.C.'s grandly restored Union Station houses shops, restaurants, and theaters. PHOTO: ASMAN CUSTOM PHOTO SERVICE, COURTESY OF UNION STATION

Union Station (Massachusetts Avenue and North Capitol Street NE) and New York, offering 15 daily departures and few stops. Passengers can also travel to such cities as Baltimore, Philadelphia, Boston, Richmond, and Atlanta. Call to obtain detailed schedule and fare information. (See our Shopping chapter for more information about Union Station.)

Dial any of the phone numbers listed above for further information about picking up Amtrak trains at Union Station or at the following suburban stations:

110 Callahan Drive, Alexandria, Virginia

Railroad Avenue, Quantico, Virginia

1040 Express Way, Woodbridge, Virginia

4300 Garden City Drive, New Carrollton, Maryland

Hungerford Drive and Park Street, Rockville, Maryland

**Maryland Commuter
Rail Service (MARC)
(800) 325–RAIL, (301) 850–5312 TDD
www.mtamaryland.com/marc/marc.htm**

Trains operate Monday through Friday between Washington's Union Station and Baltimore (including Oriole Park at Camden Yards for you baseball and Inner Harbor fans), serving many of the key commuter corridors of Prince George's County. Fares vary according to your destination; you can travel from Union Station to the Camden Yards station for $5.75 one way, and $10.25 round-trip; $43 for a week's fares or $143 for a month's worth. MARC also links the region with Martinsburg, West Virginia and Frederick, Maryland. Call the numbers listed earlier for detailed, automated information about stations, schedules, and fares. Two children younger than age six can travel free with a rider paying full fare.

**Virginia Railway Express (VRE)
1500 King St., Ste. 202
Alexandria, VA
(703) 684–1001
www.vre.org**

The region's newest commuter rail service hit the tracks in 1992. It's a unique public-private transportation partnership, offering convenient, economical alternatives to car commuting. VRE operates two lines: the Manassas Line, between Manassas and the District, and the Fredericksburg Line, from Fredericksburg to the District.

Manassas Line stations are located in Manassas, Manassas Park, Burke, Springfield, Alexandria, Arlington, and the District. Fredericksburg Line stations are in Fredericksburg, Falmouth, Stafford, Quantico, Woodbridge, Lorton, Springfield, Alexandria, Arlington, and the District. As with Metro, VRE has easy-to-spot roadside directional signs to help guide travelers to the stations, four of which are just a short walk from easy connections with Metrorail at L'Enfant Plaza and Union Station in the District, and at Crystal City and King Street (Alexandria) in Northern Virginia. Single-ride fares range in price from $2.15 to $7.00, depending on your travel route. You can buy discounted 10-trip and monthly passes. Senior citizens, riders ages 21 and younger, and dis-

abled people can ride for 50 percent off the regular fare. Call for detailed trip information.

Taxicabs

District taxi fares are based on a zone pricing system, ranging from $5.00 for a single zone to $15.60 for an eight-zone ride. You'll pay an extra $1.50 per additional person. A rush-hour surcharge of $1.00 from 7:00 to 9:30 A.M. and 4:00 to 6:30 P.M. on weekdays. If you're planning an interstate trip, call (202) 331-1671. Contact the D.C. Taxicab Commission, 2041 Martin Luther King Jr. Avenue SE, Washington, D.C., (202) 645-6018, dctaxi.dc.gov, with questions or complaints.

You shouldn't have any trouble hailing a cab in the District. In the suburbs you'll most readily find them at Metro stops and the airports; otherwise, you'll need to call to arrange a pickup. Cabs in the suburban jurisdictions still use a traditional meter system.

Numerous cab services are available in Metro Washington. PHOTO: COURTESY OF WASHINGTON DULLES INTERNATIONAL AIRPORT

Commuter Aids

Arlington County Commuter Assistance Program
Arlington County Deptartment of Public Works, Planning Division
2100 Clarendon Blvd., Ste. 717
Arlington, VA
(703) 228–3725
www.commuterpage.com

If your commute takes you to or through Arlington, check out CommuterPage.com for comprehensive information on transportation alternatives, traffic, weather, and fare purchasing information.

Commuter Connections
Metropolitan Washington Council of Governments
777 N. Capitol St. NE, Ste. 300
Washington, DC
(800) 745–RIDE
www.commuterconnections.org

Are you interested in joining a car pool? Missed your ride home because you had to work late? Need information about local mass transit? Commuter Connections, a regional transportation information network, is ready to come to the rescue with solutions to common dilemmas. If you regularly travel to work via car alternatives, your can join the Guaranteed Ride Home program, which provides free rides home from work, up to four times annually, in cases of emergencies, illnesses, or unscheduled overtime. The network's rideshare database also helps people find car pools or van pools in their neighborhoods. Commuter Connections helps companies implement commuting and "telework" programs; provides information about Park-and-Ride lots, HOV locations, and public transit options; and publishes a quarterly newsletter.

Prince George's County Ride Finders
Prince George's County Department of Public Works and Transportation
9400 Peppercorn Pl., Ste. 320
Landover, MD
(800) 486–RIDE, (301) 925–5167 TDD

Fill out an application and you'll receive a car pool/van pool match list with names of other commuters with whom you may wish to arrange transportation.

SmarTraveler Information System
400 Virginia Ave. SW., Washington, DC
(301) 628–4343
www.smartraveler.com

Call this automated service before you leave for work or home and you'll have an idea of what to expect in traffic and transit conditions. The free service—operated by Partners in Motion, a partnership of several public agencies and private businesses—provides constant updates from 5:30 A.M. to 7:00 P.M. on weekdays, as well as construction and events information all the time. Mobile phone users can dial 211.

Airport Options: Reagan, Dulles, and BWI

Washington ranks as one of the top five domestic and international air travel markets, according to the Greater Washington Board of Trade. Naturally, air travel to and from Washington-area airports has been a shaky proposition for many passengers following September 11, 2001, when terrorists hijacked and crashed four jets, including one that had taken off from Washington Dulles International Airport. Air travelers now can expect long lines and more thorough inspections at security checkpoints. In fact, most airlines strongly recommend arriving at least two hours before your scheduled departure time. (For more specifics about security measures and passenger restrictions, visit the airport's Web site.)

When traveling requires you to leave the ground, however, you'll be glad that Metro Washington is served by not one, but three major airports: Ronald Reagan Washington National; its sister facility, Washington Dulles, and Baltimore/Washington International, commonly called BWI. This situation offers travelers some real advantages in scheduling, carrier selection, and, to a lesser degree, fares. Combined, the three airports handle about 42 million passengers annually and are served by nearly 50 scheduled airlines.

Washington is served by three major airports: Ronald Reagan Washington National, Washington Dulles International, and Baltimore-Washington International. PHOTO: COURTESY OF VIRGINIA TOURISM CORPORATION

The region is a major cargo hub as well, with more than a billion pounds of airfreight transported annually. Dulles, with four air cargo buildings, gets most of the region's cargo business.

While BWI is state-owned and -operated, Reagan and Dulles are managed by the Metropolitan Washington Airports Authority (MWAA), an agency created by an act of Congress in 1987. Before the dawn of MWAA, whose board of directors features equal representation by Virginia, Maryland, and District residents, Reagan and Dulles were the only two civil airports in the nation run by the federal government. Contrary to public perception, MWAA is self-financed; no state or local tax revenues are used to fund airport activities or construction. Reagan and Dulles are very much in Northern Virginia, despite the announcement you may hear on the plane flying in, or the occasional Washington, D.C. address or phone number you may see.

For general information on Reagan and Dulles, call the Metropolitan Washington Airports Authority at (703) 417-8000. Both Reagan and Dulles are served by the authority's Washington Flyer Ground Transportation System, (703-685-1400), a network of buses, taxis, and limousines. Regular bus service is offered between each airport, to and from the Downtown Terminal at 15th and K Streets NW, as well as to and from the West Falls Church Metrorail station. Read on for more information about each individual airport.

Baltimore-Washington International Airport
Anne Arundel County, MD
(800) I–FLY–BWI
www.bwiairport.com

Baltimore-Washington International often seems overshadowed by Reagan and Dulles, but that's changing. BWI is modern, easy to get to, easy to use, and ably serves both of its namesake markets with all major domestic carriers. A 370,000-square-foot International Pier opened recently, garnering high praise from the local media. Other recent projects include parking garage expansion, motorized pedestrian walkways, and a recreational trail.

Arlington-based US Airways in particular offers extensive service, and BWI is the only local airport served by wildly popular Southwest Airlines. The airport boasts a handful of foreign airlines, including Air Canada, Air Jamaica, British Airways, and Icelandair. BWI also has taken the lead in offering regional residents the most choices in low-cost flights, with Southwest and Continental in particular slugging it out in fare wars.

The fact that BWI is so user-friendly, boasts ample parking, and is served by both the Amtrak and MARC rail lines gives the airport added clout with the flying public. Garage parking is free for the first half-hour, a welcome bonus if you're just dropping off a passenger. Rates after the first 30 minutes are $2.00 per half-hour, with a maximum $30.00 for the day. A new daily parking lot opened at Elm Road and Aviation Boulevard in November 2001. Parking in one of Lot B's 1,400 spaces costs $2.00 per hour or $11.00 maximum per day. Other parking options include ESP Parking across from the Air Cargo Complex, with on-demand shuttle service at $3.00 per hour, with a $13.00 daily maximum; and Satellite Parking, with many shuttles, at $1.00 per hour, with a $7.00 daily maximum, and the seventh day free. Eight car rental companies are on the premises, and visitors will find plenty of taxis and limousines.

While you wait, grab a bite to eat at one of the airport's fast-food restaurants or bars, or browse one of the specialty shops like the Smithsonian Museum Shop. The airport also has a game room

Insiders' Tip
Traffic delays are not uncommon on the routes to area airports, so leave for the airport with time to spare.

and observation gallery to keep fidgety kids happy.

Count on driving for nearly an hour to BWI from downtown Washington or Northern Virginia—and that's without heavy traffic! The airport is in Anne Arundel County just off the Baltimore-Washington Parkway, but is also easily accessible from I-95. Ample signs posted along the Maryland portion of the Capital Beltway clearly show you which exit to take for BWI.

Ronald Reagan Washington National Airport
Arlington County, VA
(703) 417-8000
www.metwashairports.com/national/index. html

The September 11 terrorist attack on the Pentagon, just a few miles away, greatly impacted Reagan National, as President George W. Bush decided to exercise extreme caution and close the bustling airport. It remained at a standstill from September 11 to October 4, when it reopened with limited services. As of March 2002, the airport had gradually resumed most flights and was operating at 77 percent of its business prior to September 11. The recent precautions unfortunately overshadow the airport's triumphs of recent years.

The $400 million main terminal that opened at Reagan in July 1997 is a dazzling new landmark—the cornerstone of the airport authority's hefty modernization and improvement program for both Reagan and Dulles. Designed by award-winning architect Cesar Pelli, the spacious terminal, with its scalloped roof and striking control tower, proves as convenient as it is eye-catching. As passengers follow clearly marked paths to their gates, they can enjoy the sky-lit views in the high, vaulted ceiling; admire tiled floor medallions, colorful railing panels, murals, glass friezes, and sculpture designed by nationally known artists; browse in shops like The Disney Store and the National Geographic Store; and grab snacks or meals at various sit-down and take-out restaurants.

Joined to the terminal by a covered walkway, one of three new parking garages offers quick access. A stone's throw from

Dulles Airport is the area's full-service domestic and international hub. PHOTO: COURTESY OF WASHINGTON DULLES INTERNATIONAL AIRPORT

the pedestrian bridge, Metro's Blue and Yellow lines pick up and deposit riders. Add a revamped road network to these innovations and you've got an airport that's finally reversing its long-held reputation for being difficult. Reagan, which has served the region since 1941, will only get better, not bigger, as airport officials like to say.

Reagan is the region's close-in, short-haul airport; it handles domestic traffic only, with nonstop flights limited to 1,250 miles. The number of landings and take-offs each day is tightly controlled by federal regulations to limit noise. In Arlington County just off the George Washington Memorial Parkway and abutting the Potomac River (from which much of the airport's land mass was claimed), it couldn't be much closer to the heart of Washington, D.C. Under normal traffic conditions, it's about a 10-minute ride from the airport, up the parkway, over the 14th Street Bridge, and into the District. It's only about another five minutes to Capitol Hill. Reagan is unbeatable for convenience. Just ask a member of Congress or anyone who works or lives in nearby Crystal City, Rosslyn, or Alexandria. The airport is served by

all the major domestic carriers and a host of commuter airlines, as well as the popular US Airways and Delta shuttles that ferry passengers hourly between Washington, New York, and Boston.

Hourly parking is $2.00 per half-hour for the first two hours, then $4.00 an hour. There's a $28-per-day maximum. Park in the daily garage for $5.00 per hour, with a $14.00 daily maximum. Parking at long-term lots, with free shuttles, costs $1.00 an hour, and $7.00 maximum per day.

Washington Dulles International Airport
Fairfax and Loudoun Counties, VA
(703) 417–8000
www.mwaa.com/dulles/index.html

Dulles, at the end of the airport-only access road 26 miles (about 45 minutes) from downtown Washington, is the area's full-service domestic and international hub. Dulles was the first airport built for the jet age, opening in 1962 and named after John Foster Dulles, secretary of state under President Eisenhower. Finnish-born architect Eero Saarinen sought to convey the movement of flight in his design of the stunning main terminal, which the American Institute of Architects has recognized as one of the greatest architectural achievements of the twentieth century. Beauty wasn't a harbinger of immediate success, however. Plagued by a "white elephant" label virtually from day one, Dulles languished severely until the mid-1980s, when a concerted effort was made to market and promote the airport and its rich, untapped potential.

Airlines and passengers have since been flocking to Dulles in increasing numbers as the airport further establishes itself as a major player in international aviation. Fifteen major domestic airlines (United has a substantial presence) and twenty foreign carriers serve Dulles. The roster continues to grow as the airport expands and bolsters its role as an East Coast hub for travel to Europe and the Far East. Its 10,000-acre site on the Loudoun-Fairfax border, a broad expanse of meadows and forest near established residential areas and a booming business corridor, provides room for enlargement that few airports in the world can match.

The airport authority's $2 billion Capital Development Program, targeting 159 improvement projects at National and Dulles, is producing splendid results: Dulles boasts a new International Arrivals Building, expanded parking, new roads and overpasses and, most notably, doubling of the main terminal's length to 1,240 feet. More new projects are in the works, with work expected to continue for the next few years.

With any luck, a rail line will be constructed in the median of the airport access road as was intended when the federal government purchased the property in the late 1950s. Such a line would conceivably link up with Metrorail's West Falls Church station, providing Dulles with the long-needed access befitting an airport that's billed as the world's gateway to the nation's capital.

Meanwhile, many people still find Dulles easily accessible, thanks to the access road, which connects to I-66. Parking proves relatively hassle-free, with close-to-terminal and various reduced-price satellite options available. The terminal houses a variety of eateries and shops to keep passengers occupied while waiting.

Dulles passengers can choose from numerous parking options. The hourly lot costs $3.00 for the first hour, $4.00 each hour for the second through fourth hours, up to $27.00 for 24 hours. Daily parking costs $5.00 per hour, with a maximum of $10.00 for 24 hours. If you'll be gone several days, opt for long-term parking, which costs $1.00 per hour, with a maximum of $6.00 for 24 hours. Your first 20 minutes are free in any of the lots. If you're running hopelessly late, you can get valet parking right in front of the main terminal. It will cost you, however: $25 for the initial 24 hours, and $12 for each day after that. At least you'll catch your flight!

Other Area Airports

Northern Virginia

Leesburg Municipal Airport
1001 Sycolin Rd. SE
Leesburg, VA
(703) 737-7125
www.flyvirginia.com/airport/jyo

The Leesburg Airport—also known as Godfrey Airport as a tribute to famous former resident Arthur Godfrey—boasts an FAA Automated Flight Service Station, three professional flight schools, and a variety of aircraft available for rent. A Reliever Airport for nearby Dulles International, Leesburg has a 5,500-foot runway. The airport offers full aircraft maintenance services, an on-site conference room, and courtesy features for both passengers and flight crews.

Manassas Regional Airport
Off Rte. 28, 4 miles SE of Manassas, VA
(703) 361-1882
www.manassascity.org/reg-airport

One of the busiest airports in Virginia, this 830-acre airport founded in 1964 handles about 140,000 takeoffs and landings annually. It has a 5,700-foot by 100-foot primary runway with Instrument Landing System and a new terminal building that opened in September 1996. It houses the Freedom Museum (703-393-0660, 877-393-0660), which opened in July of 1999. The patriotic museum honors Americans who fought and died for freedom. Hours are 9:00 A.M. to 5:00 P.M. Monday through Saturday and noon to 4:00 P.M. Sunday. Admission is free.

The airport boasts more than 300 based aircraft, the most of any airport in the state.

The FAA Level 2 Tower is open 6:30 A.M. to 10:30 P.M., and the facility is open 24 hours a day. Two fixed-base operators, Jet Services FBO (703-361-7267, UNICOM frequency 122.95); and Dulles Aviation Inc. (703-361-2171, UNICOM frequency 123.0), offer flight instruction and other services. Other flight schools on the premises include Flightech (703-257-9999) and Manassas Aviation Center Inc. (703-361-0575). Amenities include three pilot supply shops, a restaurant, maintenance services, and hangar space for rent. Owned and operated by the city of Manassas, the airport generates an annual economic impact of more than $41 million.

Insiders' Tip

If you're thinking of bicycling to work, call the Bike Commuter Hotline at (202) 628-2500. In Fairfax County, the Department of Comprehensive Planning offers a map of bicycle trails. Call (703) 324-1210 for information.

Suburban Maryland

College Park Airport
1909 Corporal Frank Scott Dr.
College Park, MD
(301) 864-5844
www.pgparks.com/places/historic/hist.cpair.html

This airport in Prince George's County boasts a museum dedicated to its storied past. College Park is the world's oldest continuously operating airport and plays nearly as important a role in aviation history as does Kitty Hawk, North Carolina. In 1909 Orville Wright came here to teach the first Army officers how to fly, and between 1909 and 1934, the airport was the site of many aviation firsts. The airport also offers instructions, sales, and a restaurant.

George Washington, shown here as a bust sculpted by Jean Antoine Houdon in 1785, surveyed the land that became the nation's capital. PHOTO: COURTESY OF MOUNT VERNON LADIES' ASSOCIATION

History

You could read dozens of volumes about Washington, D.C., and merely scratch the surface of the rich history associated with our Nation's Capital. From high-profile local incidents to the federal government's role in national and global affairs, events emblazoned on today's front pages frequently turn up in tomorrow's historical tomes. In this chapter we won't attempt a scholarly discourse on the people and episodes that shaped our fair city. Rather, we offer a thumbnail sketch of Washington history, featuring landmark events from the District's shaky beginnings to its even shakier recent past. (For more about current conditions here, see the Overview chapter.)

Don't fret: You won't be quizzed! You may, however, learn a few intriguing facts about places you'll undoubtedly encounter during your forays into this unique city.

Creating a Capital

He's not only the Father of Our Country. George Washington also is the Father of Washington, the District of Columbia, in the sense that our first president chose the site for the Nation's Capital that later would be named in his honor.

During the years immediately following the Revolutionary War, Northerners and Southerners held fierce debates over where to put the permanent capital city. Philadelphia proved a top contender, along with New York and Charlestown. The two sides finally struck a deal in 1790, an agreement forged between two of the greatest political leaders in America: Alexander Hamilton, a New York Federalist and fiscal conservative, and Thomas Jefferson, a Virginia agrarian liberal. Under the straightforward terms, Jefferson's Southerners agreed to support Hamilton's proposal that the federal government assume the war debts of the 13 original states if, and only if, Hamilton's Northerners would agree to move the capital city south, from Philadelphia to a veritable wilderness along the banks of the Potomac River.

President George Washington, a surveyor by profession, honed in on what he deemed an ideal site in 1791: a central location that proved convenient to the states and close to the Potomac River, which he considered a likely boon for commerce. Never mind that the area consisted of scattered farms and murky riverside corridors that resembled swamps to most who saw them. Washington could picture in its place a magnificent city, and he knew just the person to put his dream to paper: Pierre Charles L'Enfant, a French-born architect who had volunteered in the American Continental army. When presented with the task, L'Enfant—who had spent his childhood in the palace at Versailles, where his father served as an artist—conjured up visions of grandeur that rivaled royal European cities and raised the eyebrows of government officials. The plan he mapped out contained wide, tree-lined streets, including a mile-long avenue with a Congressional building at one end and a presidential "palace" at the other. He imagined large parks adorned with statues and fountains.

L'Enfant had his own ideas of how to do things, and he increasingly ruffled

41

Historical Resources

Historical societies and offices can help you dig up facts about local people and places. Following are some local resources:

Historical Society of Washington, D.C. (202–785–2068, www.hswdc.org),
Montgomery County Historical Society (301–762–1492, www.montgomeryhistory.org),
Prince George's County Historical Society (301–464–0590, www.pghistory.org),
Office of Historic Alexandria (703–838–4554, ci.alexandria.va.us/oha/oha.html),
Arlington Historical Society Museum (703–892–4204, www.arlingtonhistoricalsociety.org),
Fairfax County History Commission (703–246–2123),
Historic Prince William, Inc. (www.historicprincewilliam.org).

feathers as he refused to follow government-ordered instructions and deadlines. Eventually, Washington had no choice but to fire him. L'Enfant's original plan remained largely intact, however. Surveyor Andrew Ellicott and his African American assistant, Benjamin Banneker, who had mapped out the district's 10-mile-square boundaries, continued laying out the city's gridlike street designs.

The City Slowly Takes Shape

The grand city L'Enfant and Washington envisioned didn't spring up overnight. On the contrary, people were in no great rush to settle into a place characterized by damp, mosquito-infested areas, free-roaming farm animals, and more muddy roads than elegant boulevards. Even in 1800, with the Capitol's north wing completed and the government relocated from its temporary Philadelphia headquarters, one local citizen described the capital as "a town of streets without houses." George Washington also had selected the location for the White House, and although he laid the cornerstone in 1792 and lived to see the building's completion, he never occupied the presidential residence. The honor of being first to live at the historic address fell upon second President John Adams and his wife, Abigail, who found the mansion to be an inconvenient work in progress for quite some time after they arrived in 1800.

Washington, D.C. received its city charter in 1802 along with a local government that included a mayor appointed by the president and a council chosen by the residents. Although officially a city, it remained a scourge to many Congress members, who found it crowded, dirty, and unbearably hot and humid in the summer. Even Thomas Jefferson, president from 1801 to 1809, retreated to his Charlottesville home to escape the heat. From 1800 to 1803, the population rose from 3,000 to only 8,000 people.

A Devastating Fire

The city still possessed an ambience of incompleteness in 1814, when, two years after the start of the War of 1812, British troops invaded the city and set fire to most of the public buildings. They set the Capitol on fire, as well as the President's House, (the White House's name until the Roosevelt administration). First Lady Dolley Madison, waiting for husband James to return from a trip, hesitated to leave their home even after James sent orders for her to evacuate. She refused to go before securing some of her husband's papers and Gilbert Stuart's portrait of George Washington, which has continued to hang in the White House throughout the years. Although rainy weather helped contain the fires, the Capitol and President's House received extensive damage. The Madisons finished out James's term in temporary residences, as the President's House repairs weren't complete until

James Monroe took office in 1817. The Capitol took even longer to rebuild: It wasn't finished until 1830.

The Capital Grows

As rebuilding progressed over the next few years, more and more people began to move to Washington. By 1822, the population had increased to more than 15,000 people, including many free Blacks. Over the next several years, citizens saw the beginnings of what would become some of the area's best-known attractions.

An Act of Congress in 1821 created George Washington University, which would grow into a nationally recognized school of higher education (see our Education chapter for more on the university today). The National Theater, founded in 1835, was one of the city's first cultural attractions. It suffered through five fires and a partial collapse over the years, but still continues to entertain Washingtonians with Broadway-caliber plays and concerts (see The Arts chapter). In 1846 the government founded the Smithsonian Institution with money willed to the country by James Smithson, a British scientist who wanted the United States to build an establishment to promote knowledge. (You'll find more on Smithsonian museums and events throughout this book.)

Construction began in 1848 on the Washington Monument, deviating greatly from the proposed equestrian statue included in L'Enfant's original plan. Due to a lack of finances, the 555-foot-tall obelisk wasn't completed until 1884, and it didn't open to the public for four years after that. The city's first art gallery, the Corcoran Gallery of Art, got its start in 1859. Today, it ranks not only as the oldest, but also as one of the finest and largest. (See the Arts and Attractions chapters for more about visiting these places.)

On a sad historical note, 1841 saw the first death of a president in office. William Henry Harrison delivered his inaugural address while standing outside in cold drizzle—for about 90 minutes. One month later, he succumbed to pneumonia and Vice President John Tyler took the oath of office, during an *indoor* ceremony.

Colvin Run Mill is one of the many historic sites in the Washington area. PHOTO: COURTESY OF FAIRFAX ECONOMIC DEVELOPMENT AUTHORITY

The Civil War Takes Its Toll

Washington, D.C. found itself in a precarious position as the Civil War raged from 1861 to 1865. Located 60 miles south of the Mason-Dixon Line and just 100 miles north of Richmond, the Confederate capital, the city was pulled in both directions. Washington became overcrowded with camps, temporary shelters, and hundreds of soldiers and escaped slaves who flocked to the city. Housing grew scarce and disease ran rampant. (See the Civil War Sites chapter for a more detailed description of the war's effects on Washington and its neighboring states.) Even though the war ended in 1865, the year proved tumultuous for the city. The budding Smithsonian Institution lost its original collection of artifacts in a fire at its castle headquarters. And the country suffered a loss even more devastating: President Abraham Lincoln, attending a performance at Ford's Theatre, was fatally shot by the deranged Confederate activist John Wilkes Booth.

Changes in Government

Through the remainder of the 1800s, the city took shape, in terms of government and appearance, as a capital in which the nation could take pride. In 1871, Congress took control of the District, initiating plans to improve the streets and add sewers along with water and gas lines. It also annexed the neighboring tobacco port town of Georgetown, popular for its taverns and residential district. The city in 1872 began planting trees systematically, creating the beginnings of many of Washington's current vistas. The White House brightened up with electric lights in 1890, the same year that cable cars began operating. Congress changed the city's government again in 1878, creating a municipal corporation with three presidentially appointed, Senate-approved commissioners.

Washington and the nation endured yet another tragedy in 1881, when angry civil servant Charles Guiteau shot President William Garfield. Although the president hung on for two months while doctors tried to help him recover, he eventually died as a result of his two wounds, and Guiteau was executed.

On the cultural front, this period saw the 1871 founding of Howard University, now the nation's largest predominantly African American university (see the Education chapter). The Smithsonian expanded with the addition of artifacts from Philadelphia's Centennial Exposition of 1876. The National Zoological Park found a home at Rock Creek Park in 1890, and the Library of Congress opened seven years later (see Attractions). The *Washington Post*, now the city's oldest daily newspaper, first went to press in 1877 (see the Media chapter).

A New Century

The 1900s brought still more changes to the Nation's Capital. Cars took to the now-paved roadways, and in 1908 the city opened a splendid new railroad terminal, Union Station. (Read more about this still-grand hub in the Getting Around and Shopping chapters.) The city's first park commission, created in 1901, strove to improve the city's appearance, in accordance with L'Enfant's original plan. In 1912, Washington received what would become one of its internationally known trademarks: Japanese cherry trees, a gift from the city of Tokyo. The delicate blossoms continue each spring to transform the shores of the Tidal Basin—created in

1900—into a frothy cloud of pale pink and white. By 1910, Washington's population had grown to 330,000. As the country entered World War I in 1917, new workers arrived in droves, driving the population up to more than 430,000 by 1920.

Another famous landmark made its debut in 1922: the Lincoln Memorial, with its majestic statue of the seated president, designed by American sculptor Daniel Chester French. (Seventeen years later, the memorial steps served as a concert stage for contralto Marian Anderson, who performed a free concert after the DAR refused to allow an African American woman to sing in their Constitution Hall.) The year 1922 also brought one of the city's worst tragedies: As Knickerbocker Theater patrons watched the final few minutes of a silent movie, the building's roof suddenly collapsed under the weight of piles of heavy snow. Caught off-guard, the audience couldn't escape in time, and 96 people perished.

A New Deal and Beyond

In 1932, following the Great Depression, President Franklin D. Roosevelt promised the nation a New Deal, and his Works Progress Administration program did indeed create many new jobs in the city. The '30s marked a boom in Washington construction that included many of the city's now familiar landmarks. In 1932, the Folger Shakespeare Library opened, and the Supreme Court moved into its majestic new quarters in 1935. The National Archives Building—which houses our country's most treasured documents, the Declaration of Independence, Constitution, and Bill of Rights—also opened its doors in 1935. The government workforce grew again when we entered World War II in 1941, ushering in the city's modern era. The West Building of the National Gallery of Art, containing some of the world's greatest art treasures, welcomed its first visitors in 1941. (The East Building addition opened 30 years later, fittingly exhibiting more modern works.) In 1943, the Pentagon, the nation's largest and now infamous office building, sprung up just across the river in Arlington, Virginia. In 1942, another striking monument, the Jefferson Memorial, joined the ranks of the city's best-loved landmarks. Renovations of the Capitol and White House ushered in the '50s. (Read more about all of these famous sites in the Arts and Attractions chapters.)

Civil Rights

With the nation still divided on issues regarding race, Washington acted as a major player in the civil rights struggles of the '50s and '60s. In 1954, the U.S. Supreme Court's ruling in the *Brown v. Board of Education of Topeka* led Washington to become one of the first major cities to integrate its schools. In 1963, around 200,000 civil-rights supporters participated in the peaceful, historic March on Washington, which culminated at the Lincoln Memorial, as Martin Luther King Jr. delivered his stirring "I Have A Dream" speech. (The event set the stage for later, larger marches, from the 250,000-person anti-Vietnam war demonstration in 1969 to the Million Man March staged by 800,000 or more African American men and boys in 1995. In 1997, approximately

> ## Insiders' Tip
> Edward Kennedy Ellington—better known as "Duke"—was born in Washington, D.C. in 1899. Today, a public magnet school for the arts and a bridge are named in honor of the jazz composer, musician, and band leader, whose boyhood home still stands in northwest Washington.

500,000 Christian men converged on the National Mall for a six-hour Promise Keepers' rally, perhaps the country's largest religious gathering ever.)

Later in 1963, the assassination of President John F. Kennedy in Dallas cast a pall over Washington and the entire nation. Five years later, King again offered a memorable speech in the capital city: his final sermon. Just days after addressing the congregation of Washington National Cathedral, King was assassinated in Memphis. The sad event triggered deadly, destructive riots here and in other cities.

The Watergate Era

The report of a 1972 break-in by Republican campaign workers at the Democratic Party headquarters in the Watergate Hotel signaled the beginning of an embarrassing tale of corruption that would reach all the way to the White House. *Washington Post* reporters Carl Bernstein and Bob Woodward earned a Pulitzer Prize for their investigative work uncovering the country's biggest political scandal. The revelations forced President Richard M. Nixon to resign from office in August 1974.

Along with the nationally oriented changes that took place in Washington in the '60s and '70s came an evolution in the city's government. In 1961, the 23rd Amendment to the Constitution granted District residents the right to vote in national elections. Three years later, they voted in their first presidential election. A charter change in 1967 allowed the city a chief executive, assistant, and nine council members. In 1970, Washington residents elected a nonvoting representative to the U.S. House of Representatives, and 1973 brought about the Home Rule Charter, allowing the city to elect a mayor and 13-member council, but giving Congress the power to veto legislation. Under the charter, the president appoints local judges, and local criminal cases fall under the jurisdiction of the Office of the U.S. Attorney General.

The 1970s also brought positive cultural additions to Washington. The beautiful Kennedy Center for the Performing Arts opened in 1971, and the National Air and Space Museum—now the Smithsonian's most popular attraction—began welcoming visitors in 1976.

The nation held its collective breath in 1981, when John Hinckley Jr. shot President Ronald Reagan outside the Washington Hilton. The assassination attempt failed, and the president recovered quickly, but press secretary James Brady, shot in the head, suffered permanent brain damage. The incident served as the catalyst for the introduction of the Brady Bill, which led to a law requiring a waiting period before handgun purchases.

The following year brought the District a pair of tragedies. An Air Florida plane crashed into the Fourteenth Street Bridge shortly after takeoff, killing most of its passengers. That same day, a Metro train crashed, causing three fatalities.

Washington Today

Life is never dull in Washington, D.C. The Nation's Capital regularly makes headlines, not only for its role in the national and international political scenes, but also for its local events. In 1990, stunned TV audiences watched a surveillance videotape of Washington Mayor Marion Barry caught smoking crack cocaine in a Washington hotel room. Not surprisingly, Barry lost reelection, as voters chose instead Sharon Pratt Dixon, the first African American woman to become mayor of a major U.S. city. Barry made a comeback, however, winning reelection in 1994, even after having served time in federal prison.

Violence, drug use, and city mismanagement continue to plague Washington, and the troubled District government is, for all intents and purposes, being run by a Congressionally mandated control board. Things are looking brighter, however, with the 1999 election of Mayor Anthony A. Williams, who proposes to make Washington "the best city in America" by improving such areas as community safety and cleanliness, education, housing, transportation, and employment.

The Pentagon, as it looked before September 11, 2001, is the headquarters for secretaries of the U.S. Department of Defense, Army, Navy, Air Force, and Coast Guard. PHOTO: COURTESY OF WASHINGTON, DC CONVENTION AND TOURISM CORPORATION

The Nation's Capital—and its most prominent resident, then-President Bill Clinton—stood awkwardly in the international spotlight for months on end in 1998 and 1999 as the country's leader faced impeachment, the result of his controversial efforts to cover up his dalliance with former White House intern Monica Lewinsky. Only the second president in United States history to be impeached by the House of Representatives, Clinton—and countless embarrassed Americans—breathed a sigh of relief when the Senate acquitted him.

Of course, no events in the city's or country's complicated history compare with the devastating happenings of September 11, 2001. When terrorists slammed jets into the World Trade Center in New York City and the Pentagon in Arlington, Virginia, everyone in Washington, D.C. braced for more turmoil. The city went into immediate high-alert mode, and many of the increased security measures continue to this day. As the region continued to reel from the reality of the plane crash, which killed nearly 200 people and destroyed a section of the Penta-

gon, a new round of terror began when anthrax-laced letters showed up in government office buildings and postal facilities. Although many of the problems have been resolved, Washingtonians remain in a state of heightened alert, always bracing for a new wave of trouble. (For more on the recent happenings and their effects on the city, see the Overview chapter.)

Washington remains a city of contrasts, and problems aside, the Nation's Capital also deserves to be in the spotlight for many of its innovations and contributions. The '90s witnessed the third Super Bowl victory for the Washington Redskins football team, the opening of the distinguished National Holocaust Memorial Museum, and the 150th birthday of the Smithsonian Institution. Milestones of the late '90s include the grand reopening of the renovated Library of Congress, dedication of the inspiring Franklin Delano Roosevelt and Women in Military Service memorials, a $400 million facelift for Ronald Reagan Washington National Airport, opening of the 20,000-seat MCI Center sports/entertainment arena, and construction of the huge Ronald Reagan

Building and International Trade Centre. A new convention center is in the works.

The city also continues to serve as an esteemed meeting place. In April of 1999, representatives from 19 nations converged on Washington for the 50th Anniversary Summit meeting of the North Atlantic Treaty Organization (NATO). The massive event went off without a hitch, even through local residents anticipated massive traffic tie-ups and impenetrable crowds of tourists.

Whether you live here or are just passing through, now is your chance to take a closer look at Washington, D.C. and create your own personal history in this intriguing city.

The District's Neighbors

The areas that lie just beyond the District's borders—the city of Alexandria and counties of Arlington and Fairfax in Virginia, and the counties of Montgomery and Prince George's in Maryland—are themselves rich with history.

Alexandria was, until 1846, included in the Washington boundaries. Founded in 1749 by Scottish merchants along the banks of the Potomac, Alexandria served as a chief port of trade during the Revolutionary years. George Washington was a prominent town figure, active in Christ Church Parish and other civic organizations.

Another resident, esteemed soldier and statesman "Light-Horse" Harry Lee, in 1799 delivered the now-famous eulogy that described Washington as "First in war, first in peace, and first in the hearts of his countrymen." Lee's son Robert Edward, commander in chief of the Confederate armies during the Civil War, spent his childhood in Alexandria. Much of colonial Alexandria still stands, and its brick side streets and quaint town houses make Old Town Alexandria a popular tourist destination.

You'll also find remnants of Northern Virginia's past in the independent city of Falls Church, which celebrated its 300th birthday in 1999. Its historic namesake, The Falls Church, dating to 1769, stands at the corner of Fairfax and Washington Streets. People still worship in the building, which also served as a colonial recruitment facility and Civil War hospital. Falls Church's surrounding counties of Arlington and Fairfax also retain vestiges of earlier times. Robert E. Lee's Arlington House, Arlington National Cemetery, and in Fairfax City and County, several houses and fort sites still draw visitors interested in the Civil War. (Read the Civil War Sites chapter for more about these locations.) Glimpse the agrarian lifestyles that once flourished in these parts by watching living history programs at Fairfax County's Historic Sully, a 1794 plantation, and Claude Moore Colonial Farm at Turkey Run.

Amidst the residential developments, shopping centers and office buildings that proliferate in the modern-day counties of metro Maryland, you'll still find traces of the prehistoric wilderness once roamed by Native Americans and discovered by English settlers like Captain John Smith in the 1600s. Prince George's County, which celebrated its tricentennial in 1996, originally included land that's now part of Washington, D.C. Once a thriving tobacco society, P.G. County still boasts historic homes and plantations, like the circa-1811 Marietta in Glenn Dale, the 1780s' Montpelier Mansion in Laurel, and, dating to 1694, Darnall's Chance in Upper Marlboro. The circa-1828 White's Ferry on the Potomac River and the C&O Canal's mule-pulled boats transport visitors to bygone days in Montgomery County, which has evolved from an agrarian community to an industrial center nicknamed "gateway to the nation's capital."

(Read more about D.C.'s neighbors in our Metro Washington Overview chapter.)

International Washington

The original plans for the Nation's Capital were drafted by a Frenchman, Pierre L'Enfant, so it seems only logical that Metro Washington would develop into a vibrant international crossroads. You don't have to look far to find some of the ingredients for this melting pot of people and traditions.

It's Chinatown, where the spirit of cross-cultural friendship is symbolized in the glittering archway that spans the width of a thoroughfare. It's Adams Morgan, where native Latinos, Ethiopians, Nigerians, Jamaicans, and others have forged a neighborhood of extraordinary contrasts, a place where many of the 100 or so restaurants serve global cuisine. It's Embassy Row, where the diplomatic corps—several thousand strong from over 150 nations—embodies the meaning of international communication, cooperation, trade, and goodwill. It's Arlington, where Vietnamese, Laotians, Cambodians, Koreans, Thai, Filipinos, and other Asian groups have prospered as merchants and small business owners. It's virtually anywhere in the region where you'll find proud people who fled war-torn, famine-ravaged, economically distressed, or brutally oppressive homelands to begin life anew here in professions as disparate as cab driver, banker, store clerk, police officer, computer technician, engineer, maintenance worker, craftsperson, scientist, and artist. It's the presence of institutions such as the World Bank, the International Monetary Fund, and the Organization of American States that speaks volumes about living and working in a global economy and a drastically shrinking world.

During the 1990s, the immigrant population boomed in the Washington area, with most jurisdictions doubling the number of residents born outside of the United States living within their borders. And unlike previous immigrants, who mainly settled inside the city, most have made the suburbs home. From 1990 through 1999, immigrants took up residence in Montgomery County, Maryland, and Fairfax, Virginia, at a rate of about 10,000 in each county, each year. Immigrants now account for 26 percent of Montgomery County's population and 23 percent of Fairfax County's residents, according to the *Census 2000 Supplementary Survey,* a national sample of households taken along with the census. These two counties rank near the top nationally for the percentages of households where foreign languages are spoken, from Korean to Farsi. By comparison, immigrants make up only 12 percent of the residents of the District of Columbia.

Patterns of immigration become apparent as you drive around the metro area and simply look out the window. In Annandale, Korean restaurants and shops line the roads. Langley Park in Prince George's County is overwhelmingly Latino. Falls Church's Seven Corners is home to what is reportedly the nation's largest Asian-oriented shopping center, Eden Center, with more than 100 Vietnamese and Chinese stores and restaurants. The largest immigrant population in the area, some 75,000, hail from war-ravaged El Salvador.

This chapter offers a glimpse of Metro Washington's colorful and diverse character. Note that diversions such as ethnic dining are not covered here, so please see the Restaurants chapter for suggestions on gastronomic globetrotting.

The Organization of American States (OAS) is the oldest international regional organization in the world. PHOTO: COURTESY OF ORGANIZATION OF AMERICAN STATES

Resources for International Visitors

International Monetary Fund Center
700 19th St. NW
Washington, DC
(202) 623–6869
www.imf.org

This intergovernmental agency's 156 member nations promote international monetary cooperation and assist in the expansion and balanced growth of global trade. The IMF also oversees the international monetary system and helps member nations overcome short-term financial problems. A new visitor center has exhibits on the history of the international monetary system and IMF's role, video programs, a bookstore, and a host of educational programs for school groups.

Meridian International Center
1630 Crescent Pl. NW
Washington, DC
(202) 667–6800, (202) 939–5544
www.meridian.org

This nonprofit educational and cultural institution, located in two splendid mansions, has a number of educational outreach programs, both for international visitors to the United States and for United States citizens interested in other cultures. It offers seminars on international political issues, intercultural briefings for those relocating or visiting a foreign country (including those coming to the United States), educational workshops, and arts programs.

Perhaps most valuable to the non-English speaker is Meridian's language bank, a service open during weekly business hours and providing immediate help for visitors trying to make themselves understood. Washington museums and Metrorail tap into the bank when at a loss for a translation. Meridian then transfers the tourist to a three-way telephone call with a native speaker of his or her language.

Organization of American States (OAS)
17th St. and Constitution Ave. NW
Washington, DC
(202) 458–3000
www.oas.org

Formed in 1890, the OAS is the oldest international regional organization in the world, providing a forum for political, economic, social, and cultural cooperation among the member states of the Western Hemisphere, including nations in North, Central, and South America and the Caribbean. The headquarters are in a magnificent white marble building just opposite the Ellipse. OAS offers free tours of its beautiful grounds and gardens and also maintains a speakers bureau. Latin American art and antiquities are showcased in the OAS Gallery as well as at the Art Museum of the Americas, an OAS annex at 201 18th Street NW, between Constitution Avenue and C Street. The museum offers slide sets, videocassettes, and publications on Latin

American art. Admission is free, and tours are available. Call (202) 458-6016 for more information.

Travelers' Aid Society
1612 K St. NW, Ste. 506
(202) 546–1127
www.travelersaid.org/ta/dc.htm
The society maintains information desks at all Washington airports as well as Union Station (AMTRAK rail arrivals). Special assistance for U.S. and foreign travelers is available at the airports from 9:00 A.M. to 9:00 P.M. weekdays and 9:00 A.M. to 6:00 P.M. on weekends.

Washington Convention and Tourism Corporation
1212 New York Ave. NW
Washington, DC
(202) 789–7000
www.washington.org
This association serves as a clearinghouse for all tourist information and can direct you to useful foreign language resources, tours, and phone numbers, either in their own organization or elsewhere.

Washington Metrorail
600 5th St. NW
Washington, DC
(202) 637–7000
www.wmata.com
Call this number to obtain free subway and bus maps in a variety of languages or go to the Web site for help with trip planning. Routes are clearly marked, as are transfer points—a useful tool for any tourist.

World Bank
1818 H St. NW
Washington, DC
(202) 477–1234
www.worldbank.org
Officially named the International Bank for Reconstruction and Development, the World Bank's main goal is to promote long-term economic growth that reduces poverty in developing nations. A major way of doing this is by providing loans and financing investments that contribute to economic growth. Although it does not provide the community outreach and one-stop shop for resources that the IMF provides, anyone research-

Washington Metro provides free subway and bus maps in a variety of languages to assist international travelers who use the transportation system. PHOTO: COURTESY OF WASHINGTON METROPOLITAN AREA TRANSPORTATION AUTHORITY

ing international economic issues should contact the bank.

The Allure of Embassy Row

Few aspects of life here are more strongly identified with international Washington than the diplomatic community. The images—stereotypical but fairly accurate in most cases—are easy to conjure up: elegant residences in fashionable neighborhoods, lavish receptions and other power social functions, limousine motorcades, large and attentive staffs, instant access to political leaders, and other establishment players and, of course, perhaps the ultimate perk: diplomatic immunity.

Ambassadors and their staffs do enjoy many special privileges, one of which is protection from many of the laws that the rest of us have to obey. This isn't to say that diplomats abuse the system and intentionally break laws knowing that they won't have to make amends, but in the event that things do happen, suffice it to say they receive considerations that go beyond the realm of even preferential treatment. Occasionally, you'll read stories of a particular embassy that has amassed, let's say, several thousand dollars worth of parking tickets and other minor violations and is being asked by the city to fork over the dough. Don't bet the mortgage on how those cases turn out.

It's tough to explain the degree to which diplomatic coddling is taken, so who better than the U.S. State Department to offer a summary explanation. Quoting Article 29 of the *Vienna Convention on Diplomatic Relations,* as found in the official Diplomatic List: "The person of a diplomatic agent shall be inviolable. He/she shall not be liable to any form of arrest or detention. The receiving State shall treat him/her with due respect and shall take all appropriate steps to prevent any attack on his/her person, freedom, or dignity." Make of it what you will.

Approximately 150 "embassies" (by law, the private residences of ambassadors and family) and "chanceries" (offices where all the work gets done) are in D.C., including those representing such geographic mind-benders as Burkina Faso, Cape Verde, Myanmar, Benin, Belarus, Mali, and the former Soviet republic of Kyrgyzstan. Chanceries are often staid and

Embassy Row on Massachusetts Avenue is where the majority of the capital's 140-plus embassies are located. PHOTO: COURTESY OF WASHINGTON, DC CONVENTION AND TOURISM CORPORATION

Embassy Listings

Unfortunately, there's no central telephone number the public can call for general information on embassies and their resources. But you can log onto www.embassy.org to get general information on each embassy. We've listed the chancery addresses, phone numbers, and Web sites of the 25 most prominent diplomatic missions. Public- or cultural-affairs personnel can help with questions and referrals. Because the turnover rate in the diplomatic corps is rather high (the diplomatic list is updated every three months), we didn't include names.

Argentina, 1600 New Hampshire Avenue NW, (202) 939–6400,
   www.embajadaargentina-usa.org
Australia, 1601 Massachusetts Avenue NW, (202) 797–3000, www.austemb.org
Brazil, 3006 Massachusetts Avenue NW, (202) 238–2700, www.brazilemb.org
Canada, 501 Pennsylvania Avenue NW, (202) 682–1740, www.canadianembassy.org
China, 2300 Connecticut Avenue NW, (202) 328–2500, www.china-embassy.org
Egypt, 3521 International Court NW, (202) 895–5400,
   www.embassyofegyptwashingtondc.org
France, 4101 Reservoir Road NW, (202) 944–6000, www.info-france-usa.org
Germany, 4645 Reservoir Road NW, (202) 298–4000, www.germany-info.org
Great Britain, 3100 Massachusetts Avenue NW, (202) 462–1340, www.britain-info.org
Greece, 2221 Massachusetts Avenue NW, (202) 939–5800, www.greekembassy.org
India, 2107 Massachusetts Avenue NW, (202) 939–7000, www.indianembassy.org
Israel, 3514 International Drive NW, (202) 364–5500, www.israelemb.org
Italy, 3000 Whitehaven St., NW, (202) 612–4400, www.italyemb.org
Japan, 2520 Massachusetts Avenue NW, (202) 238–6700, www.embjapan.org
Mexico, 1911 Pennsylvania Avenue NW, (202) 728–1600, www.embassyofmexico.org
Netherlands, 4200 Linnean Avenue NW, (202) 244–5300,
   www.netherlandsembassy.org
Philippines, 1600 Massachusetts Avenue NW, (202) 467–9300
Russia, 2650 Wisconsin Avenue NW, (202) 298–5700, www.russianembassy.org
Saudi Arabia, 601 New Hampshire Avenue NW, (202) 342–3800,
   www.saudiembassy.net
South Africa, 3051 Massachusetts Avenue NW, (202) 232–4400
South Korea, 2370 Massachusetts Avenue NW, (202) 939–5600, www.koreaemb.org
Spain, 2375 Pennsylvania NW, (202) 452–0100, www.spainemb.org
Sweden, 1501 M St. NW, (202) 467–2600, www.swedenemb.org
Switzerland, 2900 Cathedral Avenue NW, (202) 745–7900, www.swissemb.org
Turkey, 1714 Massachusetts Avenue NW, (202) 659–8200, www.turkey.org

rather industrial looking, while many of the embassies are gracious old mansions, painstakingly restored, complete with manicured lawns and gardens and massive gates. Diplomatic residences are clustered primarily in the historic northwest neighborhood of Kalorama, located north of Dupont Circle, and along Massachusetts Avenue northwest between Sheridan and Observatory Circles, thus the common reference to the area as Embassy Row. Some embassies, however, are scattered throughout other parts of town. Coats of arms and flags identify each diplomatic mission, though not all are easy to spot from the street.

Although you're unlikely to have much success walking up to an embassy and asking for a peek inside, some swing their doors open to the public a few times a year during organized tours, often as important fundraisers for charitable causes (see Annual Events). The walking/bus tours are a great way to see some beautiful homes and get a rare up-close look at a unique world.

Embassies are wonderful, often overlooked sources of information on culture, customs, history, and other facets of a nation, as well as on a broad range of travel and tourism topics, and it's all usually free. Many diplomatic missions, particularly some of the larger ones representing Canada, Mexico, Australia, and western European nations, also offer wonderful outreach programs, lectures, art exhibits, and more that are open to the public. In any one month, you might find a series of Aboriginal films at the Australian Embassy, a symposium at the Canadian Embassy on implications of the North American Free Trade Agreement, or a lecture on gourmet cooking at the French Embassy. Embassies can also direct citizens to area social clubs and various ethnic organizations.

Hurdling Monetary Barriers

Besides most major banks and airports, local firms specializing in currency exchange include:

Thomas Cook Currency Services. This service is a subsidiary of the large British-based travel and currency-exchange company. Aside from the usual posts at the airports, Ronald Reagan Washington National and Washington Dulles International, there are also two offices in Washington, D.C.: Union Station, 50 Massachusetts Avenue NE, Washington, D.C., (202) 371-9219; and 1800 K Street NW, Washington, D.C., (202) 872-1233. For more information, visit the Web site at www.us.thomascook.com.

American Express Travel Service. There are several locations throughout the metropolitan area. The Washington, D.C. locations are at 1150 Connecticut Avenue NW, Washington, D.C., (202) 457-1300; and at 5300 Wisconsin Avenue NW, Washington, D.C., (202) 362-4000.

In Virginia American Express can be found at Pentagon City Mall, 1100 South Hayes Street, Arlington, Virginia, (703) 415-5400; Springfield Mall, exit 169A off I-95, Springfield, Virginia, (703) 971-5600; and at Tysons Galleria, exit 11 B off I-495, 2001 International Drive, McLean, Virginia, (703) 893-3550.

Speaking the Language

If words, not money, are the problem, there are several major translation services available:

Berlitz Translation Services, 1050 Connecticut Avenue NW, Washington, D.C., (202) 331-1160; Tysons Corner Center, 2070 Chain Bridge Road, McLean, Virginia, (703) 883-0627; or 11300 Rockville Pike, Rockville, Maryland, (301) 770-7550. The Web site is at www.berlitz. com.

The Interpreters Bureau, 1660 L Street NW, Washington, D.C., (202) 296-1346.

The Language Exchange, 2305 Calvert Street NW, Washington, D.C., (202) 328-0099, www.languageexchange. com.

Meridian International Center Language Bank, 1630 Crescent Place NW, Washington, D.C., (202) 667-6800, (202) 939-5544, www.meridian.org.

Insiders' Tip

Don't overlook the sometimes-forgotten wealth of resources offered by embassies and numerous international organizations in Washington.

Ethnic Neighborhoods

Adams Morgan is one of the Washington, D.C., neighborhoods you don't want to miss touring. Its hub is at 18th Street and Columbia Road NW. The area is alive with restaurants, bars, nightclubs, shops, boutiques, and a host of other attractions, many of which revolve around the community's Caribbean, Latin American, and African roots.

Chinatown encompasses 8 blocks bordered by H Street and 6th and 9th Streets NW. It is 3 blocks from the D.C. Convention Center, 7 blocks from Capitol Hill, and sits conveniently atop the Gallery Place station on Metrorail's Red Line. You will again see restaurants and shops galore.

The social highlight of the year is undoubtedly the Chinese New Year celebration each January and February. Perhaps the neighborhood's most visible symbol, the glittering jewel-tone Friendship Archway spans H Street at 7th. Decorated in the classical art of the Ming and Ch'ing dynasties and featuring four pillars and five roofs, the $1 million project was paid for and built jointly by the D.C. government and Beijing in 1986. The two capital cities pledged in 1984 to create a mutually beneficial relationship emphasizing cultural, economic, educational, and technical exchanges with a goal of making Washington's Chinatown a world-class center for Asian trade and finance.

International Landmarks

Landmarks, both natural and man-made, are as much a part of Washington's international landscape as its people. Here's a quick look at a few of the monuments and landmarks that have a distinct international flavor. Countries of all sizes are an integral part of the Nation's Capital. Among the most prominent influences:

Japanese cherry trees were a gift from the city of Tokyo in 1909. More than 3,000 of these gorgeous specimens dot the landscape near the Jefferson Memorial, the adjacent Tidal Basin, and nearby Hains Point. Because the original trees were

> **Insiders' Tip**
>
> If you're in search of a number of international dining options near one another, consider spending an evening in Arlington, Bethesda, Wheaton, Adams Morgan, or Chinatown.

infected by a fungus, the Department of Agriculture had them destroyed. Replacements arrived in 1912 and were officially welcomed by First Lady Helen Taft and the wife of the Japanese ambassador. Several of these specimens were lost in 1999 after a family of eager beavers had their way with them. After weeks of effort and headline attention, officials finally snared the beavers and moved them upstream to a more rural location.

Saving the trees was deemed a national priority. You see, each April (with a little cooperation from Mother Nature), in what is surely one of the most welcome harbingers of spring, the trees sprout their brilliant pink-and-white blossoms. Thousands of passersby enjoy seeing the blooming trees during the weeklong National Cherry Blossom Festival, but the dazzling "peak" period lasts only a few days. The weather greatly affects the arrival, brilliance, and longevity of the blossoms, so listen for the National Park Service's blossom forecasts as spring approaches.

The Netherlands Carillon is an often-overlooked landmark that has strong foreign ties. After World War II the Dutch government gave the 49-bell tower to the United States in gratitude. Looming over Arlington near the Marine Corps War Memorial (Iwo Jima statue) and Arlington National Cemetery, it is surrounded by a sea of tulips. It is also the site of numerous summer and holiday concerts.

Even Washington's most famous landmark, the Washington Monument, has global influence. The 555-foot obelisk—the world's largest masonry structure—contains nearly 200 memorial stones in its interior walls. Among the stones are a block of lava from Italy's infamous Mount Vesuvius, a mosaic block from the ruins of Carthage (present-day Tunisia), a stone from the Swiss chapel of William Tell, and a stone praising George Washington in Chinese. There is also a replica of the stone given by Pope Pius IX. The original stone was stolen by a radical anti-Catholic group in 1854 and dumped in the Potomac. The replacement, a gift to the National Park Service in 1982, is Italian marble inscribed in Latin with the phrase *A Roma Americae,* meaning "From Rome to America."

Heritage Festivals

What better way to honor the diverse heritage of Metro Washingtonians than with parties, parades, festivals, and other such events. Each year literally starts with a bang as the colorful Chinese Lunar New Year parade draws thousands with music, firecrackers, and colorful costumes. In spring several metro-area municipalities celebrate St. Patrick's Day with their own parades. You can binge on traditional green beer and corned beef and cabbage.

Choose any month of the year and you're likely to find an ethnic celebration in Washington. The Greek, British, Hispanic—they're all ready to party in their unique ways. For a great mix of them all, catch the popular Smithsonian Festival of American Folk Life, which highlights our diverse cultural background. The annual festival is held over a 10-day period in late June and early July (always including the 4th). (For more on these and other celebrations, turn to the Annual Events chapter.)

Cultural Immersion

Almost every nation has an interest group located in Washington, but most of them focus on promoting their agendas to the media and the U.S. government. If you want to delve deeper into the multicultural side of Washington, many organizations provide public outreach. For more information, contact the following:

Washington, D.C.

Alliance Française de Washington
2142 Wyoming Ave. NW
Washington, DC
(202) 234–7911
www.francedc.org

This organization has branches throughout the world and in other major U.S. cities. Native speakers provide French lessons and cultural and social activities are available, all at a reasonable cost.

Association of American Foreign Service Women
5125 MacArthur Blvd. NW
Washington, DC
(202) 362–6514
www.kreative.net/fslifelines

Foreign service families moving in and out of Washington are often strangers to the city and its international resources. This organization provides a home base for such families and helps them cope with their itinerant lifestyles. As the name implies, it has close ties with the U.S. State Department and can serve as a resource for those stationed in Washington and abroad.

> ## Insiders' Tip
> Parking is scarce and traffic can be a hassle, so take Metrorail or some other form of public transportation to downtown monuments like the Lincoln Memorial or to annual festivals such as the Chinese New Year parade.

Central American Resource Center
1459 Columbia Rd. NW
Washington, D.C.
(202) 328–9799
www.incacorp.com/carecen

This advocacy organization provides direct legal services on immigration issues to the enormous Latino community in the D.C. area.

Goethe Institut
814 7th St. NW
Washington, DC
(202) 289–1200
www.goethe.dc/uk/was

This active nonprofit organization's mission is promoting the German language and culture worldwide. It is run with impressive Teutonic efficiency and offers a wide variety of cultural activities, media outreach, and German language classes.

Hispanic Service Center
1805 Belmont Rd. NW
Washington, DC
(202) 234–3435

Not a tourist organization, nor exactly one for cultural exchange, this service center is instead a resource for Spanish speakers in America who need help with government documents, translation, housing, and other daily life issues.

The Hospitality Information Service (THIS)
1630 Crescent Pl. NW
Washington, DC
(202) 232–3002
www.meridian.org

THIS is like a Welcome Wagon for foreign diplomats stationed in Washington. It serves as a valuable source of information as they settle here, providing lists of schools, stores, hospitals, and other crucial information. THIS also sponsors social and cultural events to help introduce diplomatic community members to one another.

Islamic Center
2551 Massachusetts Ave. NW
Washington, DC
(202) 332–8343

The Islamic Center's primary mission is managing the Washington mosque, which is in the same building (see the Worship chapter). The center also offers Arabic language classes and periodic cultural events.

Japan Information and Culture Center
1155 21st St. NW
Washington, DC
(202) 238–6900
www.embjapan.org

There is perhaps no diplomatic outlet in Washington quite like the expansive Japan Information and Culture Center, an adjunct of the Japanese Embassy and definitely the top local authority on all things Japanese. The center offers a friendly, helpful staff; permanent exhibit space for showings by a wide range of Japanese artists; and a calendar of events filled with programs about Japan and its people.

Japan-America Society of Washington
1020 19th St. NW, LL Ste. 40
Washington, DC
(202) 833–2210
www.us-japan.org/dc

Japan is an enigma to most Americans, and the Japan-America Society seeks to bridge the gap of understanding with exchanges of information on business, culture, and the arts. The society promotes several concerts and performances a year at venues throughout Washington, as well as smaller gatherings aimed at those doing business in or touring Japan. It can also direct you to Japanese language classes by native speakers.

Meridian International Center
1630 Crescent Pl. NW
Washington, DC
(202) 667–6800, (202) 939–5544
www.meridian.org

Please refer to the beginning of this chapter, where we have included a full listing for the Meridian International Center.

National Council for International Visitors
1420 K St. NW
Washington, DC
(202) 842–1414
www.nciv.org

The council is a national network of program agencies and community-based organizations that provide services to participants in international exchange programs. These nonprofit groups design and implement professional programs and internships and provide cultural activities and home hospitality opportunities for foreign officials and international scholars.

Suburban Maryland

Italian Cultural Society of Washington, DC
4500 North Park Ave., Ste. 806N
Chevy Chase, MD
(202) 333–2426
www.italianculturesociety.org

This group provides language lessons and once-a-month social gatherings for Italians or anyone practicing the language.

Muslim Community Center
15200 New Hampshire Ave.
Silver Spring, MD
(301) 384–3454
www.mccmd.org

This is the largest Muslim Center in Maryland, providing a wide range of services for the Muslim community. The center operates a full-time school, the Islamic Academy of MCC, and plans to expand its facilities and services even further.

Accommodations

Extended-Stay Hotels
and Inns

Full-Service Hotels

On a Budget

Hostels/University Inns

Finding a room at the inn isn't a difficult task in Metro Washington. Hotels, motels, and special extended-stay lodgings are almost as common a sight in the Nation's Capital as lawyers and lobbyists . . . well, almost.

All kidding aside, the lodging industry is a big, big business here. Hotels and motels are the single largest contributor to the region's approximately $5.2 billion tourism industry. All told, there are about 65,000 hotel and motel rooms in the metro area, ranging from the ultra luxurious to the merely functional.

As a general rule of thumb, hotels in the suburbs, even close-in areas, are priced less than D.C. properties. That's not always the case, but it's pretty safe to say you can find a slew of real values out there as long as you don't mind being a bit off the beaten path. No matter where you stay, the area's comprehensive public transportation system (especially Metrorail and Metrobus) does an excellent job linking hotels with business and tourist areas. You'll discover that many hotels also offer their own shuttle and limousine services to destinations around the area.

Another rule of thumb is that the Washington tourism industry reaches its peak in spring and fall. Occupancy rates are at their highest during these months, and so too are room prices. Planning ahead is never a bad idea.

No matter what time of year, Metro Washington hotels do the bulk of their business Monday through Thursday hosting the area's business travelers. Many hotels cut their rates on weekends, sometimes as much as 50 to 60 percent. With that in mind, always feel free to negotiate for the best deal and always inquire about weekend, off-season, holiday, corporate, and family rates.

The best source we know to keep you informed of the latest seasonal rate discounts and other special hotel package programs is the Washington, D.C. Convention and Tourism Corporation (202–789–7000). When in town, also be sure to stop by the new D.C. Chamber of Commerce Visitor Information Center, located on the street level of the Ronald Reagan Building and International Trade Center at 1300 Pennsylvania Avenue NW (across from the Federal Triangle Metro Center). You can make hotel and restaurant reservations there, as well as buy tickets for local tours and even send an e-mail postcard back home. The center's number is (202) DC–VISIT. Its Web site is www.dcvisit.com.

We've divided this chapter into several categories, beginning with a section on extended-stay accommodations. For those of you who plan to house hunt in the area, who might be on a short-term work assignment, or just simply need a place to call home for a while, the extended-stay section is intended to give you an overview of some of the region's best options. Almost all the choices here include properties that have kitchenettes, many with separate living areas as well.

We follow with a section called Full-Service Hotels. This is intended for tourists, newcomers, and longtime residents alike who are looking for, or need to recommend, interesting, practical, and/or memorable places to spend a night in Metro Washington.

If you look hard enough, you'll find that the District, Northern Virginia, and Suburban Maryland all have more than their share of hotel bargains—some you might even call steals. To help you along, we've listed some of our favorite values in the On a Budget section. Believe us, no one appreciates a bargain more than writers.

A short section on hostels and university inns lists some of the unsung and nontraditional accommodations found only in Washington, D.C.

Although the following lists are by no means exhaustive, we feel they represent some of the best and most viable choices available in each category.

Price Code

To give you an idea of what to expect price-wise, we've provided the following scale as a very general guide. It is based on the average cost for double occupany, during peak season.

$ . . . . .Under $100
$$ . . . .$100 to $149
$$$ . . . .$150 to $200
$$$$ . . . . .More than $200

All hotels listed accept most major credit cards. Virtually every establishment listed also extends some kind of weekend or off-season rates.

Extended-Stay Hotels and Inns

Washington, D.C.

Best Western New Hampshire Suites Hotel
1121 New Hampshire Ave. NW
Washington, DC
(202) 457–0565
www.bestwestern.com/newhampshire
suiteshotel
$$–$$$$

This newly renovated property offers 76 suites with kitchenettes, complimentary continental breakfasts, and valet parking. Bring along the jogging shoes and shorts, for you're only a hop and a skip from Rock Creek Park and its miles and miles of gorgeous wooded trails and running paths.

Capitol Hill Suites
200 C St. SE
Washington, DC
(202) 543–6000, (800) 424–9165
$$$$

You can stay a night, a week, a month, or a year at this flexible, all-suite property just a short walk from the Capitol, the Library of Congress, the Supreme Court, Metro, and other "Hill" destinations. All 152 suites have kitchens. It's a popular extended-stay choice among government and private sector workers with ties to Capitol Hill. To accommodate that clientele, the hotel offers complimentary continental breakfast and newspaper, valet parking, and lunch or dinner delivery from area restaurants.

Carlyle Suites Hotel
1731 New Hampshire Ave. NW
Washington, DC
(202) 234–3200, (866) HOTEL–DC
www.carlylesuites.com
$$$

This art deco, all-suite hotel in the trendy Dupont Circle area offers rooms with fully equipped kitchens, a health club, a coin-operated laundry, and free parking. From here, you're just a 2-block walk from the Dupont Circle Metro station and tons of galleries, restaurants, boutiques and bars. Pets are accepted.

Embassy Square, Summerfield Suites by Wyndham
2000 N St. NW
Washington, DC
(202) 659–9000, (800) 424–2999
www.staydc.com
$$$

This 278-suite facility offers efficiencies, suites, and even two-bedroom, two-bath apartments. Popular with relocating families and executives on short-term assignments, Embassy Square sits in the heart of the Dupont Circle neighborhood, about equal distance from the White House and Georgetown. Each suite comes with a kitchenette, and guests are given free reign of an off-premise health club as well as an on-site swimming pool. There's a free continental breakfast, same-day valet service, and an on-site convenience store.

Embassy Suites Hotel Downtown
1250 22nd St. NW
Washington, DC
(202) 857–3388
www.embassysuitesdcmetro.com
$$$$

This West End addition to the national chain boasts two-room suites with separate living rooms (including queen-size sofa beds) and bedrooms. Standard in each suite are two color TVs, two phones with voice mail, data-port hookup, a kitchenette, iron, and hair dryer. The upscale 318-suite property is close to everything: downtown, Dupont Circle, Foggy Bottom, and Georgetown. Guests receive complimentary cooked-to-order breakfasts, and there's room service available from the Italian restaurant on-site. Both an indoor swimming pool and health club are on the grounds. This is an especially popular place with families, which is not surprising because kids 12 and under eat for free.

Georgetown Suites
1111 30th St. NW
Washington, DC
(202) 298–7800, (800) 348–7203
www.georgetownsuites.com
$$$

This is an ideal choice for extended stays that require you to be in or near Georgetown. All 214 suites have kitchenettes with refrigerators and coffeemakers, and come equipped with irons, hair dryers, and computer outlets. The facility has a health club and a multilingual staff. Georgetown Suites is frequented by corporate managers and government employees on short-term assignment. The surrounding Washington Harbour complex is a stunning waterfront development that also houses restaurants, gift shops, boutiques, and the like.

Lincoln Suites Downtown
1823 L St. NW
Washington, DC
(202) 223–4320
www.lincolnhotels.com
$$$

Somewhat of a sleeper (no pun intended), the Lincoln Suites, formerly known as

Insiders' Tip
Book hotels early if you plan to come during the first week of April when the cherry trees bloom. This is peak tourist season.

Hotel Anthony, shouldn't be overlooked. This moderately priced, all-suite hotel is in the middle of downtown, only 5 blocks from the White House and convenient to monuments, museums, and Metro. Kid-friendly, all suites have VCRs, and there's a large stock of children's movies for the asking, along with free cookies.

One Washington Circle
1 Washington Circle NW
Washington, DC
(202) 872–1680, (800) 424–9671
$$$$

All 151 units here include kitchens and some feature balconies. Just across the circle is George Washington University and Foggy Bottom Metro. Also in walking distance are the Kennedy Center, Georgetown, Dupont Circle, and parts of downtown. This property is often frequented by performers from the Kennedy Center who drop into the on-site West End Cafe and piano lounge (see Restaurants and Nightlife chapters).

The River Inn
924 25th St. NW
Washington, DC
(202) 337–7600, (800) 424–2741
www.theriverinn.com
$$$

It's not on the Potomac, but the river's not too far away. Nor is most of Georgetown and all of Foggy Bottom. All 126 units in this former apartment house are suites, each with a full kitchen. Small pets are welcome. It's a nice place to unwind after an evening at the Kennedy Center, just a couple of blocks away.

St. James Suites
950 24th St. NW
Washington, DC
(202) 457–0500, (800) 852–8512
www.stjamessuiteswdc.com
$$$

The St. James is an upscale all-suite property that can be checked into for a night, a month, or longer. It's near 24th and K Streets, just off Washington Circle and near Foggy Bottom Metro and George Washington University. Georgetown and Dupont Circle are also close. Full kitchens, marble baths, robes, child care, computer outlets, voice mail, a concierge, and a health club are among the numerous amenities. Not only do they serve a complimentary breakfast, but also complimentary hors d'oeuvres and cocktails. On nice days you can also enjoy the outdoor pool and sundeck.

Savoy Suites Georgetown
2505 Wisconsin Ave. NW
Washington, DC
(202) 337–9700, (800) 944–5347
www.savoysuites.com
$$$

This recently remodeled 150-suite hotel is in earshot of the inspiring Washington National Cathedral and is largely insulated from the hustle and congestion of closer-in lodgings. Many suites have in-room Jacuzzis and full kitchens, and you can request fridges and microwaves. There's also a swimming pool, coin-operated laundry, Metro shuttle, and on-site parking. Pets are welcome, too.

The State Plaza Hotel
2117 E St. NW
Washington, DC
(202) 861–8200, (800) 424–2859
$$$

Don't let the harried urban setting fool you. The State Plaza Hotel, across from the State Department in Foggy Bottom, is a quiet, self-contained world unto itself. The former apartment building now houses 225 spacious suites featuring separate kitchens and dining rooms, same-day valet, shoeshine, safety deposit boxes, garage parking, and fitness center. The

hotel is often frequented by government employees, especially State Department types, on short-term assignments.

The Swissôtel Washington—The Watergate
2650 Virginia Ave. NW
Washington, DC
(202) 965–2300
www.swissotel.com
$$$$

The new owners of the Watergate complex were smart to keep the name; they know the hotel will forever be known best as the site of the infamous "break-in" that ultimately ended the political career of President Richard M. Nixon. There's nothing suspicious about the hotel, however, one of the most luxurious in the District. Gracing the banks of the Potomac River, adjacent to the Kennedy Center, the Watergate has kitchenettes, personal valet service, complimentary limousine service, a swimming pool, and a health spa. There are 232 rooms, of which 85 are suites and 60 are junior suites. It's pricey, yes, but the experience is one that's quintessentially Washington.

Northern Virginia

Alexandria
The Executive Club Suites
610 Bashford La.
Alexandria, VA
(703) 739–2582, (877) 316–CLUB (2582)
www.dcexeclub.com
$$–$$$

This upscale all-suite property is at the north end of Old Town and is only a couple of minutes drive to National Airport. Various options are available, but the best values are with extended stays. The handsome rooms feature nineteenth-century reproductions, rich jewel tones, and the kind of comfortable furniture you might find in a very nice home. What's more, you have a separate living room, kitchen, and master bedroom, just like a true apartment. Other amenities include free continental breakfast, evening reception, health club with sauna, shuttle service, and outdoor pool.

Infamous as the site of the break-in that began the Nixon administration scandal, The Swissôtel Washington—The Watergate, is a favorite among tourists.

Sheraton Suites Alexandria
801 N. Asaph St.
Alexandria, VA
(703) 836–4700
www.sheraton.com
$$$

The Sheraton (once a Marriott) commands a superb location and has numerous amenities. Each newly renovated suite has a wet bar, refrigerator, coffeemaker, iron and ironing board, two TVs with remote-control, a VCR in the bedroom, and two telephones with call waiting. Guests also enjoy a pool and a health club. It's a 10-minute walk away from lower King Street, the nerve center of Old Town, and a five-minute drive from National Airport.

Arlington

The Executive Club Suites
108 S. Courthouse Rd.
Arlington, VA
(703) 522–2582, (877) 316–2582

1730 Arlington Blvd.
Rossyln, VA
(703) 525–2582
www.execlub.com
$$–$$$

Please see the Alexandria listing.

The Virginian Suites
1500 Arlington Blvd.
Arlington, VA
(703) 522–9600, (800) 275–2866
www.virginiansuites.com
$$

Specializing in month-to-month suites, the low-cost Virginian offers hotel convenience and basic comfort. The Rosslyn location is close to Metro, Georgetown, and most of Arlington and Alexandria. Guests receive Metro and grocery store shuttle service, maid service, cable TV, free utilities and parking, and access to an on-site swimming pool, fitness center, and saunas.

Fairfax County

Embassy Suites/Tysons Corner
8517 Leesburg Pike
Vienna, VA
(703) 883–0707
www.embassy-suites.com
$$$$

A Tysons Corner location—about halfway between Washington and Washington Dulles International Airport—makes this 232-suite property convenient to most points in Northern Virginia. Suites come with refrigerators and microwaves, and guests can help themselves to a free breakfast. There's also complimentary shuttle service, a fitness center, and indoor pool. The hotel is close to one of the world's largest office and shopping complexes, and just a few minutes drive from Wolf Trap, the nation's only national park for the performing arts (see The Arts chapter for more information on Wolf Trap).

Marriott Residence Inn Herndon/Reston
315 Elden St.
Herndon, VA
(703) 435–0044
www.residenceinn.com
$$$

Short- and long-term stays are made easy at this all-suite Marriott property about 5 miles east of Dulles Airport in the town of Herndon. One- and two-bedroom suites come with fireplaces. Pets are permitted. The Marriott has a pool and fitness area and also offers free parking and shuttle service to the Dulles airport. It's near AOL and numerous other high-tech companies.

Marriott Suites/Washington Dulles
13101 Worldgate Dr.
Herndon, VA
(703) 709–0400
www.marriott.com
$$$$

A turnkey home base for house-hunters in Fairfax and Loudoun counties, Marriott Suites/Washington Dulles is, as the name suggests, close to the airport but also within a few minutes drive of some of the most desirable suburban neighborhoods in Northern Virginia. Besides all the perks you'd expect from this national chain, the hotel is adjacent to Worldgate Athletic Club, one of the nation's largest, and close to the new Dulles Town Center, with numerous shopping, dining, and nightlife options.

Suburban Maryland

Montgomery County

Marriott Suites Bethesda
6711 Democracy Blvd.
Bethesda, MD
(301) 897–5600
www.marriott.com
$$$$

House-hunters in Montgomery County and upper Northwest Washington would do well to consider Marriott Suites Bethesda as a temporary command center. It's near the intersection of the Beltway and I–270, Marriott Corporation's world headquarters, and IBM. Guests here enjoy free parking, an indoor/outdoor swimming pool, health club, restaurant, and all the amenities you'd expect from this service-oriented national chain.

TownePlace Suites by Marriott
212 Perry Pkwy.
Gaithersburg, MD
(301) 590–2300, (800) 257–3000
www.towneplace.com
$$

With studio, one-bedroom, and two-bedroom suites, TownePlace provides a moderately priced home base for extended stays in Washington's northern suburbs. TownePlace has an exercise room, pool, and coin laundry. The hotel is located near Montgomery County's booming technology corridor along I–270 and Lakeforest Mall. Pets are allowed.

Prince George's County

Comfort Inn and Suites College Park
9020 Baltimore Blvd.
College Park, MD
(301) 441–8110
www.hotelchoice.com/hotel/md611
$$–$$$

The renovated hotel offers regular rooms as well as 33 suites. It's convenient for parents of University of Maryland students as well as travelers who need access to Baltimore-Washington International Airport, 25 miles away. Suites offer fridges, in-room coffeemakers, and complimentary breakfast with newspaper. You'll also find a coin-operated laundry, health club, and outdoor pool.

Full-Service Hotels

Washington, D.C.

Capital Hilton Hotel
16th and K Sts. NW
Washington, DC
(202) 393–1000
www.capital.hilton.com
$$$$

The 12-story, 543-room Capital Hilton is a short walk to most points downtown and just 2 blocks north of the White House. A massive renovation a few years ago resulted in new guest rooms with multiline phones and voice mail, business amenities on the top four floors, and a new health club. Not surprisingly, the hotel handles a large convention and tourist trade. Fran O'Brien's Steak House in the hotel is a hopping bar and restaurant, but more of a meet-and-greet place than a gourmet restaurant.

Channel Inn Hotel
650 Water St. SW
Washington, DC
(202) 554–2400, (800) 368–5668
www.channelinn.com
$$

This basic 100-room hotel is perched right on the Southwest waterfront, with beautiful views of East Potomac Park and nearby marinas. You're also a short walk to the venerable Arena Stage Theater, the National Mall, and the Smithsonian museums. Free parking is available, and guests can enjoy indoor as well as outdoor pools. This is also the home of the Pier 7 restaurant (see our Nightlife chapter), which features dining and dancing.

The Churchill Hotel
1914 Connecticut Ave. NW
Washington, DC
(202) 797–2000, (800) 424–2464
www.churchillhotel.com
$$$$

New owners recently changed the name of the former Hotel Sofitel Washington, but little has been altered in this large, elegant Dupont Circle hotel. The hotel boasts, and rightly so, a full-service business center and meeting rooms. There's a health club on the premises as well as a restaurant and piano lounge (see our Nightlife chapter). The hotel, which was renovated several years ago, has public rooms that are very impressive, guest rooms that are comfortable and geared to the business traveler, and an Embassy Row location that is equally accessible to Dupont Circle and downtown. It has 144 units, including 36 suites.

Four Seasons Hotel
2800 Pennsylvania Ave. NW
Washington, DC
(202) 342–0444
www.fourseasons.com
$$$$

Like so many of Washington's premium hotels, the Four Seasons is often frequented by the rich and famous. Rock stars are a common sight here, and a few years ago Donald Trump and Marla Maples staged a much-publicized brouhaha in the lobby. Despite the occasional weirdness, the Four Seasons is all class. Guests of this Georgetown gem can expect some of the best service in Washington, an outstanding concierge, a top-rated restaurant (Seasons), and a premiere fitness center with spa services, including herbal message and aromatherapy. The piano lounge is a hot spot for cocktails among the Washington business elite.

The Georgetown Inn
1310 Wisconsin Ave. NW
Washington, DC
(202) 333–8900, (800) 424–2979
www.georgetowninn.com
$$$$

If it's Georgetown you want, the Georgetown Inn is the place to be. Right in the nerve center of Washington's most popular nightlife district (the daylife ain't bad either), this intimate 96-unit inn offers complimentary coffee and the *Washington Post* every morning, overnight shoeshines, turndown service, and business services. Valet parking is available, an added plus in parking-scarce Georgetown.

The Grand Hyatt Washington
1000 H St. NW
Washington, DC
(202) 582–1234
www.washington.hyatt.com
$$$$

The Grand Hyatt covers all the bases. It sits across the street from the Convention Center and a half block from bustling Metro Center. Within a short walk are Pennsylvania Avenue and the White House, the National Theater, the Shops at National Place (see our Shopping chapter), and the Smithsonian museums. This gigantic 900-room property is built around a 7,000-square-foot lagoon with waterfalls, with a 12-story atrium glass roof overhead. Camp Hyatt facilities accommodate children, and of course there's a swimming pool and health club, not to mention five restaurants and a cigar bar. Extra perks include a kosher kitchen and a video checkout service.

The Hay-Adams Hotel
1 Lafayette Sq. NW
Washington, DC
(202) 638–6600, (800) 853–6807
www.hayadams.com
$$$$

One of our personal favorites, this ultra-luxurious, ultrahistoric property overlooks Lafayette Park and the White House to the south. Diplomats, politicians, and the who's who of the Washington elite, including former presidents and presidents-elect, bunk and dine at the Hay-Adams regularly. This is the ultimate Insiders' hotel but always accommodating to all. Valet parking, a full-time concierge, nightly turndown service, and butler service are just some of the amenities. Some rooms come with kitchenettes.

The Henley Park Hotel
926 Massachusetts Ave. NW
Washington, DC
(202) 638–5200, (800) 222–8474
$$$$

The Henley Park has emerged as one of the city's leading European-style hotels. This decorative 96-room property (formerly an apartment building) is less than

Former presidents and diplomats have been guests at the Hay-Adams Hotel, which overlooks the White House and Lafayette Park. PHOTO: COURTESY OF THE WASHINGTON, DC CONVENTION AND TOURISM CORPORATION

2 blocks from the Convention Center and near Union Station, Capitol Hill, and the National Mall. Guests are treated to express check-ins, minibars, complimentary limousine service on weekday mornings, overnight shoeshines, and health club privileges.

Hilton Washington Embassy Row
2015 Massachusetts Ave. NW
Washington, DC
(202) 265–1600
www.hilton.com
$$$$

Location, location, location is the theme here. In the city's embassy district, near Dupont Circle, the Embassy Row handles a large, well-heeled international clientele, including newcomers shopping for more permanent residences. A massive renovation several years ago spruced up this already-nice hotel with 193 rooms. The rooftop bar and pool is a great warm-weather hangout. There's also a health club on the premises.

Holiday Inn Capitol at the Smithsonian
550 C St. SW
Washington, DC
(202) 479–4000
www.holiday-inn.com
$$$$

A colleague visiting from South Dakota summed this place up best: "It's nothing super fancy, but it's a location you can't beat—right up close to the [National] Air and Space Museum." Indeed, the Holiday Inn Capitol knows its market. Tour groups take advantage of the takeout deli and moderate prices, considering the location. Kids pack the rooftop pool in summer. Not even Fido or Puff will be turned away here. Nonguests can park in the hotel's garage for $12 a day, a convenience if you prefer to drive rather than take Metro into the city for a Smithsonian visit.

Hotel Lombardy
2019 I St. NW
Washington, DC
(202) 828–2600, (800) 424–5486
www.hotellombardy.com
$$–$$$

An innlike hotel for those who want to be near everything, the Hotel Lombardy has 125 rooms with kitchenettes and mini-bars, free newspapers, VCRs, children's movies, and turndown service. Walk to the White House, West End, Foggy Bottom, downtown, and the National Mall. The Hotel Lombardy is an excellent value, when you consider its location.

Hotel Washington
15th and Pennsylvania Ave. NW
Washington, DC
(202) 638–5900, (800) 424–9540
www.hotelwashington.com
$$$$

One of the city's oldest hotels, the Hotel Washington sits across the street from the Treasury Department and around the corner from the White House. It is registered with the National Trust for Historic Preservation. You might find tour groups here; accordingly, ask about discounted room prices. The hotel's Roof Terrace lounge is and always has been, bar none, the best public place in the city to watch fireworks on July 4th or any of the annual parades along Pennsylvania Avenue. Bring your out-of-town guests here for an alfresco lunch with an awe-inspiring view. All 340 rooms, including 16 suites, have been renovated, and the hotel includes a fitness center with saunas.

Howard Johnson Plaza and Suites of
Washington, DC – A Taj Hotel
1430 Rhode Island Ave. NW
Washington, D.C.
(202) 462–7777
www.hojo.com
$$$

This convenient midtown hotel is popular with tour groups, thanks to its convenient location near two metro stops (DuPont Circle and McPherson Square) and just 5 blocks north of the White House. The neighborhood here is gracious by day, but borders a red-light district by night, so cab it when you go out to dinner. Still, the amenities of this 184-suite property are impressive, including walk-in kitchens, in-room safes, coin-operated laundry, underground valet parking, and outdoor rooftop pool.

One of the city's oldest hotels, the Hotel Washington sits across the street from the Treasury Department and around the corner from the White House. PHOTO: COURTESY OF HOTEL WASHINGTON

Hyatt Regency Washington on Capitol Hill
400 New Jersey Ave. NW
Washington, DC
(202) 737–1234
www.hyatt.com
$$$$

The Capitol Hill edition of this international chain comes with everything you'd expect: valet parking, video checkout service, a game room and children's suite, a beauty salon, swimming pool, and health club. The massive 834-room property is a block from the Capitol and 2 blocks from Union Station. The rooms are standard Hyatt, which means all the business-related amenities, but nothing fancy. Thirty-one of the units are suites. As you can imagine—given its size and location—the hotel commands a huge convention and tourist business.

The Jefferson Hotel, a Lowe's Hotel
1200 16th St. NW
Washington, DC
(202) 347–2200, (800) 368–5966
www.thejeffersonhotel.com
$$$$

A small and gracious hotel refuge amid the hustle of downtown, the Jefferson is popular with the old money elite who from time to time join the roster of presidential appointees. Many have taken apartments here, and it's no wonder, considering the understated, elegant surroundings. Each room offers complimentary bathrobes, hair dryers, one-hour pressing, multiline phones, minibars and VCRs, CD and cassette players, and 24-hour concierge. Swimming pool and health club privileges are available at the nearby University Club. Pets are accepted.

Jury's Normandy Inn
2118 Wyoming Ave. NW
Washington, DC
(202) 483–1350, (800) 424–3729
www.jurysdoyle.com
$$

The 75-room Normandy, in upper Northwest, is lodged between Rock Creek Park and Dupont Circle. This is an intimate, European-style inn in a residential neighborhood that includes a slew of embassies. Underground parking is available, as are on-site limousine and car-rental services. Rooms come with minifridges and coffeemakers, as well as valet service and a continental breakfast.

Jury's Washington Hotel
1500 New Hampshire Ave. NW
Washington, DC
(202) 483–6000
www.jurys.com
$$$

Recently purchased and renovated by Ireland's largest hotel group, Jury's Washington Hotel is right across the street from the Dupont Circle Metro station, close to some of the city's best art galleries, bookstores, boutiques, and restaurants. The 314 businesslike rooms come with wet bars, and there's a restaurant on the premises. This hotel caters to a lot of international groups.

JW Marriott
1331 Pennsylvania Ave. NW
Washington, DC
(202) 393–2000
www.marriott.com
$$$$

Part of downtown Washington's renaissance of the 1980s, this entry boasts 772 rooms as well as a passageway to The Shops at National Place (see our Shopping chapter). Just steps from the White House and the National Mall, the Marriott is big with conventions, tourists, and business travelers. There's a huge, marbled, multilevel lobby and lots of meeting and eating places. Not only are there a swimming pool and health club on the premises, but many business amenities, including a copy center, video messaging, and video check out. The hotel is directly across from the Ronald Reagan International Trade Center.

Loews L'Enfant Plaza Hotel
480 L'Enfant Plaza SW
Washington, DC
(202) 484–1000
www.loewshotels.com
$$$$

The Loews L'Enfant is a pleasant, airy hotel near the pulse of bureaucratic Washington. Its best feature, though, is its location directly above a Metro subway station and shopping promenade. Within a short walk are the offices of NASA, the Department of Housing and Urban Development, the Transportation and Agriculture Departments, and the Federal Aviation Administration. Expect to find all the amenities for business and pleasure at this 370-room property, including a rooftop swimming pool and health club. All rooms come with VCRs, minibars, stocked refrigerators, three phones, in-room safes, and a TV/radio in the bathroom. Some also have kitchens. Pets are allowed.

The Madison
15th and M Sts. NW
Washington, DC
(202) 862–1600, (800) 424–8577
www.dcmadisonhotel.com
$$$$

Elegant is the only way to describe this downtown institution featuring 353 rooms appointed with French and Asian antiques acquired by renowned collector and hotelier Marshall B. Coyne. This hotel is consistently rated in national travel magazines as a top choice of business executives. To give you an idea, it's where David Rockefeller stays when he comes to Washington. Guests should expect refrigerators and stocked bars in each room, as well as indoor valet parking and all the business amenities. What's more, it's convenient to everything in federal and corporate Washington.

Marriott Wardman Park
2660 Woodley Rd. NW
Washington, DC
(202) 328–2000
www.marriott.com
$$$$

At 1,350 rooms, this is Washington's largest hotel, a sprawling behemoth of brick, white columns, French doors, endless corridors, and room-sized chandeliers. The setting is a grand expanse of parkland at the edge of Rock Creek. The National Zoo is 3 blocks to the north. This hotel, which offers all sorts of convention and tourist services, includes a post office, pool, health club, shoeshine stand, and hair salon. Rooms come with Starbucks coffee/tea service, voice mail, video check out, and every other amenity imaginable for the comfort of the business traveler. Pets are allowed.

The Morrison-Clark Inn
**11th St. and Massachusetts Ave. NW
Washington, DC
(202) 898–1200, (800) 322–7898
wwwmorrisonclark.com
$$$**

This inn would be a $$$$ property were it almost anywhere else in the city. However, as luxurious as it is, it is in a neighborhood undergoing gentrification, at the eastern edge of downtown near the Convention Center. Occupying one of the oldest buildings in Washington, the Morrison-Clark features authentic Victorian decor with all the modern amenities, including computer ports, and all the old-fashioned luxuries like complimentary newspaper and shoeshine. The restaurant here is renowned for its fine American cuisine.

Park Hyatt Washington
**24th and M Sts. NW
Washington, DC
(202) 789–1234
www.hyatt.com
$$$$**

Another in a long list of competitive West End hotels, the Park Hyatt is one of the most elegant in the Hyatt chain. Three blocks from Georgetown, it features a wonderful restaurant and sidewalk cafe (see the Restaurants chapter). In the rooms you'll find the usual Hyatt amenities plus some four-star touches, including multiline phones, minibars, and complimentary fresh fruit. The hotel boasts an on-site swimming pool and a health club, as well as a beauty salon.

Phoenix Park Hotel
**520 N. Capitol St. NW
Washington, DC
(202) 638–6900
www.pparkhotel.com
$$$**

For a touch of the Emerald Isle right here in Washington, check into the Phoenix Park. A newly built wing brings the total number of rooms to 150. It is 2 blocks from the Capitol and a block from Union Station and Metro. The hotel's Dubliner Pub is widely regarded as one of the best Irish bars in Metro Washington (see the Nightlife chapter).

Radisson Barcelo Hotel
**2121 P St. NW
Washington, DC
(202) 293–3100
www.radisson.com
$$$$**

This 300-room property is close to both Georgetown and Dupont Circle, right in the middle of a row of wonderful restaurants and cafes, including the hotel's own Gabriel (see the Restaurants chapter). The rooms are nicely appointed, in line with the Radisson standard, and there's a business center, sauna, swimming pool, and health club. Nearby Rock Creek Park beckons joggers, strollers, and romantics.

Renaissance Mayflower
**1127 Connecticut Ave. NW
Washington, DC
(202) 347–3000, (800) 228–7697
www.renaissancehotels.com
$$$$**

This much-revered Stouffer hotel is a Connecticut Avenue landmark, a place to see and be seen, and a Washington institution. The Mayflower's lobby takes up an entire block, and the property has two good restaurants and a lounge. Some of the rooms in this 660-unit-plus hotel have kitchenettes. The White House is only 4 blocks away, and just outside the bank of brass-and-glass doors is one of Washington's nicest shopping and restaurant districts.

Renaissance Washington, D.C. Hotel
**999 9th St. NW
Washington, DC
(202) 898–9000
www.renaissancehotels.com
$$$$**

Rapidly becoming one of the District's premiere convention and trade show sites, the Renaissance is across from the Convention Center, about halfway between the White House and Capitol Hill, and about 4 blocks from the MCI Center.

Since 1926, every U.S. president has visited The St. Regis Washington, D.C., which is just 2 blocks from the White House. PHOTO: COURTESY OF THE ST. REGIS WASHINGTON, D.C.

Twenty-five retail shops, a fitness center, food court, post office, hair salon, and indoor pool complement the 801 rooms. In each room expect all the business amenities related to computers and telephones. There's valet parking and a convenient Metro station nearby (Gallery Place). Pets are allowed.

The St. Regis Washington, D.C.
923 16th St. NW
Washington, DC
(202) 638–2626
www.luxurycollection.com
$$$$

A 192-room luxury hotel just 2 blocks from the White House, The St. Regis is a member of ITT Sheraton's distinguished Luxury Collection. Built in 1926—and beneficiary of a $27 million renovation that restored it to its original grandeur—it was designed to resemble an Italian Renaissance palace, as evidenced by its gilded ceilings, magnificent lobby, and elegantly appointed guest rooms and suites. Its array of amenities, including a 24-hour health club, 24-hour room service and concierge, and convenient location have established it as a consistent headquarters for the business, political, and social elite.

Washington Monarch Hotel
2401 M St. NW
Washington, DC
(202) 429–2400
www.washingtonmonarch.com
$$$$

Formerly the ANA Hotel, the grand 415-room Washington Monarch is known for its outstanding service. The lobby is a plush, airy hall of marble, plants, and Oriental rugs, and the guest rooms mirror the decor. The real highlight here though is the 14,000-square-foot fitness center, popular with big-bucks Washingtonians and visiting celebrities. You can also get your exercise with a jog through nearby Rock Creek Park. Georgetown's dining and shopping are a five-minute walk away.

Westin Fairfax Washington, D.C.
2100 Massachusetts Ave. NW
Washington, DC
(202) 293–2100
www.westin.com
$$$$

The name of this Embassy Row landmark has changed quite a few times, but it continues to be opulence personified. The Westin Fairfax was previously The Luxury Collection, before that the Ritz-Carlton, and even earlier, the Fairfax Hotel. Whatever its name, the quality remains the same. Here you can lounge in your complimentary terry robe after a hot bath in a marble tub. Newspapers are delivered to your door, and shoeshine and limousine services are available. Some rooms come with kitchenettes. As might be expected, it is popular with CEOs and guests of Washington officialdom. The Jockey Club restaurant is typically rife with stars of industry, government, and the entertainment world (see the Restaurants chapter). The 24-hour fitness center with sauna keeps the night owls happy.

The Westin Grand Washington, D.C.
2350 M St. NW
Washington, DC
(202) 429–0100, (800) 848–0016
www.westin.com
$$$$

This hotel has had several names, but it has remained a grand hotel throughout

The Westin Fairfax, an Embassy Row landmark, offers opulent surroundings to area visitors.
PHOTO: COURTESY OF WESTIN FAIRFAX

With its ornately decorated lobby and luxurious lounges, the historic Willard Inter-Continental is a Washington landmark. PHOTO: COURTESY OF THE WASHINGTON, DC CONVENTION AND TOURISM CORPORATION

the years. The 263 newly renovated rooms feature marble bathrooms, minibars, and all sorts of luxurious toiletries. All the premium services are offered too, as well as a swimming pool and health club. If you really want to splurge, try one of the eight suites with wood-burning fireplaces and Jacuzzis. Wedged between downtown and Georgetown in the West End neighborhood, the Grand is also close to Rock Creek Park, George Washington University, and the Foggy Bottom Metro.

The Willard Inter-Continental
1401 Pennsylvania Ave. NW
Washington, DC
(202) 628–9100, (800) 327–0200
washington.interconti.com
$$$$

Along with the Hay-Adams, the Four Seasons, and a select few other properties, the Willard is among the crème de la crème of Washington hotels. Ironically, this stunning historical landmark almost fell victim to the wrecking ball before it was renovated and reopened in grand fashion in 1986. The 341 newly renovated rooms

and suites are as plush as you'd expect, with lots of mirrors, marble, and good reproduction furniture. Within a one- or two-minute walk are the White House, the Treasury Department, the National Theater, the Department of Commerce, and the National Mall. The hotel has two elegant lounges, a cafe, and a formal restaurant, the Willard Room (see Restaurants chapter).

Wyndham Bristol
2430 Pennsylvania Ave. NW
Washington, DC
(202) 955–6400
www.wyndham.com
$$$$

Service is key at this classic West End hotel that's just a few strides away from Georgetown. The 239-room Wyndham offers valet parking, complimentary newspapers, a shoeshine service, and rooms with hair dryers and coffee machines. Classic English and contemporary decor accentuates the already classy atmosphere of this discreet, European-style hotel.

Wyndham Washington, D.C.
1400 M St. NW
Washington, DC
(202) 429–1700
www.wyndham.com
$$$$

We tainted locals still know this best as the former Vista International Hotel, the place where former D.C. Mayor Marion Barry got busted—and videotaped, no less—for using crack cocaine. (After serving time in prison, he was, remarkably, reelected in 1994, succeeding Sharon Pratt Kelly, the woman who succeeded him four years earlier.) That's not to knock the Wyndham, however. This is a fine, centrally located hotel that offers guests three telephones in every room and voice mail, as well as minibars, refrigerators, and all the other business amenities. It's an impressive sight, too, with its 14-story glass atrium draped in greenery. There's a fitness room with sauna, restaurant, and lounge.

Northern Virginia

Fairfax County

Hilton McLean at Tysons Corner
7920 Jones Branch Dr.
McLean, VA
(703) 847–5000
www.hilton.com
$$$$

A Tysons Corner landmark, the 458-room McLean Hilton features a glass-domed atrium and a splashy lobby filled with marble, brass, and live plants. The rooms here are ordinary contemporary-style Hilton, but the 43 concierge-level Tower rooms offer some extras like in-room faxes and coffeemakers plus complimentary continental breakfast and evening hors d'oeuvres. There's a fully equipped health club, an indoor pool, minibars in each room, bathroom phones as well as all the amenities business travelers expect. You'll find a restaurant, bar, and drug store on the premises, and you're close to shopping, movie theaters, and still more shopping at the two nearby megamalls that are the retail focal point of Tysons Corner. (See our Shopping chapter.)

Ritz-Carlton Tysons Corner
1700 Tysons Blvd
McLean, VA
(703) 506–4300
www.ritzcarlton.com
$$$$

As they are so apt to do with many of their newer properties, the folks behind the Ritz-Carlton chain like to make sure their moneyed customers have easy access to fashionable shopping areas. In this case it's the attached and oh-so-exclusive Galleria at Tysons II (Saks Fifth Avenue, Neiman-Marcus, etc.), in the heart of Fairfax County's mecca of consumerism, Tysons Corner (see our Shopping chapter). As for the hotel itself, it's typical Ritz-Carlton, fancy to the nth degree: Expect the usual grand decor, attentive service, and fine dining, as well as indoor pool and health club.

Its location is on one of the highest points in the area—all the better for a great view of some D.C. landmarks on a clear day, because there isn't much in the way of scenery in the immediate area, unless you count high-rise office buildings, stores, and a patchwork of busy roads. The 399 rooms feature classic English antique reproductions, marble bathrooms, safes, minibars, and all the toiletries and business amenities. In addition, there's a business center on the premises, as well as a choice of free self-parking or valet parking and complimentary transportation within a 3-mile radius. If you want to be closer to downtown D.C., check into the Ritz-Carlton Pentagon City, attached to the Fashion Centre at Pentagon City shopping mall and offering the same amenities; 1250 South Hayes Street, Arlington (703) 415–5060.

Sheraton Premiere at Tysons Corner
8661 Leesburg Pike
Vienna, VA
(703) 448–1234
www.sptc.com
$$$$

One of Northern Virginia's most luxurious hotels, and one of the nicest in the Sheraton chain, the towering Sheraton Premiere extends to guests such perks as golf privileges, a fitness center, indoor and outdoor pools, free parking, an on-site airline ticket office, racquetball courts, and free transportation to nearby Dulles Airport. You can't miss it—it's the glass tower at Route 7 and the toll road and one of the tallest buildings in Tysons Corner, a city in itself. It's also close to I-66 and the Beltway. There are restaurants and lounges on premises (see the Nightlife chapter).

Washington Dulles Airport Marriott
45020 Aviation Dr.
Dulles, VA
(703) 471–9500
www.marriott.com
$$$

Talk about the Marriott advantage: This is the only hotel on the grounds of Washington Dulles International Airport. A large pond and acres of wooded landscaping almost belie the location of this 368-room hotel, though. There's an indoor and outdoor pool, tennis courts, fitness center, and free parking. The terminal is a two-minute drive away, and complimentary shuttle-bus service is provided. Business travelers will appreciate the video checkout.

Westfields Marriott
14750 Conference Center Dr.
Chantilly, VA
(703) 818–0300
www.marriott.com
$$$–$$$$

You'd never know this 335-room hotel was part of a chain, and indeed, Marriott only became involved a few years ago. Westfields' stately Georgian facade and 1,100 manicured acres give the impression of an old established Virginia resort. The facility, however, is the product of the boom days of the 1980s. It exudes elegance, from its state-of-the-art conference rooms to its outstanding restaurant and ornate guest rooms decorated in marble, country prints, and rich carpets. Dulles Airport is 7 miles to the north along Route 28. The hotel is also about equal distance from U.S. 50 and I-66. This is an ideal venue for a corporate retreat, large

Insiders' Tip

Save yourself time and trouble by using a local reservation service to secure a hotel room during peak season, such as cherry blossom weekend. Reputable businesses such as Washington, DC Accommodations (800-554-2220, www.wdchotels.com), will find out what you're looking for, verify availability, and book your room, often at a lower rate than you can get on your own.

or small; a wedding reception; or any other special occasion. Don't miss dinner at the Palm Court (see the Restaurants chapter). Rooms feature three multiline phones and refrigerators. There's a tourist desk, pro shops, a business center, free valet parking, an indoor heated pool, outdoor pool, health club with steam bath, tennis courts, an on-call physician, and nearby championship golf.

Alexandria

Hilton Alexandria Mark Center
5000 Seminary Rd.
Alexandria, VA
(703) 845–1010
www.hilton.com
$$$$

From I-395 you can't possibly miss the Hilton Alexandria, a tower of concrete and glass that emerges from the surrounding woodlands like a futuristic sentinel. The 500-room hotel, big with convention and conference folks, is surrounded by a manmade lake and about 80 acres of woods—a nice buffer from the traffic and congestion of Alexandria's West End. The former Radisson hotel comes with an indoor/outdoor swimming pool, health club, game room, barber shop, and free parking. There's complimentary transportation to Reagan Washington National Airport, 10 minutes away.

Holiday Inn Select Old Town Alexandria
480 King St.
Alexandria, VA
(703) 549–6080
www.sixcontinenthotels.com/holiday-inn
$$$$

A tourist mecca, especially on weekends, the 227-room Old Town Holiday Inn offers one of the best locations in Alexandria's famed historic district. From here you're right across the street from the town square, the site of a colorful street market held every Saturday morning, and a short walk from galleries, shops, bars, restaurants, and the Potomac waterfront. This recently renovated property is one of the top hotels in the Holiday Inn chain. Colonial-themed guest rooms offer speakerphones with computer-modem capability and voice mail, safes, and coffeemakers. As you would expect, there's video checkout and a business center, indoor parking, indoor pool, and exercise room. There's also free transportation to Ronald Reagan Washington National Airport and Metro subway stops.

Morrison House
116 S. Alfred St.
Alexandria, VA
(703) 838–8000, (800) 367–0800
www.morrisonhouse.com
$$$$

This elegant eighteenth-century–style mansion in the center of Old Town is one of the region's most-celebrated inns. Each of the 45 rooms is individually decorated with Federal-period antiques and chandeliers, and several rooms come with fireplaces and four-poster mahogany beds. The inn's cozy restaurant and lounge enhance an already intensely romantic

atmosphere. Morrison House is the perfect urban getaway and the site of many honeymoons.

Arlington County

Holiday Inn National Airport
2650 Jefferson Davis Hwy.
Arlington, VA
(703) 684–7200, (703) 684–7200
www.sixcontinentshotels.com/holidayinn
$$$

In a corridor of concrete, glass and steel, the hotel is close to Reagan National Airport, the Pentagon, Arlington National Cemetery, the Fashion Centre at Pentagon City, Crystal City Underground (shopping) and, 10 minutes to the south, Old Town Alexandria. Guests receive complimentary shuttle service to the airport and Metro, as well as laundry and valet service, voice mail, a health club, pool, and free parking. Try the 50s-style diner inside the hotel.

Hyatt Regency Crystal City
2799 Jefferson Davis Hwy.
Arlington, VA
(703) 418–1234
www.hyatt.com
$$$$

Crystal City, a conglomeration of office buildings, fast-food restaurants, high-rise condos, and big hotels, isn't going to win any awards for aesthetics, but it sure is convenient. Same can be said for the Hyatt Regency here, a 685-unit hotel that offers a health club, an outdoor swimming pool, and a lounge and rooftop restaurant with a view of D.C. Guests receive complimentary shuttle service to Reagan National Airport or Metro, barely three minutes away. Crystal City is also close to the Pentagon, downtown D.C., and Old Town Alexandria.

Key Bridge Marriott
1401 Lee Hwy.
Arlington, VA
(703) 524–6400
www.marriott.com
$$$$

About as close to Washington as you're going to get in Virginia, the 585-room Key

Bridge Marriott is a short walk (or shorter jog) across its graceful namesake span from Georgetown and just 2 blocks from the Rosslyn Metro. The hotel's riverside location affords spectacular views of the Potomac and the District beyond. There's free on-site parking, an indoor/outdoor pool, and health club. Each morning, guests are treated to complimentary coffee and newspapers. Rooms have all the usual business amenities.

Ritz-Carlton, Pentagon City
1250 S. Hayes St.
Arlington, VA
(703) 415-5000
www.ritzcarlton.com
$$$$
See preceding description under Ritz-Carlton Tysons Corner.

Sheraton National
900 S. Orme St.
Arlington, VA
(703) 521-1900
www.starwood.com
$$-$$$
This 417-room hotel is just a mile from the Pentagon and less than a 10-minute drive from Reagan Washington National Airport. Don't expect anything stylish—rather it's a functional meeting place for those with business at the Pentagon or downtown D.C. There's an on-site fitness center and pool, as well as a complimentary shuttle to Reagan Washington National Airport, Pentagon City shopping mall, and Metro. You'll also find a rooftop restaurant and lounge, neither particularly distinctive, an indoor pool, and health club.

Loudoun County

Lansdowne Conference Resort
44050 Woodridge Pkwy.
Leesburg, VA
(703) 729-8400, (800) 541-4801
www.lansdowneresort.com
$$$-$$$$
In a resortlike setting north of Dulles Airport, Lansdowne attracts a growing share of meetings and conventions, especially among international firms. Luxurious

rooms are complemented by an attentive staff, state-of-the-art meetings technology, an 18-hole golf course, indoor and outdoor pools, and a fitness center and spa. Lansdowne is part of Loudoun County's burgeoning Route 7 corridor, one of the region's fastest-growing commercial districts. You don't have to leave the premises for anything, and the fine restaurant is a special treat.

Suburban Maryland

Montgomery County

Bethesda Marriott
5151 Pooks Hill Rd.
Bethesda, MD
(301) 897-9400
www.marriott.com
$$$-$$$$
This 407-room property is high atop a hill near the Capitol Beltway, the National Institutes of Health, and White Flint shopping mall. It's a sprawling place with all manner of eateries—and we're talking exceptional cuisine, an indoor/outdoor pool, tennis courts, and exercise room. There's also free parking and a shuttle to the Metro.

Courtyard by Marriott Silver Spring
12521 Prosperity Dr.
Silver Spring, MD
(301) 680-8500
www. courtyard.com
$$-$$$
This recently built hotel is located in a rapidly developing area of northeastern Montgomery County, closer really to College Park and the University of Maryland than downtown Silver Spring. A few of the 146 units are suites with refrigerators and microwaves. There's an indoor pool and exercise room.

Holiday Inn Bethesda
8120 Wisconsin Ave.
Bethesda, MD
(301) 652-2000
www.holiday-inn.com
$$$
It's hard to get closer to the Bethesda Naval Hospital and the National Insti-

tutes of Health than this hotel, a Wisconsin Avenue landmark for two decades. You're about equal distance from the Beltway and the District line. The main distinction of this hotel, however, is The Yacht Club, a singles spot for those 30 and older (see the Nightlife chapter).

Hyatt Regency Bethesda
1 Bethesda Metro Center
Bethesda, MD
(301) 657–1234
www.hyatt.com
$$$

This bustling hotel in the heart of Bethesda's business district is atop a Metro subway station, so it couldn't be more convenient. Both Washington and the surrounding suburbs are just a few Metro stops away. Rooms come with all the business amenities now standard at most Hyatts, including video checkout, voice mail, minibars, and a striking atrium-style lobby full of shops and services. The shopping malls at White Flint and Mazza Gallerie are only a couple of subway stops away (see our Shopping chapter).

Prince George's County

Greenbelt Marriott Hotel
6400 Ivy La.
Greenbelt, MD
(301) 441–3700
www.marriott.com
$$$

This is one of the nicest full service hotels near the University of Maryland and NASA Goddard Space Flight Center. There are 283 standard rooms in this hotel as well as concierge-level and extended stay accommodations. You'll find a restaurant, pub, free parking, indoor and outdoor pools, a health club, tennis courts, and a business center.

Ramada Inn New Carrollton
8500 Annapolis Rd.
New Carrollton, MD
(301) 459–6700
www.ramada.com
$$

This small hotel near the US Airways Arena has been newly renovated to answer the needs of business travelers. Rooms feature kitchenettes with fridges, computer outlets, free shoeshine, and newspaper. On premises you can avail yourself of a business center that provides fax and copy services. There's a complimentary shuttle within a 10-mile radius and an on-site car rental service, gift shop, restaurant, and lounge. The 238 rooms are functional and convenient.

On a Budget

Washington, D.C.

Allen Lee Hotel
2224 F St. NW
Washington, DC
(202) 331–1224, (800) 462–0186
www.allenleehotel.com
$

Rooms at the Allen Lee in Foggy Bottom can start as low as $45 for a single with a bathroom down the hall, which partly explains why it does a brisk business with students and young international tourists. The very basic 85-room hotel is right on the beaten path—close to Metro and 6 blocks from the White House, the Kennedy Center, and the Lincoln Memorial. It is ideal for tourists not dependent on a car.

Days Inn Connecticut Avenue
4400 Connecticut Ave. NW
Washington, DC
(202) 244–5600
www.daysinn.com
$$–$$$

In the city but away from the masses, this 155-room edition of the national chain comes with free on-site parking, in-room safe, and voice mail. It's in upper Northwest D.C., a safe and exclusive neighborhood, and is made even more convenient by the presence of the Van Ness/UD.C. Metro 2 blocks away. Also close by are American University, the National Zoo, Rock Creek Park, and the restaurants and shops of Tenleytown and Cleveland Park.

Hotel Harrington
11th and E Sts. NW
Washington, DC
(202) 628–8140, (800) 424–8532
www.hotel-harrington.com
$

The no-frills Harrington is for the budget conscious who want to be in the thick of it. It's a half-block away from Pennsylvania Avenue, about equal distance from the White House and the Capitol. There's nearby parking for $8.50 a day, a restaurant, bar, barber shop, and laundry room. Pets are welcome. The Harrington has always done a strong business with Europeans. More Americans should follow their lead. Families may want to try one of the 26 suites in the 260-unit hotel.

The International Guest House
1441 Kennedy St. NW
Washington, DC
(202) 726–5808
$

The International Guest House is a nonprofit facility maintained by the Mennonite Church to provide clean, inexpensive lodging for international visitors in a homey atmosphere. Indeed, the large brick home with its wraparound porch is in a pleasant residential area off 16th Street Northwest, across the street from Rock Creek Park. Breakfast is served family style at 8:00 A.M., with guests and staff eating together. There is a large living room for lounging and reading, and a television is in the basement. Single guests are asked to share a room with another person. Another restriction that might cramp your style is the 11:00 P.M. curfew, after which the house is closed. However, for the rock-bottom rates of $25 per person per night, you can hardly find a more reasonable bargain in a nice, safe area.

Red Roof Inn Downtown D.C.
500 H St. NW
Washington, DC
(202) 289–5959
www.redroof.com
$$

Anyone who's ever stayed in a Red Roof Inn knows what to expect. The neighborhood is not the most scenic, but the hotel is less than 2 blocks from the Metro and MCI Arena, 4 blocks to the Washington Convention Center, and 7 blocks to Capitol Hill. The inn also offers a restaurant, exercise room with sauna, and guest laundry. Small pets are allowed.

Windsor Inn
1842 16th St. NW
Washington, DC
(202) 667–0300, (800) 423–9111
$–$$

This is called an inn, but with 45 rooms, it's a bit large to fit into that category. The rooms are pleasant and neat, but not luxurious. The location, though a bit off the beaten path from midtown and the sights, is convenient enough to Metro. On a nice day, you can walk the 12 blocks to the White House—a pleasant stroll past some handsome buildings. Your room comes with complimentary continental breakfast and evening sherry.

Windsor Park Hotel
2116 Kalorama Rd. NW
Washington, DC
(202) 483–7700, (800) 247–3064
windsorparkhotel.com
$$

The Windsor Park in Washington's exclusive Kalorama neighborhood is another great European-style bargain. Close to the bustle of Adams Morgan and the shopping of Dupont Circle, the innlike setting is perfect for families with young children. All 43 simple rooms come with a small refrigerator, complimentary continental breakfast, and newspaper.

Northern Virginia

Alexandria

Hawthorn Suites Alexandria
420 N. Van Dorn St.
Alexandria, VA
(703) 370–1000
www.hawthorn.com
$$

If it's important to be near shopping malls and right off the interstate but not too far from D.C., then the Hawthorn should fit

Linking to the Chains

Many of the hotels listed in this chapter belong to national chains. For your convenience, we've listed their toll-free telephone numbers below.

Best Western (800) 762–3777
Comfort Inn (800) 228–5150
Days Inn (800) 329–7466
Econo Lodge (800) 553–2666
Embassy Suites (800) 362–2779
Hilton (800) 445–8667
Holiday Inn (800) HOLIDAY
Howard Johnson (800) 654–2000
Hyatt (800) 233–1234
Marriott (800) 228–9290
Park Inn International (800) 670–PARK
Radisson (800) 333–3333
Ritz-Carlton (800) 241–3333
Sheraton (800) 325–3535
Travelodge (800) 578–7878
Wyndham (800) WYNDHAM

the bill. The 186-suite hotel in Alexandria's West End is within striking distance of I–395, one of the region's busiest arteries, and Landmark Shopping Center, one of the region's busiest malls. D.C. is just 9 miles up the road, while Old Town is but 5 miles east. The area is a fast-food mecca, but you can take solace in that all suites here come with kitchens. This place could use a renovation, but you can't beat it for the price.

Arlington

Econo Lodge Metro
6800 Lee Hwy.
Arlington, VA
(703) 538–5300, (888) 987–2555
www.econolodge.com
$$

Don't let the name rule out this property for you. This member of the popular national budget motel chain has consistently been rated as one of the best Econo Lodges in the country. Why else would inner-Beltway politicians and dignitaries and celebrities like Shirley Maclaine choose to stay here? The location couldn't be bet-

ter. The 47-room lodge is at the junction of I–66 and Lee Highway, the first interchange you'll come to when entering Washington from Dulles Airport. It also puts you in proximity to the amazing French cuisine of La Cote d'Or Cafe (see Restaurants) and within about eight minutes of the East Falls Church Metro station. About half the rooms are nonsmoking, and several are wheelchair accessible.

Quality Hotel Courthouse Plaza
1200 N. Courthouse Rd.
Arlington, VA
(703) 524–4000, (888) 987–2555
www.qualityhotelarlington.com
$$

A huge but pleasant hotel in an urban setting, the Quality Arlington is a real bargain—a nice, clean, modern facility that won't break the bank. Its location can't be beat either—near the Court House Metro, which means shops, restaurants, a movie theater, and all kinds of family amusement options. What's more, a complimentary shuttle will take you there. A bit further is the Rosslyn business district and Georgetown. At the Quality Hotel you'll find amenities like in-room coffee, free local calls, a sauna, coin-operated laundry, in-room Nintendo, a huge outdoor pool, health club, and free parking. Suites have full kitchens. The place is crawling with families during the spring and summer months, testament no doubt to its budget prices and ease.

Quality Inn Iwo Jima
1501 Arlington Blvd.
Arlington, VA
(703) 524–5000
www.hotelchoice.com
$$

Popular with tourists, this 141-room edition of the national chain is within an easy walk of Arlington Cemetery, the Iwo Jima Memorial, the National Mall, and even Georgetown. Rosslyn Metro is 3 blocks away. The hotel, though a bit worn, offers low prices as well as free parking, free local phone calls, in-room coffeemaker, laundry facilities, and an indoor/outdoor pool, but this is an older property and you should expect only the basics insofar as rooms are concerned—nothing fancy here.

Travelodge Cherry Blossom Motel
3030 Columbia Pike
Arlington, VA
(703) 521–5570
www.travelodge.com
$

For the basics the Travelodge Cherry Blossom Motel is hard to beat, especially for families and solo travelers on a budget. Prices start at $79 a night, and besides a place to sleep you get complimentary coffee, juice, and doughnuts in the lobby from 6:00 to 10:30 a.m. daily, use of a fitness center and laundry facilities, free on-site parking, and free local phone calls. Adding to its convenient Arlington location (a great base for D.C. sightseeing), there's a Metro station less than 2 miles away. You'll have to do without a swimming pool on site, but with this much bang for your buck, you probably won't even miss it. And if you do, you're welcome to use a pool located 2 blocks down the street.

Suburban Maryland

Bethesda
American Inn of Bethesda
8130 Wisconsin Ave.
Bethesda, MD
(301) 656–9300, (800) 323–7081
www.american-inn.com
$–$$

Much closer to the District than the Park Inn, the American Inn is in the middle of downtown Bethesda, about a 10-minute walk from the Bethesda Metro and only a couple of minutes drive from NIH. This is a simple property, nothing fancy, but it has a great location not far from Bethesda's famed restaurant row. Guests of the American can get microwave ovens upon request, and there's a pool for cooling off.

Park Inn and Suites
11410 Rockville Pk.,
Bethesda, MD
(301) 881–5200, (800) 752–3800
www.parkinnwashdc.com
$

It's not exactly the most scenic place around (this is the land of strip centers and fast-food restaurants), but then again you're not paying for the view. This 159-room motel in North Bethesda recently underwent a $5 million renovation. It is clean, safe, and close to White Flint Mall, the epitome of suburban shopping malls. What's more, it offers an hourly shuttle service to the National Institutes of Health, so don't be surprised if you see a lot of doctors and scientists running around.

Gaithersburg
Red Roof Inn Gaithersburg
497 Quince Orchard Rd.
Gaithersburg, MD
(301) 977–3311
www.redroof.com
$

It's nothing fancy, but even during the Cherry Blossom Festival, double rooms go for $79. Business king rooms come with an enhanced work area, data port, and speaker phone.

The National Institute of Standards and the Montgomery Fairgrounds are within walking distance. The Shady Grove Metro stop is couple miles away, and it's about a 40-minute ride to tourist attractions downtown. Free coffee and newspapers are available in the lobby. One small pet per room is permitted.

Silver Spring

Days Inn Silver Spring
8040 13th St.
Silver Spring, MD
(301) 588–4400
www.daysinn.com
$

This Days Inn provides the basic comforts and is is near much of upper Northwest D.C. and close-in areas of Montgomery County. Walter Reed Army Hospital is a mile to the south, and Takoma Park, to the immediate east, has some interesting Bohemian-tinged shops, restaurants, and nightclubs. It's also in walking distance to the National Oceanic and Atmospheric Administration.

Holiday Inn Silver Spring
8777 Georgia Ave.
Silver Spring, MD
(301) 589–0800
www.holiday-inn.com
$$

An easy walk to the Silver Spring Metro and the District line, this Holiday Inn sits in the center of one of Suburban Maryland's oldest and most established neighborhoods. The 231-room hotel's been here a long time, but it was gutted in 1996 and totally renovated. It's a great base for house hunters in Silver Spring or neighboring Takoma Park. Downtown Washington is a good 20-minute drive by way of 16th Street.

Hostels/University Inns

George Washington University Inn
824 New Hampshire Ave. NW
Washington, D.C.
(202) 337–6620, (800) 426–4455
www.gwuinn.com
$$$

Formerly the Inn at Foggy Bottom, this newly renovated hotel is within walking distance from George Washington University, Georgetown, and much of the Smithsonian. Some of the hotel's 95 rooms have kitchens and there's also a restaurant on site. Discounts are available to G.W. students and alumni.

Georgetown University Conference Center
3800 Reservoir Rd. NW
Washington, D.C.
(202) 687–3200
www.conferencecenters.com/wasgu
$$$

The nation's oldest Catholic university is the obvious main attraction of this on-campus hotel run by Marriott. Mostly frequented by guests of the university and seminar participants, the conference center offers some rooms with kitchenettes plus a swimming pool and health club. All of the Georgetown neighborhood is within a few minutes walk, and the business district of Rosslyn (Virginia) looms just across Key Bridge. Don't worry about nonstop college parties keeping you up at night; the hotel is at the far-north end of campus, in a relatively quiet residential area.

Washington International American Youth Hostel
1009 11th St. NW
Washington, D.C.
(202) 737–2333
www.hiwashingtondc.org
$

A clean, safe alternative for young travelers on a budget, this 250-bed dorm-style hostel is 1 block north of the Washington Convention Center—not the greatest neighborhood, but one undergoing a renaissance. There's a large common area for meeting other travelers (lots of Europeans here), a huge kitchen for groups, and a coin-operated laundry. Free movies and tours are available and, as you can imagine, security is very tight. The price is rock bottom—$22 for members of the hostelling association and $24 for nonmembers.

Bed-and-Breakfasts and Country Inns

Washington, D.C.
Northern Virginia
Suburban Maryland

Whether you're a newcomer or a Washington area resident, inns and bed-and-breakfasts are an escape from the rush of everyday life. They provide a more intimate alternative to large, busy hotels and may sometimes, but not always, be less expensive. A recent trend among stressed urbanites has been to book a long weekend at one of these hideaways, even if it's 10 minutes from home! It's cheaper than an out-of-town trip, takes less time, and yet it's so hassle-free that the sense of relaxation can be every bit as profound.

Given the historical nature of Metro Washington—and the number of large homes, former embassies, and other spacious structures—it's surprising there aren't more highly publicized bed-and-breakfasts in the area. Maybe it's because Washington and the surrounding suburbs host so many tours, school groups, and conventions that the most obvious accommodations are in big, full-service hotels. Bed-and-breakfasts do exist in Metro Washington, and you'll find them most easily through a reservation service. Many area bed-and-breakfasts are represented by agencies that match the guest with the right accommodation—often a lovely room in someone's private residence. We highly recommend that you contact one of these reservation services if you wish to have a broad selection from which to choose. Your host may be the homeowner, and if both parties are willing to mingle, you'll have a chance for an intimate look at the lives of Washingtonians. These locals are also a good source of information on neighborhood restaurants, entertainment, shopping, and the latest museum exhibits. They're pleased to share their knowledge and will often help you make arrangements, just like a concierge in a big hotel would. The charm of smaller hostelries is, of course, the personal touch.

The immediate metro area doesn't offer the selection of bed-and-breakfasts that you'll find in the surrounding countryside of Maryland and Virginia and their neighboring states. If you don't mind driving a greater distance or if you're looking to get out of the area for a weekend hideaway, check the Daytrips chapter for further recommendations.

That said, the bed-and-breakfasts that do exist locally are often magnificent. Some are housed in historic buildings, others in stately Federal-style town homes, and most are furnished in grand style. Rooms are individually decorated and varied, with some offering luxuries like two-person Jacuzzis, down comforters, and fireplaces.

Bed-and-breakfasts, as the name implies, generally include a full breakfast for two in the room tariff, though a few restrict themselves to continental breakfasts. Some also serve afternoon tea or evening hors d'oeuvres. Inns, on the other hand, may charge extra for all meals.

These intimate bed-and-breakfasts usually provide all the amenities of home—and then some—or they may purposefully eschew such modern-day intrusions as in-room phones, VCRs, and televisions. If you require the modern conveniences, be sure to ask whether they're provided when you make your reservation.

One final note: inns and bed-and-breakfasts usually require a deposit to hold a reservation and they often have strict cancellation policies requiring plenty of advance notice. You can't blame them—they're small businesses and every room counts.

Nearby bed-and-breakfasts offer guests an escape from the fast pace of Washington, D.C. PHOTO: COURTESY OF VIRGINIA TOURISM CORPORATION

Price Code

The price code is based on average room cost per night based on double occupancy.

$	Less than $100
$$	$100 to $149
$$$	$150 to $200
$$$$	More than $200

Washington, D.C.

Bed & Breakfast Accommodations, Ltd.
P.O. Box 12011
Washington, DC 20005
(202) 328–3510
www.bedandbreakfastdc.com
$–$$$$

From budget to luxury offerings, Bed & Breakfast Accommodations, Ltd. will connect you with an array of private-home lodgings and inns. Some apartments are even available for family groups and extended-stay guests. Choices include historic properties with antiques and gardens, and some with pools. They offer more than 35 selections such as the Victorian-furnished Aaron Shipman House

near Dupont Circle and the "Painted Lady" of Capitol Hill; convenient contemporaries like the Gallery Inn near Dupont Circle and Adams Morgan, and the "Arlington" Bed and Breakfast near the Ballston Metro. Various types of breakfast are included.

Bed & Breakfast League/Sweet Dreams & Toast
P.O. Box 9490
Washington, DC 20016
(202) 363–7767
$–$$$

This is a reservation service specializing in bed-and-breakfasts in Washington's historic districts. All guest houses have easy access to public transportation and many offer on-site parking. Some of the 135 rooms offer kitchenettes.

The Dupont at The Circle
1604 19th St. NW
Washington, DC
(202) 332–5251, (888) 412–0100
www.dupontatthecircle.com
$$–$$$$

Just a block from the bustle of Dupont Circle, this upscale Victorian charmer sits on a tree-lined residential street just steps from the Dupont Metro stop. The eight luxurious guest rooms and suites are decorated with antiques; many have fireplaces and antique writing desks. Every room has a full private bath with a clawfoot or whirlpool tub and is provided with sumptuous Egyptian cotton linens. All the rooms are nonsmoking and have telephones with voice mail and data ports. Services include a complimentary continental breakfast, newspaper, and limited parking.

Kalorama Guest House at Kalorama Park
1854 Mintwood Pl. NW
Washington, DC
(202) 667–6369
www.washingtonpost.com/yp/kgh
$–$$

In the lively Adams Morgan neighborhood, just a block from the restaurant district, this elegant 30-room inn is furnished in Victorian antiques. Once inside, expect peace and quiet. Fifteen of the rooms, including the five suites, have private baths. The suites contain TVs and phones. Complimentary continental breakfast and afternoon aperitifs are served in the parlor and garden.

Kalorama Guest House at Woodley Park
2700 Cathedral Ave. NW
Washington, DC
(202) 328–0860
www.washingtonpost.com/yp/kgh
$

This Victorian townhouse (two on the same street, actually) is in northwest Washington, in the gorgeous Woodley Park neighborhood. It's close to Washington National Cathedral and the National Zoo. The Woodley Park/Zoo Metro is 3 blocks away. The 18 rooms are similar in atmosphere and amenities to the Kalorama Guest House, which is not surprising because they are owned by the same innkeepers.

Northern Virginia

Bed & Breakfast Association of Virginia
P.O. Box 791
Orange, VA 22960
(888) 660–BBAV
www.bbonline.com/va/bbav/index.html

Contact this association for a free directory of more than 200 member inns throughout the state, including several in the Northern Virginia area. All BBAV inns offer guest comment cards and submit to on-site inspections.

Fairfax County

Bailiwick Inn
4023 Chain Bridge Rd.
Fairfax, VA
(703) 691–2266
www.bailiwickinn.com
$$$–$$$$

This early nineteenth-century brick house is wedged in the center of Fairfax City's charming but often overlooked historic district, just across Route 123 from the old courthouse. The Bailiwick has 14 guest rooms, each named for a local historical figure, all with feather beds and some with Jacuzzis and fireplaces. George Mason University and its beautiful Center for the Arts are right up the road, and the Vienna Metro station is less than 10 minutes away. The rate includes a filling gourmet breakfast, which one morning might feature French toast filled with cream cheese and apples, and another morning eggs Benedict.

Insiders' Tip

If you drive, be sure to ask about parking at in-town bed-and-breakfasts. Many are in residential areas with limited parking.

Prince William County

Sunrise Hill Farm Bed & Breakfast
5590 Old Farm La.
Manassas, VA
(703) 754–8309
www.bbonline.com/va/sunrise
$–$$

Civil War buffs, naturalists, and horse-lovers will fall for this cozy bed-and-breakfast inside the Manassas National Battlefield Park, just 30 miles west of Washington, D.C. Hiking and horseback-riding trails abound at the park, and Sunrise Hill will even board your horse. Manassas's historic district, home to the much-acclaimed Manassas Museum, is also nearby. (See our Civil War chapter for information on these historic sites.)

Loudoun County

The Laurel Brigade Inn
20 W. Market St.
Leesburg, VA
(703) 777–1010
www.loudouncounty.com/dining/inn.htm
$–$$

Rooms here start at $95 a night, making this old colonial stone inn one of the better bed-and-breakfast bargains around. Guests can choose from five tastefully appointed rooms, each with a private bath. Guests receive a continental breakfast and complimentary newspaper. Children can be accommodated. The house restaurant specializes in Virginia country dining and is reasonably priced.

Loudoun County Bed & Breakfast Guild
108–9 Loudoun St. SW
Leesburg, VA
(703) 777–1806, (800) 644–1806
www.vabb.com

Visit the organization's Web site to find information about nearly 20 inns found around Loudoun County. Accommodations range from historic farmhouses to elegant estates.

The Norris House Inn
108 Loudoun St. SW
Leesburg, VA
(703) 777–1806, (800) 644–1806
www.norrishouse.com
$$–$$$

The historic Norris House Inn and its adjacent Stone House Tea Room date from the pre–Revolutionary War era. PHOTO: THE NORRIS HOUSE INN

Right in the middle of Leesburg's historic district, The Norris House Inn (built in 1760) has guest rooms with canopied beds, antiques galore, and fireplaces. It's a nice spot for a romantic night away but also conducive to small meetings and family celebrations. Guests have full use of the stately dining room, parlor, library, sunroom, and a rambling veranda overlooking beautiful gardens. Its Stone House Tea Room, next door, is open by reservation and on special weekends each month. Washington is about an hour away.

Suburban Maryland

The Davis Warner Inn
8114 Carroll Ave.
Takoma Park, MD
(301) 408–3989
www.daviswarnerinn.com
$–$$$$

Guests enjoy homemade, hot breakfasts with entrees such as crepes or eggs Benedict at this bed-and-breakfast in charming little Takoma Park. Afternoon tea is available on request. Listed on the National Registry of Historic Places, the 1855 house is the oldest residence in the area. The second floor, for guests ages 18 and older, boasts three rooms with a shared bath and one with a private bath that includes a Jacuzzi. The third-floor family suite includes three bedrooms, a kitchen, laundry facilities, a full bath, dining and living rooms, and amenities such as satellite TV, a phone, and computer. The nearest Metro stop is about a mile away, accessible by a bus that stops just outside the inn.

Longwood Manor Bed and Breakfast
2900 DuBarry La.
Brookeville, MD
(301) 774–1002
www.bbonline.com/md/longwood
$–$$$

Only 16 miles from Washington, D.C., Longwood Manor features three guest rooms, all with private baths, cable TV, and individual air-conditioning. Built in 1817, the large, formal residence, complete with a white-columned facade, orig-inally served as the home of Thomas Moore, who invented the first refrigerator. Special features include a spacious outdoor swimming pool, a large meeting room, and event catering. Guests receive an expanded continental breakfast.

Pleasant Springs Farm Bed & Breakfast
16112 Barnesville Rd.
Boyds, MD
(301) 972–3452
www.PleasantSpringsFarm.com
$$$

Surrounded by 30 acres of gardens, meadows, nature trails, and streams, this restored log cottage can accommodate a couple or a family with well-behaved children. Dating to 1768 and recently featured on HGTV, the cabin includes two log sitting rooms, one of which boasts a fireplace. One bedroom has a queen-size bed and full bath, while a second offers a full bed and half-bath. The building has window air-conditioning. Full homemade breakfasts, delivered by the innkeepers, include such dishes as eggs Benedict, scalloped potatoes and quiche seasoned with herbs grown on site. Guests can purchase farm products such as hand-spun and -dyed wool yarn, and cheese and soap made from goat milk. The inn closes January through March.

The Reynolds of Derwood Bed and Breakfast
16620 Bethayres Rd.
Derwood, MD
(301) 963–2216
www.reynolds-bed-breakfast.com
$

Conveniently located in a quiet suburban neighborhood just minutes from the Shady Grove Metro station, this two-room, family-oriented inn without age restrictions features several amenities for active guests. Highlights include a putting green, driving range, exercise room, sauna, and two outdoor hot tubs; a park is right across the street. The President's Room showcases authentic memorabilia from the many years when innkeeper Joan Reynolds's parents worked for the White House. The window offers a view of the 25-foot, illuminated waterfall outside. An adjoining Quilt Room, stocked with toys, can be added for guests with children. The downstairs Williamsburg Room is wheelchair accessible. Both rooms include TVs with VCRs, and guests have access to a collection of 450 videos. Continental breakfasts—custom ordered on the inn's Web site—can be eaten in the sunroom or outdoors at tables near the waterfall. Reynolds, whose art studio is on-site, sells her paintings, drawings, and notecards of local historic places.

Restaurants

From Chinatown to Adams Morgan, Capitol Hill to
Georgetown, Rockville to Old Town Alexandria, and Tysons Corner to Bethesda, a veritable dining world in miniature awaits you. Whatever cuisine you crave, you're likely to find it in Metro Washington, mainly because so many residents are originally from elsewhere. Despite this, Washington has only recently begun to be recognized as a city for fine dining. Compared with San Francisco, say, or New Orleans, the Metro area's culinary stars are few, but they are growing in prominence.

Magazines like *Gourmet, Bon Appétit*—and their readers—have begun to sit up and take notice, and several Washington chefs have won international reputations. It had to happen sooner or later, given the area's demographics. Metro Washington offers a customer base that is diverse, well traveled, and affluent. Suffice it to say there are plenty of folks here who appreciate good food and who can afford to dine out regularly. Not to say that you can't dine reasonably. There are some bargains, especially among Washington's ethnic eateries. You'll also find the national chains, from the economical Chili's to the deluxe steak houses like the Palm, Morton's, and Ruth's Chris Steak House. But if you're from anywhere except New York, Tokyo, or London, get ready for sticker shock. Even the folksiest eateries are likely to be pricier than you'll find back home.

Before we get into the meat of this chapter, though, a few words about the ingredients.

Please keep in mind: This is in no way an exhaustive listing. We'd probably still be writing if that was the objective! Instead, we've dished up an eclectic buffet, if you will—a little of this and a little of that—to give you a taste for what's available. Still, we've barely scratched the proverbial surface—or rather, removed that first delicious layer—of what Metro Washington has to offer in the way of calories, carbohydrates, and cholesterol.

The restaurants that made the cut are a mix of recognized local favorites (in some cases, institutions), very personal choices and a smattering of others in the District, Suburban Maryland, and Northern Virginia. With a few exceptions, none of the major national chain establishments (including fast-food outlets, sandwich/pizza joints, and full-service family restaurants such as Bennigan's, Ruby Tuesday, Chi-chi's, Outback Steakhouse, etc.) are represented. We want to introduce you to places you're unlikely to find anywhere else.

(Be sure to check out our Close-up on kids' dining in the Kidstuff chapter also.)

All establishments listed accept most major credit cards unless otherwise noted.

Restaurants are divided first by geographic areas: Washington, Northern Virginia, and Maryland. Within each area we've broken down the list by ethnic cuisine, and restaurants under each ethnic heading are in alphabetic order. One final note—seafood restaurants used to be a separate category, but fish is now so prevalent on most menus that we've simply grouped these restaurants according to the type of ethnic cuisine they specialize in.

Bon appétit!

Price-Code

To give you an idea of what to expect price-wise, we've provided the following scale as a very general guide. Prices shown are for a complete dinner for two including appetizers, wine, beer or spirits, and dessert, but excluding tax and tip. All, of course, are subject to change.

$ . . . .$40 or less
$$ . . . .$40 to $65
$$$ . . . .$65 to $100
$$$$ . . . . .More than $100

Washington, D.C.
American/Continental

Blackie's House of Beef
1217 22nd St. NW
Washington, DC
(202) 333–1100
$$

Opened in 1946, Blackie's has established itself as a Washington landmark, and it's an easy one to find. A white building dripping with New Orleans–style black wrought iron, Blackie's sits just off M Street between Georgetown and downtown. This place is a bit kitschy and very cozy, with fireplaces and all the warming touches you could ask for. Not a gourmet mecca, but rather a place for hearty appetites, Blackie's features generously thick steaks and roast beef, as well as some standard seafood dishes. They are open for lunch weekdays and dinner nightly.

California Grill
1090 Vermont Ave. NW
Washington, DC
(202) 289–2098
$

If you're near the White House or other downtown tourist sites and are looking for a fresh alternative to fast food, try the California Grill. This self-serve cafeteria-style restaurant offers oodles of fresh vegetables, salads, tostados (one even with mahimahi), and espresso bar. Prices are only a little higher than fast food. Open for breakfast and lunch only, Monday through Saturday.

Capital Grille
601 Pennsylvania Ave. NW
Washington, DC
(202) 737–6200
www.thecapitalgrille.com
$$$$

Yes, Capital Grille is part of a chain, but since it was only the third link, we've decided to include it. Why? In a very short time it has become one of the trendiest places around Capitol Hill, the kind of establishment where you're likely to run into the town's top lobbyists, along with the legislators they're trying to influence. Nowadays, some of Washington's most important powerbrokers are women, and you'll find them here, too, but this place has the atmosphere of a men's club—dark wood, dark green, and, yes, even hunting trophies. From the street you're greeted with a view of the meat-aging room, complete with moldy rinds that will be expertly cut away to provide you with flavorful—and humongous—cuts of beef. Even vegetarians will find something to like here if they are able to overlook the carnivorous atmosphere. The baked potatoes weigh a pound and salads are a meal in themselves. Capital Grille is open for lunch weekdays and dinner nightly.

Cashion's Eat Place
1819 Columbia Rd. NW
Washington, DC
(202) 797–1819
$$$

Ann Cashion is one of the town's most innovative chefs, and she has won many honors to prove it, both locally and nationally. Her namesake restaurant serves dinner nightly and Sunday brunch but is closed Monday.

The dining room is curved and spills into the street on warm summer evenings, thanks to a front wall of sliding glass doors that open onto the patio. The crowd is as eclectic as the Adams Morgan neighborhood that is home to the restaurant. There are sleek women in black dresses—and black lipstick to match—along with young execs in khakis and the occasional business-suited lawyers. The real attraction, however, is the food. It has a down-home, southern touch, but there's always an interesting fillip, often in the chef's choice of vegetable accompaniments.

The menu changes regularly; recently, the salmon was served on buttery summer cabbage with a sherry vinegar beurre blanc and the grilled swordfish in tomato-lime salsa came with a side of fried yucca and cubanelle peppers. There are all kinds of exotic meats, like buffalo, sweetbreads, and guinea hen. What really makes dining here memorable, though, is Cashion's flair for seasoning. She manages to make her dishes distinctive, but she's so skilled at combining flavors, that you're not quite sure what the ingredients are.

Chadwicks
3205 K St. NW
Washington, DC
(202) 333–2565
$$

It's tough to avoid comparisons with the local Clyde's chain (see subsequent entry), but Chadwicks should view it as a compliment. It's easy to find something to like in this warm, inviting Georgetown saloon/restaurant, be it the woodsy atmosphere, the selection from the bar, or the hamburgers. Indeed, this may be one of the best burgers in town, thick and charbroiled to your taste. The rest of the menu is the usual saloon fare, served in generous portions: seafood, soups, salads, pasta, and the like. Chadwicks serves lunch and dinner daily, and Sunday brunch. The only hard part for the uninitiated may be finding this place, which sits literally beneath the Whitehurst Freeway near the foot of Wisconsin Avenue.

Clyde's of Georgetown
3236 M St. NW
Washington, DC
(202) 333–9180
www.clydes.com
$$

Here's a D.C. institution that was smart enough to bring its success to the suburbs. Although all of the locations outside the Beltway have proven to be a hit, none have quite the charm as this streetfront saloon in the very crux of trendy Georgetown. Serving lunch and dinner daily, and Sunday brunch, it's a raucous, lively place—a little bit meat market, a little bit family fun center—all housed in nooks and alcoves that feature touches of stained glass, extravagant art, and, often, wall-to-wall people. Beyond the irresistible bar area, Clyde's beckons with its own brand of award-winning chili, steaks, burgers, salads, sandwiches, and homemade desserts. Clyde's makes a special effort to buy its produce from local farmers, so the veggie dishes can be among the freshest in town. The food's not always perfect—and almost never exceptional—but the place is a blast, and its appeal is broad. Patrons include college students, families, and business types.

Dean & DeLuca Cafe
3276 M St. NW
Washington, DC
(202) 342–2500
$

Shopping in Georgetown and want to grab a quick bite? Do you need some takeout to stock your hotel room? This self-service counter, serving lunch and dinner daily in one of D.C.'s premier gourmet markets, will fit the bill with passable-to-yummy soups, sandwiches, salads, and fresh baked goods. The Cafe also provides classy catering for cocktail parties and wedding receptions. For those who need an extra shot of energy, there's also an espresso bar.

Georgia Brown's
950 15th St. NW
Washington, DC
(202) 393–4499
www.gbrowns.com
$$$

If upscale soul food's your bag, this is the place, but if you prefer traditional preparations, you may be startled by some of the innovations at Georgia Brown's. You'll find black-eyed peas, grits, and collards—but they may not taste familiar. A few years back, in fact, Washington's food community was embroiled in debate about Georgia Brown's crispy collards, anathema to southern cooks who leave 'em simmerin' all day 'till they melt in your mouth. In response Georgia Brown's added the traditional collards to their menu, but kept the crispy greens for those who preferred them. Give the brown-sugar grilled pork chops and hearty Carolina gumbo a try. Georgia Brown's serves lunch weekdays, dinner nightly, and Sunday brunch.

Kinkead's
2000 Pennsylvania Ave. NW
Washington, DC
(202) 296–7700
www.kinkead.com
$$$

Seafood is the specialty of imaginative Robert Kinkead, one of Washington's premier chefs, and a Boston transplant. His casual restaurant serves lunch Monday through Saturday, Sunday brunch, and dinner nightly. Just 4 blocks from the White House, Kinkead's is always packed, and the wooden booths and floors make for some noisy rooms. The atmosphere, however, is beside the point in a place that transforms seafood into such a melting, rich, heavenly experience. Kinkead runs this restaurant with military precision, as you can see through the open kitchen. The kitchen staff wear headphones to communicate above the clatter, turning out seafood timed to perfection. Try the skate wing if they have it or, in season, the soft-shell crab. The seasonings are bold and exotic, and the appetizers are almost too pretty to eat.

Melrose Restaurant at Park Hyatt
1201 24th St. NW
Washington, DC
(202) 955–3899
$$$$

Melrose breaks the mold of hotel restaurants, which aren't generally regarded as serious eateries (though that is changing). There's an Asian influence to some of the cooking here, but also several traditional, luxurious Continental dishes. Every ingredient is top quality, as are the artistic presentations. On a warm day the outdoor terrace garden with its fountain and wide canvas umbrellas is great for people watching, thanks to its location on a busy corner of M Street. The marble and brass dining room, with its plush banquettes and floor-to-ceiling windows, makes you feel pampered, as does the gracious service. The prices are as high as the very best restaurants in town, and although Melrose is very good, you may not feel it warrants a budget-busting evening. They are open for breakfast, lunch Monday through Saturday, dinner, and Sunday brunch.

Mr. Smith's of Georgetown
3104 M St. NW
Washington, DC
(202) 333–3104
www.mrsmiths.com
$$

You won't be able to see the lovely patio garden from the street, yet it's the main draw at this saloon/eatery in Georgetown. You'll find standard pub fare here at reasonable prices and, at night, a piano bar. In fact, Maryland-raised Tori Amos sang here as a teenager. If you like fancy cocktails, this place features daiquiris and other frozen drinks in a dozen varieties. Mr. Smith's serves lunch and dinner daily and Sunday brunch.

New Heights
2317 Calvert St. NW
Washington, DC
(202) 234–4110
www.newheightsrestaurant.com
$$$$

This second-floor charmer overlooks the massive Omni Shoreham Hotel and Rock

Creek Park. Serving dinner nightly and Sunday brunch, it has the warm, casual feel of an artsy neighborhood bistro, but don't be deceived. It has been home to some of the hottest young chefs in the country. As befits such an avant-garde kitchen, the menu is full of surprising combinations, most of which succeed. It's hard to recommend any particular dish because the menu is revised on a regular basis, but be assured whatever you order will be cooked properly.

Old Ebbitt Grill
675 15th St. NW
Washington, DC
(202) 347–4801
www.clydes.com
$$

When they say old, they mean it—since 1856. Old Ebbitt Grill bills itself as "Washington's oldest saloon," and although that may be subject to argument, especially since its renovation (handsome forest green upholstery, mahogany booths, and Victorian lamps), its stellar reputation and prime location are not. Just 2 blocks from the White House, this casually elegant establishment long ago made a name for itself with roasts, steaks, fresh seafood, homemade pastas, soups, burgers, deli-style sandwiches, and homemade desserts. Check out the famed Oyster Bar—even if you don't a have a taste for this particular Chesapeake Bay delicacy.

Old Ebbitt Grill is open for lunch Monday through Saturday, dinner nightly, and Sunday brunch. With a 3:00 A.M. closing time on Friday and Saturday, it's understandably popular with the hungry after-theater crowds. In the Grill's atrium you'll find Ebbitt Express, serving freshly prepared, wholesome takeout food for breakfast, lunch, and dinner.

Old Glory
3139 M St. NW
Washington, DC
(202) 337–3406
www.oldglorybbq.com
$$

Great barbecue, sandwiches and burgers; a lively, casual atmosphere; and fascinating history-rich decor combine to make Georgetown's Old Glory something to shoot fireworks about. If you take your barbecue seriously, you'll want to sample all six of the sauces here: Each follows the recipe of a different barbecue region, like Memphis and Texas. Corn muffins, biscuits, and hush puppies are the real thing, but save room for the mouth-watering desserts. This is a noisy, fun spot, so be sure to add it to the list of places to consider for birthday celebrations or other get-togethers. Old Glory is open for lunch Monday through Saturday, dinner nightly, and Sunday brunch.

Polly's Cafe
1342 U St. NW
Washington, DC
(202) 265–8385
$

Polly's Cafe typifies the ethnically diverse, rapidly gentrifying Shaw/Cardozo neighborhood along U Street. It's a restaurant and bar where bikers and brokers seem to feel equally at home. There's the usual range of burgers, chicken, and seafood, with a revolving selection of specials, such as chicken stuffed with spinach. Open for dinner daily and for brunch on Saturday and Sunday. For night owls and folks who've just been to the nearby Lincoln Theater, Polly's Cafe stays open until 3:00 A.M. on Friday and Saturday nights.

Prime Rib
2020 K St. NW
Washington, DC
(202) 466–8811
$$$$

This is a place for high rollers, and you'll sense it as soon as you see the flashy blondes at the lively bar and lots of fit, fiftyish men . . . with lots of money. People dress up for dinner here: dark suits, slinky black dresses, and even a bit of glitter. The dining room has the feel of an old-time lovers' rendezvous, with its draperies and martinis and baby-grand piano—but it's too crowded for an effective hideaway. The food here is as much an attraction as the ambience. You won't find better prime aged beef, and there's live Maine lobster and fresh Florida seafood flown in daily. Don't forget the traditional accompaniments either: mouth-watering mashed potatoes and creamed spinach. Prime Rib is open for lunch weekdays and dinner Monday through Saturday.

Restaurant Nora
2132 Florida Ave. NW
Washington, DC
(202) 462–5143
www.noras.com
$$$$

Nora Pouillon, the chef and founder of Restaurant Nora, was one of the first in the city to insist on organic ingredients. From free-range poultry to farm-fresh chévre, Nora has always produced the best and most healthful food. Her cozy restaurant has the same honest, farmhouse feeling, with its decorative handicrafts, dark wood floors, and Windsor chairs. As is often the case with simple beauty, this eatery attracts the rich and famous, from former President Clinton to media mogul Barry Dillard. Dishes are sophisticated without necessarily being too calorie laden, with influences from India, France, and, of course, the United States. In general the cuisine will suit those who prefer their foods less seasoned. Those who savor strong flavors may even find some dishes a bit bland. If you go, be sure to save room for one of the special fresh-fruit desserts. Restaurant Nora is open for dinner Monday through Saturday, and closed on Sunday. (See our Close-up on Nora in this chapter.)

Rupperts
1017 7th St. NW
Washington, DC
(202) 783–0699
www.rupperts.com
$$$$

This top-notch restaurant is in a part of town that is, to put it kindly, in transition. The new $300 million Washington Convention Center is under construction across the street and across 5 entire blocks. So how does Rupperts continue to draw well-heeled customers from all over the city? It's simple—the food is irresistible. Plus, the restaurant's a tranquil spot at night, because there's no construction then.

Step through the front door and a romantic refuge complete with flowers, crisp white linens, and candlelight greets you. But the food is what's important here. The menu changes according to what's available at market, and that can mean foie gras, osetra caviar with tiny French green beans, squab, and several kinds of uncommon fish. Vegetarians will have no trouble eating here, thanks to all sorts of interesting produce.

Stop right now if you're getting full though, because you are forbidden to miss dessert! It's worth every calorie. Though the dessert menu changes as often as the dinner menu, and what we had may not be available when you go, do not pass up the brown sugar ice cream swamped in plump raspberries and apples. The other members of your party will just have to settle for the sculpture of blackberries and white chocolate mousse or the figs and chocolate.

Lunch is served on Thursday only. Dinner is served Tuesday through Saturday; the restaurant is closed on Sunday and Monday.

1789 Restaurant
1226 36th St. NW
Washington, DC
(202) 965–1789
www.clydes.com
$$$$

Perhaps it's the location, a two-story Federal townhouse in a quiet residential area of upper northwest in the shadows of Georgetown University. Then, once you treat your palate to the food, that immediately carries equal weight. Whatever the reason, 1789 captivates with its country-inn charm and elegance and the efficient, first-class service. Although named for the year the university was founded, 1789 offers a truly Modern American menu, serving dinner nightly, with such classic treats as pheasant, venison, fish, veal, soft-shell crabs, lobster, and homemade soups. Top Washington chef Ris Lacoste makes daily menu changes to accommodate what's fresh at market. Be sure to leave room for the breads and desserts, all whipped up on the premises. Those seated before 6:15 P.M. can enjoy a three-course meal for $29. 1789 is open for dinner nightly.

Starland Cafe
5125 MacArthur Blvd. NW
Washington, DC
(202) 244–9396
$

Remember the hit song "Afternoon Delight" by the Starland Vocal Band in the 1970s? The Starland Cafe is co-owned by Washingtonian Bill Danoff, who was in the group and also penned other songs, such as "Take Me Home Country Roads." The cafe is located in a comfortable residential neighborhood near the Potomac, northwest of Georgetown. Brunch on Saturday or Sunday offers Belgian waffles, smoked salmon, and eggs Benedict. Or go for the live acoustic jazz and blues on Friday nights. You may just get a table next to Danoff himself.

Vidalia
1990 M St. NW
Washington, DC
(202) 659–1990
$$$

You'd never guess there was a sunny farmhouse dining room in the basement of this midtown office building, but that's just the impression you'll get when you walk through the door of Vidalia. The bright yellow surroundings pique the appetite, as do the heavenly aromas from the kitchen. Here you'll find haute Southern cuisine with accents of whatever else inspires the chef, and whatever is fresh at market. Unlike much Southern cooking, which relies on frying and slow simmering, Vidalia serves dishes with real finesse and its own creative touches. You'll be off to a good start with a basket of cornbread and buttermilk biscuits so sinful you may be tempted to make a meal of them. For a main course you'll find all sorts of great, rich Southern-influenced dishes. The seafood is juicy and prepared just right, and these may be the best sweetbreads in town. Vegetable accompaniments are always unusual, but rarely low-cal, so don't look for salvation here. It may be

wise to wear something loose; you may feel a size larger at meal's end. Vidalia is open for lunch weekdays, dinner Monday through Saturday, and is closed on Sunday.

West End Cafe
Washington Circle Hotel
1 Washington Circle NW
Washington, DC
(202) 293–5390
www.onewashcirclehotel.com/wec.htm
$$$

A great place for a pre- or posttheater dinner, the West End Cafe is an adventurous but comfortable dining spot. One of the two dining rooms features plenty of greenery and glass; the other doubles as a piano bar and has a darker, more intimate feeling with its earth-toned walls and upholstery. There's a lot of leeway for mixing and matching meals here, and many types of cuisine influence the menu. Choices range from simple fare like pizza and omelettes to more elaborate main courses that highlight interesting spices or a mix of exotic ingredients. Vegetarians, too, will appreciate the extra effort that has gone into dreaming up some of the meatless dishes. There's a little something for everyone at the West End Cafe, serving breakfast and lunch on weekdays, dinner nightly, and Sunday brunch.

Willard Room
Inter-Continental Hotel
1401 Pennsylvania Ave. NW
Washington, DC
(202) 637–7440
www.washington.interconti.com/dining
$$$$

The Willard Room is almost daunting in its grandeur: soaring ceilings decorated with medallions and carved moldings, elaborate chandeliers, silken draperies, and table settings fit for royalty. The cooking is also rich and elaborate—a cuisine that hearkens back to the turn of the century when course after lavish course was served. You'll find all the rare epicurean treats here—game, truffles, and vegetables in fancy shapes and combina-

Nora Pouillon: A Pioneer in Healthy Cooking

Nora Pouillon is a groundbreaker. When she was named 1996 Chef of the Year by the San Francisco–based American Tasting Institute, she became the first woman ever to receive the award. That was only one in a long career of firsts, though. Twenty years ago, when Pouillon opened her small Restaurant Nora in a Washington, D.C. town house, it immediately became all the rage. No other fine chef in the city insisted on organic vegetables or meats unadulterated by hormones and antibiotics. Nora's was crowded for lunch and crowded for dinner. Two decades later, its popularity hasn't waned a bit. If anything, it's grown.

The Viennese-born chef is always on a mission, always striving to get out the message about organic foods, even now that they are so popular. Typical of Pouillon is her role as a founding member of Chef's Collaborative 2000, which promotes the use of food from growers who practice organic agriculture. The water she uses at her newest restaurant, Asia Nora, comes from an Aquapure system especially designed for Pouillon. "It is essential that our water is free of chlorine, calcium, magnesium, bacteria, and all metals. We feel that our water is better than any bottled brand. Just taste it!" says Pouillon. One thing is certain, after the recent scares in D.C. resulting from bacteria-contaminated water, systems like Pouillon's are more important than ever.

Nora Pouillon strives to get the message out on organic foods. PHOTO: COURTESY OF CAMILLA ROTHWELL, ASSISTANT TO NORA POUILLON

As for the wine list at Nora's restaurants, many offerings are organic. And it doesn't end there. Her dairy products are from The Organic Cow of Vermont. Her herbs come from her own patio garden at Restaurant Nora, a little patch of green carved out of the sidewalk near the entrance. The beef she serves is from cattle fed a high fiber diet of organic hay and cereal grains. Her soft-shell crabs are still moving when they're delivered each morning. Pouillon is quick to stress that she practices what she preaches, even in her private life. Chefs are notorious for their late hours and indulgent diets, but Pouillon, a mother of four, says she has always been conscious of a healthy lifestyle for the sake of her family. Her daily ritual begins with either yoga or aerobic dance, and she's a regular participant in sports ranging from in-line skating to swimming.

Fitness magazine honored her as one of America's healthiest chefs and her unique organic lifestyle was the topic of a feature article in Japan's top food and living magazine. Such accolades are nothing new to Pouillon, who has been praised in publications as diverse as *Gourmet, USA Today, Travel & Leisure,* the *Washington Post, Food & Wine,* the *San Francisco Examiner,* and *Vegetarian Times.* Pouillon's career has been crowned by two events monumental in the life of any chef: the publication of her first cookbook and her Chef of the Year award from the prestigious International Association of Culinary Professionals. Pouillon's goal in writing *Cooking with Nora* (Park Lane Press, May 1996) is to demonstrate how easy it is to cook foods that are both organic and low in fat. "I hate hidden calories in restaurants and try not to do the same to my customers," she told *Washington Woman* magazine. "Being a woman I think makes me more sensitive to the 'fat' subject." And that's a philosophy we can all appreciate.

tions. Eye-popping desserts are wheeled to your table on a dessert cart that looks like it came straight from Paris, both in its construction and its contents. It's all lovely, and yet no one dish is a standout. If you're out to impress a client or a date, you couldn't choose better surroundings, but if it's a truly memorable meal you're after, there may be better choices for the money. The Willard Room is open for breakfast and lunch weekdays, and dinner Monday through Saturday.

African

Fasika's
2447 18th St. NW
Washington, DC
(202) 797–7673
www.fasikas.com
$$

This recent entry into the Ethiopian restaurant scene offers an upscale atmosphere. In summer, the patio, with its linen-covered tables, offers a fascinating vantage point for people watching. Inside, the room is decorated with huge African baskets and tambours covered in colorful prints. The lights are flattering and there are plenty of plants in the front windows. Go for the fixed price, eight-course dinner accompanied by live music. The food is standard for Ethiopian—spicy stews of seafood, meat or poultry, large flat breads, greens, yams, and other vegetarian main courses. Lunch is served on Satur-

days and Sundays and dinner is served nightly.

Meskerem
2434 18th St. NW
Washington, DC
(202) 462–4100
www.meskerem.net
$$

National recognition and awards galore have done a lot to enhance the reputation of this Ethiopian restaurant, which some critics rank as the nation's finest. If you enjoy such dining adventures, one visit will have you singing its praises too. Enjoy the big floppy crepelike bread for scooping up the various hot and mild meat dishes (including beef, lamb, and chicken), the lentils and green vegetables, and all that glorious sauce. You can't beat the prices. Lunch and dinner are served daily.

Red Sea
2463 18th St. NW
Washington, DC
(202) 483–5000
$

Serving lunch and dinner nightly, Red Sea is also a heavyweight contender in the local arena of award-winning Ethiopian kitchens. It's the mother of all Ethiopian restaurants in the Adams Morgan neighborhood, the first to open its doors 17 years ago. Succulent lamb and beef, delicious poultry and seafood, irresistible spices and stews, and an excellent vegetarian menu combine to rank Red Sea as yet another Adams Morgan stalwart. Open for lunch and dinner daily.

Zed's Ethiopian Cuisine
1201 28th St. NW
Washington, DC
(202) 333–4710
www.zeds.net
$$

Only alphabetical order put Zed's at the end of the list for recommended Ethiopian dining. Although it offers less ambience than some of its competitors, it always scores high where it matters the most for a restaurant: food. In particular the rich sauces, beef dishes, and a unique offering of broiled short ribs help place Zed's ahead of many of its contemporaries. Zed's serves lunch and dinner daily.

Asian (includes Chinese, Japanese, Vietnamese, and Thai)

Asia Nora
2213 M St. NW
Washington, DC
(202) 797–4860
www.noras.com
$$$$

Before the sushi craze Americans equated Asian restaurants with budget fare, and most do still prove relatively economical. This is not so at Asia Nora. The setting is a breathtaking cocoon of rosy wood, gold pillars, intimate lighting, and eye-catching art—and the food lives up to the surroundings. You'll find precious Japanese-style plates decorated with art of the edible kind.

Since the owner is the same Nora (see the Close-up in this chapter) who began the organic food craze in Washington two decades ago, you can be sure of fresh fish and vegetables. You'll find dishes that tend more toward the Japanese or Thai, like the ginger-flamed filet mignon and shichimi onions, as well as those with a more Indian influence, like the curry served with traditional accompaniments like chutney and basmati rice. Asia Nora is open for dinner but closed on Sundays.

Ching Ching Cha
1063 Wisconsin Ave. N.W.
Washington, DC
(202) 333–8288
$

This serene little tea room is a welcome respite from the crowded hustle of Georgetown. Guests partake of the classic Chinese tea ritual here, choosing from 33 teas from China and Taiwan. There's a raised platform with two low tables and lots of pillows for sitting and laid-back sipping. Sweets and snacks are available, as well as light "Tea Meals" that include a choice of three vegetables and one of the three feature dishes, with jasmine rice and a bowl of soup.

Cities
2424 18th St. NW
Washington, DC
(202) 328–7194
www.citiesrestaurant.com
$$$

We've categorized this as a $$$ restaurant, but you could get away with spending a lot less by composing a meal of hot and cold appetizers. Cities changes the national origin of its menu every year. It recently abandoned its Barcelona cafe fare for elegantly served sushi, teriyaki, and other Tokyo cuisine. With plenty of intimate alcoves, it has a romantic, candlelit atmosphere perfect for special evenings. It serves dinner nightly.

Haad Thai
1100 New York Ave. NW
Washington, DC
(202) 682–1111
$$

Not only is this one of the most popular Thai restaurants in downtown Washington, it's also one of the most vibrantly decorated. Big windows, room-sized murals, and artistic fixtures make for a lively, trendy atmosphere, and being near the Washington Convention Center is a big plus. The food is just as vibrant as the space. Flavors explode in your mouth, not

Washington's Chinatown, whose entrance is marked by an ornate arch, is home to numerous Chinese restaurants. PHOTO: COURTESY OF THE WASHINGTON, DC CONVENTION AND TOURISM CORPORATION

just with hot chilis, but also with lemon grass and all those other wonderful Thai spices. Like most Asian restaurants, Haad Thai offers a menu with a mind-boggling array of selections, but any of the curries and coconut-based dishes will please lovers of Thai cuisine. Haad Thai is open for lunch Monday through Saturday, and dinner nightly.

Hunan Chinatown
624 H St. NW
Washington, DC
(202) 783–5858
$$

The competition is fierce in the Asian restaurant-rich H Street thoroughfare, but Hunan Chinatown is a standout for its refined atmosphere and its excellent ingredients. Serving lunch and dinner nightly, the restaurant offers such specialties as smoked duck and plump, juicy dumplings. The sauces are excellent, without the greasiness you may find in lesser Chinese cuisine. Open for lunch and dinner daily.

Japan Inn
1715 Wisconsin Ave. NW
Washington, DC
(202) 337–3400
www.japaninn.com
$$$

Serving lunch weekdays and dinner nightly, this authentic Japanese inn has been a Washington mainstay for years, and it remains an elegant landmark at the edge of Georgetown, in an unmistakably Japanese building. Inside, you'll find serene rooms, each offering a different dining option, such as tabletop grilling or sushi—unusual for Japanese restaurants in Washington, which are often cramped. The cuisine is standard fare, and the setting makes for a complete Japanese experience. An evening here is an event.

Makato
4822 MacArthur Blvd. NW
Washington, DC
(202) 298–6866
$$$

It's likely no one will recommend this tiny

Japanese gem, but that's because few people know of it. It's hard to find, even when you do know where to look, but it's worth the trouble. The door is your first hint that this is the real thing. It's made of pale wood and rice paper and is unmistakably Japanese. Inside, you must remove your shoes before you enter the minuscule dining area. The seats are padded stools unless you sit at the sushi bar. Here, your best bet is to go for the tasting menu, a 10-course meal of specialties that you may never see outside Japan. You'll get a chance to sample everything from soup to a delicate, perfect serving of exotic fruit or homemade fruit ice at meal's end. Lunch is served Tuesday through Saturday, dinner is served Tuesday through Sunday and they are closed on Monday.

Oodles Noodles
1120 19th St. NW,
Washington, DC
(202) 293–3138
$

This stylish fusion eatery is open for lunch Monday through Saturday and dinner nightly. For more information, see the listing under "Suburban Maryland."

Perry's
1811 Columbia Rd. NW
Washington, DC
(202) 234–6218
$$$

An Asian restaurant named Perry's? Well, yes, in a way. Perry's, at the throbbing heart

of Adams Morgan, offers pretty darned good sushi and other Asian dishes along with international standards like pasta. Some dishes are a wonderful fusion of East and West. Perry's is for those who like to party hearty and, in summer, there's no better place than the rooftop garden sparkling with fairy lights. Inside, there's sleek decor reminiscent of those decadent '80s. Speaking of decadence, there's a drag show at Sunday brunch. They are open for dinner and the Sunday brunch.

Star of Siam
1136 19th St. NW
Washington, DC
(202) 785–2838
$
2446 18th St. NW
Washington, DC
(202) 986–4133
$

Competition in the Thai restaurant scene has become considerably stiffer in recent years, but Star of Siam hasn't been fazed. It's consistently good, consistently popular, and consistently top-rated region-wide—hard to improve on that. Whether the location is downtown (19th Street), or in Adams Morgan (18th Street), expect satisfaction at Star of Siam. The fish and curry selections are especially good, and happy hour sushi bargains are quite good for a midtown location. They are open for lunch weekdays and Saturdays at 19th Street, lunch on Saturdays and Sundays at 18th Street, and for dinner nightly at both locations.

Sushi-Ko
2309 Wisconsin Ave. NW
Washington, DC
(202) 333–4187
$$$

As the name implies, sushi is the word at Sushi-Ko, and few in town do it better: eel, toro, sea urchin, shrimp, salmon, quail eggs, flying-fish roe, and even monkfish liver. In fact, when Japanese dignitaries come to Washington for official visits, Sushi-Ko does the catering. Although many people have been converted by the "Try it, you'll like it" urging of their fellow diners, not everyone has embraced the sushi phenomenon. Not to worry—Sushi-Ko also offers decidedly tasty and non-sushi creations, many of which are the chefs' own fusions of Japanese and American cooking styles and ingredients. This is a cramped, no-frills place, but it's always packed with people who know Japanese cuisine. Sushi-Ko is open for lunch Tuesday through Friday and dinner nightly.

Tony Cheng's Mongolian Barbecue
619 H St. NW
Washington, DC
(202) 842–8669
$

To be certain, there's no shortage of barbecue joints in Metro Washington, but you'll be hard pressed to find the Mongolian style (yes, Mongolian) offered anywhere but Tony Cheng's. Here's how it works: you fill your plate with the raw ingredients of your choice from a buffet, then you take it to the chef who grills it. It's as good as it is different, but don't just take our word as gospel. Tasting is believing. Expect generous offerings of meat, vegetables, and tangy sauces, and if you have trouble deciding, opt for the all-you-can-eat deal. Tony Cheng's is open for lunch Monday through Saturday, dinner nightly and Sunday dim sum (Chinese dumplings filled with a variety of delectable meats and vegetables), served from 11:00 A.M. to 3:00 P.M.

Vietnam-Georgetown
2934 M St. NW
Washington, DC
(202) 337–4536
$$

This was one of the first Vietnamese restaurants in Washington, and it remains popular, perhaps in part because of the appealing garden in back that, on summer evenings, is strung with fairy lights. The food is quite tasty—the usual Vietnamese restaurant fare of spring rolls and sweet and sour dishes and fresh grilled seafood. If you enjoy Southeast Asian food and the bustle of downtown

Washington, then you won't be disappointed. It is open daily for lunch and dinner.

French

Gerard's Place
915 15th St. NW
Washington, DC
(202) 737–4445
$$$$

Chef and owner Gerard Pangaud is a true luminary, having won two Michelin stars in France at a very young age. In the United States he has won equal acclaim. His namesake restaurant near the White House is a pretty, unpretentious, very pleasant place in which to spend an evening, but it's not where you'd bring a date you want to impress with fancy surroundings.

Gerard's is for serious gourmets. The food is as refined and as carefully prepared as in the most highbrow eatery. Roasts are juicy; seafood is cooked to that perfect temperature at which it retains its moisture but imparts its full flavors. Dessert may offer some items you've never seen before, like fruit soups or unusually flavored soufflés. This is the place to try something different, safe in the knowledge that it will be a pleasurable experience. Lunch is served weekdays, dinner Monday through Saturday, and it's closed on Sunday.

La Chaumiére
2813 M St. NW
Washington, DC
(202) 338–1784
$$$

This country inn/bistro in the heart of Georgetown is a perennial favorite in the competitive, come-and-go world of French restaurants. With its midroom fireplace and its walls decorated with antique farm tools and copper molds, this is the perfect spot to come in out of the cold. Expect attentive and warm service, and hearty and reliable French peasant fare like cassoulet and couscous, tripe, quenelles of pike, and choucroute garnie. If these earthy offerings don't tempt,

Authentic, fresh ingredients yield an exquisite dining experience. PHOTO: UPS PHOTO GALLEY, COURTESY OF CESCO TRATTORIA

there is more conventional fare, often rich with garlic, butter, and other delicious staples of French country cooking. Lunch is served weekdays, dinner is served Monday through Saturday, and La Chaumiére is closed on Sunday.

La Colline
400 N. Capitol St. NW
Washington, DC
(202) 737–0400
$$$

This Capitol Hill restaurant lacks a bit in atmosphere—it's more executive than romantic—but makes up for it with reliable, classic French cooking. It's been around for more than 20 years, but the menu is regularly updated and always fresh. The rich, traditional French standards are there along with some modern innovations, like creative pastas and lively salads. For the quality of the service and

cuisine, the prices are very good, and if you're sightseeing on Capitol Hill, this is a good place to stop for a meal. La Colline serves breakfast and lunch on the weekdays, dinner Monday through Saturday, and is closed on Sunday.

La Fourchette
2429 18th St. NW
Washington, DC
(202) 332–3077
$$

You'll think you're in Montmartre at this quaint little spot in Adams Morgan. Walk past the entrance and the garlic wafts out, inviting you in. As befits a French restaurant, there are tables outside where you can watch the wide cross-section of humanity on busy 18th Street. Inside, murals of cafe scenes dominate the walls. The tables are tiny and the chairs are the kind you'd find in a Paris bistro. The menu, too, looks like it came straight from Paris: cheese-filled onion soup, crepes, bouillabaisse, escargots, and pâtés. You can't go wrong. La Fourchette is open for lunch weekdays and dinner nightly.

Lavandou
3321 Connecticut Ave. NW
Washington, DC
(202) 966-3002
$$

This adorable neighborhood restaurant, serving lunch weekdays and dinner nightly, is tucked away in a strip of old shops north of the National Zoo, but don't let the facade fool you. Inside, you'll find hearty provençale bistro cooking in a dollhouse setting that may be a little too close for those seeking complete privacy, but just right for those who want the full flavor of casual French dining. This is the kind of homey cooking that carries the punch of garlic and balsamic vinaigrette, cured meats, white beans, and wine. The pork tenderloin is wrapped with bacon and served with a hearty red wine sauce. The Daube Provençale is beef marinated in red wine and oranges, and then cooked with bacon and walnuts; or try the Carbonado, a lamb stew with artichokes, beans, tomato, and celery. Open daily for lunch and dinner.

Le Rivage
1000 Water St. SW
Washington, DC
(202) 488-8111
$$$

For some reason fine cuisine seems to elude those waterfront restaurants with the great views, but not at Le Rivage. This little gem, tucked away among the tour group meccas on the Maine Avenue wharf, offers seafood dishes that are absolutely reliable in quality and taste. There is some creativity among the daily specials, but even if you choose a traditional favorite, you are sure to enjoy it at Le Rivage. As a special treat the restaurant offers a dessert sampling that consists of several of its homemade goodies in one dish. It's open for lunch weekdays and dinner nightly.

German

Cafe Berlin
322 Massachusetts Ave. NE
Washington, DC
(202) 543-7656
$$$

No, you haven't been transported from Capitol Hill to Germany; it just feels that way when you step into Cafe Berlin. Like most restaurants located in town houses, this one has that cozy, warm feeling that immediately charms. The hearty fare—good and reasonably priced—and, of course, the beer selection make this eatery worth a try for those who enjoy German food, both new and traditional, in an Old World setting. Lunch is served Monday through Saturday, and dinner is served daily.

Old Europe
2434 Wisconsin Ave. NW
Washington, DC
(202) 333-7600
www.old-europe.com
$$$

Praise and popularity are old hat for Old Europe, unwavering in its appeal, at the same spot for more than half a century in upper Georgetown. This place, some will contend, embodies all that an Old World German restaurant should be, except maybe for the American locale. Just use your imagination, though, and enjoy various wursts, schnitzel, dumplings, pork, and other filling creations, not to mention the homemade pastries and an extensive wine and beer list. And we can't forget the lively, infectious music. Lunch is served daily except Sundays, and dinner is served nightly at Old Europe.

Hispanic/Caribbean/ Tex-Mex

Cactus Cantina
3300 Wisconsin Ave. NW,
Washington, DC
(202) 686-7222
$$

Lively crowds flock to this funky Cleveland Park retreat with their sights set on

Tex-Mex delights, and Cactus Cantina doesn't disappoint. Standard fare includes generous portions of enchiladas, tacos, ribs, and fajitas. There's also a mesquite grill that turns out tasty salmon, shrimp, ribs, and quail. It's open daily for lunch and dinner.

Coco Loco
810 7th St. NW
Washington, DC
(202) 289–2626
$$

Coco Loco is such a hopping nightspot (see our Nightlife chapter) that some may forget it is also a top-notch choice for Latin American cuisine. The decor immediately spells fun: Floors are Mexican tile, asymmetrical pillars are painted in bright colors, and festive paper lanterns and green plants hang from the rafters. You can start off the evening with Mexican tapas, those minidishes that give you the chance to taste a bit of everything. The array is seemingly endless, ranging from familiar quesadillas to a Latin American version of lobster.

When it comes to main courses, you'll find the Brazilian influence heavy, and it's a welcome one. This is the place to try churrascaria—a banquet of Brazilian roasted meats and salads. Or you may want to choose from the eye-popping buffet of cold dishes or the variety of rotisseried meats circulated to tables by a contingent of waiters. It's an experience not to be missed, especially on Friday and Saturday nights, when the dancers emerge at eleven. It's open for lunch Monday through Friday and dinner nightly.

Enriqueta's
2811 M St. NW
Washington, DC
(202) 338–7772
$$

This charming whitewashed restaurant decorated with Mexican crafts has endured in Georgetown far longer than most of the surrounding restaurants, and there's a reason. The food is authentically Mexican, refined Mexican. The menu may even seem unfamiliar if you've only fre-quented those chains that heap their plates with a mélange of sauces, beans, and tortillas. Even the familiar standards here, such as enchiladas, will taste different than in the Americanized Mexican restaurants. Enriqueta's food, although not exactly gourmet fare, is a cut above, and certainly worth a try if you've never tasted the real thing. Enriqueta's is open for lunch weekdays and dinner nightly.

Gabriel Restaurant
2121 P St. NW
Washington, DC
(202) 956–6690
$$

Tucked into the lower level of the Radisson Barcelo Hotel, Gabriel is a surprise for a hotel restaurant, and a chain hotel at that. It doesn't look like a Latin restaurant—the furnishings are standard hotel dining room, yet there's a tapas buffet at lunch and during the cocktail hour, and the menu is unmistakably south of the border. The seafood has been very good, and the empanadas stuffed with plantains and a variety of other fillings are interesting and tasty. All fried dishes are not executed with equal skill however. If you want to sample it all and decide for yourself, go for the buffet at lunch or brunch. Both are a bargain. Breakfast and dinner are served daily, and lunch is served daily except for Saturdays.

Red Sage
605 14th St. NW
Washington, DC
(202) 638–4444
www.redsage.com
$$$$

All the rage since debuting in 1992, Red Sage quickly established a distinctive presence at Washington's ever-growing table of dining spots. How did it happen? Quite simply through a compelling combination of innovative Southwestern-style food served in what has been called a "showplace" of museum-quality architecture, design, and handicrafts. Look for light fixtures encircled by metal buffalo silhouettes, Indian wool rugs on the hardwood floor, alcoves for wine displays lit

Red Sage serves innovative Southwestern fare with a flair in a restaurant decorated with handcrafts.
PHOTO: COURTESY OF THE WASHINGTON, DC CONVENTION AND TOURISM CORPORATION

with an amber glow, and russet leather booths. Savor especially the cinnamon-smoked quail with pecans and ham or the wild mushroom and Swiss chard-filled ravioli. If nothing else, Red Sage, serving lunch weekdays and dinner nightly, is worth a try just to see if so many people could possibly be so right in their bountiful praise.

Taberna del Alabardero
1776 I St. NW
Washington, DC
(202) 429–2200
$$$$

Taberna del Alabardero, in the minds of many critics and everyday patrons alike, is considered a serious candidate for the title of nation's finest Spanish restaurant. Although traditional cuisine from Spain may be a new dining experience for many, one visit will reveal a cuisine of refinement and elegance unimagined by those who think Spanish food is pretty much like Tex-Mex. Recipes are from the Iberian peninsula, which means fresh sardines, roasted duck, whole suckling pig, rabbit, and several kinds of paella. The setting is

as upscale as in any French restaurant, and the service is top drawer. This is not casual dining. Lunch is served weekdays, dinner is served Monday through Saturday, and it's closed Sunday.

Italian

Al Tiramisu
2014 P St. NW
Washington, DC
(202) 467–4466
$$$
www.altiramisu.com

You'll feel like you're in one of those whitewashed underground wine cellars that they so cleverly convert into restaurants in Europe. The effect is romantic and oh-so-intimate. This Dupont Circle restaurant is the brainchild of Chef Luigi Diotaiuti, Italian born, and trained in some of the best restaurants in the world, not to mention the Ritz Escoffier Ecole de Gastronomie Française in Paris. Your first course should be pasta—it's like silk here, both in terms of the subtle melding of flavors and the just-right texture. Next should be a dish of fish, the restaurant's specialty. Try the linguine with baby clams. The desserts are all delicious, and this small, friendly place is eager to please. They serve lunch on the weekdays and dinner nightly.

Galileo
1110 21st St. NW
Washington, DC
(202) 293–7191
$$$$

Galileo's Roberto Donna is one of Washington's stars. He is in demand all over the world as a guest instructor, speaker, and—of course—chef. Aside from Galileo, he owns a slew of other restaurants in town, many less expensive. Galileo is his flagship, however, and it continues to be one of the city's premier Italian restaurants. You cannot be certain that every detail of every meal will be flawless, but when this restaurant is on point, it's stellar. What's more, Donna is a trendsetter, a visionary, and that makes his restaurant worth a splurge. As for specifics, if you love vegetables, you won't be able to resist some of the versions here, such as the asparagus in black truffle vinaigrette or the grilled exotics. If you're a fan of risotto, you won't find any better version outside of Italy. Galileo is open for lunch weekdays and dinner nightly.

i Ricchi
1220 19th St. NW
Washington, DC
(202) 835–0459
www.iricchi.net
$$$$

Why go to Florence when you can taste the fortunes of her cuisine right here in the District? This bright, airy restaurant takes pride in serving an authentic taste of Tuscany. The setting is inviting country-casual with some luxurious touches: pink tablecloths, flowers, wooden chairs with rush seats, and lots of copper and plants. As for food, it's tough to go wrong here, especially if you try the cheeses, the pasta, the olive oil, the quail, veal, rabbit, and the pork. Especially popular, though, is the fish cooked on a wood-burning grill. i Ricchi has taken Tuscan cuisine in

a classy setting to new heights. i Ricchi is open for lunch weekdays, dinner Monday through Saturday, and closed Sunday.

Obelisk
2029 P St. NW
Washington, DC
(202) 872–1180
$$$$

Now, for something completely different. You won't find a wide range of choices here; in fact this restaurant offers a fixed price menu from which you choose one of three items for each course. How can they get away with such restraint? This tiny town house dining room is always full, so it must be the cooking. You sense that the people who put this together take artistic pride in their creation, and so they should, from the decor of elegant rusticity to the food. Let's start with the bread: It's crusty and aromatic, accompanied by top-shelf olive oil. It's also, of course, made in-house. It's hard to recommend any one dish because the menu changes all the time, and if you're looking for flashy, extravagant cooking, you won't find it here. For subtle, genuine quality Obelisk is a sure bet. The restaurant serves dinner Tuesday through Saturday and is closed on Sunday and Monday.

Sesto Senso
1214 18th St. NW
Washington, DC
(202) 785–9525
www.sesto.com/sesto
$$$

This chic restaurant of dark wood and mirrors has a split personality. At lunch and weeknight dinners, it's crowded with suits from the surrounding office buildings. Weekend diners may be either pleased or disappointed (depending on the company) to discover that they're eating alone. But wait an hour or two and the long, polished bar will be jumping with a crowd of young Europeans and Euro lookalikes who are there to flirt, drink, and party. Make no mistake, though, Sesto Senso has serious dining. The carpaccio here is the real thing, thin-sliced filet rather than beef cut from a pre-

pressed loaf. It is garnished with exquisite olive oil and huge shavings of Parmesan—it may be the best in town. The menu is extensive and tempting, but make friends with any of the kindly staff—the maître d', the waiter, the bartender—and they'll persuade the chef to concoct something just for you. Your new friend will play 20 questions to discover your likes and dislikes, and then you'll be treated to a custom-made meal that contains all your favorite ingredients. It's open for lunch weekdays and dinner Monday through Saturday.

Middle Eastern/ Mediterranean/Indian

Bacchus
1827 Jefferson Pl. NW
Washington, DC
(202) 785–0734
$$

In the minds of many Washingtonians, the art of Middle Eastern cooking—in this case Lebanese—begins and ends at Bacchus, whether you choose the original location here or the offshoot in Bethesda, Maryland, 7945 Norfolk Avenue, (301) 657-1722. Count on quality and satisfaction in whatever menu selection catches your eye at this whitewashed, bustling restaurant. Bacchus specialties include the creative kebabs of beef, chicken, and lamb; savory sausages; stuffed cabbage; and baby eggplant. Bacchus knows how to mix spices and textures for a knockout effect. The absolute must here is the assortment of mezze, appetizers like fragrant hummus with ground beef and toasted almonds on top, baba ghanouj, or hot, flaky phyllo stuffed with cheese. You can make a complete dinner of appetizers and not feel deprived. Dessert? You won't have room. Bacchus in D.C. is open for lunch weekdays, dinner Monday through Saturday, and is closed Sunday. The Bethesda spot is open for lunch on weekdays and dinner nightly.

Bombay Club
815 Connecticut Ave. NW
Washington, DC
(202) 659–3727
$$

That a restaurant this elegant should also be something of a bargain is remarkable, especially when you consider it's just a block from the White House. Bombay Club is not what we in America think of as your typical Indian restaurant. Imagine instead colonial India and all its privilege, and you'll have it right. You can find the "usual" Indian fare here, and it is good, but why not zero in on the dishes that you don't find in other Indian restaurants, such as the seafood appetizers or salads? Seafood also stars as a main course, especially when cooked in a tandoori oven. So often tandoori dishes are overcooked in other Indian restaurants, but here you'll find an unusual refinement. The Bombay Club is an exotic way to spend an evening, and your pocketbook won't feel the punch as much as in other restaurants of this caliber. Lunch is served weekdays and dinner daily.

Lebanese Taverna Restaurant
2641 Connecticut Ave. NW
Washington, DC
(202) 265–8681
$$

This lively, attractive establishment has served notice as a serious contender in the Middle Eastern market, a category that seems either to enchant diners or completely turn them away. For the faithful Lebanese Taverna will surely please with its own brand of moussaka (a Greek staple)—sans the usual ground beef—and other delicious eggplant dishes, spicy sausages, a variety of vegetable kebabs, and, of course, a wood-fired oven that brings out all the right aromas. Also, be sure to sample the wonderful Lebanese breads. It's hard to complain, given the reasonable prices, good cooking, and the cordial and efficient service. There's also a Virginia location at 5900 Washington Boulevard, Arlington, (703) 276-8681. Lunch is served Monday through Saturday and dinner nightly.

Marrakesh
617 New York Ave. NW
Washington, DC
(202) 393–9393
$$$

Dinner at Marrakesh is an event and a festival of new sensations. First, there are the low, cushy sofas and the equally low tables; then, there's the bit about eating with your hands. At the beginning of the meal, the waiter brings water and towels to accommodate the custom. Finally, there's the teasing belly dancer who, of course, selects several men from the audience as stage props to the hilarity of everyone else. The food? Oh, yes, it's good, too. The roasted chicken in preserved lemons and olives, the lamb bursting with spices, the flaky bastilla (a savory-sweet concoction of phyllo pastry and meat dusted with sugar) all serve to make the seven-course meal an exotic foray. Marrakesh is open for dinner daily and will open at lunch for parties of 10 or more. This restaurant does not accept credit cards.

Taj Mahal
1327 Connecticut Ave. NW
Washington, DC
(202) 659–1544
$

The vegetarian crowd won't have any complaints about this place; yet Taj Mahal also does right by nonvegetarians, serving imaginative selections of Mogul and tandoori cuisine with all the right spices. This casual Dupont Circle favorite lays out a tremendous lunch buffet weekdays. Perhaps the overall appeal has something to do with Taj Mahal's claim to being "Washington's oldest authentic Indian restaurant" (since 1965). You can also visit its newer Northern Virginia location at 7239 Commerce Street, Springfield, (703) 644–2875. Taj Mahal serves lunch weekdays and dinner nightly.

Insiders' Tip

Dining havens such as Arlington, Bethesda, Adams Morgan, and Georgetown have scores of restaurants representing every nationality in short distance of one another.

Northern Virginia

American/Continental

Amphora Restaurant
377 Maple Ave. West
Vienna, VA
(703) 938–7877
$$$

Amphora's Diner Deluxe
1151 Elden St.
Herndon, VA
(703) 925–0900
$-$$

If you've got a late-night craving, you'll probably find just the right dish at one of these popular diners, open 24 hours and usually bustling no matter what time of day. The menus feature a huge selection of treats, from a la carte and breakfast items to filling Greek specialties. We love the mouth-watering moussaka, but if we're in need of comfort food, we can't resist the open-faced roast beef or turkey sandwiches, served with mashed potatoes and gravy. Many folks visit for the desserts alone, particularly the decadent layer cakes, pies, and pastries, baked at the neighboring Amphora Bakery at 403 Maple Avenue West, Vienna, (703) 281–5631, or in the Herndon restaurant.

The Herndon location boasts an added bonus: It looks like an eatery right out of a movie. Built just a few years ago, it's probably the most gorgeous diner you'll ever see. Sleek neon lights accent the facade, while inside, smooth, dark wood gives the place a surprising air of elegance.

The Amphora chain also includes several fast-food Knossos and Village Chicken restaurants, specializing in great-tasting, budget-priced Greek food and rotisserie chicken dinners. Locations are sprinkled throughout Northern Virginia.

Carlyle Grand Cafe
4000 28th St.
Arlington, VA
(703) 931–0777
$$

One of the cornerstone establishments in the tidy, compact urban village of Arling-

Delicately flavored and gracefully presented, the simple strawberry becomes an elegant dessert.

PHOTO: R. HOLDEN, COURTESY OF CESCO TRATTORIA

ton, Carlyle Grand Cafe is convenient city dining without parking headaches (ample, free, and convenient spaces nearby). Just a stone's throw from I-395, the restaurant features fresh, modern, and simple decor and quality food (meats, seafood, pasta, sandwiches, etc.). The hot beignets served in lieu of bread for Sunday brunch are impossible to resist. As for the menu, it offers a wide variety of New American cuisine, from Thai-flavored dinner salads to garlicky pastas. Choose to dine downstairs, where the popular bar limits the seating and makes for a livelier time, or upstairs where it's decidedly quieter but equally enjoyable. Carlyle Grand Cafe is open for lunch Monday through Saturday, dinner nightly, and Sunday brunch.

Chutzpah Deli
12214 Fairfax Town Center
Fairfax, VA
(703) 385-8883
www.chutzpahdeli.com
$

The Chutzpah Deli brings a little slice of New York to the Virginia suburbs. Owners brag that the bagels are imported from New York, and Chutzpah's menu brims with what the deli calls "Jewish soul food." Regulars rave about the chicken soup (better than Mom's?), tasty corned beef sandwiches, and lox, eggs, and onions. Enjoy complimentary bowls of pickles and coleslaw on your table while you wait for your order. Chutzpah is open for breakfast, lunch, and dinner Monday through Saturday and closes at 3:00 P.M. on Sunday.

Clyde's
11905 Market St.
Reston, VA
(703) 787–6601
8332 Leesburg Pike
Vienna, VA (Tysons Corner)
(703) 734–1900
$$

These suburban versions of the original District Clyde's have done well, to say the least. The older Tysons location and the newer one in Reston—a cornerstone establishment in the impressive and still-developing Town Center—have faithful patrons and are wildly popular happy-hour, late-night, and brunch destinations. (See the Washington listing for details.) Like the downtown and Chevy Chase, Maryland branches, these two, especially Tysons, are decorated with lavish amounts of glossy wood and glass. The menus are pretty much alike at all branches. Clyde's is open for lunch and dinner nightly and Sunday brunch.

Fish Market
105 King St.
Alexandria, VA
(703) 836–5676
$$

Like hundreds of other Old Town buildings, the one that houses the ever-popular Fish Market has a storied past. It was at one time a focal point of the Colonial-era seafaring trade, when Alexandria was a port city and market of widespread importance. The city still buzzes here in the lower King Street area, but these days the activity is centered around the flourishing restaurant and small-retail business. Fish Market consists of several rooms, including a packed raw bar and a balcony overlooking the heavy pedestrian traffic on King Street. Waiting in line here is not at all uncommon, especially on weekends, so plan accordingly. The raw bar is stocked with spicy shrimp, oysters on the half shell, and all manner of fresh seafood. The restaurant proper offers lots of fried specialties, often accompanied by that southern favorite, hush puppies. Chowders, too, are thick and hearty here. You can get more low-calorie fare, but it

somehow doesn't seem to match the raucous, checkered tablecloth ambience. It's open for lunch and dinner daily.

Hard Times Cafe
3028 Wilson Blvd.
Arlington, VA
(703) 528–2233
1404 King St.
Alexandria, VA
(703) 683–5340
428 Elden St.
Herndon, VA
(703) 318–8941
6263 Springfield Plaza
Springfield, VA
(703) 913–5600
www.hardtimes.com
$

Chili in one of a dozen incarnations is the best reason to go to Hard Times Cafe. But there's nothing wrong with that reason, is there? Visit one of these down-home joints, which are dark and loud and lots of fun, for a casual—very casual—evening or a quick bite accompanied by Hank Williams tunes on the jukebox. No one will frown if you wipe your bowl clean with a chunk of yummy cornbread. We're partial to the Cincinnati-style chili, served with shredded cheese and onions atop a dish of spaghetti. They are open for lunch and dinner daily.

Heart in Hand
7145 Main St.
Clifton, VA
(703) 830–4111
www.heartinhandrestaurant.com
$$$

A favorite of former First Lady Nancy Reagan, romantic Heart in Hand specializes in American cuisine with a Southern touch. The bread basket at the beginning of the meal may be the highlight, but soups are hearty and good, and the restaurant features great homemade desserts. You can't help but get sentimental and warm all over as you're served in this historic farmhouse in the quaint one-stoplight community of Clifton, the heart of Fairfax County's affluent horse country. Heart in Hand is open for lunch and dinner Tuesday through Saturday and Sunday brunch. It's closed Mondays.

Hermitage Inn
7134 Main St.
Clifton, VA
(703) 266–1623
www.hermitageinnrestaurant.com
$$$$

Just across the street from the village of Clifton's other top restaurant, Heart in Hand, Hermitage Inn offers romance that's more Continental than country. Housed in a white, two-story former hotel once visited by Presidents Grant and Hayes, Hermitage Inn features a wide veranda and second-story balcony, along with a beautifully landscaped patio garden just right for warm summer evenings. Inside, you'll find a plantation-style dining room cooled by softly whirring ceiling fans and French doors, and warmed by flattering pastel decor and fireplaces. In winter you may prefer to dine instead in the publike wine bar/restaurant on the first floor, complete with its own wood-burning fireplace.

The food here is a mixture of New American and French, with a number of daily specials. Salads, even the most basic, are creative and tasty. There are interesting game specials from time to time that are worth a try, but the real treat here is the wine list, which offers nearly 20 different selections by the glass as well as some unusual bottles. Enjoy soaking in the atmosphere and leave renewed by the peaceful, romantic setting. It's open for dinner Wednesday through Sunday, Sunday brunch, and is closed Monday and Tuesday.

J. R.'s Stockyards Inn
8130 Watson St.
McLean, VA (Tysons Corner)
(703) 893–3390
$

There's Morton's of Chicago across the street and then there's J. R.'s, the budget alternative. At this casual, kid-friendly restaurant, the beef is fresh from the family-owned packing plant, and it's aged and cut in-house. Try their fresh seafood, chicken, lamb chops, barbecue, or gour-

> ## Insiders' Tip
> If you've had it with trying to park your own car in Bethesda's popular restaurant district, spend an extra $3.00 or $4.00 on valet parking and save yourself a headache. Public and private lots fill up fast and are so crowded they are difficult to navigate.

met salads. Nothing fancy here, just good food and lots of it. It's open for lunch weekdays and dinner nightly.

Kenny's Pit Bar-B-Que
3060 Duke St.
Alexandria, VA
(703) 823–3330
$

You wouldn't expect to find such a tasty barbecue joint in such an obscure place, but there Kenny's sits, wedged between an auto repair place and a doughnut shop. It's not the easiest place to spot, but make the effort to slow down and find it. Grab a chair in the dinky, sparse, and often drafty dining area and enjoy the tangy and cooked-to-perfection pork, beef, and chicken barbecue sandwiches and platters. And don't forget the side orders such as corn bread, beans, coleslaw, and chunky French fries, which are good enough to be main courses. It's open for breakfast Monday through Friday and for lunch and dinner Monday through Saturday.

Kilroy's
5250-A Port Royal Rd.
Springfield, VA
(703) 321–7733
www.kilroys.com
$

Whether you come with your kids for the Sunday brunch buffet, to watch Monday Night Football, or dance to live bands playing '80s and '90s tunes, Kilroy's has it all. There are a total of 29 TVs in its lounge and dining room, and you can reserve one to watch your favorite team. Kilroy's is open for lunch and dinner daily and may be most popular for its moderately priced brunch, which includes omelettes to order, Belgian waffles, eggs Benedict, and nearly a dozen other items.

Market Street Bar & Grill
1800 Presidents St.
Reston, VA
(703) 709–6262
www.msbg.net
$$$

The Hyatt Regency resides in Reston's impressive Town Center, which makes it easy to find your way to the hotel's first-rate restaurant, the Market Street Bar & Grill. Accented by an open grill and colorful paintings, the contemporary wood-floored dining area serves remarkably good pasta, seafood selections, and soups. Visible through the curved wall of windows is an inviting terrace where meals are also served.

The chef here is creative, and at suburban prices, this place can be a bargain. Not to say that it's inexpensive. It's just that some of the menu items would cost far more downtown. Try the appetizer of lobster and grits or the Japanese-style sushi trio. A lot of the seafood dishes have Asian accents that the chef executes with finesse. If your tastes are more American, try the pumpkin seed-dusted breast of turkey with butternut squash risotto, rotini, and hard cider jus. The meat dishes here are all high quality, and vegetable accompaniments can be as tempting as the main course. Desserts here are a treat: creme brûlée, fruit cobblers, or tarts, and a sinful chocolate praline torte.

At Market Street, there's always a unique twist on the old standards. It's open for breakfast daily, lunch Monday through Saturday, dinner nightly, and Sunday brunch. Also, you can enjoy live jazz there on Friday, Saturday, and Sunday nights.

Morton's of Chicago
8075 Leesburg Pk.
Vienna, VA (Tysons Corner)
(703) 883–0800
11956 Market St.
Reston, VA
(703) 796–0128
www.mortons.com
$$$$

Here's one of the exceptions to our no-national-chains pledge made at the beginning of this chapter. We didn't list Morton's location in D.C. because there are so many superb steakhouses in the District, but if you want this kind of quality in Northern Virginia, there's only Morton's. It's a big-night-on-the-town kind of place without the commute and parking hassles. If this legendary steakhouse can't satisfy that hankering for prime dry-aged beef, you might as well buy some cattle and a do-it-yourself guidebook. The waiter who brings the cuts of meat to your table on a trolley presents the menu with drama. Along for the ride is a live lobster just waiting for someone to soak it in butter. As with other Washington area steakhouses, the vegetable accompaniments and salads (all a la carte) are served in portions generous enough to satisfy a sumo wrestler. Our favorite here is the Delmonico or, for bigger appetites, the porterhouse. But other meats and seafood are also top drawer. For dessert Morton's soufflés are always popular, but must be ordered with the meal, and by the time you've made your way through the entree, you may regret the extra course. If you want to try the D.C. locations, one is in Georgetown at 3251 Prospect Street NW (202–342–6258), and the other at 1050 Connecticut Avenue (202–955–5997). The Virginia locations are open for lunch weekdays and dinner nightly.

The Palm Court
Westfield's Marriott Conference Center
14750 Conference Center Dr.
Chantilly, VA
(703) 818–3522
$$$$

Housed in the magnificent Georgian-style mansion that is the heart of the Westfield's conference center and hotel, The Palm Court is worth the drive into western Fairfax. Before you sit down to eat, enjoy the rolling, manicured lawns and the building's extravagant antique furnishings and custom-made Oriental carpets. Expect dining at its most formal, with live piano music, lavish place settings, and tableside preparation. This is a place that keeps up with all the culinary trends while offering a reassuring selection of Continental and American favorites, including Caesar salad, lobster bisque, rack of lamb, veal, duck, and a bevy of sinful desserts.

There are some surprises on the menu, too. On one recent outing, we tasted a combination of bear and boar. The bear was delicious and tender, and the boar was as gamey as you would expect, but interesting nevertheless. A top-drawer restaurant in the suburbs is a rare treat. Westfield's is open for breakfast, lunch, and dinner Monday through Saturday and for Sunday brunch.

Phillips Seafood Grill
8330 Boone Blvd.
Vienna, VA (Tyson's Corner)
(703) 442–0400
www.phillipsfoods.com
$$$

This is the seventh of the popular Phillips seafood restaurant family, but it's the first of its kind in a new concept for the chain: a fashionable bar and grill in contrast to the traditional family seafood house that has become the Phillips trademark. Surely the upscale Tysons Corner location had something to do with the change, but it's a hit just the same and little wonder why more are planned. Tucked in an office park at Routes 7 and 123, the 300-seat restaurant dishes out filling tossed salads, seafood, fish, beef and pasta entrees, and dramatic desserts, all with an emphasis on freshness and creativity. A seat in the main dining room affords a view of the display kitchen and its wood-burning grills. There's outdoor seating in the summer and a raw bar and happy hour specials all the time; private dining rooms are available. Phillips is open for lunch weekdays, dinner nightly, and Sunday brunch.

Portner's
109 S. Saint Asaph St.
Alexandria, VA
(703) 683–1776
$$

Although it may seem hard to distinguish among some of Old Town's numerous dining spots in beautiful old brick buildings, there's just something about Portner's that helps it stand out. There are four dining areas, each appealing in its own way. The brick garden patio behind a wrought-iron gate is prime seating in summer; the pub with its dark wood booths and old-fashioned bar is great for a quick bite or an evening of socializing. Lunch or Sunday brunch is cheery in the sun-filled atrium; and for dinner, the upstairs dining room decorated with grand bronze lamps, polished wood, and etched glass, is a setting of festive elegance. As for the food, it's perfectly good and filling American fare ranging from steaks to grilled fish to tasty pasta standards. Desserts are extravagant concoctions and definitely worth saving room for. But Sunday brunch may be where Portner's really shines, from the sourdough French toast, to the eggs Benedict and smoked salmon frittatas. Portner's is open for lunch Monday through Saturday, dinner nightly, and Sunday brunch.

Red, Hot & Blue
1600 Wilson Blvd.
Arlington, VA
(703) 276–7427
208 Elden St.
Herndon, VA
(703) 318–7427
4150 Chain Bridge Rd.
Fairfax, VA
(703) 218–6989
1701 Clarendon Blvd.
Arlington, VA
(703) 522–3355
www.rhnb.com
$$

Barbecue fan? You won't find better than Red, Hot & Blue. By now a Washington institution, this crowded joint in Arlington serves succulent ribs, pulled pork and chicken, and brisket. The ribs are served wet (with sauce) or dry (rubbed with spices, no sauce). Sauces and seasonings are perched on each table so you can customize your order. There are other locations in the Metro area (see Suburban Maryland listings), but we think the original one on Wilson Boulevard in Arlington is best. Open for lunch and dinner daily.

Silver Diner
3200 Wilson Blvd.
Arlington, VA
(703) 812–8600
14375 Smoketown Rd.
Dale City, VA
(703) 491–7376
12251 Fair Lakes Pkwy.
Fairfax, VA
(703) 359–5999
8101 Fletcher Ave.
McLean, VA
(703) 821–5666
8150 Porter Rd.
Merrifield, VA
(703) 204–0812
11951 Killingsworth Ave.
Reston, VA
(703) 742–0805
6592 Springfield Mall
Springfield, VA
(703) 924–1701
www.silverdiner.com
$

Like the Maryland locations (see our entry under Suburban Maryland) these restaurants have the feel of an old-time diner. We especially like the Silver Diner for breakfasts and desserts. Waffles and French toast are great here. If you're visiting later in the day, try their meatloaf and mashed potatoes, burgers and shakes, or humongous sandwiches. The 3:00 A.M. closing time on weekends makes Silver Diner a favorite stop for night owls. Silver Diner is open for breakfast, lunch, and dinner daily.

Tuscarora Mill
203 Harrison St.
Leesburg, VA
(703) 771–9300
www.tuskies.com
$$

Tuscarora Mill is one of Leesburg's best-loved dining spots. Soaring beamed ceilings, dark wood, and old farm tools let you know you're in horse country. This casual spot is great for thick sandwiches, burgers, fries, and other well-executed American dishes. The desserts of the mile-high, fudgy ilk, are the highlight. You wouldn't make a special trip to Leesburg to eat here, but the town is crammed full of history, boutiques, and antique shops, so go exploring before or after your meal. Tuscarora Mill is open for lunch and dinner nightly.

Union Street Public House
121 S. Union St.
Alexandria, VA
(703) 548–1785
www.usphalexandria.com
$$

Union Street is one of the area's most popular neighborhood saloons and restaurants. Choose a lively and often-crowded bar scene downstairs, quieter dining in the raw bar and grill room upstairs, or something in between in the sometimes overlooked backroom oyster bar. An array of huge dinner salads and sandwiches grace the menu, along with the usual saloon fare like buffalo wings, fritters, pastas, burgers, and some grilled meats. Highlighted here are a dozen or so draft beers including the house exclusive—the rich and delicious Virginia Native. It is open for lunch and dinner daily and Sunday brunch.

Warehouse Bar and Grill
214 King St.
Alexandria, VA
(703) 683–6868
www.warehousebarandgrill.com
$$

This pleasant restaurant bills itself as New Orleans–style and offers Louisiana specialties, but the decor is casual, understated classic American, with the exception of the nice gallery on the second floor overlooking the space below. The place has a fun atmosphere, a hopping bar scene, and is a great place to drop in if you're in the neighborhood. Snag a window table to take in the interesting sights along King Street. Open for lunch Monday through Saturday, dinner nightly, and Sunday brunch.

Asian

Bee-won Secret Garden
6678 Arlington Blvd.
Falls Church, VA
(703) 533–1004
$

We dare you to try and find this restaurant in any other guide, because it is truly a secret in this area. Tucked into a strip mall, this is not a place you'd wander into by accident. Once inside, the decor is pleasant but simple, with a sushi bar, a scattering of booths, a long table in the center, and smaller tables against the wall—all in light wood. The reason to come here is the sparkling fresh sushi as well as Korean and Japanese cooked dishes, all at rock-bottom prices.

The fresh fish tank at the entrance is not just for show. There is an Asian custom that many Westerners find abhorrent—that of serving whole fish that are still alive. Vital organs are separated from the meat but left intact enough so the fish lives as it is eaten, assuring the ultimate in freshness. This is definitely not for everyone, but some Asians consider it a delicacy, and at Secret Garden you can have it. As you might imagine, this is a restaurant that caters to a great many Asians, so if it's authenticity you want, this is the place. Bee-won is open for lunch and dinner daily.

Busara
8142 Watson St.
McLean, VA
(703) 356–2288
www.busara.com
$$

Fans of the downtown Busara, with its wild murals and ultramodern seating, have quickly made a hit of the Tysons Corner shopping center branch of this innovative Thai restaurant. On the menu are all the traditional Thai favorites like curries, pad Thai, or larb gai, but there are also some imaginative fusion dishes. For lunch or dinner try one of the meal-sized salads or make a meal of the dough-wrapped appetizers that range from shrimp to chicken to veggies. If you order curry or one of the other sauced dishes, specify how hot you want it to be or use the chili-pepper scale on the menu as a guide. It's especially nice to sit in the outdoor garden on a fine day. Busara serves lunch and dinner daily.

Duangrat's
5878 Leesburg Pk.
Falls Church, VA
(703) 820–5775
$$

New Thai restaurants spring up all the time in Metro Washington, but Duangrat's continues to shine. Maybe it's the gracious, almost formal decor, with its rosy tablecloths, flowers, and generously upholstered chairs; then again, it's probably the food as much as anything. There are always interesting daily specials—try the spicy soft-shell crab if it's available—and the menu is as long and varied as in any Thai restaurant, with a few extra soups and stews thrown in. Compare the standard Thai dishes here with those in other restaurants, and you'll see why

Daring diners can trade their forks for chopsticks at Washington's numerous Asian restaurants.

Duangrat's is so popular. Batters are always light and fresh, peanut sauce is never cloying, and the crab-stuffed chicken wings are head and shoulders above anyone's in town. Duangrat's serves lunch and dinner daily.

Hee Been
6231 Little River Tnpk.
Alexandria, VA
(703) 941–3737
$$

This is where Northern Virginia's large Korean community comes to celebrate special occasions, and you'll understand why once you've experienced Hee Been. Korean barbecues are always fun, grilled at the table and accompanied by a dozen condiments. The difference at Hee Been is that nothing is done by rote, and no one is rushed. Let the waiter be your guide as to what's good. You're sure to have an adventure. If language is a barrier and you want to venture beyond barbecues, try the soups—some as thick as stews, others brothlike and delicate. Whatever you choose, don't miss the short ribs, which are a star here. Hee Been is open for lunch and dinner daily.

Matuba
2915 Columbia Pk.
Arlington, VA
(703) 521–2811
$

Matuba is open for lunch weekdays and dinner nightly. Please see the Suburban Maryland listing.

Nam Viet
1127 N. Hudson St.
Arlington, VA
(703) 522–7110
$

The name may be turned around, but we've figured it's for a reason: That's exactly what you'll be inclined to do after your first dining experience at Nam Viet. Go back again. And soon. The food is as consistently good as the atmosphere is relaxing and unpretentious, and the prices reasonable. Don't miss the bon dun, the great selection of soups, or the

skewered meats grilled with fragrant herbs. You can enjoy your meal outside in warm weather, but the indoor dining room is several steps above the utilitarian atmosphere found in some of the other low-cost neighborhood restaurants. Nam Viet is open for lunch and dinner daily.

Peking Gourmet Inn
6029-6033 Leesburg Pk.
Falls Church, VA
(703) 671–8088
www.pekinggourmet.com
$$

This used to be a favorite of the first President Bush, and it still has plenty of good things to offer on the menu, but the Peking duck remains the standard against which to measure all others—crispy on the outside, lean on the inside, and carved at tableside. The appetizers are very good, too, especially the dumplings, the sesame shrimp toast, and the hot and sweet cabbage. Peking Gourmet Inn takes pride in growing its own leeks and garlic sprouts, and they are featured in several main courses, but the meats can sometimes be flabby—it's often hit or miss here. Still, the place has kept its prices low enough so that mistakes won't spoil your evening, and if you choose right, you'll love your meal. Be sure to make reservations for dinner. Despite the endless array of dining rooms, it's always crowded and there's always a line. That should tell you something right there. They serve lunch and dinner daily.

Pho 75
1711 Wilson Blvd.
Arlington, VA
(703) 525–7355
3103 Graham Rd., Ste. B
Falls Church, VA
(703) 204–1490
382 Elden St.
Herndon, VA
(703) 471–4145
www.pho75.net
$

You don't choose this Vietnamese restaurant for the atmosphere. It's basic, very basic. And you don't go for variety. The only thing you can order, appropriately enough, is pho. But you can bet the pho's darned good here. In case you haven't tried it, pho is a soup based on beef broth and studded with wonderfully aromatic Asian spices like lemon grass, coriander, and anise. But lest you think you'll leave hungry, imagine a soup so thick with noodles, meat, and veggies that it easily makes a meal. If you want to spice it up even more, there's a variety of condiments that comes with each order, as well as bottles of sauce on the tables. Price-wise, the whole thing just barely breaks into the double digits, so it's an unbeatable bargain. (See the Surburban Maryland section for locations in Langley Park and Rockville.) Pho 75 is open for breakfast, lunch, and dinner nightly until 8:00 P.M.

Tachibana
6755 Lowell Ave.
McLean, VA
(703) 847–1771
$$$

Tachibana, in upscale McLean, is a low-key, western-style dining room curved around a sushi bar. Although there are many Japanese specialties, the point is the sushi, which is well executed, fresh, and often displays a variety not found elsewhere in the suburbs. Try any of the sushi chef's specials and you won't be disappointed. Unlike many Asian restaurants, the service is unhurried, and the plush carpeting and upholstered chairs lend themselves to long, quiet conversations. You can also sit at the surprisingly roomy sushi bar and watch the master at work. Tachibana is open for lunch weekdays and dinner daily.

Tara Thai
226 Maple Ave.
Vienna, VA
(703) 255–2467
7501-E Leesburg Pike
Falls Church, VA
(703) 506–9788
4001 North Fairfax Drive
Arlington, VA
(703) 908–4999
www.amir.org
$$$

The decor here makes a statement. It looks like an aquarium: deep blues and greens,

very moody, very pretty. There's also a touch of Africa in the zebra-striped banquettes. It's all very young, fun, and vibrant. The food is vibrant, too, bursting with chilis, lemon grass, lime, and cilantro. A standout is the shrimp—big, juicy, and cooked just right. If you like whole fish, this is the place to have it. It is smothered in all those tongue-teasing spices, and even after you're full, you can't stop picking at it, the flavor's so memorable. All the seafood is good here, befitting the aquarium theme. After dinner, Tara Thai pays tribute to America's endless sweet tooth by offering a variety of unusual desserts. Most feature tropical fruits and flavorings, and all are delectable, though some may not suit western palates. Owner Nick Srisawat has also expanded his concept into suburban Maryland: One shining new Tara Thai is at 12071 Rockville Pike (301–231–9899), and another is in downtown Bethesda at 4828 Bethesda Avenue (301–657–0488). Tara Thai is open for lunch and dinner every day.

Woo Lae Oak
1500 S. Joyce St.
Arlington, VA
(703) 521–3706
$$

This is a great stop if you happen to be shopping at Pentagon City, but Woo Lae Oak alone is also worth a trip. Step inside this long, crowded room and you'll know from the fragrant smoke that there's a whole lot of grilling going on. Korean-style barbecue is a favorite here, and the sushi is a good way to start the meal. It's served on ice and portions are generous. This eatery has a long menu featuring many noodle dishes and soups, so ask your waitress for recommendations or watch what the Koreans around you are ordering. They serve lunch and dinner daily.

Young Chow
420 S. 23rd St.
Crystal City, VA
(703) 892–2566
www.youngchowrestaurant.qpg.com
$

This is a great place to kill some time during a long layover at very nearby Reagan

National Airport. Young Chow is a mere five minutes away (even less with a little luck), barely a block off Jefferson Davis Highway, but whether you're a local or a visitor, you can depend on tasty Chinese food of the Szechuan, Hunan, and Cantonese varieties. Of course, being in a veritable mecca of corporate and government offices, Young Chow's take-out business is substantial. Open for lunch and dinner nightly.

French

Cafe Rochambeau
310 Commerce St.
Occoquan, VA
(703) 494–1165
$$

The tiny village of Occoquan draws people from the Washington area who want to step back to a more serene time and enjoy a small town atmosphere enhanced by a river view. At the northern end of Prince William County on Route 123, Occoquan attracts thousands each year with its craft shows and antique shops—and hungry shoppers have to eat. There's no more inviting spot on a summer evening than the wide, flower-filled veranda of Cafe Rochambeau. In a country-style white Victorian, the place positively exudes old-time romance. Inside, there are wooden floors and simple, country-style decorations—nothing cutesy. The food is good country French, and the menu sticks to a few standards: a beef dish, a couple of fish preparations, chicken, and often veal or lamb. The food is always tasty, but stick to the grilled dishes if you don't really like sauces. For dessert the lemon silk pie is outstanding by any measure. The cafe is open for lunch and dinner daily except Mondays, during the summer months, they're open Mondays, too.

La Bergerie
218 N. Lee St.
Alexandria, VA
(703) 683–1007
www.labergerie.com
$$$

La Bergerie is an old classic that always pleases. After two decades you might expect it to fade or get sloppy, but the food here is always a delicious surprise. The origins are Basque, that region between Spain and France that produces food rich with garlic, tomatoes, bell peppers, and seafood. There are also the elegant French standards like sole in creamy sauce or coq au vin. All this is served in a setting that is cozy and formal. The walls are brick, lending warmth. As in the best restaurants, the tables are generous and well spaced, and there are leather banquettes scattered about the dining room. Service is very proper and traditional, and some of the waiters are of the European breed that makes a lifelong career in elite restaurants, taking great pride in their professions, as they should. End your meal with one of La Bergerie's desserts—many of which are made in-house. The tarts are particularly good. They serve lunch and dinner Monday through Saturday and are closed Sunday.

La Cote d'Or Cafe
6876 Lee Hwy.
Arlington, VA
(703) 538–3033
$$$

This place is a jewel in the rough, with the "rough" being its location right off I-66, next to a garage. It's not a dangerous neighborhood, but it doesn't give a clue as to the lavishly romantic setting that awaits you inside. Striking arrangements of roses, pretty table settings, and intimate lighting all add up to a downtown atmosphere—at downtown prices—right in the Virginia suburbs. The food lives up to the surroundings, as befits highly esteemed Washington chef, Raymond Campet, who decided to set up shop in Virginia.

There are all sorts of elegant classics featuring game, duck, and high-quality beef. The daily specials are particularly good but often pricier than the regular menu. The dishes are expertly sauced, such as the game meats with savory berry glazes or the seafood with buttery garlic accents. Desserts, even the simple berries in sabayon sauce, can be a real treat. Several critics consistently rate this restaurant among the best in Washington. They serve lunch and dinner daily.

L'Auberge Chez François
332 Springvale Rd.
Great Falls, VA
(703) 759–3800
www.laubergechezfrancois.com
$$$

Accessible only by a twisting two-lane road—one of many in woodsy, fashionable and oh-so-affluent Great Falls—L'Auberge Chez François continues to reap awards and praise as the years go by, and it never seems to falter in its appeal. There's an unmistakable country inn warmth and romance that permeates the soul. The French cuisine hails from Alsace, that province along the German border that specializes in game and richly sauced vegetables. The wait staff is dressed in keeping with the theme: dirndl skirts, colorful vests, and the whole bit. Menu selections are endless, all accompanied by garlic bread, salad, after-dinner sweets, and a slew of side dishes. Stick with traditional Alsatian fare—duck, pork, or anything in puff pastry—and you can't go wrong. Desserts are equally representative of the region, with lots of fruit tarts and soufflés that are definitely worth a try. Reservations for weekends should be made a month in advance (unless you want to wait till the last minute and hope for a cancellation), but it's worth the wait. L'Auberge Chez François is the kind of place you anticipate with a smile. It's open for dinner Tuesday through Sunday and is closed Monday.

Le Gaulois
1106 King St.
Alexandria, VA
(703) 739–9494
$$

The minute you walk through the door and onto the hardwood floors at Le Gaulois, you feel as though you've found refuge from the city bustle in a country French auberge—no easy feat for a streetside restaurant. Friendly, quiet, and accommodating to a new degree, Le Gaulois serves creative and very reliable French-influenced cuisine at reasonable prices. The menu changes here with the seasons, and as you'd expect, winter entrees are hearty offerings in warm sauces infused with wine and garlic. Summer is the time to try seafood poached or grilled, then spiked with zesty herbs. If you're seeking authentic French peasant fare, try the organ meats. Not many places offer such a wide selection. Accompaniments can range from crisp, buttery veggies to those homey parsleyed potatoes. This is country French cooking at its best, with prices that don't break the bank. Le Gaulois is open for lunch and dinner Monday through Saturday and is closed Sunday.

Le Refuge
127 N. Washington St.
Alexandria, VA
(703) 548–4661
$$

If Le Gaulois is peaceful, then Le Refuge is the exact opposite. It's a wild place where you may feel as though you're dining in your neighbor's lap. It makes for lots of conversations and laughter between tables though, and you'll have a good time. The food here is typical brasserie fare, with good, solid cooking that is quick and inexpensive. Veggie accompaniments are French classics like calorie-laden Lyonnaise potatoes (deliciously sinful!) or green beans swimming in butter. You really can't go wrong here when the bill is so very reasonable. Le Refuge is open for lunch and dinner Monday through Saturday and is closed on Sunday.

Hispanic/Caribbean/ Tex-Mex

Anita's
9278 Old Keene Mill Rd.
Burke, VA
(703) 455–3466
13921 Lee Jackson Hwy.
Chantilly, VA
(703) 378–1717
701 Elden St.
Herndon, VA
(703) 481–1441

10880 Lee Hwy.
Fairfax, VA
(703) 385–2965
10611 Lomond Dr.
Manassas, VA
(703) 335–6400
521 Maple Ave. E.
Vienna, VA
(703) 255–1001
147 Maple Ave. W.
Vienna, VA
(703) 938–0888
$

Vienna was the original home of this popular local chain of "New Mexico"–style Mexican food outlets, but the town couldn't keep Anita's to itself for long. Soon, other suburban communities began to experience what they were missing. Although the fare may not satisfy Tex-Mex aficionados used to the zestier, eye-watering concoctions, it is nevertheless consistently good and inexpensive, the service is efficient, and the setting is relaxed and inviting. You can't help but overdo it on the homemade chips and salsa before the entrees arrive, but be sure to leave room for the sweet, puffy sopaipillas that beg to be topped with honey. They serve lunch and dinner nightly.

El Pollo Rico
2917 N. Washington Blvd.
Arlington, VA
(703) 522–3220
$

This modest, Peruvian-owned cafe is among the best of the area's bargain rotisserie-chicken restaurants. El Pollo Rico ("Delicious Chicken") does a brisk carryout business, but you can also sit at one of the handful of small tables scattered around the simple room. The menu is limited, and the only real reason to come is the house specialty: marinated, charcoal-fired rotisserie chicken that's perfectly flavored and practically melts in your mouth. With it, you can have fries, empanadas, or tamales. If you're in Maryland, try the Wheaten location at 2541 Ennalls Avenue (301-942-4419). El Pollo Rico serves lunch and dinner nightly. They do not accept credit cards.

La Cantinita's Havana Cafe
3100 Clarendon Blvd.
Arlington, VA
(703) 524–3611
$$

This sleeper has finally received the notice it deserves from Washington food critics. You'll find authentic Cuban cuisine here, quite different from Tex-Mex, but containing many of the same spices. The roast pork is especially good, robust and zinged with a combination of hearty seasonings. If you want something lighter, try the red snapper served with an addictive vinegar-based sauce that'll make your tongue do a salsa. Havana Cafe is also a step-up from Washington's Tex-Mex restaurants in terms of decor. It's a light, airy space, where lunch is served weekdays and dinner nightly.

Rio Grande Cafe
4301 N. Fairfax Dr.
Arlington, VA
(703) 528–3131
1827 Library St.
Reston, VA
(703) 904–0703
$$

Please see Suburban Maryland listing.

Santa Fe East
110 S. Pitt St.
Alexandria, VA
(703) 548–6900
$$

This Old Town Alexandria restaurant couldn't be more inviting, with its whitewashed walls, French doors, old bricks, and beamed ceilings. Inside, it looks like an Architectural Digest photo shoot of a Santa Fe hacienda, though it is actually a historic, Federal-style town house dating from colonial times. The food is a departure from the normal Tex-Mex fare. This is creative Southwestern. That means white chili, roasted pork and chicken, and complex sauces over good fish. Try one of the dishes that is slow cooked, like the chilis. In keeping with the sophisticated surroundings, the wine list is what you'd expect of an upscale restaurant, and, except in the bar area, the tables are set with linens and placed far enough apart for privacy. If you want Southwestern cuisine that's a bit creative, in a setting a bit more formal than the norm, Santa Fe East is the answer. Open for lunch and dinner daily.

South Austin Grill
801 King St.
Alexandria, VA
(703) 684–8969
Austin Grill Springfield
8430 Old Keene Mill Rd.
Springfield, VA
(703) 644–3111
$$

This Old Town Alexandria Tex-Mex spot is always jumping, and there's a reason why. The bar downstairs is crammed with attractive 20- and 30-somethings, and the margaritas are good and plenty. Upstairs, there's almost always a wait for a table. Those in the know appreciate the authenticity of Austin Grill. To be won over requires a mere sample of any of the expertly prepared and presented enchiladas, fajitas, burritos, chili, and even the zesty appetizers. Wash it all down with something frosty, then sit back and enjoy the sights and sounds. You'll surely understand why this restaurant is a hit. The Austin Grill can also be found in D.C. in Glover Park at 2404 Wisconsin Avenue (202-337-8080) and in the heart of Bethesda at 7278 Woodmont Avenue (301-656-1366). Open for lunch and dinner nightly.

Sweetwater Tavern
14250 Sweetwater Ln.
Centreville, VA
(703) 449–1100
3066 Gatehouse Plaza
Falls Church, VA
(703) 645–8100
$$

The same team who dreamed up such popular eateries as the Carlyle Grand Cafe and Best Buns Bread Company has ventured into Southwestern cuisine with Sweetwater Tavern. As usual, these owners know how to do it right, with high quality, imaginative variations on the old standards. The decor glows with rich wood and

leather, amber lighting, and Indian rugs. Wrought-iron chandeliers feature Western scenes, as do the etched glass dividers on the booths. There's a highly rated microbrewery on premises, not to mention the spicy, smoky dishes such as ribs, quesadillas with poblanos, black bean chili with smoked chicken, and grilled smoked salmon. Desserts are big and mouth watering. Don't even try to resist the chocolate waffle filled with the richest of chocolate ganache—that's pure chocolate, butter, and cream to you and me. Sweetwater Tavern is open for lunch and dinner nightly and Sunday brunch.

Tortilla Factory
648 Elden St.
Herndon, VA
(703) 471–1156
$

Other parts of the region will hopefully have a Tortilla Factory to call their own some day, but until then, it's worth a trip to this small town near Dulles Airport. Tacos, fajitas, enchiladas, burritos, nachos, salsa—the Tortilla Factory prepares them all in the zesty Sonoran tradition—and the results are memorable. Plus, you get a ton for the money in this casual, friendly setting. Let the branching out of the Tortilla Factory begin! The restaurant serves lunch and dinner daily and also hosts live folk music—sometimes by renowned acts—on Tuesdays.

Italian

Generous George's Positive Pizza and Pasta
3006 Duke St.
Alexandria, VA
(703) 370–4303
$

It's an odd name indeed, but the gigantic portions of superb pizza and pretty good pasta—served atop a pizza crust—are nothing to laugh at. You'll be too busy chewing, swallowing, and smiling in between. The pizza's the whole point of coming here, and at least one member of your party should order it. The toppings are all fresh and high quality. This is no run-of-the-mill sausage! If you pass on the pizza, try the chicken Florentine. The quirky, eclectic decor—a true mishmash of the odd, the colorful, and the bizarre—and a fun family atmosphere, for kids in particular, makes Generous George's a hit every time. One visit and you'll understand why people gladly sweat the lines on weekends. They are open for lunch and dinner daily. (See our Kidstuff chapter for more on family dining here.)

Geranio Ristorante
722 King St.
Alexandria, VA
(703) 548–0088
$$

Year after year, this Old Town restaurant stays fresh. The atmosphere bursts with good-fellowship and vitality, and the decor is cheerful, particularly on cold winter nights when the fire roars. Geranio feels like the authentic Italian trattoria that it is, with rustic floors of tile or hardwood, ceramic art on the walls, and friendly waiters. The menu lists more than a dozen pastas available for either the first course or as entrees, such as lobster risotto with lobster oil and penne with seared fresh tuna, black olives, tomatoes, and capers.

Surprisingly for a restaurant this modest, the seafood dishes are very good as well, especially any of the fish prepared with lemon and capers. There are lots of interesting veal, lamb, and chicken entrees as well. The fried baby squid with caper sauce and the grilled Portobello mushroom with arugula and Parmesan stand out as appetizers. Everything is satisfying and simply prepared. Especially tasty is the olive oil served with the bread—it's full of fragrant herbs. Desserts aren't the strong point here but, again, they're competent. Instead, top off your meal with a cup of espresso. It is open for lunch weekdays and dinner nightly.

Il Cigno
1617 Washington Plaza
Reston, VA
(703) 471–0121
$$$

The food here is less special than the setting, which is worth the trip if dining alfresco is what you have in mind. There's plenty of outdoor seating overlooking Reston's beautiful Lake Anne. If that weren't enough, Il Cigno's neighboring cafes, in a fan-shaped row, lend an air of festivity to the scene. This pedestrian square (actually, it's a circle) seems very European and escapist on a warm evening. Musicians often play at one end, and the neighborhood's residents come out in full force to enjoy a lakeside promenade or casual dining by the water. In summer there are good appetizers that feature fresh produce, but the menu is pretty much like any other Italian restaurant. It's the setting that's extraordinary, and you're sure to leave with a feeling of well-being. Il Cigno is open for lunch weekdays, dinner nightly, and is closed Sunday in winter.

Il Radicchio
1801 Clarendon Blvd.
Arlington, VA
(703) 276–2627
www.robertodonna.com
$

Another offshoot of a downtown location, Il Radicchio is a bargain-priced eatery that still manages to seem trendy. The concept here is simple: Order an all-you-can-eat bowl of spaghetti and pair it with one of a dozen or so sauces offered. There's variety enough to satisfy anyone, from those who prefer simple pesto to those who think spaghetti ain't spaghetti unless it has tomato sauce. You won't find the haute cuisine of Roberto Donna's downtown flagship, Galileo (see the D.C. listings), but then you won't pay the prices he charges there either. At Il Radicchio, Donna caters to a whole different crowd: families, busy bees in need of a quick meal, and young up-and-comers who want lots to eat and don't want to pay a lot. The pizzas are good, too. Lunch is served lunch Monday through Saturday and dinner nightly.

Paolo's Ristorante
1898 Market St.
Reston, VA
(703) 318–8920
www.paolosristorante.com
$$

Paolo's Reston branch is inviting, with its outdoor tables in the town square, its cafe-style seating just outside the front doors, and the curved, sunny room within. There's also a bar that hops on weekends, complete with loud music and attractive guys and gals out on the town.

As soon as you're seated, you'll be served Paolo's signature breadsticks, soft and warm, along with a zesty green-olive tapenade. The main courses feature lots of pastas, some quite imaginative, along with meat that's mostly grilled and infused with light sauces. Balsamic vinaigrette plays a big role in the cooking here, and that's just great as far as we're concerned. Pizzas cooked in wood-burning ovens are a house specialty, and the crusts are smoky, thin and delicious, just as you'd expect. You can make a meal of Paolo's salads—which range from steak over greens to grilled chicken with Greek-style accompaniments—and you'll always be offered fresh grated Parmesan as a garnish. Also try the Georgetown location, at 1303 Wisconsin Avenue (202-333-7353). Paolo's serves lunch and dinner daily and Sunday brunch.

Tivoli Restaurant
1700 N. Moore St.
Rosslyn, VA
(703) 524–8900
$$$

It's a tribute to Tivoli's quality that it has managed to endure for two decades hidden away in this Rosslyn high-rise. Perhaps it helps to have a bakery and carryout service of the same name on the ground floor—advertisement for the good things to come upstairs. This handsome dining room, rendered even more inviting by the wraparound windows and the strategically placed mirrors, is one of the more formal restaurants in the Virginia suburbs. It's a good place to take clients or a first date. Tivoli bills itself as a northern Italian restaurant, and you'll find many dishes napped in the rich sauces of that region. There are risottos and stuffed pastas, as well as old standards of the fettucine Alfredo ilk. You'll also find some Continental classics that you don't often see anymore, like veal Oscar. This is a

place to linger and enjoy your meal, an elegant, leisurely experience at prices that are surprisingly reasonable. They serve lunch weekdays and dinner Monday through Saturday. The Tivoli is closed Sunday.

Middle Eastern/ Indian/Afghan

Bombay Bistro
3570 Chain Bridge Rd.
Fairfax, VA
(703) 359–5810
www.bombaybistro.com
$$

You could come to Bombay Bistro every day for a month and never exhaust the menu possibilities. This is superb and very serious Indian cuisine, with some prepared in a tandoori oven, some curried, and some grilled over charcoal. The main courses are so filling that there is always some left over. The solution? Bring a large group, split the main courses, and sample the appetizers and those wonderful, smoky Indian breads (which you do have to order—they aren't free). The standouts among the main courses are the lamb dishes. Lamb nilgiri khorma is an irresistible type of curry served with green masala alive with fresh coriander. Whole fish is enhanced by a marinade that features ginger, garlic, and yogurt. Tandoori specialties can sometimes be a bit dry, but they're so tasty that you can almost overlook the flaw. This is a casual, fairly nondescript place, but there are some low tables in a back nook that are very romantic, and the food makes every meal seem special. This location is less crowded than the Bombay Bistro in Rockville, Maryland, at 98 West Montgomery Avenue (301-762-8798). Lunch and dinner are served daily.

Connaught Place
10425 North St.
Fairfax, VA
(703) 352–5959
$$

This tiny Indian restaurant is tucked into a group of storefronts between a parking

The popular Bombay Bistro started out as a favorite of expatriates but now attracts a variety of diners from around the area. PHOTO: COURTESY OF BOMBAY BISTRO

lot and a house in Fairfax. But it's worth the trouble of finding it. The curries, Indian breads, and appetizers are served with style and attention to detail—you'll never be rushed here. The cooking can be as good as at its Fairfax neighbor, Bombay Bistro. The menu contains all the Indian standards, but the execution and personal warmth make all the difference here. Ask your waiter to guide you, and you'll be treated to intricate descriptions that answer your every question. Lunch and dinner are served daily.

Nizam's
523 Maple Ave. W.
Vienna, VA
(703) 938–8948
www.nizamsrestaurant.com
$$

You'll find plenty of people who will argue that Nizam's is the region's best Turkish restaurant. Small and attractive as a jewel box, Nizam's is famous for its house special, doner kebab. Slices of lamb are marinated in yogurt and Turkish spices, then stacked on a vertical rotisserie spit and slow-roasted. The result is fragrant, crusty, juicy slices of meat served with pita bread and yogurt seasoned in the Middle Eastern style. Because doner kebab is such a major project, Nizam's prepares it on Tuesday, Friday, Saturday, and Sunday evenings. You'll also do fine with the regular menu, which features such delicacies as marinated lamb in a variety of styles, beef tenderloin, stuffed grape leaves, and assorted eggplant preparations. Nizam's is open for lunch Tuesday through Friday, dinner Tuesday through Sunday; it is closed Monday.

Pasha Cafe
2109 Pollard St.
Arlington, VA
(703) 528–2126
$$

The cuisine here harks from Egypt and is very similar to other Middle Eastern cuisine, so expect the usual array of delicious appetizers like hummus, tabbouleh, and baba ghanouj. The fun is in mixing and matching dishes. The menu suggests various combinations that provide a taste of just about everything. Meals are filling and delicious, though somewhat over-salted. Try the kofte, kebabs, or on the lighter side, lemony chicken. The waiters, many of whom are Egyptian, are warm, hospitable, and happy to guide you. One problem: Waits for a table can be long, and the line crowds into the front end of the one-room dining area. Ask for a table away from the door and arrive early or late to avoid a long spell of standing. Pasha Cafe serves lunch Monday through Saturday and dinner nightly.

Suburban Maryland

American/Continental

Bethesda Crab House
4958 Bethesda Ave.
Bethesda, MD
(301) 652–3382
$$

They offer famed Chesapeake Bay crabs, yes, but Bethesda Crab House is also a popular late-night dining option; they are open till midnight seven days a week. If you order the crabs, you'll be given a tableful along with the implements to crack 'em open, so wear washable duds. Be aware that dwindling crab catches are forcing prices higher quickly.

Clyde's of Chevy Chase
76 Wisconsin Circle
Chevy Chase, MD
(301) 951–9600
www.clydes.com
$$

We've told you about Clyde's in D.C. and Clyde's in Virginia, so why gild the lily by going on about the Chevy Chase location? Well, you've gotta see it to believe it. This is as much an elegant entertainment center as a restaurant. There's a model train that circles overhead, and the theme is carried through in the booths, which are replicas of Orient Express parlor cars.

Gleaming model airplanes hang from the ceiling, and stunning posters, prints, and hand-painted murals adorn the walls. This place must've cost a fortune to build, with its cushy leather seats and sumptuous woodwork, but Clyde's can afford it. The Chevy Chase location is a hit, as are the other branches. The food here is good and varied, but a special treat is the vegetarian platter, offering all sorts of gems at a very reasonable price; otherwise, as at the other Clyde's locations, you do best when you stick to pub fare—steak, salads, and sinful desserts—all particularly festive in a setting like this. They serve lunch Monday through Saturday, dinner nightly, and Sunday brunch.

Crisfield's
8012 Georgia Ave.
Silver Spring, MD
(301) 589–1306
Crisfield's at Lee Plaza
8606 Colesville Rd.
Silver Spring, MD
(301) 588–1572
$$

Crisfield's used to be one of those seafood places so basic and utilitarian in decor that you knew the food had to shine—especially at these downtown prices. Well, it's lost some of its luster, but if your namesake is the tiny Maryland community that claims to be the crab capital of the solar system, you'd better serve some world-class crabs. And Crisfield's still does. Maybe that's why it's still going strong after nearly 50 years in business, although the two restaurants went under separate ownership a few years ago. If you're in the neighborhood, there's no better place for crab and crab dishes, but it's not worth a trip. Crisfield's serves lunch weekdays and dinner nightly. The Georgia Avenue location is closed Monday.

The Inn at Glen Echo
6119 Tulane Ave.
Glen Echo, MD
(301) 229–2280
$$$

In its previous lives The Inn at Glen Echo served as a boarding house and a rowdy biker bar. But since 1985 the rambling

Washington's proximity to the Chesapeake Bay allows restaurants and markets to provide fresh seafood like the Maryland blue crab. PHOTO: COURTESY OF MARYLAND OFFICE OF TOURISM

pink house at the edge of Glen Echo Park has focused on serving up fresh seafood, steaks, and other American cuisine in a warren of dining rooms, porches, and patios. Its brunch buffet draws legions of loyal patrons, and a line sometimes snakes out the door Sunday mornings. The best all-weather seats in the house are on the two side porchlike rooms, one upstairs and one down. On mild days the wide windows slide open and a light breeze wafts in as green leaves rustle overhead. An outdoor patio is also available. In late spring and summer, the inn's soft-shell crabs and crab cakes are its biggest draw. It's open for breakfast Saturday only, for lunch Monday through Saturday, for brunch on Sunday, and for dinner nightly.

Louisiana Express Company
4921 Bethesda Ave.
Bethesda, MD
(301) 652–6945
www.louisianaexpresscompany.com
$

No, you haven't been transported back to "Lew-zee-ann-uh." It just seems that way at Louisiana Express Company, where authentic Cajun treats—crawfish, po' boys, jambalaya, soft-shell crab sandwiches, the works—are served up in a down-home atmosphere. Stop by early for a full breakfast or on Sunday for a knockout brunch. They serve lunch Monday through Saturday, dinner nightly, and bunch on Sunday.

Normandie Farm
10701 Falls Rd.
Potomac, MD
(301) 983–8838
www.popovers.com
$$$

You're not far away at Normandie Farm. It just feels that way. This Potomac landmark has lost nothing through the years; you can still count on delicious American cuisine in a gracious setting reminiscent of a country inn. Every meal begins with a basket of puffy, hot popovers—heavenly! The menu goes on to include some rich, old-fashioned specials. Last time we looked, they were still doing beef Wellington—not for those watching their weight. Over the years the cuisine has become more sophisticated, and there are Continental touches on the menu, particularly among the seafood dishes. This is still the place to come for traditional holiday meals. Normandie Farm is open for lunch and dinner Tuesday through Saturday, Sunday brunch, and is closed Monday.

O'Brien's Pit Barbecue
387 E. Gude Dr.
Rockville, MD
(301) 340–8596
www.obrienspitbarbecue.com
$

Casual and inexpensive, O'Brien's has endured for years as a popular stop for some of the tastiest Texas-style barbecue around. There is other, newer, competition, but O'Brien's holds its own with favorites like chili dogs, pork spareribs, and beef brisket. Side orders like beans and rice and spicy onion rings have plenty of pizzazz, too. O'Brien's is open for lunch and dinner nightly.

Old Angler's Inn
10801 MacArthur Blvd.
Potomac, MD
(301) 299–9097 or 365–2425
www.oldanglersinn.com
$$$$

Old Angler's Inn sits snugly in the woods across the lane from the C&O Canal towpath. It looks like an enchanted cottage from a fairy tale, with its half-timbered accents and stone walk. You can cozy up next to the roaring fireplace in fall and winter or enjoy patio dining by a fountain in spring and summer. Back inside, the spiral staircase leads from a sitting area featuring big, soft couches, to an intimate, albeit bustling, dining room where the mood continues to captivate. The prices at Old Angler's Inn may give you a little predinner heartburn—this is a "jackets required" kind of place—but then again, when you consider the setting, service, and wonderful menu selections such as rack of lamb, venison, quail, and rabbit, the financial bite seems somehow less painful. Seafood is treated with respect, carefully herbed and never overcooked. Seared tuna and several other dishes feature Asian spices that show the chef's range of skill with any number of cooking styles. If you just can't decide what looks best, let the chef choose for you with his nightly tasting menu. Sated, you can relax into one of those down-filled couches and enjoy an after-dinner digestif. They serve lunch and dinner Tuesday through Saturday, Sunday brunch, and are closed Monday.

Red, Hot & Blue
16809 Crabbs Branch Way
Gaithersburg, MD
(301) 948–7333
677 Main St.
Laurel, MD
(301) 953–1943
$$

If you like barbecue, this is the place to come for lunch or dinner. Please see the Virginia listing.

Silver Diner
11806 Rockville Pk.
Rockville, MD
(301) 770–1444
14550 Baltimore Ave.
Laurel, MD
(301) 470–6080
www.silverdiner.com
$

This is a recent Washington-based chain that looks like an old-time diner. The Silver Diner sits at the edge of a busy Rockville shopping center, and is almost always crowded. Breakfasts and desserts are tops here, with the rest being pretty standard stuff. In keeping with the diner theme, there's meatloaf and mashed potatoes, burgers and shakes, and humongous sandwiches. Waffles and French toast are great here and can be had at any time of the day. The 3:00 A.M. closing time on weekends makes Silver Diner a favorite stop for night owls. There are also six Silver Diners in Virginia (see our listing under Northern Virginia). Silver Diner is open for breakfast, lunch, and dinner daily.

Thyme Square Cafe
4735 Bethesda Ave.
Bethesda, MD
(301) 657–9077
$$

Whimsical painted pea pods curve around the windows, and giant pears and peppers flank the door. Inside, more larger-than-life veggies form a mural, giant paper peppers are suspended from the ceiling, and the booths are upholstered in a cherry and pear print. For those striving for five fruits and vegetables a day, this is a good place to meet that nutritional quota. The restaurant is largely vegetarian, with a smattering of fish and chicken entrees. But there's no granola or tempeh in sight. Instead, the cafe offers a global cuisine—from China to Cuba—that's low on fat and high on flavor. There's crisp artichoke polenta with spinach, roasted vegetable ratatouille and garlicky white beans, spicy pad Thai noodles, and wood-oven-roasted chicken pizza with sun-dried tomatoes and shaved artichokes. It's open Monday through Saturday for lunch and Sunday for brunch, and nightly for dinner.

Asian

Benjarong
885 Rockville Pk.
Rockville, MD
(301) 424–5533
$

This Thai restaurant in a Rockville shopping center is unexpectedly elegant. The

A waiter at a local restaurant prepares for one of Washington, D.C.'s numerous large gatherings.
PHOTO: COURTESY OF FAIRFAX COUNTY ECONOMIC DEVELOPMENT AUTHORITY

decor is pastel and cheery with linen covered tables set comfortably apart to allow for private conversation. There are almost 100 items on this menu: 10 soups, 15 appetizers, and the rest as main courses. Spices here are combined masterfully, and you really can't go wrong no matter what you order. Shrimp is presented in almost a dozen ways, as are whole fish, squid, and soft-shell crab. Pork and beef play a lesser role, but there are several interesting duck dishes, including a shredded duck appetizer with lemon grass, pepper, onion, and chili. If you want incendiary spicing, you'll have to ask, because dishes have been toned down a bit for Western palates. Benjarong serves lunch Monday through Saturday and dinner nightly.

Good Fortune
2646 University Blvd. W.
Wheaton, MD
(301) 929–8818
www.goodfortunerestaurant.com
$
Good Fortune has earned a name for itself in the local world of Cantonese cuisine.

It's so affordable that it's almost too good to be true. An exhaustive menu may require more time than usual to peruse, but if you lack the patience, you can't go wrong with any of the selections featuring lobster, duck, and fish, or the interesting casserole creations and spectacular stuffed mushrooms. Good Fortune is open for lunch and dinner nightly.

Hunan Pearl
12137 Darnestown Rd.
Gaithersburg, MD
(301) 330–8118
$
Hunan Pearl is one of those neighborhood places that consistently wins high marks from the community, but isn't that well known farther afield. You'll find consistently good Chinese fare at this location, convenient to I-270 commuters exhausted from the long trek to D.C. As crowded a field as it is, Hunan Pearl manages to distance itself just a bit from some of the formidable suburban competition. It serves lunch and dinner daily.

Mama Wok and Teriyaki
595 Hungerford Dr.
Rockville, MD
(301) 309–6642
$

If nothing else, you gotta love the name. This restaurant—which features Chinese and Japanese cuisine—has more to offer than that, however. If you're not squeamish, there's live seafood prepared to your liking, and the selection's not limited to fish, as in many other restaurants. According to the season, you're likely to find oyster, clams, crab, or shrimp. Even if you don't want to meet your meal before you eat it, the other seafood items are sparkling fresh, and simple preparations show them to good advantage. The decor here is as plain as could be, but when there's such fresh seafood to be had at rock-bottom prices, who cares about atmosphere? It's open for lunch and dinner daily.

Matuba
4918 Cordell Ave.
Bethesda, MD
(301) 652–7449
$

For top-notch Japanese cuisine at bargain prices, Matuba can certainly dish it out. Budget sushi is almost an oxymoron, but not at Matuba, which offers sushi and sashimi in a large variety of combinations. Sushi rolls are a special treat, executed with flair. At Matuba, you can afford sushi as a first course and go on to sample tempting cooked seafood as a second course—the soft-shell crab, for example. There's another Matuba in Arlington (see our listing under Northern Virginia). Matuba is open for lunch Monday through Saturday and dinner nightly.

Oodles Noodles
4907 Cordell Ave.
Bethesda, MD
(301) 986–8833
$

The downtown branch of Oodles Noodles (see our Washington, D.C. section) often has a long line at lunch, but the Bethesda location is a bit less frenetic, albeit popular. This stylish fusion eatery features a decor with lots of sunshine and gleaming surfaces. It looks upscale, so the decidedly scaled-down prices are a surprise. Japanese, Malaysian, Thai, and Chinese cuisine get equal time here, with appetizers ranging from satays to Japanese dumplings stuffed with meat and served with sesame soy sauce. There are only three soups on the appetizer menu, one Chinese, two Thai, and all are good. Glance at the extensive list of entrees and you'll find other soup selections worthy of a meal. They're really bowls crammed with goodies, then spooned over with aromatic broth. The heat quotient of the chilis here will be altered to your liking. Oodles Noodles offers lots of adventure for very little money. They serve lunch Monday through Saturday and dinner nightly.

Pho 75
1510 University Blvd.
Langley Park, MD
(301) 434–7844
771 Hungerford Dr.
Rockville, MD
(301) 309–8873
www.pho75.net
$

See the Virginia listing for information on this no-frills local chain that serves hearty aromatic bowls of this Vietnamese soup.

Sabang
2504 Ennalls Ave.
Wheaton, MD
(301) 942–7859, (301) 942–7874
$

If you enjoy Thai, Vietnamese, or virtually any other Asian cuisine, you'll like Indonesian. The trouble is in finding a restaurant that serves it. There's a lovely one downtown (see Washington listing for Sarinah), but in the suburbs you needn't look any farther than Wheaton's Sabang for inexpensive, interesting creations in this unique gastronomic genre. Like the downtown Sarinah, Sabang is an exceptionally pretty and festive space—maybe it's the Indonesian aesthetic of jewellike colors, handmade textiles, and intricately carved furniture. In mundane Wheaton this place is an oasis. As for the cooking, Indonesian is so unfamiliar to most Westerners that it's not a bad idea to order the rijstaffel, an amalgam of dishes that allows you to sample a broad range. If that doesn't appeal, try the satays, skewered meats with dipping sauce of peanuts and chilis. If you're still confused, ask your server; the staff here is warm, helpful, and eager to share this cuisine with you. They serve lunch and dinner daily.

Sam Woo
1054 Rockville Pike
Rockville, MD
(301) 424–0495
$$

Sam Woo's selections are among the area's best in Korean cuisine (grilled at your table if you'd like), and you'll know it at once when you walk in and see all the Korean diners there. There's a broad selection of main course soups and casseroles, many that are sure to please seafood lovers—or choose from an extensive selection of Japanese entrees including chicken teriyaki, sushi, and tempura. Try the weekday buffet for a truly different kind of lunch break. Sam Woo is open for lunch and dinner daily.

Seven Seas Chinese Restaurant
1776 E. Jefferson St.
Rockville, MD
(301) 770–5020
$$

This restaurant is well known in the Washington area for its seafood, and you know it's fresh from the minute you walk in and spot the large fish tank full of ocean delicacies. Seven Seas serves both traditional Chinese and Japanese fare, including dim sum and sushi. This small storefront restaurant has also branched out even more into calorie-conscious offerings, both vegetarian and with meat. Seven Seas is open for lunch and dinner daily.

Sunny Garden
1302 E. Gude Dr.
Rockville, MD
(301) 762–7477
$

Taiwanese food seems a likely candidate for that hard-to-find restaurant category, but one visit to Sunny Garden and you'll wonder why. In fact, you'll probably find more familiar items than you expect, because Taiwanese cooking incorporates some of the Chinese-American style so familiar to so many people. Seafood and vegetable specialties, in particular, help make Sunny Garden a bright spot on the list. It's open for lunch and dinner daily.

Suporn's
2302 Price Ave.
Wheaton, MD
(301) 946–7613
$

You've probably gathered by now that Wheaton and Rockville are meccas for Asian restaurants, and there are many Thai offerings among them. Suporn's is a bargain-priced eatery that offers some interesting dishes and a great deal of range. Start with one of Suporn's many salads, some flavored with lime, cilantro, anise, chilis, peanuts, or in most cases, a combination of several harmonious seasonings. Go on to hot, spicy soup or skip to a main course that features noodles, curries, or stir-fry. The prices here are so low, you can try it all. Suporn is open for lunch Tuesday through Saturday, dinner Tuesday through Sunday, and it's closed Monday.

Tako Grill
7756 Wisconsin Ave.
Bethesda, MD
(301) 652–7030
$$

As the name implies, Tako Grill ventures beyond its considerable sushi menu to feature an equally wide array of grilled foods. There are grilled meats, seafood, and a surprising variety of vegetables, many so exotic that they're not found elsewhere in Washington—certainly not grilled. At one time fans would stand in line to eat here because the restaurant accepts no reservations, but Tako Grill was recently expanded, so the wait shouldn't be as long. Try going on a weeknight just to be sure. Open for lunch weekdays and dinner nightly.

An aquarium theme and a vibrant menu attract Maryland and Virginia diners to Tara Thai.
PHOTO: COURTESY OF TARA THAI

Tara Thai
4828 Bethesda Ave.
Bethesda, MD
(301) 657–0488
12071 Rockville Pike
Rockville, MD
(301) 231–9899
www.amir.org
$$

The Maryland suburbs around Washington have lots of good, basic Asian restaurants, but here's one with glamour. For more on Tara Thai, please see their Virginia listing. They serve lunch Monday through Saturday and dinner nightly.

Taste of Saigon
410 Hungerford Dr.
Rockville, MD
(301) 424–7222
$$

This light, pretty Vietnamese restaurant is always crowded despite its hard-to-find location in the middle of a Rockville parking lot. The prices are good—which accounts for some of its popularity—but

with so many reasonably priced Asian restaurants in Rockville, that's not all there is to it.

There's the fashionable contemporary dining room with plenty of light and cheery linens on the tables, the outdoor patio with stylish umbrellas, and there's the food. Try the whole fish bathed in spices and scallions, intriguing soups crammed with noodles and meat, and stir-fries bursting with fresh veggies. There's also a location at 8201 Greensboro Drive in McLean, Virginia. Both serve lunch and dinner daily.

French

Jean-Michel
10223 Old Georgetown Rd.
Bethesda, MD
(301) 564–4910
$$$

This restaurant may be located in a shopping center, but it's a very classy one and this is a classy restaurant. Step through the door and you'll think you're in one of those chic Paris eateries that tourists never find.

The crowd is well heeled, the room is alive with conversation, and the lighting is flattering and rosy. Owner Jean-Michel has been a presence in Washington for decades, and he once reigned supreme in one of those downtown French restaurants that bit the dust with the three-martini lunch. He now offers cuisine on a slightly more modest scale, but you won't feel shortchanged. Try any of the beef or seafood dishes here—they're especially good. They serve lunch weekdays and dinner nightly.

La Ferme
7101 Brookville Rd.
Chevy Chase, MD
(301) 986–5255
www.lafermerestaurant.com
$$$

La Ferme is nestled into a wealthy residential section of Montgomery County, one of the few commercial enterprises in the neighborhood, but it's hardly a drop-in kind of place. There's something both fresh and luxurious about the country French decor—you couldn't ask for a more inviting setting. As befits a restaurant in this cosmopolitan and very upscale area, the food is excellent. Cuts of meat are well trimmed for the utmost in tenderness and taste. Veal is often pallid elsewhere but at La Ferme it shines. Seafood classics like Dover sole are done right here, but you can also find more modern, simply grilled fish. Restaurants that serve Châteaubriand aren't exactly rare in the Washington area, but they aren't common either. La Ferme does it and does it well. This is the kind of spot that's lovely for a special occasion or for an escapist lunch on a lazy, summer day. Lunch is served Tuesday through Friday and dinner Tuesday through Sunday. La Ferme is closed Monday.

La Miche
7905 Norfolk Ave.
Bethesda, MD
(301) 986–0707
www.users.erols/bitebyte/la-miche.htm
$$$

Think of dried flowers, lively prints, and baskets, and you've pictured La Miche. This French charmer, near the National Institutes of Health, has stayed ahead of the competition for more than two decades by sticking to the basics of French cooking, like lobster bisque, cream sauces, puff pastries, and meats redolent of garlic. You probably won't find anything unfamiliar on this menu—just calories-be-damned French cooking that takes you back to the old days. La Miche is open for lunch Tuesday through Friday and dinner nightly except for Sunday.

Le Vieux Logis
7925 Old Georgetown Rd.
Bethesda, MD
(301) 652–6816
$$$

Even in restaurant-packed Bethesda, Le Vieux Logis makes you do a double take. That's because it looks like a slice of Alsace with its half-timbered facade and flower-filled window boxes. Flowers are everywhere, and what a nice greeting! Inside, there are other reminders of Alsace in the cooking, which has a somewhat German accent; for example, many of the meat dishes are paired with sauces that contain fruit or mustard. Mushrooms are used liberally in both appetizers and main courses. Try the mushroom soup, a creamy concoction with a haunting flavor. If seafood's your fancy, you'll find several dishes infused with citrus. They are lighter than the meat dishes and also very good. This is interesting, unusual French cuisine, and you won't find a more pleasant setting. They serve dinner nightly except for Sunday.

Italian

Cesco
4871 Cordell Ave.
Bethesda, MD
(301) 654–8333
www.robertodonna.com
$$

There's no more agreeable patio on Bethesda's restaurant row than that at Cesco, and the interior decor is just as inviting, with wonderful arches and plenty of windows. The menu here departs a bit from the Italian standards—there are some interesting ingredients

Chef Francesco Ricchi creates Italian dishes that have been described as works of art. PHOTO: UPS
PHOTO GALLEY, COURTESY OF CESCO TRATTORIA

and presentations. For example, one of the appetizers is a delectable work of art: a cylinder of baked Parmesan cheese filled with endive and other greens. The bruschetta brings to mind the Italian flag: red, white, and green. One piece has a fresh tomato topping, another is punctuated with broccoli rabe, and another with cannellini beans. If it's meat you're craving, try the sinful filet of beef layered with eggplant and tomato in a Gorgonzola cheese sauce. Cesco is open for lunch weekdays and dinner nightly.

C. J. Ferrari's
143111 Baltimore Ave.
Laurel, MD
(301) 725–1771
www.cjferraris.com
$

There's nothing fancy about this bargain-priced eatery in Prince George's County, but surprising care is taken with several dishes. Anything tomato-based is a good bet here—the sauce is springy and flavorful. Try one of the seafood dishes, like scallops in a delicious wine sauce, zinged with a bit of mustard. You'll want to sop up that extra sauce with a slice of the restaurant's crusty bread. What put Ferrari's on the map though is the white pizza, a garlicky, cheesy version that puts others to shame. For dessert, try the homemade ice cream. Ferarri's is open for lunch Tuesday

through Friday, dinner Tuesday through Sunday. It is closed Monday.

Fratelli
5820 Landover Rd.
Cheverly, MD
(301) 209–9006
$$

You don't expect to find style like this in Cheverly, and you especially don't expect it at these low prices. Although Fratelli's doesn't merit a special foray into Prince George's County, it's a nice place to stop if you're already there. This isn't gourmet Italian, but rather good hearty cooking. Don't miss the bargain-priced antipasto, which contains all manner of seafood from clams to shrimp. Pizzas here are a safe bet when it comes to choosing a main course—there's no scrimping on the cheese here. Or if you don't want finger food, try one of the pastas in red sauce. Fratelli is open for lunch on weekdays and dinner nightly.

Geppetto's
10257 Old Georgetown Rd.
Bethesda, MD
(301) 493–9230
$

Imagine pepperoni piled so high it's hard to see the pizza itself. Although such generosity seems terribly wasteful except for perhaps eaters of above-average girth, it's tough for lovers of deep-dish pizza and pasta not to adore Geppetto's. The pleasure begins from the moment you step inside this casual cafe at the upscale Wildwood Shopping Center and take in the delightful aroma. This is not a place for those seeking delicate refinements in Italian cooking. It's Italian-American abbondanza at its best. You can order takeout and delivery at the Georgetown location at 2917 M St. NW, Washington, D.C. (202–333–2602). Lunch and dinner are served daily.

Il Pizzico
15209 Frederick Rd. (also known as Rockville Pike)
Rockville, MD
(301) 309–0610
$$

Outside Il Pizzico's windows, traffic on Route 355 in northern Rockville careens past strip malls and car dealerships. Inside the restaurant, though, faux windows set in the walls offer painted views of sunlit terraced Italian hillsides. And the small storefront with a generic sign outside belies the white linen tablecloths and white-coated waiters within. Although the menu is not expansive, you can hardly go wrong, especially with the veal, fish, and pasta that is made on site. The wild mushroom-stuffed ravioli with pistachio cream sauce is rich and satisfying—coupled with an icy glass of Pinot Grigio, it's pure heaven. Ask about the daily specials, the wine list and, lest we forget, the desserts. Il Pizzico is open for lunch weekdays Monday through Saturday and is closed Sunday.

Pines of Rome
4709 Hampton La.
Bethesda, MD
(301) 657–8775
$

Pines of Rome has stuck to its guns through cooking fads from nouvelle to northern Italian to fusion. Never has it deviated from the old Italian-American standard: pasta with heavy, red sauce served on checkered tablecloths. Sure, there's a white pizza that's pretty good and a robust spaghetti carbonara, but that's about as adventurous as you want to get here. This is a place to bring kids when you want to eat cheaply, quickly, and plenty. It's open for lunch and dinner nightly.

That's Amore
15201 Shady Grove Rd.
Rockville, MD
(301) 670–9666
1699 Rockville Pike
Rockville, MD
(301) 881–7891
www.thatsamore.com
$$

You'd better pack an appetite when you go to That's Amore. Even then, one dish may be enough to serve your entire party. For cheap eats, the food here is very good, and the atmosphere is raucous and friendly, with lots of families. The cooking is heavy on the garlic, tomato sauce, and cheese—nothing subtle about this place. The menu contains all the Italian standards like egg-

plant and veal parmigiana, but the underlying ingredients hardly matter when the toppings are so robust. Try anything that features lemon-butter sauce and you'll probably be happy. The meal-sized salads are stocked with lots of goodies like olives, onions, and tomatoes. If you want to sample everything from soup to nuts, bring your extended family and share, or you'll never get through it. There is also a Virginia location at 150 Branch Road, SE in Vienna (703–281–7777). Open for lunch on weekdays and dinner nightly. The Rockville Pike location is also open for lunch on the weekend.

Tragara
4935 Cordell Ave.
Bethesda, MD
(301) 951–4935
$$$$

This may be the most extravagant—and the most formal—Italian restaurant in the Maryland suburbs, and it's one of the prettiest, with two levels, generous floral arrangements, and light, bright decor. The food is mostly northern Italian, which means rich white sauces, grilled meats, and a delicate hand with seasoning. You may end up spending more here than you think you should, but if you're looking for a special occasion Italian restaurant in Maryland, nothing comes close in terms of overall atmosphere and cuisine. Tragara is open for lunch weekdays and dinner nightly.

Middle Eastern/Indian

Aangan Indian Restaurant
4920 St. Elmo Ave.
Bethesda, MD
(301) 657–1262
$$

In Hindi, the word "aangan" means courtyard, and with its potted palms, climbing vines, and flickering lanterns, Aangan Indian Restaurant recreates a lush patio. The enveloping rattan chairs, stone archways set into the stucco walls, and wicker blinds enhance the tropical feel and impart a welcome, warm atmosphere in the dead of winter. The food also plays its part in heating the place up. Aangan concentrates on the cuisine of northern India, its spice palette filled with ginger, garlic, cumin, and curry. Many of the dishes focus on lamb or chicken, often cubed and served as kabobs. Open daily for lunch and dinner. The weekday lunch buffet is a particular bargain.

Bacchus
7945 Norfolk Ave.
Bethesda, MD
(301) 657–1722
$$

Bacchus is open for lunch weekdays and dinner nightly. Please see their listing in the D.C. section.

Bombay Bistro
98 W. Montgomery Ave.
Rockville, MD
(301) 762–8798
$$

Bombay Bistro is open for lunch and dinner nightly. Please see their listing in the Virginia section.

Hispanic/Tex-Mex

Andalucia
12300 Wilkins Ave.
Rockville, MD
(301) 770–1880
9431 Elm St.
Bethesda, MD
(301) 907–0052
$$$

Rockville has a Spanish star in Andalucia, which serves consistently good food (emphasizing the gastronomic delights of southern Spain) with the grace and flair of a matador. This place, with its wonderful guitar music in the evenings, isn't nearly as informal as the other restaurants in the Hispanic category. Don't overindulge in the good and garlicky appetizers—you have to save room for such specialties as paella and zarzuela. Don't overdo it on those tasty entrees either; the desserts—especially the cakes—are a delightful way to top it all off. They

are open for lunch and dinner every day except Monday at the Rockville location. In Bethesda they serve lunch on weekdays and dinner nightly.

Cottonwood Cafe
4844 Cordell Ave.
Bethesda, MD
(301) 656–4844
$$

The popular Cottonwood Cafe showcases cuisine that is truly indigenous to the American Southwest. It has a style and taste all its own. The secret: traditional herbs and spices combined with an open-grill preparation. It may not be much of a secret, but it helps Cottonwood Cafe stand out in a crowd. The menu here ventures far beyond the normal Southwestern fare we've come to expect in Metro-area restaurants. You can find beef tenderloin, pasta, duck, and shrimp, all prepared with a spicy punch. The setting and the service are more sophisticated than the competition and the margaritas sizzle. They are open for lunch Monday through Saturday and dinner nightly.

Rio Grande Cafe
4919 Fairmont Ave.
Bethesda, MD
(301) 656–2981
231 Rio Blvd.
Gaithersburg, MD
(301) 632–2150
$$

It used to be that an hour-long wait was standard for a table at Rio Grande Cafe. Some of the furor has died down, perhaps eased by the two Virginia locations, but this casual eatery remains popular. One of the highlights here is the tortilla machine, which produces warm, fresh . . . you guessed it . . . tortillas to accompany the fajitas and other Tex-Mex fare. You'll find the usual tacos, enchiladas, burritos, plus a few unexpected items like frog legs and quail. This place is loud, busy, and frenetic, so it might not be the place for an intimate evening. They are open for lunch Monday through Saturday dinner nightly and Sunday brunch.

Nightlife

In a place where shuffling papers and climbing corporate ladders are forms of recreation, and starched shirts and leather pumps are considered de rigueur fashions, nightlife may not seem like a top priority for many people. Believe it or not, even stressed-out, career-minded Washingtonians know how to have a good time away from the office, embracing the work hard/play hard philosophy with ample gusto.

Although the nightlife here is plentiful and diverse, don't expect a heavy dose of Los Angeles-style glitz or New York–style up-'til-dawn decadence. Instead, like the dining scene, after-hours diversions in Metro Washington include a little bit of everything, from cutting-edge music halls and stand-up comedy venues, to funky watering holes, sports saloons, yuppified fern bars, and high-energy dance clubs.

First, here are a few things to keep in mind before venturing out for an evening on the town. As a general rule, the District offers the widest variety of nightlife, but you can almost always expect to pay a bit more for such things as drinks, cover charges, and live entertainment. Case in point: Single beers approaching the $5 mark are common, especially at some of the city's tonier clubs—and if they don't get you at the bar, there's a good chance you paid for it at the door. Sometimes, you may get nailed at both places, but then, no one ever recommended barhopping as a way to save money.

Suburban establishments are generally a bit less expensive, but in some cases they lag well behind their urban counterparts in the character and atmosphere departments. Whether you live in the Virginia exurbs or far-flung Maryland counties, chances are your nightlife will occur in one of three places: Montgomery County, Maryland; Washington, D.C.; or the Northern Virginia suburbs immediately surrounding Washington—that is, Arlington or Fairfax Counties and Old Town Alexandria. Accordingly, we've used only three geographical divisions in the listing below: Washington, D.C., Northern Virginia, and Suburban Maryland.

"Last call for alcohol," as the saying goes, is typically around 2:00 A.M. in the city, and 1:00 to 1:30 A.M. in the 'burbs. Some of the downtown haunts may not finish shooing people out the door until 3:00 or 4:00 A.M., but alcohol cannot be legally served after 3:00 A.M. in the District.

Incredibly, soft drinks aren't always that much cheaper than booze at many bars and clubs in Metro Washington, although they certainly should be in this age of heightened awareness about the lunacy of drinking and driving. Some places do, however, occasionally offer free, unlimited nonalcoholic beverages to the designated driver in a group, so it pays (in more ways than one) to inquire.

The scourge of underage drinking and the increasingly tough penalties levied against those who serve minors have convinced many business owners—grocery, convenience, and liquor store operators included—to be extra cautious about who's buying. So take the request to see your driver's license as a compliment, not an insult. On your drive home don't be surprised if you encounter roadblocks where police check for drunk drivers—it's a common practice on weekends in the Metro Washington area.

For weekly updates on what's happening on the local nightlife scene, we highly recommend the "Weekend" and "Washington Weekend" sections of the *Washington Post* and the *Washington Times,* respectively. Both supplements include expansive listings of clubs, shows, special events, and other pertinent information. The *Post* publishes its guide on Friday, and the *Time* prints its on Thursday, a strategy that the paper says helps you get a jump on planning those blessed two days of freedom. It makes sense. We know some people who start thinking about the upcoming weekend on Monday.

As with the dining section, this is far from an exhaustive roundup of Metro Washington nightspots, and again we've tried to emphasize the local places. Entries bearing an asterisk (*) beside their name are also covered in the Restaurants chapter, so please refer to that section for more details.

Washington, D.C.

Live Music and Dancing

Badlands
1415 22nd St. NW
Washington, DC
(202) 296–0505

Badlands is one of the gay dance clubs that newcomers to Washington will hear of first. That's because it's always crowded and always rocking. There's a little something for everyone, from a music video room to pool tables. The crowd is fairly young, in shape, and attractive. There are often theme nights ranging from country and western to karaoke. The club is open Thursday through Sunday nights, with a weekend cover charge of up to $10.

Black Cat
1811 14th St. NW
Washington, DC
(202) 667–7960
www.blackcatdc.com

This eclectic nightclub ranges from swing music to alternative rock, depending on which night you go. On swing music nights you'll find people sipping champagne and smoking cigars. On rock nights it's a whole different crowd—a very young one, with lots of black jeans in evidence. To keep up with what's going on here, you'll need to call for the weekly schedule. They are open nightly, and tickets are $5.00 to $15.00.

Blues Alley
1073 Wisconsin Ave. NW
Washington, DC
(202) 337–4141
www.bluesalley.com

You could easily miss the aptly named Blues Alley, as it's hidden in a Georgetown alley, halfway between K and M Streets off Wisconsin Avenue. For decades this intimate supper club has been the city's top spot for the best in local and national jazz and blues acts, including the likes of Tony Bennett, Wynton Marsalis, and Charlie Byrd. Reservations are a must, especially on weekends and when top talent is on the bill. Blues Alley is open nightly, and tickets are $10 to $30.

Some of the biggest blues and jazz artists have played at the aptly named Blues Alley. PHOTO: COURTESY OF THE WASHINGTON, DC CONVENTION AND TOURISM CORPORATION/T. KEENS

Bukom Cafe
2442 18th St. NW
Washington, DC
(202) 265–4600
www.bukom.com/bukom

Washington has a large community that hails from Africa, and many of its members can be found at this hot spot in Adams Morgan when the place rocks with live reggae music from Wednesday to Saturday. The atmosphere starts out relaxed, but it picks up as the band plays on and the night progresses. Dress is casual as could be. There is no cover charge.

Chief Ike's Mambo Room
1725 Columbia Rd. NW
Washington, DC
(202) 332–2211
www.greatidea.com/chiefike

This funky Adams Morgan nightclub draws a casual crowd ranging in ages from 20-something to around 40. On weekends there's some very hip live music. Bands vary from reggae to rock. If you don't like the music here, you can wander down the street to any number of other locales for live tunes. They are open nightly, with a weekend cover charge of $3.00 to $5.00.

Coco Loco*
810 7th St. NW
Washington, DC
(202) 289–2626
www.cocolocodc.com

A great Latin restaurant, Coco Loco is transformed into a wild nightclub when the clock strikes 11. There's live entertainment on Saturdays, which segues into dancing on one of two floors: one is for Latin music, and one is for "international," which basically means updated disco with a Euro beat and a smattering of American favorites. If you're rusty—or a neophyte—Thursday is Latin dance-lesson night. They are open Monday through Saturday for dinner, with live entertainment only on Friday and Saturday. The cover charge is $10.

Dubliner Pub
520 N. Capitol St. NW
Washington, DC
(202) 737–3773
www.dublinerdc.com

For a taste of the Emerald Isle without stepping on a plane, head for this popular pub. The Dubliner is in the Phoenix Park Hotel and is considered by many to be the region's most authentic Irish pub and dining experience. Although Irish cuisine may be beside the point, Irish folk music appeals to many and is featured here nightly. They are open nightly, with no cover charge.

The Fireplace
2161 P St. NW
Washington, DC
(202) 293–1293

The Fireplace has been around for decades, first as a bar and lounge for all sorts, now as a bar and lounge for a mostly gay crowd. The salient feature of this place is, in fact, the fireplace visible at the corner of the building (it looks like an outdoor fireplace at first) on P and 22nd streets. Inside, you'll find a very dark series of rooms and a couple of bars on two stories. The clientele here is definitely on the prowl, so if you're looking for a place to meet new people, this may be it. You'll find a mix of neighborhood locals and tourists from nearby hotels, along with a somewhat raffish element. The Fireplace is open nightly, with no cover charge.

Irish Times
14 F St. NW
Washington, DC
(202) 543–5433
www.kellysirishtimes.com

This low-key pub features live Irish music Thursday through Saturday. Entertain-

> ## Insiders' Tip
> The newest hot strip for Washington night-clubs is U St. NW. New clubs seem to spring up monthly here.

ment is mostly of the acoustic guitar variety, and the crowd is an easy mix of downtown suits, chinos, and bluejeans. Irish Times is open nightly, with no cover charge.

Kramerbooks & Afterwords Cafe
1517 Connecticut Ave. NW
Washington, DC
(202) 387–1400
www.kramers.com

Here's a fun twist: a bookstore with live music from Wednesday to Saturday. Long before Borders and the other big chains came along and tried it, this Dupont Circle mainstay dreamed up the idea of teaming these two great forms of entertainment. Expect a laid-back approach with lots of acoustic guitar and folk music—nothing too intrusive. The cafe serves three meals a day and has great coffee and desserts. They are open nightly (24 hours on Fridays and Saturdays), with no cover charge.

Melrose*
1201 24th St. NW
Washington, DC
(202) 955–3899

There aren't too many places in Washington for adults who prefer the fox trot to freestyle flailing. Melrose, with its Saturday evening band music in an elegant setting at the Park Hyatt Hotel, fills the gap. This is a pricey restaurant, and drinks here don't come cheap, but the room is glamorous with marble, plush banquettes, and extravagant flower arrangements. It's a dressy place, and a great way to top off a special evening. Melrose is open nightly, with no cover charge.

Nation
1015 Half St. SE
Washington, DC
(202) 554–1500
www.nation-cc.com

Nation opened in 1999 in what was formerly called The Ballroom, a space where international rock stars like David Bowie have enthralled crowds. The new Nation benefits from a $2 million renovation, including a cutting-edge sound system,

new lounges, high-tech lighting, and an enormous outdoor patio. The club is already attracting some big names, including Eminem and the reunited Blondie. The crowd is young and hip and not afraid to venture into this iffy part of town, home to a number of clubs where anything goes. The schedule is determined by show times. Tickets are $10 to $30.

9:30 Club
815 V St. NW
Washington, DC
(202) 393–0930
www.930.com

If alternative rock is your thing, you won't want to miss the 9:30 Club. The crowd here is young and pierced, and the atmosphere is dark and intense. Playing in this redesigned space are cutting-edge bands. They are open nightly, and ticket prices range from $5.00 to $10.00, depending on the show.

Pier 7
650 Water St. SW
Washington, DC
(202) 554–2500
www.channelinn.com

Pier 7, at the Channel Inn Hotel, is a pleasant waterfront restaurant. Here you can enjoy live music and dancing with the baby-boomer-and-up crowd Wednesday through Sundays. Dress is conservative, ranging from business suits to sportswear—this is a white tablecloth kind of place. Plenty of tourists make the stop here, because the riverside restaurants bring them in by the busload. Pier 7 is open nightly, with no cover charge.

Nightclubs

The Brickskeller
1523 22nd St. NW
Washington, DC
(202) 293–1885
www.thebrickskeller.com

On the fringes of Georgetown, The Brickskeller remains the city's consummate beer-lover's nirvana, offering more than 700 brands from around the world.

The Adams Morgan neighborhood is a bustling area of restaurants, bars, nightclubs, shops, and boutiques. PHOTO: COURTESY OF WASHINGTON, DC VISITORS INFORMATION CENTER

It's handy for washing down fare like pizza, sandwiches, and buffalo burgers. Be sure to check out the unbelievable beer can collection lining the walls. They are open nightly, with no cover charge.

Coco Loco*
810 7th St. NW
Washington, DC
(202) 289–4386
www.cocoloco.com

Coco Loco is open Monday through Saturday and closed Sunday. The cover charge is $10 Friday and Saturday. (Please see the listing under Live Music.)

Modern
3287 M St. NW
Washington, DC
(202) 338–7027

This new addition to Georgetown's club scene may be modern, but it's not postmodern. No techno DJs or light show wizardry here. There are, however, some funky touches, with a bubble chair suspended in air in the corner and retro mod plastic couches scattered around. The DJs spin a familiar range of funk, soul, disco, and pop, and Georgetown University students and 20-something professionals crowd the small dance floor. Open nightly with no cover charge.

Polly Esther's
605 12th St. NW
Washington, DC
(202) 737–1970
www.pollyesthers.com/dc

There's nothing else quite like this place in D.C. Note the last four digits of the phone number—not to mention the club's name—and you'll have a hint as to Polly Esther's theme. Yes, it's a retro-'70s disco, complete with a Saturday Night Fever dance. Not your favorite decade? Okay, step up to the Culture Club (remember Boy George?), another room featuring dance music and memorabilia from the '80s. If you don't want to look back at all, head up to the third floor club, Generations, for current music. This place is a scream—be sure to wear your platforms and white polyester three-piece suit for the best effect. They are open Thursday through Saturday, with a cover charge of $7.00 on Thursday and $10.00 on Friday and Saturday. (See Suburban Maryland for Rockville location.)

Third Edition
1218 Wisconsin Ave. NW
Washington, DC
(202) 333–3700

Nightclubs come and go in Washington, but the Third Edition in Georgetown has managed to pack 'em in for over two decades. Maybe it's the Wisconsin Avenue location right near the busy M Street intersection, or maybe it's the glass doors, thrown open to let the music out and the crowd in. Whatever the reason, Third Edition draws a fairly well-groomed crowd of mostly 20- and 30-somethings, including lots of students from nearby Georgetown University. They are open nightly, with a cover charge of $5.00 on Friday and Saturday.

Zei
1415 Zei Alley NW
Washington, DC
(202) 842–2445
www.zeiclub.com

Just off I Street, between 14th and 15th Streets NW, the glamorous crowd at Zei ranges from fat cats—who head straight for the members-only room on the third level—to the young and hip who jam the dance floor below. The music is very loud and hi-tech, with lots of Euro sound thrown in. There are video screens, of course, and house dancers, along with a roving band of cigarette girls. They are open Thursday through Saturday, with a cover charge of $10 on the weekends.

Sports Bars

Buffalo Billiards
1330 19th St. NW
Washington, DC
(202) 331–7665
www.bedrockdc.com

Cowboys would feel right at home here with the pinto-printed upholstery, peeled log chairs, and, of course, a Southwestern menu of bar munchies and a few more substantial dishes. As the name implies, this is primarily a pool hall. There are the requisite music and TVs, of course, and a singles bar atmosphere. They are open nightly, with no cover charge.

Champions of Georgetown
1206 Wisconsin Ave. NW
Washington, DC
(202) 965–4005

Tucked at the end of a short alleyway in Georgetown, near the famed intersection of Wisconsin and M Street, Champions, as its name implies, is a true sports bar. Expect the usual saloon beverages and chow in this sports junkie's paradise, crammed with memorabilia, souvenirs, photos, posters, and the like. This is a great place to watch the hometown Redskins, Wizards, and Capitals, or any televised sporting event for that matter. At night and on the weekends, dancing is de rigueur as a DJ spins popular tunes for the 20s and early 30s set. Big crowds are standard. They are open nightly, with no cover charge.

Fanatics
1520 K St. NW
Washington, DC
(202) 638–6800

This sports bar advertises itself as having plenty of babes, beers, and billiards. All three are probably true, because it is connected to Archibald's—a strip joint that's been around since 1969. For those whose idea of entertainment involves spectator sports of a different kind, however, there are 30 TVs, seven satellites, five pool tables, and darts. One oddity: This place sits on the edge of Washington's red-light district and evening restrictions against left and right turns, depending on where you're coming from, are strictly enforced to curtail soliciting. Observe traffic and parking rules carefully or you could be hit with a hefty fine. They are open nightly, with no cover charge.

The Rock Sports Bar and Restaurant
717 6th St. NW
Washington, DC
(202) 842–7625
www.rockdc.com

The neighborhood is undergoing gentrification, and The Rock has played no small part in drawing people to the area after dark. Near the new MCI Center, this sports bar features an eye-popping 27 televisions, a billiards room, a dance floor with DJ music, and a rooftop Tiki Bar. There is something for everyone at this rowdy, yet upscale, spot. Dress ranges from casual to business attire, and the crowd is a mix of yuppies, preppies, and young singles on the prowl. They are open nightly, with no cover charge.

Piano Music

Kinkead's*
2000 Pennsylvania Ave. NW
Washington, DC
(202) 296–7700

Upstairs is one of Washington's best restaurants; downstairs is a spacious, woodsy bar with a jazz combo Tuesday through Saturday. Despite the proximity to George Washington University, this is a crowd of adult professionals. Yet it's a casual scene, rarely jam-packed, and quiet enough for conversation. Drop in after dinner in the restaurant or when you're in the neighborhood. There is no cover charge.

Mr. Smith's of Georgetown*
3104 M St. NW
Washington, DC
(202) 333–3104

This may be Washington's most popular piano bar—it's certainly the oldest. It's also a piano bar in the traditional sense, with everyone gathering 'round the player and chiming in. The lights are low, the drinks include every fancy concoction imaginable (and some that aren't), and the crowd is convivial. You'll fit right in, no matter where you come from or what you're wearing. They are open nightly, with no cover charge.

West End Cafe*
One Washington Circle NW
Washington, DC
(202) 293–5390

This marvelous, but casual, eatery features an intimate lounge with piano music on the weekends that's good enough to impress the performers who drop by after their gigs at the nearby Kennedy Center. It's great for a postthe-ater nightcap, but you may need reservations on weekends. The room is decorated in cool neutrals and the seating is in comfortable banquettes, a small bar, or at linen-covered tables. They are open nightly, with no cover charge.

Cigar Bars

Butlers, The Cigar Bar
1000 H St. NW
Washington, DC
(202) 637–4765

This glitzy Art Deco bar, in the Grand Hyatt Hotel, is the place to go for cigars and martinis when you're in the neighborhood of the Washington Convention Center. (The state-of-the-art ventilation system keeps the room from reeking.) The crowd is well-heeled business travelers and Washington business types from the surrounding office buildings. They are open nightly, with no cover charge.

Chi-Cha Lounge
1624 U St. NW
Washington, DC
(202) 234–8400
www.chi-cha.com

This ever-so-hip place is in D.C.'s hottest new club district. The crowd is mostly young and Euro—and just about everyone is smoking something, whether it be cigarettes, cigars, or even, on certain nights, a hookah. On Tuesdays live jazz adds to the cool (attitude, not temperature), dark atmosphere. They are open nightly, with no cover charge.

Off the Record
16th and H Sts. NW
Washington, DC
(202) 942–7599
www.hayadams.com

The Hay-Adams is one of Washington's most historic and luxurious hotels—they know how to do things right here. Off the Record, with its low-lit, men's club atmosphere, offers not only cigars, but a generous selection of single-malt scotch, champagnes, and wines by the glass. Many are hard-to-find labels and can cost as much as $20. The Hay-Adams is right across Lafayette Square from the White House, and the patrons here look like the kind of successful folk who may have come from an appointment at 1600 Pennsylvania Avenue. They are open Monday through Saturday, with no cover charge.

Ozio Martini & Cigar Lounge
1835 K St. NW
Washington, DC
(202) 822–6000

Ozio's may be the hippest of the town's cigar bars and it was one of the first. It's a very dark lounge with booths and tables placed around a small dance floor. The place starts to rock after midnight, when a mix of Euro types and K Street expense account executives crowd the dance floor. There's a wide selection of gin and vodka martinis, including a couple of original Ozio recipes. The waiter will bring the humidor to your table, and the cigar smoke will be sucked into special ashtrays in the center. They are open Monday through Saturday.

Comedy Clubs

The Improv
1140 Connecticut Ave. NW
Washington, DC
(202) 296–7008
www.dcimprov.com

This club—yes, we admit, it's part of a national chain—brings top acts to Washington in a convenient midtown location. You can have dinner if you attend the early shows or wait for the 10:30 performance on weekends and dine at one of the great restaurants nearby. Acts here are often comedians you've seen on TV, and you'll recognize most of the names. They are open Tuesday through Saturday, and tickets are $15 to $20.

Northern Virginia

Alexandria's Old Town area is Northern Virginia's answer to Georgetown. That ought to give you an idea of the richness of the nightlife in this charming and beautiful area. As with Georgetown, a sidewalk

Georgetown is a vibrant hub of nightclubs, specialty shops, boutiques, and restored homes.
PHOTO: COURTESY OF WASHINGTON, DC CONVENTION AND TOURISM CORPORATION

stroll along the narrow, sometimes cobblestone streets will reveal a world unto itself. The hub of Old Town's nocturnal activity is located on the river side (east) of Washington Street, also known as the George Washington Memorial Parkway, especially lower King Street and the surrounding few blocks.

Not all of Virginia's nightlife is in Old Town, though. There are also pockets of activity in Rosslyn and just 10 minutes farther west in Clarendon. People who are serious about nightlife still head into D.C., but the suburbs have enough to keep you occupied for at least a few evenings on the town. Because of the more limited offerings, we haven't created as many categories as for downtown Washington, D.C. For example, piano lounges are not a category, but are rather listed under live music. One category you will find here that's missing from D.C. is dinner theaters—we haven't found any in Washington D.C., whereas Northern Virginia has a couple. As we mentioned in the introduction, we have not broken down Northern Virginia by county for two reasons: The first is that distances are insignificant for the most part, and the second is that nightlife is limited enough that any further breakdown would result in some categories having only one listing—or perhaps none. That isn't to say that fun can't be found in the 'burbs, though. Just read on if you want proof.

Live Music and Dancing

America Restaurant
Intersection of Rtes. 7 and 123
McLean, VA
(703) 847–6610
On Friday nights America features the 16-piece Tom Cunningham Orchestra, one of the most popular big bands in the Washington area. They play all the swing classics: Glen Miller, Benny Goodman, Tommy Dorsey, and on and on from 9:00 P.M. to midnight. Because this spot is located right in Tysons Corner Center, the clientele varies from drop-ins to jitterbug wannabes dressed for the occasion. They are open nightly, with a cover charge of $12.

The Birchmere
3701 Mount Vernon Ave.
Alexandria, VA
(703) 549–7500
www.birchmere.com
In an area known as Arlandria (Arlington/Alexandria border), this has become one of the top national venues for bluegrass, zydeco, country, folk, pop, and blues performers, all in a down-to-earth, casual setting. The once crowded space has undergone a major expansion and renovation. Now you'll find a pool hall, German beer garden, and plenty of room for the crowds that gather here for top-of-the-line performers such as David Crosby, Doc Watson, and The Nighthawks. The schedule is determined by show times, and tickets are $10 to $30.

Clarendon Ballroom
3185 Wilson Blvd.
Arlington, VA
(703) 469–2244
www.clarendonballroom.com
It's new, it's art deco, it's smoke-free, and it's huge. There's a lot going for the Clarendon Ballroom. The 20,000-square-foot former carpet outlet now hosts swing dances twice a week and has live rock and DJs on the weekends. The building retains its original 1930s pressed-tin ceiling in

gold leaf, and the 1,000-person capacity ballroom is decked out in art deco touches, from lamps to mirrors. It also rents out to private parties, complete with catering. Closed Monday.

Cowboy Cafe North
4792 Lee Hwy.
Arlington, VA
(703) 243–8010

Cowboy Cafe South
2421 Columbia Pike
Arlington, VA
(703) 486–3467
Country and western is king at Cowboy Cafes, and, on weekends, there's live music. You'll find a lot of military personnel from nearby Fort Myers at the South location, along with young singles, but as with most country music venues, fans of all ages come to line dance and two-step. Both venues are open nightly, with no cover charge.

Fat Tuesday's
10673 Braddock Rd.
Fairfax, VA
(703) 385–8660
www.fatsfairfax.com
Near George Mason University, Fat Tuesday's is another major force in live rock and R&B music on Wednesday to Sunday nights. This is a much smaller setting than some of the concert halls listed in this category, and it couldn't be more casual. The crowd is a mix of blue-collar workers and students. Take pitchers of beer; hot music; a dark, noisy bar; and a location at University Mall and you get the idea of what kind of atmosphere to expect at Fat Tuesday's any day of the week. It is open nightly, with a cover charge of $3.00 to $5.00 Wednesday through Sunday.

Fish Market*
105 King St.
Alexandria, VA
(703) 836–5676
This Old Town spot always seems to be full of jolly people ready to party, and the ragtime piano player adds to the mood on Wednesday through Saturdays. You can

dine on seafood while you enjoy the old-time saloon atmosphere, the humor, and the cheerful music. They are open nightly, with no cover charge.

Hero's
9412 Main St.
Manassas, VA
(703) 330–1534

Manassas is a sleepy little town, but there are several clubs and eateries on Main Street. What's notable about Hero's is the live music on Saturdays. You'll find mostly jazz trios or quartets in this laid-back spot. Given the small-town location, it is as casual as you'd expect and the night tends to end early, even if the official business hours are standard for Virginia. They are open nightly, with a $5.00 cover charge on weekends.

Ireland's Own
132 N. Royal St.
Alexandria, VA
(703) 549–4535

Fans of live Irish-themed acoustic music, Irish food, and Irish drink can get their fill at Ireland's Own in Old Town Alexandria. St. Patrick's Day, in particular, is an occasion at this bar. This is a casual, neighborhood place, comfortable for people of any age. They are open nightly, with a $5.00 cover charge on weekends.

Jaxx
6355 Rolling Rd.
Springfield, VA
(703) 569–5940
www.jaxxroxx.com

You wouldn't expect to find a progressive rock concert hall in suburban Virginia,

especially conservative Springfield, but Jaxx is just such a place. Patrons are young college students, grunge wannabes, and others in that general age group. On occasion former big names like Johnny Winter and Eddie Money appear. Show times determine openings, with cover charges from $5.00 to $25.00.

Lobby Lounge
1700 Tysons Blvd.
McLean, VA
(703) 506–4300
www.ritzcarlton.com

The Ritz-Carlton at Tysons Corner is a showplace of antiques, art, and Oriental rugs, and the Lobby Lounge is as lovely a refuge as the rest of the hotel. Tables are spaced for intimacy and the piano music is low key but high quality. The pianist here has a range from gospel to classic, but the playing is never intrusive. They are open nightly, with no cover charge.

Murphy's of Alexandria
713 King St.
Alexandria, VA
(703) 548–1717
www.murphyspub.com

As if it weren't cozy enough to have an intimate sweaters-and-jeans type place along the cobbled walks of Old Town, this place also features a wood-burning fireplace and Irish music nightly. Like Ireland's Own, listed earlier, this is a hot spot on St. Patrick's day after the parade. They are open nightly, with no cover charge.

The Shark Club
14114 Lee Hwy.
Centreville, VA
(703) 266–1888
8411 Lee Hwy.
Falls Church, VA
(703) 641–8888
8794 Sacramento Dr.
Alexandria, VA
(703) 360–8283
www.sharkclubonline.com

With four D.C.-area locations (including one in Bethesda at 4915 Street Elmo Avenue (301–718–4030), the Shark Club offers casual dining and billiards all

---

Insiders' Tip

Although last call in Washington dance clubs is usually 2:30 A.M. on weekends, most places don't pick up speed until at least 11:00 P.M.

under the watchful eyes of Jaws-like creatures painted on the walls. All but the Falls Church location include a restaurant called the Pacific Grill, where you can order everything from bar food appetizers to filet mignon. DJs spin dance music on the weekends. Live bands at some locations. Try the salsa dance lessons on Thursdays at the Falls Church location.

Tiffany Tavern
1116 King St.
Alexandria, VA
(703) 836–8844

This cozy spot at the west end of Old Town isn't very well known outside the neighborhood, but it's usually crowded, thanks to the intimate space. It's the only bar in the Washington area that hosts bluegrass bands every weekend. Dress down or dress up as you please. There is no cover charge, and they are closed on Sundays.

219 Basin St. Lounge
219 King St.
Alexandria, VA
(703) 549–1141

For a more formal setting than some of those listed previously, 219 Basin St. Lounge in Old Town offers live jazz and Louisiana cuisine one floor below the 219 restaurant. The decor here is particularly inviting, featuring a brick courtyard and wall accents; a dark, sophisticated lounge; and a restaurant upstairs furnished in New Orleans–style French reproductions. It is open in the evenings Tuesday through Saturday. The cover charge is $5.00 on Friday and Saturday.

Whitey's
2761 N. Washington Blvd.
Arlington, VA
(703) 525–9825
www.whiteyseat.com

Arcade games, live music, and a casual setting—it all comes together at Whitey's, an Arlington neighborhood watering hole that oozes with character. The hole-in-the-wall, sports-themed charm of suburbia was never better represented than here. Live rock 'n' roll and R&B help keep the place jumping on Tuesday through Saturday nights. They are open nightly, with a cover charge of $4.00.

Meet and Greet

You won't find live music at these places except on special occasions. However, you may find dancing, and, if so, we've indicated it; otherwise, the point is to check out the crowd, have a few drinks, and maybe even strike up a conversation with a stranger.

Bullfeathers
112 King St.
Alexandria, VA
(703) 836–8088

One of the most popular nightspots for singles in particular, Bullfeathers is tucked away from streetview save for its sidewalk canopy, so look for the distinctive maroon awning that announces its presence to passersby. Although some windows would help temper the cave-like ambience, Bullfeathers has long been a preference of Old Town barhoppers in a wide range of age and dress. To the right of the bar is a large dining area with food ranging from burgers to swordfish. If you want to avoid the lines on Friday and Saturday nights, you can have a bite earlier in the evening, and then drift over to the bar. Bullfeathers is open nightly, with no cover charge.

Chadwicks*
203 S. Strand St.
Alexandria, VA
(703) 836–4442

Chadwicks is as inviting as the Georgetown original, with bars upstairs and down. On weekends, 20- and 30-somethings pack the place. Beer is the drink of choice and the dress is khakis to business suits. They are open nightly, with no cover charge.

Champion Billiards
2620 S. Shirlington Rd.
Arlington, VA
(703) 521–3800

Pool halls have caught on in the Washington area, and one of the places that's been around longest is Champion Billiards. This is a very casual place where enjoying a few games, drinking beer, and listening to the CD jukebox make for a welcome alternative to the traditional night out. Nonpool shooters in particular will appreciate the video arcade. They are open nightly, with live local bands on Saturday nights, with no cover charge. (See Suburban Maryland for more locations.)

Clyde's*
8332 Leesburg Pike
Vienna, VA (Tysons Corner)
(703) 734–1901
11905 Market St.
Reston, VA
(703) 787–6601
www.clydes.com

Whether you choose the location in Reston Town Center or the one in Tysons Corner, Clyde's is a hopping place for the check 'em out crowd. Tysons is more upscale, with the peak action on weeknights for after-business, 30-plus patrons. The decor is extravagant art nouveau and business suits are the norm—it's a prosperous-looking bunch here. Reston, which runs a more family-oriented eatery, also has a handsome, lively bar, but expect chinos rather than custom-made suits, and leggings rather than dresses. Clyde's is open nightly, with no cover charge.

Dr. Dremo's Taphouse
2001 Clarendon Blvd.
Arlington, VA
(703) 528–4660
www.drdremo.com

The eclectic, offbeat bars Bardo Rodeo and Ningaloo occupied this space before it was transformed into Dr. Dremo's Taphouse recently. The new management jettisoned the small art gallery and sushi and added more pool tables. But one thing remains the same: The place still sells Bardo beer brewed in Virginia's Rappahannock County. Open nightly.

Fast Eddie's Billiards Cafe
9687 Lee Hwy.
Fairfax, VA
(703) 385–7529
7255 Commerce St.
Springfield, VA
(703) 912–7529
www.fasteddies.com

This is a fun hybrid of pool hall, bar, and restaurant. It's hard not to have a good time here, even if shooting pool isn't your thing. If it is, there are plenty of tables, but you can almost always count on a wait during prime time on Friday and Saturday nights. Also expect efficient, cheerful service; tasty chow; and a better singles atmosphere than one might expect. It's best to go in a small group to make it easier to meet the attractive group shooting a round at the next table. They are open nightly, with no cover charge.

Joe Theismann's
1800 Diagonal Rd.
Alexandria, VA
(703) 739–0777
www.joetheismanns.com

This restaurant and bar, named after the former Redskins' quarterback and current football announcer, offers great sports viewing and karaoke. On Friday nights expect a dark, clubby scene for the over-30 set. Dress ranges from casual to business suits. The Old Town location attracts a clientele that's a bit more affluent than that of the original restaurant in Baileys Crossroads, which was sold to another company and is now called Bailey's Tavern. It is open nightly, with no cover charge.

P. J. Skidoos
9908 Lee Hwy.
Fairfax City, VA
(703) 591–4515

This restaurant and bar has become something of a contemporary disco when it comes to music and the dance atmosphere. It boasts a busy club scene and rates as a prime spot for singles—professionals and students—in their 20s and 30s, not to mention anyone with a hankering for hearty munchies. There's sometimes a decent live rock band on Saturday nights. They are open nightly, with no cover charge.

Portner's*
109 S. Saint Asaph St.
Alexandria, VA
(703) 683–1776

Portner's is popular with a 30-plus group

that flocks here for lively happy hours, a gorgeous setting, and an ambience that's conducive to—surprise!—the lost art of carrying on a conversation. This also doubles as a sports bar on days when the Redskins are playing. Forget conversation then: The TVs above the bar become the focal point. They are open nightly, with no cover charge.

Rocket Grill
1319 King St.
Alexandria, VA
(703) 739–2274

Rocket Grill has been transformed into a club for young singles. There are karaoke nights along with dancing to DJ music. The Old Town Alexandria crowd is pretty tame—the type you wouldn't mind bringing home to Mom—and the age range is 20s to 30s, with the dress as anything you please. You won't find nearly as much grunge here as in downtown spots, however. They are open nightly, with no cover charge.

Sweetwater Tavern*
14250 Sweetwater La.
Centreville, VA
(703) 449–1100
3066 Gatehouse Plaza
Falls Church, VA
(703) 645–8100

Neither Centreville nor Falls Church are hot spots for nightlife, so Sweetwater Tavern—a new restaurant and brewpub—is a welcome addition in both locations. The restaurant features very good Southwestern cuisine and sinful desserts, while the bar attracts singles and couples alike, not to mention folks who want to watch sports in a convivial atmosphere. You'll find a handsome, Wyoming-style ambience with big wrought-iron chandeliers, vaulted ceilings, and all manner of Wild West art. These are casual, suburban places, so dress down. They are open nightly, with no cover charge.

Union Street Public House*
121 S. Union St.
Alexandria, VA
(703) 548–1785
www.usphalexandria.com

This has long been one of Old Town's most popular singles spots, and there seems to be no end in sight for the accolades. Crowded? Yes. But the wait that's not unusual during prime time is worth it, if only for the spirited bar ambience, the extensive and offbeat beer selections, and the friendly help. If the front bar is too much, try the often-overlooked oyster bar in back. It's smaller and less lively, but the beer is just as good and it's easier to find a seat or a quiet corner. They are open nightly, with no cover charge.

Dinner Theater/ Comedy Clubs

Lazy Susan Dinner Theater
U.S. 1 at Furnace Rd.
Woodbridge, VA
(703) 550–7384

Lazy Susan has been around forever and it remains a popular destination for residents of Northern Virginia who enjoy musicals. Dinner and the show together make for a nice evening. They are open nightly, except on Monday. Tickets are $32.95, except on Saturdays, when they cost $34.95.

West End Theater
4615 Duke St.
Alexandria, VA
(703) 370–2500

Some of the plays here, mostly musicals, are very well reviewed by Washington critics, and the location at the west end of Alexandria means that you can venture into Old Town after the show to make a night of it. Besides evening performances, there are Sunday and Wednesday lunch matinees. They are open nightly, except on Monday. Tickets range from $29 to $35. (See the Kidstuff chapter for information about shows for children.)

Suburban Maryland

The Maryland suburbs don't possess quaint pedestrian areas like Georgetown in Washington, D.C., or Old Town Alexandria in Virginia; as a result, there are few clubs. But that doesn't mean you can't find nightlife. There are essentially two hubs of nighttime activity in the Maryland suburbs, each radically different from the other. For affluent Montgomery County, Bethesda, and Rockville have grown into a sprawling "downtown" of sorts, so it's not surprising that this urban-style suburban core offers its share of nighttime diversions. A little farther from Washington is College Park, the home of the 35,000-student University of Maryland. Here, too, the nightlife rocks, with partying students filling the bars along U.S. 1, also known as Baltimore Avenue. We've also mentioned some notable places outside both hubs.

Live Music and Dancing

Bethesda Marriott
5151 Pooks Hill Rd.,
Bethesda, MD
(301) 897–9400
www.marriott.com

This is a sprawling hotel that draws lots of conventioneers. It's also one of the few in the Maryland suburbs to consistently offer live piano music. The crowd here is mature, and the dress is casual to business suits. This isn't a raucous piano bar, but rather a spot for conversation and easygoing entertainment. There's also a dance spot in the hotel, which can be lively when the hotel is full. They are open nightly. There is no cover charge.

Flanagan's Irish Pub
7637 Old Georgetown Rd.
Bethesda, MD
(301) 986–1007
www.irishusa.com/flanagans

Flanagan's features acoustic and folk music Tuesday through Saturday in a comfy pub setting. Food isn't bad here either, and the dress is casual, so it's a great stop for a lazy weekend evening or a bite after work. They are open nightly, with no cover charge.

The Royal Mile Pub
2407 Price Ave.
Wheaton, MD
(301) 946–4511
www.royalmilepub.com

This attractive and comfortable oasis in downtown Wheaton features live Celtic music and jazz four to five times a month. Every third Sunday, a traditional Irish session is led by well-known local musician Dennis Botzer. Most Saturdays also feature traditional Irish or Scottish music. Rarely is there a cover charge. The pub is open seven nights a week and has a surprisingly interesting menu. Berry salad on wild greens with goat's cheese isn't your usual pub fare. The owner's son is a culinary school graduate and has helped shape the menu.

Meet and Greet

Champion Billiards
1776 East Jefferson St.
Rockville, MD
(301) 231–4949
904 Upper Fairlawn Ave.
Laurel, MD
(301) 604–1300
www.championbillards.com

See Northern Virginia listing for further information.

Dave and Buster's
White Flint Shopping Center
11301 Rockville Pike
Rockville, MD
(301) 230–5151
www.daveandbusters.com

Dave and Buster's is a multimedia, multi-sensation event. It's almost too much to absorb in one visit. An 11-screen video wall in the Players Bar, a mystery theater with audience participation on weekends, virtual reality, billiards, and all manner of games attract families, singles, and date-night couples. Dave and Buster's serves weekday lunches until 5:00 P.M., dinners until late into the night, giant servings, giant drinks, . . . and the list goes on. Dress is casual, though the neighborhood is one of the most upscale in the country, so you don't have to worry about being over-dressed if you've just come from work. They are open nightly, with no cover charge except on Friday and Saturday after 10:00 P.M., when the cover is $5.00.

The Hangar Club
6410 Old Branch Ave.
Camp Springs, MD
(301) 449–6970

How do you categorize a place like this? We haven't included strip joints for male clients, so why The Hangar Club, which features male strippers on Thursday to Saturday nights? Well, it's the only club we know in the area that caters almost exclusively to straight women, so it's unique. Its decency level, as some might put it, is a notch above many of the clubs for men featuring female dancers—here they don't take quite everything off, but it's indeed enough to send the female patrons into a tizzy. Dancing and gawking—and plenty of high-pitched screaming—are the norm here.

This cavernous establishment hosts hundreds of bachelorette parties and girls-night-out get-togethers each year. More than 30 brands of beer help keep the whistles wet. If you're a woman, however, be warned: They feature exotic female dancers Sunday through Wednesday and Monday through Saturday during the day. They are open nightly, with an admission charge of $15.

Hollywood Contemporary Ballroom
2126 Industrial Pkwy.
Silver Spring, MD
(301) 622–5494
www.hollywoodballroom.com

Dancing is the point here. It's a 6,800-square-foot, floating maple dance floor, where ballroom lessons (rumba, swing, tango, fox trot) are offered each night for an hour until the dancing-in-earnest takes over. The group is old, young, and everything in between—people who love to dance and those who want to learn. There are also special nights just for singles. Dress is mostly casual, but don't be surprised if a couple in formal wear float by. They are open Wednesday through Sunday, with a cover charge of $10.

Jokes On Us Comedy Club
312 Main St.
Laurel, MD
(301) 490–1993
www.jokesonuscomedyclub.com

In stuffy, button-down Washington, things can seem a bit humorless at times. There are few comedy clubs here, but that doesn't mean people don't like to laugh. Featuring local comedians to nationally known acts, Jokes On Us is a recent addition to the Washington area's paltry assortment of comedy offerings. It has two comedy shows nightly Friday through Sunday, with ticket prices ranging from $10 to $30, along with a jazz happy hour on Thursday for $10, including a buffet.

94th Aero Squadron
5240 Paint Branch Pkwy.
College Park, MD
(301) 699–9400

This dance club's intriguing aviation/military theme—a nod to the nearby College Park Airport, which is the nation's oldest in continuous operation—includes a prop plane outside and a World War I ambulance inside. A mix of white-collar patrons and, of course, plenty of students from the nearby University of Maryland help keep the place hopping. There is no cover charge, and they are open seven nights a week.

Polly Esthers
1750 Rockville Pike
Rockville, MD
(301) 881–7340
www.pollyesthers.com/rockville

Like its downtown Washington location,

the newer Rockville Polly Esthers, located inside the Doubletree Hotel, offers plenty of funky '70s and '80s nostalgia. It's open Wednesdays through Saturdays, with cover charges ranging from $5.00 to $8.00.

The Yacht Club
8111 Woodmont Ave.
Bethesda, MD
(301) 654-2396

Washington impresario "Tommy the Matchmaker" Curtis has been a presence in the nightlife scene since the 1970s, and he's launched many projects, some of which haven't lasted. With The Yacht Club, though, he's got a hit. This is a singles club for the over-30 crowd, a dress-up place (jacket required), except on one of the countless theme nights. Every once in a while there's live music—often dating from the '60s—but it's mostly DJ-driven dance tunes. Curtis brags about the number of matchmaking successes he's had—more than 100 engagements or marriages began here so far, he says. Some of those couples supposedly still drop in here for old time's sake, but this is very definitely a strut-your-stuff atmosphere for those still looking. They are open Wednesday through Saturday. The cover charge is $3.00 to $8.00.

Uncle Jed's Roadhouse
7525 Old Georgetown Rd.
Betheda, MD
(301) 913-5886
www.unclejeds.com

Upscale downtown Bethesda is hardly the place you'd expect a Southern-style roadhouse. But Uncle Jed's provides a good alternative to the sometimes studiously nouveau cuisine establishments nearby. There's pool and pinball and cheap happy hours nightly, often featuring the place's own brew, Uncle Jed's Hooch. There's more than bar food here, too, with such specialties as pinebark stew, a Southern-accented amalgam of catfish and shrimp, along with po' boys and meatloaf. Open nightly.

Dinner Theaters

Blair Mansion Restaurant
7711 Eastern Ave.
Silver Spring, MD
(301) 588-6646
www.mansionmysteries.com

This restaurant, which for years was a special occasion family place, fell out of style a few years back, but it caught a second wind when the management dreamed up the Blair Mansion Mysteries. These shows will never see Broadway, but they should appeal to the whole family with lots of laughs and audience fun. Ticket prices include full dinner, tip, tax, and even hors d'oeuvres. Performances are held every Friday and Saturday and occasionally on Thursday and Sunday. Tickets are $37.95. (See the Kidstuff chapter for information about Now This! Kids! performances here.)

Burn Brae Dinner Theater
3811 Blackburn La.
Burtonsville, MD
(410) 792-0290
www.burnbrae.com

This spot in the exurbs of Maryland has long been a destination for Metro Washingtonians wanting something different from the usual dinner and a movie. It's a bit of a haul from downtown, but the shows here are well run. You'll find musical standards like *Fiddler on the Roof, A Chorus Line,* and *Singin' in the Rain,* featuring solid casts. The schedule of dinner at 6:00 P.M., show at 8:00 P.M. (or similar scheduling for matinees) ensures that there's enough time to clear the tables and eliminate cutlery noise. Ticket prices include the works. They are open nightly except Monday. Tickets are $32.95 on weekdays and $33.95 on Friday and Saturday.

Palm trees accent an atrium at popular Tysons Corner Center in McLean, Virginia. PHOTO: COURTESY OF FAIR-
FAX ECONOMIC DEVELOPMENT AUTHORITY

Shopping

If you're a shopaholic looking to kick your habit, forget about coming to the Nation's Capital! Whatever the object of your desire, you're certain to find it here. Metro Washington's thousands of retail establishments include everything from megamalls, factory outlets, and neighborhood shopping centers to department stores, tony designer boutiques, discount retailers, bulk-buy membership warehouses, and antique havens.

In this chapter we offer a shopping tour of Metro Washington, spotlighting major malls and popular retail districts as well as some of the D.C. area's most interesting specialty stores, with categories listed alphabetically. Don't overlook the small merchants in your particular community when deciding where to spend those hard-earned dollars. They're often the hardest hit during shaky economic times, and they rely heavily on faithful local patrons to keep them afloat. For some items, these places can be just as competitive—and often far more convenient—than their larger rivals.

Malls and Prime Shopping Districts

Metro Washington

Washington, D.C. boasts a glamorous mall in almost every corner of town, from Chevy Chase to Northeast. They're thriving places, attracting both tourists and city residents. We'd be remiss, however, if we didn't also mention several strips of prime shopping that don't classify as malls.

For example, Connecticut Avenue from Dupont Circle south to Pennsylvania Avenue NW and the blocks surrounding it offer a delightful mix of boutiques, salons, bookstores, and very pricey designer shops, such as Burberrys Ltd. of London. Farther east, one of Washington's largest department stores, Hecht's, takes up a city block at 12th and G Streets NW. The area also includes plenty of smaller stores and restaurants, as well as the convenient Metro Center Metrorail station.

Georgetown's Wisconsin Avenue and M Street NW serve as the hub for dozens of boutiques, antique shops, bookstores, art galleries, restaurants, and jewelry stores stretching north to New Mexico Avenue, south to K Street, east to 28th Street, and west to 34th Street. Visitors often compare Georgetown to Greenwich Village, and the place is a party, day or night. Don't miss an excursion here.

Besides the great districts we've described, Washington's malls are destinations in and of themselves. Here are some of the biggest and best.

Mazza Gallerie
5300 Wisconsin Ave. NW
Washington, DC
(202) 966–6114
www.mazzagallerie.net

This glass-fronted structure is home to upscale retailer Neiman Marcus. You'll find more than 20 other posh stores and boutiques here—including a fabulous jewelry store, Pampillonia. New arrivals include Williams-Sonoma Grande Cuisine, the Saks Fifth Avenue Men's Store, and Villeroy and Boch. General Cinemas' 11-screen luxury theater features leather seating and cafe meals. Friendship Heights is the closest Metro station. Parking in the remodeled garage is $1.00 per hour.

The Old Post Office Pavilion
1100 Pennsylvania Ave. NW
Washington, DC
(202) 289–4224
oldpostofficedc.com

If it's souvenirs or Washington memorabilia you want, this is the place to be. Rescued from demolition in the 1960s and later transformed into a shining star of the city's retail and tourism sectors, this historic destination offers the city's second-highest vantage point. Take the glass elevator up to the 315-foot clock/bell tower and enjoy the view! The pavilion, near the Federal Triangle Metro stop, also features more than a dozen shops and services along with a large food court.

The Shops at Chevy Chase Pavilion
5335 Wisconsin Ave. NW
Washington, DC
(202) 686–5335

A lot of people think this mall, and its neighbor across the street—Mazza Gallerie—are in Maryland, but they're right over the line. And they're top of the line, too. The Pavilion houses the exclusive day spa and beauty salon, Georgette Klinger (see Salon listings in this chapter), as well as a number of artsy boutiques for women's clothing, housewares, gourmet foods, and shoes. Anchored by the popular Pottery Barn, the 40-store mall also features Joan and David, Talbots, the Cheesecake Factory, Starbucks, and a food court. Take Metro to the Friendship Heights station.

The Shops at Georgetown Park
Wisconsin Ave. and M St. NW
Washington, DC
(202) 298–5577
www.shopsatgeorgetownpark.com

There is no question that this is downtown's (as opposed to Chevy Chase, D.C.'s) most posh and complete mall. It's right in the heart of Georgetown and features four floors decorated in lavish Victorian style. Standard mall stores here includes the likes of the upscale Ann Taylor, Caché, and J. Crew. The mall also houses designer boutiques like Ralph Lauren's Polo Shop. Recent additions

include the Creighton-Davis Gallery, featuring original artwork, and the GIA & Co. boutique. If you get hungry, stop at one of eight eateries discreetly tucked away on the bottom floor, or pop next door for a quick bite at gourmet grocery, cafe, and carry-out Dean & DeLuca. The mall's multilevel underground garage offers discounted parking: $1.00 an hour during the first two hours, with a $10 purchase.

The Shops at National Place
1331 Pennsylvania Ave. NW
Washington, DC
(202) 662–1250

This mall adjacent to the massive J. W. Marriott Hotel and the National Press Building bustles with more than 90 shops, including some fascinating independent boutiques, mostly featuring women's clothing and jewelry. Office workers crowd the big food court during the noon hour. Take Metro to the Metro Center hub.

The Shops at National Press
529 14th St. NW
Washington, DC
(202) 662–7000

Like the connecting National Place, this small mall proves convenient to theatergoers and D.C. tourists. Anchored by discount fashion giant Filene's Basement, three-level National Press features stores and restaurants that complement the offerings next door. Specialty shops include the likes of Easy Spirit-9 West. As with adjacent National Place, skip the expensive on-site parking if you can. Take Metro to the Metro Center station.

Union Station
Massachusetts Ave. and First St. NE
Washington, DC
(202) 371–9441
www.unionstationdc.com

Housed in the glorious 1908 Beaux Arts train station, the mall here features national chain clothing boutiques, a bookstore, a record store, a nine-screen cinema, restaurants, and a food court—more than 120 shops in all. A separate

The Shops at Georgetown Park are lavishly decorated in Victorian style. PHOTO: COURTESY OF THE SHOPS AT GEORGETOWN PARK

section, the East Hall, offers a variety of jewelry and craft stalls, many selling unique ethnic merchandise. You'll find souvenirs and memorabilia at the U.S. Mint shop (specializing in unique coin-themed items), Political Americana (American political collectibles galore), and Made in America (brass and pewter Washington-themed desk accessories, patriotic gifts, jewelry, and apparel).

Despite its additional role as a shopping hub, Union Station chugs on as a working railroad station too, accommodating not only Metrorail but several commuter lines and Amtrak (See the Getting Around chapter). Although the station operates around the clock and the restaurants and theaters stay open fairly late, the stores operate during regular mall retail hours. (So much for that 3:00 A.M. credit-card fix.) Visit during December, when Union Station holds its annual Christmas in Norway celebration and colossal model trains exhibit. (Our Kidstuff chapter's dining guide describes the mall's family-oriented restaurants and food court.)

Northern Virginia

The most varied and interesting shopping district in northern Virginia isn't even a mall—it's Old Town Alexandria. Begin at the easternmost end of King Street and work your way up. Most intersecting streets, including major thoroughfare Washington Street, also contain a seemingly endless array of stores. You'll find antique shops, clothing boutiques for kids and adults, book stores, art galleries, craft shops, gourmet food emporiums, and, when you get hungry, all manner of restaurants (see the Restaurants chapter).

The flagship of the area is the waterfront Torpedo Factory Art Center and the adjacent minimall, at the intersection of Union and King. (See our Arts chapter for more information.) Local artists feature their work in side-by-side galleries, all housed under one roof. Painters, sculptors, photographers, potters, and jewelers all showcase their talents here. On weekends look for street performers who enjoy entertaining the passersby.

One of the nation's most extensive historic districts, Old Town Alexandria combines specialty shops, boutiques, restaurants, and nightclubs with eighteenth-century cobblestone streets and architecture.

PHOTO: COURTESY OF VIRGINIA DEPARTMENT OF ECONOMIC DEVELOPMENT

Some of Old Town's most popular and charming shops include Hats in the Belfry, 112 King Street, (703) 549-2546, specializing in funky and fun cranial creations; Unique, 213 King Street, (703) 836-6686, which features unusual gift items, jewelry, and greeting cards; and the Winterthur Museum Store, 207 King Street, (703) 684-6092, an extension of the Winterthur Museum in Delaware, stocking elegant American decorative-art houseware reproductions from 1640 to 1860. (See our Kidstuff chapter for information about children's specialty stores.)

In the northwestern part of the county, Reston Town Center (off Reston Parkway between the Dulles Toll Road and Baron Cameron Avenue; www.reston towncenter.com) resembles a new downtown business district, with its striking architecture, pedestrian-friendly layout, and numerous public gathering spots, including a large fountain. Nearly 60 shops and restaurants—mostly specialty retailers such as The Gap, Banana Republic, and Victoria's Secret—line the broad avenues. The food scene includes outdoor cafes like Clyde's and Paolo's (see Restaurants). The Equity Office Garage features 550 free parking spaces as well as retail stores and restaurants.

Still growing, Town Center also contains office space, a residential section (condo mania), a 13-screen cinema, and the posh Hyatt Regency Reston Town Center. The open-air Equity Office Pavilion houses free concerts during the summer and an outdoor skating rink during the winter (see the Parks and Recreation chapter).

Not far from Reston, rapidly growing Loudoun County boasts one of the area's newest regional malls, a large outlet center and lots of big shopping plazas, especially in the Highway 7 corridor that includes the communities of Ashburn, Sterling, and Sterling Park.

You'll also still find small towns and villages alive with their own brand of retail activity. Historic downtown Leesburg (intersection of Highways 7 and 15) offers more than 100 merchants, primarily specialty retailers stretching along Market and King Streets. (See the Antiques section in this chapter.)

Virginia's Prince William County offers two fun and funky shopping districts. Old Town Manassas (Highway 29, 7.5 miles off I–66 in the city's downtown area), features nearly two dozen merchants, mostly of the crafts and antiques variety. It's worth a stroll if you're in town to visit the Civil War sites. Also in Prince William County, the historic riverfront community of Occoquan (just off I–95, about 10 miles south of the Capital Beltway, but also accessible from the extreme southern end of Highway 123), boasts more than 100 merchants in a charming Victorian setting. You'll find lots of collectible bears and antiques here.

Northern Virginians do most of their shopping at malls, however, and they have several from which to choose.

Ballston Common Mall
4238 Wilson Blvd., at N. Glebe Rd.
Arlington, VA
(703) 243–8088
www.ballston-common.com

Just a 1-block walk from the Ballston Metro station (Orange Line) at Fairfax Drive and North Stuart Street, the mall features nearly 100 stores, including anchor Hecht's. The ground level of the four-story mall boasts a food court. A recent major expansion included the opening of Regal Cinemas Ballston Common 12, a posh movie theater featuring stadium seating and state-of-the-art sound.

Specialty stores here include the likes of Britches of Georgetowne, Claire's Accessories, Rainbow, and Record Town. Among the many restaurants, you'll find Memphis Bar-B-Q Company and trendy Rock Bottom Restaurant & Brewery.

The Crystal City Shops
U.S. 1, between 15th and 23rd Sts.
Arlington, VA
(703) 922–4636
www.thecrystalcityshops.com

In the concrete and steel maze known as Crystal City, just off Jefferson Davis Highway (Route 1), are Crystal City Shops

North (on Crystal Drive, between 15th and 18th Streets) and Crystal City Plaza Shops (corner of Crystal Drive and 23rd Street), two subterranean shopping experiences linked by a climate-controlled walkway. Visit more than 130 stores, cafes, and restaurants. Specialty stores include Geppi's Comic World and Mad About Bears, a store featuring popular Boyd's Bears, as well as Ship's Hatch, carrying hard-to-find nautical items. Because these stores are covered by high-rise apartment and office buildings, they're hard to find, so it's good they're connected to Metrorail's Crystal City station (Blue and Yellow Lines) at 18th Street and Jefferson Davis Highway. Parking in two underground garages is free on weekends and after 4:30 P.M. weekdays.

Dulles Town Center
21100 Dulles Town Circle
Dulles, VA
(703) 404–7120
www.shopdullestowncenter.com

Loudoun County residents no longer have to travel to neighboring Fairfax County, Virginia, or Frederick, Maryland, to shop at a regional mall. Just up the road from Washington Dulles International Airport, this huge, two-story complex opened in the summer of 1999. Anchored by Hecht's, Lord & Taylor, JCPenney, and Sears, the mall also houses 125 specialty shops, restaurants, and entertainment. Nordstrom is set to open in the fall of 2002.

Fair Oaks Mall
Intersection of U.S. 50 and I–66
Fairfax, VA
(703) 359–8300

Macy's, Lord & Taylor, Hecht's, Sears, and JCPenney anchor this megamall of 185 stores and services, including an office for laser eye surgery. Specialty retailers include the likes of Papyrus (gifts and stationery), Sephora (cosmetics), People's Pottery, and standard mall favorites like the Gap, Laura Ashley, Talbots, and Bath & Body Works. The mall features several dining options, but no food court. Visit during the holiday season for the annual

ing has left you too pooped to drive home, the snazzy Ritz-Carlton Hotel is right next door. In fact, it's joined to the mall and has its own entrance right off the promenade; however, you'd better have plenty of cash or credit left over if you plan on getting a room for the night. If you're a frequent customer here, sign up for the free shopper incentive program. You can take Metro right to the mall, making it a popular shopping destination for commuters.

display of lifelike stuffed animals, adored by kids.

If you can't find what you're looking for at Fair Oaks, supplement your shopping spree at several shopping centers within a couple of miles. Fairfax Town Center, just across the street at the intersection of U.S. 50 and West Ox Road., Fairfax, houses Tower Records, Bed Bath and Beyond, Zany Brainy (a children's educational superstore profiled in our Kidstuff chapter), and a United Artists movie theater. The neighboring Fair Lakes area includes a two-story Kohl's department store, featuring clothing and housewares, 12551 Fairlakes Circle, Fairfax. Right next door to Kohl's, Galyan's offers just about anything you'd ever want in the way of sporting or outdoor goods. Down the street, you'll find Fairlakes Shopping Center, with a Toys Я Us Kids World superstore, Target, and Walmart.

Fashion Centre at Pentagon City
1100 S. Hayes St.
Arlington, VA
(703) 415–2400
www.fashioncentrepentagon.com

Arlington County's premier retail showcase, Pentagon City, as it's customarily called, is one of the area's most exciting and dynamic shopping showplaces, a visual wonderland complete with towering skylights, palm trees, a sunlit food court, six-screen cinema, and 170 stores spread over four levels. Anchor tenants are Macy's and Nordstrom; specialty shops include The Nature Company, Victoria's Secret, Bath & Body Works, The Disney Store, Discovery Channel Store, and Britches of Georgetowne. If all that walking and buy-

Landmark Mall
5801 Duke St. at I–395
Alexandria, VA
(703) 941–2582

Alexandria's only enclosed shopping mall is Landmark Mall, which some residents of neighboring Fairfax County happily call their own as well. Landmark underwent an extensive renovation, expansion, and general marketing makeover several years ago that has done wonders for aesthetics and business. The "new" three-level Landmark offers a wealth of (free) covered and surface parking and some 120 stores and restaurants (but no movie theaters), including anchor tenants Hecht's, JCPenney, and Sears. You'll find specialty stores like Antiques of Essence, an emporium featuring lots of fun surprises; Firefly, an upscale women's clothing store; and mall favorites like the Gap. New stores include Macy's, Lord & Taylor, and Old Navy. Special programs include live music every Wednesday night in the food court, and a collectors' market on Saturday mornings. The mall is conveniently located right off I–395.

Springfield Mall Regional Shopping Center
Intersection of Franconia and Loisdale Rds.
Springfield, VA
(703) 971–3000
www.springfieldmall.com

This mall has local bragging rights when it comes to sheer size: It houses 230 stores, including three anchors, Macy's, JCPenney, and Target. Largely geared toward families, it features a Planet Play games arcade, laser tag, play tower, and beautiful carousel. It also sponsors more than 20 family-oriented events annually, including a monthly kids' club and, during the holiday season, a store just for children. The mall offers two food courts, a multiscreen movie theater, and specialty stores like the Gap, the Disney Store, Aeropostale men's and women's clothing, and the Virginia Department of Transportation Informational Store, where shoppers can get the latest information about the "Mixing Bowl" construction project. (See the Getting Around chapter.) Due to its convenient southeastern Fairfax location, just a few hundred yards off I-95 near the I-395 interchange, Springfield Mall is popular with District residents as well as shoppers from points south including Woodbridge, Fredericksburg, and the large military community in Quantico.

Conveniently, just across Frontier Drive (by Macy's) from the mall is a mini shopping center that opened in late 1994. It's anchored by Best Buy, one of the growing number of retailers offering rock-bottom prices on major appliances and consumer electronics. You'll also find Kohl's just minutes away.

Tysons Corner Center
Intersection of Hwys. 123 and 7
Vienna, VA
(703) 893-9400
www.shoptysons.com

Tysons Corner is one of the shining jewels in Fairfax County's economic crown. Shoppers from throughout the region flock to Tysons Corner Center and its nearly 250 stores including Nordstrom, Bloomingdale's, Lord & Taylor, Hecht's, JCPenney, Brooks Brothers, and Eddie Bauer. LL Bean, the Maine-based catalogue company, opened a large retail outlet here in the summer of 2000. Check out the waterfall, fish pond, and climbing wall!

Newer businesses include the Discovery Channel Store, Jessica McClintock, Chiasso, and Build-a-Bear Workshop, where shoppers can create their own stuffed animals. The mall's restaurants include the megapopular Rainforest Cafe, described in our Kidstuff chapter.

Tysons is one of the area's oldest shopping malls (opened in the 1968), but you wouldn't know it. Like so many of its peers, Tysons experienced a rebirth during the mid-1980s with a major renovation and expansion that dramatically enhanced its look and customer friendliness. Among the most welcome changes were the addition of parking decks and the conversion of underground truck tunnels into rows of specialty shops.

Tysons Galleria
2001 International Dr.
McLean, VA
(703) 827-7730
www.tysonsgalleria.com

Just across Chain Bridge Road (Route 123) from Tysons Corner Center and adjacent to the Ritz-Carlton Hotel, this 100-store showplace is upscale to the nth degree. Its anchors include Macy's, Saks Fifth Avenue, and Neiman Marcus. Other retailers include an FAO Schwarz superstore, Hugo Boss, Elan salon and day spa, and the only Vidal Sasson salon in the D.C. market. The restaurants here are first-rate, including the likes of Maggiano's Little Italy, Legal Sea Foods, and P.F. Chang's China Bistro.

If the two Tysons malls don't hold your interest, cross Highway 7 and you'll discover a series of strip malls housing car dealers, restaurants, hotels, specialty stores, and large chain outlets such as Tower Records, Borders Books & Music, and Marshall's.

Suburban Maryland

Maryland's got malls all right, but it also has some of the priciest shopping streets around.

D.C.'s answer to Michigan Avenue, the Chevy Chase Shopping District features more than 200 stores and restaurants along Wisconsin Avenue, where Chevy Chase, Maryland, and the Chevy Chase district of D.C. meet. At 5555 Wisconsin Avenue, Saks Fifth Avenue has anchored the upscale area for more than three decades. This huge, stately store possesses almost all the cachet of the original on New York's Fifth Avenue, and its very presence has served as a catalyst for dozens of other exclusive shops to locate nearby, including the likes of Tiffany & Co., Cartier, Lord & Taylor, and Gianni Versace. Across Wisconsin Avenue you'll find women's shops where clerks bring dresses out from the back for you to try on, and service is always the utmost in personal courtesy. Saks-Jandel, 5510 Wisconsin Avenue, is a Washington retailer known worldwide as a premier furriery and designer boutique. Wander south from there, or cross the street, and you'll be immersed in yet more glamour, culminating in D.C.'s Mazza Gallerie and The Shops at Chevy Chase Pavilion (see this chapter's listings), just across the state line, and only 2 blocks away. The Friendship Heights Metro station is right next door.

Drive north from Chevy Chase on Wisconsin Avenue, and you'll hit Bethesda. No matter which way you look, you'll see blocks and blocks of stores, selling furniture, Oriental rugs, furs, art, clothing, shoes, toys, books, and anything else you can dream up. This shopper's paradise goes on for approximately 2 square miles, culminating at Wilson Boulevard to the west, and Cordell Avenue to the north.

No matter how great a shopping district, on a blowy, winter day or a sticky, summer day, a mall can be a refuge. Here are some of the biggest and best in metro Maryland.

Beltway Plaza Mall
6100 Greenbelt Rd.
Greenbelt, MD
(301) 345–1500
www.beltwayplazacenter.com

Serving nearby University of Maryland and Prince George's County, this mall features stores like Target, Sports Authority, Burlington Coat Factory, Marshalls, and Value City. Children can play games and ride rides at Jeepers!, and adults can work out at a Gold's Gym with a glass-enclosed basketball court. As an added convenience, the mall boasts the area's largest Giant Food grocery. In all, the mall houses more than 100 fashion and specialty stores as well as 14 movie theaters.

Lakeforest
701 Russell Ave.
Gaithersburg, MD
(301) 840–5840
www.shoplakeforest.com

In northern Montgomery County, two-story Lakeforest Mall offers anchor stores Lord & Taylor, Hecht's, Sears, and JCPenney, plus a whopping 160 other stores, five theaters, and more than a dozen restaurants. Specialty stores are along the lines of Banana Republic, Ann Taylor, Talbots, Brookstone, and Mastercraft Interiors. The mall is sister to Fair Oaks Mall in Fairfax, Virginia (see earlier).

Landover Mall
2103 Brightseat Rd.
Landover, MD
(301) 341–3200

This is by far the biggest mall in Prince George's County, offering more than 100 stores and specialty shops, including anchors Hecht's, Sears, and JCPenney. Specialty stores at the two-story mall include Lerner New York, Stride Rite, and Suncoast Motion Pictures.

Westfield Shoppingtown Montgomery Mall
7101 Democracy Blvd.
Bethesda, MD
(301) 469–6000
www.montgomerymall.shoppingtown.com

With 200 specialty stores, Montgomery Mall may require a full day to explore. Check out anchors Nordstrom, Sears, and Hecht's, along with specialty stores like Crate and Barrel, J. Crew, Guess?, Ann Taylor, and The Limited. The mall also houses a movie theater and restaurants like California Pizza Kitchen and Slade's American Grill. Special events include a kids' club on Wednesday mornings and an annual charitable shopping night in November.

Westfield Shoppingtown Wheaton Plaza
Shopping Center
11160 Viers Mill Rd.
Wheaton, MD
(301) 946–3200
wwwwheaton.shoppingtown.com

This mall houses more than 120 stores, including anchors Hecht's and JCPenney.

It features the usual mall specialty stores, as well as cinemas and several restaurants. Wheaton Plaza underwent remodeling in 2000.

White Flint
11301 Rockville Pike
North Bethesda, MD
(301) 468–5777
www.shopwhiteflint.com
Once considered one of the area's most upscale malls, White Flint now caters mostly to families, with features such as KidZone and an on-site children's theater, Bethesda Academy of the Performing Arts (BAPA). (See Kidstuff for more information.) Anchored by Bloomingdale's, Lord & Taylor, a giant Borders Books, and Music & Cafe, the three-level mall houses 125 stores and restaurants. In addition to mainstream stores like the Gap and Banana Republic, White Flint also features the trendy adult amusement center/restaurant Dave & Buster's (see the Nightlife chapter), a five-theater Loews Cineplex, and the Roxsan Day Spa. The mall holds annual programs such as camp, health, and bridal expos, and offers a VIP frequent shoppers program. You don't even have to drive: Free shuttle buses transport shoppers from the nearby White Flint Metro station.

Outlet Malls

They literally bring 'em in by the busloads at outlet malls, particularly huge Potomac Mills near Woodbridge, Virginia, and its new sibling, Arundel Mills in nearby Arundel County, Maryland. Because people are willing to drive long distances to visit these places, and because there aren't too many of them in Metro Washington, we haven't broken them down by geographic region, but we've listed them alphabetically. All of the following destinations are within an hour of the Washington area.

Arundel Mills
7000 Arundel Mills Circle
Hanover, MD
(410) 540–5100
www.millscorp.com/arundel/index2.html

> **Insiders' Tip**
> Turn a daytrip into a weekend getaway when visiting some of the popular outlet malls in Pennsylvania and West Virginia—maybe you can even fit in some skiing.

Although slightly smaller than its Virginia counterpart, newcomer Arundel Mills, which opened in November 2000, also specializes in name-brand outlet stores, including some places you won't find anywhere else in the region. Anchors include the recently opened, 130,000-square-foot Bass Pro Shops Outdoor World, featuring everything for fishing and hunting enthusiasts; Off 5th—Saks 5th Avenue Outlet; Books-a-Million; Old Navy; and Muvico Egyptian 24 Theaters, the area's largest movie theater, which even features a children's playroom. Among clothing and specialty stores you'll find a Banana Republic Factory Store, Ann Taylor Loft, Jones New York Country, Skechers USA, Kirkland's Outlet, and the Flag Shop. Grab a bite to eat at the large food court.

City Place Mall
8661 Colesville Rd.
Silver Spring, MD
(301) 589–1091
City Place (Colesville Road and Fenton Street) is an outlet-shopper's paradise, with five levels of off-price shopping. Among the 63 stores you'll find here are Nordstrom Rack, Marshalls, Ross, 9 West, Fashion Warehouse (women's apparel for as little as $10), and Burlington Coat Factory. The mall also houses a food court and a 10-theater cinema.

Leesburg Corner Premium Outlets
Hwy. 7 and U.S. 15
Leesburg, VA
(703) 737–3071
www.premiumoutlets.com

Potomac Mills is one of Virginia's top tourist attractions. PHOTO: COURTESY OF POTOMAC MILLS SHOPPING CENTER

This outdoor outlet center features 60 stores, including designer clothing names like Saks Fifth Avenue, DKNY, Tommy Hilfiger, Polo Ralph Lauren, Liz Claiborne, and Burberry. Other specialty stores feature housewares, country decorating accessories, party goods, jewelry and hair accessories, and gourmet food items.

Potomac Mills
2700 Potomac Mills Circle
near Woodbridge, VA
(703) 643–1054
www.potomacmills.com

It says something about the power of shopping when one of the most popular tourist destinations in history- and scenery-rich Virginia is an outlet mall, namely Potomac Mills. Several million people shop here annually.

Just 12 miles south of Washington off I–95 (you can't miss the signs), Potomac Mills more than lives up to its billing as a paradise for shoppers, especially those with a penchant for savings. More than 230 off-price and outlet stores include the likes of L.L. Bean, Saks Fifth Avenue, Polo Ralph Lauren, Tommy Hilfiger, Nautica, and Laura Ashley. You'll also find a large JCPenney outlet, Old Navy, T. J. Maxx, Marshalls, SYMS, and the Sports Authority. The mall houses the 62,000-square-foot Vans SkatePark, touted as the world's largest facility of its kind for skateboarding and Rollerblading. A large game arcade and 15-screen theater also provide entertainment. Potomac Mills also offers more than 20 restaurants and food-court eateries and full concierge service, including foreign currency exchange.

Swedish furniture retailer IKEA, previously one of Potomac Mills's biggest anchor stores, moved in November 2001 to a new building just a few feet outside the mall. With 300,000 square feet of retail space, double the size of the old location, IKEA features more than 10,000 furnishings, housewares, toys, accessories, and gourmet food items. The new store even showcases its products in three complete model homes. The restaurant serves delicious Swedish meatballs and other specialties as well as children's meals. While parents shop, kids can hang out in a large play area with a Swedish farmhouse theme.

Prime Outlets Hagerstown
495 Prime Outlets Blvd.
Hagerstown, MD
(888) 883–6288
www.primeoutlets.com

Conveniently located just off I–70 West, this collection of more than 80 outlet stores features such names as Gap, Bass, Black and Decker, Bugle Boy, Jones New York, Brooks Brothers, DKNY, Polo Ralph Lauren, and Dockers. Folks in the far reaches of Montgomery County may find this place more convenient than the Virginia centers.

Antique Districts

Washingtonians have an insatiable appetite for antique paintings, furniture, and bric-a-brac, as demonstrated by the numerous districts and shops specializing in such merchandise. Maybe folks are inspired by the many historic buildings and neighborhoods in the region, or maybe they've just got to have accessories to accent the conservative colonial architecture prominent in even the newest homes. The region offers antique emporiums for the most serious of collectors as well as those who just like to dabble.

Antique shops often buy at public auctions, then mark up the items as much as 100 percent, a necessity when you consider that they must pay rent, salaries, insurance, and all the other incidentals associated with owning a business. Still, antique shops are a good place to get an education on quality and construction. Many are sleepy little stores where the proprietors are happy to share their knowledge. Owners realize that a browser today may be a paying customer tomorrow, so don't be shy about asking questions.

If variety is what you're after, you'll want to stroll through one of Washington's several antique districts. One of the foremost is Georgetown in Washington, D.C., which has stores on every block offering serious furniture and accessories like grandfather clocks, nineteenth-century paintings, and sterling. These are the shops that furnish those mansions hidden along the side streets, so expect to fork over major bucks.

If your budget is more restrained, you might venture to Howard Avenue in Kensington, Maryland. This is one of the foremost antique districts in the mid-Atlantic, with store after store featuring genuine antiques, reproductions, lighting, and other accessories. It's serious, but not as rarefied as Georgetown. Head to the lower, warehouse end of Howard Avenue for serious antique shopping, expecially if you are looking for big pieces and a wider selection. The downtown Antique Row, by contrast, has lots of cute, smaller shops full of collectibles. On the streets branching out from Howard, you'll discover furniture makers and restoration experts who provide value for the money. Nothing here is cheap, but the quality is good and the service excellent.

In Virginia, Loudoun County is making an effort to become the antiques capital of the Old Dominion. You'll find well-stocked shops throughout historic downtown Leesburg, as well as dozens of dealers grouped in antiques malls on the outskirts of town. Along the western stretches of U.S. 50 in Loudoun, hunt country delights are the name of the game in the Middleburg Historic Shopping District. The tiny burg offers a fair number of stores for its size, many along Washington and Madison Streets. Middleburg's antique specialties run the gamut from hunt prints and accessories to period furniture and jewelry.

The cobbled streets of Old Town Alexandria in Virginia will lead you to dozens of antique shops. King Street from the west end of town to the river offers stores that stock everything from genuine Persian rugs (preembargo antiques), to French, English, and American period furniture. The streets that intersect King (Washington, Asaph, Royal), as well as those parallel to it (Cameron, Prince), likewise have many specialty antique stores with merchandise such as chandeliers, mirrors, tableware, and art. Quality varies from store to store, and the search here could easily occupy several days, depending on how long you linger at each shop.

Adam Weschler & Son Fine Art Auctioneers and Appraisers
909 E St. NW
Washington, DC
(202) 628–1281
www.weschlers.com

Since 1890, Weschler's has been a premier spot for those interested in fine antique furniture, jewelry, paintings, and decorative items. Auctions take place every Tuesday, and the business also holds special catalogue events. This highly reputable house offers some very nice pieces, but the people who shop here—including dealers—usually know what they're doing, so bargains may be snapped up from under your nose if you're an amateur.

Featherstone Square Antique Mall & Collectibles
14567 Jefferson Davis Hwy.
Woodbridge, VA
(703) 491–9099

You ought to find something to your liking at this 100,000-square-foot mall, one of the largest of its kind in the D.C. area and all of Virginia. More than 200 dealers carry an eclectic array of antiques, from primitive to retro, as well as contemporary collectibles along the lines of Beanie Babies and Barbies. You'll find lots of furniture, books, china, silver, textiles, coins, and bric-a-brac. As an added bonus for true shopaholics, Potomac Mills outlet mall (see previous listing) is just 1½ miles from here!

Laws Auctioneers Inc.
7209 Centreville Rd.
Manassas, VA
(703) 631–0590
www.lawsauction.com

Auctions take place several days a week here, and a lot of the merchandise might be classified as junk—which the owners unabashedly admit during the proceedings. You'll also find bargains, particularly when there's a catalogue auction. At such times, you may discover some fine early twentieth-century and nineteenth-century furniture and decorative items. More often, you'll find decent reproductions and lots of rococo, European-style

furniture. Across the gravel drive from the auction gallery, a large antiques mall houses shops ranging from serious purveyors of nineteenth-century furniture to those selling cutesy country-style pieces.

Old Market Antiques
442 S. Washington St.
Falls Church, VA
(703) 241–1722

This 10,000-square-foot space features more than 30 shops offering furniture from Mission style to European style. You'll also find antique tools, trunks, and textiles.

Sloan's Auction Galleries
4920 Wyaconda Rd.
N. Bethesda, MD
(301) 468–4911
www.sloansauction.com

Sloan's offers everything from nice reproductions to serious furniture, paintings, and jewelry. Major antiques are featured at multiday catalogue auctions with plenty of advance notice and several days set aside for previewing. Less valuable items are sold every Thursday in what Sloan's calls "attic" auctions. This business is family owned and highly respected, though no Washington auctioneers are considered to be on a par with New York's Sotheby's or Christie's.

Thieves Market Antiques Center
8101 Richmond Hwy.
Alexandria, VA
(703) 360–4200

This 20,000-square-foot, dusty warehouse on raffish Richmond Highway has been around for nearly 50 years, and every Washingtonian who collects antiques

> **Insiders' Tip**
> Scoop up bargains at local estate and yard sales held on Saturday mornings throughout the metro area.

knows about it. It's only open on weekends, and you have to sift through a lot of merchandise to find something truly worthwhile, but it's fun to poke around among the old paintings, rugs, furniture, coins, china, and other bric-a-brac.

Bookstores and Newsstands

We thought it appropriate to offer a handy guide to some of the area's best bookstores and newsstands—those places with such a wealth of resources (including maps, out-of-town newspapers, and local see-and-do/history guides) that they're invaluable to newcomers. Visit them often enough and you'll make friends with some of the most helpful and knowledgeable people around. Remember, too, that Washington's many museums and universities feature gift shops and bookshops worth exploring. We've listed a couple of noteworthy ones in this category as well as the section on museum shops.

Of course, you've heard of the large chains—and they're wonderful in terms of size and variety of stock. In Washington, Maryland, and Virginia, you'll find numerous branches, mostly in malls, of superstores like B. Dalton Bookseller, Barnes & Noble, Borders Books & Music, Brentano's, Tower Records and Books, and Rand McNally Map & Travel Store. Most of these places have cushy reading chairs, coffee shops, and plenty of special events—they're great places to while away a lazy afternoon. You'll find one nearby whether you're in Washington, Maryland, or Virginia, so consult the phone directory. Also, if you happen to be in either Ronald Reagan Washington National or Washington Dulles International Airports, check out the wide selection at Benjamin Books, a national chain that has upgraded the standards for airport bookstores.

Aside from these excellent chains, Washington is also blessed with a wealth of fine independent bookstores, many of which offer similarly inviting atmospheres. Check them out. The following are among those we especially enjoy.

Washington, D.C.

AD.C. Map and Travel Center
1636 I St. NW
Washington, DC
(202) 628–2608, (800) 544–2659

This little shop has been around for about a third of a century and continues to be a popular browsing spot for those who love to travel. Not only does the store carry every kind of map imaginable, but it also features a nice selection of travel books, including narratives and guides. The store is closed on Sundays. Located on Farragut Square, the store is right next door to the Farragut West Metro station.

Bridge Street Books
2814 Pennsylvania Ave. NW
Washington, DC
(202) 965–5200

This intimate bookstore at the edge of Georgetown specializes in humanities and social science topics such as politics, cultural theory, literature, philosophy, poetry, and history. It's open daily.

Chapters: A Literary Bookstore
1512 K Street NW
Washington, DC
(202) 347–5495
www.chaptersliteracy.com

Chapters, an independent book store, specializes in poetry, literary fiction, and foreign language books. Conveniently located in the downtown office corridor along K Street, Chapters also has a small gift section, as well as books on tape. It's open daily. McPherson Square is the closest Metro stop.

Cleveland Park Bookshop
3416 Wisconsin Avenue NW
Washington, DC
(202) 363–1112
www.clevelandparkbooks.com

On upper Wisconsin Avenue, this friendly neighborhood spot features all kinds of highbrow specialty volumes as well as picture books on travel and gardening. Like most independents, they're happy to order what you can't find on the shelves. Definitely part of the surrounding community, this store draws customers with regular author signings as well as conveniences like shipping, wrapping, and book accessories. It also specializes in stationery. It's open daily. Take Metro to the Tenleytown-AU station.

Franz Bader Bookstore
1911 I St. NW
Washington, DC
(202) 337–5440

If it's a gorgeous picture book you're after, this is the place. Franz Bader specializes in books on the visual arts—design, graphics, photography, and architecture—and most of their selections are breathtaking. Even if you don't buy, this place is worth a look for the sheer beauty of the photographs you'll see. It's closed on Sundays. Farragut West is the closest Metro station.

Glover Books & Music
2319 Wisconsin Ave. NW
Washington, DC
(202) 338–8100

Not only does this store have a wide selection of popular books for adults and children, but it also features sheet music, videos, computer software, and tickets for shows and sports events. Conveniently located in the cozy Glover Park neighborhood of upper Georgetown, Glover's is open daily.

International Language Centre
1803 Connecticut Ave. NW
Washington, DC
(202) 332–2894
www.newsinform.com/ilc-main.html

If you're a foreign tourist in Washington, you may want to stop in here for books, magazines, videos, and newspapers in more than 200 languages. If you're an American going abroad, drop by to get a feel for the culture you'll be visiting. Open daily, it's just 2 blocks from the Dupont Circle Metro stop.

Kramerbooks & afterwords Cafe & Grill
1517 Connecticut Ave. NW
Washington, DC
(202) 387–1400
www.kramers.com

This Washington mainstay is crowded day and night, thanks to its great, full-service restaurant and outdoor cafe, and its central location at the hub of Dupont Circle activity. Political books and big bios are always featured in the window, as are tomes on economics, philosophy, religion, and gay/lesbian studies. The selection here is large enough to include plenty of beach reading and guides to everything under the sun. It's open daily. Take Metro to the Dupont Circle station.

MysteryBooks
1715 Connecticut Ave. NW
Washington, DC
(202) 483–1600, (800) 955–2279
www.killerbooks.com

Don't know where to go for a great selection of whodunnits? Mystery solved: Head for this fun store near the Dupont Metro station. It carries more than 18,000 titles and frequently features book signings.

Olsson's Books & Records
1239 Wisconsin Ave. NW
Washington, DC
(202) 338–9544 (Books only)
1307 19th St. NW
Washington, DC
(202) 785–1133
1200 F St. NW
Washington, DC
(202) 347–3686 (Books only)
418 7th St. NW
Washington, DC
(202) 638–7610 (Books only)
www.olssons.com

In the heart of Georgetown, as well as in other convenient spots, this popular shop is the oldest and one of the largest independents in the Washington Metro area, with more than 100,000 titles in stock. You're bound to find what you're looking for in both the music and book departments. Check out the large cookbook section, as well as plenty of selections on subjects ranging from the military to psychology and self-help. If a suburban location is more convenient, visit their store in Bethesda, Maryland, at 7647 Old Georgetown Road (301-652-3336), or in Old Town Alexandria, Virginia, at 106

South Union Street (703-684-0077), or in Arlington, Virginia, at 2111 Wilson Boulevard (703-525-4227). Some locations have cafes.

Politics & Prose Bookstore & Coffeehouse
5015 Connecticut Ave. NW
Washington, DC
(202) 364-1919
www.politics-prose.com

This bookstore is very highly thought of by Washington's intelligentsia, thanks to the personal touch of the owners and their savvy blend of the latest and most popular books, as well as the obscure. Washington authors always get the spotlight here, and there are frequent readings, coffees, and signings by local and national celebrities. The store takes pride in being the city's largest independent bookseller. As an added bonus, it's got free parking behind the store.

Reiter's Scientific & Professional Books
2021 K St. NW
Washington, DC
(202) 223-3327
www.reiters.com

Reiter's claims to have more than 60,000 scientific and technical books, including tomes on computers, math, physics, engineering, medicine, nursing, business, and psychology. They'll also make a special effort to hunt down anything not in stock. It's open daily, and close to both the Farragut North and Farragut West Metro stops.

Reprint Bookshop
455 L'Enfant Plaza SW
Washington, DC
(202) 554-5070

Ignore the name, which originates from the fact that the shop only sold paperbacks when it opened 40 years ago (and paperbacks are, of course, reprints of hardcover books). Now, the store sells all kinds of popular fiction, nonfiction, literature, and, naturally, paperbacks. Specialties include African American literature as well as computer guides. Convenient to the L'Enfant Plaza Metro station, the store is closed on Sundays.

Second Story Books Inc.
2000 P St. NW
Washington, DC
(202) 659-8884
www.secondstorybooks.com

Another Dupont Circle institution—the store's been here for more than 25 years—Second Story features old and rare books, first editions, fine bound volumes, or those that are just plain used. If you're looking for something unique or just hard to find, try this shop. If a branch in Maryland is more convenient, drop in at 12160 Parklawn Drive, Rockville (301-770-0477), or 4836 Bethesda Avenue, Bethesda, (301-656-0170).

Trover Shop
221 Pennsylvania Ave. SE
Washington, DC
(202) 547-BOOK
1706 G St. NW
Washington, DC
(202) 789-2290
1031 Connecticut Ave. NW
Washington, DC
(202) 659-8138
www.trovershop.com

This independent has been around for more than 40 years. It continues to be popular with busy Capitol Hill office workers as well as the lobbyists, lawyers, and White House types who frequent the midtown location. Right near the Library of Congress, the Pennsylvania Avenue shop specializes in political science, though you also can find plenty of lunch-hour escape reading. All three locations are close to Metro stops.

Northern Virginia

The Book Chase
102 W. Washington St.
Middleburg, VA
(540) 687-6874, (800) 373-7323

This small bookstore makes a nice browsing break from the shopping in Middleburg's antique district. You'll find horse-related books, English publications, guidebooks, popular fiction, magazines, and volumes on topics of local interest. It's open daily.

George Mason University Bookstore
Student Union Building 2
4400 University Dr.
Fairfax, VA
(703) 993–2666
www.bkstore.com/gmu/index.html

There aren't many bookstores in this section of Fairfax, so the university bookstore is quite a blessing—a well- stocked emporium that also carries accessories and stationery. Not only will you find textbooks, but also popular and classic fiction as well as nonfiction. It's closed on Sundays.

Olsson's Books & Records
106 S. Union St.
Alexandria, VA
(703) 684–0077
www.olssons.com

To learn more about this Old Town location overlooking the Potomac River, please see the Washington, D.C. listing.

Suburban Maryland

Maryland Book Exchange
4500 College Ave.
College Park, MD
(301) 927–2510
www.marylandbook.com

University of Maryland is one of the largest in the nation, with some 40,000 students, so it makes sense that this bookstore would be equally comprehensive. You'll find more than 125,000 titles here—that's right, we haven't mistakenly added any zeroes. The store stocks plenty of text and reference books, fiction and nonfiction best-sellers, used books, and school supplies.

Olsson's Books & Records
7647 Old Georgetown Rd.
Bethesda, MD
(301) 652–3336
www.olssons.com

Please see the Washington, D.C. listing.

Second Story Books
12160 Parklawn Dr.
Rockville, MD
(301) 770–0477

4836 Bethesda Ave.
Bethesda, MD
(301) 656–0170

Please see the Washington, D.C. listing.

Metro Area Newsstands

A special note should be made of the following stores that do a good job of specializing in those hard-to-find newspapers and magazines, including those in foreign languages.

Book-N-Card
8110 Arlington Blvd.
Falls Church, VA
(703) 560–6999

This convenient shop in the Yorktowne Center, at the intersection of I-50 (Arlington Boulevard) and Gallows Road, stocks some 5,000 magazine titles—all English language—and a number of mid-Atlantic daily newspapers. The 33-year-old store, the metro area's oldest independent book dealer, also carries greeting cards and a wide array of books.

Glover Books & Music
2319 Wisconsin Ave. NW
Washington, DC
(202) 338–8100

See the listing under Washington, D.C. bookstores.

International Language Center
1753 Connecticut Ave. NW
Washington, DC
(202) 332–2894

See the listing under Washington, D.C. bookstores.

The Newsroom
1753 Connecticut Ave. NW
Washington, DC
(202) 332–1489

This spot features newspapers from most major U.S. cities as well as a huge variety of periodicals, including publications written in foreign languages. It also specializes in maps of major cities. Its Dupont Circle location draws a colorful mix of browsers—and the management tolerates lengthy browsing.

News World
1001 Connecticut Ave. NW
Washington, DC
(202) 872–0190

Like The Newsroom, this store features thousands of titles—magazines and newspapers from around the world.

Old Town News
721 King St.
Alexandria, VA
(703) 739–9024

This spot, conveniently located amidst the boutiques and restaurants of Old Town Alexandria, carries a wide variety of international newspapers and international magazines, as well as a large stock of those published in the United States. It's a sister store of Book-N-Card, listed earlier.

Furniture and Home Decorating

With so many people moving in and out of the D.C. area all the time, it's no wonder that furniture stores here thrive. You'll find stores to fit every budget—sprawling furniture warehouses to high-style designer shops.

Of course, nearly every mall has a Pottery Barn or Crate & Barrel, both great stores for picking up smart home accents at reasonable prices. If you've lived in the United States within the last five years, you know all about these places, so we won't waste space on descriptions. Instead, we'll try to give you an overview of stores particular to the region, hit the highlights, and get you started. By no means is this a comprehensive list, and for more ideas, consult your telephone directory, the home section in Thursday's *Washington Post*, the ads in *Washingtonian* magazine, and the regional advertising pages in *Architectural Digest*. Note that our list is alphabetical rather than geographical. If you're like us, borders don't matter in your quest for just the right piece!

Country Curtains Retail Shop
Arlington Forest Center
Arlington Blvd. (U.S. 50) at Park Dr.
Arlington, VA
(703) 522–7111
www.countrycurtains.com

Fans of the Stockbridge, Massachusetts-based curtain company's cheerful catalogues should visit the D.C. area's only immediate Country Curtains shop. You'll view lots and lots of inspiring window displays as well as coordinating furnishings and accessories.

Danker Furniture
1211 S. Fern St.
Arlington, VA
(703) 416–0200
10670 Lee Hwy.
Fairfax, VA
(703) 691–4333
1500 Ritchie Hwy.
Annapolis, MD
(410) 757–1674
120 Halpine Rd.
Rockville, MD
(301) 881–6010

This place is as swank as a large furniture store gets. It specializes in high-style and high-quality pieces, ranging from Chippendale to ultracontemporary. The showroom is beautifully decorated—inspiring, in fact, and designers on the premises can help you envision what the pieces will look like in your own home.

The Hardwood Artisans
3622 King St.
Alexandria, VA
(703) 379–7299
14080-E Sullyfield Circle
Chantilly, VA
(703) 803–7785
15005 Farm Creek Dr.
Woodbridge, VA
(703) 643–1044
605 Hungerford Dr.
Rockville, MD
(301) 340–0998
www.hardwoodartisans.com

Are you short on space? Consider drop-down, foldout furniture. The store specializes in cabinets primarily and can construct a multipurpose piece to fit the tiniest studio apartment. Merchandise includes entertainment units, dressers, bookcases, and Murphy, trundle, and platform beds—or you can have it all combined in one wall system. The solid hardwood pieces don't come cheap, but they're built to last. The Woodbridge store is closed on Sundays.

Marlo Furniture Warehouse & Showroom
5650 General Washington Dr.
Alexandria, VA
(703) 941–0800
3300 Marlo La.
Forestville, MD
(301) 735–2000
13450 Baltimore Ave.
Laurel, MD
(301) 419–3400
725 Rockville Pike
Rockville, MD
(301) 738–9000
www.marlofurniture.com

You won't be in Washington a day before you see or hear ads for Marlo. This store seems to be open around the clock, seven days a week, and is always pushing a special sale. It's no wonder—there's room after room of merchandise here, and it's gotta be moved! You really will find some good bargains, in styles ranging from colonial to contemporary.

Mastercraft Interiors, Ltd.
10390 Lee Hwy.
Fairfax, VA
(703) 273–7800
Intersection of I–66 and U.S. 50
Fair Oaks Mall
Fairfax, VA
(703) 385–8822
1405 Forest Dr.
Annapolis, MD
(410) 269–5530
Lake Forest Mall
701 Russell Ave.
Gaithersburg, MD
(301) 417–9259
1428 Rockville Pike
Rockville, MD
(301) 770–0400
www.mastercraftinteriors.com

If you favor Mission- or Williamsburg colonial-style furnishings, you'll be in hog heaven at Mastercraft. The stores also showcase Country French, Shaker, and other styles of good-quality furniture from names like Thomasville and Stickley, along with posh accessories. You'll find lots of silky mahogany, fluffy down, solid brass—and it's not cheap. The sales offer great bargains, however.

Persnickety
Wildwood Shopping Center
10305 Old Georgetown Rd.
Bethesda, MD
(301) 530–8805
Tysons Corner Center, Intersection of Hwys.
123 and 7
McLean, VA
(703) 760–8996
www.persnickety.com

These genteel little shops stock furniture and fabrics that seem meant for a lady's boudoir or a sunroom. Look for cheery French provincial-style flowers and stripes by Pierre Deux, Nina Campbell, and Colefax & Fowler, to name just a few. They're meant to be draped over the cushy sofas, ottomans, and easy chairs that decorate the store. You'll also find whimsical lamps and four-poster beds of decorative wrought iron and brass.

Saah Unfinished Furniture
2330 Columbia Pike
Arlington, VA
(703) 920–1500
5641-F General Washington Dr.
Alexandria, VA
(703) 256–4315
14802 Build America Dr.
Woodbridge, VA
(703) 494–4167
811 Hungerford Dr.
Rockville, MD
(301) 424–6911
www.saahfurniture.com

If you're a do-it-yourselfer, then Saah may have just what you want. This 48-year-old, family-owned business carries unfinished armoires, hutches, shelves, entertainment centers, tables, and chairs in pine, oak, aspen, and birch. Prices are reasonable, value is good, and you'll have the satisfaction of seeing your handiwork every day. The Arlington store is closed Sundays, and the Woodbridge store is closed Wednesdays.

Sofas By Design Fast
7305 Arlington Blvd.
Falls Church, VA
(703) 698–7632

The name is misleading, because this shop sells much more than sofas, including stylish lamps, tables, and all sorts of eye-catching accent pieces. Naturally, you will find sofas, and they are made relatively fast, for custom design. You pick the frame and fabric from hundreds of choices, and in four to six weeks, you have your merchandise. Of course, the pieces in the showroom are delivered much more quickly. What's more, the quality down and wood here cost less than you would expect.

Theodore's
2233 Wisconsin Ave. NW
Washington, DC
(202) 333–2300
www.theodores.com

Theodore's has been at the vanguard of Washington's contemporary furniture scene for 32 years. No fake colonial stuff here—just sleek, eclectic, innovative pieces that you won't find just anywhere. Its location in upper Georgetown makes it a popular spot for trendies in the surrounding neighborhood, but people are also willing to travel to this one-of-a-kind shop.

Urban Country Designs Ltd.
7801 Woodmont Ave.
Bethesda, MD
(301) 654–0500

This eclectic design studio features top-quality furniture that's a blend of antique, ethnic, and a touch of contemporary. Here, they strive for an entire design concept rather than simply a sofa or a dining room table, so you'll find wall, window, and floor treatments, as well as decorators to help you pull it all together.

Museum Shops

Any overview of shopping in our Nation's Capital has to include a mention of the city's great museum and gallery shops, particularly those at any of the Smithsonian's vast collection of properties. These places aren't just for tourists. Locals love them as well, especially for gifts that are hard to find anywhere else, including books, jewelry, china, framing-quality posters and prints, and assorted novelties. (See our Arts and Attractions chapters for more on the museums that house these shops.)

Bureau of Engraving and Printing
14th St. and Independence Ave. SW
Washington, DC
(202) 874–3019
www.bep.treas.gov

Buy sheets of uncut $1.00 and $2.00 bills, always fun for the kids to see.

Decatur House Museum
748 Jackson Pl. NW
Washington, DC
(202) 842–0920
www.decaturhouse.org

This museum on Lafayette Square, across from the White House, sells reproduction home accessories of the eighteenth and nineteenth centuries.

Hillwood Museum and Gardens
4155 Linnean Ave. NW
Washington, DC
(202) 686–8500
www.hillwoodmuseum.org

This former residence of Marjorie Merriweather Post (the cereal heiress) features a large collection of French and Russian decorative arts, and reproductions are on sale in the gift shop. You'll remember your visit with the Fabergé-style egg pendants and other items relating to the permanent collection.

Hirshhorn Museum
950 Independence Ave. NW
Washington, DC
(202) 357–1300
hirshhorn.si.edu

The Hirshhorn Museum features modern art, and the jewelry in the gift shop reflects it. It's quirky and interesting, especially the earrings, which are not the kind of merchandise you'll find in a shopping mall.

John F. Kennedy Center for the Performing Arts
Rock Creek Pkwy. and New Hampshire Ave. NW
Washington, DC
(202) 467–4600
www.kennedy-center.org

Visit the Kennedy Center for a good selection of gifts with music, dance, theater, and opera themes.

Mount Vernon Inn Gift Shop
George Washington Memorial Pkwy.
Alexandria, VA
(703) 780–0011
www.mountvernon.org

The gift shop at George Washington's estate has reproductions of his key to the Bastille, Martha Washington's cookbook, china and silver, and toys and souvenirs. The Christmas ornaments make nice mementos.

National Air and Space Museum
6th St. and Independence Ave. SW
Washington, DC
(202) 357–1300
www.nasm.si.edu

Kids love the stuff here, from the freeze-dried ice cream like the astronauts eat to the kites and other flight-related objects. Books and videos also will appeal to the aspiring pilots and astronauts on your gift list.

National Archives Museum Store
7th St. and Constitution Ave. NW
Washington, DC
(202) 501–5000
www.nara.gov

Here you'll find great replicas of the Declaration of Independence, the U.S. Constitution, and the Bill of Rights, along with posters and postcards. These make wonderful learning tools and souvenirs for kids. The shop also stocks a variety of games, gifts, greeting cards, books, clothing, and crafts.

National Building Museum
401 F St. NW
Washington, DC
(202) 272–2448
www.nbm.org

Some folks visit this museum especially to browse the Museum Shop, which is widely known for its wonderful selection of unusual building toys and other architecture-oriented gifts.

National Gallery of Art
600 Constitution Ave. NW
Washington, DC
(202) 737–4215
www.nga.gov

The basement shops of the National Gallery carry a vast collection of inexpensive prints and postcards of masterpieces that are suitable for framing. You'll also find stationery, jewelry, scarves, and glorious picture books.

National Geographic Society
17th and M Sts. NW
Washington, DC
(202) 857–7000
www.nationalgeographic.com
For superb wall maps, globes, books, and educational children's toys, the National Geographic Society can't be beat.

National Museum of African Art
950 Independence Ave. SW
Washington, DC
(202) 357–2700
www.nmafa.si.edu
Every home could benefit from a few eclectic accents, and you'll find just the right touch of ethnic artistry here. Look for textiles, dolls, crafts, and jewelry from Africa. You're sure to get compliments on these exotic items.

National Museum of Women in the Arts
1250 New York Ave. NW
Washington, DC
(202) 783–5000
www.nmwa.org
The shop just inside the museum's front doors features several cases of unique jewelry designed by artists. Decorative objects, books, stationery, clothing, and other gifts also cram the shelves in this tiny but well-stocked store.

Navy Museum
901 M St. SE
Washington, DC
(202) 433–4882
www.history.navy.mil/branches/nhcorg8.htm
Kids love the hands-on nature of this museum, with its uniforms, medals, guns, and ship parts. The shop stocks small souvenirs and elegant gifts relating to the U.S. Navy, Coast Guard, Marine Corps, and Merchant Marines.

Washington National Cathedral
Wisconsin and Massachusetts Aves. NW
Washington, DC
(202) 537–5766
www.cathedral.org/cathedral
The shop here stocks unusual Gothic and Medieval products such as stuffed gargoyles, colorful window decorations, and stained-glass-patterned scarves. If you're home decorating, pick up one of the dramatic tapestries or Gothic stone garden accessories.

Secondhand Stores

Outlet malls may offer bargains, but if you want something more economical—or more offbeat—you may want to check out the area's numerous secondhand shops.

Clothing

Many shops in the area offer great bargains in designer clothing. Expect to pay about one-third of what you'd shell out for a comparable new item. Some of the more upscale include the following:

Encore Resale Dress Shop
3715 Macomb St. NW
Washington, DC
(202) 966–8122
This 32-year-old store on a genteel Cleveland Park side street features great bargains on designer clothes, furs, and accessories. You'll find names like Chanel, Escada, and Ungaro, and glamorous accessories like scarves, handbags, leather goods, and unworn shoes. Don't expect "vintage" here: Nothing is older than two years. Open Monday through Saturday; the store accepts clothing by appointment.

Inga's Once Is Not Enough
4830 MacArthur Blvd. NW
2nd Fl., Washington, DC
(202) 337–3072
Socialites from ritzy Foxhall bring their once-used gowns and designer suits here for resale. Expect some real bargains,

including barely worn Chanel, Christian Lacroix, Armani, Bill Blass, Ungaro, and more. Accessories include handbags by the likes of Gucci and Prada. The store is closed on Sundays.

Second Chance
7702 Woodmont Ave.
Bethesda, MD
(301) 652–6606

Second Chance features only top-quality, contemporary designer clothes and accessories. You'll find a room packed with glamorous evening wear, funky, fashionable shoes, furs, sportswear, and all manner of jewelry, purses, belts, and scarves. The store is closed on Mondays.

Second Hand Rose
1516 Wisconsin Ave. NW
Washington, DC
(202) 337–3378

If current designer clothing is your thing, check out this boutique, which features modern items by such designers as Armani, Versace, and Donna Karan. You'll also find furs and accessories. It's open Monday through Saturday.

Secondi
1702 Connecticut Ave. NW
Washington, DC
(202) 667–1122

You'll find high-style consignment clothing for women at this small boutique, tucked away 2 blocks north of Dupont Circle. Look for designers like Donna Karan, Coach, Banana Republic, Ann Taylor, Country Road, Kate Spade, and Prada. The store is open daily.

Furniture

Consignment Galleries
3226 Wisconsin Ave. NW
Washington, DC
(202) 364–8995

This shop displays quality furniture and accessories in a charming showroom that gives you a good idea of how the other half lives. The nice thing is that you can have a piece of the good life for less-than-new prices. Even if you're only looking for something small, this place is worth a stop. You'll find French and Italian accessories, oil paintings, many styles of lamps, Oriental screens, sterling, crystal—just about any style and period you can imagine. Consignment Galleries also stocks a variety of traditional-style furniture pieces. The store is closed on Sundays.

The Cordell Collection
4911 Cordell Ave.
Bethesda, MD
(301) 907–3324
www.cordellconsign.com

In the heart of Bethesda, you'd expect to find the best in used furniture, and this shop delivers. Artfully blended antiques, reproductions, and collectibles inspire the imagination. Prices are not cheap, but some of the pieces are in the category of "they just don't make 'em like that any more." The store is closed on Sundays.

Upscale Resale
8100 Lee Hwy.
Falls Church, VA
(703) 698–8100
www.upscale-resale.com

Maybe it's the catchy name, but this has become one of the premier shops in Metro Washington for high-quality secondhand furniture. This store is picky about what it carries, and its showroom is attractive and classy. A lot of wealthy people live in Washington, and some of them appear to have left their discards here on consignment—maybe the remainder have picked up a few pieces here?

Spas and Salons

Beauty products are easy to find—any department store or salon has them. If you're like most people, you stick to certain brands and you know where to find them. What about beauty services? If you're looking for sessions that can last anywhere from an hour to a day, and that may include manicures, waxing, facials, and massage, you'll need a day spa—a wonderful place to unwind from Washington's frenetic pace. Here are some of the top names in the Washington area. Most serve both men and women and offer gift certificates to give as special presents. Expect to pay anywhere from $60 to more than $100 for a facial, $80 for an hour-long massage, and $250 to $300 for a whole day of pampering.

Beauty Spas

Elizabeth Arden Red Door Salon & Spa
5225 Wisconsin Ave. NW
Washington, D.C.
(202) 362–9890
www.reddoorsalons.com
Fairfax Square, 8075 Leesburg Pike
Vienna, VA
(703) 448–8388
Spectrum Center
Reston, VA
(703) 467–8488

Remember those 1940s movies where women would sit in a steam box with their cold-cream slathered faces poking out? Chances are, they were in Elizabeth Arden, who started the whole day spa concept decades ago. Well, the Washington salon is still going strong, though a lot of competition has come along in the interim. Maybe it's because of that same competition that this salon, once so pricey, is now relatively reasonable.

Georgette Klinger
Chevy Chase Pavilion,
5345 Wisconsin Ave. NW
Washington, DC
(202) 686–8880
www.georgetteklinger.com

The Hungarian-born Klinger founded her first salon in New York and was an immediate hit with all manner of celebrities. She has since brought her skincare methods and products to Washington, where the salon is equally successful. Whatever beauty treatment you can imagine, you can find at Klinger. On your first visit you'll be asked to fill out a skincare questionnaire, much as you would in a dermatologist's office. The questionnaire becomes part of your "chart," which is kept on file for future reference.

The atmosphere at Klinger is soothing, feminine (though there are male clients, too), and ultraclean. The specialty here is facials, some of which last more than an hour and involve the use of aromatic herbs or fruit acids. There are also manicures, pedicures, and haircuts and cosmetic makeovers available. Ask about packages, and you'll save some money.

Jacques Dessange
5410 Wisconsin Ave.
Chevy Chase, MD
(301) 913–9373
www.dessange.com

This full-service salon has it all, and you don't even need to venture into downtown. You can have a facial, bodywrap, haircut, makeover, manicure, pedicure, waxing, and massage. The atmosphere of this Parisian salon is energetic, trendy, and upscale.

Lillian Laurence Ltd.
2000 M St. NW
Washington, DC
(202) 872–0606

Lillian Laurence was a day spa before the term was invented. It's always been on the cutting edge of beauty treatment and continues to be so, offering facials, massage, body wraps, mud packs, body polishing, waxing, and nonsurgical face-lifts. It's a pleasant refuge, conveniently located in the lower level of a midtown office building.

Petra's Skin Spa
3915 Old Lee Hwy., Ste. 21A
Fairfax, VA
(703) 385–6800
www.eurodayspa.com

This sweetly scented hideaway in the heart of Fairfax specializing in "European Aesthetics," stays on the cutting edge of all beauty developments. There are therapies for every problem: toning facials that stimulate with light electrical pulses, fruit-acid peels to exfoliate, aromatherapy massages, hydradermie facials, and anti-stress treatments. None of it comes cheaply, but you save a bit when compared to downtown salons. The atmosphere is both intimate and elegant, with a stylish sitting area and spotless therapy rooms.

s/p/alon
1605 17th St. NW
Washington, DC
(202) 462–9000
www.spalon.net

This trendy day spa and salon offers massages, haircutting and coloring, facials, alpha-hydroxy treatments, makeup, manicures, pedicures, sea-water gel wraps, body polishing, organic peeling, and body- and eye-firming treatments. You also can shoot the works and go for a package.

The Washington Institute for Skin Care
2311 M St. NW, Ste. 200
Washington, DC
(202) 785–8855
www.skinlaser.com

If we could go anywhere in the world for a facial, this would be the place. Its decor is hushed, spare, and elegant, not frilly or trendy like many day spas—maybe because it's associated with a doctor's office, the Washington Institute of Dermatologic Laser Surgery—but the sterile atmosphere is very reassuring. Facials cost plenty here, but you can get glycolic peels, extractions, and acid treatments with complete assurance that the job will be done right and your skin won't be damaged. Waxing, makeup, manicures, and pedicures are also available, as are a wide assortment of skincare products found only in doctors' offices.

Hair Salons

Following is a list of Washington salons most often mentioned in national beauty magazines. They serve both men and women.

Daniel's Salon
1831 M St. NW
Washington, D.C.
(202) 296–4856

In a handsome townhouse, Daniel's is three stories packed with beauty services.

It's always bustling with patrons of both sexes, generally up-and-coming executives from the surrounding office district.

La Coupe
1775 K St. NW
Washington, DC
(202) 775–1934

Near the White House, La Coupe bustles with a young, business-oriented clientele and a slew of Eurostyle hairdressers.

Okyo Beauty Salon
2903 M St. NW
Washington, DC
(202) 342–2675

This bright, spare-looking loft attracts all sorts of Washington celebs. It's acclaimed for fine cuts and coloring, as well as long waits for appointments. Call well in advance.

Roche Salon
3050 K St. NW, Washington Harbour Plaza
Washington, DC
(202) 775–0775
www.rochesalon.com

This salon is a fantasyland, complete with paintwork to simulate blue skies and brightly colored cabanas (changing rooms) that make you think of a day at the beach. Don't let the whimsy fool you though: Cuts and color are taken seriously here, and the salon is regularly named in national magazines as one of Washington's best. What's more, they won't try to chop off your long hair or give you an unsuitable, hard-to-manage style. *InSalon* magazine named Roche Salon's informative Web site the best in the beauty industry. It even offers cyberspace makeovers!

Salon Jean Paul
4820 Yuma St.
Washington, DC
(202) 966–4600

This has been a favorite of the Washington establishment for many years. In upper Northwest, D.C., Salon Jean Paul attracts a number of patrons from the affluent residential area surrounding it.

Unique Stores

Some stores just don't fit into any category, or if they do, they're the only ones in it. The stores listed below either offer more of their specialty than anyone in Metro Washington, or they offer obscure merchandise.

Ademas
816 N. Fairfax St.
Alexandria, VA
(703) 549–7806
If you like unique flooring, head for this Old Town designer showroom, where you can choose from handmade tile, marble, granite, terra-cotta, and limestone. You'll be amazed at the variety of colors, textures, and patterns.

Art to Wear . . . and Gifts to Share
10455 North St.
Fairfax, VA
(703) 691–9000
Local artists work and display their wares at this pleasant shop in the heart of Fairfax City. The store carries lots of handcrafted jewelry, pottery, stained glass, and as the name implies, wearable designs such as dresses, vests, and printed T-shirts. The children's section offers lots of great baby gifts. Art to Wear also offers sewing and craft classes for kids and adults. It's open daily.

The Artisans
Langley Shopping Center
1366 Chain Bridge Rd.
McLean, VA
(703) 506–0158
www.artisansofmclean.com
The artistry of American craftspeople highlights this shop in McLean. You'll find wearable art, gifts, housewares, and jewelry—all of it unique. Candlesticks are sculptures containing glass and semi-precious stones, and brooches are striking enough to make a memorable outfit of any little black dress. Not everything here is costly, though. Polymer clay jewelry starts at $15, and you'll also find a nice selection of hair accessories and journals.

Backstage—The Performing Arts Store
545 8th St. SE
Washington, DC
(202) 544–5744
This newly relocated, expanded costume store, 2 blocks from the Eastern Market Metro station, will actually make your costume to order, if you wish. Or you can choose from the large selection of ready-made disguises and all kinds of accessories, including wigs, masks, makeup, and dancewear. The shop is closed on Sundays.

The Brass Knob
2311 18th St. NW
Washington, DC
(202) 332–3370
www.thebrassknob.com
You've selected the perfect furniture, wall coverings, and draperies for your new house, but how do you pull it all together? It's the details that count, and The Brass Knob can provide them. The store carries a wide variety of antique lighting fixtures, stained and beveled glass, doorknobs, and hardware. You'll also love the architectural accents here, such as fireplace mantles, porcelain sinks, tiles, ornamental ironwork, and carved stone. Visit the sister store, The Back Doors Warehouse, 2329 Champlain Street NW, Washington, D.C. (202–265–0587), for larger items such as claw-foot bathtubs and fences. The stores are within walking distance of each other.

The Christmas Attic
125 S. Union St.
Alexandria, VA
(703) 548–2829
House in the Country
107 N. Fairfax St.
Alexandria, VA
(703) 548–4267
www.christmasattic.com
Christmas lasts year-round in these two magical Old Town shops. The Christmas Attic features hundreds of gorgeous ornaments and decorated trees with themes ranging from Victorian lace to gold-and-glass, musical instruments, and toys. Its sister store, House in the Country, carries country-style gifts, collectibles, and decor items as well as Christmas merchandise.

Both stores even smell like Christmas, thanks to strategically placed potpourri and, during the fall, bushels of apples at the doors.

The Counter Spy Shop
1027 Connecticut Ave. NW
Washington, D.C.
(202) 887–1717

Are you sure your conversations are private? Find out with wire tap and bug detection devices from The Counter Spy Shop. The store stocks all sorts of gadgets for the aspiring 007. Choose from night-vision goggles, a parabolic mike that claims to pick up sound from miles away, the so-called Truth Phone, which is meant to act as a lie detector by measuring voice stress, and many more secret agent items. The store is closed on Sundays.

Distinctive Bookbinding and Stationery
1150 Connecticut Ave. NW
Washington, D.C.
(202) 466–4866

This shop will take you back to an era when people prided themselves on the quality of their stationery and penmanship and on the leather-bound volumes in their libraries. You'll find exotic Florentine writing paper of the highest quality here, as well as all sorts of writing accessories, including scented ink. If you already own some worn first editions, this is the place to have them rebound and restored. The store is closed on Sundays.

Fahrney's Pens Inc.
1317 F St. NW
Washington, D.C.
(202) 628–9525, (800) 624–PENS
www.fahrneyspens.com

Other stores in Washington sell fine pens and pencils, but Fahrney's is an institution. Appropriately located near the National Press Building, this shop has been around since 1929, and the service is just as personal today as it was then. It specializes in writing instruments from Montblanc, Parker, Cross, Sheaffer, Waterman, and Pelikan. The store is closed on Sundays.

Mark Keshishian & Sons Inc.
Oriental Rugs
4507 Stanford St.
Chevy Chase, MD
(301) 654–4044, (301) 951–8880
www.orientalcarpets.net

Sometimes it seems as though there's an Oriental rug dealer on every corner in Washington and the surrounding 'burbs. Many of them are excellent, but Keshishian is widely considered the cream of the crop when it comes to appraising, variety of merchandise, and restoration. The store carries antiques of the first quality as well as more contemporary pieces. The staff is friendly, knowledgeable, and what is most important, willing to share information.

Modigliani
Georgetown Park, 3222 M St. NW
Washington, D.C.
(202) 333–0406

You'll find lingerie shops galore in every Washington area mall—the national chains are well-represented here. Modigliani, however, is in a class by itself when it comes to quality and selection. This quiet, elegant boutique specializes in top-of-the-line European dainties by La Perla, Nina Ricci, Lejaby, and others. It also carries hard-to-find sizes.

Music Box Center
1920 I St. NW
Washington, D.C.
(202) 783–9399

Choose from more than 1,500 music boxes, both antique and modern, and then personalize your choice with one of more than 500 melodies. Browse through the selection and you'll be surprised at the variety of shapes and sizes of these pretty boxes.

Palais Royal
1125 King St.
Alexandria, VA
(703) 549–6660
Wildwood Shopping Center
10231 Old Georgetown Rd.
Bethesda, MD
(301) 897–5009
6651 Old Dominion Dr.
McLean, VA
(703) 356–3085

For the best in French linens for the bed, bath, and table, head straight for this classy emporium. The high thread count in their sheets will make you think you're sleeping on silk, but it's cool crisp linen and cotton instead. The table displays are inspiring, but bring your gold card.

Park Place
2251 Wisconsin Ave. NW
Washington, DC
(202) 342–6294

You won't believe the selection of garden furniture, fixtures, and accessories here. Browse among classic styles in teak, wicker, and metal, and decorative pieces like lampposts, massive flower pots, and stained-glass panels. The shop also carries Tiffany-style interior lamps. Whether you have an estate or a tiny kitchen garden, you're sure to find the whimsical or dramatic touch you need here.

The Surrey
10107 River Rd.
Potomac, MD
(301) 365–1250

Potomac is traditional horse country, and this high-toned shop caters to those wealthy enough to belong to that set. You'll find all manner of riding clothes and equipment, including leather jackets and pants, boots, riding crops, and cold weather gear.

Tennis Factory
2500 Wilson Blvd., Ste. 1000
Arlington, VA
(703) 522–2700
www.tennisfactory.com

Tennis players will be agog at the selection of women's, men's, and children's clothing, shoes, and rackets here. Trained staff help shoppers choose from every brand imaginable. Still not sure? Rent a demo racquet. Get your own racquet restrung overnight.

Tiny Jewel Box
1147 Connecticut Ave. NW
Washington, DC
(202) 393–2747
www.tinyjewelbox.com

Yes, there are dozens of jewelry stores in Metro Washington, and every mall seems to have at least three, but the Tiny Jewel Box is special. It carries modern designer jewelry, of course, but the real attraction here is the area's largest collection of antique and estate jewelry. The business has bought and appraised such items since 1930. You can find Art Nouveau brooches, rings, and earrings for as little as $200, but you also can spend tens of thousands of dollars for some of the shop's diamond and platinum pieces.

Veneman Music & Sound
12401 Twinbrook Pkwy.
Rockville, MD
(301) 231–6100
8319 Amherst Ave.
Springfield, VA
(703) 451–8970
www.musicemporium.com

A look in the Yellow Pages will show you lots of stores specializing in musical instruments and sheet music, but Veneman has been around longer than most, and it is highly respected in the Washington area. The store buys and sells used instruments, does all sorts of repairs, and carries a wide selection of new instruments and accessories.

Yes Natural Gourmet
3425 Connecticut Ave. NW
Washington, DC
(202) 363–1559
1825 Columbia Rd. NW
Washington, DC
(202) 462–5150

A lot of mainstream grocery chains have jumped on the organic food/herb/vitamin bandwagon, and they do a wonderful job. A look at the telephone directory will reveal dozens of listings for health food stores, but we have to takes our hats off to one of the most long-lived and consistent shops in the Washington area, Yes Natural Gourmet. Its two locations prove its success—many health food boutiques fade away after a couple of years. Yes sells organic produce and groceries, diet products, bulk food, and herbs, vitamins, and bodycare items. Refuel at the deli and juice bar.

ZYZYX Inc.
Wildwood Shopping Center, 10301A Old Georgetown Rd.
Bethesda, MD
(301) 493–0297

It may be the very last entry in a Maryland suburban phone book, but ZYZYX is tops with shoppers seeking unique gifts and home accents. The colorful store carries unique pottery, jewelry, and other artistic, fun stuff.

Annual Events

How many times have you seen photos of the president emerging from the massive portals of the Washington National Cathedral, surrounded by Secret Service and cabinet officials? Imagine attending Christmas Eve services in that same house of worship, surrounded by the very newsmakers you've glimpsed on CNN. If that doesn't sound like your cup of tea, rest assured that in Washington, D.C., you'll have plenty to do and see. Year-round you'll find parades, festivals, and ceremonies, many of which you may have seen on television—like the annual lighting of the national Christmas tree.

Many who come to Washington plan their trips around special celebrations and exhibitions. From the exuberance of the Chinese New Year to the ceremonial splendor of the Marine Color Guard on parade, Washington visitors and residents can choose from an endless variety of fascinating, amusing distractions. The beauty of touring the area is that some of the most exciting and well-known events are free and open to the public.

Here you'll find a month-by-month calendar of events in the Washington Metro area. In the monthly categories you'll find geographic subdivisions: Washington, D.C., Northern Virginia, and Suburban Maryland. Most events are free, but 2001 adult admission fees are shown for those that aren't. Please note that for the most part we have not included dates and times because they so often change from year to year. Instead, you'll find contact numbers for people and organizations who can provide a wealth of information.

January

Washington, D.C.

Chinese New Year Parade
H St. NW, between 5th and 8th Sts.
Washington, DC
(202) 638–1041

The Lunar New Year is a time to close accounts, pay debts, clean house, honor ancestors, prepare exotic foods, and thank the gods for a prosperous year. The residents of Washington's Chinatown do it all in style, with traditional firecrackers, drums, and colorful dragon dancers that make their way through the streets flanked typically by more than 10,000 onlookers. The date of the event varies according to the new moon, and sometimes happens in February.

Martin Luther King Jr.'s Birthday Observance
Lincoln Memorial
23rd St. and Independence Ave.
Washington, DC
(202) 619–7222
www.nps.gov/ncro

Local choirs, guest speakers, and a military color guard salute the memory of the influential civil rights leader at the site where, on a sweltering summer afternoon in 1963, he led one of the largest public demonstrations ever held in Washington. King delivered his famous "I Have a Dream" speech from the memorial steps.

Northern Virginia

Robert E. Lee's Birthday Celebration
Arlington National Cemetery
Memorial Dr.
Arlington, VA
(703) 557–0613

In tribute to one of Virginia's and the South's greatest military heroes, the doors of Lee's cherished Arlington House open wide for an afternoon of nineteenth-century music, samples of Civil War–era food, and displays of restoration work.

Suburban Maryland

Annapolis Heritage Antique Show
Medford National Guard Armory
Hudson St.
Annapolis, MD
(410) 435–2292
www.armacostantiqueshows.com

This giant of an antiques show—7,700 square feet of exhibit space—is set most appropriately in a city that's one of the nation's premiere antique meccas. You'll find dealers from all over the United States showing wares as varied as nineteenth-century French furniture to Shaker, Chinese export, and American country styles. You'll also find, appropriately enough (Annapolis is a yachting capital), marine artifacts and maps and a myriad of other decorative items, such as porcelains, Oriental rugs, and paintings. The show runs for three days and opens with a preview party for serious private collectors, charging a $50 admission fee that allows you into the following day's shows. The show benefits The London Town Foundation, which supports historic preservation, research, and interpretation in Maryland. Admission to the Annapolis Heritage Antique Show is $7.00.

February

Washington, D.C.

Abraham Lincoln's Birthday
Lincoln Memorial
23rd St. and Independence Ave. NW
Washington, DC
(202) 619–7222
www.nps.gov/ncro

A wreath-laying ceremony and reading of the Gettysburg Address are highlights of the 16th president's birthday celebration on February 12, at his namesake memorial. The site is inspiring with its view of the Reflecting Pool, the Washington Monument, and the U.S. Capitol. Inside, the 19-foot marble statue is set against inscriptions of Lincoln's second inaugural address and the Gettysburg Address.

International Tourist Guild Day
Old Post Office Pavilion
Pennsylvania Ave. and 12th St. NW
Washington, DC
(202) 298–1474
www.washingtondctourguides.com

Meet at Old Post Office Pavilion on Pennsylvania Avenue and 12th Streets NW. Admission is $2.00. This one-day-only event is sponsored by The Guild of Professional Tour Guides of Washington, D.C. and features a professionally narrated three-and-a-half-hour tour of the U.S. Capitol and memorials. Drive by the White House, Washington Monument, Smithsonian Museums, Washington National Cathedral, and Embassy Row. They do not take reservations or sell advance tickets. Call for dates and times.

Washington Boat Show
Washington Convention Center
900 9th St. NW
Washington, DC
(703) 823–7960
www.washingtonboatshow.com

Surrounded by rivers, and with the Chesapeake Bay just a short drive away, Metro Washington is boat-crazed. This five-day event has become a tremendous draw in a town where people have the money to spend on grown-up toys. It showcases next year's models of hundreds of boats from dinghies to motor yachts. If you're a serious buyer, you can often snag great buys at the show. Flash your wallet and representatives from the big boat makers will be ready to negotiate. If you're not in that league, you can still purchase nautical accessories and pick up brochures from yacht charter companies.

Northern Virginia

George Washington's Birthday Parade
Wilkes and St. Asaph Sts.
Old Town Alexandria, VA
(703) 838–4200
ci.alexandria.va.us

Old Town plays host to the nation's largest birthday parade, honoring a native son and America's first president. The cobbled streets of Old Town, flanked by eighteenth- and nineteenth-century historical buildings, including private residences, make a perfect backdrop for the celebration. The route begins in a beautiful residential section of town, and ends at Gadsby's Tavern, a nationally designated historical building dating from the eighteenth century. It is now a restaurant with costumed servers and eighteenth-century–style minstrels. Make sure to bundle up because it can be cold and windy in February.

GMC Capital Home & Garden Show
Expo Center
Willard Rd. and Rte. 28
Chantilly, VA
(800) 274–6948
www.capitalhomeshow.com

The Capital Home Show is a good place to see what's new in remodeling and decorating products and services. The show offers more than 300 exhibitors for homeowners to speak with to receive free expert advice, helpful hints, and tips for projects for inside and out. Admission to the three-day event is $8.00 for adults.

Mount Vernon Open House
Mount Vernon Estate
George Washington Memorial Pkwy.
Alexandria, VA
(703) 780–2000
www.mountvernon.org

After the parade in Old Town, head south to George Washington's lovely estate on the Potomac for an afternoon of period costumes, music, and food. Admission is free of charge on this special day, which usually includes a performance on the bowling green by the U.S. Army Old Guard Fife and Drum Corps and the Commander-in-Chief's Guard. A tour of the house is worth the wait, and "George Washington" will be on the grounds all day to receive your birthday wishes.

March

Washington, D.C.

D.C. Spring Antiques Fair
The D.C. Armory
2001 E. Capitol St. SE
Washington, DC
(301) 924–5002

The area's most popular antique show, this three-day display features almost 200 dealers from the United States, England, France, and Canada. You'll find an eye-popping array of collectibles from delicate sterling, porcelains, Oriental rugs, and fine furniture. Browsers are welcome, but it's also a good place to connect with dealers in far-flung areas who will be more than happy to ship you their wares as well as notifications of their latest finds. Admission is $6.00. The event also takes place in October and December.

National Cherry Blossom Festival
Various parks and downtown locations
Washington, DC
(202) 619–7222
www.nationalcherryblossomfestival.org

Perhaps Washington's most visible fete, the National Cherry Blossom Festival honors the extraordinary blooming of the city's 3,000 Japanese cherry trees—surely one of the most beautiful sights in Amer-

The National Cherry Blossom Festival celebrates the blossoming of more than 3,000 Japanese cherry trees in downtown D.C. PHOTO: COURTESY OF WASHINGTON, DC CONVENTION AND TOURISM CORPORATION

ica. The capstone event is the Cherry Blossom Festival Parade (usually the first Saturday in April), but scores of related parties and ceremonies begin the last week of March. The trees bloom anywhere from late March to early April, depending on Mother Nature. A word to the wise: If at all possible, take Metrorail into Washington and walk to the Tidal Basin. It's a short jaunt from most stops downtown, and you'll save yourself the agony of trying to find a parking space.

St. Patrick's Day Parade
7th to 17th Sts. and Constitution Ave. NW
Washington, DC
(202) 637–2474
www.dcstpatsparade.com
Salute the Irish and sport the green in style during this always-festive downtown parade that features traditional dancers, bagpipers, and floats galore. The parade, which lasts about three hours, has been a major Washington event for more than 30 years. Afterwards participants and spectators alike spill into the bars and eateries that flank the parade route. High school bands from around the country join in, as well as bands from Ireland. It's not nearly as big as the one in New York, but it manages to clog traffic for most of the day, so take the Metro.

Smithsonian Kite Festival
15th St. and Constitution Ave. NW
Washington, DC
(202) 357–2700
kitefestival.org
Cherry blossoms excepted, nothing signals the dawn of spring quite like the sight of colorful kites dipping and soaring next to the Washington Monument. Kite makers and flyers of all ages compete for prizes and trophies.

Washington Home & Garden Show
Washington Convention Center
900 9th St. NW
Washington, DC
(703) 823–7960
www.washingtonhomeandgardenshow.com
This extravaganza of color and scent features gardening experts, landscape design-

ers, and, of course, masses of flowers and plants. This four-day show features almost 600 exhibitors in a space larger than two acres. Over half of that space is filled with gardens that have been forced into bloom—breathtaking gardens that can include waterfalls and bridges, magnificent statuary, and dramatic trees. The home show component includes decorating and remodeling exhibits and information. Cost is $9.00.

Northern Virginia

St. Patrick's Day Parade
King and West Sts., Old Town
Alexandria, VA
(703) 237–2199
www.ballyshaners.org
Usually held a day or two before the D.C. parade, Old Town's festivities extend beyond the parade route and into the city's extremely popular Irish pubs, such as Murphy's and Ireland's Own.

Woodlawn Plantation Annual Needlework Exhibition
George Washington Memorial Pkwy. and U.S. 1
Alexandria, VA
(703) 780–4000
Needlework crafts from the eighteenth century to the present day are on display at this lovely plantation, about 3 miles east of the Mount Vernon estate. The exhibition includes works by amateur and professional stitchers, as well as celebrities like Maureen Reagan, the former president's daughter. Admission is $7.00 and $5.00 for children 12 and under.

Suburban Maryland

Annual Quilt Show
C. Elizabeth Reig School
2614 Kenhill Dr.
Bowie, MD
(301) 262–3314
Heirloom and contemporary quilts are showcased in this popular Prince George's County show. Admission is $4.00.

Windy March is the time for the annual Smithsonian Kite Festival. PHOTO: COURTESY OF THE WASHINGTON, DC CONVENTION AND TOURISM CORPORATION

April

Washington, D.C.

Shakespeare's Birthday Celebration
Folger Shakespeare Library
201 E. Capitol St. SE
Washington, DC
(202) 544–4600
www.folger.edu

The Capitol Hill building is an attraction in itself, with its replica of Shakespeare's Globe Theatre, but during the birthday celebration, the library also offers music, theater, children's events, food, and special exhibits. Admission is free.

Smithsonian Craft Show
National Building Museum
401 F St. NW
Washington, DC
(888) 832–9554
www.smithsoniancraftshow.org

Some 100 juried exhibitors show their crafts at this wildly popular event, which features fiber, ceramics, glass, jewelry, leather, metal, paper, textiles, and wood. Admission is $10.

Washington International Film Festival
(Filmfest D.C.)
Theaters and reception halls
Washington, DC
(202) 724–5613
www.filmfestdc.org

All of Washington is the focus of the cinematic world during this two-week festival of international and American film. Washington is one of the top U.S. movie markets and one of the most filmed cities in the world.

White House Easter Egg Roll
The White House (Southeast Gate)
E. Executive Ave. NW
Washington, DC
(202) 456–7041
www.whitehouse.gov/history/tours/special-events.html

Children ages three through six, accompanied by adults, gather on the White House South Lawn for the annual Easter Egg Roll. This is easily the best opportunity in town for youngsters—and for that matter, parents—to play at the president's house. Each child receives a commemorative wooden egg and other free souvenirs. The event also includes concerts by nationally known family entertainers like Tom Chapin, storytelling by celebrities like Jamie Lee Curtis, strolling costumed characters, and educational exhibits. Similar festivities for older children and those who miss out on tickets for the White House activities take place on the Ellipse, located just across E Street from the executive mansion. Arrive as early as you can. It's not uncommon for the line to start before dawn. Free tickets usually run out well before 9:00 A.M.

White House Spring Garden and House Tours
The White House
1600 Pennsylvania Ave.
Washington, DC
(202) 456–7041

The spectacular gardens of the presidential home are open to the public during these annual tours (usually for two days during the second week of the month). Highlights include the Jacqueline Kennedy Rose Gardens and the spectacular West Lawn Gardens.

Northern Virginia

Easter Sunrise Service
Arlington National Cemetery
Memorial Dr.
Arlington, VA
(703) 607–8052
www.arlingtoncemetery.org

The cemetery's Memorial Amphitheatre, an inspiring setting, awaits early-morning worshipers. The service is conducted by a changing roster of prominent Washington ministers and includes a moving, dignified tribute by the Army's Old Guard.

Historic Garden Week in Virginia
Statewide
(804) 644–7776
www.vagardenweek.com

The finest in Virginia homes and gardens are spotlighted during this week-long festival. Our favorites include the gardens at such area plantations as Mount Vernon, Gunston Hall, and Oatlands. Call to find out more about tours in Northern Virginia. Admission is $10 to $30 depending on tour chosen.

May

Washington, D.C.

"The Commandant's Own"
U.S. Marine Corps Barracks
8th and I Sts. SE
Washington, DC
(202) 433–6060
www.mbw.usmc.nil/parades/parade_
evening.asp

Reservations are recommended, but admission is free to these extraordinary Friday night parades, beginning in May and running through August. Here is your chance to see the elite of the United

Insiders' Tip

While attending summer outdoor concerts, consider applying bug spray to keep the gnats and mosquitoes away. They can be fierce!

States military in a 75-minute performance of music and precision marching. The evening parade begins with a concert by "The President's Own" United States Marine Band. After the concert, "The Commandant's Own" United States Drum and Bugle Corps and the Marine Corps Silent Drill Platoon perform.

Reservations must be made in writing and requested at least three weeks in advance. Address requests to Protocol Office, Marine Barracks, 8th and I Streets SE, Washington, D.C. 20390–5000. The request should include the name of the party (either group or individual), the number of guests, a complete return address, and a point of contact with a telephone number.

Georgetown Garden Tour
Various locations
Washington, DC
(202) 333–4953

The private gardens of this famous neighborhood are on display in this inspiring tour. You'll be surprised at the extensive landscapes hidden behind Georgetown's walled courtyards and gardens. Some go an impossibly long way—you'd never guess it from the outside. Guided and self-guided tours are available. Admission for the 2001 tour was $20.

Goodwill Embassy Tour
Starting spot determined each year
(202) 636–4225, ext. 1257
www.dcgoodwill.org/pages/special_events_
et.htm

An event held each spring, the embassy tour benefits Davis Memorial Goodwill Industries. It's a grand opportunity to view places you would otherwise be unlikely to see, complete with art, furniture, architecture, and decor representing the best of their respective nations. You will see some priceless items and catch a glimpse into the way the world's most rarefied society lives. Tour tickets include shuttle-bus transportation. Reservations are required. Admission is $30 in advance, and $35 on the day of tour.

Memorial Day Ceremonies
Vietnam Veterans Memorial
Constitution Ave. and Henry Bacon Dr. NW
Washington, DC
(202) 619–7222
www.nps.gov/ncro

Speeches, military bands, and a keynote address are the centerpieces of this solemn event. Directories help you find names on the walls, and you can request a name rubbing.

Memorial Day Weekend Concert
West Lawn of the Capitol, Capitol Hill
Washington, DC
(202) 619–7222
www.nps.gov/ncro

As a kickoff to the summer tourist season, this popular concert features the globally acclaimed National Symphony Orchestra in an unforgettable setting under the stars.

"The President's Own"
U.S. Marine Chamber Orchestra Concert Series
National Academy of Sciences
2101 Constitution Ave. NW
Washington, DC
(202) 433–4011
www.marineband.usmc.mil

The free Sunday concerts, held all month, are rare opportunities for the public to enjoy the orchestra, which frequently performs at state dinners and diplomatic receptions. These are talented professional musicians, and Washingtonians normally crowd the hall, so come early. The concerts are also held free of charge on Wednesdays throughout the year.

Washington National Cathedral Flower Mart
Massachusetts and Wisconsin Aves. NW
Washington, DC
(202) 537–6200
www.cathedral.org

Each year, the mart's theme is a salute to a different country, featuring flower booths, entertainment, and decorating demonstrations.

Northern Virginia

"The Commandant's Own"
Iwo Jima Memorial
U.S. 50 at Arlington National Cemetery
Arlington, VA
(202) 433–4173
www.mbw.usmc.mil/organizations/silent_drill_platoon.asp

Beneath the shadows of the dramatic Marine Corps War Memorial, commonly known as the Iwo Jima Memorial, you'll be awed by the precision and discipline of the Marine Corps Silent Drill Platoon, stirred by the patriotic music of the Drum and Bugle Corps. These concerts will rivet you, and your children will remain fascinated for the entire hour. The site itself offers an inspiring view of the Nation's Capital and the Potomac River in the setting sun. Bring a picnic dinner and blanket—there's plenty of space on the lawn. See this event weekly, May through August.

Memorial Day Ceremonies
Arlington National Cemetery
Memorial Dr.
Arlington, VA
(703) 697–2131
www.arlingtoncemetery.org

Wreath layings at the John F. Kennedy grave site and the Tomb of the Unknowns are part of the ceremonies that wind down with a service at the Memorial Amphitheatre. The president usually delivers the keynote address.

The Virginia Gold Cup
5089 Old Tavern Rd.
The Plains, VA
(800) 69–RACES
www.vagoldcup.com

The Virginia Gold Cup Race is run every spring and fall. PHOTO: COURTESY OF BECKY SWINEHART

Usually held the same day as the Kentucky Derby, this premier steeplechase of Virginia and the international community has blossomed into one of the largest sporting and social events in Metro Washington. Held at Great Meadow, riders compete for a $50,000 purse which, if they win the Gold Cup's counterpart in England, nets them another 30,000 pounds. Great Meadow is in the heart of the state's gorgeous hunt country, about an hour west of Washington in Fauquier County. In 2001 admission was $60 per car in advance. The International Gold Cup takes place at Great Meadow on the third Saturday in October.

Suburban Maryland

Andrews Air Force Base Open House
Andrews Air Force Base
Camp Springs, MD
(301) 981–4511
www.andrews.af.mil
This air show is an impressive display of American military and technological might. You'll see all those bombers and fighter planes you read about in the news, as well as precision formation flying by the crack Air Force Thunderbirds. As is often the case with sites and events in Metro Washington, you need to be early to avoid traffic.

Chesapeake Bay Bridge Walk
Chesapeake Bay Bridge
Annapolis, MD
(410) 288–8405
www.mdtransportationauthority.com
Here's your opportunity to take in the magnificent vistas of the Chesapeake Bay, but at a leisurely pace several hundred feet above the water. The 4.3-mile jaunt, enjoyed by thousands of all ages and fitness levels, goes from east to west and occupies an entire span of the twin-span Bay Bridge. For those who are truly in shape and looking for a different way to cross the bay, an organized run precedes the official walk. Whatever the mode of transport, buses take participants to the bridge from a staging area in the stadium parking lot at the Naval Academy in nearby Annapolis.

Drama on Parade: Silent Drill at Sunset

These U.S. Marines move in such crisp and perfect unison that they almost look like robots. The hush of the audience is absolute. Faces are rapt, awestricken at the finesse of the Silent Drill Platoon. In the setting sun, the bayonets fixed atop the M-1 rifles gleam like mirrors. The platoon stands erect and still—not a muscle seems to twitch.

Despite the heat of the summer evening, they are in full dress: white gloves, white caps and slacks, and the famous navy jackets. Above the scene towers the U.S. Marine Corps War Memorial, the famous bronze sculpture that captures the moment in World War II when U.S. Marines raised the flag on the Japanese island of Iwo Jima. It's a perfect backdrop for the dramatic demonstration that takes place at sunset on the green lawn below. The marines hold the sunset parades here, each Tuesday evening in summer, in tribute to the men who fought at Iwo Jima, as homage to those whose "uncommon valor was a common virtue." (The base of the sculpture bears the quotation in gold lettering.)

The parade begins with the platoon marching onto the green from an area behind the memorial. First come the Battle Colors, the Official Colors of the Corps. The streamers and silver bands that grace the Colors represent every battle, campaign, and expedition the corps has participated in since its founding more than two centuries ago. The Color Sergeant has the responsibility of carrying the National Colors, and by virtue of that billet is considered the senior sergeant in the Marine Corps. Then, clad in red jackets and white slacks, the U.S. Marines Drum and Bugle Corps, known as "The Commandant's Own," parade to a series of toe-tapping marches and popular tunes. Their choreography is intricate, and the marching patterns are fascinating to watch.

The climax of the evening is unquestionably the Silent Drill Platoon, a corps of elite military performers. They stand on the field alone, their bearing ramrod straight, their positioning accurate to a hair's breadth. Their silent exercise begins, a breathtaking drill punctuated only by the sound of the rifles thumping into their owners' gloved hands. The Rifle Inspector, who stands facing his 24-person team, issues no verbal commands. The rifles twirl, change hands, and come to rest in a ruler-straight row pointing at the evening sky. Onlookers gasp with each twirl of the bayonets—risky maneuvers that miss the marines by only centimeters.

Each member of the platoon has spent six weeks training for 12 to 14 grueling hours a day. Training doesn't end there. New members must practice for six months before they are permitted to perform before the public. The goal is to spin the rifle and march without looking at the weapon. The group makes it look effortless, but around 50 percent of the marines recruited for the Silent Drill Team fail to graduate to the ranks. Mistakes during the parades are seldom seen, although if one does occur, it is then up to the marine to save face with another dazzling maneuver.

The highlight of the 11-minute drill is the moment when the Rifle Inspector comes to a stop before a single member of the team. The marine throws his rifle, spinning it into the air. The Rifle Inspector catches it with one hand, and there is the

The marching platoons emerge from behind the U.S. Marine Corps War Memorial in Arlington, Virginia, to take their places for the Tuesday evening Sunset Parade. PHOTO: COURTESY OF MCGEHEE & ASSOCIATES

sharp report of metal as it hits. It's a strong, authoritative sound. Not a breath is heard from the audience as the two marines exchange the rifle, tossing it, spinning it, twisting it in different patterns and directions. When it is over, the audience exhales in relief that there were no mishaps, and then erupts in giddy applause.

The Tuesday evening Sunset Parades have been a summer tradition in Washington since 1956. They are free and no reservations are required, because there is only lawn seating. Those who plan ahead, however, can make reservations to attend the somewhat more elaborate Friday Evening Parades, held at the Marine Barracks in Washington, D.C. The Friday Evening Parades are 15 minutes longer than the Sunset Parades and searchlights add to the drama. More marines also participate, including Private First Class Chesty XI, a brindle-and-white pedigreed English bulldog who serves as the official mascot of the Marine Barracks of Washington, D.C.

During the closing ceremony, the marines march away and the searchlights are extinguished as a lone bugler comes out and plays "Taps."

For information on parking, reservations, and transportation, contact the marine barracks at (202) 433–6060.

Kemper Insurance Open
TPC at Avenel, 10000 Oaklyn Dr.
Potomac, MD
(301) 469–3737
www.kemperopen.com

The Pro-Am classic features some of the brightest stars on the PGA Tour plus a handful of local celebrities. Former Redskins quarterback Mark Rypien made the rigorous final cut several years ago but met his match against the likes of Greg Norman and John Daly. Admission is $35 to $290, depending on the number of days covered.

June

Washington, D.C.

Carnival Extravaganza
Emery Park, Georgia and Missouri Aves. NW
Washington, DC
(202) 726–2204
www.dccaribbeancarnival.com

Washington's large Caribbean population turns out in full force for this annual carnival that is reminiscent of Caribbean and Brazilian celebrations, though on a smaller scale. Participants wear elaborate costumes with sequins and peacocklike feather headpieces.

Dupont-Kalorama Museum Walk Day
Various locations on Dupont Circle
Washington, DC
(202) 667–0441
www.dkmuseums.com

D.C.'s most famous arts district extends a gracious welcome through house tours, craft demonstrations, and concerts on the first Saturday in June. A shuttle service is provided.

Festival of American Folklife
National Mall
Between Independence and Constitution Aves.
Washington, DC
(202) 357–2700

The rich cultural and folklife heritage of the Americas is played out on the National Mall in the form of lectures, concerts, working villages, and hands-on exhibits. You'll see performances and exhibits from obscure societies you may not have known existed, as well as the more familiar ones, like Cajun or Navajo Nation. The festival runs through the 4th of July and attracts upward of 1 million people.

Marine Band's Summer Concert Series
The U.S. Capitol's West Terrace and Ellipse
Next to the White House
Washington, DC
(202) 433–4011
www.marineband.usmc.mil

Free concerts are held on Wednesday and Sunday evenings through August. These are concerts only, as distinct from the parades/concerts/military drills held at Iwo Jima and the Marine Barracks from May to August (see pertinent listings under the month of May).

The Shakespeare Theater Free-for-All
Carter Barron Amphitheatre
16th St. and Colorado Ave. NW
Washington, DC
(202) 334–4790
www.shakespearedc.org

Carter Barron and D.C.'s Shakespeare Theater collaborate to stage free, professional performances of Shakespearean masterpieces for two weeks every June. These open-air productions draw huge crowds, in spite of the fact that you have to drive into D.C. to pick up those free tickets the same day of the performance.

Northern Virginia

Antique Car Show
Sully Plantation
Rte. 28 (Sully Rd.)
Chantilly, VA
(703) 437–1794

A car-lover's fantasyland unfolds at this historic plantation in western Fairfax County, in the shadows of Washington Dulles International Airport. You'll find about 450 cars, ranging from the era of the Model-T to 1954. Admission is $6.00.

Fairfax Fair
Fairfax County Government Center Grounds
Government Center Pkwy.
Fairfax, VA
(703) 324-3247
www.fairfaxfair.com

This is not exactly a country fair, but then again, Fairfax County hasn't been rural for quite some time. Instead of livestock and produce, you'll get your fill of high-tech laser shows, fireworks, arts and crafts, business, government service, and community information booths. There's also plenty of music, games, and rides along the midway for the kids and the young at heart.

Red Cross Waterfront Festival
Oronoco Bay Park
Base of Oronoco St. at the waterfront
Old Town Alexandria, VA
(703) 549-8300
www.waterfrontfestival.org

One of Alexandria's top summer events, the Red Cross Waterfront Festival brings in a weekend full of music (including some top-name rock, country, folk, and reggae acts), ethnic foods, canoe rides, juried arts and crafts, fireworks, tall ships and even a 10K run to work off all the

calories. Admission is $5.00 to $8.00 for adults, and practically free for kids.

Suburban Maryland

Annapolis Waterfront Festival
Annapolis Yacht Basin
Compromise and Main Sts.
Annapolis, MD
(410) 268-8828
www.showsinc.com

The capital city honors its maritime heritage during this three-day festival, which features handicrafts from around the nation. Exhibitors displaying handmade materials fill an entire block at the foot of Main Street and a tented area adjacent to the City Dock, which is flanked by Compromise Street. You'll find wearable art, paintings, carvings, and all manner of decorative items.

July
Washington, D.C.

Annual Soap Box Derby
Begins at Constitution Avenue NW
Between Delaware and Louisiana Aves.
Washington, DC
(301) 670-1110

It takes an Act of Congress each year to close the easternmost section of Constitution Avenue for this race, and each year Congress passes a joint resolution enabling the event—which proves that po-liticians aren't all sourpusses. Approximately 50 children from ages 9 to 16 participate in the "Gravity Grand Prix," as it's sometimes called, racing a course from Constitution and Delaware Avenues NW to Louisiana Avenue NW. The route runs between the Russell Senate Office Building and the U.S. Capitol, and the event lasts all day. The kids build their own cars, some from kits and some not, and many have even recruited local businesses as sponsors. Participants take this 60-year-plus tradition seriously and put a lot of effort into their entries, but the event couldn't be more fun.

Bastille Day
12th St. and Pennsylvania Ave. NW
Washington, DC
(202) 234–7911
www.francedc.org

Washington has a large French-speaking community, plus many French restaurant fans, so this Gallic Independence Day celebration on July 14 draws plenty of participants. Enjoy live entertainment and watch waiters bearing trays race to the Capitol and back.

Latin American Festival
Adams Morgan
Columbia Rd. NW and the National Mall
Washington, DC
(301) 588–8719

Latin American music, dance, art, food and theater are the focus of a two-day heritage festival that takes place in the eclectic Adams Morgan neighborhood and on the grounds of the Washington Monument.

National Independence Day Celebration
The National Mall
Between Independence and Constitution Aves. NW
Washington, DC
(202) 619–7222
www.july4thparade.com

Washington fittingly plays host to the nation's largest 4th of July party, with a parade down Constitution Avenue, colonial military maneuvers, concerts at the Sylvan Theatre next to the Washington Monument, and an evening performance by the National Symphony Orchestra on the west steps of the Capitol. The day ends with a spectacular 45-minute fireworks exhibit that has been known to draw more than a million onlookers—on both sides of the river.

Northern Virginia

Vienna's Fourth of July Celebration
Waters Field
Cherry and Center Sts.
Vienna, VA
(703) 255–6300
www.ci.vienna.va.us

One of suburban Washington's oldest July 4th celebrations, Vienna presents a viable small-town alternative to the pressing crowds and traffic associated with the downtown D.C. festivities. There's music and also some surprisingly good fireworks.

Virginia Scottish Games
Episcopal High School
3901 W. Braddock Rd.
Alexandria, VA
(703) 912–1943
www.vascottishgames.org

Northern Virginia (Alexandria in particular) shows off its proud Scottish heritage at this weekend fete, which features Highland dancing, bagpiping, fiddling, and traditional athletic events. Scottish foods, crafts, and genealogy exhibits are also an integral part of the popular festival. Admission is $10 to $15.

Suburban Maryland

Wheaton Sparkles
Westfield Shoppingtown Wheaton
Intersection of Veirs Mill Rd. and University Blvd.
Wheaton, MD
(240) 777–6804
www.co.mo.md.us/services/rec/WtnSpkls.html

If you want a somewhat lower-key version of the downtown July 4th festivities, try this suburban version, with activities for children, capped by a decent fireworks display that draws thousands each year.

Insiders' Tip

A great way to view Independence Day fireworks is from a boat on the Potomac River, but whether you intend to make a group tour or hire your own, try to make reservations months in advance.

August

Washington, D.C.

U.S. Army Band's "1812 Overture"
The Ellipse, behind the White House
Washington, DC
(202) 208–1631

Guaranteed to get the patriotic juices flowing, the "1812" gets a dose of firepower from the Salute Gun Platoon of the Third U.S. Infantry.

Northern Virginia

Arlington County Fair
Thomas Jefferson Center
3501 S. 2nd St.
Arlington, VA
(703) 228–6407
www.arlingtonfair.com

Arlington's urban multicultural heritage is the reason for this four-day fair typically held the third week of the month. Craftspeople and exhibits are indoors, while food vendors are outside.

Civil War Living History Day
Fort Ward Museum and Park
4301 W. Braddock Rd.
Alexandria, VA
(703) 838–4848
www.fortward.org

Fort Ward was one of several Union fortifications that encircled Washington during the Civil War. This living history reenacts Union and Confederate camp life, complete with artillery drills. (See our Civil War Sites chapter for more on this park.)

Suburban Maryland

Kunte Kinte Heritage Commemoration and Festival
St. John's College
60 College Ave.
Annapolis, MD
(410) 349–0338
www.kuntekinte.org

Made into a household name with the airing of TV's 1977 landmark miniseries *Roots*, recently rebroadcast on its 25th anniversary, Kunte Kinte was brought into the harsh New World at the Port of Annapolis. The festival honors his legacy and the rich traditions of generations of succeeding African Americans. There are educational programs for children and adults, as well as African American crafts exhibits and demonstrations. Food vendors represent many ethnic backgrounds, and entertainment ranges from gospel singers to calypso. Admission is $5.00 for adults and $3.00 for seniors and children.

Maryland Renaissance Festival
Crownsville Rd., off Md. Hwy. 450 E.
Crownsville, MD
(410) 266–7304
www.rennfest.com/mrf

The Free State slips into a medieval state of mind during this well-attended festival usually held the last weekend of August and extending into October. Jousting events, jugglers, and medieval foods and crafts are just some of the many delights awaiting visitors at this 20-acre "village" located in the heart of suburban Crownsville. Admission is $14.95 for adults, $5.95 for children ages 7 to 15, and free for kids 6 and under.

Montgomery County Agricultural Fair
Montgomery County Fairgrounds
Exit 10-11 off I–270
Gaithersburg, MD
(301) 926–3100
www.mcagfair.com

There's still plenty of rural character in this highly urbanized county, as evidenced by the size and popularity of this old-fashioned country fair. You'll find livestock judging, pony rides, a petting zoo, gardening displays, old-time handcraft and baking exhibits, amusement park rides, games of chance, concerts, and plenty of food concessions. Admission is $5.00 for adults and free for children under 12. Parking costs $2.00.

Rotary Crab Feast
U.S. Navy-Marine Corps Stadium
Farragut Rd.
Annapolis, MD
(410) 841–2841
www.annapolisrotary/com.

Lovers of Maryland's prized crustacean should bring a hefty appetite to the world's largest crab feast, held for over 50 years. More than 185,000 gallons of crab soup and 325 bushels of Maryland blue crabs are consumed at this spicy event, which benefits the Annapolis Rotary Club.

September

Washington, D.C.

Adams Morgan Day
Columbia Rd. and Florida Ave. NW
Washington, DC
(202) 789–7000
www.adamsmorganday.org

This giant ethnic festival, a salute to Adams Morgan's multicultural character, is a hot ticket with the city's young and hip crowd. Expect to hear great music—reggae, jazz, R&B, and salsa—and be tempted by some of the city's best international cuisine.

Ambassadors' Ball and Benefit
Grand Hyatt Hotel
1000 H St. NW
Washington, DC
(202) 296–5363
www.msandyou.org

One of Washington's premier dress-up events, and the kickoff to the Washington social season, the Ambassadors' Ball benefits the National Multiple Sclerosis Society. Chairwomen for the event invariably include the wives of national politicians. For a few hundred bucks, you too may attend—and it's all for charity. Admission is $300.

Hispanic Designers Gala Fashion Show and Benefit
1000 Thomas Jefferson St. NW
Washington, DC
(202) 362–8010
www.hispanicdesigners.org

This event draws Hispanic entertainers and politicians. Proceeds fund scholarships for young Hispanic designers. Admission is $350.

Kalorama House and Embassy Tour
Kalorama Neighborhood, Woodrow Wilson House
2340 S St. NW
Washington, DC
(202) 387–4062

Historic Kalorama is still one of D.C.'s most exclusive and interesting neighborhoods. Homes and gardens in this area are lavish and beautifully maintained. You begin at the Woodrow Wilson House, a museum property of the National Trust for Historic Preservation. Admission is $18 in advance, and $20 on the day of the tour.

Kennedy Center Open House
John F. Kennedy Center for the Performing Arts
2700 F St. NW
Washington, DC
(202) 467–4600
www.kennedy-center.org

Stroll the towering red-carpeted halls of Washington's premier performing arts center, and then enjoy the free concerts and performances at this annual open house.

Labor Day Weekend Concert
West Lawn of the Capitol
Capitol Hill
Washington, DC
(202) 619–7222

The National Symphony Orchestra officially closes Washington's summer tourist season with a rousing selection of classical and patriotic arrangements. This event is packed, so plan to come early, maybe with a blanket and a picnic, and take public transportation or you'll be caught in the mother of all traffic jams.

National Frisbee Championships
Washington Monument grounds
15th St. and Constitution Ave. NW
Washington, DC

This annual contest featuring disk-catching canines never fails to make the evening news. The dogs are amazing, and you'll wonder how the owners trained them to make some of those catches. Dogs are judged on showmanship, leaping agility, and execution.

Rock Creek Park Day
Nature Center, Rock Creek Park
5200 Glover Rd. NW
Washington, DC
(202) 426–6829
www.nps.gov/rocr

The nature center is headquarters for a slate of environmental, recreational, and historical programs during this daylong tribute to one of the world's largest and most beautiful urban parks. Each year, Rock Creek Park Day commemorates the founding of the park in 1890. There's cake, a raffle, and a program in the nature center.

Northern Virginia

Historic Homes Tour of Old Town Alexandria
Meet at the Gatsby Arcade at King St. across from City Hall
Alexandria, VA
(703) 838–4200

Much of Old Town dates from the eighteenth century, but this is a chance to see homes still used as private residences. The tour is a one-day-only event benefiting the Inova Alexandria Hospital. Admission is $20.

International Children's Festival
Wolf Trap Farm Park for the Performing Arts
1624 Trap Rd.
Vienna, VA
(703) 255–1892
www.wolftrap.org

At America's only national park for the performing arts, kids take center stage for a three-day outdoor festival celebrating the global arts. Sponsored by the Arts Council of Fairfax County, the popular event features a variety of performances

Each September, Adams Morgan Day draws a diverse crowd to sample the neighborhood's international cuisine and listen to everything from live blues to salsa music. PHOTO: COURTESY OF THE WASHINGTON, DC CONVENTION AND TOURISM CORPORATION

and educational workshops presented by groups from the local area, throughout the U.S., and around the world. Most of the performance groups are largely made up of children. Admission is $10.00 for adults and $8.00 for children age three and older.

Occoquan Fall Craft Show
Mill, Union, Washington, and Commerce Sts.
Old Town Occoquan, VA
(703) 491–2168
www.occoquan.com

More than 350 juried artisans, representing 30 states, exhibit their wares in front of some 100,000 shoppers in this tidy and historic waterfront community. This weekend fair just might be the largest craft show on the East Coast. Admission is free.

Oktoberfest
Reston Town Center
Market St.
Reston, VA
(703) 787–6601
www.clydes.com

More than 20,000 people usually attend this four-day beer, polka, and sauerbraten festival in lively Reston Town Center. This is a big, open area where you can let the kids run, and there's plenty to amuse them, from balloons to dancers and musicians. Admission is free.

Old Town Chili Cook-Off
Oronoco Bay Park
Oronoco St. at the waterfront
Old Town Alexandria, VA
(703) 863–8545
www.hardtimes.com

This annual event featuring chili and other comestibles from local restaurants benefits the National Kidney Foundation of the National Capital area. It's held at the edge of the Potomac River in Old Town Alexandria, near the many shops and restaurants of the charming historic district. Admission is $5.00.

Vienna Fall Carnival
Vienna Community Center
120 Cherry St. SE
Vienna, VA
(703) 281–1333

The magnificent Hall of Flags is a popular tour during the annual Kennedy Center Open House. Free concerts and performances bring visitors from all around to view the towering red-carpeted halls of the center. PHOTO: COURTESY OF THE KENNEDY CENTER

Carnival rides, popcorn, funnel cakes, and hot dogs are what this four-day event is all about. You can enjoy all the rides you want for $12.50 the first night of the event, which falls on September 6th in 2002. Admission is free the remaining three days, but you have to pay for all the rides.

Suburban Maryland

Maryland Seafood Festival
Sandy Point State Park
U.S. 50 at the Chesapeake Bay Bridge
Annapolis, MD
(410) 268–7682
www.mdseafoodfestival.com
The bounty of the Chesapeake Bay is baked, steamed, grilled, broiled, sautéed, and fried at this waterside park, next to the western end of the towering Bay Bridge. Admission is $7.00 for adults and free to children under seven.

Prince George's Community College Blue Bird Blues Festival
Prince George's Community College
301 Largo Rd.
Largo, MD
(301) 322–0853
pgweb.pg.cc.md
It's a blues festival, but there are also children's activities, food, and crafts. The one-day event features a half-dozen or so local bands. Admission is free.

Prince George's County Fair
Prince George's Equestrian Center
U.S. 4
Upper Marlboro, MD
(301) 952–7900
www.countyfair.org
Like neighboring Montgomery County, urbanized Prince George's still holds on to its rural origins. Begun in 1842, this county fair is the oldest in the state of Maryland, and you'll find many old-time traditions like livestock contests, 4-H shows, and horticultural displays. (The county was once a major producer of tobacco, and vestiges of that tradition can still be seen in areas far beyond the Beltway.) Admission is $5.00.

October

Washington, D.C.

Annual Lombardi Gala
Various locations throughout Washington, DC
(202) 687–1067
lombardi.georgetown.edu
All proceeds from this benefit go to the Lombardi Cancer Center at Georgetown University Medical Center. The Lombardi Center is one of only 40 centers in the nation designated as a comprehensive cancer center by the U.S. National Cancer Institute, a part of the National Institutes of Health. The gala features a dinner and a silent auction of many high-ticket items. Admission is $350.

Taste of D.C. Festival
Freedom Plaza, Pennsylvania Ave.
Between 9th and 14th Sts. NW
Washington, DC
(202) 724–5430
www.washington.org/taste
Washington's top restaurants lay it on the line in this public tasting, which also includes free concerts, arts and crafts exhibits, and games for the kids. Proceeds go to various charities. Admission is free, but food samples start at $4.00.

Theodore Roosevelt's Birthday Celebration
Theodore Roosevelt Island
George Washington Memorial Pkwy.
Arlington, VA
(703) 289–2530
www.nps.gov/this
The scenic urban wilderness sanctuary of Roosevelt Island plays host to this birthday party honoring the nation's first environmental president. Hike along trails in this 88-acre preserve, view the 17-foot bronze statue of Roosevelt, then stop and chat with the Roosevelt look-alike who plays the former president for the day. There's even birthday cake!

Washington International Horse Show
MCI Center
Washington, DC
(301) 840–0281
www.wihs.org

Equestrian teams from the United States and Europe compete in a week of events, with plenty of sideline shows for laypeople and kids. There are competitions in dressage and jumping and exhibition events. Admission ranges from $10 to $60, depending on dates and seat locations.

Northern Virginia

Marine Corps Marathon
Iwo Jima Memorial
U.S. 50 at Arlington National Cemetery
Arlington, VA
(703) 784-2225
www.marinemarathon.com
Thousands of world-class runners snake through the downtown streets and parks in what has become one of the nation's most prestigious marathons. Although most of the action takes place in Washington, the race begins and ends at the Iwo Jima Memorial in Arlington. Registration is $50 for runners.

Vienna Halloween Parade
Branch and Maple Aves.
Vienna, VA
(703) 255-6300
www.ci.vienna.va.us
Vienna claims the region's oldest (since the 1940s) and largest (several thousand strong) Halloween Parade, which wends its way along a stretch of the town's main thoroughfare.

Waterford Homes Tour and Crafts Show
I-662 to High St.
Waterford, VA
(540) 882-3018
www.waterfordva.org
About 50 years ago a group of Waterford residents had the foresight to set up a preservation foundation in Loudoun County to save this picturesque National Historic Landmark village from suburbia. The annual event, which features over 100 juried artisans, benefits ongoing restoration and preservation efforts. Admission is $12 in advance and $14 on the day of tour and show. Children 12 and under are admitted free.

Suburban Maryland

Taste of Bethesda
Fairmont, Norfolk, and St. Elmo Sts.
Bethesda, MD
(301) 215-6660
www.bethesda.org
Tens of thousands of food experts flock to this food and music festival showcasing more than 40 prime restaurants from Bethesda. Admission is free, and food samples start at $2.00.

U.S. Sailboat Show/U.S. Power Boat Show
Annapolis City Dock, Dock St.
Annapolis, MD
(410) 268-8828
www.usboat.com
Held on consecutive weekends, with the sailors going first, these are the largest in-water boat shows in the nation. With boats and nautical products from the world's leading manufacturers, Annapolis turns into a festival for the water-loving set. General admission is $4.00.

November

Northern Virginia

Alexandria Antiques Show
Holiday Inn Hotel and Suites
625 First St.
Old Town Alexandria, VA
(703) 838-4554
You guessed it—more antiques and crafts from the heirloom gold mine of the mid-Atlantic. The furniture here is often quite formal, in keeping with the Old Town setting, with lots of oil paintings and European pieces. Admission is $8.00.

Veterans Day Ceremonies
Vietnam Veterans Memorial
Constitution Ave. and Henry Bacon Dr. NW
Washington, DC
Arlington National Cemetery
Memorial Dr.
Arlington, VA
(202) 619-7222
www.nps.gov/ncro

Both solemn and celebratory, the ceremonies attract thousands of veterans, military VIPs, general spectators, and, often, the commander-in-chief of the armed forces (a.k.a. the president).

Suburban Maryland

Sugarloaf's Autumn Crafts Festival
Montgomery County Fairgrounds
Exit 10 or 11 off I–270
Gaithersburg, MD
(301) 990–1400
www.sugarloaf.com
This is it, the granddaddy of all Metro D.C. craft shows, featuring 575 juried artisans. It'll take you two hours just to walk the grounds, let alone browse and shop. Admission is $7.00. Other, smaller shows are offered throughout the year.

December

Washington, D.C.

National Christmas Tree Lighting/
Pageant of Peace
The Ellipse, behind the White House
Between 15th and 17th Sts. NW
Washington, DC
(202) 619–7222
www.nps.gov
The president lights the giant National Christmas Tree and officially kicks off the Christmas season. From early December to New Year's Day, the Ellipse is the site of nightly choral concerts, a nativity scene, live reindeer, a burning yule log, and lighted Christmas trees from each of the nation's states and territories.

Washington Auto Show
Washington Convention Center,
900 9th St. NW
Washington, DC
(301) 670–1110
www.washingtonautoshow.com
Each year, this massive exhibition introduces car buffs to next year's models, as well as wildly imaginative concept cars that may one day come to market in mod-

ified form. There are often autograph signings by Washington celebrities, live radio broadcasts, and, of course, those glamorous human models in their glittering outfits. Admission is $8.00.

Washington National Cathedral Christmas
Celebration and Services
Washington National Cathedral
Massachusetts and Wisconsin Aves. NW
Washington, DC
(202) 537–6200
www.cathedral.com
The Christmas Eve service here, at Washington's answer to the great cathedrals of Europe, is simply breathtaking; however, passes are required to attend, and you should write for them in November if you expect to snag one of the 3,400 seats available for either the 6:00 P.M. or 10:00 P.M. service on Christmas Eve. At the earlier service the cathedral's 24-member girls' choir performs; the later service features 40 singers of the men's and boys' choir.

Up to six tickets per person may be requested by sending a self-addressed stamped envelope to Christmas (the year), Washington National Cathedral, Massachusetts and Wisconsin Avenues NW, Washington, D.C. 20016. Be sure to include your own name, address, and a daytime phone number with your request. Also specify which service you would like to attend. On Christmas Day, there are services at 9:00 A.M., noon, and 4:00 P.M., and none require passes. The 9:00 A.M. is televised and features a choir, while the two later services have only organ music and hymns.

Northern Virginia

Alexandria Scottish Christmas Walk
Campagna Center
418 S. Washington St.
Alexandria, VA
(703) 549–0111
A gathering of the clans—bagpipes and all—takes over the streets and alleys of Old Town for one of the holiday season's most festive events. Adjunct activities include a designer tour of homes and a Christmas marketplace of decorations

and ornaments at the Campagna Center (no admission fee). The Historic Alexandria Candlelight Tours continue the magic the very next week. Call (703) 838-4554 for information or check its Web site at www.historicalexandria.org.

Northern Virginia Christmas Craft Market
Expo Center
Willard Rd. and Rte. 28
Chantilly, VA
(757) 417-7771
www.emgshows.com

More than 350 fine artists and craftspeople display their work, including Christmas collectibles and a seemingly infinite number of home decorating ideas for the holidays. Specialty food vendors also offer gift food packages and stocking stuffers. Admission to the three-day show is $6.00.

Suburban Maryland

Christmas Lights Parade
Annapolis City Dock
Dock St.
Annapolis, MD
(410) 280-0445
www.visit-annapolis.org

Annapolitans decorate their yachts with Christmas lights for this highly visual, and often chilly, evening on the Chesapeake Bay.

Festival of Lights
Washington Mormon Temple Visitors' Center
9900 Stoneybrook Dr.
Kensington, MD
(301) 587-0144
www.washingtonlds.org

Tens of thousands of lights adorn the grounds of this Oz-like temple looming above the Capital Beltway. Inside the visitor center are Christmas trees bearing decorations from around the world. The temple itself is open only to those of the Mormon faith. (See the Worship chapter for more information.)

Attractions

Washington, D.C.
Northern Virginia
Suburban Maryland
Tour Operators

You'll never lack for something to do in Metro Washington.
Just when you think you've seen it all, a new monument opens or the Smithsonian Institution hosts a special exhibition. In this chapter we fill you in on some of the region's most popular attractions, from monuments and museums to famous historic sites. At the end we've included information on some of the leading commercial tour operators. See the Metro Washington Overview chapter for information about the numerous convention and visitors bureaus and tourism offices that serve the Washington area.

You'll also find some important attractions featured prominently in other chapters. Washington's major art museums, such as the National Gallery, are described in our Arts chapter. Our Kidstuff chapter details the family-oriented exhibits and programs at many museums listed here. We cross-reference such entries where applicable.

Washington, D.C.

Monuments

Franklin Delano Roosevelt Memorial
West Potomac Park, along the Tidal Basin
1850 W. Basin Dr. SW
Washington, DC
(202) 426–6841
www.nps.gov/fdrm/home.htm

Dedicated in May of 1997, this tribute to FDR's presidency is notable for being the city's first completely wheelchair-accessible monument. It's also the subject of mild controversy, with some critics expressing disappointment that the statue of the seated president fails to depict him in his *own* wheelchair. It's an eye-catching representation nonetheless, complete with FDR's little terrier, Fala. A statue of Eleanor Roosevelt stands nearby, marking the first time a presidential memorial includes a first lady.

On seven and a half acres near the Jefferson Memorial, the monument features

Two visitors get a first-hand look at a sculpture in the Franklin Roosevelt Memorial in downtown Washington, D.C. PHOTO: COURTESY OF WASHINGTON, DC CONVENTION AND TOURISM CORPORATION

four outdoor "galleries" representing each term of FDR's presidency. Gardens, pools, and fountains accent the pathway that connects the different sections; in fact, early visitors found the water so inviting on hot summer days that park police issued an order banning people from splashing in the fountains! Photo opportunities abound here: Tourists especially enjoy posing with the life-size figures in the breadline sculpted by George Segal. You'll find the memorial right off the path that circles the Tidal Basin, which is a must-see during cherry blossom season in April. Rangers staff the site from 8:00 A.M. to midnight daily, except on December 25. Admission is free. The site has special parking for disabled visitors, but regular spaces in the vicinity fill up quickly. If you don't mind walking, take Metro to the Smithsonian station.

Korean War Veterans Memorial
French Dr. SW
Washington, DC
(202) 426–6841
www.nps.gov/kwvm/home.htm

The Korean War Veterans Memorial is one of the city's newest memorials, dedicated in 1995. This startling tribute to the 1.5 million U.S. men and women who served during the Korean War features a stainless-steel patrol of 19 lifelike statues, designed by World War II veteran Frank Gaylord. Depicting members of the four branches of the armed forces, the scattered sculptures face a black granite wall that's etched with photographic images of actual American service men and women. The site, featuring a circular Pool of Remembrance and grove of trees, is near the Lincoln Memorial Reflecting Pool. Staffed hours are 8:00 A.M. to midnight daily, except December 25. Admission is free. Smithsonian is the closest Metro stop.

Lincoln Memorial
On 23rd St. and Independence Ave. NW
Washington, DC
(202) 426–6841
www.nps.gov/linc/home.htm

The somber, seated Civil War president looks past the stairs that have served as a site for many public demonstrations and across the vast Reflecting Pool. An equally captivating vista is the one in the opposite direction, straight across Memorial Bridge and up to Arlington House on the hill overlooking Arlington National Cemetery.

Completed in 1922 and modeled after the Parthenon in Athens, the memorial, designed by architect Henry Bacon, includes walls that are inscribed with the Gettysburg Address and Lincoln's Second Inaugural Address. Daniel Chester French's 19-by-19-foot marble statue has eyes that really do seem to follow you as you walk past, gazing up at the serious face. The free attraction, staffed by National Park Service rangers from 8:00 A.M. to midnight daily except December 25, includes a bookstore on the lower level. To avoid parking hassles, take Metro to the Smithsonian stop.

The National Law Enforcement Officers Memorial
605 E St. NW
Washington, DC
(202) 737–3400
www.nleomif.com/

The National Law Enforcement Officers Memorial features a tree-lined pathway leading past a granite wall displaying the names of fallen officers. Tragically, the list is expansive, with more than 14,000 names, including the first police officer ever killed in the line of duty, back in 1794. The memorial, open 24 hours daily, is at Judiciary Square, between E and F Streets and 4th and 5th Streets NW, right next to a Metro station. A visitor center features exhibits relating to many of the slain officers. It also houses a gift shop. Hours are 9:00 A.M. to 5:00 P.M. Monday through Friday, 10:00 A.M. to 5:00 P.M. Saturdays, and noon to 5:00 P.M. Sundays and holidays, except New Year's Day, Thanksgiving, and Christmas. Admission is free.

Theodore Roosevelt Memorial
Theodore Roosevelt Island in the Potomac River
Washington, DC
(703) 289–2500
www.nps.gov/gwmp/tri.htm

The Lincoln Memorial's 36 outer columns represent the states of the Union at the time of Lincoln's assassination in 1865. PHOTO: COURTESY OF WASHINGTON, DC CONVENTION AND TOURISM CORPORATION

This obscure, enchanting monument to America's environmental president is set amid a densely wooded island in the middle of the Potomac River between the Roosevelt and Key Bridges. Besides a giant statue of the gregarious 25th president, the island is laced with 2½ miles of trails—perfect for jogging or a leisurely walk. Its marshy shoreline offers excellent views of the Washington and Northern Virginia skylines. Open from sunrise until dark, Roosevelt Island is accessible only from the Virginia side via a footbridge. A bicycle/pedestrian bridge spanning the G.W. Parkway near the north end of the parking lot offers an easy connection to Rosslyn, Key Bridge, and Georgetown, just beyond. Admission is free.

Thomas Jefferson Memorial
Southern end of 15th St. SW
Washington, DC
(202) 426–6821
www.nps.gov/thje/home.htm
Breathtaking any time, but especially at night, the Jefferson Memorial has an undeniable aura, sensed by locals and tourists alike. Inspired during our first visit to the city, we huddled with our touring high school youth group on the memorial's moonlit front steps and harmonized on "Let There Be Peace on Earth."

The architectural firm that blueprinted the National Gallery of Art also designed this memorial, built in the style of Jefferson's Rotunda at the University of Virginia and dedicated in 1943 on Jefferson's 200th birthday. Marble walls inscribed with Thomas Jefferson's writings surround the 19-foot bronze likeness of our third president. Created by Rudolph Evans, the statue crowns a 6-foot pedestal. Looking from the memorial across the Tidal Basin affords an unforgettable illuminated view of downtown Washington. Add blossoming cherry trees and a warm, sunny spring day and you're talking tingles up and down the spine.

The memorial is open 24 hours a day, staffed from 8:00 A.M. to midnight daily, except on December 25. You can purchase Jefferson-related books and other items in the bookstore on the lower level and in the gift shop upstairs near the rotunda. Admission is free. Parking, as usual, is scarce, so think about taking Metro to the Smithsonian station.

U.S. Navy Memorial and Naval Heritage Center
Pennsylvania Ave. NW, Ste. 123
Washington, DC
(202) 737–2300
www.lonesailor.org/nmf.php

This interesting memorial at Market Square, open 24 hours, features the largest map of the world, inlaid in granite on the plaza. The Lone Sailor, a beautiful Stanley Bleifeld sculpture, keeps sentry. Nearby, two walls hold 22 bronze-sculpture panels, a representation of American naval history, and a salute to those who have served or will serve in the navy. Fountains and pools further accent the plaza. Inside the adjacent Naval Heritage Center, guests can view free movies, daily at noon. The center, which also features interactive videos, a log room, and a gift shop, is open 9:30 A.M. to 5:00 P.M. Monday through Saturday, March through October, 9:30 A.M. to 5:00 P.M. Tuesday through Saturday, November through February. Admission is free. The closest Metro station is Archives/Navy Memorial.

Vietnam Veterans Memorial
Bacon Dr. and Constitution Ave. NW
Washington, DC
(202) 426–6841
www.nps.gov/vive/home.htm

Just a short walk from the Reflecting Pool and the Lincoln Memorial, the Vietnam Veterans Memorial, or simply "The Wall," has become one of the most visited monuments in the city since its controversial opening in 1982, attracting more than 1.7 million people annually. Built with private funds, the structure—designed by a young architecture student named Maya Ying Lin—is composed of simple black granite panels embedded in the earth and etched (in chronological order) with the names of the more than 58,000 Americans who perished in the war. A few steps away, a pair of amazingly lifelike bronze

sculptures depict servicemen and women in wartime action scenes. The Wall is often the site of some of the most moving personal tributes ever witnessed at a very public place. It's staffed from 8:00 A.M. to midnight daily, except on Christmas. Admission is free. The closest Metro station is Foggy Bottom.

Washington Monument
15th St. NW
Washington, DC
(202) 426–6840
www.nps.gov/wamo/home.htm

Even newcomers can't miss this 555-foot signature landmark. A monumental renovation began with interior improvements in January 1998 and continued into the fall of 2001.

Certainly one of the most photographed icons anywhere, the marble tower—the tallest free-standing masonry structure in the world—contains nearly 200 memorial stones from all 50 states as well as numerous countries and organizations. An elevator ride to the 500-foot level rewards visitors with an unsurpassed view of Washington and environs.

You need a free ticket to go inside the monument. Pick up as many as six from the kiosk on 15th Street, normally open 8:30 A.M. to 4:30 P.M. Or, make reservations in advance by calling the National Park Reservation service at (800) 967–2283 or visiting reservations.nps.gov. The monument's regular hours are 9:00 A.M. to 4:45 P.M. September through March and 8:00 A.M. to midnight April through August. The site is closed December 25. The Smithsonian Metro is the closest station. (See our Civil War chapter for more on the monument's history.)

Federal Sites

* Bureau of Engraving and Printing
14th and C Sts. SW
Washington, DC
(202) 874–3188
wwwmoneyfactory.com

Few people ever get closer to so much money than they do at the Bureau of

Visitors and locals take photos, stroll the grounds, and admire the view near the reflecting pool in front of the Washington Monument. PHOTO: COURTESY OF WASHINGTON, DC CONVENTION AND TOURISM CORPORATION

Engraving and Printing, which boasts a recently renovated gallery from which to watch currency being printed. A 35-minute guided tour, one of the most popular in Washington, offers visitors a look at the fascinating process involved in the production of U.S. currency as well as stamps. Tours start every 20 minutes from 9:00 A.M. to 2:00 P.M. Monday through Friday, except federal holidays. They also take place from 5:00 to 7:00 P.M. from May through August.

Tickets, required March through September, are free but available only on a first-come, first-served basis. The ticket booth on Raoul Wallenberg Place (formerly 15th Street) is open from 8:00 a.m., until all tickets are distributed, Monday through Friday. From June through August, the booth reopens from 3:30 P.M., or until the tickets are gone, for extended hours tours. Tours end in the visitor center, open from 8:30 A.M. to 8:00 P.M. during peak season and 8:30 A.M. to 3:30 P.M. during nonpeak months, where you can purchase fun souvenirs like pens filled with shredded currency. Smithsonian is the nearest Metro station.

Congressional Cemetery
1801 E St. SE
Washington, DC
(202) 543–0539
www.congressionalcemetery.org
This cemetery on the Anacostia River in Southeast D.C. is a final resting place for more than 60,000 Americans, including more than 60 senators and representatives. Suffering from disrepair and vandalism in recent years, it made the National Trust for Historic Preservation's 11 Most Endangered list in 1997. These days, things are looking up for the 192-year-old cemetery. More than 1,000 volunteers helped with cleanup in 1997. In May 1999 Congress provided a $1 million appropriation, to be matched with funds collected by the Association for the Preservation of Historic Congressional Cemetery.

Scores of interesting American personalities found here include such notables as John Philip Sousa, J. Edgar Hoover, Mathew Brady, and several Native American chiefs. At Congressional, you also can view the grave of Vice President Elbridge Gerry of Massachusetts, the man who gave us the term *gerrymander*, a reference to voting district alterations that give one political party an unfair advantage and often result in oddly shaped jurisdictions. The cemetery is open from dawn to dusk. The office and library are open from 9:30 A.M. to 2:30 P.M. Monday, Wednesday, and Friday, and 11:00 A.M. to 3:00 P.M. on Saturday. Admission is free.

Department of State
22nd and C Sts. NW
Washington, DC
(202) 647–3241
www.state.gov/www/about_state/
diprooms/tour.html

This massive agency, responsible for creating and carrying out U.S. foreign policy, is partly accessible to the general public. A must-see for eighteenthth-century furniture aficionados, free 45-minute tours of the elegant eighth-floor diplomatic reception areas begin at 9:30 and 10:30 A.M. and 2:45 P.M. Monday through Friday, except federal holidays. The tour is not recommended for children unless they're over the age of 12, and strollers are not permitted. Call to make required reservations at least four weeks in advance, if possible. Written materials about the many interesting aspects of the department

ment are available by calling the Public Information Division at (202) 647–6575.

Department of the Treasury
1500 Pennsylvania Ave. NW
Washington, DC
(202) 622–0896, (202) 622–0692 TDD
www.treas.gov/opc/opc0006.html

This National Historic Landmark opens for guided public tours on Saturday mornings. Highlights of the 90-minute walk through the lovely building, which dates to 1836, include the elegant suite used by Abraham Lincoln's treasury secretary Salmon P. Chase; the marble Cash Room used for Ulysses S. Grant's inaugural reception (note the 1,500-pound chandelier); and a Burglar Proof Vault from 1864. The free tours begin at 10:00, 10:20, 10:40 and 11:00 A.M. You must make a reservation and provide your name, date of birth, and social security number by noon on Friday, and your reservation must be confirmed by 4:30 P.M. On arrival, you must present a photo ID. Enter through the Appointment Center on 15th Street between F and G Streets NW. Parking may be scarce, so take Metro to Metro Center or McPherson Square.

Federal Bureau of Investigation
J. Edgar Hoover FBI Bldg.
935 Pennsylvania Ave. NW
Washington, DC
(202) 324–3447, (202) 324–1016 TDY
www.fbi.gov/fbinbrief/tour/tour.htm

The J. Edgar Hoover Building is as intriguing as the man himself. The free, one-hour excursion through America's top law-enforcement agency offers an inside look at crime-fighting techniques and crime laboratories, a peek at photos of the FBI's Ten Most Wanted Fugitives, and a thrilling live firearms demonstration, viewed safely from behind glass. After the tour, visit the gift shop for FBI souvenirs. Like so many of the city's other popular tours, this one requires early arrival to ensure ticket admission. Tours take place from 8:45 A.M. to 4:15 P.M. Monday through Friday. Walk here from Metro Center, Federal Triangle, Gallery Place, or the Archives/Navy Memorial Metro stations.

Insiders' Tip

Contact your Congressional representative's office to request Congressional passes and tickets for special tours of the White House, Supreme Court, Federal Bureau of Investigation and Bureau of Engraving and Printing. They're in limited supply, and you must ask for them at least three months in advance.

The Interior Museum
1849 C St. NW
Washington, DC
(202) 208–4743
www.doi.gov/museum/museum/index.html

Housed in the Department of Interior's main building, constructed during the FDR administration, this unique museum features exhibits of surveying equipment, maps, historical documents, natural history, and American Indian cultures. Visitors can view many of the original 1930s' features, such as Art Deco-style metal silhouettes and intricately detailed dioramas that depict Interior bureaus.

The museum is free, and open from 8:30 A.M. to 4:30 P.M. Monday through Friday and 1:00 to 4:00 P.M. the third Saturday of each month. It's closed on federal holidays. Adults must show photo IDs to enter. Call two weeks in advance to arrange guided tours or to see the New Deal murals. Farragut West is the nearest Metro stop.

Library of Congress
Independence Ave. at 1st St. SE
Washington, DC
(202) 707–8000
www.lcweb.loc.gov/

Another one of Thomas Jefferson's legacies to Washington, his personal collection of books grew into the world's largest library, totaling some 120 million items in 460 languages. One million people annually visit the library's three buildings, all of which house topical reading rooms open to adults older than high-school age. The Thomas Jefferson Building reopened in May of 1997, sporting a new visitor center and 90-seat theater where you can watch a new film about the library. Don't miss the marble-floored Great Hall, where you can view such treasures as the Gutenberg Bible and the room's magnificent stained-glass ceiling. Other highlights include the main reading room, a large gift shop, a performing arts gallery, and special rooms that display some of the library's important collections. Take a free guided tour at 11:30 A.M., 1:00 P.M., 2:30 P.M., and 4:00 P.M., Monday through Saturday. Call TTY (202) 707–6362 in advance to arrange for

sign-language interpretation, available at 2:30 P.M. Monday and 11:30 A.M. Friday. The building is open from 10:00 A.M. to 5:00 P.M. Monday through Saturday, and closed on Sundays and federal holidays. Visitors should enter the Carriage entrance at 1st Street and go to the information desk, where tours start.

The library's Madison and John Adams Buildings offer reading rooms, and the Madison also contains exhibitions and a cafeteria. The John Adams Building also houses reading rooms. Call (202) 707–6400 for reading room hours and instructions on how to obtain a required Reader Identification card if you plan to do research or read at the library.

Located on Capitol Hill near the U.S. Capitol, the library is close to the Capitol South Metro stop.

* The National Aquarium
Department of Commerce Bldg.
14th St. between Constitution and
Pennsylvania Aves. NW
Washington, DC
(202) 482–2825
www.nationalaquarium.com

Not to be confused with the centerpiece of Baltimore's Inner Harbor that shares the same name, this is the nation's oldest aquarium, established in 1873. It's one of the city's lesser-known attractions, due in part, perhaps, to its basement location. Some 70 tanks house more than 270 species of aquatic creatures, including alligators, sea turtles, and denizens of the Touch Tank, a children's favorite that offers a thrilling hands-on experience with underwater life. Be sure to check on times for the popular shark feedings. (See our Kidstuff chapter for a complete description.)

* National Archives Building
700 Pennsylvania Ave., with entrance on
Constitution Ave., between 7th and
9th Sts. NW
Washington, DC
(202) 501–5000
www.nara.gov

The three most important documents in America—the Declaration of Independence, the Constitution, and the Bill of

Rights—reside in helium-filled, sealed glass encasements in the beautiful Rotunda of this well-guarded building. To keep the precious parchments out of harm's way, the Charters of Freedom are lowered 20 feet each evening into a special bombproof, fireproof vault. On July 5, 2001, the Rotunda closed for a renovation project that's set to include new encasements, a display of all four pages of the Constitution, and upgrades to make the building wheelchair accessible. The improved display should open sometime during the summer of 2003.

The Rotunda also houses the 1297 Magna Carta and the American Originals exhibit of other important historical documents. For a totally different experience, trace your family history in the cavernous Research Room, or simply take advantage of one of the free lectures, films, or other exhibits.

For a free schedule of public events, write to the National Archives Public Affairs Office, Room G6, Washington, D.C. 20408. The building is open to researchers from 8:45 A.M. to 5:00 P.M.

Monday and Wednesday; 8:45 A.M. to 9:00 P.M. Tuesday, Thursday, and Friday; and 8:45 A.M. to 4:45 P.M. Saturdays. It's closed on Sundays and federal hoildays. The nearest Metro stop is Archives/Navy Memorial.

The Old Post Office Pavilion
1100 Pennsylvania Ave. NW
Washington, DC
(202) 289–4224
oldpostofficedc.com

This 12-story landmark soaring above America's Main Street was built in 1899 as the nation's postal headquarters. Since concerned citizens stepped in to save the building from demolition in 1934, it has been masterfully renovated to feature shopping, dining, and entertainment attractions, including an annual New Year's Eve gala. Ride the glass elevator up to the tower's 12th-floor observation deck for a dramatic view. The Pavilion is open from 10:00 A.M. to 7:00 P.M. Monday through Saturday, noon to 6:00 P.M. Sunday. Admission is free. Federal Triangle is the nearest Metro station.

The National Archives building, an imposing neoclassical structure, is the storehouse of national records.
PHOTO: COURTESY OF WASHINGTON, DC CONVENTION AND TOURISM CORPORATION

Organization of American States
17th St. and Constitution Ave. NW
Washington, DC
(202) 458-3000
www.oas.org

The incredible art and culture of the Americas—Canada, the Caribbean, Latin America, and the United States—unfolds at this impressive compound across from the Ellipse. The main building boasts a monumental entrance hall and huge Palladian windows and features changing exhibitions. Be sure to visit the Art Museum of the Americas, housed in a separate building at 201 18th Street NW. Hours are 10:00 A.M. to 5:00 P.M. Tuesday through Sunday. The museum is closed Mondays, federal holidays, and Good Friday. Admission is free. To arrange a guided tour, call (202) 458-6016. Farragut West is the nearest Metro stop.

While in the vicinity, walk across Virginia Avenue and take a look at the striking statue of Símon Bolívar, the liberator of much of South America.

* Supreme Court of the United States
1st St. and Maryland Ave. NE
Washington, DC
(202) 479-3211
www.supremecourtus.gov

The weightiest legal decisions in the land are handed down behind the imposing columned facade of this renowned building. Although their work is of paramount importance, the nine justices don't deliberate for a full calendar year, but go into session only between October and June. They typically hand down orders and opinions on Mondays, an exciting time to visit. When the nation's highest court is not in session, free lectures are given on weekdays every hour on the half-hour from 9:30 A.M. to 3:30 P.M. When court is in session, line up early on the Front Plaza for limited seating. You can choose to hear a full argument, or just watch for a few minutes. The building, open from 9:00 A.M. to 4:30 P.M. weekdays except holidays, also has exhibits, a film, a gift shop, and food. Union Station and Capitol South are the nearest Metro stations.

The United States Botanic Garden
Conservatory
Maryland Ave. and First St. SW,
Washington, DC
(202) 225-8333
www.aoc.gov/USBG

Recently renovated, this showcase for living plants sits on the grounds of the U.S. Capitol. Highlights include almost 4,000 plants housed in a climate-controlled environment, a gift shop, themed gardens, and features designed for safety and accessibility. The conservatory holds numerous workshops, tours, lectures, and family activities. Hours are 10:00 A.M. to 5:00 P.M. daily. Admission is free. The nearest Metro stations are Federal Center Southwest and Capitol South.

* United States Capitol
East End of the Mall on Capitol Hill
Washington, DC
(202) 225-6827
www.aoc.gov/homepage.htm

Perhaps the strongest competitor to the Washington Monument in terms of worldwide recognition, the Capitol looms majestically over the city as its tallest building, something that will never change, thanks to the farsighted vision of early planners of the federal district. Tours of the great halls and the magnificent renovated Central Rotunda of this regal edifice have been halted indefinitely due to security concerns following the events of September 11, 2001. Guided tours, when in session, take place from 9:00 A.M. to 4:30 P.M. Monday through Saturday from September through February, and from 9:30 A.M. to 8:00 P.M. Monday through Friday and 9:30 A.M. to 4:30 P.M. Saturdays March through August. During peak season, you'll need a ticket to take a guided or self-guided tour. Wait in line at the east front staircase. Following your tour, you can visit the House and Senate chambers. A Capitol Visitor Center is in the works, with completion expected in 2005.

When the building reopens to the public, brochures will help guide visitors who prefer to meander through on their own.

You'll find plenty to look at besides the Rotunda. Don't miss the colorfully detailed Brumidi Corridors, featuring painted walls designed in the 1850s by Italian artist Constantino Brumidi. Many of the works have been restored to their original appearance. You'll also want to see such highlights as the dimly lit Old Supreme Court Chamber, restored to look just as it did in the mid-nineteenth century; the National Statuary Hall, featuring sculpted tributes to notable Americans; and the President's Room, an ornate chamber that many presidents used for late-night bill signing.

For a peek at Congress in action, obtain a pass through the office of your representative or senator. You don't need a pass to visit the House and Senate galleries when Congress isn't in session. Capitol South and Union Station are the closest Metro stations.

* U.S. Department of Agriculture
12th St. and Jefferson Dr. SW
Washington, DC
(202) 720–4197
www.usda.gov/oo/visitorcenter/
Trace America's agrarian roots at the Department of Agriculture's Visitor Information Center, located in the Administration Building. Exhibits and displays change regularly. This monolithic agency is housed in one of the largest structures in Washington, just a short walk from the National Mall. In Room 103A, the center is open from 9:00 a.m. to 3:00 p.m. Monday through Friday, except holidays. Admission is free. The Smithsonian is the closest Metro station.

* U.S. Information Agency
330 Independence Ave. SW
Washington, DC
(202) 619–3919
www.voa.gov
The American propaganda machine comes alive on the Voice of America tour at the U.S.I.A. The free tour is cancelled indefinitely due to security reasons. When the building reopens to the public and the tour resumes, it will continue to tell the story of how the VOA's shortwave radio systems and television programs, magazines and books are used to gain support abroad for American policies. Call in advance to check the schedule for resumed tours.

* The White House
1600 Pennsylvania Ave. NW
Washington, DC
(202) 456–7041, (202) 456–2121 TDD
www.whitehouse.gov
Known as the "President's Palace" in its early days, this masterpiece of Federal architecture each year hosts scores of dignitaries, entertainers, and other luminaries, not to mention more than 1 million curious tourists. Burned by the British during the War of 1812, the White House has been home to every president and his family except George Washington.

Sadly, the White House is yet another landmark forced to step up security and halt public tours indefinitely. Until tours resume, visit the Web site for a virtual look at the seven rooms normally included as part of a self-conducted free public tour offered Tuesday through Saturday, from 10:00 A.M. to noon.

If possible, take a virtual tour or actual tour during December to see the halls decked in holiday splendor.

When tours are in session, tickets are required for self-guided tours from the third Tuesday in March to the Saturday before Labor Day as well as during December. Pick up a timed ticket, available beginning at 7:30 A.M. on the day of your tour, at the White House Visitor Center, southeast corner of 15th and E Streets (800–717–1450). The ticket counter closes at noon, or whenever it has distributed all passes. Tickets aren't required during off-peak months, but you must be in line at the White House by noon. To obtain a free VIP pass that's good for a guided tour, offered from 8:15 to 9:00 A.M. Tuesday through Saturday, contact the office of your representative or senator at least 8 to 10 weeks in advance.

The visitor center, open from 7:30 A.M. to 4:00 P.M. daily, features a video presentation and exhibits about the White House, as well as a gift shop. (See our Annual Events chapter for details about the Easter Egg Roll and Spring Garden tours.)

Every president except George Washington has lived in the Palladian-influenced White House.
PHOTO: COURTESY OF WASHINGTON, DC CONVENTION AND TOURISM CORPORATION

Directly south of the White House grounds is an expanse of parkland known as the Ellipse, the site of the annual Pageant of Peace holiday celebration (see our Annual Events chapter). One of the Ellipse's little-known features is the Settlers' Memorial, a granite marker located near 15th Street. Here you will find inscribed the names of the 18 landowners whose corn and tobacco farms ultimately became the land that is today's Washington, D.C.

Federal Triangle is the closest Metro stop.

Museums and Galleries

The Smithsonian Institution—On the National Mall

Arthur M. Sackler Gallery
1050 Independence Ave. SW
Washington, DC
(202) 357–2700, (202) 357–1729 TTY
www.asia.si.edu

The Sackler features a permanent collection of Asian and Near Eastern masterpieces. (See The Arts chapter for a complete description. The Kidstuff chapter describes family programs.)

Arts and Industries Building

900 Jefferson Dr. SW
Washington, DC
(202) 357–2700, (202) 357–1729 TTY
www.si.edu/ai

You'll feel as though you've stepped back in time when you enter this Victorian-style building, next to the Castle (see following entry). Although it still shows traces of its previous incarnation as a recreation of the 1876 Philadelphia Centennial Exposition, the museum now houses various temporary exhibitions.

The museum is open from 10:00 A.M. to 5:30 P.M. daily, except December 25. Admission is free. (See Kidstuff for information about the museum's Discovery Theater.)

The Castle

1000 Jefferson Dr. SW
Washington, DC
(202) 357–2700, (202) 357–1729 TTY
www.si.edu

Take one look at its imposing reddish-brown, Norman Gothic exterior and you'll know how this building got its name. The Castle has been a fixture on the Mall since 1855 and now almost seems out of place in the company of some of the more modern architecture. But what a story it has to tell. This is the original building of the Smithsonian Institution, which now encompasses 14 museums and the National Zoo in Washington, D.C., making it the largest museum complex in the world and an unparalleled national treasure. An ideal place for newcomers to begin exploring the Smithsonian collection, the Castle houses a high-tech visitors information center, as well as the crypt of James Smithson, the Englishman whose donations led to the birth of the institution that bears his name. It's free, and open daily except Christmas, from 10:00 A.M. to 5:30 P.M.

Freer Gallery of Art
Jefferson Dr. at 12th St. SW
Washington, DC
(202) 357–2700, (202) 357–1729 TTY
www.asia.si.edu

This impressive gallery features an important collection of Asian and nineteenth- and early twentieth-century American art. (See our Arts chapter for a thorough description, and Kidstuff for information about children's activities.)

Hirshhorn Museum and Sculpture Garden
7th St. and Independence Ave. SW
Washington, DC
(202) 357–2700, (202) 357–1729 TTY
www.hirshhorn.si.edu

Visit this gallery to view works by many of the great nineteenth- and twentieth-century artists. (See our Arts chapter for a complete description, and Kidstuff for details about family programs.)

National Air and Space Museum
6th St. and Jefferson Dr. SW
Washington, DC
(202) 357–2700, (202) 357–1729 TTY
www.nasm.si.edu

Humankind's insatiable fascination with flight is dramatically underscored by the National Air and Space Museum's status as the most-visited museum in the world. Its more than two dozen galleries— including the magnificent glass-walled

This redbrick Castle on the National Mall was the first of the great Smithsonian museums. Finished in 1855, it now houses administrative offices and an information center. PHOTO: COURTESY OF WASHINGTON, DC CONVENTION AND TOURISM CORPORATION

lobby where dozens of aircraft hang in suspended animation—showcase the evolution of aviation and space technology.

The collection features history-making planes flown by the Wright brothers and Charles Lindbergh, the Apollo 11 command module, a space station, and the wiry "flying fuel tank" that was flown on a record-breaking nonstop flight around the world. Free highlights tours take place daily, starting at the tour desk in the South lobby. Special tours can be arranged by calling the Educational Services Tour Office at (202) 357-1400. Check the museum's daily events schedule for times of the exciting Samuel P. Langley IMAX Theater and Albert Einstein Planetarium shows, which require tickets. Planetarium shows are $4.00. Daytime theater admission is $6.50 for adults, $5.50 for ages 2 through 17 and 55 and older. Buy a combo ticket for $9.00 for adults, $8.00 for youths and seniors. The museum is open from 10:00 A.M. to 5:30 P.M. daily, except on December 25. Admission is free. The closest Metro stop is L'Enfant Plaza.

Since the museum no longer has room to accept large items for display, an annex has been approved for a site on the grounds of Washington Dulles International Airport, where several large aircraft wait in storage. It's slated to open in 2003.

National Museum of African Art
950 Independence Ave. SW
Washington, DC
(202) 357-2700, (202) 357-1729 TTY
www.nmafa.si.edu
This unique museum dedicated to African culture and art features permanent exhibits and rotating shows. (See our Arts and Kidstuff chapters for more information.)

National Museum of American History
14th St. and Constitution Ave. NW
Washington, DC
(202) 357-2700, (202) 357-1729 TTY
www.americanhistory.si.edu
Visitors of all ages love the exhibits of American culture, politics, and technology brought to life at this ever-popular National Museum of American History. From White House dishes to an original Model T, from Archie Bunker's armchair

to Mr. Rogers' sweater, the exhibits are as varied and interesting as history itself. The interactive Information Age exhibit is among the most popular, as is the extensively renovated display of the First Ladies' gowns. The museum also features intriguing temporary shows. Take a break in the old-fashioned ice-cream parlor downstairs, and be sure to visit the large museum shop, filled with fascinating books, recordings, toys, and unique gift items. (Our Kidstuff chapter describes features geared toward children.) The museum is open from 10:00 A.M. to 5:30 P.M. daily, except December 25. Admission is free. It's a short walk from the Smithsonian Metro station.

National Museum of Natural History
10th St. and Constitution Ave. NW
Washington, DC
(202) 357-2700, (202) 357-1729 TTY
www.mnh.si.edu
You'll know you've arrived at the National Museum of Natural History when you look up and see the colossal stuffed elephant in the rotunda—and it only gets more intriguing from there. This treasure house contains more than 81 million items documenting humankind and the natural environment. It's undergoing a massive refurbishing, so don't be surprised to find some areas temporarily off limits.

The Discovery Center, which opened in spring 1999, houses the Samuel C. Johnson IMAX theater. Watch 2-D and 3-D and interactive films on a six-story screen! Daytime tickets, available up to two weeks in advance, cost $6.50 for adults and $5.50 for ages 2 to 17 and 55 and older. Tickets for evening shows are $8.00 for adults and $7.00 for youths and seniors. Other highlights of the new addition include a cafe in a six-story, glass-domed atrium and huge gift shops. Friday nights feature live jazz performances.

Prepare to be dazzled as you enter the Janet Annenberg Hooker Hall of Geology, Gems and Minerals. It's filled with some of the most impressive jewelry most people will ever lay eyes on, as well as an enormous collection of natural gems and minerals (see the Close-up in this chapter).

The National Museum of American History houses exhibits that grab the attention of any age group.
PHOTO: DAVE PENLAND, COURTESY OF THE SMITHSONIAN INSTITUTION

The museum's other highlights include dinosaur skeletons (an even bigger hit with youngsters thanks to Barney-mania and the gargantuan success of Steven Spielberg's dino flicks), displays of early man, and a live coral reef.

The museum's immensely popular insect zoo underwent a dramatic metamorphosis that culminated in a grand reopening in late 1994 as the O. Orkin Insect Zoo. It's named after—that's right—the founder of Orkin Pest Control (Otto Orkin to be precise), perhaps the most familiar of all monikers in the bug-bagging business. The zoo includes a 14-foot model of an African termite mound that children can crawl through, a live beehive (behind glass, thankfully), a Southwest desert diorama, and a rain forest exhibit complete with live giant cockroaches and leaf-cutter ants. (See our Kidstuff chapter for more on this and other kid-pleasing attractions.)

Guided highlights tours usually take place at 10:30 A.M. and 1:30 P.M. Monday through Thursday and at 10:30 A.M. Fridays. Meet in the Rotunda. The museum is open from 10:00 A.M. to 5:30 P.M. daily,

except December 25. Admission is free. Federal Triangle is the nearest Metro stop.

The museum's Naturalist Center, a hands-on study facility, is temporarily at 741 Miller Drive, Leesburg, Virginia (703-779-9712). It's open 10:30 A.M. to 4:00 P.M. Tuesday through Saturday, closed Sundays and federal holidays.

S. Dillon Ripley Center (The Smithsonian International Gallery)
1100 Jefferson Dr. SW
Washington, DC
(202) 357-2700, (202) 357-1729 TTY
www.si.edu/ripley/start.htm

You'll find the International Gallery as well as the Smithsonian Associates membership and education branch at this underground site, between the Castle and Freer Gallery of Art. The gallery hosts a variety of traveling exhibitions. Entered through a copper-topped kiosk, it's open from 10:00 A.M. to 5:30 P.M. daily. The center also houses the Smithsonian Institution Traveling Exhibition Service (SITES), International Center, and conference rooms.

A 75 million-year-old sea turtle on display at the National Museum of Natural History intrigues a young child. PHOTO: CHARLES PHILLIPS, COURTESY OF THE SMITHSONIAN INSTITUTION

The Smithsonian Institution—Off the National Mall

Anacostia Museum and Center for African American History and Culture
1901 Fort Pl. SE
Washington, DC
(202) 357–2700, (202) 357–1729 TDD
www.si.edu/anacostia

At the small Anacostia Museum, you'll find two intriguing changing cultural and historical exhibitions focusing on regional and national topics. For example, the 1998 show *Man Made: African-American Men and Quilting Traditions,* showcased approximately 40 pieces created by African American men.

The Anacostia Museum also features changing exhibits related to African-American culture. It reopened in February 2002 following extensive renovation. It is open from 10:00 A.M. to 5:00 P.M. daily, except December 25. Admission is free.

National Postal Museum
2 Massachusetts Ave. NW
Washington, DC
(202) 357–2700
www.si.edu/postal

The newest museum in the vast Smithsonian collection, the National Postal Museum opened in July 1993 with great fanfare. Philatelists queued up for several hours get special first-day-of-issue commemorative stamps. The museum documents the founding and development of the modern postal system and features interactive displays and the largest stamp collection in the world, including all U.S.-issue stamps since 1847. The museum is open from 10:00 A.M. to 5:30 P.M. daily, except December 25. Admission is free. (See Kidstuff for more on the museum's many child-friendly exhibits.)

National Zoological Park
3000 block of Connecticut Ave. NW
Washington, DC
(202) 357–2700
www.si.edu/natzoo

Nearly 5,000 animals call the National Zoo home, including notable new additions Asian elephant calf Kandula, Sumatran tiger cub Berani, and giant pandas Mei Xiang and Tian Tian. Bison, prairie dogs, and grasses highlight one of the zoo's newest exhibitions: The American Prairie. Another recent addition, Think Tank, features interactive and observation exhibits related to how animals think. Look for the Orangutan Transportation System, a unique outdoor, overhead cable system.

Peering into the dens of prairie dogs at the National Zoological Park gives city dwellers an insight into the American prairie. PHOTO: COURTESY OF NATIONAL ZOOLOGICAL PARK

Other especially popular exhibits include the Reptile Discovery Center, Pollinarium, ape house, and the big cats. Be sure to leave time for a stroll through a recreated rain forest in the Amazonia exhibit, one of the newest additions to the zoo.

The wild animals on display aren't the only endangered species around here; ditto for parking spaces. Do yourself a huge favor and take Metro to the Cleveland Park station, a less-taxing walk than the uphill schlep from the Woodley Park/Zoo station (on the Red Line). From there it's a pleasant 10-minute walk up the street. Visit early in the morning to avoid crowds and to see the animals at their liveliest: The grounds are open from 6:00 A.M. to 6:00 P.M. daily mid-September through April, and 6:00 A.M. to 8:00 P.M. the rest of the year. Most animal buildings are open from 10:00 A.M. to 4:30 P.M. mid-September through April, 10:00 A.M. to 6:00 P.M. the rest of the year. Call (202) 673-4955 to schedule guided tours, which sometimes fill up months in advance. Friends of the National Zoo (FONZ) offers numerous special programs in the visitor center, during and after zoo hours; call (202) 673-4960 for information about membership, which includes parking privileges. Visit the gift shop for a variety of animal-related souvenirs. Admission is free. (See Kidstuff for additional information.)

Renwick Gallery
Pennsylvania Ave. and 17th St. NW
Washington, DC
(202) 357-2700
americanart.si.edu/collections/renwick

This off-the-Mall gallery showcases American design, crafts, and contemporary arts. (See our Arts chapter for a complete description.)

Smithsonian American Art Museum and
National Portrait Gallery
8th and G Sts. NW
Washington, DC
(202) 357-2700
americanart.si.edu, www.npg.si.edu

The National Museum of American Art's permanent collection features paintings, sculptures, and photographs from colonial to modern times. The National Portrait Gallery houses an array of paintings and other works depicting famous Americans. Both museums closed in January of 2000 for an extensive three-year building renovation.

Other Museums, Galleries, and Attractions

B'nai B'rith Klutznick National Jewish
Museum
1640 Rhode Island Ave. NW
Washington, DC
(202) 857-6583
bbi.koz.com

The permanent collection of this museum features items spanning some four thousand years of Jewish culture and history. Highlights include the Jewish Sports Hall of Fame, correspondence between George Washington and the sexton of a Rhode Island synagogue, a Torah cover marking the Finzi-Contini wedding, ancient bowls, seventeenth-century candlesticks, unique menorahs, and ritual objects. The museum also showcases several changing exhibitions annually. A gift shop sells a variety of Judaic merchandise. Museum hours are from 10:00 A.M. to 5:00 P.M. Sunday through Friday. The museum is closed on federal and major Jewish holidays. Admission is free. The nearest Metro stop is Farragut North.

Capital Children's Museum
800 3rd St. NE
Washington, DC
(202) 543-8600
www.ccm.org

The Capital Children's Museum offers a nice change of pace for kids and parents who need a break from Washington's heavy-duty attractions. This place makes learning fun with hands-on exhibits, interactive displays, and a special emphasis on world cultures. (See our Kidstuff chapter for a full description.)

The Janet Annenberg Hooker Hall of Geology, Gems, and Minerals

Dazzling: That's the word that immediately comes to mind when you visit the Janet Annenberg Hooker Hall of Geology, Gems, and Minerals at the Smithsonian Institution's National Museum of Natural History. After a two-year, $13-million renovation, the 20,000-square-foot hall opened in September of 1997 with new, well-lit displays of old favorites like the Hope Diamond and recent acquisitions. Many specimens underwent cleaning and repair.

Hooker, for whom the hall is named, died in 1997, just a few weeks after the new exhibit opened. She contributed $5 million to the privately funded project and also donated Cartier-designed yellow starburst diamonds and, several years ago, the Hooker Emerald, a jaw-dropping 75.47-carat stone surrounded by 20 baguette diamonds in a platinum setting.

The exhibit begins in the Harry Winston Gallery, named for the jeweler who in 1958 donated what would become the Smithsonian Institution's most popular attraction: the Hope Diamond. The flawless blue gem takes center-stage here, rotating inside a circular display vault, while surrounding onlookers marvel at the illuminated 45.52-carat stone's clarity. Written displays tell all about the Hope Diamond's intriguing history. Also, in this room you'll find such large natural treasures as a 1,300-pound slab of quartz, a sheet of nearly pure copper, and a natural sandstone formation that looks like abstract art.

The Hope Diamond is from the National Gem Collection. PHOTO: DANE PENLAND, COURTESY OF SMITHSONIAN INSTITUTION, NATIONAL MUSEUM OF NATURAL HISTORY

If you enjoy window shopping at elegant jewelry shops, you'll love the National Gem Collection. An amazing array of treasures glistens from inside illuminated display cases. The one-of-a-kind, Art Deco–style Clagett Bracelet features an exotic hunt scene, painstakingly created of 626 diamonds, 73 emeralds, 48 sapphires, and 20 rubies. Nearby, flashes of light emanating from the 22,892.5-carat American Golden Topaz may temporarily blind you. Among the collection's royal jewels, Marie Antoinette's pear-shaped diamond earrings create tiny rainbow-hued points of light throughout the case. Empress Marie-Louise's crown, a wedding gift from husband Napoleon I, contains—count 'em—more than 1,000 diamonds. An empress can never have too many diamonds, though: Celebrating the birth of the couple's first son, Napoleon presented his wife with a necklace bearing 172 of the glittering stones, weighing more than 263 carats!

The gem collection—which also includes numerous rubies, sapphires, emeralds, and aquamarines in various sizes and cuts—by itself would impress most visitors. The equally awesome Minerals and Gems Gallery follows it. Here, you'll see cases filled with more colors, shapes, and sizes of natural formations than you'd dream possible. (It's a great place to take kids for a visual scavenger hunt!) The Mineral Rainbow display showcases such samples as florescent blue azurite, purple quartz, avocado pyromophite, coral crocoite, lemon yellow sulphur, and red rhodochrosite.

The awesome Hope Diamond captures the attention of young visitors to the National Museum of Natural History. PHOTO: COURTESY OF SMITHSONIAN INSTITUTION

Elsewhere in the room, look for wulfenite that resembles a pile of peanut brittle, and precariously piled iron pyrite cubes that look like a carefully cut and stacked sculpture.

After mingling with the minerals, check out the mine gallery, where you can walk through a simulated mine and see what stones look like underground. The new hall also includes a gallery devoted to plate tectonics, the scientific concept that explains such phenomena as earthquakes and volcanos. Here, you can create your own earthquakes and touch a 3.96-billion-year-old rock, the world's oldest. You'll end your tour in the Moon, Meteorites, and Solar System Gallery, where you can look at moon rocks and stardust.

The hall also includes computer programs, films, and interactive exhibits. A Rocks Gallery contains hands-on displays. Like most Smithsonian exhibitions, the gems and minerals hall is free.

DAR Museum
1776 D St. NW
Washington, DC
(202) 879–3241
www.dar.org/museum

This museum of the Daughters of the American Revolution features state-named period rooms, decorated with lovely furnishings, china settings, and other accent pieces. Tell your docent if there's a certain room you wish to visit during your tour. The museum is open from 8:30 A.M. to 4:00 P.M. Monday through Friday and 1:00 to 5:00 P.M. Sunday, with guided tours of the period rooms given from 10:00 A.M. to 2:30 P.M. weekdays and 1:00 to 5:00 P.M. Sundays. Admission is free. The building closes on federal holiday weekends. (See our Kidstuff chapter for details about children's programs here.)

Ford's Theatre
511 10th St. NW
Washington, DC
(202) 426–6924, (202) 347–4833 (box office)
www.fordstheatre.org

Forever memorialized as the place where President Lincoln was shot by John Wilkes Booth, Ford's still is very much a working year-round professional theater. (See our Arts and Civil War chapters for complete details about the theater and its museum.)

Frederick Douglass National Historic Site
1411 W St. SE
Washington, DC
(202) 426–5960
www.nps.gov/frdo

Cedar Hill, the beautifully restored Victorian home of former slave Frederick Douglass, is the centerpiece of this slice of tranquility near the banks of the Anacostia River. A visitor center features a 30-minute film and numerous exhibits on the life of the famed abolitionist, editor, orator, and advisor to Lincoln. Take a half-hour tour and stop by the bookstore with volumes on black history. Hours are 9:00 A.M. to 4:00 P.M. daily except New Year's Day, Thanksgiving, and Christmas. The site stays open until 5:00 P.M. mid-April through mid-October. Admission is free. (Also see our Civil War chapter.)

National Building Museum
401 F St. NW
Washington, DC
(202) 272–2448
www.nbm.org

Created by an act of Congress in 1980, this is the only national museum of its kind, offering a variety of exhibits and programs about building aspects from architecture to urban planning. Housed in the beautiful 1887 structure originally occupied by the Pension Bureau, the museum is known for its spectacular 316-by-116-foot Great Hall, a frequent site of presidential inaugural balls. Its 75-foot-high Corinthian columns are among the world's tallest indoor pillars. The museum's permanent exhibitions include *Washington: Symbol and City,* a must-see for anyone interested in the stories behind the capital's monuments and famous buildings. Changing exhibitions focus on such topics as engineering and home improvement.

The museum boasts an interesting gift shop and the Blueprints Cafe featuring light meals and snacks from 9:00 A.M. to 5:00 P.M. Monday through Saturday and noon to 5:00 P.M. Sunday. Free, guided tours, which start next to the fountain in the Great Hall, take place at 12:30 P.M. Monday through Wednesday; at 11:30 A.M., 12:30 P.M., and 1:30 P.M. Thursday through Saturday; and at 12:30 and 1:30 P.M. Sunday. Other free programs include films, concerts, lectures, and family activities (see our Kidstuff chapter). Museum admission also is free. Hours are 10:00 A.M. to 5:00 P.M. Monday through Saturday, and noon to 5:00 P.M. Sunday. The museum is closed on Thanksgiving, December 25, and January 1. Taking Metro couldn't be more convenient: Walk out of the Judiciary Square station and you're right there!

National Gallery of Art
4th St. and Constitution Ave. NW
Washington, DC
(202) 737–4215
www.nga.gov

Housing one of the world's greatest art collections, the National Gallery is another of Washington's amazing free attractions. (For a complete description, see our Arts and Kidstuff chapters.)

National Geographic Society
17th and M Sts. NW
Washington, DC
(202) 857-7588
www.nationalgeographic.com/explorer

At the headquarters of this venerable institution, you'll find Explorers Hall, a geography and map lover's paradise. Exhibits, ranging from earth science and cultural geography to environmental and social issues, change regularly and never fail to fascinate. Like so many wonderful attractions in Washington, it boasts free admission. It's open from 9:00 A.M. to 5:00 P.M. Monday through Saturday and holidays, except Christmas, 10:00 A.M. to 5:00 P.M. Sunday. (See the Kidstuff chapter for more information.)

National Museum of Women in the Arts
1250 New York Ave. NW
Washington, DC
(202) 783-5000
www.nmwa.org

This is the world's first museum devoted entirely to works by women artists. (You'll find a thorough description in our Arts chapter.)

* The Navy Museum
Building 76, Washington Navy Yard
805 Kidder Breese SE
Washington, DC
(202) 433-4882
www.history.navy.mil/branches/nhcorg8.htm

Housed in the former Naval Gun Factory, this museum offers a fascinating look at United States naval history from the American Revolution to the present day. More than 5,000 artifacts on display include gun mounts, full-size equipment models, decorations and awards, uniforms, and artwork. Explore exhibits about such topics as polar exploration (including Admiral Richard E. Byrd's Antarctic hut), World War II, space travel, and undersea study.

A favorite rainy-day destination for families, the museum features hands-on activities, plenty of space for active kids,

> **Insiders' Tip**
> Become a Smithsonian Resident Associate to enjoy benefits like a subscription to *Smithsonian* magazine, discounts on museum shop purchases, and free events just for members. Annual membership is $45 for individuals. Call (202) 357-3030

and a gift shop with fun souvenirs (see our Kidstuff and Shopping chapters). Don't miss the Washington Navy Yard's neighboring attractions, including the decommissioned destroyer *Barry* (DD-933), the first marine railway, and a gate designed by Benjamin Latrobe. Museum hours are subject to change. Call in advance to arrange for an escort, a new security precaution. Admission is free. Parking is free and generally plentiful. Eastern Market is the closest Metro station.

The Octagon
1799 New York Ave. NW
Washington, DC
(202) 638-3105
www.archfoundation.org/octagon

History and architecture buffs alike will find plenty of interesting features at this National Historic Landmark, the country's oldest architecture museum. Designed by William Thornton, first architect of the U.S. Capitol, the building served as James and Dolley Madison's temporary home after the British burned the President's House during the War of 1812. In fact Madison signed the war-ending Treaty of Ghent at the Octagon. A five-year, $5 million restoration, which ended in 1996, included repainting rooms in true period hues.

The adjacent icehouse holds a gift shop, and the site's enclosed garden features a vending cart and seating for outdoor dining. Visitors can view furnished period rooms, as well as architecture- and design-related exhibitions that rotate twice a year. The American Architectural Foundation operates the museum, which is open from 10:00 A.M. to 4:00 P.M. Tuesday through Sunday. Tours begin on the hour and half-hour. Admission is $5.00 for adults and $3.00 for students and seniors. Please note that the building isn't elevator-equipped, and therefore is not completely wheelchair accessible. You should be able to find metered on-street parking. Taking Metro to Farragut North or Farragut West will require you to walk a few blocks.

The Phillips Collection
1600 21st St. NW
Washington, DC
(202) 387–2151
www.phillipscollection.org

Renoir's beloved *The Luncheon of the Boating Party* highlights the permanent collection at this intimate art museum. (Read more about it in our Arts chapter.)

Sewall-Belmont House
144 Constitution Ave. NE
Washington, DC
(202) 546–1210
www.natwomanparty.org

Almost lost amid the grandeur of Capitol Hill, this eighteenth-century building now houses the headquarters of the National Woman's Party and contains mementos of the equality movement, including writings and heirlooms belonging to Susan B. Anthony and Alice Paul, the woman who penned the Equal Rights Amendment. The mansion was once the abode of Albert Gallatin, the treasury secretary who masterminded the finances of the $15 million Louisiana Purchase in 1803.

The building also houses the country's first feminist library. Docent-led tours, which include a half-hour film about the suffragist movement, take place at 11:00 A.M., noon, 1:00 and 2:00 P.M. Tuesday through Friday, and at noon, 1:00, 2:00, and 3:00 P.M. Saturday. The tours last approximately an hour and are recommended for ages eight and older. Visit the

gift shop for history books, women's crafts, and unique souvenirs like replica jail door pins. Museum hours are 11:00 A.M. to 3:00 P.M. Tuesday through Friday, noon to 4:00 P.M. Saturday. Admission is free, but donations of $3.00 are recommended.

The nearest Metro stops are Union Station and Capitol South. Wheelchair access is limited.

The Textile Museum
2320 S St. NW
Washington, DC
(202) 667–0441
www.textilemuseum.org

You'll be amazed at the intricate handwork exhibited in this museum's collection of Oriental carpets and other important textiles. (See our Arts chapter for a description.)

United States Holocaust Memorial Museum
100 Raoul Wallenberg Pl. SW
Washington, DC
(202) 488–0400
www.ushmm.org

As compelling as it is disturbing, the U.S. Holocaust Memorial Museum—another recent addition to the city's cultural roster—documents the horrors of the Holocaust through photographs, film, interactive exhibits, and incredible artifacts. Built with private funds and opened in the spring of 1993, the museum occupies a two-acre parcel right next to the Bureau of Engraving and Printing, just off the National Mall. The five-story building, between 14th and 15th Streets, is itself a fascinating architectural statement and tribute to the victims. Due to the graphic nature of some displays, the tour is not recommended for children younger than 11. The museum also houses resource and research facilities and a theater and auditorium for special programs. Grab a light meal in the dairy cafe, open from 8:30 A.M. to 4:30 P.M. The museum shop features books and other Holocaust-related items.

Visitors must obtain tickets to tour the museum's permanent exhibition; they're free, albeit not always easy to come by. Pick them up at the 14th Street entrance, beginning at 10:00 A.M. on the day of your visit or obtain them in advance through Tickets.com (800–400–9373). The museum is open from 10:00 A.M. to 5:30 P.M. daily. The museum is closed on Yom Kippur and Christmas. Parking is scarce, so take Metro to the Smithsonian station, 1 block away.

Washington Dolls' House & Toy Museum
5236 44th St. NW
Washington, DC
(202) 244–0024

This little gem is as popular with adults as it is with children. As you view the exhibits, a tiny world unfolds, tracing the development of homes and domestic life from around the globe—all from a miniature perspective. Enjoy the amazing collection of antique dollhouses, dolls, toys, and games. The two museum shops sell hard-to-find miniatures and charming children's books written by the museum's founder, Flora Gill Jacobs. If the visit is part of a birthday celebration, the little ones can feast on cupcakes and lemonade in a special ice-cream parlor. Your best bet is to book early for parties. The museum is open from 10:00 A.M. to 5:00 P.M. Tuesday through Saturday and from noon to 5:00 P.M. on Sunday. It's closed on Mondays, New Year's Day, Thanksgiving, and Christmas. Admission is $3.00 for adults and $1.00 for children. Friendship Heights is the nearest Metro stop. (See our Kidstuff chapter for more on youngsters' favorites here.)

The Washington Post
1150 15th St. NW
Washington, DC
(202) 334–7969
www.washingtonpost.com

To get the inside scoop on how the news is gathered, disseminated, printed, and distributed, take a tour of this bastion of American journalism. Free guided tours, offered every hour except noon, from 10:00 A.M. to 3:00 P.M. on Mondays (except for federal holidays), are open to adults and children at the fifth-grade level and above. Make reservations in advance.

Neighborhoods

Embassy Row
Along Massachusetts Ave. NW
Washington, D.C.

Nearly 50 of the city's approximately 150 embassies are clustered along this 2-mile stretch of prime real estate, hence the designation Embassy Row. From the grand and ornate to the simple but elegant, the homes make for a wonderful walking tour, especially in the spring and fall. Look (very closely in some cases) for the flag and coat of arms that designate each diplomatic mission. From an architectural perspective some of the more noteworthy embassies include those of Brazil, Japan, Britain, Austria, Pakistan, and Turkey. (See our International Washington chapter for more information.)

Georgetown
M St. and Wisconsin Ave. NW
Washington, DC
(202) 789–7000

A thriving tobacco port and completely independent Maryland community when Washington was established as the Nation's Capital in the late 1700s, Georgetown is the city's oldest and best-known neighborhood and one that's synonymous with wealth, power, and

Insiders' Tip

Legend has it that Washington planner Pierre L'Enfant hated Chief Justice John Jay with such a passion that he intentionally left out the letter J in his layout of alphabetically designated streets.

prestige. Locals and out-of-towners alike come here to stroll the narrow, cobblestone streets; view the elegant homes; and sample the incredible array of nightclubs, bars, art galleries, restaurants, funky shops, and elegant boutiques. Keep an eye out for that precipitous set of steps made famous in a memorable but gruesome scene from *The Exorcist*, the classic devil flick starring Linda Blair.

The nerve center of Georgetown is at M Street and Wisconsin Avenue NW, through the years the spillover site of some spirited post–Super Bowl, New Year's Eve, and Halloween celebrations. Besides those steps we mentioned, prime attractions in this part of town include venerable and beautiful Georgetown University (whose graduates include President Clinton), described in our Education chapter, and C&O Canal National Historic Park, described in our Parks and Recreation chapter.

Amid the noisy drama of M Street lies the Old Stone House, 3051 M Street NW (202–426–6851), built in 1766 and believed to be the oldest building in the District. Step into the backyard and you'll enter another world. A quiet garden, maintained by the National Park Service, overflows with seasonal plants, exotic butterflies, and birds. It's a great place for a brown-bag lunch. When you're finished, take a tour of the historic house that many parapsychologists claim is one of the most haunted buildings in Washington. It's open 9:30 A.M. to 5:00 P.M. daily, except January 1 and December 25. Admission is free.

You'll also find Dumbarton Oaks, at 1703 32nd Street NW, (202–339–6400, www.doaks.org), the aristocratic former home of Mr. and Mrs. Robert Woods Bliss. Now owned by Harvard University, the 16-acre property features a museum with pre-Columbian and Byzantine collections, open 2:00 to 5:00 P.M. Tuesday through Sunday, with free admission. It also features beautifully landscaped gardens, accessible from an R Street entrance, open 2:00 to 6:00 P.M. mid-March through October and 2:00 to 5:00 P.M. November through early March. Admission is $5.00

for adults, and $3.00 for children and seniors. Call the docents' office at (202) 339–6409 for information about tours.

See the priceless collection of Fabergé eggs at Hillwood Museum and Gardens, 4155 Linnean Avenue NW (202–686–5807, 877–HILLWOOD; www.hillwood museum.org). This former home of cereal heiress Marjorie Merriweather Post recently reopened after an extensive renovation. Call in advance to arrange a visit. A reservation requires a refundable deposit of $10.00 per adult, $8.00 per senior age 65 or older, and $5.00 per student younger than 18.

Religious Sites

See our Worship chapter for more information about these and other historic places of worship.

The Basilica of the National Shrine of the Immaculate Conception
4th St. and Michigan Ave. NE
Washington, DC
(202) 526–8300
www.nationalshrine.com

With a lofty bell tower, ornately carved entryway, and vibrantly decorated dome, the country's largest Roman Catholic church takes your breath away even before you go inside. Enter you must, however, to see the many treasures of this Byzantine-Romanesque house of worship. Guided tours take visitors throughout the building to see stained-glass art, mosaics, and sculptures, most of which honor Mary, the Mother of Jesus. Highlights include more than 50 chapels, each designed to express a unique vision of Mary; the world's largest mosaic portrait of Jesus, the Byzantine *Christ in Majesty;* and pillars of different types of marble, symbolizing the universality of the church. Thousands of people turn out for the basilica's special worship services, such as a memorial Mass held for John F. Kennedy Jr., Carolyn Bessette Kennedy, and Lauren Bessette in July 1999.

The building is open from 7:00 A.M. to 6:00 P.M. daily November through March, and from 7:00 A.M. to 7:00 P.M. daily April through October. Free, guided tours, which last 30 minutes to an hour, take place from 9:00 to 11:00 A.M. and from 1:00 to 3:00 P.M. Monday through Saturday, and 1:30 to 4:00 P.M. Sunday. Call in advance to arrange group tours. You also can pick up a brochure for a self-guided tour. Carillon concerts are held on Sunday afternoons.

Visit the gift shop for a variety of Catholic-oriented merchandise. A cafeteria offers breakfast and lunch. Free, on-site parking is available. The nearest Metro stop is Brookland-CUA.

Franciscan Monastery
14th and Quincy Sts. NE
Washington, DC
(202) 526–6800
www.pressroom.com/~franciscan
Guided tours, lasting about 45 minutes, include a look at full-scale replicas of Holy Land shrines such as the Roman Catacombs. This is a beautiful, peaceful enclave that many Washingtonians know nothing about. Tours take place on the hour except at noon from 9:00 A.M. to 4:00 P.M. Monday through Saturday, and from 1:00 to 4:00 P.M. Sundays. Admission is free, with a suggested $1.00 donation. Brookland is the nearest Metro station.

Washington National Cathedral
Massachusetts and Wisconsin Aves. NW
Washington, DC
(202) 537–6200
www.cathedral.org/cathedral
This magnificent Gothic stone church took 83 years to build, and it's filled with unique and stunning art. The cathedral offers a wide assortment of tours on a regular basis. Your best bet is to take a general highlights tour to receive a 30- to 45-minute overview of the building's features, like its more than 200 stained-glass windows, including a Space Window, an abstract tribute to the Apollo 11 mission that contains a moon rock.

The cathedral is open from 10:00 A.M. to 5:00 P.M. Monday through Friday, 10:00 A.M. to 4:30 P.M. Saturday, and 8:00 A.M. to 5:00 P.M. Sunday. Regular tours, beginning

at the west entrance doors, take place from 10:00 to 11:45 A.M. and from 12:45 to 3:15 P.M. Monday through Saturday and from 12:30 to 2:30 P.M. on Sundays. No tours are given on Palm Sunday, Good Friday afternoon, Easter, Thanksgiving, and Christmas. The suggested donation for most tours is $3.00 for adults, and $1.00 for children. The cathedral offers specialized tours and programs like "Tour and Tea." Call for times and costs. (See our Kidstuff and Annual Events chapters for more information about cathedral programs and special events.)

Northern Virginia

Museums and Other Attractions

Alexandria Black History Resource Center
638 N. Alfred St.
Alexandria, VA
(703) 838–4356
ci.alexandria.va.us/oha/bhrc/index.html
For an introduction to the city's rich African American heritage, stop by this center, where exhibits help convey the significance of historical figures and events, while a library next door offers a wealth of information. It's open from 10:00 A.M. to 4:00 P.M. Tuesday through Saturday and 1:00 to 5:00 P.M. Sundays. Admission is free. Braddock Road is the closest Metro stop.

Arlington National Cemetery
Memorial Dr.
Arlington, VA
(703) 692–0931
www.arlingtoncemetery.org
With its sea of white headstones spread across 612 wooded, hilly acres overlooking the capital city, Arlington National Cemetery is perhaps the most famous burial site in the world, and one of Washington's most popular tourist attractions. This is the final resting place for more than 250,000 American military personnel who served in conflicts from the Revolutionary War to the present. Among the

many famous graves are those of President John F. Kennedy and his brother Robert; President William Howard Taft; 12 astronauts, including Mercury's Virgil "Gus" Grissom and those aboard the space shuttle *Challenger*; and prize-fighter Joe Louis.

It's also the site of the Women in Military Service Memorial, the country's first national memorial honoring all women who have served their country in the armed services. Dedicated in October 1997, the memorial at the cemetery's main gateway includes a hall of honor, a 196-seat theater, exhibit space, and details and photos about registered servicewomen.

Also on the cemetery grounds is the Tomb of the Unknowns, where crowds gather to view the somber Changing of the Guard every hour on the hour from October 1 through March 31 and every half-hour during the day and hourly at night from April 1 through September 30. (The tomb made recent headlines with the discovery that the "unknown" bones of a Vietnam soldier buried there actually belong to Air Force First Lieutenant Michael J. Blassie, whose plane was shot down in 1972.)

Majestic Arlington House, Robert E. Lee's former home, sits high on a hill facing the Lincoln Memorial. Arlington House is also where Pierre Charles L'Enfant, the French architect who drafted the original plans for Washington, is buried. (See our Civil War chapter for information about Civil War–related sites.)

Continuous 30-minute Tourmobile tours run daily (except on Christmas) from 8:30 A.M. to 6:30 P.M. April through September and from 9:30 A.M. to 4:30 P.M. October through March. Tours depart from the Arlington Cemetery visitor center, where you'll also find exhibits and a gift shop. Admission to the cemetery is free. Tourmobile tickets cost $4.75, and $2.25 for children ages 3 to 11. The cemetery is open from 8:00 A.M. to 5:00 P.M. October through March and 8:00 A.M. to 7:00 P.M. April through September. It has its own Metro stop.

Carlyle House
121 N. Fairfax St.
Alexandria, VA
(703) 549–2997
www.nvrpa.org/museum.html

One of the first houses built in Alexandria, this nearly 250-year-old replica of a Scottish manor home was the residence of John Carlyle and his wife Sara Fairfax. Among its other uses, the house served in 1755 as the headquarters of General Braddock, leader of the British forces during the French and Indian War. We recommend you take a guided tour of the home and its terraced garden. Hours are from 10:00 A.M. to 4:30 P.M. Tuesday through Saturday and noon to 4:30 P.M. on Sunday. Tours begin every half-hour. Admission is $4.00 for adults, $2.00 for ages 11 to 17, and free for ages 10 and younger.

Christ Church
118 N. Washington Sts.
Alexandria, VA
(703) 549–1450

George Washington and Robert E. Lee both attended this church, which dates to the mid-1700s. It's open from 9:00 A.M. to 4:00 P.M. Monday through Friday, 9:00 A.M. to 4:00 P.M. Saturday, and 2:00 to 4:30 P.M. Sunday. Admission is free, but the church welcomes contributions. (See our Worship chapter for additional information.)

Colvin Run Mill Historic Site
10017 Colvin Run Rd.
Great Falls, VA
(703) 759–2771
www.co.fairfax.va.us/parks/history.htm

Visit this working, water-powered nineteenth-century gristmill on the weekend, and you'll often find special events like

Insiders' Tip
You'll find Washington, D.C.'s central point clearly marked on the basement floor of the United States Capitol.

Civil War encampments, ice-cream making, wood-carving lessons, and outdoor concerts. Stop by the general store for old-fashioned candy, handmade crafts, and fun gift items, as well as a display of old tins, bottles, and utensils. The site is open daily from 11:00 A.M. to 5:00 P.M., except Tuesdays. Mill tours, offered on the hour from 11:00 A.M. to 4:00 P.M., cost $4.00 for adults, $3.00 for students ages 16 and up, and $2.00 for children and seniors. (See our Kidstuff chapter for information about programs for youngsters.)

Gadsby's Tavern Museum
134 N. Royal St.
Alexandria, VA
(703) 838-4242
www.gadsbytavern.org

The social nerve center of colonial Alexandria, Gadsby's is noted as "the finest tavern built in the colonies." Gadsby's was the site of numerous balls, meetings, and political functions. Among the luminaries who unwound here were the Marquis de Lafayette, John Paul Jones, Aaron Burr, George Mason, Francis Scott Key, Henry Clay, and, of course, George Washington. The tavern—now functioning as a museum—has been restored to its colonial condition and is open for tours. The 200-year-old George Washington Birthnight Banquet and Ball is still held here every year and is one of the most prestigious social events in Virginia.

Other special events include dance classes, costumed reenactments, teas for girls and their dolls, and summer camps with colonial themes. The museum is open from 11:00 A.M. to 4:00 P.M. Tuesday through Saturday and from 1:00 to 4:00 P.M. Sunday October through March, and from 10:00 A.M. to 5:00 P.M. Tuesday through Saturday and 1:00 to 5:00 P.M. Sunday April through September. It's closed on Mondays and major holidays, and occasionally during private rentals. Admission is $4.00 for adults, $2.00 for students ages 11 to 17, and free for children ages 10 and younger accompanied by a paying adult. Stop by the adjacent Gadsby's Tavern Restaurant, 138 N. Royal

Street (703-548-1288), for a colonial bite to eat, served by costumed waiters.

George Washington Masonic National Memorial
101 Callahan Dr.
Alexandria, VA
(703) 683-2007
www.gwmemorial.org

Beltway travelers passing Alexandria can't miss this tall granite tower, standing majestically atop a hill just outside of Old Town. Modeled after the ancient lighthouse in Alexandria, Egypt, the familiar landmark was erected by Freemasons throughout the nation to honor their fraternal brother, who served as Worshipful Master of the Alexandria-Washington Lodge No. 22 in 1788 and 1789. (Ironically, the very hill upon which the monument sits could have held the U.S. Capitol, but Washington vetoed the site!)

Visitors see several of Washington's personal and family possessions, portraits and Masonic relics. Among the artifacts displayed in the Replica Lodge Room are the clock that Washington's doctor stopped the moment Washington died and the little silver trowel that Washington used to lay the cornerstone of the U.S. Capitol. A Mason-led tower tour is the only way for visitors to view the nine-story memorial's upper levels, which house more Washington-related displays, Masonic organizations' exhibits, a Masonic library, and a top-floor observation deck. Children especially enjoy the detailed mechanical model of an Imperial Shrine Parade, complete with tinier renditions of those unique tiny Shriners' cars.

The memorial is open from 9:00 A.M. to 4:00 P.M. daily except New Year's Day, Thanksgiving, and Christmas. Visitors can take guided 45-minute tours of the tower and observation deck on the half-hour during the morning and on the hour during the afternoon. Note that the building is only partially wheelchair accessible, and eating, drinking, and smoking are prohibited inside. Parking is free and plentiful, and the King Street Metro station is a short walk. Admission is free, but you're welcome to make a donation.

Gunston Hall Plantation
10709 Gunston Rd.
Lorton, VA
(703) 550–9220
www.gunstonhall.org

George Mason, a framer of the Constitution and the father of the Bill of Rights whose namesake university is also in Fairfax, built this southeastern Fairfax County landmark in 1755. With its period furnishings, formal gardens, and exhibits, Gunston Hall serves as a landmark connection with the region's colonial past. The home is more than just a museum or monument, though. It's also a favorite spot for small meetings, parties, and receptions. Request a schedule of annual events, featuring such seasonal favorites as a kite celebration in March and Christmas programs in December. The plantation is open 9:30 A.M. to 5:00 P.M. daily, except New Year's Day, Thanksgiving, and Christmas. Home tours begin every half-hour. Admission is $7.00, $6.00 for seniors older than age 60 and $3.00 for children ages 6 to 18.

Iwo Jima Statue
U.S. 50 at Arlington National Cemetery
Arlington, VA
(202) 433–4173

Officially known as the U.S. Marine Corps War Memorial, this is the largest bronze statue in the world and depicts the raising of the American flag on Mount Suribachi during World War II. Presented to the nation by members and friends of the Marine Corps, the statue was created by Felix de Weldon, based on the famous photograph by Joe Rosenthal. Nearby, the Netherlands Carillon was a thank-you gift from the Dutch people for America's aid during World War II. In season a gorgeous field of tulips lies at the base of the bell tower. At night the illuminated statue proves a striking sight for passersby.

The Lyceum
201 S. Washington St.
Alexandria, VA
(703) 838–4994
ci.alexandria.va.us/oha/lyceum/index.html

Alexandria's History Museum showcases a permanent collection of city-related artifacts, including locally produced furniture and housewares. Changing exhibits focus on various cultural and historical topics. The museum also hosts special events in its lecture hall. Visit the gift shop for local souvenirs. The Lyceum is open from 10:00 A.M. to 5:00 P.M. Monday through Saturday and from 1:00 to 5:00 P.M. Sunday. It's closed on Thanksgiving, December 24 and 25, and January 1. Admission is free.

Visitors stroll the pastoral grounds of Gunston Hall, the ancestral home of George Mason.

PHOTO: COURTESY OF FAIRFAX COUNTY ECONOMIC DEVELOPMENT AUTHORITY

Mount Vernon
Southern end of the G.W. Memorial Pkwy.
Alexandria, VA
(703) 780–2000
www.mountvernon.org

One look at the view from the green expanse of lawn and you'll see why George Washington chose this site for his gracious riverside plantation, which has become America's most-visited historic house. Washington's final resting place, Mount Vernon offers a wealth of information about the life of the man as well as the turbulent colonial period. Present-day archaeological digs on the site continue to tell us more. Mount Vernon is easily one of the most popular tourist attractions—especially among foreign guests—in all of Metro Washington.

After touring the mansion, sit a spell on the long, white-columned porch, where you can take in the most glorious view of the Potomac. Garden enthusiasts will enjoy walking through the estate's many authentic gardens and looking at original trees from Washington's day. The wonderful *George Washington: Pioneer Farmer* exhibit features a round, 16-sided barn, farm animals, and fields of crops, between the mansion and the Potomac Wharf. Open year-round, the site offers hands-on activities March through November. Mount Vernon features special events throughout the year, including a wreath-laying ceremony for Washington's birthday and candlelight tours during December.

Mount Vernon is open from 8:00 A.M. to 5:00 P.M. April through August; 9:00 A.M. to 5:00 P.M. during March, September, and October; and 9:00 A.M. to 4:00 P.M. November through February. Admission is $9.00 for adults; $8.50 for seniors ages 62 and older, with identification; and $4.50 for children ages 6 through 11. Annual passes and group discounts are available. Visit Mount Vernon's gift shop for colonial-themed merchandise. Visitors can dine at the colonial Mount Vernon Inn or a snack bar at the visitor center.

Oatlands Plantation
On Rte. 15 near Leesburg, VA
(703) 777–3174
www.oatlands.org

About 6 miles south of Leesburg, in Loudoun County, this classic revival home built in 1803 is one of the state's foremost historic plantations. Four acres of formal terraced English gardens accent the grounds and architecture. Oatlands is the site of various events and gatherings throughout the year, including annual plays and a needlework exhibition. It's open from late March through December from 10:00 A.M. to 4:30 P.M. Monday through Saturday, and from 1:00 to 4:30 P.M. Sundays. Admission is $8.00 for adults, $7.00 for seniors, and $1.00 for children younger than age 12.

* The Pentagon
Arlington, VA
(703) 695–1776
www.defenselink.mil/pubs/pentagon/index. html

With $17\frac{1}{2}$ miles of corridors housing more than 23,000 Defense Department employees, the Pentagon remains the largest single-structure office building in the world. Sadly, public tours here are suspended indefinitely following the terrorists' attack of September 11, 2001. Motorists can glimpse reconstruction from the George Washington Memorial Parkway.

Potomac Mills
2700 Potomac Mills Circle
Prince William, VA
(703) 643–1770, (800) VA–MILLS
www.potomacmills.com

Forget the Civil War sites, historic homes, national parks, even Colonial Williamsburg. Incredibly, Potomac Mills, 15 miles south of the Capital Beltway (follow signs from I–95 near Woodbridge) is one of Virginia's top tourist attractions. For shopaholics and bargain seekers in general, the allure is obvious: hundreds of stores, including numerous upscale retailers, offering superb prices on clothing, household goods, appliances, and all manner of other merchandise. It ranks as one of the world's largest outlet malls. When hunger pangs strike, you can choose from more than 20 eateries. (See our Shopping chapter for more on this mall.)

Ramsay House Visitors Center
221 King St.
Alexandria, VA
(703) 838–4200
www.funside.com

Visit this historic house to peek into the life of William Ramsay, the town overseer, census-taker, postmaster, and member of the committee of safety. Ramsay was a close friend of George Washington and hosted the president-elect in his home the last night before the inauguration. You'll also find numerous free pamphlets about local tourist sites, restaurants, and lodgings.

Stabler-Leadbeater Apothecary Shop
105 S. Fairfax St.
Alexandria, VA
(703) 836–3713
www.apothecary.org

From 1792 to 1933 this early pharmacy dispensed medicine to Alexandrians, including loyal customers James Monroe, Robert E. Lee, and George Washington's family. When it closed, it was the second-oldest apothecary shop in the United States and the oldest in Virginia. Today, the shop is a museum exhibiting an array of colonial medical implements and patent medicines. It also contains the most comprehensive collection of apothecary jars in the nation.

It's open from 10:00 A.M. to 4:00 P.M. Monday through Saturday and 1:00 to 5:00 P.M. Sunday. January through March, the museum is closed on Wednesdays. Admission is $2.50 for adults, $2.00 for ages 11 to 17, and free for ages 10 and younger.

Woodlawn Plantation and Frank Lloyd
Wright's Pope-Leighey House
9000 Richmond Hwy.
Alexandria, VA
(703) 780–4000

Another of southern Fairfax County's architectural icons, Woodlawn Plantation was the Georgian estate home of Nellie Custis Lewis, granddaughter of George and Martha Washington. William Thornton, architect of the U.S. Capitol, designed the richly appointed mansion, a virtual neighbor of Mount Vernon. Our

favorite time to visit is during March, when hundreds of handstitched entries in the annual needlework exhibition decorate the rooms. Browse in the gift shop downstairs, and, only during March from 11:30 A.M. to 2:00 P.M., enjoy lunch in the Woodlawn Pub.

The spacious grounds also feature the Pope-Leighey House, designed by Frank Lloyd Wright in 1939. Hours are 10:00 A.M. to 4:00 P.M. daily during March, 10:00 A.M. to 4:00 P.M. Monday through Saturday, and noon to 4:00 P.M. Sunday April through December. Admission to one house is $6.00 for adults and $4.00 for students in kindergarten through 12th grade and seniors ages 65 and older. Admission to both houses is $10.00 for adults, and $7.00 for students and seniors.

Suburban Maryland

Museums and Other Attractions

Bay Bridge
Md. Rt. 50
Anne Arundel/Queen Anne's Counties, MD
(410) 974–0341, (888) 754–0117
www.mdta.state.md.us/facilities/
baybridge.html

Officially, the William Preston Lane Jr. Memorial Bridge, the Bay Bridge, as it's affectionately known, connects Metro Washington with the rural charms of Maryland's Eastern Shore and the Atlantic Coast resorts of the Delmarva Peninsula. The approximately 4.3-mile twin spans offer a spectacular view of the world's largest estuary. Motorists pay a $3.50 toll before heading eastbound.

Beall-Dawson House and the Stonestreet
Medical Museum
111 W. Montgomery Ave.
Rockville, MD
(301) 762–1492
www.montgomeryhistory.org

This authentically restored brick house, dating to 1815 and furnished in the Federal style, is the headquarters of the Montgomery County Historical Society.

The adjacent museum offers fascinating insight into early surgical practices and medical treatments. The site also has a gift shop. Hours are from noon to 4:00 P.M. Tuesday through Sunday. Admission is $3.00 for the general public, and $2.00 for seniors and students older than age six. Admission is free for children ages five and younger and Montgomery County Historical Society members.

Garber Preservation, Restoration and Storage Facility
3904 Old Silver Hill Rd.
Suitland, MD
(202) 357-1400
www.nasm.si.edu/nasm/garber/Garber.html

Surprisingly, few fans of the National Air and Space Museum—the most-visited museum in the world—know about this hidden gem in Prince George's County. This facility, essentially the aeronautical restoration shop for the Smithsonian Institution, houses more aircraft than Air and Space. Inside the multibuilding installation, visitors view actual restoration projects and numerous aircraft, such as a British Hawker Hurricane IIc employed in World War II's Battle of Britain and a Nieuport 28, a French-built airplane flown by American pilots during World War I. You also can see several astronautical artifacts, such as the nose cone from a Jupiter launch vehicle that carried monkeys into space. To take a guided tour, you must make a reservation, recommended at least two weeks in advance.

Tours take place at 10:00 A.M. on weekdays and at 10:00 A.M. and 1:00 P.M. Saturday and Sunday. Take heed of these caveats: Tours last three hours and are not recommended for children younger than age 14. The site has no rest rooms or water fountains, and many buildings lack heating and air-conditioning.

* Goddard Space Flight Center NASA Visitors Center
Soil Conservation Rd., Greenbelt, MD
(301) 286-8981
pao.gsfc.nasa.gov/vc/vc.htm

Visitors to this museum learn about the history of American rocketry, from its humble beginnings on Robert Goddard's Massachusetts farm in 1926 to current research involving the Hubble Space Telescope. For security reasons, public tours are suspended indefinitely. Visit the gift shop for space-related souvenirs. The center is open from 9:00 A.M. to 4:00 P.M. daily. Call for tour information. Parking and admission are free. (See our Kidstuff chapter for information about hands-on activities and model rocketry programs.)

Maryland State House
State Circle, Annapolis, Md.
(410) 974-3400
www.mdarchives.state.md.us/msa/ homepage/html/statehse.html

The beautiful Maryland State House is yet another reason to visit the historic sailing mecca of Annapolis. The focal point of Maryland's government, this is the nation's oldest state house in continuous legislative use. It even served as capitol of the United States for several months in 1783–84 and is the place where George Washington resigned his commission as commander of the Continental Army and where the Treaty of Paris was ratified, ending the Revolutionary War. Be sure not to miss the great exhibits depicting Annapolis during colonial times. The visitor center is open from 9:00 A.M. to 5:00 P.M. Monday through Friday and from 10:00 A.M. to 4:00 P.M. on Saturday and Sunday. Free 25-minute tours take place at 11:00 A.M. and 3:00 P.M. daily.

National Capital Trolley Museum
1313 Bonifant Rd.
Wheaton, MD
(301) 384-6088
www.dctrolley.org

This unique regional attraction features demonstrations and displays of antique electric streetcars from the United States and Europe. There's also an interesting audiovisual show. (See Kidstuff for information about the trolley rides here.) The museum is open from noon to 5:00 P.M. Saturday and Sunday January through November; from 11:00 A.M. to 3:00 P.M. Thursday and Friday during most of the summer; and 10:00 A.M. to 2:00 P.M. Thursday and Friday March 15 to May 15 and October 1 to November 15. It's open from noon to 5:00 P.M. Memorial Day, July Fourth, and Labor Day. It also is open 5:00 to 9:00 P.M. Saturday and Sunday in December during the annual Holly Trolleyfest. It's closed December 3, 24, and 25, and New Year's Day. Admission is free, but trolley rides cost $2.50 for adults and $2.00 for children ages two through seventeen.

* National Institutes of Health
Bldg. 10, 9000 Rockville Pk.
Bethesda, MD
(301) 496-1776
www.nih.gov

NIH is where doctors, scientists, and technicians wage war against some of society's most devastating illnesses and disorders, including cancer, AIDS, heart disease, diabetes, arthritis, and Alzheimer's disease. This sprawling federal research complex— a branch of the U.S. Department of Health and Human Services—is perhaps the nation's preeminent medical resource.

NIH's National Library of Medicine (301-496-6308), is the largest medical library in the world and features a reading room and a department specializing in historic and rare books. The NIH's visitor information center offers a slide show, films, and a "working" lab. Free tours of the grounds are available for walk-in visitors at 11:00 A.M. on Monday, Wednesday, and Friday; special-interest tours can also be arranged. The Visitor Information Center is open from 8:30 P.M. to 4:00 P.M.

National Wildlife Visitor Center
Patuxent Research Refuge
Rte. 197
Laurel, MD
(301) 497-5772
patuxent.fws.gov

There's a wildlife research facility amid the din of Metro Washington? Indeed. This agency of the U.S. Department of the Interior conducts vital investigations involving a variety of endangered species. It's open from 10:00 A.M. to 5:30 P.M. daily,

except December 25. Admission is free. Guided tram tours through the woods are $2.00, $1.00 for seniors older than age 55 and children younger than age 12. (See Kidstuff for more information.)

U.S. Naval Academy
Bordered by King George St. and the Severn River
Annapolis, MD
(410) 263-6933
www.usna.edu

It's hard not to feel exceedingly patriotic when you set foot on the gorgeous grounds of this National Historic Site where naval officers have been trained since 1845. The academy chapel dominates the scene; below the building lies the crypt of John Paul Jones. Other campus highlights include a museum featuring models, swords, and paintings; Bancroft Hall, where the Brigade Noon Formation takes place; numerous monuments dedicated to naval heroes and battles; and Navy-Marine Corps Memorial Stadium. The Armel-Leftwich Visitor Center, 52 King George Street (Gate l), houses a theater, gift shop, and exhibits. Guided tours, with times varying seasonally, are available daily except Thanksgiving, December 25, and January 1. Be prepared to show a photo ID.

Tour Operators

It takes a while to find your way around any new place, so until you get your bearings straight, what better way to get an overview of all the top attractions than to take a professionally guided tour?

The following companies provide regular, scheduled sight-seeing excursions for the general public:

All About Town
519 6th St. NW
Washington, DC
(202) 393-3696

Air-conditioned motor coaches take visitors to monuments, museums, and government and historic sites. Choose from a variety of packages, including Washington by twilight.

Bike the Sites Inc.
3417 Quesada St. NW
Washington, DC
(202) 966–8662
www.bikethesites.com

For a more leisurely way to see Washington, you might consider a bicycle tour of the C&O Canal, Mount Vernon, and other sights in and near the city.

Capitol River Cruises
Washington Harbour
3050 K St. NW at 31st St.
Washington, DC
(301) 460–7447, (800) 405–5511
www.capitolrivercruises.com

The 91-person *Nightingale II*, a riverboat originally built for sight-seeing excursions to Mackinac Island, takes passengers on 50-minute, narrated cruises along the Potomac River from Georgetown to Ronald Reagan Washington National Airport and back.

D.C. Ducks
2640 Reed St. NE
Washington, DC
(202) 832–9800
www.historictours.com/washington/dcducks.htm

Ride in the area's only amphibious touring vehicles—part bus, part boat, they must be seen to be believed.

Doorways to Old Virginia
P.O. Box 20485
Alexandria, VA 22320
(703) 548–0100

Guides attired in colonial costumes, created by company owner Stella Michals, lead candlelit Ghosts and Graveyard walking tours, recommended for ages seven and older and offered on Friday, Saturday, and Sunday nights April through October. The tours chronicle documented eerie happenings in Old Town Alexandria and end in a graveyard! Group tours are available by appointment. Tours last approximately one hour.

Gray Line Worldwide
Gray Line Terminal
Union Station, 50 Massachusetts Ave. NE
Washington, DC
(202) 289–1995
www.grayline.com

This internationally known sight-seeing tour company offers a variety of D.C. tours and packages, including trolley tours and "Washington After Dark" coach tours.

Guided Walking Tours of Washington
9009 Paddock La.
Potomac, MD
(301) 294–9514

Local historian Anthony Pitch leads two-hour walking tours of the Adams Morgan district and Georgetown on Sundays from mid-March through mid-December and by appointment. The guide specializes in "anecdotal history," focusing on homes of famous Washingtonians past and present.

Liberty Helicopter Tours
1724 S. Capitol St. SE
Washington, DC
(202) 484–8484, (800) 927–9279

These pilot-narrated tours provide great views from a different perspective.

Odyssey Cruises
Gangplank Marina
600 Water St. SW
Washington, DC
(888) 741–0282
www.odysseycruises.com

This long, sleek ship is low enough to pass under the 14th Street Bridge, so you get to travel the Potomac River from Georgetown to Old Town Alexandria. Savor an elegant meal and dance to live music as you view the passing sights from the glass atrium dining rooms, or enjoy the fresh air as you take a walk around the quarter-mile deck.

The Old Town Experience
P.O. Box 19898
Alexandria, VA 22320
(703) 836–0694
www.alexandriacity.com/tour/oldtown.htm

Carolyn Cooper, a long-time local resident, leads walking tours of Alexandria's historic district.

Old Town Trolley Tours of Washington
2640 Reed St. NE
Washington, DC
(202) 832–9800
www.historictours.com/washington/
trolley.htm

A lively, old-fashioned trolley with gold lettering will be a big hit with the kids.

Potomac Party Cruises, Inc.
Zero Prince St.
Alexandria, VA
(703) 683–6076
www.dandydinnerboat.com

The *Dandy* offers popular lunch, brunch, and dinner and dancing cruises along the Potomac, from Old Town Alexandria to Georgetown and back. The riverboat is climate-controlled for year-round tours.

Potomac Riverboat Company
Alexandria City Marina
King and Union Sts.
Old Town Alexandria, VA
(703) 548–9000
www.potomacriverboatco.com

The *Matthew Hayes* riverboat offers 90-minute narrated excursions on the Potomac between Alexandria and Georgetown. A 50-minute cruise takes passengers to Mount Vernon, where they can explore George Washington's home before reboarding for the return trip. To learn more about historic Alexandria, take the 40-minute narrated *Admiral Tilp* cruise along the waterfront area. Tours run April through October.

Scandal Tours of Washington
1602 South Springwood Dr.
Silver Spring, MD
(202) 783–7212
www.gnpcomedy.com/scandaltours.htm

Take a humorous look at landmarks involved in Washington scandals, such as Monica Lewinsky-related sites, Gary Hart's town house, and the Watergate. The tours run spring through fall.

Shore Shot
Washington Harbour
31st and K Sts.
Washington, DC
(202) 554–6500
www.shoreshot.com

Breeze past the Washington sights while cruising the *Potomac* aboard a 53-foot speedboat. The 45-minute, narrated tours travel between Georgetown to Boiling Air Force Base.

Spirit Cruises
Pier 4, 6th and Water Sts. SW
Washington, DC
(202) 554–8000
www.spiritofwashington.com

This ship seats 600 people and travels to Alexandria.

Tour D.C.
1912 Glen Ross Rd.
Silver Spring, MD
(301) 588–8999
www.tourdc.com

Two-hour walking tours of lower Georgetown feature interesting historical highlights. (See our Civil War chapter for more information.) Other tours spotlight Embassy Row and Dupont Circle.

Tourmobile Sightseeing
1000 Ohio Dr. SW
Washington, DC
(202) 554–5100
www.tourmobile.com

Free all-day reboarding is offered by this service, which is the only one authorized by the U.S. National Park Service to board and discharge people on the National Mall and in Arlington National Cemetery.

Civil War Sites

Undeniably the most tragic event in our country's history, the Civil War claimed more than 620,000 Americans and shattered the lives of millions of surviving soldiers and families.

For four harsh years the Washington area stood at the epicenter of this tragedy. Even before April 12, 1861, when Confederates fired the first shots on Fort Sumter, South Carolina, the tense capital city found itself in a most precarious location—60 miles south of the Mason-Dixon Line and just 100 miles north of Richmond, the Confederate capital. Across the Potomac River in Virginia, the Stars and Bars flew defiantly from homes and shops easily viewed by Union soldiers. Surrounding Washington on the eastern side of the river lay Maryland, the powerful border state where loyalties shifted from town to town—and often from house to house.

Even residents of the capital city grappled with the loyalty issue. Not surprisingly, many fled to join the Confederate cause, while thousands of other Southern sympathizers remained at home, many taking part in clandestine operations under the nose of the Federal military complex.

The war forever changed the complexion of this once sleepy Southern town. Temporary shelters, office buildings, camps, hospitals, and supply depots cropped up throughout the city. Each day, hundreds of new residents flocked to the District. Housing proved scarce, crime soared, slums grew up in the shadows of the Capitol and the White House, and public services all but disappeared. Tiber Creek, a marshy tributary now covered by Constitution Avenue, was an open sewer. The unsanitary conditions led to a typhoid epidemic that killed thousands of residents, including a young son of President Abraham Lincoln.

Ironically, for much of the war, Washington was a slave-holding city. Only six months before the Emancipation Proclamation became law did the District ban slavery.

If conditions were tough in Washington, then they were simply tortuous in the surrounding countryside of Virginia and Maryland. At the Battle of First Manassas in July 1861, 35,000 Union soldiers under the command of General Irvin McDowell met a Rebel force of 32,000 troops. It was supposed to be an easy Northern victory—so easy that hundreds of Washingtonians rode out to the site 30 miles west of the city to witness the festivities. First Manassas turned out to be anything but a Northern cakewalk. The Confederate army, bolstered by the brave showing of General Thomas Jackson (who earned the nickname "Stonewall" here) crushed the Union advance. By day's end, nearly 900 young men lay dead on the fields of Matthews Hill, Henry Hill, and Chinn Ridge. Ten hours of fierce fighting ended any notion that the war would be settled quickly.

First Manassas sent a shockwave through Washington, which erected forts and gun batteries at a frantic pace, encircling the anxious city that many grew to believe could be overrun by General Robert E. Lee (a native to the area) and his adept Southern army.

Indeed, the South did come close to striking the Union nerve center. At Fort Stevens, in the present-day Rock Creek Park, Confederate General Jubal A. Early led his troops into the District's northern fringes on a balmy July evening in 1864. President Lincoln was among the many spectators who witnessed the attack that the Union eventually repelled.

The Civil War ultimately devastated neighboring Virginia. In Fredericksburg and surrounding Spotsylvania County, just 50 miles south of Washington, four major battles (Fredericksburg, Chancellorsville, The Wilderness, and Spotsylvania Court House) raged

The deadliest clash of the war took place at Antietam, less than 70 miles from Washington, D.C.
PHOTO: MIDDLETON EVANS, COURTESY OF MARYLAND OFFICE OF TOURISM

between 1862 and 1864. Over a patch of land no larger than 500 square miles, some 100,000 Union and Confederate soldiers died—nearly twice the casualties of the Vietnam War. Tens of thousands more casualties would be claimed in the hundreds of skirmishes and battles, including the bloody Battle of Second Manassas (3,300 killed), that took place within a 60-mile radius of Washington. In fact more Americans perished on Virginia's Civil War battlefields than in all other American wars combined.

The single most violent day of the war took place near the rural Maryland hamlet of Sharpsburg, less than 70 miles northwest of the District. Here, on September 17, 1862, at the Battle of Antietam, more than 12,000 Federal troops and 10,000 Confederates died in some of the most gruesome hand-to-hand combat ever witnessed. Never in our history have more Americans been killed in one day.

The point here is not to be macabre or sensational in describing these events, most of which took place at historic sites easily accessible to modern-day Washington. Rather, it is to help put into perspective the full tragedy of the war, which sometimes becomes lost amid the crowds and commercialization that inevitably seize the region's battlefields and shrines during the tourist season.

The rest of this chapter offers a brief look at some of Metro Washington's fascinating Civil War sites. If you're a Civil War buff, you can look forward to a plethora of outings. If you're simply interested in learning a little more about The War Between the States, you'll find the Washington area an excellent instructor.

Those wishing to read more in-depth analyses of the Civil War in Washington, should pick up a copy of *The Insiders' Guide to the Civil War in the Eastern Theater,* by Michael P. Gleason.

If you're a Civil War purist, you may want to join one of the area's many roundtable groups or battle reenactment troupes, clubs that meet regularly at locations around Metro Washington. For more information contact any of the national battlefield parks mentioned.

Washington, D.C.

Abraham Lincoln "Emancipation Group" Statue
Lincoln Park, East Capitol St.
Between 11th and 13th Sts. NE
Washington, DC

Emancipated citizens paid for this $18,000 statue, created by prominent sculptor Thomas Ball and dedicated in 1876. The bronze work depicts the president holding the Emancipation Proclamation as a freed slave kneels at his feet.

Abraham Lincoln Statue
Judiciary Square, NW, Washington, DC

This life-sized marble statue, sculpted by Lot Flannery and dedicated in 1868, depicts Lincoln as a lawyer and statesman.

Admiral David G. Farragut Memorial
Farragut Square
17th and K Sts. NW
Washington, DC

Vinnie Ream Hoxie, the first female sculptor commissioned by the U.S. government, created this 10-foot, standing statue using metal from Farragut's flagship, *Hartford*. The statue's dedication took place in 1881. Farragut, the U.S. Navy's first admiral, captured New Orleans from the Confederates and controlled the lower Mississippi during the war. Hoxie also created the marble statue of Lincoln that stands in the U.S. Capitol's rotunda.

African American Civil War Memorial
U St. and Vermont Ave. NW,
Washington, DC
(202) 667–2667
www.afroamcivilwar.org

Unveiled with great fanfare on July 18, 1998, this memorial honors the 209,145 African American soldiers who fought in Union troops during the Civil War. It's set in the city's historic Shaw neighborhood, named for Robert Gould Shaw, the white colonel who led his 54th Massachusetts Volunteer Infantry in the ill-fated attack on a Confederate fortification depicted in the acclaimed film *Glory*. The Shaw community nearly became the site of a similar memorial in 1888, but Civil War veteran George Washington Williams's proposal failed to garner House support. The site features the *Spirit of Freedom* sculpture by Kentucky artist Ed Hamilton, as well as two curved granite walls bearing the names of the men who fought in the United States Colored Troops.

On the first Saturday of each month throughout spring and fall, the 54th Massachusetts Volunteer Infantry, Company B, of Washington, D.C., performs drills from noon to 1:00 P.M. on the Spirit of Freedom Memorial Plaza. Annual events include a Veterans Day ceremony and wreath laying to mark Martin Luther King Jr.'s birthday.

The accompanying African American Civil War Memorial Freedom Foundation Museum and Visitors Center, 1200 U Street NW, displays artifacts and photos and offers screenings of Civil War videos. Hours for the free museum are 10:00 A.M. to 5:00 P.M. weekdays and 10:00 A.M. to 2:00 P.M. on Saturday.

Take Metro's Green Line to the U Street/African American Civil War Memorial/Cardozo station.

Albert Pike Statue
3rd and D Sts. NW
Washington, DC

One of the most peculiar and controversial statues in Washington, this memorial sculpted by Gaetano Trentanove supposedly was erected to honor the man who headed the Scottish Rite of Freemasonry (the Masons) during the mid- to late-nineteenth century. Little is actually known about Albert Pike, however, other than his role with the Masons and a career that dabbled in poetry, newspaper publishing, and adventuring. Pike also served as a general in the Confederate Army, commanding an Indian Regiment. Consequently, this statue is the only such outdoor fixture in D.C. that honors a Rebel military officer. In recent years protests have called for its removal, but based on precedent, the likelihood of that ever happening is slim. Dedicated in 1901, it moved to its current site in 1977.

**Blair House
165 Pennsylvania Ave. NW,
Washington, DC**

This venerable mansion has served as a guest house for visiting heads of state and other dignitaries since the administration of Franklin D. Roosevelt. Here, Robert E. Lee received the offer to command the Union Army. As we all know, the troubled Virginian turned down the invitation extended by Francis P. Blair, a trusted Lincoln advisor. Four days later, Lee swore allegiance to his beloved Old Dominion and the rest is history. The building is not open to the public.

**The Civil War Preservation Trust
1331 H St. NW, Ste. 1001
Washington, DC
(202) 367–1861, (888) 606–1400
www.civilwar.org**

As most Civil War buffs know, many battlefields remain sites of potential destruction, this time in the form of encroaching development. The Civil War Preservation Trust, a nonprofit organization, works to preserve these hallowed grounds, including sites in Maryland and Virginia. The trust also sponsors tours, and its Civil War Discovery Trail links more than 500 museums, battlefields, cemeteries, historic houses, and other sites in 28 states. Membership is $35 annually.

**Ford's Theatre National Historic Site and The Petersen House
511 10th St. NW
Washington, DC
(202) 426–6924
www.fordstheatre.org**

The night of April 14, 1865, forever changed the face of America. At 8:30 P.M., the Lincolns and their guests, Maj. Henry Reed Rathbone and Clara Harris, arrived at Ford's Theatre to see a performance of the critically acclaimed comedy *Our American Cousin*. Less than two hours later, Confederate activist and actor John Wilkes Booth entered the presidential box, shot Lincoln, then stabbed Rathbone during a struggle as Booth tried to leave. As Booth escaped the city, the president, mortally wounded, was carried across the street to the Petersen House, where the official pronouncement of death came at 7:22 the next morning.

Today, Ford's Theatre, a National Historic Site, is largely restored to the way it looked the night of the assassination. It is still a performing theater, with plays scheduled throughout the year. (See The Arts chapter.) The lower-level museum displays Lincoln memorabilia, featuring some 3,000 items, such as the 44-caliber Derringer Booth used to shoot the president. The exhibit includes information about the conspirators tried for the assassination and details about all 12 of the president's funeral services. Visit the museum's bookstore if you want to read up on the president. At Petersen House (516 10th Street) you can view the room where the president died. The free sites generally are open daily from 9:00 A.M. to 5:00 P.M., and is closed on Christmas. Call ahead though, because the theater also closes during matinees, rehearsals, and special occasions. Ford's is a short walk from three Metro stations: Metro Center (Red and Blue/Orange Lines), Gallery Place (Green and Yellow), and Archives/Navy Memorial (Green and Yellow). You'll find parking at four garages within a couple of blocks of the theater.

**Fort Dupont Park
Minnesota Ave. and Randle Circle SE
Washington, DC
(202) 426–7723
www.nps.gov/nace/ftdupont.htm**

Nestled in the hills of Anacostia, Fort Dupont was one of 68 Union forts and 93 gun batteries that formed a ring around the city. (Visit the National Park Service's Web site at www.nps.gov/rocr/ftcircle/index.html for a detailed map and additional information about the sites. Also see the Rock Creek Park Forts entry in this chapter.) It guarded the vital 11th Street Bridge that linked the southeast neighborhood with the Federal district of Washington. Although it never saw battle, the fort served as an important sanctuary for runaway slaves, many of whom joined D.C.'s growing community of contrabands. The guns and barracks are gone, but the fort's earthworks can still be found in the 376-acre namesake park, which is run by the National Park Service. The Fort Dupont Park Activity Center is open Monday through Friday from 8:00 A.M. to 4:00 P.M., and the park is open dawn to dusk. It's also the site of summer concerts, generally held on Fridays and Saturdays from 7:00 to 11:00 P.M. during July and August. Other park features include an ice-skating rink, basketball and tennis courts, sports fields, picnic areas, community gardens, and environmental education and seasonal programs. Admission is free.

Frederick Douglass National Historic Site
1411 W St. SE
Washington, DC
(202) 426–5960/5961
www.nps.gov/fdro/freddoug.html

Former slave Frederick Douglass became a famed abolitionist, editor, orator, and advisor to Abraham Lincoln. Douglass's 21-room home, Cedar Hill, contains a vast collection of personal items and artifacts from this turbulent period in American history. Visitors watch a 17-minute film at the visitor center, which also houses a statue of Douglass, exhibits of memorabilia, and a gift shop filled with books about Douglass and his causes. U.S. National Park Service rangers lead engaging 30-minute tours of the white brick house. Cedar Hill, a National Historic Site in the southeast neighborhood of Anacostia, affords a stunning view of downtown to the north. The site is open daily mid-April through mid-October from 9:00 A.M. to 5:00 P.M.; mid-October through mid-April from 9:00 A.M. to 4:00 P.M.; and closed New Year's Day, Thanksgiving, and Christmas. Admission is free. Groups of 10 or more must make reservations.

This Victorian house was the residence of African American statesman, orator, and abolitionist Frederick Douglass. PHOTO: COURTESY OF WASHINGTON, DC CONVENTION AND TOURISM CORPORATION

Gen. George B. McClellan Monument
Connecticut Ave. and California St. NW
Washington, DC

This Antietam commander and 1864 Democratic presidential candidate sits atop his horse on a hill overlooking Connecticut Avenue in this bronze statue, sculpted by Frederick MacMonnies and dedicated in 1907.

Gen. John Alexander Logan Statue
Logan Circle, Vermont Ave. at 13th and
P Sts. NW
Washington, DC

Created by sculptor Franklin Simmons and dedicated in 1901, this bronze equestrian work honors Civil War leader and 1884 presidential candidate Logan.

Gen. Philip Sheridan Monument
Sheridan Circle
Massachusetts Ave. and 23rd St. NW
Washington, DC

This elaborate work, sculpted by Gutzon Borglum of Mount Rushmore fame, features the Union commander whose ride from Winchester, Virginia, is immortalized in Thomas Buchanan Read's poem "Sheridan's Ride." Fountains accent the equestrian bronze.

Gen. William Tecumseh Sherman Monument
Sherman Square
15th St. and Pennsylvania Ave. NW
Washington, DC

Between the Treasury Department and the Ellipse is a small park area that contains the mounted statue of General William T. Sherman, the Union commander who almost single-handedly destroyed the Deep South. A fierce soldier, Sherman was also a compassionate man who had sincere sympathies for the South. In fact many of the radical Republicans in the U.S. Senate thought he was too sympathetic, and Sherman found himself ostracized from the inner circles of power after the war.

Gen. Winfield Hancock Scott Memorial
Pennsylvania Ave. at 7th St. NW
Washington, DC

Henry Ellicott's bronze equestrian statue, dedicated in 1896, pays tribute to the general who got the better of Robert E. Lee at the Battle of Gettysburg.

Joe Hooker's Division Site
Below Pennsylvania Ave.
Between 9th and 15th Sts. NW
Washington, DC

Washington's most notorious red-light district cropped up during the Civil War, in an area wedged between Pennsylvania Avenue and the National Mall. Houses of ill-repute sprung up to cater to the growing masses of troops and administrators who were flooding the Northern capital. Along with the soldiers and bordellos came swarms of gamblers, thieves, pimps, and other unsavory characters. As legend has it, General Joseph Hooker, a onetime commander of the Army of the Potomac, took responsibility for rounding up the city's growing legion of prostitutes (some estimates ran as high as 15,000) and confining them to this area that became known as Hooker's Division. Legend also has it that this is where the slang name for prostitutes originated. The once lively district is now the site of the sterile and staid Federal Triangle, a sprawl of government offices and facilities, including the Internal Revenue Service.

Lincoln Memorial
The National Mall at 23rd St. NW
Washington, DC
(202) 426–6841, (202) 426–6895
www.nps.gov/linc/home.htm

The awesome marble shrine to perhaps the nation's greatest president is loaded with symbolism, from the wall-carved inscription of the Gettysburg Address to the 36 Doric columns representing the reunion of the 36 states at the time of Lincoln's death. Perhaps the most poignant symbol associated with the monument, however, is the nearby Arlington Memorial Bridge. The stately bridge connects the Lincoln Memorial with Arlington House, Robert E. Lee's plantation home that overlooks the monument from the Virginia side of the Potomac River. This union suggests not only the healing of the

The Lincoln Memorial honors the Civil War president. PHOTO: COURTESY OF WASHINGTON, DC CONVENTION AND TOURISM CORPORATION

Maj. Gen. James B. McPherson Monument
McPherson Square, Vermont Ave., between 15th and K Sts. NW
Washington, DC

McPherson Square may be best known as a Metro stop, but it's also the location of this equestrian statue, constructed from a captured cannon. Chief engineer for General Ulysses S. Grant, McPherson commanded the army of Tennessee and was killed during skirmishes near Atlanta. Louis Rebisso sculpted the work, which was dedicated in 1876.

Mathew Brady's Photo Studio Site
627 Pennsylvania Ave. NW, Washington, DC

The upper floors of this Pennsylvania Avenue office building once housed the gallery and studio of the nation's most celebrated Civil War photojournalist, Mathew Brady (note the single "t" in his first name, which is often seen spelled the traditional, albeit incorrect, way). Brady's haunting photographs—and those of his colleagues—have done more to unlock the mysteries and nuances of the tragic war than have all subsequent volumes of written documentation. The great and near-great of official Washington, including one of Brady's biggest admirers, President Lincoln, frequented the photographer's studio. The site is not open to the public.

The Old Capitol Prison Site
1st and E. Capitol Sts. NE, Washington, DC

After the British burned the original Capitol in the War of 1812, a temporary building sprung up across the street. The interim structure served a variety of purposes but was probably most famous as a prison for Southern spies and sympathizers, as well as your garden variety of criminals (both Yanks and Rebs), rogues, drunks, con artists, and other suspected misfits.

In 1865 the prison was the site of the hanging of Confederate Capt. Henry Wirz, commander of the Andersonville Prison in Georgia, where more than 13,000 Federal troops died of disease and hunger. The Old Capitol was demolished in 1867. The

nation but a common linkage between two great Americans. Admission is free to the memorial, which is open 24 hours and staffed by park rangers from 8:00 A.M. to midnight daily, except Christmas. (See our Attractions chapter for more information.)

Maj. Gen. George C. Meade Monument
Pennsylvania Ave. and 3rd St. NW
Washington, DC

This marble work, sculpted by Charles A. Grafly and dedicated in 1927, honors the commander of the Army of the Potomac. Meade helped defeat Confederate forces at the Battle of Gettysburg.

Insiders' Tip

The Smithsonian Associates offer frequent Civil War-related lectures, courses, and study tours. Annual resident associate membership— which also entitles you to Smithsonian shop discounts and a subscription to *Smithsonian* magazine—costs $45 for a single, $55 for a double, and $58 for a family. Contact the organization at (202) 357-3030 or Smithsonian Associates, Ripley Center 3077, 1100 Jefferson Drive SW, Washington, DC 20560. visit the Web site at smithsonian associates.si.edu.

Old Capitol Prison site is the present-day U.S. Supreme Court. (See our Attractions chapter for tour information.)

Old Corcoran Art Gallery
17th St. and Pennsylvania Ave. NW
Washington, DC
(202) 357-1300

During the first three years of the war, the Old Corcoran Art Gallery (now the Renwick Gallery) served as the Union's largest supply depot in Washington, dispensing tens of thousands of uniforms, tents, and other kinds of equipment to soldiers fighting in the Virginia countryside. General Montgomery C. Meigs, Army Quartermaster, used the building as his headquarters during the last year of the war. The gallery is open daily except Christmas, 10:00 A.M. to 5:30 P.M. Admission is free. (See The Arts chapter for more information about the Renwick and the current Corcoran Gallery.)

The Peace Monument
Pennsylvania Ave. at 1st St. NW
Washington, DC

This allegorical, 44-foot marble statue and fountain honors U.S. Navy casualties from 1861 to 1865. Franklin Simmons sculpted the work in Rome in 1877.

The Rock Creek Park Forts
Rock Creek Park, 5000 Glover Rd. NW
Washington, DC
(202) 282-1063
www.nps.gov/rocr

In and around Rock Creek Park, Washington's huge and surprisingly pristine urban forest, one can roam the grounds of a handful of strategic Civil War forts that guarded Washington from the Confederates. Fort Stevens, just to the east of the park at 13th and Quakenbos Streets NW, is where General Jubal A. Early's spirited Southern forces squared off against an aggressive Union line in July 1864. Among the battle's many spectators was President Lincoln, who only after much pleading from a Union commander reluctantly retreated to safer ground. It was the first and only battle the president ever witnessed, and it marked the only time a president in office came under direct enemy fire. A half-mile north of the fort, Battleground National Cemetery, 6625 Georgia Avenue NW, contains the graves of 41 Union soldiers who perished while defending the fort. The one-acre cemetery also holds monuments to four units that fought at the fort: 25th New York Volunteer Cavalry, 98th Pennsylvania Volunteers, 122nd New York Volunteers and 150th Ohio National Guard.

Fort Reno, at Belt Road and Chesapeake Street, no longer remains, but you can check out its key vantage point as the highest spot in the District, more than 400 feet above sea level. Fort DeRussey, meanwhile, sits right off a bike path at Oregon Avenue and Military Road NW, in the heart of Rock Creek. To the west of the park, at

Western Avenue and River Road, is Fort Bayard, now a popular picnicking site. The park is open daily during daylight hours. Admission is free. (Check out our Parks and Recreation and Kidstuff chapters for more details about Rock Creek Park features.) Remains of other forts still exist at Fort Slocum Park, bordered by Kansas Avenue, Blair Road, and Milmarson Place NE; Fort Totten Park on Fort Totten Drive, south of Riggs Road; and Battery Kemble Park, bordered by Chain Bridge Road, MacArthur Boulevard, 49th Street, and Nebraska Avenue, NW. Fort Bunker Hill, no longer visible, once stood in a Northeast section now bordered by 14th, Otis, 13th, and Perry Streets, near the current site of a Franciscan monastery.

TOUR D.C.
1912 Glen Ross Rd.
Silver Spring, MD
(301) 588–8999
www.tourdc.com

Although no Civil War battles took place in Georgetown, the city nonetheless stood in the thick of the conflict, as citizens expressed divided loyalties and Union soldiers took over schools, hospitals, and churches. Enthusiastic guide Mary Kay Ricks's 90-minute walking tours of lower Georgetown feature Civil War–related and Underground Railroad sites and stories. Here's where you may learn that the current Gap site once served as a jail for Union Army deserters, or that Confederate spies were executed at Tudor Place. The walks also include highlights from other historical periods. Tours, usually offered at 10:30 A.M. on Saturdays and by appointment for groups, cost $12 per person. Ricks recommends the tours, which cover about 2 miles, for ages older than 12. Call in advance to make reservations and find out where the tour starts. (See our Attractions chapter for other tours of D.C. and vicinity.)

U.S. Patent Office Site
8th and F Sts. NW
Washington, DC
(202) 357–1300

Today, the former U.S. Patent Office houses two of the city's greatest cultural treasures: the Smithsonian American Art Museum and the National Portrait Gallery, including a fascinating selection of Civil War-related artwork. During the war, besides being a place where inventions were inspected, the building served as temporary barracks and as an army hospital. Lincoln held his second inaugural ball here on March 5, 1865, barely a month before the war's end. See The Arts chapter for more about the galleries, which are temporarily closed for renovations.

Ulysses S. Grant Memorial
Union Square, 1st St. NW
Between Pennsylvania and Maryland Aves.
Washington, DC
(202) 426–6841

Sculptor Henry Shrady's memorial to the tireless Union general is one of the most striking images in the District. Dedicated in 1922, it's modeled after a sketch made of Grant by a young soldier from Massachusetts during the aftermath of battle at Virginia's Spotsylvania Court House. The general sits atop his war-horse, Cincinnati, and his penetrating eyes seem to survey the vastness of the National Mall unfolding to the west. The adjacent bronzed images of cavalry troops in action are some of the most moving combat sculptures ever crafted. The memorial—the largest equestrian statue in the country and the second largest in the world—looms in front of the Capitol Reflecting Pool.

The United States Capitol
Capitol Hill, 1st St. between, Independence and Constitution Aves.
Washington, DC
(202) 225–6827
www.aoc.gov/cc/cc_overview.htm

During the Civil War, the Capitol served a variety of roles, including use as a barracks and hospital for Union troops. Capitol architect Thomas Walter, in a letter written to his wife on May 3, 1861, noted that the building housed 4,000 troops "with all their provisions, ammunition and baggage, and the smell is awful. The building is like one grand watercloset."

Perhaps the Capitol's most unusual function during wartime was as a bakery. Believe it or not, during the early months of the war, bakers made some 16,000 loaves of bread each day on the ground floor of the west center building. Wagons stationed in the courtyards waited to carry loaves, passed through windows, to hungry soldiers stationed at the nearby forts that protected Washington. (See our Attractions chapter for tour information.)

Washington Arsenal Site
4th and P Sts. SW
Washington, DC

The Washington Arsenal, the largest such Federal installment of the Civil War, also served as the nearest rail and water shipping point for ammunition headed to the battlefronts in Virginia. Two days after the assassination of President Lincoln, the conspirators who aided John Wilkes Booth were brought to the arsenal's prison and tried. On July 7, 1865, the four condemned, including a woman, Mary Surratt, were hanged here and buried in the adjacent prison yard. Four years later, the bodies were released to their respective families. This is now the site of Fort McNair.

Washington Monument
Constitution Ave. and 15th St. NW
Washington, DC
(202) 426–6841
www.hps.gov/wamo/home.htm

Like just about everything else in Washington, the city's most visible landmark was greatly impacted by the Civil War. Work on the monument, which had begun in 1848, came to an abrupt halt during the war. At that time it stood only 156 feet high, or less than a third of its completed height (555 feet). One can readily see the point where work stopped on the memorial; the masonry patterns of the last two-thirds of the obelisk are different from the original section. Interestingly, former Confederate prisoners were employed to help build the final stretches of the monument, which opened to the public in 1888. (See our Attractions chapter for more information.)

The White House
1600 Pennsylvania Ave. NW
Washington, DC
(202) 456–7041
www.whitehouse.gov

America's most famous home wasn't all that majestic in the years leading up to and during the Civil War. In fact, just two years before the outbreak of the war, sewage from the White House still emptied directly onto the Ellipse (known in those days as the White Lot), the marshy park immediately to the south. Nearby, at the bottom of 17th Street, stood the city dump and a polluted, disease-ridden canal. You may remember that one of Lincoln's sons, Willie, died of typhoid fever and the president himself came down with small pox—no doubt due to the unhealthy surroundings. (See our Attractions chapter for more details.)

Willard's Hotel
1401 Pennsylvania Ave. NW
Washington, DC
(202) 628–9100
washington.interconti.com

Perhaps the grandest of Washington's grand hotels, Willard's (today known as Willard Inter-Continental Washington) was the undisputed social center of the Nation's Capital during the Civil War. Both Lincoln and Grant slept here during their first nights in the city, and Julia Ward Howe, while staying here, penned "The Battle Hymn of the Republic," the spiritual anthem of the North. Ironically, John Wilkes Booth frequented the hotel during the weeks prior to the Lincoln assassination. (See our Accommodations chapter for more about this hotel.)

Northern Virginia

Alexandria

Alexandria National Cemetery
1450 Wilkes St.
Alexandria, VA
(540) 825–0027 (information through Culpeper National Cemetery)
www.interment.net/data/us/va/alexandria/alexannat

At this small military cemetery created by President Abraham Lincoln in 1862, you'll find rows of white tombstones marking the graves of about 3,500 Civil War soldiers.

Confederate Statue
S. Washington and Prince Sts.
Alexandria, VA
(703) 838-4554 (Office of Historic Alexandria)

At the busy intersection of South Washington and Prince Streets stands Alexandria's memorial to its fallen Confederate comrades. The statue is simple enough: a single soldier standing upright and gazing steadfastly toward the south. Several years ago the statue, which stands in the middle of the street, took a tumble when accidentally knocked over by a speeding motorist, an act that set off a minor controversy. Some folks in the community claimed it was a traffic hazard, an insensitive one at that, and should be removed permanently. A legion of powerful city elders sensed an underhanded Yankee plot to rid Alexandria of part of its history. A mended Johnny Reb returned to his original position, a striking reminder that the passions of the Civil War still run deep.

Fort Ward Museum and Historic Site
4301 W. Braddock Rd.
Alexandria, VA
(703) 838-4848
www.ci.alexandria.va.us/oha/fortward

Named after the first Union officer killed in the Civil War, Fort Ward was one of dozens of Union fortifications that suddenly popped up following the North's embarrassing defeat at the Battle of First Manassas, just 30 miles to the west. Armed with 36 guns, it was the fifth-largest fort surrounding the Nation's Capital.

Today, visitors can see much of the same structure as it appeared more than 100 years ago. A self-guided walking tour takes about 45 minutes. The Fort Ward Museum contains an impressive collection of Civil War artifacts and photographs. Each August, the park holds its annual Civil War Living History Day, one of the region's better period reenactment events. The grounds of the 45-acre park are open 9:00 A.M. to sunset daily, and the museum is open 9:00 A.M. to 5:00 P.M. Tuesday through Saturday, noon to 5:00 P.M. Sunday. It's closed Thanksgiving, Christmas, and New Year's Day. Admission is free. Guided tours can be arranged, at least a month in advance, for groups of 10 or more people. Tour admission is free for city residents and $2.00 per adult, $1.00 for children younger than age 12 for other visitors.

Lee-Fendall House Museum and Garden
614 Oronoco St.
Alexandria, VA
(703) 548-1789
www.leefendallhouse.org

Built in 1785 by Philip Richard Fendall, cousin of "Light Horse Harry" Lee, this historic home served as a residence to Lee family members until 1903, with one Civil War–related exception: In 1863 the Union Army took over the property and turned it into a hospital. Today, visitors view the restored home in its 1850–1870 residential appearance.

A popular site for weddings and private parties, the house and gardens also host special holiday events and educational programs. Hours are 10:00 A.M. to 4:00 P.M. Tuesday through Saturday and 1:00 to 4:00 P.M. Sundays. Call ahead on weekends, as the museum often closes on Saturdays and Sundays for special events. Admission for guided tours is $4.00 for

> ## Insiders' Tip
> A Guidebook to Virginia's Historic Markers, published for the Virginia Historic Landmarks Commission, contains descriptions of markers throughout the state. Look for it at local libraries.

adults, $2.00 for ages 11 to 17, and free for ages younger than 11.

The Lyceum
201 South Washington St.
Alexandria, VA
(703) 838–4994
ci.alexandria.va.us/oha/lyceum

Originally a cultural and educational center for the city, the Lyceum served as a hospital for the Union Army in 1861. It now houses changing and permanent exhibitions related to local history, including events during the Civil War years. Hours are 10:00 A.M. to 5:00 P.M. Monday through Saturday, 1:00 to 5:00 P.M. Sundays. The museum also boasts a gift shop and lecture hall, the site of programs and concerts. Admission and parking are free.

Arlington County

Arlington House, the Robert E. Lee Memorial in Arlington National Cemetery
Memorial Dr.
Arlington, VA
(703) 235–1530
www.nps.gov/arho

Perched on a bluff overlooking the Potomac River, Arlington House once was the home of Robert E. Lee. When Lee left to command the Confederate forces, the neo-Classical mansion and its several thousand acres of surrounding property were seized by Federal troops and became the headquarters for the Army of the Potomac. Three Union forts were built on the land, and casualties (both Northern and Southern) from local battles were buried here beginning in June 1864.

Today, the area is known as Arlington National Cemetery and is one of the most visited burial grounds in the world. The house, under ongoing restoration, features original and period furniture, including Lee family heirlooms. From the front steps of the mansion, one can experience perhaps the most spectacular views of Washington. The house is open daily from 9:30 A.M. to 4:30 P.M., closed Christmas and New Year's Day. Admission is free.

Civil War buffs visiting the cemetery should look for the heavily symbolic, $75,000 Confederate Memorial, designed by a Confederate soldier and commis-

Robert E. Lee (1870) and Stonewall Jackson (1851) led Southern forces in the Civil War.
PHOTO: COURTESY OF THE *RICHMOND-TIMES DISPATCH*

sioned by the Daughters of the Confederacy. Other points of interest include Memorial Amphitheater, near the site of a village where 1,100 freed slaves lived after the war; Section 27, where 3,800 former slaves known as "Contrabands" are buried; and the equestrian statue honoring Major General Philip Kearny, killed during Fairfax County's only recorded Civil War battle (see Fairfax City Cemetery listing).

The cemetery is open daily from 8:00 A.M. to 5:00 P.M. October through March and 8:00 A.M. to 7:00 P.M. April through September. Admission is free. (See our Attractions chapter for more information about tours and highlights of this popular tourist site.)

Fairfax City and County

Fairfax City Cemetery
10561 Main St.
Fairfax, VA
(703) 385-8414

A gray granite obelisk marks the graves of 200 unknown soldiers of the Confederacy, including 96 Fairfax County Civil War fatalities. Nearby, a monument close to Fair Oaks Shopping Center on U.S. 50 honors two Union officers, Major General Philip Kearny and General Isaac Stevens, killed during the Battle of Ox Hill, the only documented Civil War battle fought in Fairfax County, on that site.

Fairfax County Public Library
Virginia Room
Fairfax City Regional Library
3915 Chain Bridge Rd.
Fairfax, VA
(703) 246-2123

The Virginia Room contains a variety of resources for people interested in the Civil War, other Virginia history, and genealogy. The library stocks a variety of books and computer materials, including local and church histories, building files, maps, and newspapers. Hours are 10:00 A.M. to 9:00 P.M. Monday through Thursday, 10:00 A.M. to 6:00 P.M. Friday, 10:00 A.M to 5:00 P.M. Saturday, and noon to 6:00 P.M. Sunday. Admission is free.

Fairfax Museum and Visitor Center
10209 Main St., Fairfax, VA
(703) 385-8414, (800) 545-7950
www.ci.fairfax.va.us/cityhistory/
visitorcenter_and_museum.htm

Visit the museum to pick up a "Courting History" brochure, detailing a self-guided walking tour of historic Old Town Fairfax that includes six Civil War–related sites: the Ford Building, Moore House, Dr. William Gunnell House, Fairfax Court House, Joshua Gunnell House, and Marr Monument. The museum itself chronicles local history, including Civil War events, through exhibits and programs. Visitors also can obtain numerous free pamphlets on area attractions. Hours are 9:00 A.M. to 5:00 P.M. daily. Admission is free.

Fairfax Station Railroad Museum
11200 Fairfax Station Rd.
Fairfax Station, VA
(703) 425-9225
www.fairfax-station.org

This small museum, set in a former Fairfax County railway station, features exhibits on the Civil War and the Red Cross and railroad memorabilia. Originally built in the 1850s, the station served as a Union supply base in 1862. Clara Barton attended to many wounded soldiers here, escaping with the last of them before Confederate soldiers burned the original station to the ground. Union troops constructed the station that now stands. The museum hosts a display of N-gauge model railroads every third Sunday, and it occasionally holds special events, such as the annual Civil War Living History Day in October. Public hours are 1:00 to 4:00 P.M. Sundays. A community center and caboose on the site accommodate parties and special gatherings.

Fort Marcy Park
Accessible only from northbound lanes of
George Washington Memorial Pkwy. near
McLean, VA (follow signs)
www.nps.gov/gwmp/home.htm
Fort Marcy, or what remains of it, sits atop Virginia's Prospect Hill, about a mile west of Chain Bridge. The Union earthwork defense compound acted as a buffer for both Chain Bridge, which spans the Potomac, connecting to Northwest Washington, and the vital Chesapeake and Ohio Canal, the main supply link for the wartime capital. During the war, the fort, named for General George McClellan's father-in-law, held 18 guns, including a 10-inch mortar, two 24-pound mortars, and 15 smaller cannons. Today, visitors can view the fort's remaining earthworks and take in dramatic vistas from the grounds, which sit 275 feet above the Potomac.

A morbidly ironic footnote to the history of a place associated with guns and violence: Fort Marcy assumed an unwanted notoriety with the 1993 death of Vincent Foster, a Clinton administration official whose body was found here following an apparent suicide. The park is

---

Insiders' Tip

The Virginia Civil War Trails project features detailed driving maps of more than 250 historic sites, museums, and other tourist attractions throughout the state. Call (888) CIVIL WAR to obtain free brochures.

---

open to the public during daylight hours, and admission is free.

Marr Monument
4000 Chain Bridge Rd.
Fairfax, VA
(703) 385-8414
On the lawn of the Old Fairfax Courthouse, at the intersection of Routes 123 (Chain Bridge Road) and 236, is a stone monument built in 1904 in memory of Capt. John Quincy Marr, the first Confederate officer killed in the Civil War. Marr commanded the Warrenton Rifles when, on the night of June 1, 1861, he perished in a skirmish in Fairfax City with Company B of the Union Second Cavalry. Like all Confederate cannons, those flanking this monument face north.

Loudoun County

Ball's Bluff Regional Park
Ball's Bluff Rd., off Battlefield Pkwy.
off Rt. 15
just north of Leesburg, VA
(703) 737-7800
www.nvrpa.org/ballsbluff.html
The viciously fought Battle of Ball's Bluff (October 21, 1861), won by the South, was an event of significant national importance because it raised serious questions in the U.S. Congress as to how the Civil War should be conducted. The Union suffered heavy casualties, a result of a series of strategic blunders. Shortly after the battle, Congress established the Joint Committee on the Conduct of the War, an organization charged with re-viewing all military procedures and other leadership issues that became politicized through war. The 168-acre site includes a .75-mile loop trail and the second-smallest national cemetery, in which 54 Union soldiers are buried. Interpretive signs tell the story of the battle. The park, gradually becoming surrounded by housing developments, is open to the public during daylight hours.

Free guided tours take place at 11:00 A.M. and 2:00 P.M. Saturdays and 1:00 and 3:00 P.M. Sundays from May through October. Admission is free. The site does not have restrooms or a park office.

John Singleton Mosby Heritage Area Driving Tour
John Singleton Mosby Heritage Area
P.O. Box 1497
Middleburg, VA 20118
(540) 687–6681

This free self-guided driving tour begins at Mt. Zion Church in Aldie, where Confederate officer John Singleton Mosby met with his guerrilla cavalry unit, Mosby's Rangers. The building also served as a Union hospital. The tour continues along scenic U.S. 50 to Paris, where Mosby's Rangers spent a lot of time on the property that now is Sky Meadows State Park (540-592-3556), open from 8:00 A.M. to dusk. The organization sells $17 *Prelude to Gettysburg: The Battles of Aldie, Middleburg and Upperville* audiotapes and $20 maps of the heritage area. The free tour brochure, "Drive Through History," is available through the organization or at area visitor centers.

Loudoun Museum
16 Loudoun St. SW
Leesburg, VA
(703) 777–7427
www.loudounmuseum.org

Featuring exhibits detailing county life from prehistoric Indian times to the present, this museum includes Civil War–related artifacts. Stop here to pick up brochures about self-guided walking tours of Leesburg's quaint historic district and the county's Town of Middleburg, both of which include buildings with Civil War significance.

"A Perfect Sneering Nest of Rebels: Leesburg in the Civil War," $3.50, describes a self-guided walking tour designed by an award-winning local history teacher. Meander through town to sites relating to key events in Leesburg's Civil War involvement. The museum sometimes offers guided tours during the summer. The museum is open from 10:00 A.M. to 5:00 P.M. Monday through Saturday and from 1:00 to 5:00 P.M. Sundays. Admission is $1.00 for adults, 50 cents for children ages 5 to 18, and free for children younger than 5.

Thomas Balch Library
208 W. Market St.
Leesburg, VA
(703) 779–1328
www.leesburgva.org/town_services/ Thomas_balch.cfm

Operated by the town of Leesburg, this local history and genealogy library houses a Civil War collection, including the Official Record on CD-rom. The museum's recent discoveries include a set of unpublished marriage records from 1860 to 1865. Hours are 10:00 A.M. to 5:00 P.M. Mondays, Thursdays, and Fridays; 10:00 A.M. to 8:00 P.M. Tuesdays; 2:00 to 8:00 P.M. Wednesdays; 11:00 A.M. to 4:00 P.M. Saturdays; and 1:00 to 5:00 P.M. Sundays.

The Village of Waterford
Waterford Foundation Inc.
2nd and Main Sts.
Waterford, VA
(540) 882–3018
www.waterfordva.org

This tiny and immaculate hunt country village on Route 662, about 15 minutes northwest of Leesburg, traces its roots to its 1733 founding by Amos Janney, a Quaker who had emigrated from Pennsylvania. By the time of the Civil War, the strongly abolitionist residents supported the Union—not surprisingly a very unpopular stance in Virginia. During the war the village suffered Union harassment because of its location and Confederate harassment because of its Quaker-influenced abolitionist beliefs. As a result of the Confederate backlash, Samuel Means, a resident miller, abandoned his Quaker principles to form the Independent Loudoun Rangers, the only organized troops in Virginia to fight for the Union.

The village's historical organization, the Waterford Foundation, Inc., keeps office hours from 9:00 A.M. to 5:00 P.M. Monday through Friday in the Corner Store. Stop by for brochures, books, and posters. (See our Annual Events chapter for information about the renowned Waterford Homes Tour and Crafts Show.)

Prince William County

Confederate Cemetery
Center St.
Old Town Manassas, VA

Two years after the South's surrender at Appomattox, Confederate veteran W. S. Fewell donated one acre of land in the center of Manassas for a cemetery. A year later, more than 250 Southern soldiers had been reinterred there. The focal point of the cemetery is a red sandstone monument capped by a bronze statue titled *At Rest.*

Manassas Museum
9101 Prince William St.
Manassas, VA
(703) 368–1873
www.manassasmuseum.org

The Manassas Museum (not affiliated with the battlefield park) occupies a modern and spacious building in downtown Manassas. It interprets the history and material culture of the community and the surrounding Northern Virginia Piedmont region. On display here is an array of prehistoric tools, Civil War weapons, and uniforms, railroad artifacts, Victorian costumes, quilts, and photos that collectively tell the story of this part of the Old Dominion. Of special interest is a pair of video programs describing the settlement of the Manassas area and the legacy of the Civil War. Above all, the museum helps one understand why two of the most important battles of the war were fought in this otherwise peaceful community.

Annual special events include commemoration of the museum's February anniversary, two Civil War weekends commemorating the July and August battles, and a Christmas open house on the first Saturday in December. An outdoor summer concert series takes place at 6:30 P.M. every other Saturday from Memorial Day to Labor Day. The museum is open from 10:00 A.M. to 5:00 P.M. Tuesday through Sunday, and is closed Monday, except on federal holidays when it is open during regular hours. It's also closed New Year's Day, Thanksgiving, and Christmas Eve and Day. Admission is $3.00 for adults, $2.00 for children ages 6 through 17 and seniors ages 60 and older. There is no charge for children younger than 6. Admission for groups of 10 or more is $2.00 per person. On Sunday admission is free. Visitors can shop in the museum store without paying admission.

The Manassas Museum System includes six additional sites. The Manassas Industrial School/Jennie Dean Memorial honors former slave Jennie Dean, who in 1893 founded a school for African Americans. The Manassas Railroad Depot houses the Manassas Visitor Center, open daily from 9:00 A.M. to 5:00 P.M.; and a railroad history exhibition, open daily from 10:00 A.M. to 4:00 P.M. Sites slated for restoration include the Mayfield and Cannon Branch Forts, the city's only remaining earthen fortifications; Liberia, a farmhouse used by both sides during the war; and the Candy Factory Arts Center, slated to open during the summer of 2002.

Manassas National Battlefield Park
12521 Lee Hwy.
Manassas, VA
(703) 754–1861 (park headquarters),
(703) 361–1339 (Visitor Center)
www.nps.gov/mana/home.htm

Just 30 miles west of the Nation's Capital, Manassas National Battlefield Park looks much the same as it did in 1861. Several square miles of Virginia countryside have been preserved as a memorial to the two landmark Civil War battles that took place here, the First and Second Battles of Manassas. The fighting claimed more than 4,000 lives and left 30,000 wounded. In recent years developers have had their eyes on parcels of land abutting the park. In one of the more controversial proposals, a prominent builder nearly won approval to construct a shopping mall within eyesight of these hallowed grounds. Fortunately, preservationists had more clout on Capitol Hill than did the developers. Consequently, at least for now, Manassas remains remarkably untouched given its proximity to suburbia.

The beauty of the battlefield goes beyond the rich history and graceful monuments. With more than 5,000 acres, Manassas is a park in every sense of the

Reenactors fight a Civil War battle. PHOTO: COURTESY OF VIRGINIA DIVISION OF TOURISM

word, with miles of horse and hiking trails, interpretive roadside tour markers, and picnic areas. The Stone House, a former tavern and way station that served as a temporary field hospital for Union forces, opens for tours daily during the summer and on weekends during the spring and fall. At the recently renovated visitor center, a 13-minute slide presentation shown on the hour and half-hour, a 5-minute electric map presentation, and a small museum help tell the story of the site's two great battles. A bookstore carries a large selection of Civil War–related reading materials.

Allow at least two to four hours for a visit. Park rangers can provide brochures outlining some of the more interesting walking and driving tours, including a 1-mile, 45-minute walking tour of Henry Hill; and a 12-mile, 90-minute driving tour of the Second Manassas Battlefield. The visitor center is open daily, except Thanksgiving and Christmas, from 8:30 A.M. to 5:00 P.M. (sometimes later during the summer). Grounds are open daily during daylight hours. Admission, good for three days, is $2.00 per person for ages 17 and older and free for visitors younger than age 17. An annual pass, good for family admission, costs $15. No trip to the area should be considered complete without a stop at the Manassas Museum in the neighboring city's Old Town district,

about a 10-minute drive from the battlefield (see the previous listing).

Suburban Maryland

Montgomery County

Cabin John Aqueduct Bridge
Off the Clara Barton Pkwy.
Cabin John, MD

The names of both President Lincoln and Confederate President Jefferson Davis appear together upon a plaque on the Cabin John Aqueduct in Suburban Maryland. The aqueduct, the longest stone arch bridge in the world, was commissioned in the 1850s when Franklin Pierce was president and Jefferson Davis was secretary of war. It was designed to transport water from the Great Falls of the Potomac to Washington. A commemorative marker adorned the bridge abutment on completion. When the Civil War broke out, someone discovered Davis's name and it was quickly removed. Years later, under the presidency of Theodore Roosevelt, a new plaque included the Confederate president. The bridge and the plaque remain to this day.

Clara Barton National Historic Site
5801 Oxford Rd.
Glen Echo, MD
(301) 492–6245
www.nps.gov/clba

Known as the "angel of the battlefield," Clara Barton was one of few women allowed behind the lines by the Union Army. She tended to the thousands of wounded at Antietam, the bloodiest day in American history. She also proved instrumental in helping locate and identify the graves of more than 22,000 Civil War soldiers scattered throughout eastern and southern theaters. Barton perhaps is best known, however, as the founder of the American Red Cross. This house, now a fascinating museum, originally served as a warehouse for Red Cross supplies. After Barton made it her permanent home in 1897, the house grew to 36 rooms and now is considered an important landmark in Victorian design. The site, which visitors view during guided tours, is open daily from 10:00 A.M. to 5:00 P.M. House tours begin every hour on the hour, from 10:00 A.M. to 4:00 P.M. Admission is free. The site is part of Glen Echo Park, which is described in our Kidstuff, The Arts, and Parks and Recreation chapters.

White's Ferry
24801 White's Ferry Rd.
Dickerson, MD
(301) 349-5200

White's Ferry on the Potomac River is just south of White's Ford, the site where Confederate General Jubal A. Early led 13,000 troops across the river into Maryland in July 1864. Early and his troops would eventually make their way into the present-day Rock Creek Park, thus becoming the only Rebel forces to ever come in striking distance of the Nation's Capital. This also is near the site where Robert E. Lee earlier crossed the river en route to his first large-scale invasion of the North. Today, at White's Ferry, you can load your car onto the cable-guided General Jubal A. Early ferry and cross the river into Virginia. It is the only ferryboat still operating on the Potomac and is accessible from both the Maryland and Virginia shores. Docks are 6 miles west of Poolesville on Maryland Highway 107, and 4 miles north of Leesburg, Virginia, on Virginia Route 655 off U.S. 15. The ferry operates daily from 5:00 A.M. to 11:00 P.M. Admission for cars is $3.00 one way, and $5.00 round-trip; admission for pedestrians is 50 cents each way. The boat leaves approximately every 12 minutes, ferrying up to 24 cars across a partially undeveloped, scenic area of the Potomac between Dickerson and Leesburg. The Maryland side boasts a picnic area, convenience store, canoe and boat rentals, and the C&O Canal.

Prince George's County

Fort Washington Park
13551 Fort Washington Rd.
Fort Washington, MD
(301) 763-4600
www.nps.gov/fowa

Gorgeous views of the Potomac and the District in the distance await visitors to the 341-acre national park on the Potomac River. Originally built to guard Washington from the British during the War of 1812, this impressive and fully restored masonry fort was the southern lookout for Union troops during the Civil War. In January 1861, manned by just 40 marines, it was the sole fort protecting the capital. The park offers artillery and firearms demonstrations, generally one Sunday per month, April through November. Visitors can take guided tours upon request. Admission is $4.00 per vehicle and $2.00 per pedestrian. The grounds are open from 8:00 A.M. to dark daily, and the visitor center, which includes a film, exhibit area, and bookstore, is open from 9:00 A.M. to 5:00 P.M. daily April through September, 9:00 A.M. to 4:00 P.M. daily October through March. Torchlight tours—$2.00 per person, free for ages 16 and younger—take place at 8:00 P.M. some Saturdays. Call for advance reservations. The park hosts an annual Evolution of Arms military history program on the last weekend in April.

The Surratt House Museum
9118 Brandywine Rd.
Clinton, MD
(301) 868-1121
www.surratt.org

This unassuming tavern and post office also served as the home of Mary Surratt, who was charged as a conspirator in the Lincoln assassination. On the day Lincoln was shot, Surratt supposedly left a package behind at the tavern. It contained field glasses for the fleeing John Wilkes Booth. As a result of her involvement, Mary Surratt was hanged along with three other conspirators, thus becoming the first woman ever to be executed by the federal government.

The visitor center includes an electric map display of Booth's escape route, exhibits, a gift shop, research library, and special events. The museum is open Thursdays and Fridays from 11:00 A.M. to 3:00 P.M; and Saturdays and Sundays from noon to 4:00 P.M. The last tours begin a half-hour before closing. In February, the museum displays its collection of 100 nineteenth-century Valentines. Admission is $3.00 for adults, $2.00 for seniors ages 55 and older, $1.00 for children ages 5 to 18, and free for children younger than age 5. The museum sponsors 12-hour, $50 bus tours of Booth's escape route during the spring and fall. Call to be placed on the mailing list.

Frederick County

Barbara Fritchie House and Museum
154 W. Patrick St.
Frederick, MD
(301) 698–0630

Forever immortalized in the John Greenleaf Whittier poem bearing her name, Barbara Fritchie was a staunch Union supporter who lived in Frederick, a town of split loyalties during the war. As legend has it, Fritchie proudly flew the Stars and Stripes from her upstairs window as General Stonewall Jackson and his Confederate troops marched in and captured the sleepy Maryland village. Jackson, noting the flag, confronted the 96-year-old patriot about her loyalties. The unfazed Fritchie shouted to the general: "Shoot if you must, this old gray head, but spare your country's flag." Jackson, struck by the woman's determination and bravery, proclaimed: "Who touches a hair on yon gray head dies like a dog."

The house, part of Frederick's large historic district, is filled with Fritchie heirlooms, including a poet's corner dedicated to Whittier's tribute. A visit includes a 12-minute video followed by a self-guided tour. The museum is open from April to October 1, Sunday from 1:00 to 4:00 P.M. and Monday, Thursday, Friday, and Saturday from 10:00 to 4:00 P.M. It's open weekends only during October and November and is closed from December through March, except during Frederick's annual Christmas Candlelight Tour. Admission is $2.00 for adults, $1.50 for seniors 62 and older and children ages 5 to 12, and free for children younger than age 5. Groups of 10 or more are admitted for $1.50 per person. The museum shop stocks Civil War–related items and gifts.

Monocacy National Battlefield
4801 Urbana Pike, off Md. Rte. 355
near Frederick, MD
(301) 662–3515
www.nps.gov/mono

Here, General Lew Wallace's Union forces suffered defeat by the Rebs under General Jubal A. Early, who later went on to attack Washington, D.C., at Fort Stevens (see Rock Creek Park and White's Ferry listings). Wallace probably is best remembered as the author who penned *Ben Hur*. Like Manassas, Antietam, and virtually every Civil War battlefield in the nation, Monocacy has fought off pressure from developers determined to turn the surrounding countryside into condominiums and shopping centers.

Visitors can watch an 8-minute map presentation, complete with lights and sound effects, and use a touch-screen computer to learn intriguing tidbits about local social history of the period. The site also features a half-mile loop trail and a new trail on the historic Worthington Farm, site of the Confederate advance. Visitors also can pick up brochures detailing a self-guided, 4-mile auto tour. Monocacy is open daily from 8:00 A.M. to 4:30 P.M. April through October and Wednesday through Sunday from 8:00 A.M. to 4:30 P.M. the rest of the year, except New Year's Day, Thanksgiving, and Christmas. Admission is free.

Insiders' Tip

Look for Civil War reenactors clad in authentic-looking uniforms at festivals throughout the Washington area. They often set up camps with tents and old-time supplies.

National Museum of Civil War Medicine
48 E. Patrick St.
Frederick, MD
(301) 695–1864
www.civilwarmed.org

This museum, housed in a circa-1832 building used as an embalming station after Antietam, recently completed a space-doubling major renovation. The museum features vignettes depicting the recruiting process, a surgeon's tent, a field hospital, and a fixed-bed hospital. Look for such unusual items as a real Civil War ambulance, wheelchair, and medical instruments. At least twice a month, the museum hosts living history presentations. It also offers Civil War walking tours by appointment only for 10 or more paying adults, for an additional fee.

The museum is open Monday through Saturday from 10:00 A.M. to 5:00 P.M., and Sunday from 11:00 A.M. to 5:00 P.M., except from mid-November to mid-March, when it closes at 4:00 P.M. The museum is closed January 1 and 2, Easter, Thanksgiving, and December 25 and 26. Museum admission is $6.50 for adults; $6.00 for seniors age 61 and older, military personnel, and college students with ID; $4.50 for children ages 10 to 16; and free for children younger than age 10. Don't miss the gift shop, with such items as unique clothespin dolls and tin leech boxes for storing rubber leeches.

The Arts

A rich and diverse arts scene is flourishing in Metro Washington, from repertory theaters and burgeoning artists' colonies to the esteemed National Symphony Orchestra and National Gallery of Art, not to mention such renowned venues as The John F. Kennedy Center for the Performing Arts and Wolf Trap Farm Park, the nation's only national park for the performing arts.

Washington, D.C. offers more museums and public galleries than any other North American city. Visitors come from all over the globe to view the National Gallery's many treasures and once-in-a-lifetime retrospectives. Although the National Gallery alone would be enough to secure our city's reputation as a visual arts center, Washington is also home to such esteemed galleries as the Smithsonian Institution's art museums, the Corcoran, the Phillips Collection, and the National Museum of Women in the Arts.

Up-and-coming visual artists can be found at galleries in such areas as Dupont Circle and Georgetown in D.C., and Old Town Alexandria in Virginia. In the performing arts Washington surpasses both New York and Los Angeles in per capita public performances. Our city has produced more than its fair share of past and present cultural luminaries, especially in the areas of stage, screen, and studio. Among those with ties to the area, whether by birth or stints working or attending school here, are actors Warren Beatty and big sister Shirley MacLaine, Goldie Hawn, Robert Prosky, Sandra Bullock, and Helen Hayes, for whom Washington's equivalent of the Tony Award is named; singers Pearl Bailey, Toni Braxton, Mary Chapin Carpenter, and Roberta Flack; opera stars Placido Domingo and Beverly Sills; jazz legends Duke Ellington and Ella Fitzgerald; guitar virtuoso Danny Gatton; and folk singer Tom Paxton.

No one will ever question the fact that the Washington area moves to a different beat. That includes the literal interpretation. Anchored by the aforementioned Kennedy Center and Wolf Trap, Metro Washington knows no music unfamiliar to its discerning ears. Live-music aficionados new to the Washington area should find nary a dull moment here. Each week, you can uncover at least one major concert that fits your taste or mood, whether it be rock, country, opera, classical, bluegrass, R&B, rap, world beat, or folk.

If all the world's a stage, and if Washington is indeed the nerve center of the globe, then it stands to reason that the Nation's Capital should have a relatively unparalleled theater scene. The truth is, we don't have the equivalent of the Great White Way here. If you want to see the biggest, brightest, and best in American theater and dance, New York's Broadway is only 220 miles away. Broadway touches Washington, however, whether by national touring productions of shows like *Rent* and *Contact* or pre–New York stagings of future Tony winners like *Annie Get Your Gun*.

Metro Washington is one of the most filmed communities in the world, and the city enjoys increasingly close ties to Hollywood. It only seems logical that film stars including John Lithgow, Susan Sarandon, and Jon Voight cut their theatrical teeth at Washington's own Catholic University, whose drama department is among the finest in the nation.

Hollywood has taken a liking to Metro Washington. The Washington area is one of the largest film markets in the nation, rivaling Los Angeles, New York, and Chicago.

This city of monuments and magnificent vistas is also one of the most-filmed locations in the world. Chances are you won't live here long before you spot a movie crew in Georgetown, Capitol Hill, Old Town Alexandria, Annapolis, or along the National Mall.

Recent films, such as *Traffic*, *Hannibal*, and *The Adventures of Rocky and Bullwinkle*, and TV shoes such as *The West Wing* feature Metro Washington as a backdrop.

In this chapter you'll find an overview of Metro Washington's performing arts, galleries, and movie houses. You'll also want to check out our Nightlife chapter for the lowdown on Washington's club scene, where you'll find a wide range of entertainment. Check out our Attractions chapter for profiles of museums and other cultural institutions.

Performing Arts Venues

Washington, D.C.

DAR Constitution Hall
18th and D Sts. NW
Washington, DC
(202) 628–4780
www.dar.org

Near the White House and next to the DAR National Headquarters and Museum, this recently renovated concert hall hosts a variety of musical performances, from classical to pop. Whitney Houston, Britney Spears, the Lincoln Center Jazz Orchestra with Wynton Marsalis, Rick James, Elvis Costello and Burt Bacharach, and the United States Air Force, Army, and Navy bands all have presented shows here. It's been said that Vladimir Horowitz, the legendary pianist, preferred to perform in this classy and surprisingly intimate atmosphere. Avoid parking hassles by taking Metro to Farragut West. (See our Attractions and Kidstuff chapters for information about the neighboring DAR Museum.)

Ford's Theatre
511 10th St. NW
Washington, DC
(202) 347–4833 (box office)
(202) 638–2941 (Ford's Theatre Society)
www.fordstheatre.org

Walk into this theater where John Wilkes Booth assassinated President Abraham Lincoln on April 14, 1865, and you'll view

The restored Ford's Theatre, the site of Abraham Lincoln's assassination in 1865, stages plays the president would have enjoyed. PHOTO: COURTESY OF WASHINGTON, DC CONVENTION AND TOURISM CORPORATION

a room appearing eerily the same as it did on that ill-fated night. The painstaking restoration includes the Presidential Box, adorned with patriotic bunting, gold drapes, and a portrait of George Washington. Nobody's allowed to sit in Lincoln's seat, although many visitors wish they could.

Today, Ford's remains an active and immensely popular theater, a tribute to Lincoln's love for the performing arts. The 699-seat theater each year stages four or five musical revues and plays that otherwise might not find a national showcase, and that Lincoln most likely would have enjoyed. Recent examples include *A Couple of Blaguards,* a two-person Irish comedy, and a new production of *To Kill a Mockingbird.* Annual events include a presidential gala and the holiday staging of Dickens's *A Christmas Carol.* Satirist Mark Russell usually performs during inaugural week.

Ticket prices range from $27 to $43, depending upon the seating area and performance time. Shows start at 7:30 P.M. Tuesday through Saturday, 2:30 P.M. Saturdays and Sundays and 1:00 P.M. weekdays. For tickets call Tickets.com at (703) 218-6500 or (800) 955-5566. Ford's does not offer parking, but you'll find two public lots within a block. The nearest Metrorail stops are Metro Center and Archives-Navy Memorial. For information on touring the theater and its museum, call the National Park Service (202-426-6924), and see our Civil War chapter.

George Washington University's Lisner Auditorium
21st and H Sts. NW
Washington, DC
(202) 994-1500
www.gwu.edu/~lisner

Students aren't the only listeners who flock to Lisner's eclectic lineup, from university concerts, plays, and ballets to international acts like Ondekoza: Demon Drummers of Japan and popular performers like the Pat Metheny Group. The concert hall boasts 1,490 seats, which offer good views but not a lot of legroom. Look for the whimsical hippopotamus statue out front. If you're driving, you may be lucky enough to find on-street parking. Otherwise, opt for the University Garage on I Street between 22nd and 23rd Streets, or take Metrorail's Orange or Blue Line to Foggy Bottom-GWU, just 3 blocks away. Ticket prices vary, but GW students can receive discounts of 20 percent or more by presenting their student IDs at Marvin Center Newsstand, 800 21st Street NW.

The John F. Kennedy Center for the Performing Arts
New Hampshire Ave. at Rock Creek Pkwy.
Washington, DC
(202) 467-4600
www.kennedy-center.org

Sitting majestically along the Potomac just south of Georgetown, this "living memorial" to the nation's 34th president proves even more impressive inside. Even if you don't attend a performance, you'll enjoy strolling through the Grand Foyer and flag-laden Hall of States and Hall of Nations. This unique arts center offers much more than beautiful hallways, however.

Topping the list is the center's recently renovated, 2,500-seat Concert Hall, which reopened in October 1997 to rave reviews of its improved acoustics and groundbreaking, accessible accommodations for disabled patrons. The $13 million worth of changes include such innovations as onstage boxes and lower-priced chorister seats onstage behind the musicians. An adjustable, multipaneled stage canopy enhances sound. Seats feature swing-away arms, and specially designed ramps permit easy wheelchair access. Visit the elegantly decorated Israeli Room on the Box Tier and Chinese Lounge on the Second Tier.

The world-renowned National Symphony Orchestra (202-416-8100), led by conductor Leonard Slatkin, performs in the Concert Hall from September through May. The 18-concert season typically features such guests as pianist Emanuel Ax, violinist Joshua Bell, and the Guarneri String Quartet, and such works as Mozart's Piano Concerto No. 20 in D minor, K. 466; Beethoven's Eroica symphony, and world premieres like Danielpour's Voices of Remembrance.

The Kennedy Center for the Performing Arts sits on the banks of the Potomac River. PHOTO: COURTESY OF THE KENNEDY CENTER FOR THE PERFORMING ARTS

Tickets range in price from $19 to more than $70. Consider a subscription if you plan to attend concerts frequently and want to be assured of the best seats. During the summer the symphony holds a Mozart festival at the center, performs the annual Capitol Fourth concert on the U.S. Capitol's West Lawn, and appears at Wolf Trap Farm Park for several outdoor shows.

The Kennedy Center's 2,318-seat Opera House—how about that 1,735-bulb chandelier?—primarily hosts Broadway productions such as *Annie Get Your Gun* and *Titanic,* as well as several national and international dance troupes. Shows often appear here before their Broadway premieres.

The Eisenhower Theater also showcases large-scale productions, while the Terrace Theater and Theater Lab accommodate smaller shows, like the long-running *Shear Madness,* a comic whodunit set in a beauty salon.

The Kennedy Center also is home to The Washington Opera (202–416–7800), with popular tenor Placido Domingo as its artistic director. A typical season includes seven operas, such as *Rigoletto, Le Cid,* and *Otello.* The recent production of *Le Cid,* which starred Domingo, was the first American staging of the opera in

more than 90 years. Tickets for most shows sell out, so if you plan to attend several performances, you'd be wise to purchase a subscription package. Call (202) 295–2400 or (800) 876–7372. Individual tickets, if you're lucky enough to get them, cost anywhere from $40 to $280, with the less-expensive seats often filled by subscribers.

The center also hosts numerous events sponsored by the 32-year-old Washington Performing Arts Society (202–833–9800), which brings a diverse array of international acts to performance sites throughout Metro Washington. The Washington Ballet (202–362–3606, www.washington ballet.org), presents shows here in the fall, winter, and spring, including such titles as *Carmen, Leaves Are Falling* and *The Young Lions Roar.* The company, founded by Artistic Director Emeritus Mary Day and now led by Artistic Director Septime Webre, also performs *The Nutcracker* annually at the Warner Theatre and George Mason University's Center for the Arts. Individual ticket prices generally range from $20 to $55, depending on the show and its location.

In 1997 Kennedy Center launched a new "Performing Arts for Everyone" initiative, highlighted by daily free concerts at

The Concert Hall at The Kennedy Center for the Performing Arts hosts some of the world's best performances. PHOTO: ROBERT NELSON, COURTESY OF THE KENNEDY CENTER FOR THE PERFORMING ARTS

6:00 P.M. on the Millennium Stage. You don't even need a ticket!

To get a close-up look at the center's many outstanding features, take a free, guided, hour-long tour, offered by the Friends of the Kennedy Center from 10:00 A.M. to 1:00 P.M. Saturdays and Sundays, 10:00 A.M. to 5:00 P.M. weekdays. You don't need reservations, but you can call (202) 416–8340 or TTY (202) 416–8524 for more details. The center boasts three restaurants: the Roof Terrace for elegant dinners, Hors D' Oeuverie for light refreshments, and Encore Cafe for casual dining. Visit the two gift shops, open from 10:00 A.M. to 9:00 P.M., for a variety of performing arts-related merchandise.

The center offers three levels of underground parking, priced at $8.00, but it tends to fill up quickly. Your best bet is to park at the nearby Columbia Plaza Garage, 2400 Virginia Avenue NW. You also can take Metro to the Foggy Bottom-George Washington University station and catch the Kennedy Center Show Shuttle, which operates from 9:45 A.M. to midnight Monday through Saturday, and from noon to midnight on Sunday and holidays.

Don't miss visiting the center during December, when it's all decked out for the holiday season. You'll also find some of the Kennedy Center's most popular programs, like the annual free Messiah Sing-Along (tickets are distributed early in the month—and they go fast!), the Paul Hill Chorale's Christmas Candlelight Concerts, and the Oratorio Society of Washington's Music for Christmas. December also marks the annual gala for recipients of the Kennedy Center Honors, awarded in 2001 to Julie Andrews, Van Cliburn, Quincy Jones, Jack Nicholson, and Luciano Pavarotti. (See our Kidstuff chapter for information about children's shows at the Kennedy Center.)

MCI Center
601 F St. NW
Washington, DC
(202) 432–SEAT
www.mcicenter.com

One of the city's most heralded new additions, the spacious athletic arena also hosts concerts by the likes of Bruce Springsteen, Barry Manilow, Billy Joel, and Alan Jackson. (See our Spectator Sports chapter for a Close-up and complete information on the center and the teams that play here.)

The National Theatre
1321 Pennsylvania Ave. NW
Washington, DC, 20004
(202) 628–6161
(800) 447–7400 (for ticket charges)
www.nationaltheatre.org

The National, the city's oldest theater, has been bringing stage entertainment to Washingtonians since 1835; in fact every president since then, with the exception of Dwight Eisenhower (and we're not sure why), has attended a show here at "The Theatre of Presidents." The National gives the impression of a Broadway theater. Whether you're sitting in the orchestra, mezzanine, or balcony of the 1,676-seat theater, you'll enjoy first-rate acoustics and elegant details like crystal chandeliers.

The National's forte is booking the big musicals such as *Les Miserables; Bring in 'Da Noise, Bring in 'Da Funk; Rent; Chicago;* and *Ragtime.* The theater has played host to several world premieres, including *Showboat* in the 1920s, and, more recently, *Crazy for You* and *Whistle Down the Wind.*

The National also hosts three entertainment series in its second-floor Helen Hayes Gallery. Admission is free, on a first-come, first-serve basis. Send a self-addressed, stamped envelope for a schedule. Saturday Morning at the National features family shows at 9:30 and 11:00 A.M., generally during the fall and mid-January through mid-April. Monday Night at the National showcases various performers at 6:00 and 7:30 P.M. Weekly film screenings highlight the Summer Cinema series.

Arrange a tour, given for groups of 10 or more, by calling (202) 783–6854. You'll view a slide show about the National's history (the theater was rebuilt five times after devastating fires in the 1800s), get a behind-the-scenes look at the theater, and even learn about friendly resident, opening-night ghost John McCullough, an actor reportedly murdered by a fellow performer in the basement.

If you're driving to the theater, you'll find convenient parking right across the street at the Ronald Reagan Building and International Trade Center. (It's a federal building, so don't be alarmed if security guards give your car a once-over.) Several nearby garages, including one right behind the theater, also offer parking, or take Metro to the Metro Center station.

Warner Theater
13th and E Sts. NW
Washington, DC
(202) 783–4000
www.warnertheatre.com

A former vaudeville and movie palace just around the corner from the National, the beautifully restored, gilt- and chandelier-accented Warner now specializes in concerts by the likes of Boz Scaggs and Tom Jones, and Broadway productions such as *Cabaret* with Teri Hatcher. The theater seats 1,850 people. Ticket prices vary according to the event. Parking and Metro opportunities are the same as those for the National.

Northern Virginia

George Mason University's Center for the Arts
Rte. 123 and Braddock Rd.
Fairfax, VA
(703) 993–8877
www.gmu.edu/cfa/

Touted as the "Kennedy Center of Northern Virginia," this showcase for local as well as nationally known acts offers a pleasant alternative for folks who'd rather avoid D.C.'s traffic and parking hassles. We've found this to be one of the area's most comfortable theaters, with roomy seating that affords excellent views and acoustics from both the balcony and orchestra levels. The center continues to attract prominent artists such as Moscow State Radio Symphony and Choruses, Vienna Radio Symphony Orchestra, Canadian Brass, Mark Morris Dance Group, Carnegie Hall Jazz Band, and Irish band Altan. Tickets, ranging in cost from $14 to $76, are available by subscription or individually, with prices varying according to the performance.

The 41-year-old Fairfax Symphony (703–642–7200), Virginia's answer to the National Symphony, performs here with such guest artists as Jean-Pierre Rampal. The center also offers a film series, with tickets priced at just $5.00, at its Cinema at the Johnson Center. The university's resident theatrical company, Theater of the First Amendment, performs critically acclaimed contemporary works, including world premieres like Anna Theresa Cascio's *Crystal*, in a building just behind the center. Inexpensive parking is available at an adjacent parking deck, which connects to the center via a pedestrian bridge.

Patriot Center at George Mason University
4400 University Dr.
Fairfax, VA
(703) 993–3000
www.patriotcenter.com

This 10,000-seat arena hosts a variety of events in addition to the men's and women's Patriots' home basketball games. The center's annual event slate features 25 shows, mostly by nationally known popular performers like Sarah McLachlan and the Barenaked Ladies.

Family programs like *Walt Disney's World on Ice* and *Sesame Street Live* take place several times a year. (See our Spectator Sports chapter for more on the center's sporting events.)

Suburban Maryland

The Prince George's Publick Playhouse for the Performing Arts
5445 Landover Rd.
Cheverly, MD
(301) 277–1710

Better known as Publick Playhouse, this Maryland-National Capital Park and Planning Commission-sponsored, 462-seat entertainment showcase specializes in family concerts and plays by visiting performers and drama troupes, including local community theater. Tickets vary in price according to the event, and discount subscriptions are available.

Strathmore Hall Arts Center
10701 Rockville Pike
North Bethesda, MD
(301) 530–0540
www.strathmore.org

In 1997 this beautiful, circa-1902 mansion underwent a 14-month, $3.2 million renovation and expansion. Originally a well-to-do private residence, Strathmore Hall now serves as an elegant setting for concerts, visual arts, and literary readings.

The Music in the Mansion series, running September through May, features esteemed classical ensembles, instrumental soloists, vocalists, and folk groups. Tickets start at $22 for adults, $19 for seniors age 60 and older, and $12 for children age 18 and younger. Subscriptions offer a discount. Strathmore's popular summer concerts feature jazz and other contemporary acts on Tuesdays, and world beat or classical performances on Thursdays. The free outdoor shows run from 7:30 to 9:15 P.M. Concertgoers can bring their own picnics or purchase food from O'Brien's Barbecue on Tuesdays and La Madeleine French bakery on Thursdays. Top off your dinner with Ben and Jerry's ice cream, available both nights. Parking is $3.00, or walk from the nearby Grosvenor Metro station.

The center also presents monthly concerts by professional musicians in the Friday Morning Music Club. Changing exhibits of visual arts can be seen in the second-floor Gudelsky Gallery Suite, first-floor Invitational Gallery, and along hallways and stairways. Strathmore promotes the literary arts through its Friends of the Library lunchtime lecture series, $15 each or $55 for a four-event series. The Strathmore Library features more than 500 works by Montgomery County residents, as well as a collection of children's books on the arts. It's open from noon to 3:00 P.M. Saturdays. Among the center's other programs are Afternoon Tea at 1:00 P.M. Tuesdays and Wednesdays, with instrumental performances in the Dorothy M. and Maurice C. Shapiro Music Room, at $10 per person; and Art After Hours, featuring performances in the cafe beginning at 9:00 P.M. Wednesdays. The galleries and gift shop are open from 10:00 A.M. to 4:00 P.M. Mondays, Tuesdays, Thursdays, and Fridays; from 10:00 A.M. to 9:00 P.M. on Wednesdays; and from 10:00 A.M. to 3:00 P.M. on Saturdays.

Outdoor Stages

Washington, D.C.

Carter Barron Amphitheatre in Rock Creek Park
4850 Colorado Ave. NW
Washington, DC
(202) 619–7222,
(202) 426–6837 (during summer)
www.nps.gov/rocr/cbarron.htm

In beautiful Rock Creek Park, this popular outdoor stage sponsors an annual summer musical festival, including many top names in jazz, soul, and R&B, Saturday and Sunday nights. The theater seats 3,700. Annual free events include performances of a Shakespearean work by the Shakespeare Theatre, the D.C. Blues Festival, and National Symphony Orchestra concerts. Note that tickets for paid concerts are nonrefundable, rain or shine. Plenty of free parking is available.

RFK Stadium
2400 E. Capitol St. SE
Washington, DC
(202) 547–9077
www.rfkstadium.com

Due east of the Capitol, this 56,000-seat former home of the Washington Redskins and current site of professional soccer games also is used for huge rock concerts and musical events. In October 2001 RFK hosted an all-day benefit for victims of the September 11 attacks. Michael Jackson headlined the all-star event, which also featured such performers as 'N Sync, Bette Midler, Aerosmith, P Diddy, and Destiny's Child. Acoustically, well, RFK is a football stadium, but as a venue for megaconcerts, it plays its role rather well.

Sylvan Theatre
The National Mall
Washington, DC
(202) 426–6839

With the Washington Monument looming in the background, this outdoor theater stages a number of military, Big Band, and pop concerts during warm-weather months.

Northern Virginia

Nissan Pavilion at Stone Ridge
7800 Cellar Door Dr.
Bristow, VA
(703) 754–6400
www.cellardoor.com/npsr

The state-of-the-art, 25,000-seat amphitheater made its debut in June 1995, presenting Metro Washington music fans with yet another attractive warm-weather venue for rock, pop, and country music concerts. It's three times the size of the more prominent Wolf Trap Farm Park (see the following listing) and features two 30-by-40-foot video screens, the largest in any U.S. amphitheater. It also offers a separate sound system just for the lawn. Concerts feature such performers as Shania Twain, Cher, Lauryn Hill, Bob Dylan, Paul Simon, Jimmy Buffet, and James Taylor. It even hosted the Spice Girls during the British lasses' brief heyday. Nissan also holds all-day events, like Farm Aid with Willie Nelson and John Mellencamp and the annual Capital Jazz Festival, held in early June, a veritable who's who of contemporary jazz artists.

Ticket prices range from free (for radio-sponsored festivals and occasional National Symphony shows) to $50. Children 12 and younger are admitted free to some shows, like those given by James Taylor and Aretha Franklin. Give yourself plenty of time to travel, as traffic on I–66 frequently backs up for miles, causing many a frustrated concertgoer to miss out on part of the show. Your best bet is to call the pavilion for alternate directions. As an added convenience, some events offer valet parking.

Wolf Trap Farm Park
1551 Trap Rd.
Vienna, VA
(703) 255–1860
www.wolf-trap.org
This beautiful National Park Service facility, with its open-air Filene Center wooden pavilion and lawn seating, brings to the Virginia suburbs some of the world's leading musical entertainers during the spring and summer. The park's annual summer concert series is virtually free of musical boundaries. Mary Chapin-Carpenter may perform on a Friday night, followed by a Saturday afternoon blues festival, a Sunday journey through Lake Wobegon with Garrison Keillor, and a Monday evening with Peter, Paul, and Mary. Concerts by the National Symphony Orchestra sometimes accompany films: NSO recently performed Holst's *The Planets* while the audience watched NASA footage on a big screen.

Concertgoers often tote elegant picnics, turning the lawn into a patchwork quilt of blankets and baskets. Ticket prices vary, starting at about $14 for some lawn seats. Note that everyone, regardless of age, must have a ticket to enter. Also, be forewarned that rarely does rain drown out a concert: If you have lawn seats during a downpour, prepare to get soaked or pay extra to upgrade your tickets to pavilion seats—if they're still available.

A smaller indoor concert hall just down the road, the intimate Barns of Wolf Trap (703–938–2404), serves primarily as a

Wolf Trap Farm Park's spring and summer concert series draws crowds to enjoy the lawn seating, the open pavilion, and some of the world's leading musical entertainers. PHOTO: COURTESY OF WOLF TRAP FARM PARK

fall-and-winter showplace for folk and acoustic musicians. (See our Kidstuff chapter for information about children's programs at Wolf Trap.)

Suburban Maryland

Merriweather Post Pavilion
10475 Little Patuxent Pkwy.
Columbia, MD
(301) 596–0660
www.mppconcerts.com

In the Howard County planned community of Columbia, a short drive from Montgomery County, Merriweather is Maryland's answer to Wolf Trap. One of the country's pioneer outdoor music halls, Merriweather is one of six locations to receive a 1998 nomination for "Best Large Outdoor Concert Venue" from the concert industry trade magazine *Pollstar*. Its summer rock and pop concert series (harder-edged than Wolf Trap's) attracts enormous crowds from the Washington-Baltimore corridor. The lineup features from 20 to 65 shows, including hot acts like Alanis Morrissette, the Brian Setzer Orchestra, Phish, Barenaked Ladies, and Steely Dan. Boomers also can count on a few old favorites, however, like Rod Stewart, the Allman Brothers Band, and the ever-popular Jimmy Buffet. Admission prices range from about $20 for lawn seats to $40 or more for pavilion tickets.

Theater

Washington, D.C.

Arena Stage
1101 6th St. SW
Washington, DC
(202) 488–3300
www.arenastage.com

Across the street from the Southwest waterfront, the nationally recognized and critically acclaimed Arena Stage presents a mix of classical and contemporary shows, including the provocative works of David Mamet and August Wilson and even occasional musicals like *Sunday in the Park with George*. The three-theater complex has

proven to be a hotbed for emerging talent and previously untried productions and boasts more than 50 Helen Hayes awards—including two in 2001—for its efforts. It's also the first theater outside of New York City to receive a Tony Award for Theatrical Excellence, awarded in 1976. The theater in 1998 hired a new artistic director, Molly D. Smith.

Recent productions ranged from the Washington premiere of Paula Vogel's explicit comedy *Hot 'n' Throbbing* to new productions of such classics as William Gibson's *The Miracle Worker* and Arthur Miller's *All My Sons*. Maurice Hines starred in the musical *Guys and Dolls*. Tickets, available by subscription, range in price singly from $32 to $54. Arrive ticketless 90 to 30 minutes before a show, and you might get lucky: During this time period, most Fichandler and Kreeger performances offer a limited number of half-price tickets. Arena's "fivetwentyfive" program features $10 tickets for patrons between the ages of 5 and 25 with valid IDs. They go fast, but if you call or drop by before 5:25 P.M. the day of the show (or the day before a weekend matinee), you may be able to get your hands on a couple. Call (202) 488-3300 for further details. The theater seats 800 in its Fichlandler theater in the round, and 500 in the Kreeger. A third stage, the Old Vat, features works by visiting troupes. Free, on-street parking usually is easy to find in the neighborhood. Disabled patrons can park in the theater's lot. Waterfront is the closest Metro station.

The Folger Shakespeare Library
201 E. Capitol St. NW
Washington, DC
(202) 544–4600
www.folger.edu

If you're a fan of the master British playwright, get thee to the Folger, where you can watch innovative productions of the Bard's plays and other works presented by visiting troupes. The intimate wooden theater on Capitol Hill, modeled after a true Shakespearean stage, seats 250 people. Expect shows like the recent production of *Hamlet* directed by 1998 Helen Hayes winner Joe Banner and also featuring the talents of 1999 Scenic Design winner Tony Cisek and 1998 Sound Design winner Scott Burgess.

Theater is just the tip of the arts iceberg here, however. The library itself, open only by appointment to scholars, features the largest collections of early editions of Shakespeare. The public can visit the reading rooms annually during Shakespeare's Birthday Open House in April (see Annual Events). The Folger holds rotating exhibits on period topics such as old-fashioned remedies. The PEN/Faulkner Novel Reading Series features nominees for the nation's largest juried fiction award, and a poetry series includes poets of national fame. The library also sponsors family programs on such topics as "Exploring Shakespeare's Plays." The Folger Consort Group, meanwhile, presents a slate of concerts of medieval, Renaissance, and baroque music.

Admission is free. Public tours take place at 11:00 A.M. Monday through Friday and 11:00 A.M. and 1:00 P.M. Saturdays, and tours of the Elizabethan Herbal Knot Garden take place at 10:00 and 11:00 A.M. every third Saturday from April through October. Shakespeare etc., the library's gift shop, sells Folger editions of Shakespeare's plays and other merchandise related to the Bard. The building is open from 10:00 A.M. to 4:00 P.M. Monday through Saturday, and is closed on federal holidays. On-street parking is available,

and the nearest Metro stations are Capitol South and Union Station.

GALA Hispanic Theatre
Warehouse Theatre
1021 7th St. NW
Washington, DC
(202) 234–7174
www.galatheatre.org

The city's only Spanish-language theater offers both classic and contemporary plays by Spanish and Latin American playwrights, including some premieres. Hugo Medrano is the artistic director.

¿No habla español? Not to worry: You can hear a simultaneous English translation through a headset. Tickets cost $27, with discounts available for seniors, children, and groups of 10 or more. The theater also sometimes features community nights, with greatly reduced ticket prices.

The Shakespeare Theatre
450 7th St. NW
Washington, DC
(202) 547–1122
shakespearedc.org

Buy your tickets early for productions of this critically acclaimed theater company, which specializes in Shakespearean and other classic drama by the likes of Ibsen and Williams. The company performs five main-stage plays annually, under the artistic direction of Michael Kahn, a five-time Helen Hayes Award recipient. Recent productons have featured such plays as *The Country Wife, Camino Real,* and a surreal version of *Twelfth Night* attended by then-President Clinton and his family.

Shows such as *Othello,* featuring Patrick Stewart in the title role, sell out quickly, with just $10 standing-room-only seats available at the last minute. (SRO tickets are available one hour before sold-out shows for cash only, with a limit of two per person.) Regular tickets, if you're lucky enough to get them, range in price from $14.50 to $64.

In a revitalized section of downtown near the National Gallery of Art, the 449-seat theater is home to Washington's resident Shakespeare company. It's housed at the Lansburgh, a former department store building that is a longtime Washington icon. Parking is available on-site for $10 in a garage accessible from 8th Street. The nearest Metro Stations are Gallery Place-Chinatown and Archives-Navy Memorial. The theater also presents two weeks of free performances of a Shakespearean play each June at Carter Barron Amphitheatre in Rock Creek Park.

Source Theatre Company
1835 14th St. NW
Washington, DC
(202) 462-1073
www.sourcetheatre.org

This innovative, 25-year-old theater company stages new plays and musicals, as well as reinterpretations of classics like *The Cherry Orchard*. Joe Banno is artistic director. The 101-seat theater's month-long, midsummer Washington Theatre Festival showcases 70 full-length plays and one-acts written primarily by local playwrights.

Tickets are $20 to $25 for main stage productions, $15 for festival performances. Parking is available at an attended lot at 1914 14th Street. If you prefer to take Metro, the U Street/Cardozo station is 1½ blocks away.

The Studio Theatre
1333 P St. NW
Washington, DC
(202) 332-3300
www.studiotheatre.org

This 22-year-old regional theater strives to combine quality and affordability in its broad range of productions. With two 200-seat theater spaces, it offers an intimate setting for plays like Athol Fugard's *Master Harold and the Boys* and Harold Pinter's *Betrayal*. Joy Zinoman is founder and artistic director of the theater, which produces five to six plays annually on its main stage. The Studio Theatre Acting Conservatory offers professional instruction, and Secondstage features works by emerging playwrights. Ticket prices range from $19.50 to $36.50. Limited free parking is available at a store lot at 15th and P Streets. The nearest Metrorail station is Dupont Circle.

Woolly Mammoth Theatre Company
917 M St. NW
Washington, DC
(202) 393-3939
www.woollymammoth.net

This cutting-edge theater specializes in world and national premieres, including recent offerings such as Regina Porter's *Man, Woman, Dinosaur* and *Dead Funny* by Terry Johnson. Howard Shawlwitz is artistic director. Productions take place on various stages. Tickets generally cost from $10 to $30, but each show also features two "pay what you can" previews. The theater also offers a variety of acting classes at $260 for eight weeks.

Northern Virginia

Le Neon Theatre
The Rosslyn Spectrum
1611 N. Kent St.
Rosslyn, VA
(703) 243-NEON
www.leneon.org

Critically acclaimed for its creative, visually interesting productions, Le Neon stages French plays in English, such as *Cyrano de Bergerac* and *Les Princesses*. Regular ticket prices range from $19 to $25, with discounts available for students, seniors, and season pass holders. Park in the free garage or take Metro to the Rosslyn station.

Signature Theatre
3806 S. Four Mile Run Dr.
Arlington, VA
(703) 820-9771, (703) 218-6500 (box office)
www.sig-online.org

This highly acclaimed 12-year-old company performs in an intimate, 136-seat black-box theater, a mere six-minute drive from the Kennedy Center. Signature, under the artistic direction of Eric D. Schaeffer, is well regarded for its productions of Sondheim shows and other musical theater revivals, as well as new plays. It has garnered 100 Helen Hayes nominations and 28 Helen Hayes Awards, including six in 1999, and twice been reviewed by *The New York Times*. The company performs three musicals and two plays annually, including such productions as *Side Show* and the world premiere of *Available Light*. Single-show tickets are $28 to $30, but nonsubscribers often find that performances sell out early. Free, on-street parking is available.

The company also holds *STAGES*, a series of free public readings of new plays at 7:30 P.M. on most Mondays. Signature also offers a drama education program for high school students.

Suburban Maryland

Olney Theatre Center for the Arts
2001 Olney-Sandy Spring Rd.
Olney, MD
(301) 924-3400
www.olneytheatre.org

Suburban Maryland's best-known playhouse, this nonprofit, professional theater in the Montgomery County countryside is a staple for quality theater. Expect solid productions of favorites the likes of *Death of a Salesman* and *Peter Pan*. Ticket prices range from $25 to $34 for adults, with discounts for students and seniors. Shows take place Tuesday through Sunday and include matinee performances on Thursdays and weekends.

The center also houses the country's oldest theatrical touring company, the 52-year-old National Players; the Potomac Theatre Project, which specializes in experimental works; school performances; acting workshops; and a free Summer Shakespeare production. In the midst of a $12 million expansion, the center is poised to become one of the region's premiere performing arts sites.

The suburban location offers a welcome bonus: lots of free, on-site parking!

Round House Theatre
12210 Bushey Dr.
Silver Spring, MD
(301) 933-1644
www.round-house.org

Celebrating its 24th season, this Montgomery County repertory company specializes in contemporary works and new translations of classics such as *The Glass Menagerie* and *The Fantasticks*. The 218-seat

theater presents four to six shows annually, under the artistic direction of Jerry Whiddon. Tickets range in price from $10 (for ages younger than 30) to $31.

The theater also conducts classes for adults and children and participates in a school outreach program. Free, on-site parking is available.

Major Galleries and Museums

Washington, D.C.

Arthur M. Sackler Gallery
1050 Independence Ave. SW
Washington, DC
(202) 357-2700
www.si.edu/asis

Distinctively international, the Sackler Gallery features a permanent collection of masterpieces of Asian and Near Eastern art that spans from the beginning of civilization to the present. Works include jades, bronzes, lacquerware, sculpture, paintings, and furniture. Many of the exhibits are on loan from various sources, while nearly 1,000 are gifts from museum namesake Dr. Arthur M. Sackler. This Smithsonian museum, which opened in 1987, connects underground with the neighboring Freer. The museum also houses a comprehensive research library and hosts numerous public programs. Admission is free, and it's open from 10:00 A.M. to 5:30 P.M. daily, except December 25. The museum is close to the L'Enfant Plaza and Smithsonian Metro stations. (See the Kidstuff chapter for details on family programs.)

Corcoran Gallery of Art
500 17th St. NW
Washington, DC
(202) 639-1700
www.corcoran.org/museum

Of all the fine arts showcases that the nation's capital has to offer, the Corcoran ranks as the largest and oldest private gallery. It boasts an amazing selection of American paintings and sculpture and a smaller assortment of European pieces. It also hosts numerous special solo and group exhibitions, featuring a wide array of works by local, national, and international artists. Some shows feature students of the Corcoran School of Art, the city's sole professional school of art and design.

Recent exhibitions included, among others, the enormously popular *Norman Rockwell: Pictures for the American People.*

The gallery also hosts frequent concerts, lectures, and family programs (see the Kidstuff chapter). Visit the gift shop and cafe, which features a popular brunch on Sundays. The Corcoran is open from 10:00 A.M. to 5:00 P.M. Friday through Monday and Wednesday, and 10:00 A.M. to 9:00 P.M. on Thursday. Admission is $5.00 for adults, $3.00 for students and seniors, $1.00 for students ages 13 to 18, and $8.00 per family. The nearest Metro stations are Farragut West (17th Street exit) and Farragut North (K Street exit).

Freer Gallery of Art
Jefferson Dr. at 12th St. SW
Washington, DC
(202) 357-2700, (202) 357-1729 TDD
www.si.edu/asia

An extensive renovation several years ago did wonders for the Freer Gallery of Art, which showcases a world-renowned collection of Asian works such as Chinese paintings, Japanese screens and Egyptian glass, and nineteenth- and early-twentieth-century American art by painters such as John Singer Sargent and James McNeill Whistler. The granite and marble building, one of the Smithsonian Institution's museums on the National Mall, opened in 1923. The undisputed highlight is Whistler's gorgeous Peacock Room, a lavish dining room designed by the artist for Frederick R. Leyland during the nineteenth century.

The museum regularly hosts special events like concerts and films; pick up a schedule or call Dial-a-Museum, (202) 357-2020, for information about upcoming programs here and at other Smithsonian museums. Tours of special exhibitions usually take place at 11:30 A.M. daily, while highlights tours begin at 12:30 P.M. Museum hours are 10:00 A.M. to 5:30 P.M.

daily except December 25. Admission is free. Your best bet is to take Metro to the Smithsonian station, practically right outside the museum's door. (See the Kidstuff chapter for information about family programs.)

Hirshhorn Museum and Sculpture Garden
7th St. and Independence Ave. SW
Washington, DC
(202) 357-2700
hirshhorn.si.edu

This striking doughnut-shaped building is yet another hard-to-miss Smithsonian landmark along the National Mall. The Hirshhorn, established in 1974, specializes in modern art, including nineteenth- and twentieth-century paintings and sculpture by such greats as de Kooning, Pollock, and Rothko.

Adjoining the building and just to the north, the idyllic Sunken Sculpture Garden features works by the likes of Matisse, Moore, and Rodin. Like all Smithsonian museums, the Hirshhorn offers special programs such as film screenings and lectures. Call Dial-a-Museum at (202) 357-2020. Take a free, walk-in tour, offered at 10:30 A.M. and noon daily except

Insiders' Tip

You'll find some of Washington's most intriguing artwork in the city's historic houses of worship. See our Attractions and Worship chapters for more about the stained-glass windows at Washington National Cathedral and mosaics at the Basilica of the National Shrine of the Immaculate Conception.

holidays and also at 2:00 P.M. on Saturdays and Sundays. Sculpture Garden tours take place at 12:15 P.M. Monday through Saturday, May through October. Hours are 10:00 A.M. to 5:30 P.M. daily except December 25. The museum is a short walk from the L'Enfant Plaza or Smithsonian Metro stops. (Our Kidstuff chapter describes family activities here.)

National Gallery of Art
4th St. and Constitution Ave. NW
Washington, DC
(202) 737–4215
www.nga.gov

The past few years have proven abundantly kind to the National Gallery of Art. First, record numbers of visitors queued clear around the building nearly every day from early October of 1998 to January 1, 1999, just to see Van Gogh's *Van Goghs: Masterpieces from the Van Gogh Museum.* The exhibition featured 70 paintings by the Dutch artist. When National Gallery benefactor Paul Mellon died at the age of 91, he left nearly 200 works of art to the gallery—on top of more than 900 pieces he donated during his lifetime!

As the icing on the cake, the gallery in May 1999 opened a 6.1-acre Sculpture Garden at 7th Street and Constitution Avenue NW, next to the West Building. Beautifully landscaped with 35 native species of trees, shrubs, and other plants, the garden features 17 modern sculptures and a central fountain/ice rink. A pavilion includes rest rooms and a cafe.

Visitors enjoy strolling curving pathways to view such works as Barry Flanagan's *Thinker on a Rock,* a pensive hare who serves as a whimsical homage to Rodin's familiar sculpture. Roy Lichtenstein's *House I* looks like a cartoon abode come to life. *Typewriter Eraser, Scale X* by Claes Oldenburg and Coosje van Bruggen resembles a giant-sized rolling eraser, complete with curved bristles. The garden, a gift of the Morris and Gwendolyn Cafritz Foundation, also contains sculptures by such artists as Alexander Calder, Louise Bourgeois, Joan Miró, and David Smith.

Actually two buildings, the National Gallery of Art is one of the world's preeminent cultural attractions, housing a collection vast and rich enough to command repeated visits. Created in 1937 by a joint resolution of Congress, the gallery grew from the bequest of prominent financier Andrew Mellon (Paul Mellon's father) and opened in 1941. You'll not find a better cultural bargain anywhere: Admission is always free.

The gallery's magnitude and diversity of exhibitions can make a visit daunting, especially for the first-time tourist. We recommend starting at the Micro Gallery, conveniently located off the West Building's main entrance off the National Mall. Here, you can preview more than 1,700 works on an interactive computer screen and design a personalized tour, complete with a map, of art you'd especially like to see. Search for works categorized according to artists, subjects, or time periods, and learn more about the artists' backgrounds.

The original West Building features some of the best in American and European painting, sculpture, and graphic arts from the thirteenth through nineteenth centuries, including works by Botticelli, Raphael, and Rembrandt, and the only da Vinci painting on exhibit outside Europe. The popular impressionism collection includes famous works by Renoir, Monet, Manet, Cassatt, Pissaro, and others. You'll also see well-known American works like Gilbert Stuart's presidential portraits. The East Building, designed by I. M. Pei and completed in 1978, showcases modern art, including a giant Calder mobile. This building also hosts many of the museum's major exhibitions, such as recent shows featuring retrospectives of works by Vermeer, Cassatt, Picasso, Whistler, Escher, and American landscape artist Thomas Moran.

A dramatic fountain- and skylight-enhanced underground, automated walkway connects the two buildings. Here you'll also find informal dining and a great gift shop featuring beautiful books and postcards and reasonably priced, framing-quality prints. Another gift shop, featuring an even more extensive selection of prints and postcards, is on the West Building's ground floor. Other dining options include the Garden Cafe in the West Building and a coffee bar in the East

Building. Call (202) 216-5966 for restaurant information and (202) 842-6466 for gift shop details.

The museum holds numerous special programs, most of which are free of charge. Obtain information by calling (202) 737-4215, or you can request a free monthly calendar of events by calling (202) 842-6662. A Sunday evening concert series (202-842-6941), features free performances by the National Gallery Orchestra at 7:00 P.M. on most Sundays, October through June. Arrive at the West Garden Court as early as 6:00 P.M.; admission is first-come, first-served. The East Building Auditorium offers free screenings of art films on weekends and some weekdays. Admission is also on a first-come, first-served basis. Call (202) 842-6799 for a schedule. (See our Kidstuff chapter for a description of family-oriented features.)

Enhance your visit with a free, guided tour of the West or East Buildings, or the Italian Renaissance, Nineteenth Century French, and American collections. Dates and times are subject to change, so visit an information desk to find out about the current schedule.

You can rent audiotours in the Rotunda, at $4.00 for adults, and $3.50 for seniors and students.

The National Gallery of Art and Sculpture Garden hours are 10:00 A.M. to 5:00 P.M. Monday through Saturday, and 11:00 A.M. to 6:00 P.M. Sundays. Take Metro to the Judiciary Square, Archives, or Smithsonian stations.

National Museum of African Art
950 Independence Ave. SW
Washington, DC
(202) 357-2700
www.nmafa.si.edu

This is a fascinating highlight on any Smithsonian tour if only for one reason: It's the one national museum dedicated solely to the collection, study, and exhibition of the art and culture of Africa. Established in 1987, it's also one of the Smithsonian's newest and most modern-looking museums. The gallery's permanent exhibitions include *Images of Power and Identity*, featuring visual arts from south of the Sahara; aesthetic, everyday African objects such as chairs, snuff containers, and drinking horns; and treasures from the ancient city of Benin. Visit the

The National Museum of African Art is one of the Smithsonian museums on the National Mall.
PHOTO: FRANK KHOURY, COURTESY OF NATIONAL MUSEUM OF AFRICAN ART

The National Museum of African Art displays many colorful masks, such as this beautiful example from Zaire. PHOTO: FRANK KHOURY, COURTESY OF NATIONAL MUSEUM OF AFRICAN ART

museum's gift shop for hard-to-find art objects and books. The museum is open from 10:00 A.M. to 5:30 P.M. daily, except on December 25. It's close to the Smithsonian Metro station. (See Kidstuff for information on family activities.)

National Museum of Women in the Arts
1250 New York Ave. NW
Washington, DC
(202) 783–5000
www.nmwa.org

Four centuries of works by women artists, including O'Keeffe, Cassatt, and Le Brun, highlight this exquisite museum, the first of its kind. Recent special exhibitions have featured works with a travel theme, sculptures by Nancy du Pont Reynolds, sixteenth-century paintings by Lavinia Fontana and other women artists of Bologna, and photographs by Sarah Charlesworth. The museum marked its 10th anniversary in 1997. In what could be the answer to a trivia question, the collection is housed, ironically enough, in a former Masonic temple. Highlights include frequent education programs, a library and research center (by appointment only), a quarterly magazine called *Women in the Arts*, a cafe, and a gift shop that specializes in unique jewelry. Metro Center is the closest Metro stop.

Hours are from 10:00 A.M. to 5:00 P.M. Monday through Saturday and noon to 5:00 P.M. Sunday. It's closed January 1, Thanksgiving, and December 25. Admission is $5.00 for adults and $3.00 for seniors and students; children ages 18 and younger get in free. (You'll find additional information in Kidstuff.)

The Phillips Collection
1600 21st St. NW
Washington, DC
(202) 387–2151
www.phillipscollection.org

In the shadows of Embassy Row, the former home of Duncan Phillips features a diverse collection of masterpieces of French impressionism, postimpressionism, and modern art. In 1997, the museum held an enormously popular Impressionism on the Seine exhibition, built around Renoir's *The Luncheon of the Boating Party,* the Phillips' best-known work from its permanent collection.

Be sure to inquire about the museum's wonderful free Sunday concerts, gallery talks, and tours. The museum has a small eatery and a gift shop. Admission is $7.50 for the general public, $4.00 for seniors and students, free for ages younger than 18, and is voluntary on weekdays. The museum is open 10:00 A.M. to 5:00 P.M. Tuesday, Wednesday, Friday, and Saturday; 10:00 A.M. to 8:30 P.M. Thursday; and noon to 5:00 P.M. Sunday. The Dupont Circle Metro stop is just a block away.

Renwick Gallery
Pennsylvania Ave. and 17th St. NW
Washington, DC
(202) 357–2700
americanart.si.edu

Leave the present and step into the late nineteenth century. The Renwick Gallery, a Smithsonian museum established in 1972, is a showcase of American design, crafts, and contemporary arts. The Grand Salon and the Octagon Room boast period furnishings and decorations from the 1860s and 1870s. The building itself dates to 1859 and is the original site of the Corcoran Gallery. (See our Civil War chapter for more on the building's historical significance.) The museum, which has a gift shop, is open from 10:00 A.M. to 5:30 P.M. daily, except on December 25. It's near the Farragut West Metro station.

Smithsonian American Art Museum and
National Portrait Gallery
8th and G Sts. NW
Washington, DC
(202) 357–2700
americanart.si.edu and
http://www.npg.si.edu/

These side-by-side museums are closed for extensive renovation and probably won't reopen until 2004. In the meantime, you can check out their Web sites for information about their collections, virtual exhibitions and touring programs.

The Smithsonian American Art Museum's permanent collection of more than 37,000 works, including paintings, sculptures, folk art, and photographs, offers a rich panorama of the nation's artistic heritage, from colonial times to the twentieth century. Look for James Hampton's *The Throne of the Third Heaven of the Nations Millenium General Assembly*, an elaborate, room-size piece constructed of recycled materials and aluminum foil. Even on-line it's impressive!

The adjacent National Portrait Gallery features likenesses of individuals who have made significant contributions to the development of the nation, including each president and such cultural icons as Elvis Presley, Babe Ruth, and Marilyn Monroe. The gallery often features themed exhibitions, such as shows highlighting George and Martha Washington and Benjamin Franklin and his cohorts.

The Textile Museum
2320 S St. NW
Washington, DC
(202) 667–0441
www.textilemuseum.org

This small, elegant museum houses renowned collections of textile art,

The National Museum of Women in the Arts displays work in a variety of media. PHOTO: COURTESY OF NATIONAL MUSEUM OF WOMEN IN THE ARTS

Famed Mexican artist Frida Kahlo completed this self-portrait in the late 1930s. PHOTO: COURTESY OF NATIONAL MUSEUM OF WOMEN IN THE ARTS

including rare oriental carpets. Visitors can explore hands-on activities in an interactive gallery. The museum also offers frequent lectures and monthly family programs. Suggested admission is $5.00 per person. Hours are from 10:00 A.M. to 5:00 P.M. Monday through Saturday, and from 1:00 to 5:00 P.M. Sundays.

The Gallery Scene

Metro D.C.'s flourishing arts community and gallery scene sometimes get overlooked due to some of the region's more internationally visible art treasures. Here we list galleries from the area's most prominent art districts.

Washington, D.C.

Affrica
2010 R St. NW
Washington, DC
(202) 745–7272
www.affrica.com

This 23-year-old Dupont Circle Gallery, unique to Washington, showcases traditional, authentic African artwork, including masks, textiles, figures, furniture, implements, pottery, currency, and adornments. Hours are noon to 6:00 P.M. Wednesday through Saturday, 2:00 to 6:00 P.M. Tuesdays, and other times by appointment.

Foundry Gallery
9 Hillyer Ct. NW
Washington, DC
(202) 387–0203
www.foundry-gallery.org

One of the Dupont Circle galleries, this 30-year-old artists' cooperative features abstract and experimental, as well as representational contemporary art. It's open from 11:00 A.M. to 5:00 P.M. Tuesday through Saturday, and from 1:00 to 5:00 P.M. on Sunday.

Galleries of Dupont Circle
(202) 232–3610

Call this information line for details about upcoming programs at the 20 diverse galleries in Washington's Gallery District. The "First Friday" evening of each month, the galleries stay open late, from 6:00 to 8:00 P.M., to mark new exhibition openings. All galleries are in walking distance of the Dupont Circle Metrorail stop.

Touchstone Gallery
406 7th St. NW
Washington, DC
(202) 347–2787
www.art-smart.com

This multiartist cooperative gallery each month features two single-artist shows of contemporary, modern work. The 26-year-old gallery also occasionally hosts invitational shows featuring international artists. Its hours are 11:00 A.M. to 5:00 P.M. Wednesday through Friday, and from noon to 5:00 P.M. Saturdays and Sundays. The gallery is part of the Pennsylvania Quarter District, between the White House and Capitol Hill. It's one of several galleries participating in a gallery walk from 6:00 to 8:00 P.M. every third Thursday.

Troyer Gallery
1710 Connecticut Ave. NW
Washington, DC
(202) 328–7189
www.troyergallery.com

This 19-year-old Dupont Circle gallery features new works by Washington and national painters, sculptors, and photographers. The business also offers art consulting for local law firms and corporations. Hours are from 11:00 A.M. to 5:00 P.M. Wednesday through Saturday and by appointment.

Veerhoff Galleries
Canal Square, 1054 31st St. NW
Washington, DC
(202) 338–6456

Established in 1871, Veerhoff is the oldest commercial gallery in the city, and one of the oldest family-run businesses, now operated by the original owner's great-granddaughter, Margaret Veerhoff. It specializes in realistic oils and pastels and original graphics and also carries many antique prints. New shows open the third Friday of each month. The gallery is one of nine at picturesque Canal Square in Georgetown. Hours are 11:00 A.M. to 6:00 P.M. Tuesday through Saturday. Customer parking is available in the retail center's basement.

Northern Virginia

Arlington Arts Center
3550 Wilson Blvd.
Arlington, VA
(703) 524–1494
www.onwashington.com/Groups-ArlingtonArtsCenter

This gallery, in a renovated schoolhouse, showcases ambitious works of regional artists. The building also contains studio space for up to 14 artists. Hours are from 11:00 A.M. to 4:00 P.M. Tuesday through Friday, and from 1:00 to 5:00 P.M. Saturdays.

First Friday Gallery
Walk Downtown
Downtown Leesburg, VA
(888) 478–1758
loudouncounty.com/art/walk.htm

The Loudoun Tourism Council and Town of Leesburg sponsor this ongoing event, held from 6:00 to 9:00 P.M. the first Friday of each month except January. Visit nine galleries and specialty shops in historic downtown Leesburg for show openings, wine, and hors d'oeuvres and book signings. Pick up a map at the Tourism Council Office, 108-D South Street SE, Leesburg, Virginia, or at any participating merchants.

The Greater Reston Arts Center (GRACE)
11911 Freedom Dr., Ste. 110
Reston, VA
(703) 471–9242
www.restonart.com

In Reston Town Center, the lively downtown hub of one of the nation's first planned communities, this gallery features changing exhibitions of contemporary works. It sponsors an annual summer arts festival and sells unique artistic holiday gifts each December. Hours are from 11:00 A.M. to 5:00 P.M. Tuesday through Saturday.

Elisabeth Vigée-Lebrun painted portraits of Russian aristocrats, like this powerful image of Princess Belozersky, completed in 1798.

PHOTO: COURTESY OF NATIONAL MUSEUM OF WOMEN IN THE ARTS

McLean Project for the Arts
McLean Community Center
1234 Ingleside Ave.
McLean, VA
(703) 790–1953
www.mcleanart.org

MPA presents themed exhibitions of works by regional and international artists in its Emerson Gallery. The non-profit organization also sponsors community classes for adults and children, and special events such as lectures and tours. The gallery is open from 11:00 A.M. to 4:00 P.M. Tuesday through Friday and 1:00 P.M. to 5:00 P.M. Saturdays.

Medlin Art Ltd.
2 Loudoun St. SE
Leesburg, VA
(703) 771–8696
loudouncounty.com/art/medlin.htm

This 17-year-old gallery, which recently relocated, specializes in limited edition prints by such artists as P. Buckley Moss and Paul Zandry. Hours are 10:00 A.M. to 6:00 P.M. Tuesday through Saturday. The gallery closes on Sundays and Mondays.

The Potomac Gallery
17 S. King St.
Leeburg, VA
(703) 771–8085
thepotomacgallery.com

This 12-year-old gallery in the heart of historic downtown Leesburg carries originals and limited editions, specializing in local art and Civil War–themed works. The store also offers custom framing. It's open

10:00 A.M. to 5:30 P.M. Monday through Saturday, noon to 4:00 P.M. Sundays.

Torpedo Factory Art Center
105 N. Union St.
Alexandria, VA
(703) 838–4565
www.torpedofactory.org

If you enjoy watching artists at work, you'll love visiting this nationally known attraction in historic Old Town Alexandria. Once a waterfront munitions factory, the massive building now houses studio and gallery spaces for more than 160 professional artists, including painters, sculptors, glass makers, jewelry makers, and potters. The view of the Potomac and bustling harbor provides an added bonus as you observe and chat with artists. Most work is for sale, including bargains like pottery seconds.

The Art League (703–683–1780), a local arts organization headquartered here, offers classes for children and adults. The Art League gallery holds juried exhibitions and sells a wide variety of affordable original works by regional artists. The building also houses Alexandria Archaeology, Room 327 (703–838–4399), where visitors can look at museum exhibits on the city's history and watch archaeologists at work in the laboratory. The organization also offers hands-on courses. The museum is open to the public from 10:00 A.M. to 3:00 P.M. Tuesday through Thursday, from 10:00 A.M. to 5:00 P.M. Friday and Saturday, and from 1:00 to 5:00 P.M. on Sunday.

Admission to the Torpedo Factory is free. The building is open from 10 A.M. to 5 P.M. daily, although individual studio hours vary. The building is closed on New Year's Day, Easter, July Fourth, Thanksgiving, and Christmas.

Suburban Maryland

The Glass Gallery
4720 Hampden La.
Bethesda, MD
(301) 657–3478
www.artline.com/galleries/glass/glass.html

As its name implies, the gallery focuses on glass in its many forms: blown, cast, fused, etc. It features about nine openings annually and carries works by artists from throughout the United States and five or six countries. It's open from 11:00 A.M. to 5:00 P.M. Wednesday through Saturday.

Glen Echo Park
7300 MacArthur Blvd.
Glen Echo, MD
(301) 492–6282
www.nps.gov/glec

"Unique" describes in a nutshell this National Park Service arts site, which began as a National Chautauqua Assembly in 1891, evolved into an amusement park, and now promotes visual and performing arts. You can watch artists work in their studios inside yurts, funky little huts topped with rounded, grass-covered roofs. Other studios fill space in buildings that once served as game arcades, rides, and concessions. You'll also find resident artists' and instructors' works exhibited in the Gallery and Bookshop in the Stone Tower, one of the site's original buildings. It's open from noon to 5:00 P.M. Tuesday through Sunday and closed Mondays and holidays.

The annual Labor Day Art Show fills the park's 65-year-old Spanish Ballroom with a variety of works by local artists. The park also hosts music festivals, such as WAMU-FM's Pickin' in the Glen, a bluegrass event. Pick up a free quarterly catalog for information about special events and scheduled art, music, and dance workshops, and classes for adults and children. To learn more about the park's history, watch the 60-minute Glen Echo on the Potomac at 2:00 P.M. on Saturdays, or take a ranger-conducted tour at 2:00 P.M. on Sundays. Plenty of free parking is available. (See our Kidstuff chapter for information about the park's antique carousel and children's theaters, then check out Parks and Recreation for details on dances held in the restored ballroom.)

At the Cinema

If you're a film buff, you'll want to check out the following events and theaters. Also, contact the city's major art museums, described earlier in this chapter, for information about their film series.

Washington, D.C.

American Film Institute and the AFI Theatre
John F. Kennedy Center, Hall of States
Washington, DC
(202) 785–4600
www.afionline.org

The prestigious AFI, which also publishes a magazine for members, appeals to film buffs and those who appreciate the cinema as an art form. AFI champions film preservation. Each year, its 224-seat theater screens more than 600 movies: silent years and early talkies, films from Hollywood's Golden Age, and the work of avant-guarde directors. The theater doubles as home to special film revivals, festivals, and premier showings. Order tickets ($6.50, $5.50 for members) in advance by calling (202) 785–4601 from 5:00 to 9:00 P.M. weekdays and 1:00 to 9:00 P.M. Saturdays and Sundays.

The AFI Silver Complex, slated to open late in 2003 in Silver Spring, Maryland, will feature the restored 1938 Silver Theatre as well as two new theaters with stadium-style seating, exhibit space, meeting rooms, and a store. The site will host film education programs for students of all ages.

Insiders' Tip

Free outdoor concerts take place every summer weekend at such locations as Reston Town Center's Equity Office pavilion, the courthouse lawn in downtown Leesburg, and the C&O Canal in Georgetown. Check the *Washington Post*'s weekend section on Fridays for a schedule.

Cineplex Odeon Uptown Theatre
3426 Connecticut Ave. NW
Washington, DC
(202) 333–FILM, #799

Don't let the boxlike, drab facade fool you. Inside, this theater offers what you'd expect from the heyday of Hollywood: velvet-backed seats, an ornate and towering proscenium, a plush reception area, and a huge screen. It's easily the area's best film-watching venue. The theater is a quick walk from the Cleveland Park Metro station.

Cineplex Odeon Wisconsin Avenue Cinemas
4000 Wisconsin Ave. NW
Washington, DC
(202) 244–0880

This six-screen complex, built in the late '80s, offers cutting-edge sound and screen technology, as well as a palatial interior that reminds you that movie-going can still be a memorable event. The theater is 6 blocks from the Tenleytown Metro station.

Washington International Film Festival (Film-fest D.C.)
D.C. Commission on the Arts and Humanities
415 12th St. NW, Ste. 803
Washington, DC
(202) 628–FILM
www.filmfestdc.org

This two-week celebration of American and international film, from the alternative to the mainstream, takes place in late April to early May. The city becomes the focus of the movie world, with scores of screenings, seminars, and receptions held throughout town. Screenings take place at theaters, museums, and auditoriums throughout town and most cost $7.00.

Washington Jewish Film Festival: An Exhibition of International Cinema
Morris Cafritz Center for the Arts
Irwin P. Edlavitch Bldg.
1529 16th St. NW
Washington, DC
(202) 518–9400, ext. 248
www.wjff.org

This weeklong December event in the District of Columbia Jewish Community Center's Cecile Goldman Theater includes feature and short films, as well as

documentaries, plus talks with filmmakers and scholars. Tickets cost $5.50 to $8.00. The center also sponsors repertory screenings all year.

Northern Virginia

Arlington Cinema 'n' Drafthouse
2903 Columbia Pk.
Arlington, VA
(703) 486–2345

At this popular moviehouse/restaurant, you can sit at a table munching nachos, pizza, and Buffalo wings; throwing back a beer or two; even smoking, while watching second-run films on a big screen. Admission is $3.99. Special features include midnight flicks and big-screen Redskins games.

Cinema Arts Theatres
Fair City Mall
Rte. 236 (Main St.) and Pickett Rd.
Fairfax, VA
(703) 978–6991
www.cinemaartstheatre.com

We head to this friendly neighborhood theater, owned by local film buffs, when we want to catch the latest art release or first-rate mainstream flick. The remodeled theaters feature amenities like loveseat-style chairs, seats with attached trays, and an eclectic menu offering freshly made deli sandwiches (a quick sell-out), sushi, cracker and cheese plates, gourmet desserts, and fancy coffees. The cinema hosts a popular Sunday morning film club, which screens upcoming indie and foreign films.

Suburban Maryland

Cineplex Odeon Shirlington 7
2772 S. Randolph St.
Shirlington, VA
(703) 671–0910

Here's another hot spot for new independent and foreign films, notable for its location in the village of Shirlington. Before or after the show, grab a bite at one of the trendy sidewalk cafes featuring anything from sushi to tapas.

Muvico Egyptian 24 Theatres
Arundel Mills
7000 Arundel Mills Circle
Hanover, MD
(443) 755-8992
muvico.com

Although located in Anne Arundel County just outside Metro D.C., this posh, enormous complex is worth the drive. With 24 screens, it's easily the largest theater in the area, and it boasts amenities galore. Check out the Egyptian-themed decor, stadium seating, and supervised children's playroom, where kids get to hang out while their parents enjoy a movie. While you're there, visit the mall's designer outlet stores.

Literary Arts

Suburban Maryland

The Writer's Center
4508 Walsh St.
Bethesda, MD
(301) 654-8664
www.writer.org

This 25-year-old nonprofit organization for people in the literary and graphic arts fields sponsors poetry, fiction, and play readings by local and nationally known writers. The center also hosts workshops and events like the annual Mid-Atlantic Small Press Conference and Book Fair, offers a book gallery of literary magazines and works by local authors, gives technical assistance, and publishes a newsletter for members. Most events are open to the public; members receive admission discounts. Membership is $40 annually for individuals, $25 for students, and $50 for families.

A Word about Tickets

The most convenient way to get tickets to Washington area shows is over the phone via TicketMaster at (202) 432-7328, or on the Web, www.ticketmaster.com; or (703) 218-6500, www.tickets.com. Unfortunately,

Insiders' Tip

Volunteers—like you, perhaps?—lead tours at the National Gallery of Art. Call (202) 842-6247 for information about training.

with any of these services, expect to fork over a surcharge of a few dollars. You can always buy at the box office, but sometimes finding same-day tickets, especially during the tourist season and for big shows, can be tricky. Your best bet is to reserve seats as far in advance as possible.

If you're like us, though, and place a premium on discount tickets, then head over to TICKETplace (202-842-5387, www.cultural-alliance.org/tickets), on the ground floor of the Old Post Office Pavilion, 1100 Pennsylvania Avenue NW, Washington, D.C., right across from the Federal Triangle Metro Station's Orange and Blue Lines. (Take Metro if you want to avoid parking hassles!) Here you can find reduced-rate tickets for day-of-performance shows only; the cost is typically half the regular price plus a service charge of 10 percent of the full ticket price. You can't make advance purchases, with the exception of a few Sunday performance tickets available on Saturday, and you must conduct all transactions by cash, travelers checks, or debit cards. The outlet is open from 11:00 A.M. to 6:00 P.M. Tuesday through Saturday, and it's closed Sunday and Monday, Thanksgiving, Christmas, and New Year's Day. You never know exactly what you'll find available, but sometimes that's part of the fun! If you're a student, senior, or enlisted military employee, you may not have to venture to TICKETplace for half-price tickets. Inquire at the box office or ticket charge service about availability. Some theaters also offer last-minute "student rush" and "standing room only" tickets.

Kidstuff

Marvelous Museums
Fabulous Farms
Rainy-Day Raves
Artful Adventures
Awesome Amusements
Sensational Shows
Perfect Parks

Washington may be filled with politicians, lawyers, and lobbyists, but any parent knows that the capital's real movers and shakers aren't even old enough to vote. Endlessly energetic and inquisitive, kids are always ready to leap into action, while moms and dads scramble to arrange safe, educational, and—most of all—fun outings. In this chapter you'll find dozens of destinations listed under a variety of categories. Whether you're passing through or planning to stay awhile, you're sure to find adventures just right for your family.

Marvelous Museums

Your kids just want to have fun; you want them to learn too. They can do both at these great museums, where hands-on activities and special family programs make visits entertaining and enlightening. And here's a bonus: Many feature free admission, so you needn't feel obligated to stay for hours if the little ones get fidgety. (Be sure to check our Attractions and Arts chapters for more information on many of these and additional museums and galleries you may find intriguing.) Please note that asterisked attractions may be closed for security reasons.

Washington, D.C.

The Smithsonian Institution

The Smithsonian museums continuously add more and more interactive exhibits and special activities with kid appeal. Start at the Castle to collect information and devise a sight-seeing plan. Above all, don't expect to see it all in one outing. Your best bet is to limit a visit to two or three hours, avoiding crowds by arriving first thing in the morning or late in the afternoon

Most Smithsonian museums are open from 10:00 A.M. to 5:30 P.M. daily, except Christmas. Admission is free. The Smithsonian Metro stop is a quick walk from most Smithsonian museums. (See our Attractions, Arts, and Annual Events chapters for additional information.)

The Smithsonian Information Center
1000 Jefferson Dr. SW
Washington, DC
(202) 357–2700
www.si.edu/activity/planvis/museums/
aboutsib.htm
Before you visit, call or stop by the Smithsonian Information Center (a.k.a. the Castle) at the listed address, and ask for *10 Tips for Visiting Smithsonian Museums with Children* and *The Smithsonian Quiz for Children*. You'll also find helpful touch-screen computers and a variety of brochures. Hours are 9:00 A.M. to 5:30 P.M. Outside, stroll through beautiful gardens or go for a whirl on the circa 1940s Allan Herschell carousel in front of the neighboring Arts and Industries Building. The ride operates daily, 10:00 A.M. to 5:30 P.M. (11:00 A.M. to 5:00 P.M. October through February), weather permitting. A ticket costs $1.75.

Freer Gallery of Art
Jefferson Dr. and 12th St. SW
Washington, DC
(202) 357–2700
www.asia.si.edu

Arthur M. Sackler Gallery
1050 Independence Ave. SW
Washington, DC
(202) 357–2700
www.asia.si.edu
Visit the information desks at these two connected museums of Asian art to obtain a variety of free children's activity sheets on such subjects as Japanese screens, scrolls,

Hindu gods, and gallery terminology. The museum gift shops carry *The Princess and the Peacocks,* a children's book about the Freer's ornate Peacock Room, designed by James McNeill Whistler. The popular ImaginAsia program, for youngsters ages 6 through 14 and their parents, features a different themed tour and related craft each month. Drop-in sessions generally take place Saturday and Sunday afternoons, with additional days available during summer.

Hirshhorn Museum and Sculpture Garden
7th St. and Independence Ave. SW
Washington, DC
(202) 357–2700
www.si.edu/hirshhorn/

You may need to caution your kids not to touch the assorted pieces in the outdoor Sculpture Garden, which looks a lot like a funky playground. Children can do lots of looking, however, and they'll see and learn plenty of interesting things about modern art by using the museum's wonderful *Family Guide*, available free of charge at the information desk. The eye-catching folder contains a dozen or more colorful "artcards," each of which features a picture of an art work, information about the artist, observations about the piece, and at least one activity.

Look for kid-pleasers like Alexander Calder's fish mobile, Andy Warhol's *Marilyn Monroe's Lips,* and Joan Miró's sculpture, *Lunar Bird.* The museum hosts free, monthly "Young at Art" family programs on Saturdays, featuring hands-on activities for children ages six to nine accompanied by adults. Call (202) 357–3235, extension 114, for reservations, which are required. Free, drop-in activities for families take place in the museum's Improv Art Room 11:00 A.M. to 2:00 P.M. Saturdays. (Also see The Arts chapter for more information about this museum.)

National Air and Space Museum
7th St. and Independence Ave. SW
Washington, DC
(202) 357–2700
www.nasm.si.edu

Voted Best Museum for Children by the readers of *Washington Families* newspaper, this most popular Smithsonian museum awes kids as soon as they walk in and spy all the hanging aircraft. They can experience firsthand the principles of flight by visiting the interactive How Things Fly gallery, where they can work the controls on a real Cessna and perform numerous experiments, like sending Gumby aloft in a miniature hot-air balloon. Related activ-

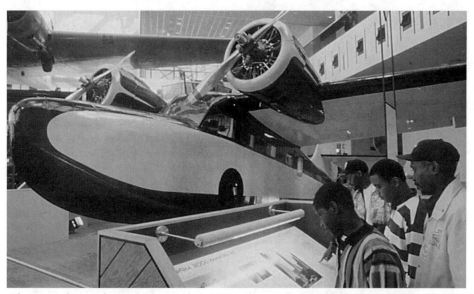

The National Air and Space Museum—the most visited museum in the world—showcases the evolution of aviation and space technology. PHOTO: COURTESY OF SMITHSONIAN NATIONAL AIR AND SPACE MUSEUM

ity sheets describe additional fun to try at home.

Elsewhere in the museum, kids enjoy walking through a space lab and touching a moon rock. The museum offers free highlights tours, which can be tailored toward children, daily at 10:15 A.M. and 1:00 P.M. Check the daily schedule for IMAX theater and planetarium shows, which require tickets.

National Museum of African Art
950 Independence Ave. SW
Washington, DC
(202) 357–2700
www.si.edu/nmafa

Kids like looking at kinetic sculptures, colorful masks, and patterned clothing. The museum regularly offers drop-in, family-oriented events, such as story-telling and the Let's Read About Africa

A young visitor to the National Museum of African Art bangs a drum during a hands-on workshop for children. PHOTO: HUGH TALMAN, COURTESY OF NATIONAL MUSEUM OF AFRICAN ART

reading program. Kids' activity sheets related to special exhibits sometimes are available at the information desk.

National Museum of American History
14th St. and Constitution Ave. NW
Washington, DC
(202) 357–2700
www.si.edu/nmah

Are the kids getting restless from too much looking and not enough touching? Head for one of the museum's two hands-on rooms, open to visitors "from ages 5 to 105" but especially geared toward young-sters, who must be accompanied by adults. In the Hands On History Room on the second floor, children can pedal a high-wheeled bicycle, try on old-fash-ioned clothing, rummage through a ped-dler's pack, and decorate a paper pot with Indian symbols, among more than 30 activities. All subjects relate to museum exhibits. The center is open free of charge Tuesday through Sunday, noon to 3:00 P.M., and it's closed on federal holidays. Tickets, available at the door, may be required on weekends and during other busy times.

Part of the *Science in American Life* exhi-bition in the first floor's west wing, the Hands On Science Center lets children five and older try such experiments as test-ing food additives, unraveling DNA genes, measuring with lasers, and determining their sunglasses' UV ratings. Hours are 12:30 to 5:00 P.M. Tuesday through Friday and 10:00 A.M. to 5:00 P.M. Saturdays and Sundays. Tickets may be required during busy periods. Adults must accompany youngsters ages 5 to 12.

Elsewhere in the museum, children like to scan bar codes at the interactive *Information Age* exhibition, and discover what modern things are made of in *A Material World.* Kids also enjoy looking at the collection of First Ladies' gowns, the Bradford Doll House, and familiar pop culture items such as Oscar the Grouch, Fonzie's leather jacket, Mr. Rogers' sweater, and Dorothy's ruby slippers. Visit the Victorian-style Palm Court ice cream parlor on the first floor for a light meal or frosty treat. The large gift shop carries interesting children's books and toys.

Children learn how to harness a mule at the National Museum of American History.
PHOTO: CHARLES PHILLIPS, COURTESY OF SMITHSONIAN INSTITUTION

National Museum of Natural History
10th St. and Constitution Ave. NW
Washington, DC
(202) 357–2700
www.nmnh.si.edu/

Kids love this museum from the moment they walk in and spot the rotunda's giant elephant. From there, head for the popular dinosaur hall, where you'll find a diplodocus, an allosaurus, and other prehistoric skeletons. The Discovery Room, also on the first floor, features hands-on activities for all ages using a variety of items like quartz, seashells, and native crafts from the museum's collections. Regular hours are Tuesday through Friday, noon to 2:30 P.M. and Saturday and Sunday, 10:30 A.M. to 3:30 P.M. Hours may increase during the summer. Obtain free passes at the door. Upstairs, the Number 1 kid-pleasing attraction is the O. Orkin Insect Zoo, filled with live creepy crawlies. Look for bugs and their relatives, such as hissing cockroaches and centipedes, and don't miss the tarantula feedings, weekdays (except Mondays and Thanksgiving)

at 10:30 and 11:30 A.M. and 1:30 P.M. and weekends at varying times. Many youngsters also enjoy discovering the many shapes, colors, and textures of gems and minerals in an exhibit that includes a few interactive components. The museum also boasts a six-story Discovery Center, which houses an IMAX theater, an interactive Immersion Cinema, a cafe in a glass-domed atrium, and a huge gift shop with lots of cool stuff for kids.

National Postal Museum
2 Massachusetts Ave. NE
Washington, DC
(202) 357–2700
www.si.edu/postal

Right across the street from Union Station (see this chapter's dining guide), this entertaining museum usually proves much less crowded than Smithsonian museums on the mall. Visit the information desk for a brochure highlighting exhibition elements children appreciate. Older kids can search for answers to true-or-false questions in the *Check It Out!* pam-

When children need a break from the museums, it's time to visit the carousel on the National Mall.

PHOTO: JIM TKATCH

phlet. The museum's many kid-pleasing exhibits include a "wooded" trail that simulates a colonial mail route, a stage coach that's a great prop for photos, interactive computer games, a puzzlelike stamp collection, and a railway mail car to explore. Children also like to look at Owney, a taxidermy postal dog who collected more than 1,000 "dog" tags during his travels aboard mail trains. Computer kiosks in the lobby create postcards that can be mailed from the museum.

If you visit on the third Saturday of the month, drop into the Discovery Center for free hands-on activities, such as designing stamp-covered bookmarks.

Other Kid-Friendly Museums in Washington

Capital Children's Museum
800 3rd St. NE
Washington, DC
(202) 675–4120
www.ccm.org

Here's your itinerary: Drink hot chocolate in Mexico, create a colorful carp kite or origami in a Japanese Tatami Room, hide in a prehistoric cave, and pal around with Bugs Bunny. You don't need a passport to do these and lots of other cool hands-on activities at the Capital Children's Museum, which adheres to the motto, "Where learning is an adventure." One of the oldest and largest children's museums in the country, CCM features nearly 40,000 square feet of exhibits on three floors. The circa-1873 former convent's exterior looks rather dreary to first-time visitors, who are quickly reassured when they spot the entrance courtyard's giant Cootie and whimsical sculpture garden made from recycled odds and ends. Inside, kids often travel first to Mexico, the museum's original and most popular exhibit, which includes a festive marketplace with a fountain and dress-up clothing. Volunteers show you how to grind chocolate and make crafts like tissuepaper flowers. Preschoolers especially enjoy the sandy "beach" in the Yucatan room, which also features a Mayan pyramid to climb. (Go inside to visit a tiny secret room!)

In the museum's Chemical Science Center, children don goggles and lab coats to conduct nifty experiments, like making foam "packing peanuts" disappear! In another favorite exhibit, *Animation: The World of Chuck Jones,* amazed kids co-star in cartoons with Warner Brothers characters, thanks to a magical blue wall. Visitors can create their own designs for experiments using early animation techniques, and discover the instruments behind cartoon sound effects.

Other interactive highlights include a Maze of Illusions, a city scene featuring a Metro bus and Metro train car, giant soap bubbles, a puppet play room, and an exhibit about Japan. The museum holds frequent story times, workshops, and guest appearances by authors and entertainers. Popular birthday party rooms feature such themes as Under the Sea and Winnie the Pooh.

Visit the museum daily, 10:00 A.M. to 6:00 P.M. during the summer, 10:00 A.M. to 5:00 P.M. Tuesday through Sunday and Monday holidays the rest of the year. (It's closed on New Year's Day, Thanksgiving, and Christmas.) Admission is $7.00 per person, $5.00 for seniors, and free for children younger than age two. Admission is half-price on Sundays before noon. Ask about one-year family memberships, which entitle the bearers to unlimited visits.

Corcoran Gallery of Art
17th St. and New York Ave. NW
Washington, DC
(202) 639–1700
www.corcoran.org

The city's oldest private art gallery is small enough not to overwhelm youngsters, who enjoy its large landscape paintings and works featuring children and animals. Visit the information desk for a free brochure, *Musing for Myths,* a scavenger hunt for pictures with mythological themes, geared toward kids ages 6 to 12.

The museum's free, ongoing Sunday Traditions program, held at 2:30 on some Sunday afternoons, features performances, workshops, and storytelling designed for families with children four and older. Call (202) 639–1725 for a schedule of upcoming events or to make required reservations. Occasional day-long, drop-in Family Day celebrations include workshops, storytelling, and other activities built around a theme such as "Artists of Our Town." (See The Arts chapter for a complete description.)

DAR Museum
1776 D St. NW
Washington, DC
(202) 879–3254
www.dar.org/museum/

Docents lead guided tours of the museum's period rooms, which are tailored to visitors' ages and interests. Pick up a free family guide to enhance your visit. Children especially enjoy the Touch of Independence area, where they can play with a genuine nineteenth-century, hand-painted Noah's Ark; roll a hoop with a stick; and enjoy a tea party with dolls, using a miniature Blue Willow china set. Nearby, the New Hampshire Toy Attic displays numerous antique toys, dolls, and games. Other period rooms feature musical instruments, tea party settings, and children's furniture that appeal to kids. Tours are held on weekdays from 10:00 A.M. to 2:30 P.M. and Sundays from 1:00 to 5:00 pm.

Call the museum for information about children's programs, such as the popular Colonial Adventure for ages 5 to 7 and summer quilt camp for kids ages 9 to 12. (See our Attractions chapter for more.)

National Aquarium
Department of Commerce Building,
Rm. B-077
14th St. between Constitution and
Pennsylvania Aves. NW
Washington, DC
(202) 482–2825
www.nationalaquarium.com

Children have an easy time seeing exhibits at the nation's first public aquarium, now more than 125 years old, and smaller and less crowded that the better-known National Aquarium in Baltimore. Kids can observe more than 270 species of fish, invertebrates, amphibians, and reptiles. A Touch Tank features horseshoe and hermit crabs, starfish and pencil urchins, all of which may be handled by little hands.

Look for the electric eel, which emits an audible charge, and the recently renovated alligator exhibit. Kids also enjoy watching shark feedings Saturdays, Mondays, and Wednesdays at 2:00 P.M. The annual summer Shark Day includes hands-on activities and costumed characters.

The aquarium is open 9:00 A.M. to 5:00 P.M. daily, except Thanksgiving and Christmas. Admission is $3.00 for adults, and 75 cents for children ages 2 to 10, and free for ages younger than 2. Visit the gift shop for fun and fishy souvenirs. The aquarium is adjacent to the Ronald Reagan International Trade Center, which houses a popular food court, and is close to the Federal Triangle Metro stop.

National Building Museum
401 F St. NW
Washington, DC
(202) 272–2448
www.nbm.org

Kids love to roam the open space in the museum's great hall and touch tactile models of Washington monuments in the *Washington: Symbol and City* exhibit.

Free children's activity booklets, available at the front desk, feature such topics as patterns, building history, architectural terms, and museum treasure hunts. Visit on Saturdays at 2:30 P.M. to learn about bridges through hands-on activities. At 2:30 P.M. on the first and third Sunday of each month, visitors discover how to build arches and trusses during a demonstration suitable for ages five and older. Call for a schedule, costs, and registration information regarding the museum's monthly family programs. The gift shop is well known for its vast selection of intriguing building toys, among other unusual items. (See Attractions for additional museum information.)

National Gallery of Art
4th St. and Constitution Ave. NW
Washington, DC
(202) 737–4215
www.nga.gov/kids/kids.htm

Kids will be less intimidated by this awe-inspiring, free museum's large scale if you start your family outing in the Micro Gallery in the West Building Art Information Room. Here, visitors can have fun using the touch-screen computer monitors to view art works featuring their favorite animals or other subjects and learn more about the artists. Design a personalized tour featuring a printed map showing the locations of works your children want to see.

Stop by an art information desk, on the main level of the West Building or on the East Building's ground level, to pick up a Postcard Tour. Two family-oriented sets, which visitors may borrow while touring the museum, include "American Art Search" for use in the West Building and "Things That Walk, Talk and Squawk" to accompany viewing of twentieth-century works in the East Building. Among children's favorite works in the West Building are Sir Peter Paul Rubens's *Daniel in the Lions' Den,* John Singleton Copley's *Watson and the Shark,* and Gilbert Stuart's presidential portraits. In the East Building children like the untitled red Alexander Calder mobile and Jackson Pollock's splattered *Lavender Mist.* Call (202) 789–3030 for a schedule of family programs held in conjunction with special exhibits. The museum also hosts a monthly, Saturday children's film series and Sunday Stories in Art.

The museum shops sell a family guide, West Building Highlights ($2.50 each), containing activities geared toward kids preschool-age and older. The shops also carry a 112-page *National Gallery of Art Activity Book* ($16.95) and other children's books about works here, as well as an abundance of postcards, perfect for designing your own museum scavenger hunt.

Bringing a baby or toddler? Free strollers for museum use are available at every entrance in both buildings. Hungry kids enjoy visiting the Cascade Cafe/Espresso Bar to eat a snack or meal while they watch a mesmerizing waterfall outside a large window. (See the dining guide in this chapter.) Outside, visit the sculpture garden, which includes a kid-pleasing giant spider. (See The Arts for a complete description.)

National Geographic Society's Explorers Hall
17th and M Sts. NW
Washington, DC
(202) 857–7588
www.nationalgeographic.com/explorer

Geographica: The World at Your Fingertips features numerous kid-pleasing hands-on exhibits, including video touch screens exploring assorted topics, a simulated tornado, and a black-box aquarium containing lifelike images of different fish for children to "catch." An interactive amphitheater, Earth Station One, boasts an impressive 11-foot globe and simulated space flight. The free museum also offers changing exhibits as well as family-oriented presentations during its midday Passport Friday program. Hours are 9:00 A.M. to 5:00 P.M. Monday through Saturday and holidays, 10:00 A.M. to 5:00 P.M. Sundays, closed Christmas. The closest Metro stop is Farragut North.

National Museum of Women in the Arts
1250 New York Ave.
Washington, DC
(202) 783–5000
www.nmwa.org

Visit the information desk for a free *Art Ventures* booklet that includes activities related to kid-pleasing works such as Lilly Martin Spencer's realistic painting *The Artist and Her Family at a Fourth of July Picnic*, Frida Baranek's untitled abstract wire sculpture, and Gabriele Munter's landscape *Staffelsee in Autumn*. Call (202) 783-7370 for recorded information about upcoming events, including family programs held monthly on Sundays. (See the Arts chapter for more information.)

* The Navy Museum
Building 76, Washington Navy Yard
805 Kidder Breese SE
Washington, DC
(202) 433–4882
www.history.navy.mil/branches/nhcorg8/htm

Ships ahoy! Kids may not care much about the U.S. Naval history presented at this recently renovated museum, but they love to climb aboard the hulking antiaircraft guns. Young visitors enjoy other hands-on activities, such as the popular submarine room, where children can pretend to steer a sub and operate assorted buttons and toggle switches on genuine instrument panels. Two periscopes offer a revolving view of the Navy Yard outside. Kids also like to drive their parents crazy by repeatedly sounding the Klaxon, a diving alarm that blares an ear-piercing "WhaOOOOOOga!" throughout the museum.

Call, preferably with three weeks' notice, to arrange a free, themed group tour, ideal for children's birthday parties. In "Ships to the Sea," children create their own ship models after looking at the museum's collections. Another tour, "Hats Off," looks at different styles of sailor hats and concludes with a hat-making session. Visitors also can take self-guided scavenger hunts using brochures obtained at the information desk. See Attractions for more information about Navy Yard hours and other attractions, such as the USS *Barry* navy destroyer.

Important: call before your visit to arrange for an escort, a recent security precaution.

Washington Dolls' House and Toy Museum
5236 44th St. NW
Washington, DC
(202) 244–0024

Although it lacks hands-on activities, this sweet little museum charms all ages with its thoroughly researched displays of nineteenth-century dolls' houses, dolls, toys, and games from the collection of founder and director Flora Gill Jacobs. Kids especially enjoy the turn-of-the-twentieth-century Mexican mansion and seasonal displays such as a revolving musical Christmas tree surrounded by toys in their original boxes. Old-fashioned birthday parties include cupcakes and lemonade in the Edwardian Tea Room, a tour and scavenger hunt, and a demonstration of antique windup toys. Look in the gift shop for Jacobs's children's books, *The Toy Shop Mystery* and *The Doll House Mystery*, both featuring objects from the museum's collection. (See Attractions for a complete description.)

The D.C. Miniguide to Kids' Dining

"I'm tired! I'm thirsty! I'm hungry!"

What parent doesn't dread these words, especially when they're pronounced by a whining child in the middle of a sight-seeing expedition? Here's your challenge: Find a restaurant—now!—with kid- and adult-pleasing food, fast and friendly service, reasonable prices, and diversions to keep your youngster entertained until the meal arrives.

Such a task can prove difficult even when you're close to home, let alone touring a new city. Fortunately, Washington and its surrounding suburbs offer countless options for family dining, from neighborhood eateries to familiar chains. Follow our tips and recommendations and you'll find that eating out with kids can be fun—really!

- Build mealtimes into your itinerary, and try to find out in advance if kids' meals or favorite a la carte items are available at whatever attraction you're visiting. With planning, you won't be caught off guard by a hungry child in the middle of touring a museum that doesn't have a restaurant.
- Eat at "off" times to avoid unsettling crowds. You'll find restaurants in popular tourist areas packed to the gills during the noon hour and between 6:30 and 8:30 P.M. Eat a late lunch or early dinner and you'll have a much shorter wait for your food.
- Find out if a restaurant features free or discounted children's meals during certain times. Many chains in the Washington area offer great specials during the week to entice families to dine on otherwise slow nights.
- To reduce the waiting time, especially when a restaurant is crowded, order the kids' meals or an appetizer such as soup as soon as you're seated. A cup of ice and a spoon also help stave off boredom for a while.
- Traveling with an infant or toddler? Avoid restaurants with few or no high chairs and booster seats, as such establishments generally aren't used to accommodating young children. Find out if the women's and men's rooms have changing tables, and ask whether the dining area or rest room offers a discreet place to nurse a baby. Many restaurants with salad bars allow toddlers to eat for free, a welcome option for parents whose children like to nosh on cheese, crackers, and fresh fruit or sliced vegetables.
- Carry a small backpack with a few emergency snack items like crackers, cereal bars, and packets of juice-fortified gummy treats. Also include some small games or toys and a pad of paper and pen or pencil for each child. Elementary-age youngsters can hone their reading and writing skills by copying everyone's orders from the menu. Or, have your youngster draw or write about someplace you've just visited. You can also use your waiting time to write postcards to mail to friends or to your child as a unique way of recording the trip.
- As soon as you enter an eatery, locate the rest rooms. Some kids enjoy visiting restaurant bathrooms just to check them out.
- Have realistic expectations. Don't count on a child to tolerate sitting for more than 45 minutes.
- Ask for a souvenir menu or place mat, inexpensive collectibles that prove easy to display or store. You might wish to circle and label each family member's meal.
- Kids love the decor, fish tanks, and fortune cookies at Chinese restaurants. Order steamed chicken and vegetables, sauce on the side, and let the youngsters poke around with chopsticks. (You'll be surprised at how much they eat!)
- The following restaurants are favorites of Metro Washington families, who appreciate their dependable service and kid-pleasing food. Note that, contrary to our usual policy, we do include some chains here because of their special features for kids. In general expect to pay from $2.50 to $6.00 for a child's meal featuring a burger or chicken fingers, fries, and drink.

Washington, D.C.

Hard Rock Cafe
999 E St. NW, Washington, DC
(202) 737–7625
www.hardrock.com
Where else can children order guitar-shaped chicken tenders? They're among several choices offered on the back of the coloring book/menu. Big kids have a blast exploring the restaurant's rock 'n' roll memorabilia, heavy on Jimi Hendrix, Elvis, and the Beatles. Many youngsters collect Hard Rock pins, available in the gift shop. Watch for Breakfast with Santa in December.

National Gallery of Art
4th St. and Constitution Ave. NW, Washington, DC
(202) 737–4215
www.nga.gov
If you're visiting museums on the National Mall, the Cascade Café/Espresso Bar in the gallery's Concourse is a good bet for a quick bite. We've watched one of the world's pickiest little eaters polish off a meal of favorite à la carte items like fresh fruits and french fries. Lines at the various self-service stations—salads, sandwiches, hot meals, desserts, etc.—usually move quickly once diners figure out what they're doing. Look for a seat near the huge window with a view of a mesmerizing waterfall outside.

Union Station
50 Massachusetts Ave. NE, Washington, DC
(202) 371–9441
www.unionstationdc.com
This bustling, beautifully refurbished train and Metro station also holds a shopping mall and numerous restaurants, including a huge food court with a wide selection of kid favorites. (Pick up a bag of freshly baked cookies at Vaccaro's Italian Pastry Shop.) If you prefer a full-service restaurant, visit America (202–682–9555), which offers great views of the U.S. Capitol upstairs. Downstairs, children can color on white butcher paper table coverings. The menu of more than 200 à la carte items, about $3.00 and up, features state specialties such as Maryland crab cakes and Virginia chicken pot pie. Kids can get a half-sized portion of any pasta dish, including plain spaghetti. Young diners also like peanut butter and jelly, hot dogs, grilled cheese, macaroni and cheese, and miniature hamburgers. The National Postal Museum, with many hands-on exhibits, is right across the street, and the Capital Children's Museum is a few blocks away. (See listings in this chapter.)

Northern Virginia

Calvert Grill
3106 Mt. Vernon Ave., Alexandria, VA
(703) 836–8425
When restaurant owners also happen to be parents of twins, a kid-friendly atmosphere just comes naturally. Young visitors enjoy coloring while waiting for their kids' menu meals. Check out the nightly specials for grown-ups.

IKEA Washington
Potomac Mills
2900 Potomac Mills Circle, Woodbridge, VA
(703) 643–2687
www.ikea-usa.com
The restaurant in this huge, popular Swedish furniture and housewares store features a brightly decorated children's dining area, kids' bag lunches, and baby food for the littlest

gourmets. The store also offers a free supervised ballroom and play area, where young-sters can romp while parents shop.

Paradiso Ristorante
6124 Franconia Rd., Franconia, VA
(703) 922–6222
Can't get a babysitter? This restaurant just down the street from Springfield Mall is your dream come true: Kids ages 3 to 10 eat at plastic picnic tables, color, and watch the latest videos in a children's dining area while their parents enjoy a quiet meal in an adjacent room. A waitress/babysitter supervises the youngsters, and parents keep an eye on things from a picture window that's a mirror on the kids' side. Children's meals, which include ice cream, are $5.99. We recommend you call ahead for reservations and availability.

Rainforest Cafe
Tysons Corner Center
1961 Chain Bridge Rd., McLean, VA
(703) 821–0247
www.rainforestcafe.com/rfc
Voted Best Restaurant for Families by readers of *Washington Families* newspaper, this so-called Wild Place to Shop and Eat captivates kids from the moment they catch the lifelike crocodile in front. Don't expect things to quiet down once you're inside: The dining areas feature animatronic gorillas who periodically holler and beat their chests, elephants who screech and raise their trunks, and flashes of realistic lightning, among other special effects and sounds that create a tropical atmosphere. A favorite destination for birthday celebrations, the restaurant offers a kids' menu with such fun selections as dinosaur-shaped chicken nuggets and Chocolate Banshee Screamer Sundaes. Don't miss the talking tree, real aquarium, and assorted surprises in the fun but pricey gift shop.

Suburban Maryland

B. J. Pumpernickel's New York Style Deli & Diner
18169 Town Center Dr., Olney, MD
(301) 924–1400
www.bjpumpernickels.com
Kids eat free at dinner, Monday through Wednesday, at this deli-diner. While the young-sters pick a meal, including a drink and cookie, from the Kids' Korner selections, you'll have to make up your mind over which of more than 300 items to choose from the regu-lar menu.

Franklins General Store and Delicatessen
5121 Baltimore Ave., Rte. 1, Hyattsville, MD
(301) 927–2740
Kids love eating at the New York-style deli, which offers inexpensive children's meals, and shopping in the newfangled, old-fashioned store, set in a building that used to house Hyattsville Hardware. The store's original fixtures, including nail bins and wooden boxes, now hold such items as candy, toys, and cooking gadgets.

Geppetto Restaurant of Bethesda
10257 Old Georgetown Rd., Bethesda, MD
(301) 493–9230
If your children like puppets, they'll enjoy looking at the glass cases displaying marionettes from Pinocchio and other classic tales. The coloring menu placemat features a Pinocchio scene from a rug hanging in the restaurant.

Stained Glass Pub Too
3333 Olney Sandy Springs Rd., Olney, MD
(301) 774–3778
This friendly neighborhood eatery features a clown performance from 6:00 to 8:00 P.M. Fridays. Kids often get balloon animals and can order from a children's menu.

Multiple Locations

We also recommend the following chains, with multiple locations throughout the metro area. Check the phone book for the nearest spot.

Bertucci's Brick Oven Pizzeria
www.bertuccis.com
Here's a novel way to stave off boredom: Children can fiddle with a ball of dough while waiting for their entrees. The finished creations can be cooked in the oven and taken home as keepsakes.

Clyde's
www.clydes.com
This popular local chain specializes in fresh, seasonal dishes. Kids enjoy looking at the decorations, such as model airplanes, and coloring on placemats.

Fuddruckers
www.fuddruckers.com
Families flock to these burger restaurants where youngsters enjoy free cookies, balloons, game rooms, funky decors, and on some nights, clowns.

Romano's Macaroni Grill
www.macaronigrill.com
The servers write their names upside down on the white paper tablecloths, upon which kids enjoy doodling as they await their meals. Don't be surprised if your waiter or waitress bursts into song or tap dances. Children get a kick out of the rest rooms, where they listen to an audio Italian lesson. Visit early, especially on weekends, when the wait for tables often runs 40 minutes or more.

Shoney's
www.shoneysrestaurants.com
These family restaurants often offer Kids' Night promotions, including free or discounted meals, balloons, lollipops, and visits from a costumed Shoney Bear.

Silver Diner
www.silverdiner.com
Resembling old-fashioned diners, complete with at-the-table jukeboxes, these friendly eateries feature kids' meals served with cardboard cars and coloring placemats.

Suburban Maryland

Discovery Creek Children's Museum of Washington
The Stable at Glen Echo
7300 MacArthur Blvd., Glen Echo Park
Glen Echo, MD
(202) 364–3111
www.discoverycreek.org

Set in one of the area's most intriguing parks (see related entries later in this chapter), this unique, program-based museum serves as a hands-on science, natural-history, and art-learning lab for families and school groups. Visitors participate in workshops related to elaborate exhibits replicating actual environments. One recent exhibit included a simulated wetlands, while a desert theme featured sand, a hut, and real cacti. Transformed into a living rainforest, the museum held such activities as Tagua Nut Treasures and Canopy Critters. Children visiting during the coral reef exhibit made their own coral creations. Live animals further enhance the programs. Hours are 10:00 A.M. to 3:00 P.M. Saturdays and noon to 3:00 P.M. Sundays. The museum reserves other times for school programs and popular birthday parties. Most activities are geared toward children ages 3 to 11 and cost $3.00 per child for museum members, and $4.00 for nonmembers. Adults get in free of charge. A one-year family membership is $50 and includes members-only programs, a subscription to the programming newsletter, and discounts.

ExploraWorld
6570 Dobbin Rd.
Columbia, MD
(410) 772–1540
www.exploraworld.com

This hands-on museum/indoor play center in Howard County, a short drive from D.C.'s neighboring Maryland suburbs, features lots of themed play stations for young children. With 24,000 square feet of space in which to roam, it labels itself "Maryland's largest activity center of its kind." It's open from 9:30 A.M. to 6:00 P.M. Sunday through Thursday and 9:30 A.M. to 8:00 P.M. Fridays and Saturdays. Admis-

sion is $2.00 for adults, $7.95 for children ages 2 and older, $3.95 for children age 1, and free for babies younger than 12 months. A popular party site, it features rooms with themes like The Polar Icecaps and Ocean Treasures.

* NASA Goddard Space Flight Center Visitors Center
Soil Conservation Rd.
Greenbelt, MD
(301) 286–8981
pao.gsfc.nasa.gov

Kids interested in space and rocketry will enjoy the museum's interactive exhibits pertaining to Goddard's involvement in the space program. Visitors can build and launch a space satellite via a computer game and sit in a Gemini space capsule that includes an audio recording simulating liftoff in a Titan rocket. Model rocket enthusiasts hold launches the first and third Sundays of each month at 1:00 P.M. The museum also arranges educational birthday parties. (See Attractions for more information about the center.)

National Capital Trolley Museum
1313 Bonifant Rd.
Wheaton, MD
(301) 384–6088
www.dctrolley.org

All aboard for an old-fashioned trolley ride! Most kids probably won't be too interested in the museum's collection of streetcar memorabilia, but they'll enjoy riding an American trolley, European tram, or Washington streetcar along the museum's demonstration railway that runs through Northwest Branch Park. Along with exhibits, the Visitors Center features a model streetcar layout and museum shop. Birthday rides are available for groups of 20 or more. (See Attractions for a complete description.)

National Wildlife Visitor Center
10901 Scarlet Tanager Loop
Laurel, MD
(301) 497–5760
patuxent.fws.gov

Budding naturalists will have fun pushing buttons and playing with interactive videos in exhibits that focus on global environmental problems, habitats, endangered species, and life cycles. A guided electric tram tour travels through the woods and around the lake of the surrounding Patuxent Research Refuge (described further in our Attractions chapter), operated by the U.S. Fish and Wildlife Service. Tram tickets are $2.00 for teens and adults, $1.00 for seniors 55 and older and children 12 and younger.

Fabulous Farms

Leave the bustling city and suburbs behind and head for a close-at-hand yet more pastoral experience at one of the following historic sites or working, pick-your-own produce farms.

Farm Museums and Plantations

Northern Virginia

The Claude Moore Colonial Farm at Turkey Run
6310 Georgetown Pk.
McLean, VA
(703) 442–7557
www.1771.org

Your kids will think they've stepped back in time as they watch a poor farm family of 1771 work their land, tend to their livestock, and perform their chores at this living-history site. The authentic-looking reenactors, often including children, are happy to answer the questions of curious, modern-day visitors. Youngsters enjoy looking at the farm animals and participating in special events like harvest time and periodic eighteenth-century market fairs. Be prepared for a lot of walking on gravel paths that wind around the six-acre farming area. (Take a tip from the staff and don't even bother trying to push an umbrella stroller along the frequently muddy paths.)

Hours are 10:00 A.M. to 4:30 P.M. Wednesday through Sunday, early April through mid-December. The farm is closed during bad weather and on Thanksgiving. Admission is $2.00 for adults and teens, $1.00 for seniors and children ages 3 to 12; tots 2 and younger

get in free. Admission for special programs usually is $3.00 for adults, $1.50 for seniors and children.

Kidwell Farm at Frying Pan Park
2709 West Ox Rd.
Herndon, VA
(703) 437–9101
www.co.fairfax.va.us/parks/
fryingpanpark.htm

Children love visiting this small, working model of a 1930s family farm, which features a barnyard full of pigs, goats, dairy cows, sheep, draft horses, chickens and peacocks, and many baby animals in the spring. It's also home to the official Presidential Turkey, which arrives after its traditional Thanksgiving pardon. Special programs include hayrides, blacksmithing demonstrations, and occasional "Putting the Animals to Bed" story times for children. Events are free or require a nominal charge. Call (703) 324–8588 for a schedule. Daily farm hours are 10:00 A.M. to 6:00 P.M. Admission is free.

Mount Vernon
Southern end of the George Washington
Memorial Pkwy.
Mt. Vernon, VA
(703) 780–2000
www.mountvernon.org

George Washington's historic estate and gardens are becoming increasingly kid-friendly, with year-round interactive programs. Throughout the summer children can visit the Hands-On History Tent to harness a fiberglass mule, play Colonial games, try on period clothing, and make wooden buckets, among other activities. They also can measure themselves next to a life-size likeness of the first president. Year-round, kids can visit the *George Washington: Pioneer Farmer* exhibit, which features, March through November, hands-on activities such as fence building, corn cracking, and fishnet making. Youngsters especially like looking at the farm animals, including such rare breeds as Ossabaw hogs and Hogg Island sheep. Even a visit to the mansion and outbuildings becomes fun for kids when they follow the Treasure Map of Mount Vernon, a souvenir brochure available free of charge at the main gate. Admission is $9.00 for folks 12 and older, $8.50 for seniors 62 and older, and $4.50 for children ages 6 through 11. (See our Attractions chapter for a complete description.)

Sully Historic Site
Rte. 28, across from Washington Dulles International Airport
Chantilly, VA
(703) 437–1794
www.co.fairfax.va.us/parks/sully

Young visitors to this restored 1794 plantation home of Northern Virginia's first congressman enjoy year-round family-oriented weekend programs on such topics as Toys and Games of Yesteryear, Quill Pen Writing, and Ice-Cream Making. During the summer, Sully offers a variety of hands-on educational activities for children ages 8 to 12. See the summer issue of Parktakes, a guide to Fairfax County parks, for details. To obtain a copy, call (703) 222–4664. Admission to the site is

$5.00 for adults, $4.00 for students 16 and older, and $3.00 for children and seniors. Hours are 11:00 A.M. to 4:00 P.M. daily, except Tuesdays.

Suburban Maryland

National Colonial Farm of the Accokeek Foundation
3400 Bryan Point Rd.
Accokeek, MD
(301) 283–2113
www.accokeek.org

Mount Vernon's neighbor directly across the Potomac River, this colonial tobacco farm, part of the National Park Service, features many barnyard animals such as cows, sheep, geese, chickens, roosters, and lovely EllieMae, the Ossabaw hog. Look for baby critters in the spring. Weekend tours feature rotating demonstrations about such topics as herbs, Colonial lighting, and textiles. Call for information about upcoming special programs such as Children's Day and seasonal celebrations. Admission is $2.00 for adults and

Young visitors to Sully Historic Site get a lesson in Colonial crafts. PHOTO: COURTESY OF FAIRFAX COUNTY PARK AUTHORITY

50 cents for children younger than 12, with a maximum of $5.00 per family. Hours, subject to seasonal changes, generally are 10:00 A.M. to 4:00 P.M. Saturdays and Sundays spring through fall. Staff members who serve as docents are available only during weekends. Visitors can take a ferry across the river to Mount Vernon during the summer; call for times.

Oxon Hill Farm
6411 Oxon Hill Rd.
Oxon Hill, MD
(301) 839–1177
www.nps.gov/nace/oxhi.htm
This turn-of-the-century working farm, owned by the National Park Service, offers daily hands-on events for children, who enjoy seeing the many barnyard animals. Kids can help milk a cow, feed chickens, and gather eggs. Call for more information about these and special weekend events. Admission is free. The farm is open daily, 8:00 A.M. to 4:30 P.M., closed New Year's Day, Thanksgiving, and Christmas.

Farm-Fresh Fun

Visit these farms in October for special children's activities, usually requiring a weekend admission fee of $6.00 to $8.50 per person. They also feature fresh or pick-your-own crops in the spring and summer.

Northern Virginia
Cox Farms
15621 Braddock Rd.
Centreville, VA
(703) 830–4121
www.coxfarms.com
The annual fall festival, throughout October, features numerous slides, climbable hay bales, hay swings, animals, face painting, and live entertainment on weekends, along with cider, apples, and pumpkins for visitors. A tractor-drawn hayride drives through a pond and includes an encounter with a spaceship, complete with "aliens" who chase after gleefully screaming kids aboard the hay wagon. The hours are 10:00 A.M. to 6:00 P.M. (or dark) daily in October. Plan to spend several hours!

Suburban Maryland
Butlers Orchard
22200 Davis Mill Rd.
Germantown, MD
(301) 972–3299
Butlers holds one of the area's most popular pumpkin festivals on weekends during October. Kids love to go for rides in a hay wagon and Cinderella's fiberglass mouse-pulled pumpkin coach, feed billy goats and other farm animals, jump in a hayloft, navigate a tunnel and straw maze, and look at the many characters who populate Pumpkin Land. The orchard is open 10:00 A.M. to 5:30 P.M. Tuesday through Sunday, with the festival held from 10:00 A.M. to 5:00 P.M. Saturdays and Sundays.

Cherry Hill Farm
12300 Gallahan Rd.
near Oxon Hill, MD
(301) 292–1928
www.cherryhillfarm.com
Weekend Halloween tours feature a hayride to the pumpkin patch, visits to a petting zoo, slides, tunnels, a 5-acre corn maze, and a Fun Barn. Visitors of all ages enjoy looking at more than 450 scarecrow characters displayed along the hayride path. Don't leave without treating the kids, and yourself, to homemade cider doughnuts or apple-pie flavored ice cream.

The market is open from 8:30 A.M. to 6:30 P.M., Monday through Saturday, 8:00 A.M. to 6:30 P.M. Sundays.

Darrow Berry Farm
Bell Station Rd.
Glenn Dale, MD
(301) 390–6191, (301) 390–6611
Take hayrides to the pick-your-own pumpkin patch, visit a haunted house, ride a pony, get your faces painted, and watch apple butter-making demonstrations. The farm is open 10:00 A.M. to 6:00 P.M. Saturdays and Sundays, beginning the second Saturday in October. Most activities are free or require a small admission fee.

Rainy-Day Raves

Actually, you needn't wait for a rainy day to visit these children's stores and craft places, big and small, all of which offer indoor fun through story times, creative activities, and other special events.

Books and Toys

Barnes & Noble Booksellers
3040 M St. NW
Washington, DC
(202) 965-9880
555 12th St. NW
Washington, DC
(202) 347-0176
5345 Wisconsin Ave. NW
Washington, DC
(202) 686-6542
3651 Jefferson Davis Hwy.
Alexandria, VA
(703) 299-9124
12193 Fair Lakes Promenade Dr.
Fairfax, VA
(703) 278-0300
6260 Arlington Blvd.
Falls Church, VA
(703) 536-0774
1851 Fountain Dr.
Reston, VA
(703) 437-9490
6646 Loisdale Rd.
Springfield, VA
(703) 971-5383
4801 Bethesda Ave.
Bethesda, MD
(301) 986-1761
21 Grand Corner Ave.
Gaithersburg, MD
(301) 721-0860
12089 Rockville Pk.
Rockville, MD
(301) 881-0237
www.bn.com

Free story hours, young adult book clubs, interactive music and movement classes, and craft sessions take place regularly in the children's departments of most stores in this large chain. Costumed characters and well-known authors also make occasional appearances. Visit to obtain a monthly events calendar.

Borders Books & Music
600th 14th St. NW
Washington, DC
(202) 737-1385
18th and L Sts. NW
Washington, DC
(202) 466-4999
5333 Wisconsin Ave. NW
Washington, DC
(202) 686-8270
1201 S. Hayes St.
Arlington, VA
(703) 418-0166
5871 Crossroads Center Way
Baileys Crossroads, VA
(703) 998-0404
11054 Lee Hwy.
Fairfax, VA
(703) 359-8420

6701 Frontier Dr.
Springfield, VA
(703) 924–4894
8311 Leesburg Pk.
Vienna, VA
(703) 556–7766
4420 Mitchellville Rd.
Bowie, MD
(301) 352–5560
534 N. Frederick Ave.
Gaithersburg, MD
(301) 921–0990
11301 Rockville Pike
Kensington, MD
(301) 816–1067
20926 Frederick Rd.
Germantown, MD
(301) 528–0862
www.borders.com

These nationally known bookstores carry a large selection of children's volumes, and each features at least one weekly free story time for preschoolers. On Saturday many of the stores hold free special events such as craft workshops, book signings by children's authors, puppet shows, storytelling, and visits from costumed characters like Curious George and the Cat in the Hat. Times vary at individual stores; stop by for a schedule.

Zany Brainy
3901 Jefferson Davis Hwy.
Alexandria, VA
(703) 299–3083
3513 S. Jefferson St.
Baileys Crossroads, VA
(703) 998–1203
2890 Prince William Pkwy.
Woodbridge, VA
(703) 680–9870
9490 Main St.
Fairfax, VA
(703) 323–3658
12180 W. Ox Rd.
Fairfax, VA
(703) 691–1896
46262 Cranston Way
Sterling, VA
(703) 404–8850
6575 Frontier Dr.
Springfield, VA
(703) 719–9585

11870 Spectrum Center
Reston, VA
(703) 318–1875
202 Kentlands Blvd.
Gaithersburg, MD
(301) 330–5160
1631 Rockville Pike
Rockville, MD
(301) 984–0112
www.zanybrainy.com

Kids are never bored when they visit these big, bright educational toy stores, which feature a different free drop-in event every day. Preschoolers enjoy story times and character photo days, and older kids have fun making crafts or trying out the latest fads, like yo-yos and Crazy Bones. Nationally known authors and illustrators sometimes drop by to sign books, and popular recording artists occasionally perform miniconcerts. Children like to push kid-size carts alongside their parents' larger ones, which can fill up quickly with music and books as well as art supplies and Beanie Babies. When youngsters tire of browsing, they can watch ongoing videos or sample new computer software. Pick up a monthly calendar to keep track of what's scheduled.

Northern Virginia

Aladdin's Lamp Children's Books & Other Treasures
126 W. Broad St.
Falls Church, VA
(703) 241–8281

Run by a children's librarian, Aladdin's Lamp is another of the area's few remaining independent, family-owned children's bookstores. The shop carries more than 20,000 titles and hosts frequent special programs, most of which are free. Reservations are recommended for story hours, usually held Wednesdays and Saturdays at 11:00 A.M. for ages two and a half to six. Workshops for older children often feature authors or community volunteers who share special talents and feature such topics as origami, sports, and American Girls.

The store, which celebrated its twelfth year in December 2001, also carries puppets, stickers, bookmarks, and a large selection of unusual Baltic amber jewelry made by the owner's family. Hours are Monday, Wednesday, Friday, and Saturday, 10:00 A.M. to 6:00 P.M.; and Tuesday and Thursday, 10:00 A.M. to 8:00 P.M. Ask for a newsletter describing special events.

Imagination Station
4524 Lee Hwy.
Arlington, VA
(703) 522–2047
www.kinderhaus.com

This neighborhood children's bookstore holds book signings and parties with costumed characters. The store carries a large selection of foreign-language books. Hours are Monday through Friday, 10:00 A.M. to 7:00 P.M. (open until 8:00 P.M. Thursday), Saturday 10:00 A.M. to 6:00 P.M., and Sunday 11:00 A.M. to 4:00 P.M. Call for a quarterly newsletter. Visit the neighboring, affiliated Kinder Haus Toys, with two floors of playthings and children's clothing at 4510 Lee Highway (703-527-5929), which is open 10:00 A.M. to 7:00 P.M. Monday through Friday, 10:00 A.M. to 6:00 P.M. Saturday, and 10:00 A.M. to 4:00 P.M. Sunday.

A Likely Story
1555 King St.
Alexandria, VA
(703) 836–2498
www.alikelystorybooks.com

This 17-year-old, independent children's bookstore in Old Town features seasonal activities, monthly costumed-character appearances, and 8 to 10 author visits annually. The shop holds story times twice a week. A drop-in program Tuesdays and Wednesdays at 11:00 A.M. offers songs and finger plays for infants to age three. Reservations are requested for programs held Saturday at 11:00 A.M., usually with themed crafts for ages three to six. The store also holds events for parents and teachers. While grown-ups browse, kids can visit the store's hermit crabs or hang out in a play space stocked with toys. The store also carries an expanded game section, featuring Alexandria-made Binary Arts games. Hours are 10:00 A.M. to 6:00 P.M. Monday through Saturday and 1:00 to 5:00 P.M. Sundays. Call for a newsletter, published five times a year.

Once Upon a Time
120 Church St. NE
Vienna, VA
(703) 255–3285
www.once.uponatime.com

A realistic tree and beautiful displays of collectible dolls, miniatures, and stuffed animals charm visitors who enter this compact but well-stocked 20-year-old toy store. Each month, Once Upon a Time hosts at least one creative special event. Children attending Madeline Day in the spring meet the popular book character and sample French pastries. Breyer horse collectors celebrate their shared interest with a party featuring carrots, apples, and sugar cubes. A newsletter, published four or five times annually, details upcoming programs. The store is open Monday through Saturday from 10:00 A.M. to 5:00 P.M., and Sundays from noon to 5:00 P.M., except during August. Stop by after taking in a children's concert at Wolf Trap Farm Park (see the subsequent Sensational Shows section as well as The Arts chapter).

Why Not?
200 King St.
Alexandria, VA
(703) 548–4420

Kids "ooh" and "aah" over the whimsically detailed plush animal scenes in the window of this charming corner store, right in the heart of historic Old Town Alexandria. Inside, you'll find two floors of specialty clothing, books, and toys, including many display models which have been placed throughout the store for children to try; toddlers get to test some, too, in an enclosed "playpen" area while their parents shop. Hours vary seasonally, but usually are from 10:00 A.M. to 5:30 P.M. Monday, 10:00 A.M. to 9:00 P.M. Tuesday through Saturday, and noon to 5:00 P.M. Sunday.

Suburban Maryland
Bookoo Books for Kids
4945 Elm St.
Bethesda, MD
(301) 652–2794

This small, independent children's bookstore hosts a weekly story time for ages one and a half and older Wednesdays at 10:00 A.M. Reservations are recommended. The shop also holds such special events as American Girl craft parties and character appearances and specializes in storybook-themed birthday parties. While parents shop, kids can play with beanbags, puzzles, and tea sets. Hours are Monday through Wednesday, Friday and Saturday, 10:00 A.M. to 6:00 P.M.; Thursday, 10:00 A.M. to 7:00 P.M.; and Sunday, noon to 5:00 P.M. Call for a newsletter.

Whirligigs & Whimsies
Wildwood Shopping Center
10213 Old Georgetown Rd.
Bethesda, MD
(301) 897–4940
American Girl Days, costumed-character appearances, and book signings by well-known children's authors are among the free special events that take place at least once a month at this specialty toy store. Although the shop doesn't publish a newsletter, its mailing list customers receive advance notification of activities. A pleasant stop after a visit to nearby Cabin John Regional Park (see the listing later in this chapter), the store is open Monday through Wednesday, Friday and Saturday from 10:00 A.M. to 6:00 P.M. and Thursday from 10:00 A.M. to 7:00 P.M.

Artful Adventures

Pottery Painting

Creativity is the name of the game at the following studios, offering ideal outings for kids who like to say, "I made it myself." Choose a white-clay figurine or serving piece, pick your colors, and start painting; the studio staff does the cleanup, glazing, and firing. Studio fees include unlimited paint, use of supplies, and glazing and kiln firing. The bisque item(s) you pick to paint cost extra—usually anywhere from $3.00 to $45.00. All supplies are nontoxic, and most clear glazes are lead-free. Birthday party packages are available at all locations. Note that you may have to wait a few days to pick up your completed masterpiece.

Made By You
3413 Connecticut Ave. NW
Washington, DC
(202) 363–9590
2319 Wilson Blvd.
Arlington, VA
(703) 841–3533
4923 Elm St.
Bethesda, MD
(301) 654–3206
209 N. Washington St.
Rockville, MD
(301) 610–5496
Hours vary at the different locations. A flat fee, ranging from $6.00 to $65.00, covers the cost of your item, supplies, and studio time.

Northern Virginia
Paint Your Own Pottery
10417 Main St.
Fairfax, VA
(703) 218–2881
www.ciao-susanna.com
Hours are Monday through Friday, 10:00 A.M. to 6:00 P.M.; Saturday, 10:00 A.M. to 5:00 P.M.; and Sunday, noon to 5:00 P.M. The studio fee is $7.00 for the first hour, $1.00 for each additional 10 minutes. Ask about specials, such as half-price kids' days.

Educational Crafts

Cathedral Medieval Workshop
Washington National Cathedral
Massachusetts and Wisconsin Aves. NW
Washington, DC
(202) 537–2934
www.cathedral.org/cathedral
The Cathedral Medieval Workshop's seven hands-on stations give families a close-up look at the creative process behind the magnificent gothic building's art and architecture. Designed for children five and older accompanied by adults, the activity center lets visitors create gargoyles from self-drying clay, carve limestone with a mallet and chisel, design a Gothic bookmark, hammer copper on an anvil, make a crayon rubbing of a brass engraving, construct arches with blocks

and a wooden frame, and piece together stained glass.

As you leave the workshop, pick up pamphlets featuring cathedral-related family activities, from puzzles to scavenger hunts. Kids who enjoy Disney's *The Hunchback of Notre Dame* especially like *Eight Great Gargoyles—A Self-Guided Tour for the Young at Heart,* featuring some of the most popular of the 107 gargoyles and countless grotesques that adorn the building's exterior.

The drop-in workshop, in the northwest crypt, is open to the public year-round on Saturdays from 10:00 A.M. to 2:00 P.M., and Monday through Friday, 1:00 to 4:00 P.M. in July. The admission fee of $5.00 per person includes a ball of clay and paper for the bookmark and brass rubbing. The cathedral also holds a monthly Family Saturday, featuring stories, a tour, and an art project built around a theme such as Groovy Gargoyles or Beauty and the Bestiary. Geared toward ages four through eight, the $6.00 sessions take place from 10:00 to 11:30 A.M. and from noon to 1:30 P.M. Call (202) 537-2220 to make a reservation. (See the Attractions, Annual Events, and Worship chapters for other activities.)

Reston Storefront Museum & Shop
Lake Anne Village Center
1639 Washington Plaza
Reston, VA
(703) 709-7700
www.RestonMuseum.org

Visit this community museum between 10:00 a.m. and noon on Saturdays for free, drop-in children's art workshops. Local artist Pat Macintyre provides materials and encouragement as youngsters create a different project each week. Activities often relate to local historical topics or seasonal themes. Browse the free museum to learn about the unique planned community of Reston. Other family-oriented Lake Anne activities on Saturdays from spring through early fall include a farmers' market from 8:00 A.M. to noon, handcrafters, and pedal-boat rentals. The Lakeside Pharmacy next door to the museum features inexpensive meals and snacks at a soda fountain and outdoor cafe.

Awesome Amusements

When the kids need to let off some steam, visit one of these amusement places for nothing but fun and games. Unless otherwise noted, prices vary widely according to the type of activity, age of participant, and time of day. Hours also vary seasonally. Your best bet is to call ahead with specifics on your visit. (See our Parks and Recreation chapter for more ideas.)

Sportrock Climbing Centers
5308 Eisenhower Ave.
Alexandria, VA
(703) 212-7625
45935 Maries Rd.
Sterling, VA
(571) 434-ROCK
14708 Southlawn La.
Rockville, MD
(301) 762-5111
www.sportrock.com

Kids—and grown-ups too—literally climb the walls at these indoor recreation centers, where the walls resemble rocky surfaces just waiting to be scaled. Check out Kids' Nite on Fridays from 7:00 to 8:30 P.M., when children ages 6 to 14 get vertical with help from experienced instructors. The cost is $19.50 per child, $30 for two siblings, and $40 for three siblings. Call for information about regular hours and rates, summer camps, and classes. Hours are noon to 11:00 P.M. Monday through Friday, 11:00 A.M. to 8:00 P.M. Saturdays, and noon to 8:00 P.M. Sundays. Admission is $14.00 for ages 13 and older, $6.00 for ages 12 and younger.

Northern Virginia

Centreville Mini Golf & Games
6206 Multiplex Dr.
Centreville, VA
(703) 502-7888
www.planetplay.com

If you're not already on vacation, you may feel like you are when you play the 18-

hole, resort-style miniature golf course, landscaped to resemble a lush, natural setting complete with waterfalls. Ready for something completely different? Head inside for a game of Laser Storm, a futuristic tag game using laser beams and accented by special lighting effects. Active kids 10 and younger can climb all over a three-story indoor playground, while less adventurous family members try their skills at arcade games that offer redemption tickets.

Millenium DDR Techno Dance
7106 Columbia Pike
Annandale, VA
(703) 354-2003

This unique arcade features popular DDR (Dance Dance Revolution) machines, which score points based on a player's ability to execute dance moves in designated sequences. Most machines require a $1.00 coin per play. The arcade also features a few video games, a karaoke booth, and "Real Drum," a percussion variation of the dancing machines. A party room includes a wall of video screens for karaoke and DVD viewing. Smoking and alcoholic beverages are prohibited inside the building. Patrons can purchase Korean snack foods, carbonated beverages, and bottled water.

Hours are noon to midnight Monday through Thursday, noon to 4:00 a.m. Fridays and Saturdays, and noon to 1:00 a.m. Sundays.

Planet Splash & Play
4600 Brookfield Corporate Dr.
Chantilly, VA
(703) 378-6600
www.planetplay.com

The new water park, open during the summer only, features an uphill water roller coaster that uses water jets to propel thrill-seekers speedily around curves. Year-round activities include a large roller-skating rink—a favorite spot for birthday parties—and go-kart track, game arcade, and snack bar. The skating rink holds special nights for preteens and teens on weekends.

Suburban Maryland

Jeepers
6000 Greenbelt Rd.
Greenbelt, MD
(301) 982-2444
700 Hungerford Dr.
Rockville, MD
(301) 309-2525
www.jeepers.com

What's faster than a rolling grape? How about a flying banana? Banana Squadron is one ride you'll find at these indoor amusement parks, which also feature kid-size roller coasters, bumper cars, and a few other jungle-themed, moving attractions. Rambunctious youngsters enjoy climbing about the mazelike playground's many tunnels and chutes and playing arcade games for coupons to redeem for prizes.

Six Flags America
13710 Central Ave.
Largo, MD
(301) 249-1500
www.sixflags.com/america

Kids needn't fret over being too little for this theme/water park's thrill rides: Looney Tunes Movie Town features rides and a live show especially for children. Crocodile Cal's Outback Beach House, a five-story, interactive play area, offers more than 100 water-powered attractions, including a barrel that dumps 1,000 gallons of water on unsuspecting passersby every few minutes. Still not wet enough? Play on the slides and submarine in the 10,000-square-foot Kids' Cove pool. You'd be wise to avoid Six Flags on summer weekends, when lines frequently require waits of 45 minutes or longer. Park personnel tend to get cranky in the heat, too. (See our Parks and Recreation chapter for more about this park, formerly known as Adventure World.)

Sensational Shows

Watching plays, puppet shows, and other live performances stimulates children's powers of imagination and promotes a

Gravity-defying rides and superheroes beckon kids to Six Flags America in Prince George's County.

PHOTO: COURTESY OF SIX FLAGS AMERICA

love of the arts. We've selected a few of our favorite places to see entertaining, high-quality productions for families. (Check out The Arts chapter for additional ideas.)

Washington, D.C.

Discovery Theater
Smithsonian Institution's Arts and Industries Building
900 Jefferson Dr. SW
Washington, DC
(202) 357–1500
discoverytheater.si.edu

Now in its 20th year, this theater puts on 16 shows a year, including five or six original works written or directed by local actors. Popular field trips for local schoolchildren, the performances include puppet shows, dance, plays, and storytelling by various artists, many of whom are nationally known. Shows take place weekdays at 10:00 and 11:30 A.M. and some Saturdays at 11:30 A.M. and 1:00 P.M. during the school year and in June and July. Admission is $5.00 per person, and reser-

vations are recommended. Call the number above for information about upcoming programs. The closest Metro stop is Smithsonian.

John F. Kennedy Center for the Performing Arts
2700 F St. NW
Washington, DC
(202) 467–4600
www.kennedy-center.org

Think you can't afford to take the whole family to a show at this internationally renowned showcase for the performing arts? Check out the free programs offered on the Millennium Stage. The series features something different every night, including children's performers. The center also features plays and concerts for kids throughout the year. Recent Kennedy Center Youth and Family Programs, presented in the Theatre Lab, have included such favorite tales as *The Best Christmas Pageant Ever* and *Tales of a Fourth Grade Nothing*. The Washington Chamber Symphony holds an annual series of educational Concerts for Young People, featuring such themes as The Mighty Strings and Beethoven's Symphony No. 5. The symphony's Family Series includes a traditional Holiday Sing-a-Long so popular it sells out four months in advance. The center also holds Broadway-caliber musicals such as *The King and I* and Disney's *Beauty and the Beast*; tickets are pricey, but worth considering for a special occasion. (See our Arts chapter for more about the Kennedy Center's programs.)

Northern Virginia

Classika Theatre
4041 28th St. S
Arlington, VA
(703) 824–6200
www.classika.org
Founded by Russian-born actress Inna U. Shapiro, this critically acclaimed theater specializes in adaptations of beloved fairy tales like *Little Red Riding Hood* and *The Snow Queen*, as well as original works. The theater presents both live-action and puppet shows, as well as thought-provoking plays for adults. It also holds a variety of drama classes and a summer camp. Tickets for children's productions range from $10 to $15, and performances take place on Fridays, Saturdays, and Sundays. You'll find the theater in the Village at Shirlington, a retail district filled with interesting restaurants and shops.

West End Children's Theatre
Children's Theatre at the West End Dinner Theatre
4615 Duke St.
Alexandria, VA
(703) 370–2500
www.wedt.com
Look around the audience here on a Saturday afternoon and you're liable to see dozens of little girls in pretty party dresses. The children's matinees, featuring musicals such as *Winnie the Pooh* and *Cinderella*, make this a popular birthday party spot, where kids can celebrate right at their tables after shows end. Most performances take place at 2:00 P.M. on Saturdays. Tickets cost $7.00 per person and

$6.00 per person for groups of 10 or greater. No meals are served, but snacks and beverages are available before the show and during intermission. (See our Nightlife chapter for information about the theater's evening dinner shows.)

Wolf Trap Farm Park
1551 Trap Rd.
Vienna, VA
(703) 255–1860
www.wolftrap.org
The National Park Service's venue for the performing arts features many kids' shows, including those of the 27-year-old Children's Theatre-in-the-Woods outdoor summer show and workshop series. Call (703) 255–1827 in late May for a schedule of puppet shows, plays, songs, stories, dancing, and clowning. Admission $3.00. Reservations for the series fill up quickly. The park's primary summer concert series in the open-air Filene Center sometimes includes children's performers like Raffi or Sharon, Lois, and Bram. Kids' shows also take place during the fall and winter in the Barns of Wolf Trap just down the road. The park's International Children's Festival, held annually during a September weekend (see our Annual Events chapter) features an eclectic array of young performers from around the world. Kids can also create a variety of beautiful craft projects in a hands-on tent staffed by adult volunteers. Call (703) 642–0862 for more details. Admission is charged. (See The Arts chapter for additional information about Wolf Trap.)

Suburban Maryland

Adventure Theatre
Glen Echo Park
7300 MacArthur Blvd.
Glen Echo, MD
(301) 320–5331
www.nps.gov/glec/adtheat.htm
Headquartered in a former amusement park penny arcade, 50-year-old Adventure Theatre is the oldest continuous children's theater in the Washington area. Semiprofessional actors annually perform eight shows, many of which are

based on classic stories for young people and recommended for ages 4 to 12. Recent and upcoming offerings dramatize such tales as *The Lion, the Witch and the Wardrobe*, *The Adventures of Beatrix Potter and Her Friends*, *Anne of Green Gables*, *Jack and the Beanstalk*, and *The Wizard of Oz*. The audience sits on carpeted steps to watch the performances, which take place Saturdays and Sundays at 1:30 and 3:30 P.M. Tickets are $5.00 a person regardless of age. After the show, kids enjoy meeting the performers, who are more than happy to sign autographs. (See the subsequent Puppet Co. Playhouse and Glen Echo Park entries for related information.)

BAPA's Imagination Stage
White Flint
11301 Rockville Pike
Rockville, MD
(301) 881–5106
www.imaginationstage.org
Conveniently located in one of the area's most popular shopping malls, this children's theater of the Bethesda Academy of Performing Arts (BAPA) presents six productions per season, ranging from adaptations of contemporary stories such as *Miss Nelson Is Missing* to classics like *Aladdin*. The 22-year-old organization also offers drama classes and camp as well as a performing company of hearing-impaired teens. Shows take place on Saturdays and Sundays. Tickets are $6.50, $5.50 each for groups of 10 or more.

Now This! Kids!
Blair Mansion Inn
7711 Eastern Ave.
Silver Spring, MD
(202) 364–8292
www.nowthisimprov.com
If you missed the debut performances of *The Ugly Princess and the Mean Carrot* and *The Duck Who Burped*, you won't get another chance to see the shows. They're among the one-time-only titles presented by Now This! Kids!, the area's only totally improvised musical theater company for kids. Using suggestions from children in the audience, the wacky adult troupe creates on-the-spot songs, comic sketches, and fairy tales. The company received the International Special Events Society's award for best entertainment and WRC-TV Channel 4's nod for Best Bet for Children's Entertainment.

The troupe works its magic on young audiences ages 5 to 12 each Saturday during a luncheon theater that attracts a lot of birthday parties. (Performers make up an original song about each birthday child.) Ticket prices range from $11 to $18, and reservations are requested.

The Puppet Co. Playhouse
Glen Echo Park
7300 MacArthur Blvd.
Glen Echo, MD
(301) 320–6668
www.thepuppetco.org
A hop, skip, and a jump from the neighboring Adventure Theatre, the Puppet Co.'s claim to fame is its status as the only East Coast theater between Atlanta and New York that performs only puppet shows. The three-person company creates unique marionettes and puppets for year-round shows, featuring both original stories and new takes on classic fairy tales like *Jack and the Beanstalk* and *Little Red Riding Hood*. The company's popular annual production of *The Nutcracker* includes stunning special effects.

Children sit on the carpeted floor, and adults squeeze in behind the kids and on the sides, where they won't block the little ones' view. *Warning:* Some toddlers and preschoolers may become frightened by the realistic witch and giant puppets used in many shows. Afterward, kids can meet the puppeteers and say hello to a marionette or two.

Shows are performed Wednesday through Friday at 10:00 and 11:30 A.M., and Saturday and Sunday at 11:30 and 1:00 P.M. Reservations are recommended. Admission is $5.00.

Perfect Parks

When the weather's great and your children get tired of their own backyard or hotel room, head for a park. We've selected a sampling of family favorites, filled with

Jack outwits the giant at The Puppet Co. Playhouse. PHOTO: COURTESY OF THE PUPPET CO. PLAYHOUSE

such dependable kid-pleasers as playgrounds, pools, merry-go-rounds, and nature centers. (Be sure and check the Parks and Recreation chapter for more information on these and other parks.)

Washington, D.C.

National Zoological Park
3001 Connecticut Ave. NW
Washington, DC
(202) 673–4800
www.si.edu/natzoo

With its 5 miles of winding, sloping pathways, the zoo proves a great destination for burning off energy. Time your visit to see a kid-pleasing animal demonstration, such as the Giant Panda interpreters' talks at 10:00 A.M. and 4:00 P.M. and elephant train-

ing at 11:00 A.M. School-age youngsters in particular enjoy hands-on attractions in the popular Amazonia, the Reptile Discovery Center, and the Invertebrate Exhibit, which features a Pollinarium filled with butterflies and hummingbirds.

The Friends of the National Zoo membership program ($47 annually) holds numerous children's programs, including camps and family overnights and camp-outs. (See the Attractions chapter for more details about zoo hours and features.)

Rock Creek Park
3545 Williamsburg La. NW
Washington, DC
(202) 426–6829
www.nps.gov/rocr

This huge, popular urban park holds a gallery, historic mill, and planetarium and nature center, all of which feature programs for children. The Rock Creek Gallery holds a children's art festival in June and a summer art camp. At Pierce Mill (202-426-6908), open noon to 4:00 P.M. Wednesday through Sunday, kids can visit an activity table to grind corn and make a model of the mill. Free story times take place twice monthly. The Rock Creek Nature Center, open 9:00 A.M. to 5:00 P.M. Wednesday through Sunday, features hands-on activities and special events for kids. Call (202) 426-6829 for information about programs there and at the Planetarium. (See the Parks and Recreation chapter for more about this park, which closes on New Year's Day, July 4th, Thanksgiving, and Christmas.)

Northern Virginia

Burke Lake Park
7315 Ox Rd.
Fairfax Station, VA
(703) 323–6601
www.co.fairfax.va.us/parks/lakefront.htm
A favorite with Fairfax County families, this park features numerous kid-pleasing

attractions, including a carousel, a *C.P. Huntington* train ride that goes through a tunnel and woods, and an ice-cream parlor for snacks or birthday parties. Youngsters also love to ride the pontoon tour boat on the lake and feed bread to the many ducks and Canada geese that flock around the marina. The park hosts a children's festival in the spring, nature camps and Saturday morning kids' concerts during the summer, and a Ghost Train Ride near Halloween. The park is open 7:00 A.M. to dark daily. Call for times and prices of the rides, which operate throughout the summer and during some weekends in the spring and fall. (See the Parks and Recreation chapter for more information.)

Colvin Run Mill Historic Site
10017 Colvin Run Rd.
Great Falls, VA
(703) 759–2771
www.co.fairfax.va.us/parks/crm
Grab some homemade ice cream at Thelma's country store just down the road, then stroll the grounds around this working, water-powered gristmill. Children enjoy feeding crushed grain to the resident millpond ducks. On many Sundays throughout the summer, the Northern Virginia Woodcarvers offer free carving lessons to kids and adults. The site frequently holds special events on weekends, including child-only holiday shopping in the old-fashioned General Store that sells candies, toys, and fun gifts. The site is open daily, 11:00 A.M. to 5:00 P.M., except Tuesdays. Mill tours, offered on the hour from 11:00 A.M. to 4:00 P.M., cost $4.00 for adults, $3.00 for any students 16 and older, and $2.00 for children and seniors.

Lake Accotink Park
7500 Accotink Park Rd.
Springfield, VA
(703) 569–3464
www.co.fairfax.va.us/parks/accotink
The new Lucky Duck Mini Golf Course highlights this kid-pleasing park, which also offers a carousel, tourboat, snack bar, and playgrounds. The park hosts a summer concert series that's popular with

The Water Mine Family Swimmin' Hole features a Lazy River with a slow-moving current.

PHOTO: COURTESY OF FAIRFAX COUNTY PARK AUTHORITY

families. (See our Parks and Recreation chapter for additional information.)

Lake Fairfax Park
1400 Lake Fairfax Dr.
Reston, VA
(703) 471–5414
www.co.fairfax.va.us/parks/lakefront.htm

The park's Western-themed Water Mine Family Swimmin' Hole features several slides, bubblers, water cannons, and shallow play areas geared toward children ages 10 and younger. The park itself is an all-round kid-pleaser, offering rides on a miniature train, carousel, and sightseeing pontoon boat for nominal fees. Call for hours, which vary throughout the summer months. Admission to the pool is $9.95 for adults, $7.95 for visitors shorter than 48 inches in height, and free for children younger than age two. Admission is $4.95 after 5:00 P.M. Admission includes unlimited rides on the park's tour boat, train, and carousel. (See the Parks and Recreation chapter for more information.)

Meadowlark Gardens Regional Park
9750 Meadowlark Gardens Ct.
Vienna, VA
(703) 255–3631
www.nvrpa.org/meadowlark.html

Here's a favorite spot for stroller-pushing parents, who get their day's exercise navigating more than 2 miles of winding walkways around landscaped gardens and three small lakes that attract ducks and geese. Kids have fun getting sprayed by a fountain, crossing stepping stones over shallow water, and watching the waterfowl and fish from a wooden gazebo overlooking Lake Caroline. Although you can't carry food into the park, you can munch in the air-conditioned visitors center snack room. Youngsters also like browsing the toys and nature-related items in the gift shop. Call for hours, which vary seasonally. Admission, charged from April through October, costs $3.00 for visitors ages 18 to 59, and $1.00 for those ages 7 to 17 and 60 and older. (See the Parks and Recreation chapter for more information.)

River Farm
7931 E. Boulevard Dr.
Alexandria, VA
(703) 768–5700
www.ahs.org/riverfarm/riverfarmhome.htm

Kids love visiting the children's gardens on the grounds of the American Horticultural Society's headquarters, just down the road from George Washington's home, Mount Vernon (see the listing under Farm Museums and Plantations, in this chapter). Among the interactive, themed plots are the crawl-through Bat Cave; a sea-themed garden in a boat; a fairy tale garden; an Alphabet Garden featuring plants starting with each letter; and Beau Beau's Garden, accented by a yellow-brick road leading to a fortlike

bridge that crosses a dry riverbed containing fun discoveries. Bring a picnic to enjoy as you gaze out at the Potomac River. The gardens are open weekdays only from 9:00 A.M. to 5:00 P.M. and, during summer, Saturdays from 9:00 A.M. to 1:00 P.M.

SplashDown Waterpark
7500 Ben Lomond Dr.
Manassas, VA
(703) 361–4451
www.splashdownwaterpark.com

At this 11-acre park, a popular family destination on sticky summer days, visitors can cool off in the 770-foot Lazy River and slip and slide through two 70-foot-tall water slides. A kids' area features four water slides. Children also enjoy getting splashed by "raindrops" and "bubblers." Umbrellas and pavilions offer much-needed shade. The park is open Memorial Day weekend through Labor Day. Hours vary while school is still in session, but during the summer the park is open 11:00 A.M. to 7:00 P.M. Sunday through Thursday, and 11:00 A.M. to 8:00 P.M. Fridays and Saturdays. Admission is $12.25 for people taller than 48 inches, $9.25 for visitors shorter than 48 inches, $5.95 for spectators, and free for children one year old and younger.

Suburban Maryland

Cabin John Regional Park
7400 Tuckerman La.
Rockville, MD
(301) 299–0024

An old-fashioned miniature train takes visitors on a 1.3-mile ride through a forest and past the large, inviting playground. Play equipment includes a complex Action Playground for school-age children plus slides, swing, and storybook-themed climbing equipment for preschoolers. Children enjoy looking for scampering chipmunks, which are in plentiful supply throughout the park. Cabin John Station, where the train boards, doubles as a garage, and kids like to watch the big metal doors roll shut after the day's last ride. The station also houses a snack bar. A nearby waste container features a talking pig that "eats" litter. (See the Parks and Recreation chapter for more information.)

Glen Echo Park
MacArthur Blvd. at Goldsboro Rd.
Glen Echo, MD
(301) 492–6282
www.nps.gov/glec/indexext.html

The sound of the antique Dentzel carousel's Wurlitzer band organ beckons visitors before they even catch sight of the prancing ponies, ostriches, and rabbits. This enchanting park, a former trolley-line amusement park now operated by the National Park Service, is full of quirky fun, from the resident artists' studios in grass-covered yurts to the Spanish ballroom that hosts Big Band and folk dancing every week. It's a nice spot for birthday parties after a show at the Puppet Co. or Adventure Theatre or a visit to Discovery Creek Children's Museum of Washington (see the previous Marvelous Museums and Sensational Shows section). Just watch out for the yellow jackets! The magnificent carousel, with rides for 50 cents, operates Wednesday and Thursday from 10:00 A.M. to 2:00 P.M. and Saturday and Sunday from noon to 6:00 P.M. May through September. Other attractions are open all year. (See The Arts chapter for more information.)

Hadley's Playground at the Falls Road Local Park
12600 Falls Rd.
Potomac, MD
(301) 770–2144
www.hadleyspark.org

This award-winning, one-acre playground features colorful, accessible, safe equipment, designed so that children of all abilities can have fun playing together. Its six themed activity zones include a frontier-style area, a castle, a pirate ship, a transportation section with a "road" for kids' ride-on toys and bikes, and sections containing assorted accessible and standard-design upper-body development activities like monkey bars. Much of the equipment, created by Little Tikes, resembles giant versions of the company's familiar toys and backyard play sets. Beneath the entire playground, rubberized material constructed from recycled tires forms smooth, springy Safety Surfacing that accommodates wheels and protects tumbling children.

The park is open during daylight hours. Shoes with cleats are not permitted, as they can damage the rubberized surface.

Robert M. Watkins Regional Park
301 Watkins Park Dr.
Upper Marlboro, MD
(301) 249–6202 (Nature Center)
www.smart.net/~parksrec/watkins.htm

Eenie, meenie, minie, moe: With so many choices, kids may have a hard time deciding what to do first. Stop at the Lottsford-Largo Train Station for tickets to take a ride on the *C. P. Huntington,* a miniature version of the classic locomotive. Grab a treat at the snack bar, then go for a spin on the antique carousel. Visit Old Maryland Farm to look at live barnyard animals, play miniature golf, or stop by the nature center. (This park also is listed in the Parks and Recreation chapter.)

Water Park at Bohrer Park at Summit Hall Farm
502 S. Frederick Ave.
Gaithersburg, MD
(301) 258–6445
www.ci.gathersburg.md.us

Gaithersburg residents flock to this pool and its special features, like two twisting 250-foot water slides, a frog slide, water fountains, and a seal that spouts water. The surrounding grounds offer a playground with a ball pit and climbing equipment, concession stand, miniature golf course, and five-hole "kiddie" course. Costs and hours vary, so please call ahead.

Wheaton Regional Park
2000 Shorefield Rd.
Wheaton, MD
(301) 680–3803

Line up at the beautiful train depot for a ride on the miniature locomotive. It's just one of many kid-friendly attractions at this popular Montgomery County park. You'll also find a snack bar and carousel (open, along with the train, throughout the summer), a huge playground and an ice-skating rink (open October through March). Walk or drive to the adjacent nature center and Brookside Gardens, both of which offer bountiful children's programs. Wherever you go in the park, expect crowds on weekends. Look for more on this park in the Parks and Recreation chapter.

Spectator Sports

Just because government and politics tend to dominate the character of Metro Washington and outsiders' perceptions of it, don't underestimate the importance of leisure activities—spectator sports especially—to residents. You'll find every level of competition here, from outstanding high school and college action to professional teams representing a variety of sports.

Sports proved a much-needed diversion during the city's recent tough times. Desperately seeking good news in the aftermath of September 11's frightening events, Washingtonians found reason to cheer when Michael Jordan announced his comeback—with the Washington Wizards! But Jordan's return to the court wasn't the only big local sports news to hit the area in 2001. Soccer lovers got a chance to root for a new home team, the fledgling Women's United Soccer Association's Washington Freedom, featuring all-star forward Mia Hamm. Hockey fans rejoiced when the Washington Capitals made a stunning trade in July and acquired the National Hockey League's leading scorer, Jaromir Jagr, from the Pittsburgh Penguins. And, as the extended baseball season finally drew to a close in early October, folks paid top dollar to watch retiring Cal Ripken Jr. take his final swings at Oriole Park at Camden Yards.

Washington has also experienced several other diverse sports milestones over the past few years. In keeping with its international presence and status as the Nation's Capital, the city recently hosted worldwide and national sporting events. RFK Stadium—former home of the Washington Redskins—was one of seven sites hosting games in the 1999 Women's World Cup soccer tournament. The same arena played a role in the 1996 summer Olympics when more than 58,000 soccer fans watched Portugal beat the United States.

In September 1997 tennis enthusiasts cheered Michael Chang and Pete Sampras to victory over Aussies Mark Philippoussis and Patrick Rafter in the Davis Cup semifinals, played at William H. G. Fitzgerald Tennis Center in Washington, D.C.'s Rock Creek Park. (The Americans lost during the finals in Sweden—oh, well!) The city also became the center of the golf universe in 1997, when TPC at Avenel in Potomac, Maryland, served as the site of the prestigious U.S. Open.

Washingtonians, by and large, hold a special place in their collective heart for one sport and one team in particular. For at least six months a year, the sports scene focuses intensely on our beloved Washington Redskins, proud member of the NFL's finest division, the NFC East. In a bittersweet turn of events in 1997, the team's new Jack Kent Cooke Stadium (later renamed Redskins Stadium and later renamed FedExField) opened—just 160 days after its 84-year-old namesake died of a heart attack. The Redskins won the stadium opener, beating the Cardinals 19-13 in overtime.

Despite its recent disappointing seasons—8 wins, 8 losses in 2001, for instance—the team enjoys an almost divine status among its faithful fans. After all, the Redskins have been in Washington for more than 60 years and boast a solid winning tradition fueled by three Super Bowl victories (all under the reign of inimitable former coach Joe Gibbs) in five appearances. Getting a ticket to a home game, however, is another matter altogether. We'll include more on this later.

Nonfans, don't despair. You'll soon discover that an ideal time to go grocery shopping or roam the malls is during a Redskins game, when a large part of the local population is at home glued to the TV.

Before becoming further immersed in Redskins mania, we should also mention Metro Washington's representatives in the National Basketball Association and Women's National Basketball Association, the Washington Wizards (formerly the Bullets) and the Washington Mystics. Hockey fans can root for the previously mentioned Capitals, the National Hockey League's local team. Conveniently, they all have the same home, the MCI Center (see our Close-up for a complete profile). Here you also can watch the popular Georgetown University Hoyas basketball team.

Soccer fans also get their kicks watching Major League Soccer team D.C. United. In October 1997 the two-year-old team won its second straight MLS championship before a capacity crowd at RFK Stadium.

Incredibly, the Nation's Capital has been without a Major League Baseball team since 1971, when the Senators moved out for a second and final time, heading southwest to become the Texas Rangers. Years before, the original version of the Senators left and turned up in Minnesota as the Twins; an expansion version of the Senators played here in the interim. Attempts to gain a team for the District or even Northern Virginia, either through league expansion or perhaps the relocation of an existing club, have proven fruitless. Organized efforts to that end persist, however, and at press time, Washington baseball supporters were hopeful that the Montreal Expos might relocate to the Nation's Capital or Northern Virginia. Fortunately, baseball junkies can get their fix with the 1997 American League Eastern Division champions, the Baltimore Orioles, whose home field sits barely an hour up the road and just blocks from the city's famous Inner Harbor.

Devotees of the diamond will also be happy to know that minor league baseball has a strong presence in Metro Washington, with the Potomac Cannons, Bowie Bay Sox, Frederick Keys, and Hagerstown Suns all within a short drive. Intercollegiate athletics are a big part of the sports scene as well, and the region's many colleges and universities afford plenty of opportunities for the spectator. Schools with the most prominent athletic programs include the University of Maryland, Georgetown University, George Washington University, Howard University, and George Mason University. Meanwhile, Johns Hopkins University, just up the road in Baltimore, is a perennial lacrosse powerhouse; and to the south in Charlottesville, the University of Virginia wields a big stick in lacrosse, as well as soccer, basketball, and football. In 1999 the United States Naval Academy of nearby Annapolis marked the 100th year of its famous Army-Navy football rivalry. They won the big game 19–9, played on December 4, in Philadelphia.

You also can live out your sports fantasies with a variety of other events, including horse and auto racing, golf, and tennis, to name a few. So, having discarded the stodgy, white-collar, work-reigns-supreme label that seems permanently affixed to Washingtonians, let's take a closer look at an abundant sporting roster. The following provides an overview of spectator sports in Metro Washington (see our Parks and Recreation chapter for general recreational pursuits).

Baseball

Major League

Baltimore Orioles
Oriole Park at Camden Yards
333 W. Camden St.
Baltimore, MD
(202) 432-7328 or (703) 573-7328 (tickets),
(410) 685-9800 (information)
www.theorioles.com

Unable to root, root, root for a home team, many Washingtonians support the Baltimore Orioles. In fact an estimated 28 to 30 percent of the home crowds travel from the Washington suburbs. The team has slipped since 1997, when it finished at the top of its division with a 98–64 record, having remained in first throughout the entire season. During that magical season, second baseman Roberto Alomar finished second in the league in individual

Oriole Park at Camden Yards, home of the Baltimore Orioles, is easily accessed by rail, bus, and automobile. PHOTO: COURTESY OF BALTIMORE AREA CONVENTION AND VISITORS ASSOCIATION

batting averages, hitting .333, and only New York topped Baltimore in American League pitching. The team also boasted the league's largest attendance, with 3.7 million people. A league championship just wasn't meant to be, however: The Cleveland Indians won the best-of-seven series 4–2.

The beloved shortstop-turned-third-baseman, Cal "Iron Man" Ripken Jr. created another personal milestone in September 1998, when he ended at 2,632 his record streak of consecutive games. The team finished its disappointing 1998 season with 79 wins and 83 loses, and no postseason play.

The O's made history in May 1999, when they hosted an exhibition game against the Cuban National Team. The Cubans won, and their pitching coach defected in Baltimore! The Orioles, under former Cleveland Indians' manager Mike Hargrove since 1999, continue to struggle, with four straight losing seasons. The team finished its 2001 season fourth out of five in its division, with 63 wins and 98 losses. Ripken, who ended his career with

more than 3,000 hits and 400 home runs and finished as the Oriole's all-time leader in nearly every major category, isn't the only popular player who won't return in 2002. The O's released outfielder Brady Anderson, the team's all-time leader in stolen bases (311) and single-season home run hitting (50 in 1996).

Going to see an O's game is much easier and more enjoyable than it used to be for Metro Washingtonians. Oriole Park at Camden Yards is a good half-hour closer than Memorial Stadium, the team's home for 38 years, and sits in a wonderful attraction-filled area easily accessed by rail, bus, and automobile.

From Northern Virginia, Suburban Maryland, and the District, just take the Baltimore/Washington Parkway north into Baltimore and the stadium is right there looming in front of you as you near the downtown area. It's a straight shot and the route is well marked. You also can take I-95 into Baltimore, but this route is a bit longer and subject to more traffic hassles. Want to ride the train? Just take Metrorail to Union Station, where you pick up a

MARC (Maryland's passenger railroad system) train to the Baltimore station literally right next to the stadium; the trip takes about 45 minutes.

Camden Yards seats about 48,000 people, a perfect size for baseball, and offers a great view from virtually every seat. Modern yet old-fashioned in an architectural sense, it's truly a ballpark designed for the way baseball was meant to be played, on real grass, with the city skyline as a backdrop. (The seating areas are smoke-free, by the way; smoking is permitted only on the concourse.) Even the stadium's location is interesting. Camden Yards sits in a historic area of downtown Baltimore and masterfully incorporates the nearly 100-year-old B&O Warehouse, which looms just beyond the right field wall. Refurbished during construction of the stadium, the warehouse now houses office space for the team, along with a cafeteria, lounge, and the exclusive, members-only Camden Club. During the early 1900s, a piece of land that's now part of the outfield was the site of a watering hole called Ruth's Cafe, operated by the father of baseball's immortal George Herman "Babe" Ruth, a Baltimore native.

Tickets, which generally go on sale during the winter for the following season, range in price from $9.00 to $40.00 for single games. Periodic bargain nights feature left field upper reserved and bleacher seats for a reduced price. Kids ages 12 and younger can join the O's Dugout Club. The $10.00 membership fee includes a membership card, player and mascot photos, and two game tickets. Call the information number above, or write to O's Dugout Club, 333 W. Camden Street, Baltimore, MD 21201.

Minor Leagues

Northern Virginia

Potomac Cannons
G. Richard Pfitzner Stadium
7 County Complex Ct.
Woodbridge, VA
(703) 590–2311
www.potomaccannons.com

Think there's no such thing as an old-fashioned, up-close baseball game? Head to Pfitzner Stadium to watch the Cannons, the Class A affiliate of the St. Louis Cardinals. These Minor League games provide inexpensive family entertainment and a chance to watch future big-leaguers in action: Past Cannons players include Bernie Williams, Barry Bonds, and Bobby Bonilla.

The Cannons play 70 games each season—mid-April to early September—at the 6,000-seat stadium off Davis Ford Road in Woodbridge. Carolina League opponents include the Durham Bulls, made famous a few years back by the hit movie *Bull Durham* that starred Kevin Costner.

Never mind that the team finished its 2001 season with a 31–39 second half record, hasn't reached a play-off since 1995, and hasn't won a championship since 1989. The Cannons still draw sellout crowds, especially on Saturday nights that feature such promotions as minibat and baseball cap giveaways. Fans enjoy the goofy between-innings contests, like mock sumo wrestling and dizzy-bat races. Ticket prices range from $5.00 ($4.00 for kids ages 6 to 14 and seniors ages 55 and older) to $10.00, with supermarket-sponsored discounts available on some weeknights. Children ages 5 and younger get in free.

The team caters to kids, with a special smoke- and alcohol-free family seating area, a kids' club, and frequent promotions. Youngsters who wait near the locker room after the game often meet players, who, unlike most Major League superstars, usually prove more than happy to sign autographs. They've even been known to supply the baseballs!

Suburban Maryland

Bowie Baysox
Prince George's Stadium
4101 Northeast Crain Hwy.
Bowie, MD
(301) 805–6000
www.baysox.com

The Baysox, a Class AA affiliate of the Baltimore Orioles, play in the Eastern League. Like the Cannons, the Baysox offer fun, family entertainment, and average right around .500 or lower. The team finished its 2001 season with a 59–82 record, in last place in the league's Southern Division. Harold Baines, Armando Benitez, and Mike Mussina all wore the Baysox uniform early in their careers. Tickets range in price from $5.00 to $14.00, with discounts available some weeknights. Children ages 12 and younger who wear their baseball or softball team jerseys get free general admission to the 10,000-plus-seat stadium Monday through Thursday, as do any kids ages 5 and younger at all games. Just for kids, the stadium includes an amusement area with a carousel, jungle gym, games, face painting, and concession stand with all food items priced at $1.00. The Junior Baysox club, $12 for youngsters ages 5 to 14, includes a T-shirt, free admission certificate, membership card, and invitation to two baseball clinics.

Frederick Keys
Harry Grove Stadium
6201 New Design Rd.
Frederick, MD
(301) 662–0013
(301) 831–4200 (from Montgomery County)
www.frederickkeys.com

The Orioles' Class A affiliate, the Keys compete in the Carolina League, which includes the rival Cannons. Fans have watched the likes of Brady Anderson, Armando Benitez, and David Segui before they were stars. Ticket prices range from $8.00 ($5.00 general admission for children ages 6 to 12 and seniors older than 60) to $11. Children ages 5 and younger get in free, and so do kids ages 12 and younger who wear their Little League shirts and caps. Popular promotions, such as fireworks nights, sell out in advance. The Junior Keys Club, $7.00 for kids ages 12 and younger, includes a T-shirt and free admission to Sunday games.

The Hagerstown Suns
Municipal Stadium
274 E. Memorial Blvd.
Hagerstown, MD
(301) 791–6266, (800) 538–9967
www.hagerstownsuns.com

Visit the Suns' 71-year-old Municipal Stadium to see a piece of baseball history: This is where Willie Mays played his first professional game. A Class A affiliate of the Toronto Blue Jays, the Suns play in the South Atlantic League. They've boasted such future stars as Curt Schilling, Mike Mussina, Arthur Rhodes, Billy Ripken and Cal Ripkin Jr., José Mesa, and Bob Milacki. Ticket prices range from $3.00 to $5.00 for general admission seating, to $7.00 for reserved seats. The Knothole Gang kids' club, $5.00 annually, features a T-shirt, certificate and card entitling the bearer to 25 cents admission to certain games.

Basketball

Professional

Washington Mystics
MCI Center, 601 F Street NW
Washington, DC
(202) 432–SEAT
www.wnba.com/mystics

If the Wizards' 1998–99 record proved disappointing, their sister team's proved downright dismal: The WNBA Washington Mystics finished their inaugural 1998 season with only 3 wins—and 27 losses! But, while the team was amassing the worst-ever WNBA record, they also were drawing the largest crowds. Go figure!

The team's terrible finish entitled them to the first pick in the WNBA draft, and they made the most of their opportunity, snagging the University of Tennessee's Chamique Holdsclaw. The 6-foot-2-inch forward racked up numerous distinctions as a Lady Volunteer, including three consecutive NCAA championships and various Athlete of the Year honors. As a Mystic, she played as the only starting rookie in the league's first all-star game, only to break her finger during the first half. The injury didn't keep her down for long, and within a few days, she was back to being one of her team's leading scorers, averaging 16.9 points and 7.9 rebounds per game. The team had a dismal season, but Holdsclaw received the league's Rookie of the Year award and made the All-WNBA Second Team.

Unfortunately, the team hasn't improved in the last two years: The Mystics finished the 2001 season tied for last place with a 10–22 record. The 2002 season, which runs May to August, looked uncertain; both Head Coach Tom Maher and General Manager Melissa McFerrin resigned in January. Fortunately, no matter how bad the team gets, boisterous crowds of mostly female fans continue to offer support. Individual game tickets range in price from $8.00 to $37.50.

The Washington Wizards
MCI Center, 601 F St. NW
Washington, DC
(202) 432–SEAT, (703) 573–SEAT
www.nba.com/wizards
Will Washington's basketball team make a name for itself? It will if Michael Jordan has anything to say about it. The former Chicago Bull became president and part owner of the team during its disappointing 1999–2000 season. Eventually, MJ decided that the best way to share his skills with young, developing players would be to join them on the court—and not just during practice. On September 25, 2001, Jordan officially announced that he was coming out of retirement. He sold his shares in the team, resigned from the presidency, and once again donned No. 23. Fans were elated, sportswriters skeptical: Could the 38-year-old Jordan still deliver the goods? Apparently he can: After 31 games in the 2001–02 season, Jordan was averaging 24.6 points and 6.2 rebounds per game, compared with 28.4 and 6.7 at the same point during his final season with the Bulls in 1997–98. He scored 51 points in a game against Charlotte and, during the highly anticipated home showdown against his former team, scored 29 points and reached a career milestone of 30,000 points. With Jordan leading the team, the Wizards waltzed into the new year in third place in the Eastern Conference, with a 17–14 record.

Expect Wizards' tickets to become increasingly hard to get. Available tickets for home games, played at the MCI Center (profiled in this chapter), cost $35 and

$45, and folks could make a convincing argument for the price being too high. But one thing's for certain about the Wizards: They play hard and they're fun to watch, winning or not. And, who knows whether Jordan will have the stamina to play another season?

Collegiate

American University
Bender Arena
Washington, DC
(202) 885–3267 (tickets)
(202) 885–DUNK (sports updates)
www.aueagles.com
The men's basketball team started it 2001–02 season under a new coach, Jeff Jones, and in a different conference, the Patriot League. (Previously, the team played in the Colonial Athletic Association.) As of early January, the team had a 7–7 record.

Led by second-year coach Shann Hart, the CAA's coach of the year in 1997–98, the women's basketball team also had a 7–7 record early in January of 2002.

Tickets for individual men's basketball games cost a maximum of $10 for adults, $8 for children. Admission to a women's basketball game is $8 for adults, $5 for children. Games take place in the newly refurbished Bender Arena.

Intercollegiate sports in which AU excels include women's volleyball, women's wrestling and lacrosse, and men's soccer, swimming, and diving.

Georgetown University
MCI Center
601 F St. NW
Washington, DC
(202) 432–SEAT, (703) 573–SEAT
www.guhoyas.com
MCI Center's other roundball tenant, Georgetown University, has earned a reputation as one of the nation's strongest programs and one that demands that athletes work as hard in the classroom as they do on the court—a rarity in major college athletics today. John Thompson, the physically imposing and highly regarded coach of the Hoyas for 27 years, deserves much of the credit. Under Thompson's direc-

tion, Georgetown won a national championship, became a regular in post-season play, and remained a force in the formidable Big East Conference.

Georgetown alumni appear on team rosters throughout the NBA. But three names, all products of the Thompson era and all dominating big men, stand out—and up: Patrick Ewing, Dikembe Mutombo, and Alonzo Mourning. Much to fans' dismay, Thompson retired for personal reasons midway through the 1999 season. He's far from forgotten: In June, he entered the Basketball Hall of Fame.

The 2001-02 men's team, under four-year GU coach Craig Esherick, boasted a promising 9-5 record as of early January. The team finished its 2000-01 season with an impressive 25-8 record, earning the Hoyas their 27th consecutive postseason tournament appearance. The team lost to Maryland in the NCAA "Sweet 16." The women's team, coached for the 15th year by Patrick Knapp, also had a winning 8-5 record at the start of the new year. The team's previous season ended with a 17-13 record, earning it a NIT bid; the postseason ended with a loss to Maryland.

Tickets to Hoyas home games cost $5.00 to $22.50. Tickets to women's games cost $2.00 to $5.00.

Other sports in which the Hoyas excel include men's and women's lacrosse and women's volleyball.

George Mason University
Patriot Center
4400 University Dr.
Fairfax, VA
(703) 993-3000
sports.gmu.edu

Patriot mania gripped George Mason University and the surrounding Fairfax community, as the men's basketball team enjoyed its first winning season in nine years during 1998-99. Under Coach Jim Larranaga, who started at GMU during the 1997-98 season, the Patriots finished with a 19-11 record, including a conference best 13-3 Colonial Athletic Association record. The team won the CAA tournament and earned the No. 14 seed in the eastern division of the NCAA Tournament, only to lose to Cincinnati in the

first round. For engineering the team's remarkable turnaround, Larranaga received the CAA Coach of the Year honor. The team finished its 2000-01 season with an 18-12 record, and boasted an 8-4 record in early January 2002.

Under Coach Debbie Taneyhill, a former Patriot point guard, the women's team finished the 2000-2001 season with an impressive 21-9 record. Early January of 2002 found the team at 8 wins, 6 losses.

Lucky for spectators trying to keep up with the action, George Mason's home arena in Fairfax is the comfy 10,000-seat Patriot Center, the only sports/entertainment facility of its kind in Northern Virginia. The men's team plays about 15 home games, with tickets selling for $10.00 each, $5.00 for youths 18 and younger. The women's team plays about 12 home games, with tickets priced at $5.00, $2.00 for youths 18 and younger. The arena hosts special sporting events such as the Harlem Globetrotters, tennis, and beach volleyball tournaments and gymnastics programs.

George Washington University
Smith Center
Washington, DC
(202) 994-6650
www.gwsports.com

Not to be excluded from Metro Washington's major college basketball lineup, George Washington University is an emerging program in its own right.

The Colonials finished their 1998-99 season with an impressive 20-9 record and the Atlantic 10 Conference West Division title. They also landed a berth in the NCAA tournament, only to get knocked out 108-88 by Indiana in the first round of play. The team has faltered in recent seasons, with a 15-15 record in 1999-2000, and a 14-18 record in 2000-01. The 2001-02 season, under new coach Karl Hobbs, got off to a promising start, with 10 wins and 4 losses going into January.

Led by 13-year Coach Joe McKeown, the women's team kicked off the 2001-02 season with a disappointing 6-7 record as of early January. The team ended its previous season with a 19-9 record, short of 20 wins for the first time in nine seasons.

Inside Washington's MCI Center

The $200 million, 1 million-square-foot, 20,000-seat MCI Center debuted December 2, 1997, to kudos all around from the fans who watched the Washington Wizards handily defeat the Seattle SuperSonics. The massive, brightly lit sports and entertainment center signals the start of a downtown revitalization, especially now that the city's crime rate appears to be on a welcome decline.

The arena's location—at 7th and F Streets NW, just a hop, skip, and jump from the Gallery Place Chinatown Metro station—proves quite convenient, particularly for those who work in the city. Most suburbanites need drive only as far as their closest Metro station.

Here are more reasons to check it out:

• Sports—The NBA Washington Wizards, WNBA Washington Mystics, NHL Capitals, and Georgetown Hoyas all play here. If you miss any action on the floor, you can look up at one of the four 12-by-16-foot screens on the 15-ton, video scoreboard cube that hangs from the center of the ceiling. It's the biggest of its kind!

The basketball playing surface dismantles to reveal a permanent ice hockey rink underneath, used by the Capitals.

• Concerts—The arena hosts some of the region's hottest concerts, including Neil Diamond in 2001. Bruce Springsteen reunited with his E Street Band to delight fans—including Al Gore and Tipper Gore—with a trio of sold-out, three-hour shows in

The NBA's Washington Wizards, shown in action against Cleveland, play in the MCI Center.
PHOTO: MARY JANE SOLOMON

August and September of 1999. A couple of weeks later, screaming preteens packed the center for two Backstreet Boys' concerts. Barry Manilow presented MCI's inaugural musical event, followed a month later by country singer Alan Jackson. Billy Joel also has appeared a few times.

• Special events—The arena hosts skating championships, professional wrestling, Disney on Ice, and the Ringling Brothers and Barnum & Bailey Circus.

• Miscellaneous features—The center—built in compliance with the Americans with Disabilities Act—features 175 to 204 wheelchair-accessible seats for disabled patrons and their companions. Call (301) 350–3400, extension 1370. Other services for the disabled include Braille signs and menus, TTY phones, 12 elevators, assisted-listening devices, and lowered counters.

The building boasts 24 rest rooms, with extra toilets in the women's rooms. Three rest rooms are designed for family use.

Your best bet, as we mentioned earlier, is to take Metro to the center. The adjacent stop, Gallery Place-Chinatown, is on the Red, Yellow, and Green Lines. If taking the Metro from the suburbs, give yourself at least an hour: Crowds can be heavy, and trains slower, before big events. If you choose to drive, you'll find 7,000 parking spaces in lots and garages within a 10-minute walk. The center's own 500 spaces, accessible on 6th Street between F and G Streets, are open to the public only during the day and nonevent weekend hours. Taxi stands for center visitors are at the corner of 5th and F Streets and 8th and F Streets. Concerned about safety? The center is equipped with a police command post, complete with two holding cells!

The arena's marketing center is at 325 7th Street NW, Washington, D.C. (202–624–9732). You can also call the MCI Center information line at (202) 628–3200.

They failed to get an NCAA bid and opted out of NIT postseason play because of injuries.

Catch the Colonials in action at the cozy Smith Center, located in the heart of the Northwest Washington campus. Tickets for men's games are $18 and $12 for adults, $10 and $6 for youths. Admission to women's games is $9 for adults, $6 for youths.

Howard University
Burr Gymnasium
6th and Girard Sts. NW
Washington DC
(202) 806–7140
www.bisonmania.com

These small but powerful Mid-Eastern Athletic Conference Bison teams have played admirably but inconsistently in recent years. Coached by Frankie Allen, the men were 16 and 12 in 2002. The Lady Bison fared better. They finished their 2000–01 season as champions and won their postseason tournament. Under coach Cathy Parson, they finished 2002 with an 18–9 record, having won all their home games. Tickets for both men's and women's Bison games are $6.00 general admission and $10.00 reserved.

University of Maryland
Comcast Center
College Park, MD
(301) 314–7070, (800) 462–TERP (tickets),
(800) 314–TERP (updates)
www.umterps.com

Another of the region's prominent basketball programs is the University of Maryland, which beginning in the 2002–03 season holds court at the brand new 17,100-seat Comcast Center.

The Terrapins enjoyed a phenomenal 2000–01 season, finishing with a 25–11 overall record and a 10–6 record in the Atlantic Coast Conference. For the first time, the Terps, coached by Gary Williams, advanced to the Final Four in the prestigious NCAA tournament, only to lose to Duke in a disappointing 95–84 game. Their fantastic season earned the team national respect, however, and fans looked forward to another great year in 2001–02. They weren't disappointed: The team finished its regular season in first place, with an astounding 25–3 overall record, 15–1 in the ACC. They were undefeated in their home games.

The Lady Terps, coached for the past 27 seasons by Chris Weller, finished their 2000–01 season 17–12 and advanced to the NCAA tournament, only to lose to Colorado State in the first round. The 2001–02 regular season found the team with a disappointing 12–16 record, 4–12 in the ACC.

Tickets to the men's games are $23 to $29, if they're available! Tickets to the women's games are $5.00 for adults and $3.00 for ages 17 and younger and senior citizens.

Football

Washington Redskins
FedExField
Arena Drive
Landover MD
(301) 276–5050
www.redskins.com

In 1999 the team sold for a record $800 million to a partnership led by 34-year-old communications mogul Daniel M. Snyder of Bethesda. The young owner began stirring things up as soon as he took over the franchise, which had been in the Jack Kent Cooke family for almost 30 years. Snyder changed the arena's name from Jack Kent Cooke Stadium to Redskins Stadium, then again to FedExField. He also made major staff overhauls, intent on turning the organization around after its disappointing 1998 season, when the Redskins opened with seven straight losses and finished with a 6–10 record.

New management lit a fire under the players, and the '99 Skins made the playoffs for the first time in six seasons but lost their second game to Tampa Bay. In 2000, the team finished 8–8, and Head Coach Norv Turner lost his job after the thirteenth game. The team finished with the same record in 2001, and new Head Coach Marty Schottenheimer's job went the way of Turner's. In 2002 the team will be coached by Steve Spurrier, who recently resigned as head football coach at the University of Florida. Many fans feel that Schottenheimer got a raw deal.

Win or lose, the Skins boast a loyal, enthusiastic following. Trying to be one of the 80,000 fans who jam the stadium for every home game, however, is tough to do, since few if any tickets are available to the general public. A limited number go on sale each summer for the one or two home preseason games in August, but they usually sell out too. So you've got to act fast. Lucky season ticket holders pay $40 to $75 per ticket (executive suites cost from $59,950 to $159,950), but don't count on season tickets' availability. You're more likely to find yourself on a waiting list. You can buy tickets through brokers, but they'll cost you a pretty penny. The good news about consistent sellouts is you never have to be concerned about home games being blacked out on local TV—an unfortunate reality in some NFL markets. Perhaps most compelling is that in a region where political party, race, gender, or socioeconomic status too often divide people, the Redskins have remained a unifying force that transcends these and other barriers.

The eye-catching, contemporary new stadium, built in just 17 months, took years of planning and false starts, but overall, fans seem pleased with the results. On the plus side, the stadium offers roomier seats, highly visible scoreboards in each end zone, 38 concession stands with food ranging from traditional stadium fare to crab cakes and Mexican food, larger rest rooms, and for those with the big bucks, two tiers of luxury seats. On the down side there's traffic, traffic, traffic! With no nearby Metrorail access, the stadium offers limited transportation options. Your best bet is to arrive early to beat the congestion and find parking.

FedEx Field is the home of the Washington Redskins. PHOTO: COURTESY OF WASHINGTON REDSKINS

Golf

Kemper Insurance Open
TPC at Avenel
10000 Oaklyn Dr.
Potomac, MD
(301) 469–3737
www.kemperopen.com

Major professional golf tournaments don't appear very often on Washington's sports calendar, so it's understandable why so many local enthusiasts of the game mark off the days in anticipation of one event: the nationally televised Kemper Open. The prestigious tournament takes place in May or June at the TPC (Tournament Players Championship) at Avenel course in beautiful Potomac, Maryland. First-time winner, Frank Lickliter earned the 2001 trophy. Tickets are available to the public, but they can go fast, especially if some of golf's big names are taking part in the tourney. Daily grounds tickets are $30, and grounds and pavilion admission is $40 through April 15; admission at the gate is $5.00 higher.

Horsing Around

Horse-racing enthusiasts are in luck. Maryland is home to several equine venues. (Virginia has approved horse betting as the latest form of gambling, but the first local tracks have yet to open; the sport is illegal in the District.)

From April through August, and again from early September through November, riders saddle up for polo most every Sunday afternoon in West Potomac Park, across from the Lincoln Memorial. General admission is free.

Steeplechase events, usually held in the spring and fall in the hunt country of Metro Washington, are as much social gatherings as they are sporting spectacles. Kentucky we're not, yet the influence of the equine industry is astounding in Virginia and Maryland. Entire towns such as Middleburg, Warrenton, and Keswick in Virginia, and Upper Marlboro and Potomac in Maryland, are dedicated to the care, training, and competition of the sport horse. Both states are home to a large number of equine-related organizations and happenings, far too many to list. Check local newspapers, especially the weekend/calendar sections, for steeplechase dates and locations.

Here are some of the region's most popular arenas and events.

Northern Virginia

Contact the Loudoun Tourism Council, 108-D South Street SE, Leesburg, Virginia, (800) 752–6118, for a free "Welcome to Virginia Horse Country" brochure. Here are two Loudoun County highlights:

The Fairfax Hunt
Belmont Plantation
Rte. 7
4 miles east of Leesburg, VA
(703) 787–6673

This annual event, usually held the third Saturday of September, features racing over hurdles and timber. Post time is 2:00 P.M.

Morven Park International Equestrian Center
41793 Tutt La.
Leesburg, VA
(703) 777–2414

Spectators enjoy tailgating parties before these steeplechase races, held the second Saturday of October.

The Virginia Gold Cup Races and The International Gold Cup Races
The Virginia Gold Cup Association
P.O. Box 840
Warrenton, VA 20188
(540) 347–2612

Virginia's premier steeplechase events take place at Great Meadow Event Center in The Plains, 40 miles west of Washington, D.C. Hobnob with the area's rich and famous at The Virginia Gold Cup Races, held the first Saturday in May, and at The International Gold Cup Races, held the third Saturday in October. Races run from 1:00 to 5:00 P.M., preceded by special events such as Jack Russell Terrier Races. Tickets run from $40 for a general car pass that admits up to six passengers, to thousands of dollars for corporate tents.

Suburban Maryland

Laurel Park
Rte. 198 and Laurel Racetrack Rd.
Laurel, MD
(301) 725–0400
www.laurelpark.com

Live thoroughbred racing takes place Wednesdays through Sundays January through March, late June through late August, and October through December. Admission is $3.00 for grandstand and clubhouse seats. Wednesdays and Thursdays, seniors get in for $1.50. Reservations are recommended for the Turf Club Dining Room, which features televised races and a view of the track and charges a $5.00 seating fee. The 9-furlong track is open all year, with simulcast racing when live races aren't held. Minimum betting usually is $2.00. A free Pony Pals kids' club features a monthly Sunday morning stable tour, craft activity, and live entertainment for children ages 2 to 12, accompanied by an adult. Preferred parking is $2.00.

Pimlico Race Course
Hayward and Winner Aves.
Baltimore, MD
(410) 542–9400
www.pimlico.com

The showcase event at this historic course (dating to 1743) is, of course, the Preakness, the second jewel in Thoroughbred racing's Triple Crown, held the third Saturday in May. Tickets are hard to come by for this prestigious event, but you can watch other thoroughbred racing during April, May, and most of June. Simulcast races are televised the rest of the year. Admission is $3.00 for grandstand seats and $5.00 for clubhouse seats. Reservations are recommended for the enclosed

dining room, which charges a $2.00 seating fee. See the Laurel Park entry for information about kids' club activities, which also take place at this course. Preferred parking is $2.00.

Rosecroft Raceway
6336 Rosecroft Dr.
Fort Washington, MD
(301) 567–4000
www.rosecroft.com

Just a few minutes from the Wilson Bridge, off Capital Beltway exit 4A, this 53-year-old raceway features live harness racing starting at 7:20 P.M. Thursday through Saturday, most of the year. Patrons also can watch simulcast thoroughbred races. Admission is $3.00, and minimum bets are $1.00. You also can watch the races from an enclosed dining room, which offers televisions at each table; reservations are recommended. Call (301) 567- 4045. Seats are $2.00. General parking is free.

Eager racing fans cheer as the horses pass the stands headed for the finish line at Pimlico.
PHOTO: COURTESY OF PIMLICO RACE COURSE

The Show Place Arena
14900 Pennsylvania Ave.
Upper Marlboro, MD
(301) 952–7900, (301) 952–7999

This 5,800-seat, multipurpose arena often plays host to horse-riding competitions. Call for a rundown of upcoming events.

The Washington International Horse Show
USAirways Arena
1 Harry S Truman Dr.
Landover, MD
(301) 840–0281, (202) 432–SEAT

This annual event, held for more than a week each fall features some of the world's top show jumpers, hunters, and dressage riders, not to mention those entertaining canine show-stealers, the racing Jack Russell terriers. This is a fun event that the whole family can enjoy. Tickets for the evening shows usually run $18 and up. Daytime event admission is $6.00. Tickets go on sale in mid-August, but also are available at the door.

Ice Hockey

Washington Capitals
MCI Center
601 F St. NW
Washington, DC
(202) 432–SEAT, (703) 573–SEAT
www.washingtoncaps.com

Like the Redskins, the Capitals also came under new ownership during the summer of 1999. Longtime majority owner Abe Pollin sold the franchise to America Online executive Ted Leonsis, local businessman Jon Ledecky, and Capitals President Dick Patrick.

Under coach Ron Wilson, now in his fifth year, the team entered 2002 in second place in the Eastern Conference. With players such as Jaromir Jagr, sharpshooter Peter Bondra, and Olaf "Oly the Goalie" Kolzig the team has a shot at a first-rate season.

As a thanks to their devoted fans, the Capitals lowered ticket prices for the 1999–2000 season and some prices still remain affordable. Single-game tickets cost $10 to $92.

Running

Marine Corps Marathon
Downtown Washington, DC
next to the National Mall
(703) 690–3431, (800) RUN–USMC
www.marinemarathon.com

This fall classic, sometimes referred to as the "People's Marathon," remains accessible to everyday runners as well as serious contenders. Registration begins in February and fills up quickly. The 2002 running is scheduled for October 27. Those who would rather watch than actually attempt to run 26 miles and 385 yards, will find abundant prime vantage points along the course, which begins and ends in Arlington but canvases a large section of the National Mall area downtown.

Soccer

D.C. United
13832 Redskin Dr.
Herndon, VA
(703) 478–6600
www.dcunited.com

Washington is well on its way to becoming a soccer town, thanks to D.C. United, its three-time Major League Soccer champion team. The 1994 World Cup games played in Washington and other U.S. cities were a huge success by any measure—a surprise, perhaps, to some people except diehard fans, including those among the region's diverse and substantial immigrant population. Now, soccer ("football" to the rest of the world) is beginning to catch on with the American public, in part because of the infant Major League Soccer league.

Washington's MLS team couldn't have gotten off to a much better start: It won three MLS Cups in four years. The team fared poorly in 2000, and its 2001 season ended prematurely when the team canceled its final games out of respect for the victims of the terrorist attacks on September 11. D.C. United finished with an 8–16–2 record and 26 points, not enough to qualify the team for the playoffs.

The team plays April through September at RFK Stadium, former home of the Washington Redskins. Tickets range in price from $16 to $36.

Washington Freedom
2400 East Capitol St. SE
Washington, DC
(202) 547–8351
www.washingtonfreedom.com

One of eight teams in the new Women's United Soccer Association, the Washington Freedom finished its debut 2001 season in seventh place, with 6 wins, 12 losses, 3 ties, and 21 points. Coached by Jim Gabarra, the team is looking to improve in 2002. Win or lose, the team draws enthusiastic crowds, especially young Mia Hamm wannabes who love to cheer on their favorite player. Fans also enjoy assorted promotions and opportunities to meet players and get autographs. The team plays April through August at RFK Stadium. Individual game tickets cost $12, $19, and $23 each. Parking is $10, or you can take Metro to the adjacent Stadium/Armory station.

Stock Car Racing

Hagerstown Speedway
15112 National Pk.
west of Hagerstown, MD
(301) 582–0640
www.hagerstownspeedway.com

Stock cars roar into action on Sunday afternoons during spring and fall, and Saturday nights late February through September. General admission for regular events is $9.00, with children younger than 12 admitted free. Special events like TNT Monster Trucks and World of Outlaw Sprints take place every other weekend. The track is a half-mile clay oval, semibanked.

Old Dominion Speedway and Dragstrip
10611 Dumfries Rd., Rte. 234
Manassas, VA
(703) 361–7753
www.olddominionspeedway.com

Stock car and drag racing take place Fridays and Saturdays, March through September.

Tennis

Washington Tennis Classic
William H.G. FitzGerald Tennis Center
16th and Kennedy Sts. NW
Washington, DC
(202) 722–5949

Tennis anyone? If the answer is yes, then the showcase event to see is the Washington Tennis Classic, held each July or August, on the fringes of beautiful Rock Creek Park. The lineup usually features several stars of the tennis world including the likes of Andre Agassi—the big winner in 1999—and Michael Chang in addition to lower-ranked players and some solid local talent. USAir Arena also hosts occasional tennis events, often for charity.

Watersports

It's free, it's exciting and it's a lot closer than you think. Here are some good bets.

> **Insiders' Tip**
> If you just can't get enough of the Redskins, pick up a copy of *Redskins—A History of Washington's Team*, published by the *Washington Post*. It's chock-full of articles by *Post* sportswriters, every stat you could ever want, loads of photos, and even trivia quizzes. You'll find it at area bookstores, supermarkets, and pharmacies.

Washington, D.C.

Washington Boat Show
Washington Convention Center
Washington, DC
(703) 823–7960
www.washingtonboatshow.com

If the water is enough to put you in the mood for looking at some larger and more expensive pleasure craft, keep an eye out for this annual trade show, held each February.

Northern Virginia

Great Falls Park
Old Dominion Dr. and Georgetown Pike
Great Falls, VA
(703) 285–2966
www.nps.gov/gwmp/grfa

For a different kind of thrill, head over to this national park in the well-heeled Fairfax County community of Great Falls and watch gutsy kayakers and occasional canoeists attempt to negotiate the wicked Great Falls of the Potomac River, just north of Washington. Definitely not for the faint of heart.

Even if you show up and don't spot any boaters, you won't have wasted a trip. The water and surrounding countryside are spectacular in themselves and worth a look any time of year. (See our Parks and Recreation chapter for more on this park.)

Suburban Maryland

United States Powerboat Show
City Dock
Annapolis, MD
(410) 268–8828
www.usboat.com/shows/pbhomes.htm

The boating mecca of Annapolis lays claim to hosting the world's largest in-the-water exhibition, held in October at the City Dock.

United States Sailboat Show
City Dock
Annapolis, MD
(410) 268–8828
usboat.com/shows/bshomes.htm

Boating purists get their due as well in October with this show also held at the City Dock.

Parks and Recreation

From small, leafy plots of land in the inner city to the giant state and regional parks found in the suburbs, our fair capital area features an abundance of lush, green spaces, beckoning both nature lovers and outdoor-sports enthusiasts. With almost 90,000 protected acres, Washington, D.C. rates as one of the country's greenest metropolitan areas, according to the Greater Washington Board of Trade. No other American urban area can claim as many National Park Service properties as can Metro Washington. It's one of the many perks of being in or near the Nation's Capital. Virginia State Parks, including four in Northern Virginia, received the Sports Foundation Inc. 2001 gold medal for most outstanding recreational management and services.

Metro Washington also boasts scores of recreation centers offering gymnasiums, swimming pools, fitness rooms, sports leagues, classes, and summer camps.

This chapter presents a brief survey of prominent national, state, regional, and local parks in the National Capital area and follows with information about recreation centers and other resources for leisurely pursuits. Note that when we don't list park hours, you'll find the park open from dawn until dark.

Parks

Washington, D.C.

Chesapeake & Ohio Canal National Historical Park
Georgetown Visitor Center
1057 Thomas Jefferson St. NW
Washington, DC
(202) 653–5190
www.nps.gov/choh/co_visit.htm

In the 1800s construction of the Chesapeake & Ohio Canal linked Washington with the western reaches of the Potomac River. The canal stretches 184 miles from Georgetown to Cumberland, Maryland, passing through 74 lift locks. In 1971 the entire length became a national park, and today the C&O Canal and Towpath are among Washington's and Suburban Maryland's most coveted recreational retreats. In 1996, in the aftermath of one of the region's biggest ever snowstorms, floodwaters devastated much of the canal and its adjacent pathways. Volunteers pitched in to help with cleanup efforts, and by the summer of 1997, bikers and joggers once again enjoyed the tree-lined gravel pathways extending along the route. The canal itself, meanwhile, makes for gentle canoeing and kayaking.

In April 1999 the park officially became a "trash-free" site with no waste receptacles: All visitors must take their garbage with them when they leave. If you forget your own bag, pick one up at designated stations in the park.

Go back in time with an hour-long, guided ride aboard the Georgetown, an authentic replica of a mule-pulled, 80-person canal boat operated by costumed interpreters. The schedule varies seasonally, but the boat generally runs from mid-April through mid-October. Admission is $8.00 for adults, $6.00 for seniors and $5.00 for children ages 4 to 14. The park also hosts frequent special events such as Civil War walks, lockhouse tours, and fishing contests. The park is closed on New Year's day and Christmas.

Visit Thompson's Boat Center, Virginia Avenue and Rock Creek Parkway (202–333–9543), to rent boats or bicycles. All-terrain bikes, which you can rent for $8.00 per hour, and cruisers, which you can rent for $4.00 per hour, are available March through November. Rent canoes, kayaks, and rowing shells for between $8.00 and $13.00 an hour, spring through mid-October.

During the summer at 4.00 P.M., every other Sunday, free concerts take place on the canal, between Thomas Jefferson and 30th Streets.

Kenilworth Park and Aquatic Gardens
Intersection of Douglas St. and Anacostia Ave. NE
Washington, DC
(202) 426–6905
www.nps.gov/kepa/index.htm

Metro Washington sits amid a region of beautiful and fragile wetlands. At this lovely site in Northeast D.C., naturalists can spend an afternoon traversing nearly 12 acres of aquatic gardens featuring dozens of species of pond and marginal plants, such as tropical and hardy water lilies and hyacinths. The park's ancient lotuses regularly draw visitors from Asia. Kenilworth is the only national park devoted to cultivating and propagating aquatic plants.

Arrive first thing in the morning in the summer to get a good look at both night- and day-blooming water lilies. More than 40 natural ponds attract water birds, frogs, turtles, and curious kids. Take a guided tour at 9:00 and 11:00 A.M. and 1:00 P.M. on weekends and holidays, Memorial Day to Labor Day. Call ahead to arrange tours at other times, depending on staff availability. The park is open daily from 7:00 A.M. to 4:00 P.M. The visitor center, featuring an exhibit area and bookstore, is open from 8:00 A.M. to 4:00 P.M. The park is closed on New Year's Day, Thanksgiving, and Christmas.

Surrounded by approximately 77 acres of marshland, Kenilworth is part of Anacostia Park, 1900 Anacostia Drive SE, Washington, D.C., (202) 690-5185. Covering approximately 1,200 acres along the Anacostia River, the park features exotic waterfowl, a boat ramp, picnic areas, playgrounds, an outdoor pool, playing fields and courts, and an outdoor pavilion used for roller skating and special events.

The National Mall
National Capital Parks-Central
900 Ohio Dr. SW
Washington, DC
(202) 426–6841
www.nps.gov/nacc

The National Park Service's D.C.-area domain begins with the National Mall, that vast esplanade as envisioned by the capital city's French designer, Pierre Charles L'Enfant. The 3-mile, 146-acre expanse of green extends westward from the foot of Capitol Hill to the Lincoln Memorial and Potomac River. It contains the highest density of museums and monuments in the world. (See our Annual Events, Arts, Attractions, and Kidstuff chapters for more on those.)

The Mall, as you'll probably discover, is every bit as humble as it is inspiring. Designed to be used by the people, it draws pet walkers, joggers, Frisbee tossers, and kite fliers. Informal games of soccer, volleyball, softball, and touch football are almost as common a sight here as the museums and monuments. From spring through fall Capitol Hill staffers, among others, use the Mall for their various athletic leagues. Less-active folks can park themselves on benches and watch the ever-changing flurry of passing activity.

The Mall is also the site of some of the nation's most important public gatherings. In 1963 Dr. Martin Luther King Jr. led one of the largest public demonstrations in U.S. history on these hallowed grounds (see our History chapter). Every four years, the East Mall, at the base of the Capitol Building, is the site of presidential inaugural swearing-in ceremonies. Whatever your political affiliation, the ceremony and the setting make for an unforgettable Washington experience.

Between the Washington Monument and Lincoln Memorial, you'll find the beautifully landscaped, 50-acre Constitution Gardens, just north of the long Reflecting Pool and near the Vietnam Veterans Memorial. Look for ducks, geese, and other water birds swimming in the gardens' six-and-a-half-acre lake, which also holds an island adorned with a memorial to the 56 signers of the Declara-

The National Mall is always fun for tossing a football or Frisbee or going for a jog. PHOTO: COURTESY OF THE WASHINGTON, DC CONVENTION AND TOURISM CORPORATION

tion of Independence. Waterfowl also frequent the Reflecting Pool and the nearby Tidal Basin, around which thousands of delicate Japanese cherry trees burst into bloom each spring (see our Annual Events chapter for details about the National Cherry Blossom Festival). Look for the Tulip Library, which boasts more colors and varieties of the flower than you'd dream possible. If you'd like to take in the sights from the water, rent a pedal boat at the Tidal Basin Boat House, 1501 Maine Avenue, (202) 484-0206. They're generally available from 10:00 A.M. to 6:00 P.M. during good weather, April through October. Rates are $8.00 for a two-seater and $16.00 for a four-seater.

On the fringes of the river end of the National Mall, West Potomac Park contains the beautifully designed Franklin Delano Roosevelt Memorial, described in our Attractions chapter. East Potomac Park, south of the Tidal Basin, features picnic areas, a playground, an outdoor pool and tennis courts, a pathway for biking and exercising, and a unique, kid-pleasing statue, *The Awakening*, which resembles a giant about to get up from his underground resting place. (See this chapter's Golfing section for information about the East Potomac Park Golf Course.)

Rock Creek Park
3545 Williamsburg La. NW
Washington, DC
(202) 426–1063
www.nps.gov/rocr
The city's second most visible green space, Rock Creek Park, covers more than 2,000 acres of rolling hills, woods, meadows, and the namesake boulder-strewn creek in the center of Northwest. President Benjamin Harrison signed the legislation creating Rock Creek Park in 1890, making it one of the nation's oldest city parks. It's also one of the world's largest urban parks, boasting plentiful amenities like its popular trails, frequented by hikers, bikers, and horseback riders. Its bike trail is also part of a larger trail network, connecting the District with both Maryland and Virginia. The park also holds picnic and play areas, an equestrian center

(202-362-0118), a golf course (see this chapter's listing under Golfing) and tennis courts.

Historic Pierce Mill (202-426-6908), is open from noon to 4:00 P.M. Wednesday through Sunday. The nineteenth-century mill holds special programs for children. Visit the Rock Creek Nature Center, 5200 Glover Road, (202) 426-6829, to explore the Discovery Room and take part in daily programs such as guided nature walks. It's open from 9:00 A.M. to 5:00 P.M. Wednesday through Sunday except New Year's Day, July 4th, Thanksgiving, and Christmas. The adjacent planetarium specializes in free educational shows for ages four and older at 1:00 P.M. on Saturdays and Sundays, and for ages seven and older at 4:00 P.M. on Saturdays, Sundays, and Wednesdays. The planetarium also holds monthly stargazing sessions. The Carter Barron Amphitheater, 4850 Colorado Avenue NW, (202) 426-0486, hosts concerts throughout the summer, as well as several performances of a free Shakespearean play each June.

(See our Attractions, Kidstuff, Sports, and Civil War chapters for more information on attractions within this urban forest.)

The United States National Arboretum
3501 New York Ave. NE
Washington, DC
(202) 245-2726
www.usna.usda.gov

The arboretum, a national site operated by the United States Department of Agriculture, showcases a lush variety of plants, flowers, and trees. The 446-acre park bursts into an incredible blaze of color during the spring azalea and summer rhododendron seasons, prime times to plan a visit. Look for one of the park's most unusual displays: 22 freestanding Corinthian columns, originally part of the United States Capitol. The arboretum's renowned annual plant sale, held during the spring, features bargains galore and many unusual species of trees, shrubs and perennials—some cultivated on site.

The park's grounds are open from 8:00 A.M. to 5:00 P.M., except on Christmas. Admission is free. The National Bonsai

and Penjing Museum is open from 10:00 A.M. to 3:30 P.M. daily. The arboretum also boasts a gift shop, open 10:00 A.M. to 3:00 P.M. daily March 1 through December 24. The administrative building is open 8:00 A.M. to 4:30 P.M. Monday through Friday and on weekends spring through fall. Free tours and classes take place on weekends.

Northern Virginia

See our Civil War chapter for information about Manassas National Battlefield Park and our Arts chapter for a description of Wolf Trap Farm Park for the Performing Arts.

Algonkian Regional Park
47001 Fairway Dr.
Sterling, VA
(703) 450-4655, (703) 430-7683 (pool)
www.nvrpa.org/algonkian.htm

Set along the Potomac in eastern Loudoun County, this Northern Virginia Regional Park Authority (NVRPA) park features an outdoor pool, miniature golf, picnic tables and shelters, a 2-mile nature trail, boat ramp, and boat and RV storage. The 500-acre park's riverfront cabins, available for rent year-round, offer a pleasant family camping experience. Call at 3:00 P.M. seven days in advance to arrange a tee time for the 18-hole, par 72 golf course.

Bull Run Regional Park
7700 Bull Run Dr.
Centreville, VA
(703) 631-0550, (703) 631-0552 (pool)
www.nvrpa.org/bullrunpark.html

Not far from Manassas National Battlefield Park, NVRPA's Bull Run features scenic hiking trails and several acres of springtime wildflowers. A large outdoor pool includes a tropical island-themed water slide. Visitors also enjoy trying their skills at miniature and disc golf and skeet- and trap-shooting at the Bull Run Shooting Center (703-830-2344), open 4:00 to 9:00 P.M. weekdays and 9:00 A.M. to 5:30 P.M. Saturday and Sunday. Avoid Thursday night when leagues meet. The park also offers group and family camping. Call (703) 352-5900 for group reservation information. The annual Bull Run Jam-

Visitors to Cameron Run Regional Park in Alexandria beat the heat by tubing in the Great Waves pool.

PHOTO: CAROL ANN COHEN, COURTESY OF NORTHERN VIRGINIA REGIONAL PARK AUTHORITY

boree features nationally known country performers. The main park is open mid-March through November. Nonarea residents must pay an entrance fee of $5.50 daily, $12.00 weekly.

Burke Lake Park
7315 Ox Rd.
Fairfax Station, VA
(703) 323–6600
www.co.fairfax.va.us/parks/lakefront.htm

A favorite with local fishing and boating enthusiasts, this 888-acre Fairfax County Park Authority (FCPA) park features a 218-acre lake. Rent rowboats or take a guided pontoon-boat tour of the lake, which includes an island sanctuary for waterfowl. (Ask your tour guide to tell you about the interesting objects at the bottom of the manmade body of water.) The park also offers a campground, picnicking, play areas, and more than 4 miles of hiking trails. (See our Kidstuff chapter for more on the park's kid-pleasing attractions. See our golf listings in this chapter for information about the park's course.)

Cameron Run Regional Park
4001 Eisenhower Ave.
Alexandria, VA
(703) 960–0767
www.nvrpa.org/cameron.html

A favorite spot for cooling off on steamy summer days, Cameron Run attracts hundreds of families to its Great Waves water park, which features a wave pool, four-story water slide, and liquid playground for youngsters. It's open 11:00 A.M. to 7:00 P.M. daily through most of the summer; admission is $10.50 for visitors taller than 4 feet, $8.50 for those shorter than 4 feet, and free for children younger than two. Batting cages and a beautifully landscaped miniature golf course are open 10:00 A.M. to 11:00 P.M. daily during the summer, and for more limited hours during the spring and fall. Golf games are $4.50 for patrons age 16 and older, $3.50 for ages younger than 16. Batting-cage tokens cost $1.00 apiece. You'll find the park just off I-495, minutes from family-geared motels and the Eisenhower Avenue Metrorail station.

**George Washington Memorial Parkway
Turkey Run Park
McLean, VA
(703) 285-2598
www.nps.gov/gwmp**

In Northern Virginia, the George Washington Memorial Parkway and its adjacent Mount Vernon Trail provide spectacular riverside hiking and biking trails extending from the river banks opposite Theodore Roosevelt Island southward 18.5 miles to Mount Vernon. You'll also find boating opportunities and nature preserves like Dyke Marsh on the river's west bank, where you may spot resident waterfowl and other critters. The 7,200-acre national park area also features such historic sites as Arlington House (see our Civil War chapter) and Claude Moore Farm (see Kidstuff).

**George Washington's Grist Mill Historic
State Park
5514 Mt. Vernon Memorial Hwy.
3 miles west of Mt. Vernon, VA
(703) 780-3383 or (703) 550-0960
www.dcr.state.va.us/parks/georgewa.html**

This interpretive historical site in Fairfax County offers tours of a reconstructed mill once used by the first president, who resided just down the road at his Mount Vernon estate. Currently, the mill is being restored and is closed to the public.

**Great Falls Park
Old Dominion Dr. and Georgetown Pike
Great Falls, VA
(703) 285-2966
www.nps.gov/gwmp/grfa**

We love to surprise our out-of-town company with a visit to one of the most impressive natural sights in Metro Washington: the cascading Great Falls of the Potomac, plunging (in some places more than 35 feet) through a series of jagged rocks and gigantic boulders that make up Mather Gorge. It's not Niagara, but it'll do! You also can view the falls from the Maryland side of the river at the C&O National Historical Park; visit both, and decide which vista you prefer. The park is a favorite with outdoor sports enthusiasts, from kayakers to rock climbers. Just

pay careful attention to the posted warning signs: The water can be as dangerous, even deadly, as it is beautiful.

Stop by the park's visitor center, open from 10:00 A.M. to 4:00 P.M., with longer hours during the warmer months, to see a 10-minute slide show, a children's area, and exhibits relating to the park's natural resources and to the Patowmack Canal, a project over which George Washington presided. The park boasts an interesting history, including a stint as an amusement park. Rangers lead daily talks as well as special programs on weekends and holidays all year. The park intermittently charges admission of $4.00 per car or $2.00 per pedestrian, jogger, or bicyclist, valid for three consecutive days and also good for entrance to the C&O Canal National Historic Park on the other side of the falls. You can obtain an annual park pass, good for Great Falls and the C&O Canal, for $15. The park is open daily from 7:00 A.M. to dusk, except on Christmas. The gates are locked at dark.

**Green Spring Gardens Park
4603 Green Spring Rd.
Alexandria, VA
(703) 642-5173
www.co.fairfax.va.us/parks/gsgp**

This garden-filled FCPA park proves a beautiful and popular spot for strolls and outdoor weddings. Demonstration gardens offer inspiration to both budding gardeners and those with green thumbs. The historic Manor House, open noon to 4:00 P.M. Wednesday through Sunday, features a gift shop, art exhibits, and special programs. Visit the Horticulture Center from

---

Insiders' Tip

Take a naturalist-led evening hike to learn about owls, bats, and other nighttime creatures. Check your local parks and recreation authority newsletter for times.

You'll forget you're in Metro Washington when hiking along the scenic paths of Great Falls. PHOTO: MIDDLE-
TON EVANS, COURTESY OF MARYLAND OFFICE OF TOURISM

9:00 A.M. to 4:30 P.M. Monday through Saturday, noon to 4:30 P.M. Sunday.

Huntley Meadows Park and Visitor Center
3701 Lockheed Blvd.
Hybla Valley, VA
(703) 768–2525
www.co.fairfax.va.us/parks/huntley.htm
This 1,424-acre park—the largest operated by FCPA—draws nature lovers of all ages, who love to explore the meadows, forests and ⅔-mile boardwalk trail through the wetlands. Keep your eyes open for wildlife, from butterflies and songbirds to deer, beaver, and waterfowl. Park naturalists conduct hundreds of programs annually at the visitor center, which features exhibits pertaining to the area's natural resources. The park also proves a popular destination for local school and Scout groups, who arrange guided tours by appointment. Visitor center hours vary throughout the year, but generally run from 9:00 A.M. to 5:00 P.M. weekdays except Tuesdays and from noon to 5:00 P.M. Saturdays and Sundays during warm weather.

Lake Accotink Park
7500 Accotink Park Rd.
Springfield, VA
(703) 569–3464
www.co.fairfax.va.us/parks/accotink
Another popular FCPA park, Lake Accotink features wetlands, streams, and a 65-acre lake with canoe, rowboat, and pedal boat rentals, along with tour-boat rides. Visitors also can fish, play miniature golf, ride a carousel, and hike trails in this 482-acre park. Special events include an annual cardboard boat race and summer concert series.

Leesylvania State Park
2001 Daniel K. Ludwig Dr.
Woodbridge, VA
(703) 670–0372
www.dcr.state.va.us/parks/leesylva.htm
This 508-acre park, off U.S. 1 in Prince William County, offers precious access to the Potomac River, upon which visitors enjoy fishing and boating. You'll even find a sandy beach for strolling and sunbathing—no swimming allowed! Hiking on 6 miles of trails and picnicking are also

popular activities. On the National Register of Historic Landmarks, Leesylvania sits on land once owned by Revolutionary War hero "Light Horse Harry" Lee and, later, the Fairfax family. The park holds frequent educational programs for all ages. A visitor center, open noon to 4:00 P.M. (weekends only during the winter), houses nature exhibits and a gift shop. Park admission, April through October, is $2.00 per car on weekdays, $3.00 on weekends. During the rest of the year, admission is $1.00 less.

Mason Neck State Park
7301 High Point Rd.
Lorton, VA
(703) 550–0362
www.dcr.state.va.us/parks/masonnec.htm

This 1,814-acre park adjoins more than 2,000 acres designated as a wildlife refuge. Mason Neck is a bird-watcher's dream: Bald eagles nest among the towering pines and hardwoods, and whistling swans and various varieties of ducks also frequent the park. Observe the resident birds unseen in blinds placed along the 3.5 miles of hiking trails. With wetlands as well as fields and forests, Mason Neck proves ideal for environmental study. Visitors also enjoy picnicking, fishing, canoeing, and windsurfing. A visitor center, open daily during the summer and on weekends during the spring and fall, offers interpretive exhibits on local plants and wildlife. The park is open 8:00 A.M. to dusk daily. Parking is $1.00 on weekdays, $2.00 on weekends.

Meadowlark Gardens Regional Park
9750 Meadowlark Gardens Ct.
Vienna, VA
(703) 255–3631
www.nvrpa.org/meadowlark.html

One of Northern Virginia's most beautiful parks, Meadowlark offers more than 2 miles of pathways through its 95 acres of gardens, small lakes, and gazebos. The beautiful landscaping showcases native plants and flowers. Here's a secret: Come here during late March and early April to see weeping cherry trees in all their glory around the main lake. It's not quite as spectacular as the Tidal Basin's famous display, but you won't have to fight traffic or hunt in vain for parking.

The regional park also boasts an atrium, which proves popular for wedding

Lakes, cooling fountains, and winding pathways beckon visitors to Meadowlark Gardens Regional Park in Vienna, Virginia. PHOTO: CAROL ANN COHEN, COURTESY OF NORTHERN VIRGINIA REGIONAL PARK AUTHORITY

receptions and other special events. (Couples sometimes wed in the park's gazebos.) The attractive visitor center houses a snack room, gift shop, rest rooms, and art exhibitions. Call for a schedule of workshops and programs. Hours vary seasonally. Admission April through October is $3.00 for visitors ages 18 to 59, $1.00 for those ages 7 to 17 or 60 and older, and free for children ages 6 and younger. Admission is free November through March. The site is closed during icy weather and on New Year's Day, Thanksgiving, and Christmas. (See our Kidstuff chapter for additional information.)

Pohick Bay Regional Park
6501 Pohick Bay Dr.
Lorton, VA
(703) 339–6104
www.nvrpa.pohickley.htm
Like neighboring Mason Neck State Park, this regional park in southeastern Fairfax County is home to nesting bald eagles. Water is the park's mainstay. Visitors can bring their own boats, or rent sailboats or pedal boats. The park also features an outdoor pool, miniature and disc golf, picnic areas, and nature trails and bridle paths. You also can camp out here year-round at the family campground. (See our Golf listings for information about the course here.) Nonarea residents must pay an entrance fee of $4.00 per vehicle.

Prince William Forest Park
18100 Park Headquarters Rd.
Triangle, VA
(703) 221–7181
www.nps.gov/prwi
Part of the Quantico Creek watershed, this national park covers more than 18,500 acres of dense pine and hardwood forests and meandering creeks. More than 30 miles of trails beckon bikers, hikers, and cross-country skiers, on those rare occasions when the region receives more than a dusting of snow. The Pine Grove Visitor Center, open from 8:30 A.M. to 5:00 P.M. daily, features exhibits about the area's resources and, on weekends, naturalist-led programs. The park offers plenty of tent sites for campers and cabins for family

camping during the summer and group camping year-round. Admission to the park, valid for three consecutive days, is $4.00 per car. An annual pass is $15.

Upton Hill Regional Park
6060 Wilson Blvd.
Arlington, VA
(703) 534–3437
www.nvrpa.org/uptonhill.html
This suburban NVRPA park is known for its challenging, lushly landscaped miniature golf course, open, along with batting cages, mid-March through October. Test your skill on hole number 10—at 140 feet in length, it's billed as the world's longest miniature golf hole. The large outdoor pool is open Memorial Day weekend through Labor Day.

Suburban Maryland

See this chapter's Dancing section and the Kidstuff and Arts chapters for information about Glen Echo Park.

Black Hill Regional Park
20930 Lake Ridge Dr.
Boyds, MD
(301) 972–3476
www.mncppc.org
With more than 1,850 acres, this Maryland-National Capital Park and Planning Commission (M-NCPPC) park attracts trail lovers and fishing and boating enthusiasts. You can rent a canoe or rowboat or ride on a guided pontoon boat, which offers Little Seneca Lake tours on the hour, noon to 6:00 P.M., on summer weekends. Admission is $2.00 per person; children younger than age 3 are admitted free. You may be lucky enough to spot beavers, muskrats, otters, or other resident wildlife. The park attracts lots of waterfowl and other birds. The visitor center, open 11:00 A.M. to 6:00 P.M. daily during the summer and 11:00 A.M. to 5:00 P.M. weekends the rest of the year, houses wildlife exhibits and is surrounded by natural gardens that attract songbirds and butterflies. Other features include playgrounds, trails, a volleyball court, and picnic shelters.

Bohrer Park at Summit Hall Farm
506 S. Frederick Ave.
Gaithersburg, MD
(301) 258–6445

Highlighted by a water park with two long slides, this site of nearly 60 acres also offers outdoor game facilities, a circular path, a miniature golf course, ponds, a playground, a concession stand, and an activity center. It's a popular summer hangout for Gaithersburg residents. Park admission is free, but pool and miniature golf prices vary, so call ahead.

Cabin John Regional Park
7400 Tuckerman La.
Rockville, MD
(301) 299–0024
www.mncppc.org

This popular M-NCPPC park features numerous recreational activities, including indoor and outdoor tennis courts, a year-round ice-skating rink (301–365–2246), handball and volleyball courts, playing fields, and trails for bikers and hikers. There's also limited primitive camping space. (See our Kidstuff chapter for more on the park's child-pleasing attractions.)

Great Falls Tavern, Chesapeake and Ohio Canal National Historical Park
11710 MacArthur Blvd.
Potomac, MD
(301) 299–3613
www.nps.gov/choh/co_visit.htm

The Maryland side of Great Falls and the C&O Canal looks remarkably similar to the way it appeared more than 100 years ago. It's a lovely park in which to bike, walk, and take a narrated, hour-long canal boat ride aboard the mule-guided *Canal Clipper,* generally offered mid-April through the beginning of November. Admission is $8.00 for adults ages 15 to 61, $6.00 for seniors, and $5.00 for children ages 4 to 14. Children younger than 3 ride for free. The park's visitor center, open from 9:00 A.M. to 5:00 P.M. daily except Christmas and New Year's Day, features exhibits and an audiovisual presentation as well as special programs. Park admission is the same as Great Falls Park admission: $4.00 per car or $2.00 per pedestrian, jogger, or bicyclist, valid for three consecutive days and also good for entrance to the park on the other side of the falls (the admission fees are charged intermittently). An annual park pass, good for Great Falls and the C&O Canal, is available for $15. The park is open daily from 7:00 A.M. to dusk, except on Christmas. The gates are locked at dark.

Greenbelt Park
6565 Greenbelt Rd.
Greenbelt, MD
(301) 344–3948
www.nps.gov/gree

Just off the Beltway in Prince George's County, this 1,100-acre national park defies its highly urban setting with 9 miles of wooded trails and special interpretive nature programs for kids, such as summer Junior Rangers activities. It also offers numerous campsites for tents and vehicles. The camping fee is just $13 per night per site. Make reservations by calling (800) 365–2267 April 1 through October 31.

Little Bennett Regional Park
23701 Frederick Rd.
Clarksburg, MD
(301) 972–6581
www.mncppc.org

This park in upper Montgomery County is a popular site for family camping from spring through fall. Make reservations by calling (301) 972–9222. The remains of historic sites accent the park's expansive network of hiking trails. Visitors also enjoy nature programs, a playground and an 18-hole, par 72 golf course (301–253–1515).

Louise F. Cosca Regional Park
11000 Thrift Rd.
Clinton, MD
(301) 868–1397
www.pgparks.com/places/parks/parks.cosca.html

This nearly 700-acre Prince George's County park features a 15-acre lake for fishing and boating. You can rent rowboats and paddle boats. It also boasts indoor and outdoor tennis courts (301–868–6462), trails for hiking and horseback riding, athletic fields, and a family campsite. Visit the Clearwater Nature Center (301-297-4575) for children's activities.

Robert M. Watkins Regional Park
301 Watkins Park Dr.
Upper Marlboro, MD
(301) 218-6700
www.pgparks.com/places/parks/parks.watkins.html

Besides the many offerings for children, described in Kidstuff, this park of more than 400 acres boasts indoor and outdoor tennis courts, playing fields, and camping sites (301-249-6900). It's a popular recreational site for Prince George's County residents.

Rock Creek Regional Park
6700 Needwood Rd.
Rockville, MD
(301) 948-5053
www.mncppc.org

Hike through the woods, picnic, visit a nature center, visit an archery range, or play golf on an 18-hole course. The park's Lake Needwood offers fishing, tourboat rides, and rental pedal boats, canoes, and rowboats. The site also has a snack bar.

Seneca Creek State Park
11950 Clopper Rd.
Gaithersburg, MD
(301) 924-2127

Near Gaithersburg, this park's 7,000 acres offer outstanding hiking, boating, and fishing opportunities almost within eyesight of suburban housing developments. The Blue Heron pontoon boat takes visitors on naturalist-guided, one-hour tours on the 90-acre lake Saturdays and Sundays during the summer and early fall months. A visitor center holds frequent programs year-round.

Wheaton Regional Park
2000 Shorefield Rd.
Wheaton, MD
(301) 680-3803
www.mncppc.org

This Montgomery County favorite bustles with activity, particularly on weekends, when families and large groups flock to the

Insiders' Tip

Look for gorgeous plantings of seasonal flowers at National Park Service-maintained sites throughout Washington. In the spring more than a million daffodils adorn the Potomac's west bank.

park. The park boasts numerous attractions and programs for children (see our Kidstuff chapter for more on those) as well as hiking and biking trails, a five-acre stocked lake for fishing, an ice-skating rink (301-649-3640), and sports courts and fields. You can walk or drive to the peaceful Brookside Gardens, 1800 Glenallen Avenue (301-949-8231), offering 50 acres of various flowers and other plants and a new visitor center for educational programs.

Recreation

We could go on forever listing and describing the thousands of recreational opportunities available to residents throughout Metro Washington. Here's a sampling of popular resources to get you started in your leisurely pursuits. If you don't see your favorite activity listed individually here, contact your local recreation department. You'll find phone numbers in this chapter. Check our Parks listings in this chapter for camping, trails, and sports court locations. Look at our Kidstuff and Senior Scene chapters for additional ideas for children and senior citizens.

Amusement Parks

Six Flags America
13710 Central Ave.
Largo, MD
(301) 249-1500
www.sixflags.com/america

The closest theme park to Washington, Six Flags America boasts such crowd-

Thrill seekers enjoy rides like the Joker's Jinx at Six Flags America in Largo, Maryland.

PHOTO: COURTESY OF SIX FLAGS AMERICA

pleasers as the Joker's Jinx steel coaster and Two Face—The Flip Side, a face-to-face roller coaster. The park features numerous Looney Tunes–themed attractions, including Looney Tunes Movietown, a rides area especially for young children. The 25-acre Paradise Island water park includes such attractions as Crocodile Cal's Outback Beach House and Monsoon Lagoon, a wave pool with waves up to four feet high.

Six Flags America is open weekends during early May and daily from Memorial Day weekend to Labor Day. Admission prices are $35.99 for adults, $26.99 for seniors ages 62 and older, $17.99 for children 48 inches and shorter, and free for children younger than age four. Parking costs $9.00. (See our Kidstuff chapter for a description of children's activities here.) The park reopens during October weekends and Halloween week for Hallowscream, featuring events such as hayrides, costume contests, and a haunted train.

We recommend avoiding Six Flags on weekends, particularly those featuring special events. Our experience on one such Saturday included long lines, malfunctioning rides, surly employees, and overflowing trash cans. Kids who visited the park during midweek camp outings, however, had no complaints.

Ballooning

How about a bird's-eye view of all that gorgeous green space we described earlier? The following FAA-certified pilots offer hot-air balloon excursions, complete with champagne and treats, at sunrise and sunset over the scenic Virginia and Maryland countrysides. Call at least a couple of weeks before the date you wish to book, and be flexible: Bad weather or high winds can whip up before you know it, forcing a postponement. Don't forget your video camera! Your pilot will be happy to recommend a bed-and-breakfast, should you want to extend your getaway.

Northern Virginia

Balloons Unlimited
2946-O Chain Bridge Rd.
Oakton, VA
(703) 281–2300
www.balloonsunlimited.com

Owner Bob Thomas has been piloting balloons above Middleburg and the Shenandoah region for 23 years. Flights cost $150 per person and last approximately an hour. You can book your trip for any day of the week, April through mid-November. Thomas also offers ballooning classes and sells balloons of the helium-filled variety at his Oakton store.

Suburban Maryland

Fantasy Flights
438 Girard St., #101
Gaithersburg, MD
(301) 417–0000
www.airtravel.com.fantasy

This 20-year-old company offers flights at sunrise in a five-person balloon above the Sugarloaf Mountain countryside between Gaithersburg and Frederick, looking out over the Potomac toward Virginia and West Virginia. Owner/pilot Randy Danneman says that on a clear day, you can

see, well, not forever, but all the way to downtown Washington. The cost is $200 per person for a one- to one-and-a-half-hour flight. You'll also get a fancy flight certificate and a color picture of the balloon. Danneman offers flight instruction also.

Sky High Adventures
17513 Soper St.
Poolesville, MD
(301) 605–0500, (301) 972–7004

Now in its 27th year, Sky High Adventures is the oldest ballooning business in the Metro D.C. area. Trips generally cost $185 to $200 a person and travel for about an hour over upper Montgomery County. Owner/pilot Pat Michaels also offers individualized flight instruction.

Bicycling

Virginia Bicycling Federation Inc.
P.O. Box 5621
Arlington, VA 22205
(703) 532–6101
www.vabike.org

This advocacy organization promotes bicycling safety, keeping its members

Washington, D.C., with its many trails winding along the Potomac and leading attractions nearby, is a great city to explore by bike. PHOTO: COURTESY OF WASHINGTON, DC CONVENTION AND TOURISM CORPORATION

informed about such issues as road and trail improvements, new riding facilities, and legislation pertinent to cyclists. The bimonthly newsletter also includes information about upcoming rides and events sponsored by bicycling organizations throughout the state. Individual membership is $18 annually, and a family can join for $30 a year.

Washington Area Bicyclist Association
733 15th Street NW, Ste. 1030
Washington, DC
(202) 628–2500
www.waba.org

Metro Washington boasts several bicycling clubs. The best way to find out more about them and discover which ones might be right for you is to contact this advocacy organization, which promotes safe bicycling conditions and greater bicycle use in the Metro Washington area.

Bird-watchers find the variety of species in the Washington, D.C. area fascinating.

PHOTO: COURTESY OF PATUXENT RESEARCH REFUGE

WABA, with more than 2,000 members, sponsors events like the National Capital Bicycle Tour and puts together newsletters and other publications. Membership is $25 per individual and $35 per family. Call to request a free copy of the *Bicycle Resource Directory,* listing clubs throughout the Washington area.

Bird Watching

Audubon Naturalist Society of the Central Atlantic States Inc.
8940 Jones Mill Rd.
Chevy Chase, MD
(301) 652–9188
www.audubonnaturalist.org

Beginning bird walks take place at Woodend, the society's headquarters and 40-acre wildlife sanctuary, at 8:00 A.M. on Saturdays from September through June. Meet at the Audubon Naturalist store entrance. Call for directions and information about other birding events. Call (301) 652–1088 to hear the Voice of the Naturalist describing recent local bird sightings.

Fairfax Audubon Society
P.O. Box 128
Annadale, VA 22003
(703) 256–6895
www.fairfaxaudubon.org

This organization sponsors frequent bird walks and educational programs, detailed in its *Potomac Flier* newsletter. Anyone is welcome to attend its free meetings at 7:30 P.M. on the third Tuesday of each month (suspended during the summer) at the Green Spring Gardens' Park Horticultural Center, 4603 Green Spring Rd., Alexandria. Society membership costs $20 annually and includes a subscription to *Audubon Magazine.*

Bowling

Duckpin Bowling Proprietors of America and National Duckpin Youth Association
2924 E. Northern Pkwy.
Baltimore, MD
(410) 254–3666
www.duckpins.org

National Duckpin Bowling Congress
4991 Fairview Ave.
Linthicum, MD
(410) 636–2695
www.ndbc.org

These organizations just outside the Washington area can provide information about local lanes featuring duckpin bowling, a unique game featuring smaller, holeless balls (between three and four pounds each) and tiny pins. This variation got its start in Baltimore and continues to be a popular pastime in the Northeast. Young children especially enjoy the game, with its easily handled balls and three tries per frame.

Nation's Capital Area Bowling Association
4710 Auth Pl., Ste. 465
Camp Springs, MD
(301) 899–5978
www.ncaba.org

Are you interested in joining an American Bowling Congress (ABC)–sanctioned league? Call for information about leagues in your community.

Washington D.C. Area Women's Bowling Association
4710 Auth Pl., Ste. 495
Camp Springs, MD
(240) 695–1985
wdcawba.org

Contact this association for information about ABC- and Women's International Bowling Congress–sanctioned leagues in your neighborhood, details about rules or a membership application. Annual dues are $16.

Chess

The U.S. Chess Center
1501 M St. NW
Washington, DC
(202) 857–4922
www.chessctr.org

Adults and children can take classes and participate in tournaments at this center in the heart of the city. It's open evenings, starting at 6:00 P.M., Monday through Thursday, and weekends, noon to 6:00 P.M. Chess enthusiasts shouldn't miss the

Interesting birds and other wildlife sometimes pose for lucky photographers visiting local parks.
PHOTO: COURTESY OF FAIRFAX COUNTY PARK AUTHORITY

center's free U.S. Chess Hall of Fame and Museum and gift shop.

Climbing

Adventure Schools Rock Climbing
7687 MacArthur Blvd.
Cabin John, MD
(301) 263–0900, (800) 39–CLIMB
www.adventureschool.com

Before you attempt to scale those inviting formations at Great Falls and other local parks, learn from an expert. Expert instructors give lessons for beginners and advanced students, generally taking folks on-site for a day of hands-on education at Carderock Park in Maryland or Great Falls Park in Virginia. They provide all the necessary equipment, too. A one-day, eight-hour course for ages 11 and older is $95; a two-day session is $175. Owner Dave Nugent also leads climbing adventures in places like West Virginia and Looking Glass, North Carolina. Call for a course catalog. The climbing school is based at Potomac Outdoors, Ltd., which also offers merchandise, white-water canoe and kayaking trips, and backcountry skiing and snow camping sessions.

Sportrock Climbing Centers
5308 Eisenhower Ave.
Alexandria, VA
(703) 212–7625
45935 Maries Rd.
Sterling, VA
(571) 434–ROCK
14708 Southlawn La.
Rockville, MD
(301) 762–5111
www.sportrock.com

These indoor climbing facilities feature 30- and 40-foot walls with a multitude of routes. Novices can learn beginning climbing skills, and more experienced climbers can hone their techniques with indoor practice sessions. The centers are open noon to 11:00 P.M. Monday through Friday, 11:00 A.M. to 8:00 P.M. Saturday, and noon to 8:00 P.M. Sunday. Daily rates are $14.00 for adults and $6.00 for ages 12 and younger. Discount passes and memberships also are available, along with rental gear and special beginners' sessions. (See our Kidstuff chapter for information about children's programs here.)

Dancing

Glen Echo Park
7300 MacArthur Blvd.
Glen Echo, MD
(301) 492–6282
www.nps.gov/glec

The 65-year-old Spanish Ballroom at this former amusement park turned national park still possesses the same 7,500-square-foot sprung maple floor upon which dancers swayed to the sounds of big bands led by the likes of the Dorseys

Insiders' Tip
Many bird-watchers enjoy participating in the annual Christmas Bird Count.

and Artie Shaw. Today, it's the local hot spot for swing dancing, but you also can take your pick from several other dances offered on a regular basis. Best of all, all events take place in a smoke- and alcohol-free atmosphere.

Friday nights feature traditional country dances like contras, squares, and mixers from 8:30 to 11:30 P.M., usually at $6.00 a person. Two left feet? Show up an hour early, March through October, and you'll get a lesson in beginning contra dancing, included in the admission fee. Call (202) 216–2116 for more information.

"Big Night Out" Saturdays attract as many as 600 people who relish swing dancing. Dances run from 9:00 P.M. to midnight, preceded by a beginners' workshop at 8:00 P.M. Admission is usually $8.00 to $10.00. The second Saturday of each month generally features Louisiana-style dancing.

The first and third Sunday afternoons feature ballroom-style dancing from 3:30 to 6:00 P.M. at $5.00 per person, preceded by waltz lessons at 3:00 P.M. The fourth Sundays feature Cajun and zydeco dances from 3:30 to 6:00 P.M., $10.00 per person, preceded by lessons from 3:00 to 3:30 P.M. Look for Western swing or ballroom dancing on the second Sunday of each month. The Folklore Society of Greater Washington holds traditional American dances on Sundays from 7:30 P.M. to 10:30 P.M. Admission is $8.00.

(Check out The Arts and Kidstuff chapters for more of this unique park's features, including an antique carousel, children's shows, a museum, and art studios.)

Northern Virginia Country Western Dance Association
P.O. Box 384
Merrifield, VA 22116
(703) 860–4941
nvcwda.com

Looking for a place to show off your Two Step or learn the latest line dance? This 500-member organization—annual membership is $18—sponsors at least two dances per month at various area community centers. Featuring a nonsmoking, family-oriented atmosphere, the events include free lessons. Admission generally runs $7.00 for members, $10.00 for non-members, and $4.00 for young people younger than 18 years.

Golfing

Our region offers numerous attractive and challenging public golf courses, many operated by local park authorities. We can't begin to list them all, but here's a representative sampling. Be sure to check our Spectator Sports chapter for information about the professional golf scene.

Washington, D.C.

East Potomac Park Golf Course and Driving Range
Hains Pt. and Ohio Dr. SW
Washington, DC
(202) 554–7660

How about a game of golf in the shadow of the Washington Monument? You'll aim right at the towering obelisk on the ninth hole of the recently renovated par 27, Red Course, which has a yardage of 5,802. You'll also see the familiar landmark in the background of the ninth hole on the 18-hole regulation, par 72 Blue Course, which has a yardage of 6,700 from the blue tees and 6,197 from the white tees. The ninth-hole regulation White Course is par 34, with a yardage of 2,480. Set on National Park Service land next to the Potomac, the flat course is open year-round, generally from dawn to dusk.

Weekday greens fees are $11 for 9 holes and $16.50 for 18 holes; weekends and holidays, fees are $14 for 9 holes and $22 for 18 holes. Power carts are available for $19 for 18 holes. Rent a pull cart for $2.50 for 9 holes and $3.50 for 18 holes. Rental clubs, available in half-sets, are $5.75 for 9 holes and $8.50 for 18. A double-deck, 100-station driving range is partially covered and heated during winter. A bucket of balls costs $4.00. The course also has a snack bar and grill and a fully stocked pro shop. Hours vary seasonally, but generally run 7:00 A.M. to 10:00 P.M. Thursdays through Tuesdays, 10:00 A.M. to 10:00 P.M. Wednesdays, May through September.

Also on site, East Potomac Mini Golf dates to the early 1920s and claims to be

How about a game of golf in the shadow of the Washington Monument? PHOTO: COURTESY OF WASHINGTON, DC CONVENTION AND TOURISM CORPORATION

the nation's longest running miniature golf operation. With each hole a par 3, it's probably one of the area's most challenging courses. The designs include such features as multiple levels and a spiraling shot. Native stonework and ponds with goldfish, water lilies, and a bridge highlight the landscaping. It's open 11:00 A.M. to 8:00 P.M. on weekdays, 11:00 A.M. to 10:00 P.M. weekends, with admission priced at $3.00 weekdays and $3.50 Saturdays, Sundays, and holidays.

Langston Golf Course and Driving Range
26th and Benning Rd. NE
Washington, DC
(202) 397–8638

This 18-hole, par 72 course features tree-lined fairways and three holes with water. The total yardage is 6,340. Look for the "Joe Louis Tree," which the "Brown Bomber" always hit, on hole number 3. The facility includes a pro shop, snack bar, and recently renovated, partially covered driving range. Fees are about the same as those at East Potomac.

Rock Creek Park Golf Course
16th and Rittenhouse Sts. NW
Washington, DC
(202) 882-7332
www.nps.gov/rocr
Here's another of Rock Creek Park's many surprises: a hilly, wooded golf course in the middle of the city. The 18-hole, par 65 course has a yardage of 4,800. Its signature hole, number 17, features a downhill par 3 to a narrow fairway. The course has a snack bar and pro shop but no driving range. Fees are similar to those at the previously mentioned courses.

Northern Virginia

Burke Lake Golf Center
7315 Ox Rd.
Fairfax Station, VA
(703) 323-1641
www.co.fairfax.va.us/parks/golf/burkegolf.htm
Adjacent to popular Burke Lake Park, this 18-hole, par 54 course with 2,539 yardage boasts a pleasant, lakeside setting. It features a putting green and lighted driving range, along with a full-service clubhouse. Tee times for this and six other Fairfax County Park Authority courses can be arranged through an automated phone-in system, with a $25 annual subscription. Burke offers private and group lessons and a Junior Golf Program for youngsters ages 5 to 17. Fees are $12 to $14 for 9 holes, and $18 to $20 for 18 holes, depending on the time you play. Rent clubs for $7.00.

Burke Lake Golf Center is one of six courses operated by the Fairfax County Park Authority throughout Fairfax County. Visit the FCPA Web site for information about the other locations.

Pohick Bay Regional Park Golf Course
10301 Gunston Rd.
Lorton, VA
(703) 339-8585
One of three Northern Virginia Regional Park Authority courses—the others are the 701-yard Algonkian in Sterling and

6,764-yard Brambleton in Ashburn—recently renovated Pohick Bay takes pride in being rated by golf magazines as one of the area's most challenging courses. The hilly 18-hole, par 72 course with narrow fairways features a 6,405 yardage. Reserve tee times by phone or in person at 3:00 P.M. seven days in advance. The course also features a driving range, pro shop and snack bar. Fees—discounted by $4.00 for 18 holes and $2.50 for nine holes for jurisdictional residents—are $29.50 Monday through Thursday, $36.50 Friday through Sunday, and holidays for 18 holes; $19.50 and $23.50 for nine holes. Juniors age 15 and younger and seniors age 60 and older can play for $23.50 Monday through Thursday. Power carts cost $26.50 for 18 holes, and $17 for nine holes; pull carts, $3.00 or $4.00.

Raspberry Falls Golf & Hunt Club
41601 Raspberry Dr.
Leesburg, VA
(703) 779-2555
www.raspberryfalls.com
Gary Player designed this 5-year-old, 18-hole, par 72 course, noted for its challenging play, abundance of bent grass, and stunning views of the surrounding Hunt Country. Yardage is 7,191, with a 134 slope. Hole number 3, a challenging par 4, features an elevated tee box with an outstanding view. Fees for 18-hole play range from $50 to $94 and include a rental cart. Call up to eight days in advance to arrange a tee time. You'll find the club off U.S. 15, just 3 miles north of Leesburg. It also houses a pro shop, full grill, and driving range with practice sand bunkers and a chipping green.

Reston National Golf Course
11875 Sunrise Valley Dr.
Reston, VA
(703) 620-9333
This 18-hole, par 71 course, noted for its tree-lined fairways, is one of the Metro Washington area's top-ranked public golf courses, according to the *Washington Post* and *Washington Flyer* magazine. Yardage from the middle tee is 6,506. The 460-yard, par 4 hole number 10 proves most challenging, with an elevated green

guarded by two bunkers. Although not required, tee times preferably are made a week in advance at this bustling course. The course has a driving range and putting and chipping greens, as well as a snack bar and pro shop. Fees, including carts, run $72 on weekends, and $49 Monday through Thursday. The course also features an enclosed deck for parties and a state-of-the-art irrigation system costing nearly $1 million.

Suburban Maryland

Needwood Golf Course
6724 Needwood Rd.
Rockville, MD
(301) 948–1075
www.mc-mncppc.org/fun/enterprise/
lakenw.htm

One of the Maryland Park and Planning Commission's eight golf courses, Needwood is a par 70, 18- and 9-hole executive course with a yardage of 6,254 from the back tee. The front is flatter than the back, and there's water on the back nine holes. Fees for 18 holes vary from $21 to $30, depending on the day and player's age, with discounts for ages younger than 18 and older than 60. The course includes a pro shop with snack bar, putting green, driving range, and a resident pro who gives lessons.

Trotters Glen Family Golf Center
16501 Batchellors Forest Rd.
Olney, MD
(301) 570–4951

On the number 11 hole at this 18-hole, par 72 course, a player must hit a perfect tee shot to avoid a water pond to the right and woods to the left. The course is 6,300 yards. Amenities include a practice area, putting and chipping greens, pro shop, snack bar, and golf school. Call seven days in advance to make a required tee time. Fees are $26 on weekends and $21 during the week.

Hang Gliding

Silver Wings Inc.
6032 N. 20th St.
Arlington, VA
(703) 533–1965
silverwingshanggliding.com

Pohick Bay Regional Park features one of Northern Virginia's popular golf courses. PHOTO: JULIE MALONEY, COURTESY OF NORTHERN VIRGINIA REGIONAL PARK AUTHORITY

If you get the urge to soar like an eagle after your visit to Mason Neck State Park, consider learning how to hang glide. John Middleton, a U.S. hang gliding certified instructor, runs the area's only hang gliding school. Beginners start at Ground School, a $10, 90-minute class in which Middleton shows videos and describes the sport. He offers flight classes, complete with essential equipment, on Saturdays and Sundays, usually from around 10:00 A.M. to 5:00 P.M. or 6:00 P.M. Students carpool to a training site, where they start on small hills. Classes are $70 each per person. Most folks need five to eight lessons before they get the "hang" of it.

Ice Skating

Fairfax Ice Arena
3779 Pickett Rd.
Fairfax, VA
(703) 323–1131, (703) 323–1132
www.fairfaxicearena.com

U.S. National Champion and World Bronze Medalist Michael Weiss trains at this popular indoor skating facility, sometimes on Friday evenings. Call for a schedule of public skating, offered daily at varying times. Sessions cost $5.75 to $6.25, and skate rental is $2.50. The arena offers private and group lessons for all skill levels, holds an annual competition and occasionally hosts ice shows. Weiss's coach, Audrey Weisiger, named 1999 Coach of the Year by the United States Figure Skating Association, is a staff member. An in-house adult ice-hockey league plays fall/winter and spring/summer seasons. The Skating Club of Northern Virginia, an organization for competitive skaters, practices here.

National Gallery of Art Sculpture Garden Ice-Skating Rink
Constitution Avenue, between Third and Ninth Streets NW
Washington, DC
(202) 737–4215
www.nga.gov/ginfo/skating.htm

Visit the area's newest outdoor skating rink and enjoy skating with a view. The rink sits amid the Sculpture Garden's intriguing works of art. Open mid-November through mid-March, the rink features two-hour sessions from 10:00 A.M. to 11:00 P.M. Monday through Thursday, 10:00 A.M. to midnight Friday and Saturday, and 11:00 A.M. to 9:00 P.M. Sunday. Admission is $5.50 for adults, $4.50 for children ages 12 and younger, seniors ages 50 and older, and students with IDs. Skate rental is $2.50, and locker rental is 50 cents. The Pavilion Cafe serves light meals and beverages.

Pershing Park Ice Rink
Pennsylvania Ave. and 14th St. NW
Washington, DC
(202) 737–6938

Skate under the stars at this popular rink, right across the street from the elegant Willard Inter-Continental hotel and just steps from the city's theater district. For a picture-perfect holiday outing in December, hit the ice after visiting the National Christmas Tree and Pageant of Peace on the Ellipse, only a couple of blocks away. The rink is open mid-December until the ice starts to melt, usually early March.

Two-hour sessions take place from 3:00 to 11:00 P.M. Monday through Thursday and from 9:00 A.M. to 11:00 P.M. Friday, Saturday, and Sunday. Admission is $5.00 for adults and $4.00 for children; figure-skate rental is $2.50. Parking is scarce, so you're better off taking Metro to nearby Federal Triangle or Metro Center.

Reston Ice Skating Pavilion
Reston Town Center, 1818 Discovery St.
Reston, VA
(703) 709–6300
www.restontowncenter.com/skating.htm

At ever-growing Reston Town Center, this elegant, glass-domed, open-sided pavilion is Northern Virginia's answer to Rockefeller Center, complete with a huge Christmas tree across the street. A visit to the rink is one of our favorite winter outings, whether we skate or just sip hot cocoa and watch those who know what they're doing. Public skating takes place usually from early November until the weather warms up. Hours are from 11:00 A.M. to 11:00 P.M. on weekends and 11:00 A.M. to 7:00 or 9:00 P.M. on weekdays. A two-hour session is $6.50 for adults and $5.50 for kids and seniors. Skate rentals are $2.50, and you can rent free helmets for the little ones. You can also purchase season passes and discount books. Lessons for various skill levels take place before and after public sessions. In the summer the pavilion hosts open-air concerts on Thursday and Saturday nights

Kites

Maryland Kite Society
10113 Lloyd Rd.
Potomac, MD
(301) 949–9078
www.kites.org/mdkites

The oldest kite club in North America, this 150-member, American Kitefliers Association–affiliated group began 30 years ago to spoof a distinguished poet's society. AKA 1998 Grand National Champion Tanna Haynes, a Pennsylvania resident, belongs to the club. Annual $10 membership includes a subscription to a quarterly newsletter. The club sponsors

Kite flying behind the Washington Monument is a popular activity. PHOTO: COURTESY OF SMITHSONIAN INSTITUTION

the Great St. John's Kite Festival, the annual Maryland Kite Retreat kite-making workshop during President's Weekend in February, and a monthly kite fly.

Winds and Rainbows
3718 Cumberland St. NW
Washington, DC
(202) 514-5942
The only East Coast kite club catering to the gay and lesbian community, Winds and Rainbows is one of two such AKA-affiliated groups. Annual $10 membership, open to anyone with an interest in kiting, includes a quarterly newsletter detailing upcoming club events.

Wings Over Washington (WOW)
2805 Hunter Mill Rd.
Oakton, VA 22124
www.kites.org/WOW
An affiliate of AKA, this active local club sponsors monthly kite flies behind the Washington Monument (look for Captain WOW, a huge soccer player) and sometimes holds kite-making workshops. Annual membership, which includes a quarterly newsletter and retailer discounts, is $15 ($10 renewal) per individual, $20 ($15 renewal) per household. Write for information.

Orienteering

Quantico Orienteering Club
6212 Thomas Dr.
Springfield, VA
(703) 528–INFO
goc.nova.org
This club sponsors map hikes and orienteering events for all ages and skill levels, throughout the Metro Washington and Baltimore area. An annual membership costs $12.50.

Outdoor Sports

Washington Women Outdoors Inc.
19450 Caravan Dr.
Germantown, MD
(301) 864–3070
www.washingtonwomenoutdoors.org

This nonprofit organization offers instruction in outdoor sports, by women and for women. All skill levels are welcome to participate in such outings as hiking and backpacking, bicycling, rock climbing, canoeing, and kayaking. Non-members are welcome, but members get discounts, as well as newsletters, use of equipment and other perks. Basic annual membership is $30.

Running

American Running Association
4405 East-West Hwy., Hwy. 410, Ste. 405
Bethesda, MD
(301) 913–9517, (800) 776–2732
www.americanrunning.org
With so many wonderful park trails and pleasant streets at their disposal, many Washingtonians choose running as their favorite way to exercise. This nonprofit, national association promotes the benefits of running and other aerobic exercise for fitness. Membership, $25 annually, includes a monthly newsletter; discounts on books, travel, and programs; free trails maps; and other benefits. Contact the organization for a list of more than 50 running clubs in Metro Washington.

Road Runners Club of America
510 N. Washington St.
Alexandria, VA
(703) 836–0558
www.rrca.org
If you're a long-distance runner, you'll be interested in this national association of nonprofit running clubs. RRCA educates runners on different facets of the sport, supports legislation that benefits runners, and publishes a quarterly newsletter. Contact the national headquarters for a list of more than 25 member clubs in the Washington/Baltimore area.

Sailing

The Mariner Sailing School
Belle Haven Marina, Inc., P.O. Box 7093
Alexandria, VA
(703) 768–0018
www.saildc.com

You'll find the biggest sailing school in the Metro Washington area just off the George Washington Memorial Parkway. Qualified sailors teach hands-on classes in adult basic sailing; youth (ages 8 to 15) basic, and intermediate sailing; windsurfing; cruising; and racing. The facility is an authorized American Red Cross provider, as well as a charter member of U.S. Sailing's Commercial Sailing Program. Call for class schedules and rates.

Washington Sailing Marina
1 Marina Dr.
Alexandria, VA
(703) 548–9027
www.guestservices.com/wsm

The Washington Sailing Marina, about 1½ miles south of Ronald Reagan Washington National Airport, will rent you a cute little Sunfish sailboat for $10 an hour.

Soccer

Northern Virginia

Fairfax Women's Soccer Association
Fairfax County, VA
(703) 541–6194
www.erols.com/fwsa

Players of all skill levels are welcome in this league of 700 women in three age groups: Open for age 18 and older, Master for age 30 and older, and Grand Master for age 40 and older. Teams play April through June and September through November, usually 10 games per season. Most games take place Saturdays on Fairfax County soccer fields. Registration is $45 for county residents, $65 for out-of-county residents.

Sports Network
8320 Quarry Rd.
Manassas, VA
(703) 335–1555
www.sports-network.com

This indoor soccer arena holds year-round leagues, mostly for adults, and winter youth leagues and summer camps. Volleyball and lacrosse teams also play here. Soccer team registration generally costs from $400 to $550 per session. Call for a schedule.

Virginia Coed Sports and Recreation Association, Inc.
P.O. Box 3050
Merrifield, VA 22116
(703) 295–0690
www.coedfun.org

Metro Washington's largest coed adult soccer league includes about 500 people on 24 teams that play outdoors March through November. Games take place seven nights a week in Burke, Virginia. Registration is available on a first-come, first-serve basis. Usually, men's spots fill up more quickly than women's. Affiliated with the U.S. Soccer Federation, the league also sponsors at least two big annual tournaments that draw approximately 45 teams from the area and other states.

Suburban Maryland

The Corner Kick
18707 N. Frederick Rd.
Gaithersburg, MD
(301) 840–5425
www.corner-kick.com

This indoor soccer facility, which also houses a bar and restaurant, holds year-round adult soccer leagues and kids' soccer leagues on weekends from November to April. Team registration is $450. Some local volleyball leagues also play here.

> ## Insiders' Tip
> Keep track of upcoming hikes, runs, and cycling events; recreational club activities; amateur sports leagues; and classes in such areas as diving and kayaking by checking out the "On the Move" listings in the *Washington Post*'s Weekend section.

Ultimate Frisbee

Washington Area Frisbee Club (WAFC)
1808 N. Quantico St.
Arlington, VA
(301) 588–2629
www.wafc.org

Kind of like football played with a flying disc, Ultimate Frisbee boasts quite a following in Metro Washington, judging from WAFC's membership of 2,300. The club sponsors spring, summer (most popular), and fall/winter coed leagues for a range of skill levels. Serious players participate in WAFC's traveling teams, while folks looking for informal play usually can find pickup games on Saturday and Sunday afternoons at the Ellipse in D.C. Most league games take place on the Anacostia Park Fields or on the Ellipse across from the White House. League fees are $5.00 to $10.00, and members can buy their own Frisbees for $5.00 each through the club. Call for more information.

Yoga

Mid-Atlantic Yoga Association, Inc.
P.O. Box 10658
Silver Spring, MD 20914
(202) 332–9401
www.mayayoga.org

Take a deep breath, relax, and contact MAYA to learn all about this unique way to exercise mind and body. Student membership is $30, while teachers pay an annual fee of $40. Benefits include the nonprofit corporation's quarterly newsletter, discounts on educational events, and opportunities to attend yoga exchanges.

Youth Sports

Ready to become a soccer mom—or dad? Your best bet for locating a youth sports organization that's just right for your child is to call your local recreation center. (See our list in this chapter.) They frequently sponsor their own leagues and can point you in the direction of groups in the area. Don't overlook smaller neigh-borhood pools and community centers, most of which offer competitive team sports and instruction.

Parks and Recreation Authorities

Many of the area's recreational opportunities can be found through national, regional, and state park authorities and through community departments of parks and recreation. Here's a rundown of Metro Washington's major parks and recreation authorities and community centers. All the recreation departments and community centers listed here, unless otherwise stated, offer after-school and seniors' activities, enrichment classes, sports instruction, gymnasiums, pools, exercise programs, leagues for kids and adults, and recreational excursions. Contact them to receive their latest programming guides.

Washington, D.C.

District of Columbia Department of Parks and Recreation
3149 16th St. NW
Washington, DC
(202) 673–7647
www.dpr.dc.gov/main.shtm

The department oversees more than 70 neighborhood recreation centers, the newly renovated Anacostia Wellness/Fitness Recreation Center, seven indoor swimming pools, 57 tennis courts, three thera- peutic recreation centers, and many park spaces.

National Capital Region, National Park Service
900 Ohio Dr. SW
Washington, DC
(202) 619–7222
www.nps.gov/nacc

The National Park Service oversees more than 6,500 acres of park space in Washington, D.C., along with such landmarks as Ford's Theatre and Frederick Douglass National Historic Sites; FDR, Korean War Veterans, Lincoln, Thomas Jefferson, and

Vietnam Veterans Memorials; the Washington Monument; and the White House.

Northern Virginia

Alexandria Department of Recreation, Parks and Cultural Activities
1108 Jefferson St.
Alexandria, VA
(703) 838–4343
www.ci.alexandria.va.us./rpca

The department has seven recreation centers, including recently renovated Mount Vernon Recreation Center and Nannie J. Lee Recreation Center. Chinquapin Park and Recreation Center boasts a 25-meter indoor pool and diving well. The department also oversees 12 major parks, the City Marina, seasonal special events, camps, and weekend nature programs at Jerome "Buddie" Ford Nature Center, 5700 Sanger Avenue, (703) 838–4829.

Arlington County Department of Parks, Recreation and Community Resources
2100 Clarendon Blvd.
Arlington, VA
(703) 228–4747
www.co.arlington.va.us/prcr

Arlington's department oversees 12 community centers, 3 year-round swimming pools, 2 nature centers, Virginia Cooperative Extension programs, a 68,000-square-foot fitness facility, and 6 parks with picnic pavilions.

City of Fairfax Parks and Recreation
John C. Wood Complex
3730 Old Lee Hwy. (U.S. 29)
Fairfax, VA
(703) 385–7858
www.ci.fairfax.va.us/ParksRec

The department sponsors 21 parks, including the 48-acre Daniels Run Park and 20-acre Van Dyck Park; a network of recreational trails for bikers, walkers, and runners; the City of Fairfax Band and other arts programs, including free summer concerts and performances at Old Town Hall, 3999 University Drive; and seasonal celebrations. The city does not have a swimming pool.

City of Manassas Department of Recreation and Parks
9027 Center St., Rm. 102
Manassas, VA
(703) 257–8237
www.manassascity.org/leisure_serv

This department sponsors tours, special events, and classes and oversees community gym programs at two local schools.

City of Manassas Park Department of Parks Recreation
99 Adams St.
Manassas Park, VA
(703) 335–8872
www.ci.manassas-park.va.us/parksrec

This department offers special events, classes, sports leagues, and two pools.

Fairfax County Community and Recreation Services
12011 Government Center Pkwy.
Ste. 1050
Fairfax, VA
(703) 222–4664
www.co.fairfax.va.us/rec/indexffxco.htm

Fairfax County Park Authority recreation centers offer many fitness opportunities. PHOTO: COURTESY OF FAIRFAX COUNTY PARK AUTHORITY

Not to be confused with the county park authority, Community and Recreation Services offers a wide variety of quarterly hobby and recreational classes—everything from aerobics and art to weight training and yoga—for Fairfax City and County residents. Most activities take place after hours at schools. The program also operates 7 community centers, 9 teen centers, 13 senior centers, therapeutic recreation services, and summer camps. The department shares its quarterly catalog with Fairfax County Public Schools' Office of Adult and Community Education.

Fairfax County Park Authority
12055 Government Center Pkwy., Ste. 927
Fairfax, VA
(703) 324–8700
www.co.fairfax.va.us/parks

This massive park authority oversees more than 350 parks on more than 16,000 acres, including 11 multiple purpose parks and numerous neighborhood and community parks. Eight full-service recreation centers, 12 historical or archaeological sites, 5 golf courses, 3 miniature golf courses, and a countywide farmers' market program also fall under the park authority's jurisdiction.

Falls Church Recreation and Parks
223 Little Falls St.
Falls Church, VA
(703) 248–5077
www.ci.fallschurch.va.us/services/park

Based at the Falls Church Community Center, the department sponsors a variety of classes, an adult gym program, a Saturday farmers' market, bike trails, nine parks, and numerous seasonal events, many of which take place at the historic Cherry Hill Farmhouse, 312 Park Avenue, (703) 248-5171. The department does not offer swimming. Its events schedule also lists offerings of the Office of Community Education, 7124 Leesburg Pike, (703) 241-7676.

Herndon Parks and Recreation
814 Ferndale Ave.
Herndon, VA
(703) 435–6868
www.herndonweb.com/rec/rec.html

Headquartered at the Herndon Community Center, this department offers extensive aquatics classes, nature walks at Runnymede Park, a children's performance series, and numerous special interest and fitness activities. A "bubble" tops the center's tennis courts from the end of October through March.

Recreation centers throughout Metro Washington sponsor Little League ball teams. PHOTO: COURTESY OF FAIRFAX COUNTY PARK AUTHORITY

Loudoun County Parks, Recreation and Community Services
1 Harrison St. SE
Leesburg, VA
(703) 777-0343
www.co.loudoun.va.us/prcs/home.htm

The department owns or oversees more than 15 parks and 11 community centers offering a variety of programs. Three developing historic sites also fall under the division's jurisdiction.

Northern Virginia Regional Park Authority
5400 Ox Rd.
Fairfax Station, VA
(703) 352-5900
www.nvpra.org

The park authority's vast network includes 17 parks, the Bull Run–Occoquan Trail, historic Carlyle House, 4 regional park swimming pools, 3 golf courses, 6 miniature golf courses and areas for boating and camping.

Prince William County Park Authority
14420 Bristow Rd.
Manassas, VA
(703) 792-7060
www.pwcweb.com/rec/parks

The park authority oversees 46 parks, 3 public golf courses, community centers, and the Chinn Aquatics and Fitness Center and Splash Down and Waterworks water parks.

Reston Community Center
2310 Colts Neck Rd.
Reston, VA
(703) 476-4500

This center serving the community in western Fairfax County includes an indoor pool, art exhibits, and a theater that hosts performances by its resident theatrical troupe and nationally known performers.

Town of Leesburg Department of Parks and Recreation
60 Ida Lee Dr. NW
Leesburg, VA
(703) 777-1368
www.parksandrec.leesburgva.org

The department's 13 parks include the

Bicyclists take to the W&OD Trail in Northern Virginia. PHOTO: CAROL ANN COHEN, COURTESY OF NORTHERN VIRGINIA REGIONAL PARK AUTHORITY

138-acre Ida Lee Park, the site of Ida Lee Recreation Center and a diverse aquatics program. The department also sponsors numerous seasonal events. In-line skaters, bikers, and skateboarders frequent the Catoctin Street Skate Park in the center of town.

Town of Vienna Parks and Recreation
120 Cherry St. SE
Vienna, VA
(703) 255-6360
www.ci.vienna.va.us/Town_Departments/Parks_and_Rec.htm

Most activities take place at the community center, which includes a teen center and boasts an outdoor bocce ball court. The department also oversees four parks, the Vienna Community Band, and numerous special events. Swimming is not available.

Lakes and rivers abound in the region surrounding Metro Washington, much to the delight of anglers like these. PHOTO: MIDDLETON EVANS, COURTESY OF MARYLAND OFFICE OF TOURISM

Virginia Department of Conservation and Recreation
203 Governor St., Ste. 302
Richmond, VA
(804) 786–1712
dit1.state.va.us/~dev/

Contact the department for information about its 43 parks and natural areas.

Suburban Maryland

City of Laurel Department of Parks and Recreation
Laurel Municipal Center
8103 Sandy Spring Rd.
Laurel, MD
(301) 725–7800
www.laurel.md.us/parks.htm

Laurel's department oversees two com-

munity centers, a golf and recreation center, an outdoor municipal pool, a senior center, playing fields, and the Granville Gude Park and Lakehouse at 8300 Mulberry Street, Laurel, (301) 490–3530.

City of Rockville Recreation and Parks
111 Maryland Ave.
Rockville, MD
(301) 309–3340
www.ci.rockville.md.us/recreaton/recleis.htm

This department oversees more than 50 parks, including a new skate park, and several community centers in Montgomery County's large city of Rockville.

Greenbelt Recreation Department
25 Crescent Rd.
Greenbelt, MD
(301) 397–2208
www.ci.greenbelt.md.us

Greenbelt's facilities include an aquatics and fitness center, community center, youth center, and recreation center, as well as two parks available for community rentals.

Maryland Department of Natural Resources/State Forest and Park Service
580 Taylor Ave., E-3
Annapolis, MD
(410) 974–3771, (800) 830–3974
www.dnr.state.md.us/publiclands

Call the department for information about its 280,000 acres of public parks and forests.

Maryland-National Capital Park and Planning Commission
Montgomery County Department of Parks
9500 Brunett Ave.
Silver Spring, MD
(301) 495–2503

Prince George's County Department of Parks and Recreation
6600 Kenilworth Ave.
Riverdale, MD
(301) 699–2407
www.mncppc.org

This massive department, covering all of Suburban Maryland, includes numerous parks and, in Prince George's County, community centers. You'll also find historic sites, nature centers, and golf courses.

Montgomery County Department of Recreation
12210 Bushey Dr.
Silver Spring, MD
(240) 777–6804
www.co.mo.md.us/rec/

Contact this department for information about its nine swimming pools, more than a dozen community centers, and numerous special programs such as summer camps.

Takoma Park Recreation Department
7500 Maple Ave.
Takoma Park, MD
(301) 270–4048
www.collabitat.com/TPRecreation

Facilities include a community center, municipal gym, four parks, and two playing fields. Swimming is not available.

Jewish Community Centers

These full-service community centers require membership, which is open to anyone. Many special events are open to non-members for a fee.

Washington, D.C.

District of Columbia Jewish Community Center
1529 16th St. NW
Washington, DC
(202) 518–9400
www.dcjcc.org

Housed in the extensively renovated original JCC building built in the 1920s, the city's modern JCC offers a wide range of programs, including an arts center, children's after-school and camp programs, an early childhood and parenting center, a library, and activities for all ages. Health and fitness features include a pool, gymnasium, racquetball and squash courts, an aerobics and dance studio, steam room, and exercise equipment and training.

Northern Virginia

Jewish Community Center of Northern Virginia
8900 Little River Tnpk.
Fairfax, VA
(703) 323–0880
www.jccnv.org

The center boasts an indoor pool, regulation-size gymnasium, fitness room, library, and auditorium for entertainment and community events. The JCC hosts a variety of programs for all ages, including an early childhood program, before- and after-school care, and summer camps. Many events are open to the public.

Suburban Maryland

Jewish Community Center of Greater Washington
6125 Montrose Rd.
Rockville, MD
(301) 881–0100
www.jccgw.org

The JCC's facilities include a sports and fitness center with indoor and outdoor pools, exercise equipment, a steam room, and courts for handball, racquetball, squash, and basketball. Men's and women's health clubs are available for additional membership fees. JCC Programs include preschool and kindergarten, summer camps and after-school activities, classes and special events for all ages, a library, and a cultural arts series.

> ### Insiders' Tip
> Call the National Park Service's Dial-A-Park (202-610-PARK) for recorded details about park events in the Metro Washington area.

YMCA

YMCA of Metropolitan Washington
1112 16th St. NW, 7th Fl.
Washington, DC
(202) 232–6700
www.ymcawashdc.org

This membership association holds a variety of fitness, recreation, camp, and child-care programs at its area branches, including five in Washington, D.C., five in Northern Virginia, and six in Suburban Maryland. Call to find the nearest location.

Insiders' Tip

Pontoon-boat tours of several parks' lakes offer excellent opportunities to view wildlife such as herons and turtles.

Daytrips and Weekend Getaways

Let's not kid ourselves. Scores if not hundreds of books have been written about daytripping and weekend frolicking in and around the Nation's Capital—and for good reason. Few areas in the United States can boast of the inexhaustible array of scenic, cultural, historic, and recreational attractions within an honest day's drive from an urban region as can Washington, D.C.

Our point here is not to rewrite what already has been inked. Instead, we want to take you to some of the most- and lesser-known nearby destinations—places we proudly put on our must-see itinerary for visiting families and relocating friends eager to discover the rich environs and folkways beyond the Beltway.

When we say "beyond the Beltway" what we really mean is away from the Metro area but close enough to more than justify a day's outing or a weekend minivacation. What a palette we have to work with! From the ancient, forest-covered Blue Ridge Mountains to the tranquil majesty of the Chesapeake Bay, the world's largest and most productive estuary, to all those points in between, the storybook quality of the mid-Atlantic countryside and all that it offers is the stuff of inspiration, rejuvenation, and endless repeat visits. It is part of the cultural fabric of being a Washingtonian.

We've begun this chapter at the beginning—our colonial roots in Virginia. From there, we travel to Virginia Hunt Country and the Blue Ridge, from West Virginia to Maryland, south to the Maryland antique mecca of Frederick County. We've touched on a few ski resorts, then, at the opposite end of the meteorological spectrum, the Chesapeake Bay and the Beaches, with special mention of those waterview towns Baltimore and Annapolis. Of course, from time to time we may have meandered beyond our geographic parameters. After all, we couldn't, in good conscience, omit such special places as the Dolly Sods Wilderness of West Virginia or the Victorian charm of Cape May, New Jersey.

We've touched on a few suggestions for overnight stays, and you can assume that rates are per room, per night unless otherwise specified. Also, bed-and-breakfasts include breakfast for two in the room rates, but if other snacks or meals are included, we've noted it. Please remember that rates can and do change with time and also with the seasons.

So let's go, weekend warriors! Put the maps in the glove box, check the fuel gauge, and fasten those seatbelts. It's time to let your imaginations and frontiers soar.

Insiders' Tip

Call the Virginia Office of Tourism in downtown Washington, (202) 872-0523, to book a room at any bed-and-breakfast in the Commonwealth.

State Tourism Offices

(All begin with (800) unless otherwise noted.)

Maryland	543–1036	• www.mdisfun.org
Virginia	934–9184	• www.virginia.org
West Virginia	225–5982	• www.callwva.com
Pennsylvania	847–4872	• www.state.pa.us\visit

State Bed-and-Breakfasts

Maryland	899–7533	• www.amandus-bbrs.com
Virginia	934–9184	• www.virginia.org
West Virginia	(304) 339–6309	• www.callwva.com/b&b

Colonial Roots

Before there was Washington, there were Williamsburg, Yorktown, and Jamestown, Virginia's historic triangle. Wedged between the James and York Rivers, arguably the Tigris-Euphrates of the South, if not the nation, **Colonial Williamsburg** (800-HISTORY, www. colonialwilliamsburg.com), **Yorktown National Battlefield** (888-593-4682, www.nps.gov/yonb), and **Jamestown Colonial National Historical Park** (757-898-3400, www.nps.gov/colo), represent, quite frankly, the best and worst of Virginia—the worst in the sense that they are obvious tourist traps, and you can't help but feel a bit regretful on seeing a McDonald's or an outlet shop within a stone's throw from some of the most hallowed ground in North America; the best in the sense that the actual historical parks are run by altruistic foundations striving for class over commercialism. It's hard not to walk out of these shrines feeling like a patriot, or at least a pioneer, and we highly recommend that you budget a full day for each locale. The drive there takes a bit more than three hours from Metro Washington, an easy shot south on I-95, then east on I-64. Once in the Williamsburg area, the three towns are easily connected by way of the Colonial Parkway, a gorgeous brick road that winds its way through forests and along the banks of the James and York Rivers.

Jamestown Island is the site of North America's first permanent English settlement in 1607, and in Jamestown Settlement, you can board replicas of the three ships that carried the settlers to the Virginia shores. Docents demonstrate typical tasks and answer visitors' questions during reenactments in the reconstructed fort and Powhatan Indian village. Kids especially enjoy learning the truth about Pocohantas, in reality a short-haired, sometimes naked young girl rather than Disney's statuesque beauty. Visit the site's attractive museum to watch a film and browse a variety of exhibits. At Jamestown's Colonial National Historical Park, you'll see thousands of items from the 1600s that have been unearthed by archeologists or preserved from the era. The equally impressive James River plantations, proud residences of three presidents and numerous statesmen, are a 40-minute drive up panoramic Route 5. These 200-year-old beauties rest gracefully on hills overlooking the James River.

It was at Berkeley Plantation, the birthplace of ninth U.S. president, William Henry Harrison, that in 1619 the first official celebration of Thanksgiving occurred. Sherwood Forest Plantation was the home of John Tyler, the 10th U.S. president, and Tuckahoe Plantation was the boyhood home of Thomas Jefferson. Tuckahoe is considered by architectural historians to be the finest existing early-eighteenth-century plantation in America.

Yorktown, due east from Jamestown on Route 31, is where the Revolutionary War ended. Important battles—including the Boston Tea Party and the British surrender at Yorktown—are depicted for tourists by actors in costume. Wherever you visit in the historic triangle, you're most likely to stay in or near Colonial Williamsburg, the area's prime attraction, and the world's largest and most extensively restored eighteenth century town. There are more than 500 original and reconstructed buildings in the square that comprises Colonial Williamsburg. You've seen the photos of the costumed actors who depict eighteenth-century townspeople and the replicas of old-time taverns, smithies, and apothecaries. It's all great fun, especially for kids, who delight in reenactments of times of yore.

Scads of hotels in the area fit every budget, but the gracious Williamsburg Inn, right in the center of the colonial section at 136 East Francis Street, will transport you to a former era when waiters wore white gloves and afternoon sherry was a daily ritual. Individually designed rooms are furnished in the Regency manner, and the formal public rooms overlook sweeping manicured lawns flanked by a broad terrace. All reservations for accommodations and dining can be made by dialing (800) HISTORY.

Mr. Jefferson's Country

We move forward in history to the time of Thomas Jefferson, arguably Virginia's favorite son. You won't live in Virginia, or for that matter in Maryland, a week before someone mentions Charlottesville, which is about three hours from Washington: south on I-95, then west on I-64. Charlottesville is popular for good reason: As home to Virginia's and the nation's most-celebrated Renaissance Man—Thomas Jefferson—Charlottesville is one of the most cherished sites in the region. Here you'll find **Monticello** (434-984-9800, www.monticello.org), Jefferson's captivating hilltop home, and the University of Virginia, one of his many intellectual and architectural achievements.

Charlottesville and surrounding Albemarle County are also about dogwood-lined country roads, hillside vineyards, funky bookstores and sophisticated galleries, museums and restaurants. At the **Boar's Head Inn** (www.boarsheadinn. com), on Highway 250 West just outside of town, you can unwind at a full-service spa and spend the night in one of its many guest rooms decorated in cozy, country English style (800-476-1988). Room prices are from $185 to $500.

For a more intimate experience check out the renowned **Clifton-The Country Inn**, 1296 Clifton Inn Drive, Charlottesville, (888) 971-1800, www.clifton inn.com. Rooms are from $175 to $425. At Clifton, there's a fireplace in every room, beds are four-posters or canopies and dressed with line-dried, cotton sheets. The decor consists of Jeffersonian antiques and reproductions, and no wonder: The estate belonged to Thomas Jefferson's daughter Martha. There's a well-regarded, full-service restaurant on the premises, and breakfast, included in the room tariff, is a calorie-busting affair that might include waffles, quiches, omelettes, fruit compote, muffins, and freshly ground coffee.

Fifteen miles east of Charlottesville is the gloriously romantic **Prospect Hill Plantation Inn**, Highway 613 at Zion Crossroads, Trevilians, (800) 277-0844, www.prospecthill.com. Set amidst rolling hills where sheep graze and wildlife wander, Prospect Hill looks like an idyllic painting. Each room is different—some have Jacuzzis and fireplaces, others are set in cabins of their own apart from the main house—so ask for descriptions. Dinners are a leisurely affair of four or five courses preceded by cocktails in the salon. Rooms are $295 to $420, including breakfast and dinner.

Mr. Jefferson's Country is also Mr. Monroe's Country and Mr. Madison's Country. Literally just down the road from Monticello is **Ash Lawn-Highland** (804-293-9539, www.monticello.avenue. org/ashlawn), James Monroe's home, and about 20 miles to the north, in Orange, Virginia, is **Montpelier** (540-672-2728, www.montpelier.org) the impressive country estate of James Madison.

Farther south, off the Blue Ridge Parkway in neighboring Nelson County, is **Wintergreen Resort** off Highway 664 (800-325-2200, www.wintergreenresort. com; see section on skiing, this chapter). The year-round facility offers a fine golf course, and the moderate climate makes it possible at times to ski in the morning and play a round of golf in the afternoon. Accommodations range from hotel-style rooms to private rental homes with walls of windows overlooking the mountains.

The Gray Lady of the Confederacy

The capital city of Virginia, and for a time, the South, is a living, breathing memorial to the Commonwealth. History isn't just a fact of life in Richmond, it's a way of life. Getting there is easy—it's 100 miles due south of Washington on I-95.

Monument Avenue, the South's answer to Pennsylvania Avenue, immortalizes the fallen sons of the Old Dominion through huge statues, tasteful gardens, and expansive greens. The newest addition—and a controversial one—is the statue of tennis legend Arthur Ashe Jr., who was the first and only African American man to win Wimbledon. His monument depicts him surrounded by children, holding books and his tennis racket overhead.

Monument Avenue cuts through the heart of "The Fan," one of Richmond's trendiest and most desirable residential areas, a la Georgetown in Washington, D.C. It is said to be the largest intact Victorian neighborhood in the United States, with approximately 2,000 houses, most of them restored.

The White House of the Confederacy (804-649-1861), and many of the original government buildings of the Confederate States of America sit within earshot of downtown and the Virginia State Capitol, yet another building designed by Thomas Jefferson. Adjacent to the White House, you'll find the **Museum of the Confederacy** (www.moc. org), the largest collection of Confederate

artifacts. One exhibit features Robert E. Lee's tent as intact as if he'd just left it. Here you will also find the **Edgar Allan Poe Museum** (804-648-5523, www.poe museum.org), which also happens to be the oldest building in the city.

Richmond is rightfully proud of its premier museum, the **Virginia Museum of Fine Arts** (804-340-1400, www.vmfa. state.va.org), housing one of the world's largest collections of Fabergé eggs as well as a stunning array of Asian antiquities and French Impressionist and British sporting art.

Richmonders are also fond of their numerous parks and cemeteries, some of the most elegant in the South. **Hollywood Cemetery** (804-648-8501, www. hollywoodcemetery.org) is the burial place of Presidents Monroe and Tyler, as well as Confederate President Jefferson Davis and more than 18,000 Confederate soldiers.

A premier place to stay in Richmond is the 275-room **Jefferson** at Franklin and Adams Streets (800-424-8014, www. jefferson-hotel.com), a grand hotel in the old style, with marble columns, palace-sized Oriental carpets, and a staircase sweeping from the mezzanine to the lounge. It also contains one of Richmond's top restaurants, Lemaire, featuring French and fusion cuisine. Rooms start at $215.

For more intimate quarters, try the **Linden Row Inn**, 100 East Franklin Street (800-348-7424, www.lindenrowinn.com). Built in 1847, the 71-room structure is listed in the National Register of Historic Places and is located in the middle of the historic district. Rooms are $89 to $189.

For hotel reservations, call (888) RICHMOND, and for general information, contact the Metro Richmond Convention and Visitors Bureau at (800) 370-9004; www.richmondva.org.

A Hunt Country Tapestry

Closer to Washington, in fact just 40 miles west of the bustle of Pennsylvania Avenue, is a quiet, rolling green land of thoroughbred horses, country squires, and antebellum stone mansions. This is hunt country, and you'll be hard pressed to find a more beautiful setting than the farms and fields of Loudoun and Fauquier Counties.

Middleburg, the self-proclaimed "Hunt Country Capital," retains its eighteenth-century charm but with new twists like gourmet bakeries, upscale restaurants, and internationally celebrated antique shops. A popular lodging and dining spot here is **The Red Fox Inn and Tavern**, 2 East Washington Street (800-223-1728, www.redfox.com), housed in a quaint stone building in the center of town. You'll find four-poster beds, fireplaces, and a full-service restaurant serving three meals a day. Room prices start at $150 and go up to $285.

The Middleburg Inn & Guest Suites at 105 West Washington Street (800-432-6125, www.middleburgonline.com /mgs), offers an eighteenth-century-style atmosphere with modern amenities, including suites with kitchens. Room prices range from $130 to $225.

To the west of Middleburg lie the lovely hill country hamlets of Upperville and Paris, where warehouse-size stables and horses seem to outnumber people five to one. Just outside Paris, meanwhile, is the public's access to hunt country living, **Sky Meadows State Park** (540-592-3556, www. dcr.state.va.us/parks/skymeadow.htm). Once a working plantation, Sky Meadows' 1,100 acres entice weekend warriors with a maze of hiking trails, including a stretch of the Appalachian Trail. By the way, Stonewall Jackson's troops camped here before leaving for the Battle of First Manassas.

Leesburg, the largest city in the area, is steeped in Virginia history; indeed, it was named after one of the most prominent families in the Old Dominion. During the War of 1812, when the British were on their way to burn Washington, the Federal Archives, including the Declaration of Independence and the Constitution, were hauled through town in 22 wagons on their way to safekeeping in an estate outside of town.

Today, Leesburg and the surrounding villages of Hamilton, Lincoln, Waterford, Hillsboro, and Purcellville are waging another successful battle for preservation, a concept near and dear to the hearts of hunt country residents who consider themselves just a few miles yet "light years" removed from Washington suburbia.

Though Leesburg is less than an hour from downtown D.C., those looking for a quick, romantic getaway might reserve a room at the **Norris House**, 108 Loudoun Street, (703-777-1806, 800-644-1806, www.norrishouse.com), a beautifully restored 1806 home. The interior is reminiscent of Colonial Williamsburg, both in the colors used and period antiques. This bed-and-breakfast has five rooms, and guests are welcomed with complimentary wine or soft drinks. Breakfast is a spread featuring fresh fruit, baked goods, and a hot entree (also see our chapter on Bed-and-Breakfasts and Country Inns).

Also less than an hour from Washington, but due south, is Fredericksburg, another popular daytrip. This historic town, now a hot spot for antiques, was founded in 1728 as a trade route for the tobacco grown in Virginia.

George Washington's boyhood home, **Ferry Farm**, is just across the Rappahanock River from Fredericksburg, on Highway 3 at Ferry Road in the village of Falmouth, (540) 373-3381 ext. 28, www.kenmore.org/farm.html. This is where he reportedly cut down the famed cherry tree, but it later became a major artillery base and river crossing point for Revolutionary forces in the Battle of Fredericksburg.

Fifth President James Monroe was also a Fredericksburg resident at one time—he practiced law here—and his office is now the **James Monroe Museum and Library** (540-654-1043, www.james monroemuseum.mwc.edu). Here, you can see the desk on which he signed the Monroe Doctrine in 1823.

A popular pastime in Fredericksburg—aside from shopping—is a 75-minute trolley tour of the historic district (540-898-0737) or, weather permitting, a tour by horse-drawn carriage (540-654-5511). There are also tour packages available, which allow admission to multiple historic sights. For information, contact the Fredericksburg Visitor Center, (800) 678-4748, (540) 373-1776; www.Fredericks burgva.com.

The Blue Ridge Mountains

Named for their pervasive blue haze, the result of a complex photochemical reaction involving trees, light, and moisture, the Blue Ridge Mountains are the nation's easternmost range, running from north Georgia to southern Pennsylvania, with Virginia claiming the largest stretch.

To give you an idea of their proximity to Metro Washington, D.C., residents of western Fairfax County can see the mountains on a clear day while driving along busy Virginia Highway 28. Conversely, Skyline Drive in Shenandoah National Park got its name because in earlier times one could make out the Washington skyline from its eastern overlooks.

It's the Big Kahuna, the Grand Poobah of the Virginia Blue Ridge: Stretching more than 130 miles along the spine of the mountains, from Front Royal south to Waynesboro, **Shenandoah National Park** (540-999-3500, www.nps.gov/shen) is a naturalist's paradise.

Each year, nearly two million people make the 90-minute pilgrimage (I-66 West from Washington) to the park and its famed **Skyline Drive** to take in dramatic vistas of the Appalachians and the rolling, fertile farmland of the Shenandoah Valley and the Piedmont. Don't let the number of visitors scare you, though: The park contains more than 195,000 acres, and once you venture off of Skyline, it's possible to hike, fish, and camp for several days without seeing another human. The same can't be said about wildlife, however. Bobcats, deer, foxes, turkeys, and bears, among other critters, are prevalent in these parts; in fact the density of deer and black bears is among the highest anywhere in the United States, so if you plan to do some backcountry trekking, be sure to check in at the ranger station to get briefed on safeguarding your camp.

For a less-rugged but equally woodsy experience, try one of the park's four drive-in campgrounds—Big Meadows, Lewis Mountain, Loft Mountain, and Matthews Arm—or two lodges, Skyland and Big Meadows. For information on any of these destinations, call (800) 999-4714.

If bed-and-breakfasts are more your style, try **Steeles Tavern Manor** on Highway 11, Steeles Tavern, (800) 743-8666, www.steelestavernmanor.com. This romantic five-room inn is a sprawling 1916 mansion on 55 acres overlooking the mountains. Coffee is brought to your door each morning prior to the candlelight breakfast served in the dining room. Or you may have breakfast served in the privacy of your room, each of which has a fireplace and Jacuzzi for two. Rooms range from $135 to $200.

Aside from the fabled **Appalachian Trail**, which runs the distance of the Shenandoah National Park, excellent hiking opportunities can be had on dozens of peaks that comprise the highest mountain range between the Catskills and the Smokies. We highly recommend a day-climb on venerable Old Rag Mountain (elevation 3,291 feet). A hike on the less-strenuous but taller Hawksbill Mountain (4,049 feet) is another favorite of daytrippers, especially in late October when the park's thick, deciduous forests turn into a technicolor fantasyland.

Above all, Shenandoah is ripe with wonderful hidden nooks and crannies. Things like abandoned settlers' cabins, cascading waterfalls, and virtually untouched trout streams brimming with native brookies are just some of the treasures awaiting those with a penchant for leaving the beaten path.

A personal favorite is the 5-mile hike to **Camp Hoover**, President Herbert Hoover's "summer White House" and austere fish camp built along the banks of the pristine Rapidan River, one of the best trout-fishing rivers in the Old Dominion. Each year around August 10, Hoover's birthday, the National Park Service hosts a "Hoover Days" weekend in which the public is allowed to visit the camp and learn a bit about the president's leisure habits and the interesting guests who frequented the remote enclave. The event offers you the option of taking a bus ride down the mountain or hoofing it, trips that both begin at the park's Byrd Visitor Center, Skyline Drive, at milepost 51.

Advance information can be obtained from the Virginia Tourism Corporation at

(800) 934–9184 or the Shenandoah Valley Travel Association, (540) 740–3132.

Little Washington, the Little Apple, and the Caverns

Blue Ridge Mountain towns move to their own whimsical, unpretentious beat. Folks still wave to strangers, and shopkeepers are gracious even if you're just browsing. Surprises abound here, sometimes bordering on the surreal.

For instance, in tiny Washington, Virginia, on U.S. 211, sits one of the most highly acclaimed restaurants and country inns in the world—**The Inn at Little Washington** (540-675-3800, www.relais chateaux.com/washington).

Well-heeled guests come from as far away as New York and Atlanta to dine on the restaurant's nouvelle French cuisine and spend a night in one of the 12 lavishly furnished rooms. Indeed, this is often a must-do for European visitors as well. On any given Sunday morning, "Little Washington," the oldest of 28 towns in the United States named for our first president, probably could claim the world's highest concentration of Jaguars and Mercedes-Benzes. Count on dropping at least a couple of hundred bucks for dinner at the inn, and several hundred for a place to lay your head, but the food and accommodations live up to their reputations. The penthouse suites, in paticular, feature living areas that look like Arabian nights fantasies—albeit tasteful. They have marble bathrooms with jetted tubs tucked into bay windows, double-headed showers as large as most normal bathrooms, and loft bedrooms with balconies overlooking a panoramic mountain vista.

Just down the road is a lesser-known, but no less delectable stop called the **Bleu Rock Inn**. Owned by the proprietors of La Bergerie restaurant in Alexandria, Virginia (see our Restaurant chapter), the Bleu Rock (800-537-3652, www.bleurockinn. com), offers a bucolic setting overlooking a pond and the inn's own vineyards. The five bedrooms here are homier than at The Inn at Little Washington, but they are charm-

ing and about half as expensive. On a summer night there's nothing more romantic than dinner on the terrace as you watch the sun set. You'll enjoy memorable French cuisine with some interesting twists, then drift up to your room for the kind of restful sleep that only country nights provide. Rooms are from $125 to $195.

Other reasonably priced (rooms between $95 and $195), charming bed-and-breakfasts in the Little Washington area include **Heritage House**, P.O. Box 90, Washington, VA 22747 (540-675-3207, www.heritagehousebb. com), in the heart of town, a country-style abode where all the knickknacks and furnishings in the room are for sale! So if you love the decor, you can take it home with you.

Sycamore Hill House, 110 Menefee Mountain Lane, Washington, (540-675-3046, www.bnb-n-va.com/sycamore. htm), about 1 mile from Little Washington atop Menefee Mountain (1,043 feet), has a more contemporary atmosphere at similar prices, with huge picture windows overlooking the Blue Ridge, cathedral ceilings (and fans to go with them), and shining brass beds. The standout here is the 75-foot veranda and patio—a perfect spot to take in the breathtaking scenery.

Down the road from Little Washington and at the base of Shenandoah National Park lies perhaps the busiest hamlet in all of Virginia. **Sperryville**, the self-proclaimed "Little Apple," is an enterprising apple-farming village; it's also a gift shop mecca that almost dares you to drive through without picking up mountain crafts, antiques, or fresh-squeezed cider from places like the Sperryville Emporium or Wolf Mountain Store. For accommodations here, try **The Conyers House**, Slate Mills Road, Sperryville (540- 987-8025, www.conyershouse.com), which features a peaceful country locale and lavish breakfasts. The 1770 manor, with rates ranging from $165 to $250, has been beautifully restored and contains such touches as beamed ceilings, Oriental rugs, stone fireplaces, and elegant country-house furnishings.

Also in the area are several vineyards where you can observe winemaking in progress, sample a bit of wine, and even have lunch or dinner. One of the best known is **Piedmont Vineyards** on Route 626, 3 miles south of Middleburg, (540) 687–5528, www.piedmontwines.com. The vineyards and winery are located on a pre-revolutionary estate called Waverly.

Across the mountain from Sperryville, the Shenandoah Valley town of Luray is home to the much-hyped, but nevertheless fascinating **Luray Caverns** (540–743–6551, www.luraycaverns.com). Take the tour—it's an hour long, and you'll see some of the most colorful and stunning stalactites and stalagmites in the East. Among the attractions is the Great Stalacpipe Organ, a natural formation that plays haunting music.

In the same complex as the caverns is the Historic Car and Carriage Caravan, an exhibit of antique cars, carriages, and coaches, some dating from the seventeenth century. You can see Rudolph Valentino's 1925 Rolls Royce here.

Of Patsy Cline, Drive-Ins, and Barbecue

If the pressures of the big city start turning you a tad cynical, take a spin out to the northern Shenandoah Valley and rediscover vintage Americana. **Winchester**, the region's largest city, is home to dozens of historical attractions, including the western frontier command office of young General George Washington and the Civil War headquarters of Thomas "Stonewall" Jackson.

Civil War buffs may remember that Winchester changed hands at least 70 times during the war, far more than any other community in the country. It is also in Winchester that the spirit of native daughter and country music legend Patsy Cline lives on. Cline, who gave us such heartfelt renditions of "I Fall to Pieces" and "Sweet Dreams," died in a plane crash in 1963 at age 30. She's buried at the Shenandoah Memorial Cemetery on Route 522, also known as the Patsy Cline Memorial Highway.

Virtually all the towns of the northern Valley are riddled with antique stores, but **Strasburg**, at the foot of Massanutten Mountain, takes the cake. Here you can find nearly 100 dealers in the downtown **Strasburg Emporium** (540–465–3711), which houses furniture from every American era, as well as intricate chandeliers, rugs, quilts, lace, old carousel horses, and pottery. Top it off with a gourmet meal at the Victorian-inspired **Hotel Strasburg**, 201 Holliday Street, Strasburg (800–348–8327, www.hotelstrasburg.com), where you can also stay the night ($75 for a regular room and $175 for a three-room suite with a Jacuzzi). For a more down-home experience, try a platter of hickory-fired ribs and chicken at **Bad Water Bill's Barbecue** (540–465–4988), which alone is worth the drive.

On the Wild Side of Front Royal

Between Strasburg and Front Royal, the heavily trafficked gateway to Shenandoah National Park, lies one of the region's truly undiscovered natural gems, the **Elizabeth Furnace Recreation Area**. Off of twisty Virginia 678, in the heart of the sprawling George Washington National Forest (540–828–2591, www.fsreb.gwjeff. r8.fs.fed.us), this rugged gorge country of spiraling limestone outcroppings and the swift-moving Passage Creek is more akin to the wilds of West Virginia than to the gentle Shenandoah Valley. It also was the site of many a clandestine military operation during the Civil War. Creekside campsites are available at the recreation area, and hikers are encouraged to make the enjoyable day-climb to the summit of Signal Knob, with its commanding views of the valley.

The Generals' City

The legacies of Stonewall Jackson and Robert E. Lee pervade their beloved Virginia, but nowhere is their presence felt more than in the scenic Shenandoah Valley town of Lexington in beautiful Rockbridge County.

Here, you can tour the only house Jackson ever owned and walk the hallowed grounds of Virginia Military Institute where he taught natural philosophy to Confederate cadets. At the **VMI Museum** (540-464-7334, www.vmi.edu/museum), displays include such objects as Jackson's bullet-pierced raincoat and his favorite war horse, Little Sorrel, preserved through taxidermy. The museum added new exhibits and updated some old ones as part of a refurbishment project several years ago.

Within earshot of VMI is the impressive **Washington and Lee University and Lee Chapel** (540-463-8768, www.wlu. edu), the still-used shrine to Jackson's confidant and the final resting place of the South's greatest hero. Don't leave Lexington without visiting the office Lee inhabited while assuming the presidency of W&L after his defeat in the Civil War. It's in virtually the same state as he left it in 1870. Buried nearby on campus is Lee's favorite mount, and maybe the most famous war horse in American history, Traveller.

You'll find several luxurious bed-and-breakfasts and inns around Lexington, three of which are owned by a single company known as **Historic Country Inns** (rates from $55 to $180). By dialing a single phone number, (877) 463-2044, you can choose among the **Alexander-Withrow** (3 West Washington Street) or **McCampbell** (11 North Main Street) inns in the center of Lexington's historic district, or **Maple Hall**, set amidst 56 acres of meadow and forest 6 miles north of town.

Maple Hall even has a restaurant serving gourmet dinner fare. The country manor looks like it belongs on the set of *Gone with the Wind*, with its massive white columns and dramatic front staircase. All three properties feature gracious, southern-style verandas, antiques, and fireplaces.

Another good choice for a beautiful bed-and-breakfast in the country is the **Inn at Union Run** (800-528-6466, www.unionrun.com), which boasts a fabulous restaurant, friendly proprietors, and antiques reportedly once owned by Winston Churchill and Henry Longfellow. Located 3 miles southwest of Lexington, the inn is situated next to a creek and

spring-fed pond on land perhaps haunted by the Union soldiers who camped there during and after the Battle of Lexington. Rates range from $95 to $175.

A Tale of Two Mountain Resorts

Lodging is in no short supply in the Virginia upcountry; however, two of the more interesting spots to rest and recreate are **Mountain Lake Hotel**, near Blacksburg, and the queen of mountain resorts, **The Homestead** in Hot Springs. Still best known as the place where the hit movie *Dirty Dancing* was filmed, Mountain Lake Lodge (rates from $135, including dinner and breakfast for two) on Highway 700 in Blacksburg (800-346-3334) sits nearly 4,200 feet up in the Allegheny Mountains of Giles County. Semirustic in nature, although a far cry from earthy, Mountain Lake caters to families in the summer and has developed quite an extensive package of theme weekends during the off-season including, of course, a "Dirty Dancing Weekend." It is isolated, yes, but once you get there expect a wealth of indoor and outdoor activities: a full spa, great hiking trails, excellent fishing in the natural spring-fed pond, and plenty of interpretive programs, such as the one on Appalachian folk art.

Up the mountains to the north, The Homestead, Main Street, U.S. 220, Hot Springs (800-838-1766, www.thehomestead.com), is consistently rated by international travel writers as one of the world's top resorts. This plush but relaxed setting is a favorite of the corporate-retreat set (as well as of members of Congress and other segments of Washington officialdom) but also is frequented by couples and families looking to pamper themselves in the resort's five-star spa, restaurants, stables, and golf courses. Golf legend Sam Snead, who grew up in the area, considers the Homestead's Cascades course one of the finest in the South. A bit on the pricey side—double occupancy during the popular month of October starts at more than $220 a night per person, with breakfast and dinner—The Homestead nevertheless is something to be experienced if just once. Our advice is to start saving now.

Wild, Wonderful West Virginia

The Mountain State just may be the best-kept secret in the nation. Its rugged terrain and inspiring mountain vistas seem to defy its proximity to the Eastern megalopolis. Within a two-hour drive of Metro Washington is a country as remote and beautiful as Montana or Idaho. The state's laid-back tenor and affordability are attracting increasing numbers of tourists, but don't ever worry about being crowded out here. In the **Dolly Sods Wilderness Area** (304-636-1800), near Petersburg, you can walk the land of the Seneca Indians, through patches of wild orchids and blueberries and huge granite boulders that afford hikers views in excess of 100 miles.

About 20 miles south of Dolly Sods is **Seneca Rocks** (304-567-2827), a gray wall of ancient sandstone that juts 1,000 feet above the floor of the South Branch Valley. For the truly adventurous, take a mountain-climbing lesson through Seneca Rocks Climbing School (800-548-0108, www.seneca-rocks.com); Seneca Rocks Mountain Guides, (800-451-5108, www. senecarocks.com); or Blackwater Outdoor Adventures (304-478-3775, www.raft boc.com).

If you'd rather keep your feet firmly on the ground, take a drive up to the Canaan Valley, the highest valley east of the Mississippi River. Spend a night or two in the cozy lodge at **Canaan Valley State Park** (800-622-4121, www.canaanresort.com), a woodsy retreat and conference center that boasts, and rightly so, the best fall colors in the United States.

If you love the outdoors, but don't like to rough it, head to the superexpensive and superluxurious **Greenbrier Resort**, 300 West Main Street, White Sulphur Springs, West Virginia. The Greenbrier (800-624-6070, www.greenbrier.com) is

considered even more upscale than The Homestead ($482 to $614 per couple, including breakfast and dinner), so know what you're getting into. If you can afford it, the experience is well worth the cost. It's a taste of the antebellum South, complete with a sprawling veranda, dancing and a black-tie affair at dinner, afternoon tea, and enough activities to keep you occupied every minute of the day: horseback riding, shooting, golf, bowling, hiking, and, of course, taking the waters and all the related spa activities.

Closer to home and easier on the pocketbook, is Berkeley Springs, West Virginia, an area that offers something for both body and spirit. As the name implies, the area revolves around the restorative hot springs and spa, and weary Washingtonians often make the two-and-a-half-hour pilgrimage to the **Country Inn and Renaissance Spa**, 207 South Washington Street (800-822-6630, www.countryinn wv.com), to be pampered by facials, body scrubs, massages, and, of course, soaks in the hot springs (rates from $85 to $210).

An attraction of equal allure is the scenery just outside of town. The Panorama Overlook on West Virginia Highway 9, four miles west of Berkeley Springs has been named by *National Geographic* magazine as one of America's most breathtaking vistas.

Coolfont Resort, 1777 Cold Run Valley Road, Berkeley Springs (800-296-8768, www.coolfont.com), near Berkeley Springs is the spa of choice for many among the Washington stress set (rates $100 to $140 per person per night, including meals). Former drug czar William Bennett kicked his cigarette habit here, and Vice President Al Gore has been a loyal customer for years, even once setting off a minipanic by getting lost in the woods with Tipper. The accommodations are modest but comfortable.

A bit farther, and just as scenic, is **Cacapon State Park**, the third largest in West Virginia (304-258-1022, www.caca ponresort.com). There are almost 30 miles of well-marked hiking trails—a great place to get your fix of fall color. Lodge rooms and cabins rent from just $62 a night. You can also reach the state park and receive loads of helpful information by calling (800) CALLWVA.

For a taste of true West Virginia hospitality, check in at the intimate and oh-so-isolated **Cheat Mountain Club**, West Virginia Highway 250, Durbin (304-456-4627, www.cheatmountainclub.com), with rates from $80 per person, including meals. Hosts Norm and Debbie Strauss will see to it that you're fed three delicious squares a day; between meals you can walk out the lodge's back door and catch native brook trout or swim in a natural pool on Shavers Fork Creek. Both Henry Ford and Harvey Firestone visited this rugged lodge, where it's as down-home as it gets.

A Tale of Two Rivers

The mighty Shenandoah and Potomac Rivers meet in **Harpers Ferry**, West Virginia, site of abolitionist John Brown's raid on the U.S. Arsenal, a spark that helped ignite the Civil War. Now operated by the National Park Service (304-535-6298, www.nps.gov/hafe), this perfectly restored village provides an excellent journey into days past, with influences spanning not only the Civil War but the founding of the nation, including a healthy dose of period architecture and steep, narrow cobblestone streets.

Craft shops abound, as do glorious views of the Blue Ridge and the wild, crystal-clear rivers running below the hilltop city. At just over 400 feet in elevation, Harpers Ferry marks the lowest point in the state of West Virginia.

When the summer steam envelopes Washington, head north approximately 65 miles on I-270 to Harpers Ferry for a day of tubing, white-water rafting, or hiking—the Appalachian Trail runs right through the town center. Trips can be arranged through **River & Trail Outfitters** (301-695-5177, www.rivertrail.com), in nearby Knoxville, Maryland.

If the hour-plus drive back to town seems much too formidable after an exhausting day shooting rapids, bunk down at one of the town's cozy bed-and-breakfast inns. The circa-1800 **Ranson-Armory** bed-and-breakfast, 690 Washington Street (304-535-2142), has only two guest rooms, but each offers a private bath and a splendid view for $80 to $90 per night, including breakfast.

If you'd like something a bit more formal, head up the road to Shepherdstown, the second-oldest burgh in the state and home to the gracious **Bavarian Inn and Lodge** (304-876-2551, www.bavarianinnwv.com), just off West Virginia Highway 480 or directly across the bridge (and state line) from Maryland Highway 34. The inn is a stone structure with a knoll-top perch above the Potomac (rates from $85 to $185, no meals). The dining room here features hearty German and game dishes. Several rooms have two-person Jacuzzis and gas fireplaces, and all are furnished with American colonial reproductions, including some four-poster beds.

Shepherdstown has one of the nation's highest concentrations of eighteenth-century buildings, making it an ideal spot to just meander. Be sure to duck into **O'Hurley's General Store** (304-876-6907, www.ohurley.com), known throughout the East for its wonderful crafts, antiques, and curios.

Just across the River: The Mountains of Maryland

On the Maryland side of the Potomac from Harpers Ferry lies Washington County, site of the Civil War's Battle of Antietam, the deadliest clash of the war and one of the bloodiest battles in American history (see our Civil War chapter for more on this battle site). It's amazing to think anything so brutal could happen in this quiet, bucolic setting of dairies, wheat fields, and vineyards.

On a more upbeat note, Washington County, the first such jurisdiction named for George, is home to four of Maryland's best state parks. **At Washington Monument State Park** (301-791-4767, www.dnr.state.md/publiclands/western/Washington.html), high atop South Mountain, you can view the first monument built in the president's honor. Originally constructed by the residents of

The restored village at Harpers Ferry National Historic Park provides a journey into days past.

PHOTO: COURTESY OF HARPERS FERRY NATIONAL HISTORIC PARK

Boonsboro, Maryland, in 1827, the stone tower has been rebuilt twice since. Climb the monument's 34 steps to take in spectacular views of the Cumberland Valley.

If you plan to stay overnight in the area, book a room at **Antietam Overlook Farm** (800–878–4241), off Highway 34 in Keedysville, Maryland. The view from the property encompasses portions of Maryland, Virginia, West Virginia, and Pennsylvania. The inn's most lavish room features a screened porch and sundeck overlooking the vista (rates from $120).

Moving south, following along the mountain, you'll hit **Gathland State Park** (301–791–4767, www.dnr.state.md. us/publiclands/western/gathland.html), which includes the ruins of Gapland, the country home of Civil War and Reconstruction journalist George Alfred Townsend. Near the entrance to the park stands the imposing War Correspondents Arch, a 50-foot structure Townsend built to honor the documentarians of the great war. Joseph Pulitzer and Thomas Edison contributed to the $5,000 building fund.

Just up the road from both Gathland and Washington Monument is **Greenbrier State Park** (301–791–4767, www. dnr.state. md.us/publiclands/western/greenbrier

.html), and its sparkling spring-fed Greenbrier Lake, said to be among the clearest in the nation. Camping, fishing, and hiking are popular activities here as well as across the county at **Fort Frederick State Park** (301–842–2155, www.dnr.state.md.us/pub liclands/western/fortfrederick.html).

Nestled along the banks of the Potomac and containing a stretch of the Chesapeake & Ohio Canal, Fort Frederick was originally built as a defense outpost on the western frontier. Still standing, although in a carefully preserved state, the fort survived the French and Indian, Revolutionary, and Civil Wars and is now honored through a series of historical reenactments each spring through fall.

The President's Mountain

Largely overshadowed by Shenandoah National Park, Maryland's **Catoctin Mountain Park** (301–663–9388, www. nps.gov/cato), is an ideal place to beat the crowds, especially during the autumn months when its 10,000-acre forest of beech, hickory, poplar, oak, and maple trees turns to brilliant shades of red, orange, and gold. Catoctin is probably most famous for being home to Camp David, the woodsy presidential retreat. Don't expect the First Family to wave you on in, though. The compound is well hidden and security, as you can imagine, is intense.

You can, however, spend the night at the park's Owens Creek Campground or in a rustic cabin at Camp Misty Mount. Catoctin's numerous trails and wild trout streams make it a great place for families and novice campers. From the park you're also within a short drive of the history-rich towns of Gettysburg, Pennsylvania, and Frederick, Maryland.

Also, near the park entrance is the quaint railroad town of Thurmont, and immediately to the south is **Cunningham Falls State Park** (301-271-7574, www. dnr.state.md.us/publiclands/western/cunninghamfalls.html), with its gorgeous namesake waterfall.

At the northern end of this area, on U.S. 15 just south of the Pennsylvania border, is the town of **Emmitsburg**, whose Main Street is still lit by gas lamps. This picturesque town, aside from its proximity to the aforementioned parks, is also an antique-lovers mecca, with its Antique Mall featuring 120 shops.

After a day of hiking or shopping, you can settle at the **Stonehurst Inn** (800–497-8458, www.emmitsburg.net/ lodging), where the owners pamper you with a lavish breakfast, afternoon tea, hors d'oeuvres, and dessert. You hardly need to go out for dinner! The inn is located in its own little private park, pond included, at 9436 Waynesboro Road in Emmitsburg (rates $75 to $105).

Just south of town on U.S. 15 is the **National Shrine of St. Elizabeth Ann Seton** (301-447-6606, www.setonshrine.org), dedicated to the first American-born saint, who lived from 1774 to 1821, and was beatified in 1963.

Maryland's Heartland

Fifteen miles south of Emmitsburg, and about one hour north of Washington via I-270, in the heart of the Free State, are two of Maryland's most endearing towns,

Frederick and **New Market**.

Both are nationally renowned antiques meccas, even more so than Emmitsburg, but they're also just great spots to unwind and enjoy the simple pleasures of graceful centuries-old buildings, perfectly manicured gardens, and friendly denizens. Frederick's 33-block historic district, punctuated by towering church spires, is a must for history and architecture buffs.

At the edge of town is **The Children's Museum of Rose Hill Manor Park**, a 1790s mansion and estate that is now a partially hands-on living museum of nineteenth-century life. Costumed guides lead you through an orchard, blacksmith shop, log cabin, and the manor house itself. You'll also see a carriage museum and farm museum where the vehicles on display are explained in depth and related to

Frederick's 33-block historic district attracts history and architecture buffs. PHOTO: MIDDLETON EVANS, COURTESY OF MARYLAND OFFICE OF TOURISM

developments today. Rose Hill Manor is at 1611 North Market Street, Frederick (800–999–3613).

To learn of more interesting sights in and around Frederick, contact the Tourism Council of Frederick County, 19 East Church Street, Frederick (800–999–3613, www.visitfrederick.org).

New Market comes alive virtually every weekend of the year with a bazaarlike setting of antique dealers and craftspeople. It is the self-proclaimed "Antiques Capital of Maryland" and is home to more than 40 shops. You'd be able to walk the length of the village in a few minutes if you didn't need to stop so often to explore the wares for sale.

Both these towns are so close to Metro Washington that an overnight stay is unnecessary; however if you're looking for a romantic getaway, consider the **Bluebird on the Mountain** bed-and-breakfast, about 25 minutes north of Frederick on Highway 550 (301–241–4161). Set into the woods like a fairy-tale cottage, the five-room inn is a light, bright home furnished with lace and wicker. Some rooms have fireplaces and Jacuzzis. Rates range from $100 to $130.

Farther south, on Highway 85, is the romantic **Inn at Buckeystown** (800–272–1190, www.innatbuckeystown.com), in the village of the same name ($140 to over $230 per couple, depending on meal plan). The eight rooms are furnished in lavish Victorian style, including crystal chandeliers, brocade upholstery, and brass-screened fireplaces. Dinner is equally lavish, with rich Continental specialties like creamy bisques, game pâtés, and homemade pastries.

Maryland's Last Frontier

High in the Allegheny Plateau, in the westernmost reaches of the Free State, sparkles Maryland's **Deep Creek Lake.** A fishing and boating dreamland (it's possible to catch walleye, bass, catfish, and trout in the same day), Deep Creek also affords weekend travelers with a number of lakeside cabin, cottage, and chalet rentals. **Railey Realty** (800–846–7368) or **Coldwell Banker Deep Creek Realty** (800–252–7335) can arrange for overnight or extended stays.

With 65 miles of shoreline, Deep Creek is best seen from the deck of a sailboat or motorboat. Rentals are available, but escalating insurance costs have made them an expensive option. Our advice is to bring your own boat or make friends with someone who has one. Honestly though, it's possible to enjoy the plentiful attractions of Garrett County without ever dipping a toe in the lake.

In nearby Oakland you can hop on the **Western Maryland Scenic Railroad** (800–872–4650, TRAIN–50; www.wmsr.com), or arrange for an afternoon of white-water rafting on the **Cheat** and **Youghiogheny** (pronounced YOK-eh-gain-e) Rivers. No trip to Western Maryland would be complete without a stop along the boulder-strewn banks of the aptly named **Savage River,** site of the 1989 World Whitewater Canoe/Kayak Championships and the 1992 U.S. Olympic Trials.

A Downhill Run

Snow? Around here? Okay, the Appalachians aren't exactly the Rockies, but you can sneak in a couple of days of passable skiing in these parts without taking the time and money for a trip out West.

In Virginia, if you're looking for full-service, hotel-style resorts, you have the option of **Wintergreen** (800–325–2200), $122 to $286 per couple, per night, off Highway 664. They also have some very nice condos about which you may want to inquire. **The Homestead** is another good choice (800–838–1766), starting at $220 per person, per night, including breakfast and dinner. Both offer all the après-ski amenities you could wish and the restaurants are very good. You could easily spend a luxurious few days at either locale, but Wintergreen has been rated by the national ski magazines as one of the best downhill spots in the South. For daytrippers or a self-catering holiday, try the modest hills at Bryce (800–821–1444, www.bryceresort.com), or Massanutten (800–207–6277 [MASS], www.massresort.com).

West Virginia's **Snowshoe** (877–441-4FUN, www.snowshoemtn.com)—a sprawling complex off U.S. 250 that spans several miles—and the smaller **Canaan Valley** off West Virginia Highway 32 (800–622-4121, www.canaanresort. com), though farther from Washington (four to five hours), are popular with more experienced skiers—trails are a bit longer and more varied. Snowshoe has the extra attraction of **The Red Fox Inn** (304–572-1111), one of the premier restaurants in the mid-Atlantic region, a surprising find for gourmets who also like to ski. Reserve ahead if you intend to eat here during your stay—all those raves in the national food magazines guarantee a packed house. Snowshoe has an extensive condo and hotel complex with rates from $142; Canaan's rates range from $70 to $100. Cross-country aficionados head to the White Grass Ski Touring Center in Canaan Valley (304–866-4114, www.white grass.com), for superb trails, friendly instruction, and a cozy lodge for hanging out, sipping cocoa, and enjoying home-cooked chili and other hearty, wholesome fare.

Just 90 minutes from Washington (about 20 miles beyond I-270, right past the Maryland-Pennsylvania border), Pennsylvania's **Ski Liberty** (717–642-8282, www.skiliberty.com) and **Whitetail** (717–328-9400, www.skiwhitetail.com), are easy daytrip destinations. Liberty is an older ski area with a simple lodge, but Whitetail is a spiffy new day resort whose design has won raves from national ski magazines. The trail selection at both places is limited, and even those ranked most difficult would be considered easy runs in Colorado, but they can't be beat for convenience. **Wisp Resort,** 296 Marsh Hill Road, McHenry, Maryland (301–387-4911, www.wispresort.com), near Deep Creek Lake, is Maryland's lone downhill ski area (room rates start at $198 on the weekends).

Maryland's only downhill ski resort is Wisp, high in the Allegheny Plateau. PHOTO: COURTESY OF MARYLAND OFFICE OF TOURISM

By the Water: Beaches and Beyond the Chesapeake Bay

Legendary Baltimore journalist and social commentator H. L. Mencken once called the Chesapeake Bay a "great big protein factory" on account of the inordinate amount of fish, crabs, and oysters found in its brackish waters. If Mencken were alive today, he would probably amend his definition to include the number of people who regularly find sanctuary on the fabled body of water. Of course, the Bay is a different creature today than it was during Mencken's time—in some ways better, in other ways worse.

Ecologically, the Bay is being tested by humanity's heavy hand. Pollution and urban sprawl have been blamed for historically low populations of oysters and some fish. Chesapeake watermen, for centuries the life and blood of the region, are slowly dying off as competition heats up in the global seafood industry.

To speak of the Bay and its rich traditions in the past tense would be foolish though. New conservation efforts, such as those of the Chesapeake Bay Foundation, have elevated awareness of this vital natural resource. As the Chesapeake, divided nearly equally between Maryland and Virginia, continues to attract record numbers of tourists to its pleasant shores and peaceful waterside villages, one can only hope that we will continue to find the energy and courage to save the Bay.

The Shore

You may have heard it called Delmarva Peninsula. Washingtonians know it as the Eastern Shore. To locals, it's simply "the Shore." For the uninitiated it's the land found on the eastern side of the Chesapeake Bay Bridge.

This fertile coastal-plain peninsula contains much of Delaware, a good chunk of Maryland, and a sliver of Virginia, thus the name Delmarva. Bounded by the Bay and the Atlantic Ocean, the Eastern Shore is the land of proud watermen, of Canada geese and duck blinds, sprawling farms, colonial villages, and what seems more water than land.

To experience the true flavor of the Chesapeake—which inspired James Michener's novel of the same name—it's imperative to "cross the bridge." Maybe you've already seen the bumper stickers proclaiming, "There is No Intelligent Life West of the Chesapeake Bay." It's a bit parochial (and tongue-in-cheek), sure, but once you catch the spirit of the place you just might start agreeing with the notion.

After crossing the bridge—the Chesapeake Bay Bridge that is—think about getting off of U.S. 50. There's nothing particularly exciting about this highway unless you're into strips of shopping centers, boat yards, and liquor stores. Our advice is to take the slower-moving but scenic Maryland Highway 213 and head north to **Chestertown**, Maryland, on the banks of the Chester River. On the way you'll pass through Centreville, government seat of Queen Anne's County and site of the oldest courthouse, circa 1792, and still in use in Maryland.

Chestertown, with its eighteenth-century waterside Georgian mansions, is best discovered on foot, like during the Candlelight Walking Tour each September. Stroll through the grounds of **Washington College**, the 10th-oldest college in

Chestertown, Maryland, is best explored on foot or by carriage. PHOTO: MIDDLETON EVANS, COURTESY OF MARYLAND OFFICE OF TOURISM

There is no weekend getaway more romantic than a trip to St. Michael's on the Eastern Shore.
PHOTO: MIDDLETON EVANS, COURTESY OF MARYLAND OFFICE OF TOURISM

America and the only one to which George Washington personally granted the use of his name. For an overnight stay consider the **White Swan Tavern** at 231 High Street (410-778-2300, www.chestertown.com/whiteswan), in the heart of the historic district and a stone's throw from the Chester River (rates from $120). Guests are welcomed with a bottle of wine in their room and, in the morning served a continental breakfast. The inn is small—only six rooms—so it's best to reserve early in summer. You'll enjoy the flower-rimmed patio and the bright antique-filled rooms.

From Chestertown, backtrack on Highway 213 and connect with U.S. 50 (but just for a short 20 miles) south to **Easton**. Now you're in the heart of Talbot County, undeniably Maryland's most aristocratic jurisdiction. Easton is the site of the massive **Waterfowl Festival** held each November, in which the world's finest wildlife artists, wood-carvers, and sculptors gather to strut their stuff along with tens of thousands of migratory Canada geese.

Easton's fabled **Tidewater Inn**, 101 East Dover Street (410-822-1300), accommodates hunters (including their dogs), sailors, antique hunters, and the occasional diplomat (rates from $110). Nearby, you can visit Third Haven Friends Meeting House, circa 1682, believed to be the oldest frame building dedicated to religious meetings in America.

Heading west, take a spin through **St. Michael's**, a waterfront hamlet that fooled the British Navy one evening during the War of 1812 when citizens placed lamplights in the tops of trees, thus giving the illusion that the village sat on a hill. The British ships fired at the tops of the trees and missed the town altogether.

You won't want to miss an outdoor crabfest at **The Crab Claw** (410-745-2900), overlooking the harbor, or a walk through the **Chesapeake Maritime Museum** (410-745-2916, www.cbmn.org), with its signature "screwpile" lighthouse, more than a century old. The place to stay in St. Michael's—if you want to splurge—is **The Inn at Perry Cabin**, 308 Watkins Lane (410-745-2200), owned and decorated by the husband of the late Laura Ashley (summer high-season rates from $295 to $695, including full breakfast and afternoon tea). This is a deluxe,

English country-house spot overlooking the water, just the getaway for a special occasion.

From St. Michael's, you're just a few minutes drive from **Tilghman Island**, a working waterman's community, and **Oxford**, arguably the most scenic town in Maryland. Tilghman is crab and oyster docks, colorful watermen, and rusted boats. It's authentic Eastern Shore. The most colorful lodging on the island can be found at **Harrison's Chesapeake House** (410-886-2121, www.chesapeakehouse. com), a traditional Chesapeake fish camp that specializes in regional cuisine and hassle-free fishing trips.

Oxford, on the other hand, is glistening million-dollar sailboats, painstakingly restored Federal-style homes, and charming bed-and-breakfasts, like **The Robert Morris Inn** at the end of Maryland Highway 333 (888-823-4012, www.robert morrisinn.com, rates from $130). Head into Oxford from the north and cross the placid Tred-Avon River aboard the Oxford-Bellevue Ferry (410-745-9023), the oldest ferry still in use in the United States. The 10-minute trip is well worth the nominal fee, especially if you're into lowering the old blood pressure.

Don't leave the region without a stop down the bay in **Cambridge**, hometown of American hero Harriet Tubman, founder of the Underground Railroad. Tubman was born on a plantation outside of town and single-handedly made her way to freedom in the North. She ventured back into the South at least 20 times to help free hundreds of other slaves during the Civil War era.

Islands in Time

Near the geographic center of the Chesapeake Bay lie two of the most intriguing islands in the area. **Smith Island**, Maryland (800-521-9185, www.intercom.net/npo/smithisland/), and **Tangier Island**, Virginia, (757-787-7911, www.tangier island-va.com), are indeed places that have defied the encroachment of modern society. Both islands, just a few square miles large, were settled by the first wave of British explorers to the Chesapeake Bay in the early seventeenth century (led by Captain John Smith). The descendants of the colonists, folks with names like Bradshaw, Harrison, Smith, and Crosby, still work the water for crabs and oysters. Other islanders make and sell high quality crafts, such as hand-carved duck decoys.

These islands are insular, as evidenced by the fact that electricity only arrived there in the 1940s. Also, the islanders' speech even today has traces of the area's Elizabethan/Cornish roots. Residents are friendly, and you may notice that those traveling in trucks and cars honk their horns and wave to greet all other vehicles and pedestrians. Visitors are greeted with good cheer to be sure, but leave your motorized vehicles and pets at home—visitors are not allowed to bring them to the islands, and, anyway, bicycles are more fun and can be easily rented (see phone numbers below). Spring is a particularly lovely time to visit, because you'll find a variety of exotic trees in bloom, including pomegranates, pears, figs, and, later in the year, mimosas.

Religion has always been a very important part of island life, ever since the Methodist Church was established in the Bay islands during the late 1800s, and tourists are welcomed at local church services. If getting as far off the beaten path as possible interests you, both islands are accessible by U.S. mail boats and other small ferries from the city dock at Crisfield, Maryland, along the far southern edge of the Eastern Shore.

Private cruise lines also provide access in season (April to October). Contact Tangier Island Cruises in Crisfield, at (800) 863-2338. To reach Crisfield from Washington, head east on U.S. 50, south on U.S. 13, and then follow Maryland Highway 413 to Crisfield. Closer to home, you can reach Smith Island from Point Lookout, Maryland. To get there from Washington, follow U.S. 301 south to Maryland Highway 235—it will lead you right to the Point, where cruises to the islands originate aboard the *Capt. Tyler* (410-425-2771). For more information on charter companies and schedules, contact the Somerset County Tourism Office at (800) 521-9189, skipjack.net/le-shere/visitsomerset/waterways.html.

The Humble Western Shore

In all fairness, you don't have to cross the bridge to enjoy the bounty of the Bay. Although less rustic and authentic than the land to the east, Maryland's Western Shore is doing a pretty good job of balancing suburban growth while retaining some of its maritime character. If you've got angling in your blood but lack a good, solid boat to grapple the Chesapeake, drive down to Chesapeake Beach's **Rod N Reel Dock** (301-855-5341), and charter a captain for a day or grab a spot on a head-boat. Either option will place you with appropriate tackle and bait and a knowledgeable skipper and first mate.

Typically, fishing on the Bay is best in the late spring and fall when bluefish and striped bass are biting. Summer is always good for panfish or redfish. South from Chesapeake Beach, head down Route 4 to **Solomons** (www.solomons-island.com), the picturesque sailing hamlet that boasts some of the finest seafood dining on the Bay, including **The RhumbLine Inn** and **Solomons Pier** (410-326-2424).

Within a short drive you can visit the crucifix-shaped Middleham Chapel, circa 1748; the fossil-lined **Calvert Cliffs State Park** (301-872-5688); and historic St. Marys City, Maryland's seventeenth-century capital (www.dnr.state.md.us/publiclands/southern/calvertcliffs.html).

If you still have energy, drive down to **Point Lookout State Park** (301-872-5688, www.dnr.state.md.us/publiclands/southern/pointlookout.html) on the southernmost tip of Maryland, and explore the remains of Fort Lincoln, one of the largest Union-run prisons during the Civil War. The park's Civil War Museum is open weekends May through September.

Charm City

In many ways **Baltimore** is the ultimate Chesapeake city. The Bay's influence is virtually everywhere, from the seafood cuisine (Ralph Waldo Emerson once dubbed the city "the gastronomic center of the universe"); to the thriving Inner Harbor area of shops, museums, and hotels; to Fells Point, the rejuvenated harborfront

Baltimore, the quintessential Chesapeake Bay city, is a short one-hour drive from Washington, D.C.
PHOTO: MIDDLETON EVANS, COURTESY OF MARYLAND OFFICE OF TOURISM

A Refuge for Solitude-Seekers

Each weekend in summer thousands of Washingtonians hit the roads and head to Ocean City, Rehoboth, and Virginia Beach. Fun spots all, but crowded with board-walks, condos, fast-food joints and . . . well, thousands of Washingtonians. Choose the road less traveled, though, and you'll be rewarded with miles of pristine beach, wide, fluffy dunes that go on forever—and sweet isolation. Too good to be true? Not on Assateague Island National Seashore, a wildlife refuge of breathtaking, unspoiled beauty, half in Virginia, half in Maryland.

Here you'll find the wild ponies made famous in Marguerite Henry's classic chil-dren's book, *Misty of Chincoteague*. A bike ride along the narrow asphalt road that borders the wetlands is the best way to glimpse these graceful herds. They are fairly accustomed to tourists and continue to graze as you look on, but don't get too near because they'll kick!

For a truly dramatic spectacle, station yourself in nearby Chincoteague, Virginia, on the last Wednesday of July, when the local fire department rounds up the ponies and swims them across the bay for auction the next day—to the delight of thousands of spectators. When the crowds depart, Assateague is left once more in tranquil-lity.

The lighthouse on Assateague Island has oper-ated as a guide for the southern end of the island since October 1, 1867. PHOTO: COURTESY OF VIRGINIA TOURISM CORPORATION

On Assateague be prepared to make your own fun. You won't find amusement parks or family-fun centers—the only facil-ities are a bathhouse and rest rooms on the Virginia side and two campgrounds on the Maryland side. What you will find, though, are more than 300 species of birds and 44 species of mammals, such as the endangered Delmarva fox squirrel and the miniature oriental deer. Scan the water and you may be lucky enough to spot a pod of bottlenose dolphins. A stroll along the undeveloped shoreline will bring you face to face with dozens of sandpipers, pelicans, and gulls. No one bothers these creatures, so they aren't overly bothered by humans.

At the southern end of the island is the picturesque red-and-white striped lighthouse, first lighted in 1867, and still in use today. The original light system, how-ever, has been replaced by a modern sys-tem, but the original remains on display in the lighthouse. The structure is operated by the U.S. Coast Guard and is accessible via a cleared trail through the woodlands.

You won't find hotels on Assateague, but a short drive to Chincoteague will lead you to some nice inns, as well as a dozen or so budget motels. The closest to Assateague—only about 100 yards away, in fact—is **Driftwood Motor Lodge** (800–553–6117), on Maddox Boulevard, right beside the bridge that connects the preserve to Chincoteauge. You'll also find bicycle rentals everywhere you turn, because that is a great way to see the area.

Assateague's two campgrounds are on the Maryland side, which takes about one hour to reach via the mainland—you can't cross over on the island in a vehicle. One campground is run by the National Park Service (410–641–1441), and the other is operated by the state of Maryland (410–641–2120). A word of advice: During the months of July and August, be prepared to battle giant mosquitoes and horse flies; however, from April through June and from September through early November, few spots can rival enchanting Assateague.

district with eclectic pubs, galleries, and Federal-style town homes.

From Fells Point, a variety of sailing trips is available through **Schooner Nighthawk Cruises** (410–276–SHIP, www.a1nighthawkcruises.com), including a three-hour buffet moonlight sail, a Sunday champagne brunch sail, a Sunday evening crab cruise, and a two-hour midnight mystery cruise on Saturdays.

If you're not on the water or at an Orioles game at the showplace **Oriole Park** at Camden Yards (www.orioles.mlb.com), the next best place to be in Baltimore is the **National Aquarium** (410–576–3800, www.aqua.org). It offers 7,000 species of aquatic life and probably the best shark tank in the nation, from nurse sharks to great whites! Inner Harbor also boasts the **Maryland Science Center** (410–685–5225, www.mdsci.org), and the **Port Discovery Children's Museum**, (410–727–8120, www.portdiscovery.org).

You can go through the **National Historic Seaport of Baltimore** (877–NHCPORT, www.natlhistoricseaport.org) for a passcard that admits you to 15 of the city's maritime attractions, including the USS *Constellation* (back in the city after a three-year restoration), Fort McHenry, and the U.S. submarine *Torsk*.

Wrap the day up with an overnight's stay at the cozy **Admiral Fell Inn**, 888 South Broadway (800–292–4667, www.admiralfell.com), overlooking the harbor in Fells Point, and you'll discover why Baltimore is called "Charm City." Rates start at $169, including continental breakfast.

Chesapeake (Largely) Undiscovered

Maryland may be for crabs, but Virginia is equally tied to the history, traditions, and fortunes of the Bay. There's no better starting place to explore the Old Dominion's maritime mystique than the Northern Neck, the verdant, five-county-long jut of land bounded by the Bay and the Potomac and Rappahannock Rivers.

Less than a three-hour drive from Washington, the tiny Northern Neck village of **Irvington** has been welcoming anglers, boaters, golfers, and antique collectors for generations. The centerpiece of the town has to be the opulent **The Tides**, 480 King Carter Drive, Irvington, Virginia (800–843–3746, www.the-tides.com), a combination resort and conference facility that claims perhaps the top golf course in the state, the world-class Golden Eagle. Waterfront rooms in the luxurious Inn are from $295 per couple, while rooms in the newly acquired Lodge across the creek begin at $149. Overlooking Carter's Creek and the Rappahannock River, the Tides is just a half-day sail from several points along the open Bay, including the equally refined resort area of Windmill Point.

Farther north up the Neck lies the sleepy little town of **Reedville**, a popular stay for bed-and-breakfast lodgers, many of whom come from as far away as the

Carolinas and New England to soak up the quiet Chesapeake atmosphere. On Reedville's shaded Main Street, visitors can choose from the **Gables** (804-453-5209), a dramatic waterside Victorian mansion, or **Morris House**, a renovated early nineteenth-century fishing captain's house (804-453-7016), (rates at both start in the $80s).

Just south of the Northern Neck is the Middle Peninsula, a region of wide-open spaces and shadowy coves; it's amazingly undiscovered given its proximity to Richmond and the Hampton Roads area. One of the more interesting sites on the peninsula is the Rappahannock River town of **Urbanna**, home to a number of antique stores and perhaps the world's largest oyster festival, scheduled every fall. The nearby communities of **Gloucester**, with its village green dating back to the early eighteenth century, and **Gwynn**, on postcard-perfect Gwynn's Island, make for interesting side trips through the peninsula's fragrant backroads.

The Urban Bay

Rivaling Baltimore in industrial stature is Hampton Roads, a booming metro area that includes the Virginia cities of Norfolk, Hampton, Newport News, Portsmouth, Chesapeake, Suffolk, and Virginia Beach. It's a region of hyperboles, beginning with the world's biggest natural harbor, Hampton Roads, and the world's largest naval installation, based in Norfolk.

A leisurely Bay cruise is mandatory here, and one of the best is offered by the

---

Insiders' Tip

To appease the kids, or simply get your quota of thrills, make a daytrip down to Paramount's King's Dominion theme park in Ashland, Virginia, just north of Richmond.

Miss Hampton II (888-757-BOAT), in Hampton Harbor. The skipper will bring you up close to some of the nation's most awesome military vessels, including Trident subs and aircraft carriers seemingly the size of Rhode Island. The region is also pocketed with great museums, including the world-class fine-art **Chrysler Museum** (757-664-6200, www.chrysler. org), in Norfolk; the **Mariners Museum** (800-581-SAIL, www.mariner.org), in Newport News; the **Virginia Marine Science Museum** (757-425-FISH, www. vmsm. com), in Virginia Beach; the **Virginia Air & Space Center** (757-727-0900, www.vasc. org), in Hampton; and the **Casemate Museum** (757-727-3391, fort.Monroe. army.mil/muse um), also in Hampton. Virginia Beach also has an environmentally oriented visitor center, the **Chesapeake Bay Center** (757-412-2300), located in First Landing/Seashore State Park. Here you'll find aquariums, exhibits, a wet lab, and touch tank—all developed by the Virginia Marine Science Center.

Also, be sure to budget time to walk through prestigious Hampton University, one of the nation's first African American colleges and easily one of the most beautiful academic settings in the Commonwealth.

Those Crazy Beaches

A cultural phenomenon strikes Washington every Friday afternoon during the summer. It seems like the whole metro area has gone to the beach, at least judging from the endless snake of traffic along U.S. 50 or down I-95. Beachgoing in these parts isn't a solitary experience, so don't expect the ambience of a deserted tropical island once you get there (the exceptions are Assateague and Chincoteague, the former described in this chapter's Close-up).

The mid-Atlantic, however, does have its share of perfectly fine beaches, each with its own distinctive personality. To beach his own, in other words. **Assateague Island National Seashore** (www.nps.gov/asis), a favorite place in the sun, is 33 miles of pristine, undeveloped beachfront stretching from nearly Ocean City, Maryland, to Chincoteague, Virginia.

Ocean City, Maryland, attracts the young and wild at heart every summer. PHOTO: MIDDLETON EVANS, COURTESY OF MARYLAND OFFICE OF TOURISM

It is much less visited than any other beach in the region and is sure to revive your spirits, with its vast stretches of pure, primitive shoreline.

Five other beaches in brief: **Ocean City, Maryland**, three hours from Washington, is a nice stretch of beach, but extremely commercial both on and away from the water (tacky boardwalk emporiums, strip malls, honky-tonks, and high-rise condos, etc.). It is, nonetheless, a huge hangout for the young and wild at heart. There are hotels, motels, and rentals galore—too many to name and in every price range—so your best bet is to contact the Ocean City (or O.C.) Visitor Information line at (800) 626-2326, www.ococean.com.

To the north, **Bethany Beach, Delaware**, attracts a much older (late 20s through retirees) crowd than O.C. but is not nearly as developed with high-rises and commercial properties. Parking is a hassle, though; it's very restricted in residential areas, and options are few so you'll probably end up walking a bit. Still, it's a great weekend destination just for the relaxed setting and comparatively pristine beaches.

Rehoboth Beach, Delaware (302–645–6660, www.Rehoboth.com/visitorservices. asp), just north of Bethany, is something of a cross between the latter and Ocean City. Plenty of families and older singles can be found roaming Rehoboth's busy, colorful boardwalk, but there are also some very posh beach homes here, as well as upscale eateries. Sometimes called the nation's summer capital for its popularity with Washingtonians, Rehoboth is the kind of resort town where you can park your car for a week and go everywhere you want to go on foot (except for the great outlet malls just outside town).

Just south, **Dewey Beach, Delaware**, is the recognized hip place for the 20- and 30-something weekenders from Metro Washington. This noisy beach has an active nightlife with lots of bustling restaurants and bars (like Mardi Gras in New Orleans, the legendary Bottle and Cork must be experienced at least once).

Finally, we have to mention **Cape May, New Jersey**, on the southernmost tip of the Garden State and a world apart from the urban corridor of the Northeast.

A ferry ride away from the Delaware shore by way of the Cape May-Lewes Ferry (302-645-6313), Cape May is a seaside dreamscape of Victorian homes, shops, and cottages. At the turn of the century, it was a gambling mecca for Southern aristocrats and sea captains but today enjoys a robust tourist trade, luring visitors to such bed-and-breakfasts as the elegant **Mainstay Inn** ($100-$295, breakfast and tea included), 635 Columbia Avenue (609-884-8690, www.mainstayinn.com), and the Gothic-style **Abbey**, Columbia Avenue and Gurney Street (609-884-4506, www.abbeybedandbreakfast.com) (rates from $100, breakfast and tea included). These bed-and-breakfasts, along with many others, require a three-night minimum stay on summer weekends. The entire town is listed on the National Register of Historic Places; it's one of those treasures of the mid-Atlantic that's not to be missed.

It is easy enough to find lodging at all these areas by searching the classified ads (rentals) or travel section of the Washington, D.C. newspapers. You can also contact the Delaware State Visitor Center at (302) 739-4266, www.visitdelaware.com.

Annapolis — Boating and Bars

Maryland's state capital is a pretty town of cobbled streets, historical sights, and glorious waterviews, but thanks to the United States Naval Academy and St. John's College, it's also a party capital extraordinaire. Just 45 minutes from downtown D.C., Annapolis is an easy daytrip, and many Washingtonians make the short trek just to browse the antique shops, walk along the harbor, or dine in one of the myriad restaurants that line the town's main arteries.

Summer or winter, you'll gravitate to the city dock at the foot of town. All roads seem to lead here, and as you might imagine, the horseshoe-shaped harbor is bor-

Sailing is a beloved pastime of many who live in or near Annapolis, Maryland. PHOTO: MIDDLETON EVANS, COURTESY OF MARYLAND OFFICE OF TOURISM

Key Attractions

Assateague Island National Seashore	(410) 641–1441	www.nps.gov/asis
Maryland State Parks & Public Lands	(888) 432–2267	www.dnr.state.md.us/publiclands
National Aquarium in Baltimore	(410) 576–3800	www.aqua.org
U.S. Naval Academy	(410) 263–6933	www.usna.edu
Colonial Williamsburg	(800) HISTORY	www.colonialwilliamsburg.org
Monticello	(804) 984–9822	www.monticello.org
Virginia Museum of Fine Arts	(888) 349–7882	www.state.va.us/vmfa/
Shenandoah National Park	(540) 635–4558	www.nps.gov/shen/
West Virginia State Parks	(800) CALLWVA	www.callwva.com
Delaware Beaches	(800) 357–1818	www.visitdelaware.com

dered by shops, bars, and restaurants for every budget and age group. You will, of course, run into plenty of cadets from the Naval Academy, spiffy in their uniforms. A favorite pastime in summer is to hang out at the water's edge, admiring the yachts that moor here. The singles scene can be very active, with fancy boats replacing fancy cars.

For more serious sight-seeing, don't miss the **Naval Academy** (www.usna. edu), a sprawling campus that dominates the town. There's a visitor center in Ricketts Hall near the entrance (Gate 1 at the base of King George Street, just past the intersection with Randall Street, overlooking the water), where you can sign up for one of four daily walking tours. You'll learn that the academy was founded in 1845 and now trains some 4,300 cadets each year. You'll see the world's largest dormitory, Bancroft Hall, and even visit a sample room. Naval hero and Revolutionary War patriot John Paul Jones is buried in the chapel, which features stained-glass windows depicting Biblical stories of the sea. Finally, you'll be left free to browse the Academy Museum, filled with model ships and nautical artifacts. For information, call (410) 263-6933.

Maryland's State House is also open for tours. It is the oldest in the nation to remain in continuous legislative use, and many historical events have occurred here, such as the ratification of the Treaty of Paris ending the Revolutionary War (1784). It also once served as the nation's capitol building, and it is where George Washington resigned as commander-in-chief in 1783. Tours, which begin with a short video, are free and conducted daily at 11:00 A.M. and 3:00 P.M., (410) 974-3400. The State House is in the center of State Circle, the confluence of Maryland Avenue, Francis Street, East Street, and West Street.

Travel east on Maryland Avenue, then make your first left onto Prince George Street to arrive at **St. John's College** (ww.sjca.edu), a small, beautiful liberal arts campus famous for teaching the great classics. Founded in 1696, it is the third oldest college in the United States. On campus is the Liberty Tree, a tulip poplar estimated to be more than 400 years old.

Another major Annapolis attraction is **William Paca House** (800-603-4020, www.Annapolis.org/paca/htm) and adjoining gardens. The grand Georgian mansion was built by Paca, who served as governor of Annapolis from 1782 to 1785; however, you won't see his handiwork if you visit Paca House. The original was torn down in the 1960s, and only through the painstaking work of preservationists and archeologists was it able to be reconstructed. It is a remarkably accurate work, and many of the original remains have been incorporated into the building. The gardens have been as beautifully restored, and they feature formal parterres, fountains, a Chinese bridge, and a miniature forest. The site can be rented for weddings and other ceremonial occasions.

When you get hungry, there's plenty to choose from in Annapolis. Opposite the city dock is the **Market House**, a restored historical structure that used to serve as a warehouse. It now is home to all sorts of fast-food eateries. For real local, try **Buddy's Crabs & Ribs** (www.buddys online.com) at the center of Market Place near the city dock, at 100 Main Street, (410) 626-1100. This big informal warehouse overlooking the waterfront is a great place for kids. You'll get crabs by the bushel or ribs by the rack and lots of news-papers and napkins so you can plunge in with no worries about the mess.

For special occasions, try the **Treaty of Paris** restaurant in the historic Maryland Inn, 16 Church Circle. The menu features Continental and New American cuisine served in a formal setting. You can also stay overnight at the inn (410-263-2641). Annapolis has plenty of chain hotels and inns. For more information, contact the Annapolis and Anne Arundel County Conference & Visitors Bureau, 26 West Street, Annapolis (410-280-0445, www. visit-annapolis.org).

Neighborhoods and Real Estate

Finding a home—whether it's an apartment, condominium, town home, or a detached house—can be one of the most stressful activities you'll ever engage in. It's tough enough if you're already familiar with the market, but for most newcomers this isn't the case.

The Metro Washington real estate scene is one of the most intimidating anywhere, given the physical expanse of the region, its exorbitant housing costs, and the subtle but important differences (political, social, demographic) that exist among Washington, D.C., Virginia, and Maryland.

This chapter doesn't promise any easy remedies for evading the house-hunting blues. Our point is simply to introduce you to the residential real estate market, the types of neighborhoods and homes available here, and the major players in the home brokerage and construction industries.

The Residential Real Estate Market

During the 1980s home prices across the metro area escalated madly, a less-than-auspicious rambler jumping in price from $90,000 in 1980 to $130,000 in 1986 and $155,000 just two years later. But in the early to mid-1990s, housing prices cooled considerably, as the economy slumped and interest prices rose.

But by the end of the 1990s, the real estate market began to make up for lost time, with multiple contracts being placed on many houses in the tony suburbs close to the city, such as Bethesda and Chevy Chase. Even houses in other suburbs and the District have been selling like hotcakes. It's not unusual to see a for sale sign posted on a Monday, only for it to be replaced by an under contract sign by the weekend.

Despite an economic slowdown that began in late 2000, which was exacerbated by the September 2001 terrorist attacks, houses are still selling at a brisk pace. This buying frenzy has been fueled in part by the lowest mortgage interest rates seen in more than 30 years, as of late 2001.

Newcomers, unless they're from San Francisco, New York, or one of the few other cities pricier than D.C., will be in for sticker shock. Sadly for the homebuyer, it's a seller's market.

There are simply not enough homes on the market for people wanting to buy or even rent them. Since the early 1990s, the number of homes on the market in the Washington area has been nearly cut in half.

Amazing stories abound of bidding wars by would-be homebuyers. One local Realtor recently put a house on the market in a prime Bethesda neighborhood for $415,000. Several days later, she had five offers for the same house. It sold to the highest bidder for $456,000.

In the most desirable communities, mid-priced home values are appreciating more than 8 percent a year, and the outlook for the next few years is for more than 5 percent annual gains, well above the national average.

To illustrate, the average price of a home sold in Montgomery County in 2001 was $273,840, while the average in 2000 was $250,538, an increase of 9.3 percent in a single year. Some of the other jurisdictions have recorded even more eye-popping price gains: House prices in the District jumped a whopping 22 percent between October 2000 and October 2001, as upscale new condos were built in the District's downtown area and more people tried to ditch their commute by moving to the city's leafy upper Northwest quadrant.

To sum up, housing is still awfully expensive in the Nation's Capital, and we doubt that will ever change. The average price of a home here is $283,540. These are steep numbers when you consider that the national average price of a house is about $210,000. According to Runzheimer International, a firm that compiles such statistics, you can expect to pay $393,500 for a four-bedroom, two-and-a-half-bath, 2,000-square-foot home in Washington's suburbs. Of major metropolitan areas, only San Jose, San Francisco, and Honolulu have a higher price for a similar house.

With that said, the Washington area still commands a high home ownership rate. An estimated 80 percent of householders own their homes, compared with 65 percent nationally. The implication is that while Metro Washington homes are expensive, many people can still afford them.

About 38 percent of owners live in detached single-family houses, while 40 percent live in town houses and 22 percent in condominiums. For those 20 percent who don't own, the fair-market rent for a one-bedroom apartment is an estimated $1,000 to $1,100, if you take the entire Metro area into consideration. For two bedrooms expect to pay $1,200 to $1,600, and for three bedrooms $1,600 and up. House rentals can range from $1,000 to $1,200 a month for a town home in the outer suburbs to $3,500 in Bethesda or $6,000 for a plush Georgetown dwelling. Why these astronomical rental prices? It's simply the law of supply and demand. More people are seeking rentals than there are rentals available and have been for several years.

One thing to keep in mind, whether you're going to buy or rent, is that the pricing rationale here is similar to other large urban areas. In other words, expect to pay a premium to be close to the Dis-

trict and near major commuting links like I-66, the Capital Beltway, and Metrorail stations. Prices drop as you move outward; commute times increase. It's the age-old tradeoff.

For more information on the local real estate market, licensing practices, ethics, and other issues involving buying or renting a home, we suggest you call one or more of the following agencies:

Greater Capital Area Association of Realtors, (202) 789-8889, www.gcaar.com

Maryland Association of Realtors, (301) 261-8290, www.mdrealtor.org

Northern Virginia Association of Realtors, (703) 207-3200, www.nvar.com

Neighborhoods and Homes

Washington, D.C.

People tend to forget that Washington, D.C., beyond the monuments, is a city of neighborhoods—communities with their own dynamics, history, and sense of place. Most of these enclaves are close knit and largely self-contained. The whole effect is something akin to a patchwork of small towns, albeit connected to an urban core.

In a city tagged for its transience, it may come as a surprise that the majority of the District's neighborhoods are home to several generations of families.

As a place to live, the District offers proximity to all major employment centers, including those in Suburban Maryland and Northern Virginia. Virtually no one here commutes longer than 40 minutes to work. Washington's prized Metro mass transit system, famed nightlife and cultural opportunities, miles of parks and forests, stately homes and shaded streets, plus its allure as the Nation's Capital, will always make it a desirable address.

That desirability comes with a price, however. The average price of a home in D.C. is $294,066. The median rent is $643, although rents of $1,500 to $2,000 are more the norm in prime neighborhoods.

The vast majority of newcomers who relocate to the District settle in **North-**

west, so we'll begin our neighborhood tour here.

Adams Morgan, which radiates from Columbia Road and 18th Street NW, is Washington's largest and most celebrated ethnic neighborhood. Its global-minded eateries are famous in these parts (see our Restaurants chapter), and it's here you'll find African clothiers next to Spanish bridal shops and Turkish shoe stores. Adams Morgan and neighboring **Mount Pleasant** have attracted a growing number of young professionals, including many tied to the White House and Capitol Hill who live in gentrified town houses and large apartment buildings. A few years ago, Mount Pleasant experienced an unfortunate riot, but the tensions have cooled and the neighborhood seems determined to carry on as one of Washington's most integrated communities.

Immediately to the south of Adams Morgan is **Dupont Circle**, Washington's answer to Greenwich Village. Interspersed among the cafes, art galleries, and boutiques are grand old brownstones and row houses. Many prominent members of the gay community, artists, young progressives, and aging bohemians call Dupont home. Although it can claim many of the same attributes as Adams Morgan, Dupont is decidedly more established and thus housing costs tend to be higher here.

Closer to downtown, and wrapping around the campus of George Washington University, are the highly urbanized neighborhoods of **Foggy Bottom** and the **West End**. Both are apartment and condo dense, with the former consisting mostly of students and professors and the latter primarily single professionals who commute by Metro or walk to nearby offices. The neighborhoods are wedged between Georgetown to the west and downtown to the east, a consolation for the area's overall lack of restaurants and nightlife.

Downtown living is enjoying somewhat of a renaissance thanks to the continued revitalization of the **Pennsylvania Avenue** corridor. Several older buildings, including the historic Lansburgh, have been revamped and now house some of the most exclusive condo units in Washington.

Anchored by a shady park-like circle, complete with fountain, the Dupont Circle neighborhood offers an eclectic mix of restaurants, offices, and townhouses. PHOTO: COURTESY OF THE WASHINGTON, DC CONVENTION AND TOURISM CORPORATION

By most measures Washington's toniest address is still **Georgetown**, with its famed M Street/Wisconsin Avenue nightlife, stylish Federal town homes, and secluded estates. The area west of Wisconsin Avenue is dominated by Georgetown University and its students; east of the avenue it's markedly quieter, with bigger homes and well-heeled residents. For those with money—tiny town houses can demand half a million dollars—and patience to bear the weekend crush of partygoers, there is simply no other close-in neighborhood that can match the charm and convenience of Georgetown.

Immediately to the north, in **Glover Park**, a more down-to-earth atmosphere pervades. Brick town homes and duplexes cluster around small parks and green

Stately brick townhouses line the residential streets of Georgetown. PHOTO: COURTESY OF THE WASHINGTON, DC CONVENTION AND TOURISM CORPORATION

spaces all within a short stroll of Wisconsin Avenue. Young families, Georgetown University professors, middle-aged empty nesters, and longtime residents live side by side and in harmony in this civic-minded and politically progressive neighborhood.

Moving farther north puts you in the land of milk and honey. The neighborhoods of **Foxhall Road**, **Spring Valley**, and **Wesley Heights** are the stuff of *Architectural Digest* photo shoots. The neighbors tend to be older than those who reside to the south, politically more conservative, and measurably wealthier. On some streets multi million-dollar homes are more the rule than the exception.

To the east, in the heart of Northwest, are **Cleveland Park** and **Woodley Park**, a checkerboard of beautiful Victorian homes with wide porches, shady yards, and sprawling square footage. You'll also find along Wisconsin Avenue numerous older apartment buildings and remodeled

town houses. Easy access to Massachusetts, Wisconsin, and Connecticut Avenues, the Metro, and such attractions as the National Zoo give the neighborhoods considerable prestige with up-and-coming professionals.

In the far stretches of upper Northwest, neighborhoods like **Tenleytown**, **American University Park**, **Barnaby Woods**, and **Chevy Chase** (not to be confused with neighboring Chevy Chase, Maryland) glow with a sense of small-town America charm, complete with quiet tree-lined streets, beautiful spacious lawns, and kids on bicycles. Along the upper western edges of Rock Creek Park, **Forest Hills** unfolds with palatial homes and tucked-away streets that allow maximum privacy for the rich and powerful.

East of Rock Creek, along upper 16th Street NW, **Shepherd Park**, **Brightwood Park**, and **Crestwood** move to a relaxed suburban beat. Homes are substantially more affordable than similar dwellings to the west of the park, and 16th Street provides a mostly hassle-free link to downtown and points south.

Two Northwest neighborhoods that are rebounding from years of neglect are **Shaw**, which straddles 14th Street above downtown, and **LeDroit Park**, just to the south of Howard University. The Metro Green Line stop at Shaw/Howard University comes with the promise of further revitalization of these Victorian neighborhoods, but crime remains an ongoing problem.

In Northeast another neighborhood on the rebound is **Brookland**, which houses an interesting mix of Catholic University students and professors, as well as elderly middle-class residents who live in well-kept row houses and Cape Cods. The university and its rolling, wooded campus dominate much of the neighborhood and bring a sense of respite from the clamor of the inner city.

The most sought-after address in **Northeast** is **Capitol Hill**, which also spreads into Southeast. As you might imagine, Capitol Hill teems with young congressional staffers, lobbyists, and members of Congress. Huge brownstones and smaller town homes are the mainstays, but a few apartment and condo units can be found. As a rule, those areas closest to the Capitol command the highest prices and are considered the safest. The higher the street numbers, however, the likelier you are to encounter crime. Even in the most exclusive sections, crime remains more of a problem than in other Washington neighborhoods of comparable price.

In **Southwest** the neighborhood of choice is the **Waterfront**, located north of the Anacostia River. A haven for federal employees, much of the Southwest Waterfront is within a short walk of Capitol Hill and L'Enfant Plaza, the massive government complex. The area boasts some fine restaurants, theaters, and pricey town homes. Seventies-style, high-rise condo and apartment buildings, however, make up the bulk of housing, which is typically more affordable than similar close-in units found to the north of the National Mall.

Anacostia, on the opposite side of the river, contains the District's largest concentration of public housing. This portion of Southeast continues to battle widespread poverty and violent crime, the worst in D.C.

Northern Virginia

Parts of Northern Virginia, such as Rosslyn, are so close to Washington that you can walk to the city in 10 minutes or, as in the case of Arlington and Alexandria, drive there in five. Other Virginia suburbs are so far flung that you need close to an hour to reach the city.

Close-in suburbs are hardly distinguishable from D.C. itself. They have high-rises, choked traffic, restaurant rows, and lots of businesses. On the other hand, there are some suburbs that seem to typify the centuries-old vision of Virginia: gracious colonial manors, lush greenery, rolling meadows, white fences, and horses. The remarkable thing is, even some of the suburbs within 40 minutes of the city have that Virginia Hunt Country atmosphere. A good real estate agent will help you narrow down your choices, weigh factors in your decision, such as distance, cost,

schools, and atmosphere. To help get you started, you may want to contact some agencies prior to your arrival. Later in this chapter, we've listed the largest ones in Metro Washington. Below is an area-by-area overview of Washington's closest Virginia suburbs.

Alexandria

Sharing ranks with Arlington County as Northern Virginia's closest-in suburb, Alexandria has strong historical and cultural ties to the District of Columbia. Make no mistake though: Although Alexandria may be a suburb of Washington, it's a Virginia city first and foremost.

Alexandria is immersed in an almost overpowering sense of place. How can it not be with George Washington and Robert E. Lee having called it home? The municipality is also characteristically Virginian in the way it is run—efficiently and pragmatically.

During rush hour no part of Alexandria is more than 40 minutes from Washington. Metrorail has three stations within the city limits. The average price of a home here is $246,878. Most newcomers' impressions of Alexandria are that it's a lot like Georgetown, but without the urban chaos. And they're right. Sort of.

Old Town, the city's most visible neighborhood, could stand double for its northern counterpart on a number of accounts. It's also pricey: town houses start at $325,000, though you're more likely to see them up in the $350,000 to $700,000 range, especially as you progress east toward the handsomely restored Potomac waterfront. Because colonial-era homes weren't designed with the automobile in mind, on-street parking is almost always the rule here, and on weekends things can get a little sticky. But Old Town is, well, Old Town, and that's the biggest selling point of all, especially among the young up-and-coming crowd that tends to migrate here.

Though some would be hard pressed to admit it, there's more to Alexandria than Old Town. Not too long ago **Del Ray**, which wraps around U.S. 1 and Potomac Yards (a massive train-switching yard), was solely a blue-collar neighbor-

The Carlyle House in Old Town Alexandria served as the headquarters of General Braddock, leader of the British forces during the French and Indian War. PHOTO: COURTESY OF VIRGINIA TOURISM CORPORATION

hood. Gentrification has set in and many bungalows and Cape Cods now command more than $300,000.

Alexandria communities that most resemble suburbia are **Rosemont**, **Seminary**, and **Beverly Hills**. Mount Vernon, to the south, has a city address of Alexandria, but is actually part of Fairfax County, so we'll cover it in that section. A lot of the homes in suburban Alexandria were built in the early 1960s on large lots; prices run from $200,000 to more than $1 million, with the greatest concentration in the $350,000 range.

Along the western edge of town are the self-contained neighborhoods of **Park Fairfax** and **South Fairlington**. The majority of housing is town homes and apartment buildings, many of which sprang up after World War II to house federal workers. Now they're popular with single professionals and first-time buyers.

Also out in the West End is **Landmark**, an area of high-rise condos, apartment buildings, and shopping centers located off I-395. Condos start at $100,000 for a one-bedroom unit and can run upward to $250,000 for deluxe models.

Arlington County

Arlington looks and acts a lot like a city. Its 26 square miles are a collage of satellite business districts, high-rise apartment complexes, and tucked-away residential neighborhoods. The county has more Metro stations per capita than any other suburb, and its population is decidedly middle-aged.

Arlington is the most urban county in Metro D.C. and it's unique in that there are no incorporated cities or towns within its borders. Like Alexandria, it was once part of the District of Columbia and many residents here are closer to downtown D.C. and Capitol Hill than are most Washingtonians. Needless to say, Arlington is a convenient and especially attractive area for single, workaholic professionals who like being less than 15 minutes from most of the area's employment centers.

The county is usually identified with its massive business/residential corridors—**Crystal City**, **Pentagon City**, **Clarendon**, **Ballston**, and **Rosslyn**. Apartments and condos are the most plentiful housing options here, with the former starting at $1,200 a month for one-bedroom units, and the latter commanding $160,000 to over $250,000.

The northern tier of the county is almost exclusively residential neighborhoods, some of the most stately areas in Metro Washington. Single-family homes in communities like **Country Club Hills** run from $500,000 for older brick colonials to $1 million and more for estate homes. The average price of a single-family home in Arlington County in 2001 was $289,120.

Despite its dense nature, Arlington has set aside hundreds of acres of park land, and its riverfront bike path, which affords stunning views of Washington and the Potomac, is a source of intense civic pride.

Fairfax County

Northern Virginia's largest jurisdiction runs the gamut on the types of neighborhoods and living options available to newcomers. In Fairfax County you'll find two-story colonials on quiet cul-de-sacs, modest Cape Cods and ramblers in older neighborhoods, lakefront town homes in new developments, California contemporaries in planned communities, giant estate homes in wooded parklike settings, and turnkey condos in high-rise buildings. If there is a common thread that runs through this massive county, it is that it's overwhelmingly middle class to upper class.

Fairfax is among the top 5 counties in the nation in median household income, at $68,000 per household (see the Metro Washington Overview chapter) and in the top 15 in median housing values. The average price for a house is $280,090. Apartments start at $800 a month in the newer complexes. Those are values if you're coming from the urban areas of the Northeast or parts of the West Coast but a shock if you hail from virtually any other part of the nation.

One affordable neighborhood inside the Beltway is **Annandale**, an area that has long been a magnet for federal workers and their families. Annandale's signature redbrick ramblers and comfortable ranch homes are priced in the $250,000 to $400,000 range. The community is one of the oldest suburbs in Northern Virginia

and is centrally located next to several busy road arteries and I–495.

To the north, **Falls Church,** an independent municipality, comes with a small-town charm and a mix of older stately Victorians and new town house developments. Single-family homes start at $250,000 and work their way up to $600,000. Route 7 (Leesburg Pike) cuts through the center of the city, offering easy access to Washington and most of Fairfax County. The average commute time to downtown D.C. is 35 minutes.

Great Falls, located in the gorgeous bluffs that tower above the Potomac River in northern Fairfax, extending through rolling countryside all the way to the Loudoun County line, is a community of large houses situated on expansive lots of a half-acre and more. Most of the homes here are colonial in design, and $500,000 to multimillion-dollar price tags are the norm. Great Falls and neighboring **McLean**, a neighborhood closer to Washington, are known for their great schools, country lanes, and serene, wooded surroundings. Horse farms, ponds, and large wildflower meadows are not uncommon here, and you can still escape the sense of overdevelopment rampant in other parts of the Metro area. Although only a 20- to 30-minute drive to D.C., the morning commutes along Chain Bridge Road (Route 123), Georgetown Pike, and the George Washington Memorial Parkway can be trying at times.

Moving outside the Beltway, the fast-growing planned community of **Burke** attracts suburbanites looking for newer houses, plenty of parks for the kids, and proximity to major shopping centers. The typical single-family home starts at approximately $280,000; town houses run from $180,000. For all its pluses, Burke commuters face a challenge each day along Braddock and Old Keene Mill Roads or via the Fairfax County Parkway to always-congested I–66. Expect a 35- to 50-minute commute into the city.

Wedged between Burke and Annandale is **Springfield**, another older community of modest ramblers on large lots mixed with newer and larger homes on small lots. Like Annandale, Springfield is

Potomac, Great Falls, and other far-flung suburbs maintain some open pastures and horse farms.
PHOTO: MIDDLETON EVANS, COURTESY OF MARYLAND OFFICE OF TOURISM

home to thousands of government and military workers. A large stock of detached homes falls into the $200,000 to $350,000 range. Town houses begin at around $150,000 and condominiums start at $100,000. Although only 15 miles south of Washington, Springfield's major link to the District is I-95, one of the region's most congested arteries. In all fairness, however, the Virginia Department of Transportation has done miracles in recent years improving existing roads and constructing convenient new secondary roads such as the Franconia-Springfield Parkway.

The parkway (as well as Franconia Road and ever-lengthening South Van Dorn Street) has become a vital transportation link for the massive yet still-developing **Kingstowne** community and its much smaller and less-exclusive neighbor, **Manchester Lakes**—places that have become especially attractive to single professionals, the newly married, and young families. Located just east of Springfield in the Franconia section of the county (which in many parts carries an Alexandria

mailing address), Kingstowne and Manchester Lakes offer a selection of nice apartments, condominiums, town houses, and (in Kingstowne only) single-family homes. Some of the smaller condos in Manchester Lakes start at $90,000. Expect to pay from $150,000 and up, meanwhile, in either community for town houses and closer to $250,000 and more for most single-family residences.

Whatever turns the housing market takes, Kingstowne and Manchester Lakes will likely only grow in popularity thanks to their appealing character, accessibility, convenience to the District and Old Town Alexandria and prime location some two miles from the shopping mecca of Springfield Mall and the Franconia-Springfield Metro station.

Mount Vernon, in southeastern Fairfax County, retains a sense of exclusivity because of its proximity to George Washington's venerable riverside estate and Old Town Alexandria. Detached homes on large lots are the backbone of this beautiful, verdant neighborhood located between U.S. 1 and George Washington Memorial

Parkway. Small side streets and country lanes lead you to manicured estates overlooking the Potomac River—many with private docks. This is a neighborhood for brisk walks on a fall day, thanks to the numerous quiet roads and bicycle paths in the area. Tucked into this affluent area are some amazing bargains—small ramblers and older homes on large lots just waiting for young families to add improvements. Traveling south on the George Washington Memorial Parkway from Old Town Alexandria, turn right on Wellington Road and take any of the side streets. You'll discover neighborhoods where children still play outside, families walk together along sleepy roads where traffic is so infrequent that no sidewalks are necessary and old, tall trees form shady canopies on even the warmest summer days.

Heading to **Oakton** and **Vienna** in the north-central part of the county (it wasn't long ago that these two were considered Fairfax's far-western suburbs), you'll encounter an area in transition from woodsy to highly developed. Located off of I-66, just a couple miles outside the Beltway, these communities are now right in the heart of the county, a factor that bodes well with commuters, many of whom use the nearby Vienna Metro station. Oakton is mostly a maze of sprawling subdivisions—albeit with larger-than-normal lots—but some parts resemble Great Falls in both topography and opulence. Vienna, an incorporated town settled by the Scots in the early 1800s, has a more established small-town feel. Homes in both Oakton and Vienna range from $300,000 to more than $1 million.

Farther west along I-66, the city of **Fairfax**, another independent municipality, boasts a fine old historic district and an ample supply of moderately priced homes. Single-family homes start at $209,000, while town houses are available from $150,000. Fairfax is at the junction of several busy roads; commutes into Washington range from 40 to 60 minutes.

In the far western reaches of the county, the rapidly growing communities of **Centreville** and **Chantilly** attract first-time homebuyers with a plentiful variety of town homes and condominiums.

Move-up buyers can purchase large colonials ($250,000 to $300,000) for 20 to 30 percent less than comparable homes closer in. Town houses begin in the $130,000s. Commuting times into downtown can run 45 to 75 minutes. Nearby, bordered by Route 123 and Route 28 are the pastoral districts of **Clifton** and **Fairfax Station**. The town of Clifton is actually a small village of white picket fences, gingerbread houses, kitchen gardens, gravel roads, and front-porch swings. You can walk through this historic little town in 15 minutes—it is surrounded by estates of five or more acres that blend into the area known as Fairfax Station.

You can hardly tell the difference between the countryside bordering Clifton and Fairfax Station: Both feature colonials of 3,000 to 7,000 square feet on five-acre tracts, private roads, abundant wildlife, unspoiled woods, and tranquil family neighborhoods. The northern end of Fairfax Station culminates at the edge of the aforementioned Burke—a decidedly middle-priced area, and the rolling hills give way to smaller lots and, in some developments, tract mansions. In fact, at the Burke-Fairfax Station border, the subdivisions are no different from elsewhere in suburbia. The Fairfax Station-Clifton area, farther south, is a version of lavish Great Falls for a cost of 20 to 30 percent less.

Out near Washington Dulles International Airport, **Herndon**, an independent town, and **Reston**, a lake- and tree-rich planned community, are populated by young professionals and their families. Detached single-family homes ($180,000 to $1 million) are the residences of choice, but a sizable number of town house and condo developments offer first-time buyers $100,000 and up alternatives. Both areas are booming, and it seems that upscale malls and pedestrian shopping and entertainment complexes are added every few months. Hidden away from the traffic are wonderful recreation areas, like Reston's **Lake Anne**, where waterside residents have docks, pontoon boats, and motorized floats. Winding along this beautiful refuge are town houses and single-family dwellings with large windows overlooking a scene right out of a Monet painting—

whimsical bridges, flower-lined canals, weeping willows, and at the center of it all, a glass-surfaced lake suitable for swimming, windsurfing, and even fishing. Also at water's edge is a town plaza featuring a crescent of restaurants and outdoor cafes.

You'd never know that these areas are bordered by the Dulles Toll Road—heavily trafficked but nonetheless functional—and just minutes from Washington Dulles International Airport.

Prince William County

In a metropolitan area where the term *affordable housing* seems like an oxymoron, Prince William County has become a sanctuary for suburbanites seeking value and space at prices that don't raise blood pressure.

At $186,110, the county's average-price home is about 30 to 40 percent lower than those in jurisdictions to the north, explaining why more first-time buyers and homeowners in the move-up market have settled in Prince William over the last decade. Simple demographics partly tell the story of the county's widespread appeal to young families: More than half of Prince William's 259,827 residents are younger than 25, according to U.S. Census Bureau estimates.

The sprawling bedroom community is one of the fastest-growing areas in the nation. In 1980 less than 150,000 residents were spread across the county's 350 square miles. By the year 2000 Prince William officials expect 350,000 people to call the county home.

Neighborhoods along the I–95 corridor such as Lake Ridge, Woodbridge, and

Montclair have been the biggest gainers so far, with most single-family homes selling between $150,000 to the upper-$200s. Town houses range from the low- to mid-$100s, while condos typically start at $70,000. The area experiencing the fastest growth is the western part of the county near Manassas and I–66 (the Gainesville area), where large single-family homes in new subdivisions can be purchased for anywhere from the mid-$100s to $400,000.

The rapid transformation from a quiet exurb to thriving suburb has come with its share of growing pains. Road congestion, while getting better, is still chronic. Prince William commuters spend more time on the road than anyone else in Metro Washington. The Virginia Railway Express, with several stops in Prince William, has lured some motorists off the road.

Loudoun County

The fortunes of this beautiful county 30 miles northwest of Washington are closely tied to the development of Washington Dulles International Airport. Loudoun County's population is growing at a rate that is among the fastest in counties across the nation. Its 2000 population of 169,600 is up 97 percent since 1990. In 2001 the average price of a single-family home was $386,462, while the average price of a town house or condo was $215,623.

Dulles's renaissance over the last 10 years has played out nicely for Loudoun, helping bring in new aerospace and international high-tech firms and boosting the population (see our Metro Washington Overview chapter). Most of the county's population lies in and around Leesburg and points east along Route 7. Single-family homes in diverse communities like Sterling, Ashburn, and Sugarland run between $170,000 to $800,000. The average town house costs between $110,000 and $160,000.

As one moves west and south of **Leesburg**, the graceful county seat, you enter hunt country, a land of blue bloods and stone fences, breathtaking country estates, Kentucky Derby-winning stables, and rolling vineyards. The most modest of

> ## Insiders' Tip
> The Washington area is so large and varied that it's not a bad idea to rent for a while before settling on a neighborhood.

homes in communities like **Middleburg, Upperville,** and **Bluemont** will cost about $180,000, and these are easily eclipsed by the number of multi-million-dollar horse farms that crisscross the pretty countryside.

Suburban Maryland

Montgomery County

Montgomery County was the first true suburb of Washington, D.C. Virginia, after all, was across the river; to get to Montgomery all you had to do was cross Western Avenue. Manmade borders, as Marylanders will tell you, are easier to cross than physical borders.

Go up to Montgomery County today and real estate agents will be the first to remind you of this. Indeed, getting into Washington is likely to be less of a hassle from the close-in suburbs because of the absence of bridges. That said, be warned that I-270, which runs north to Rockville, Gaithersburg, and Frederick County, can be a commuting nightmare. In the past few years, major improvements, including new lanes and upgraded feeder roads, have resulted in a better stretch of highway, but a look at the daily traffic reports will show that the improvements have barely kept up with demand. I-495, the Beltway into Montgomery County, is hardly better, though both are good, multilaned roads.

Like Fairfax County, Montgomery County has every type of housing and neighborhood option under the sun. You will find an abundance of quiet, tree-lined residential communities. The county's 28,000 acres of parkland are right next to many of these communities, from the poshest addresses in Chevy Chase to the lower-income neighborhoods along Veirs Mill Road in **Wheaton**. Like its Virginia cousin, however, housing doesn't come cheap in Montgomery County, with $273,840 the average price for a home as of October 2001.

The quintessential Montgomery County community has got to be **Bethesda**, a residential sanctuary for thousands of government officials and industry leaders. North Bethesda, convenient to the Beltway and Metro, is the denser section of town, chock full of town house developments and midrise condo units. To the south, in neighborhoods like **Chevy Chase**, you'll find vintage suburbia, with large Victorians and colonials situated on impeccably manicured lots.

Close to the beltway, single-family homes range between $220,000 for the tiniest Cape Cod or ranch to upwards of $2 million for a new minimansion or renovated Victorian. Commuting time into the city seldom exceeds 30 minutes.

The equestrian set is still holding on in Suburban Maryland, and nowhere is it more evident than in posh **Potomac**. In some areas subdivisions have chopped down once-magnificent farms into gaudy five-acre horse "farmettes," but the overall atmosphere remains largely pastoral. Town houses—the few that are here—start at $300,000, while single-family abodes range from $400,000 to several million. This is where many Washington sports, media, and political figures live and the name "Potomac" in your address is sure to add cachet to your image. River Road, Potomac's lovely link with the outside world, is a winding two-laner that wasn't designed for express commuting, and the moderate crowding at rush hour is testimony to that. Then again, many of the folks who live in Potomac can probably set their own schedules, which probably explains why rush hour isn't worse.

Hovering the District line east of Rock Creek Park are **Silver Spring** and **Takoma Park**, two established and quite different residential areas. Silver Spring is probably Montgomery's most ethnic community. Of late, its downtown corridor is witnessing a genuine renaissance, with the Discovery Channel building new headquarters here and the American Film Institute renovating a showcase theater. Single-family homes start at $175,000 and go up to $1 million.

Takoma Park, immediately to the south, is Metro Washington's answer to Berkeley, California, or Boulder, Colorado. Almost beyond politically correct (the entire city is designated a Nuclear Free Zone), the town is a flash point of community activism. A mix of young, free spirits; middle-aged bohemians; and elderly longtime residents live in older and mostly modest Cape Cods and Victorians, and the prices pretty much mirror those in Silver Spring, but the setting is more about trees and big yards than in neighboring Silver Spring (the latter has similar enclaves, however).

The village of **Kensington**, 8 miles north of D.C. and 1 mile north of the Beltway, defies its highly suburban location. Fewer than 2,000 people live in this half-square-mile community that is among the oldest suburbs in Metro Washington (incorporated in 1894). Many of the Victorian homes date back to the 1890s, adding a nostalgic air to the place. There are mature trees and rolling hills dotted with houses on spacious lots, as well as more typical suburban streets featuring sidewalks and closely spaced homes. Parts of Kensington border Rock Creek Park's Beach Drive, and the homes along here can be well over $500,000. For the most part, though, houses start at $300,000 and work their way upward to the $600,000s in the Kensington area.

Most of the people north of the Beltway live in or around the communities of **Wheaton**, **Rockville**, and **Gaithersburg**. Metrorail and Georgia Avenue connect Wheaton—a middle- to lower middle-class, ethnically mixed neighborhood—with Washington. In Wheaton you'll find reasonably priced apartments (from $1,000 for a two-bedroom) and small, modest brick ramblers and Cape Cods, some under $200,000. The more affluent Rockville, the county seat, and Gaithersburg, its fast-growing northern neighbor, were once serene little dairy towns whose pastures are now dotted with town homes and single-family developments. Rockville

has most of the detached housing ($250,000 to $600,000) and is family oriented. Gaithersburg has a large population of young professionals and young families who tend to migrate toward moderately priced town homes ($180,000 and up) in areas like Montgomery Village, a planned residential community.

Two northern Montgomery County communities in transition are **Germantown** and **Damascus**. Germantown is the denser of the two, with its rolling hills carpeted by new condominiums, town houses, and shopping centers. About 10 miles up Highway 27, once-sleepy Damascus is evolving into a bedroom community of first-time homeowners who are just as likely to commute to Baltimore as Washington.

Prince George's County

The average price of a home in Prince George's County was $146,645 as of October 2000, more than 40 percent less than a comparable house next door in Montgomery County.

Why the sizable price difference? Perception. Prince George's could use some good spin doctors. The county's reputation is as a blue-collar haven with subpar schools and too much crime. Yes, it's more working class than Montgomery and Fairfax, and yes, it's had its share of crime problems, especially in neighborhoods close to the District border. Prince George's is also the most racially integrated county in Metro Washington, and its schools have made tremendous progress in recent years.

Progressive communities like **College Park** teem with college students, artists, writers, and aging activists. **University Park** and **Greenbelt** (home of Goddard Space Center) have high concentrations of academicians, scientists, and engineers, while **Bowie**, **Mitchellville**, and **Upper Marlboro** attract white-collar professionals and families. Waterfront living gives Fort Washington's **Tantallon** neighborhood a distinct panache, and this is where you're likely to find some of the most expensive real estate in Prince George's, with many homes hitting the $500,000 mark.

Several major road arteries, including U.S. 50, I-295, Branch Avenue, and Pennsylvania Avenue, connect the county with nearby Washington, helping make commuting times here among the lowest in Metro D.C.

Property Taxes

In the District of Columbia, Maryland, and Virginia, homes are appraised at 100 percent of their market value. Homeowners in D.C. also get an exemption for the first $30,000 of their property's value.

For a $250,000 home—about the average price in Metro D.C.—this is roughly what you'd pay in property taxes in the following jurisdictions in 2001:

Washington, D.C.:	$3,281

Northern Virginia:	
Alexandria	$2,775
Arlington County	$2,557
Fairfax County	$2,825
Loudoun County	$2,700
Prince William County	$3,275

Suburban Maryland:	
Montgomery County	$2,700
Prince George's County	$3,368

Washington, D.C. recently enacted a tax break for owners/occupants of private residences. Called the Homestead Act, citizens may apply for a $30,000 deduction on the assessed value, then pay only $0.96 tax per $100 of assessed value, which would almost halve the above levy to $1,632.

In Maryland a state transfer and recordation tax is split 50–50 between the buyer and seller, unless otherwise negotiated. That tax is 1.94 percent on residences costlier than $70,000—which means pretty much everything in the county. If, however, the purchaser is a first-time homebuyer, the seller is required by law to pay 0.25 percent of the transfer tax.

When you look at these figures, it's important to keep in mind the type of property for which you're being taxed. A $275,000 home varies from being a condo in a premium Washington neighborhood, a modest town house in Old Town Alexandria, or a spacious colonial on a large lot in Prince George's and Prince William Counties.

Real Estate Companies

The scene in Metro Washington is changing daily, with two giants—Long & Foster and Pardoe Real Estate—gobbling up most smaller firms or crowding them out of the area market. As of this writing, the following are some of the major real estate brokerage firms doing business in the entire Metro Washington area. You will find agents at each covering Washington, Maryland, and Virginia. Any of these firms can provide you with good service in residential properties because all have various agents who specialize in different types of property, like undeveloped land or condos.

But how to choose one particular agent? Some suggestions include driving through the area you are interested in and seeing whose name appears on the most signs. That agent may be very busy, but he or she is likely a full-time real estate professional and a go-getter who knows your chosen area and is willing to invest time in prospective clients. If you're not sure of the area in which you'd like to live, browse through the classifieds of area newspapers—including the county papers and free tabloids found in supermarkets—to get an idea of pricing and types of houses available. Many real estate agents advertise in these publications, and they'll often tout their honors and awards (such as million dollar agent, president's club, or Number 1 agent in a given area, county, or state).

Another method of finding an agent is to ask neighbors or co-workers for recommendations. Remember, once you've narrowed down your choices, get three references from former clients. Find out if their agent advertised to their satisfaction, gave them the service they required, and, what's most important, sold their home or located a new one in a timely fashion. Ask the agent directly what he or she will do to market your property or help you find a new one. How much do they spend on advertising? Do they hold open houses? How often do they deal with the type of property you are hoping to buy or sell? What is the median price of the homes they deal with? If the agent specializes, for example, in condos and you're looking for a half-million-dollar home in the exurbs, then they're probably not for you.

Finally, be sure your agent is a good source of newcomer information and services, whether you're buying or selling. If you're selling, you'll want them to put together a nice introductory package on your house and neighborhood for prospective buyers. If you're a buyer, you'll want the information yourself.

Coldwell Banker Stevens Realtors
Residential Real Estate
465 Maple Ave. W.
Vienna, VA
(703) 281–1400, (800) 336–4567
www.cbstevens.com

One of the most established brokerages in Metro Washington, and indeed the nation, Coldwell Banker is another billion-dollar sales producer, with 24 offices and 1,200-plus licensed agents. The company has its own referral network service, which can be of value, since the agency was ranked num-

ber 1 in U.S. residential sales by both *Real Trends* magazine and *National Relocation and Real Estate* magazine.

Long & Foster Real Estate Inc.
11351 Random Hills Rd.
Fairfax, VA
(703) 359–1500
www.longandfoster.com

This dominant regional player in both residential and commercial markets handled about $13 billion in residential sales in the mid-Atlantic area in 2000, according to the firm. In 1998 it sold 45 percent of the homes in Metro Washington, far outdistancing its closest competitor, Weichert Realty, with 21 percent of market share. The firm specializes in new-home, high-end sales and relocation. It's also ubiquitous: Some 7,000 licensed agents work out of 160 offices scattered through the region.

Pardoe Real Estate ERA
2828 Pennsylvania Ave. NW
Washington, DC
(202) 333–6100
www.pardoe.com

This firm specializes in upper-end residential real estate, particularly in Georgetown, Potomac, and McLean. It's not unusual for Pardoe properties to sell for well over $1 million dollars, which explains why, although the firm is relatively small compared with others in Metro Washington, it ranks second behind Long & Foster in dollar amount of area residential sales. Pardoe did more than $2 billion in sales in 2000.

RE/MAX Central
6707 Democracy Blvd.
Bethesda, MD
(301) 564–9681
www.remax.com

From starter homes to mansions, RE/MAX has one of the largest listings in the market. It has dozens of offices throughout Northern Virginia, Washington, and Suburban Maryland and is part of the RE/MAX International Referral Roster System. One point about RE/MAX: Its agents keep 100 percent of their

---

Insiders' Tip

You want to look, but you don't want to hook up with a real estate agent yet? In hopes of ultimately securing you as a client, most agents will be happy to provide you with a long, computer-generated list of homes in your price range. Get a map and drive by the homes to get an idea of those you want to explore further.

commissions rather than splitting them with the company, as is typical at other companies. In exchange, they receive little administrative or advertising support. Does this make a RE/MAX agent work harder? It's difficult to say, but agents who agree to these terms are bound to be confident go-getters.

**Weichert Realty
6410 Rockledge Dr.
Bethesda, MD
(301) 718–4111
www.weichert.com**
Just a few years ago, this Maryland-based firm bought out a portion of D.C.'s Shannon and Luchs Co. and Virginia's Mount Vernon Realty (absorbing both names) and overnight became one of the largest and most powerful residential brokerage firms in Metro D.C., second behind Long & Foster. The company is particularly noted for its large inventory of luxury homes and estates.

Relocation Information

Following are some services and organizations you may wish to contact for information before you relocate. Often, your agent is the best source for general relocation information, because most real estate firms either have their own relocation department or partner with an outside relocation firm.

• Employee Relocation Council: a national organization headquartered in Washington that serves corporations that are relocating their employees. It serves as a clearinghouse of ideas, options, and services for companies interested in discovering how other companies are handling relocations. The council publishes a related monthly magazine, *Mobility*. Call (202) 857–0857 or visit the Web site at www.erc.org.

• *Welcome Newcomers Guide:* An invaluable tool for newcomers, with information on everything from schools, child care, and neighborhoods to maps, mortgage charts, and real estate tables. For a free copy, call (301) 588–0681 or log onto www.petrapub.com/newcomer/dc.

• Operation Match: A home-sharing service for the region sponsored by the Metropolitan Washington Council of Governments. This program matches singles, single parents with one child, or small families to those who have space to rent in their homes and is ideal for those who wish to "test the waters" before making a long-term buying or renting decision. Call (202) 962–3716 for a recorded list of locations.

• Corporations are the main clients of Runzheimer International, which provides cost of living data on major U.S. markets; however, individuals can also obtain less extensive information for a cost of about $20. Call Runzheimer International at (800) 942–9949 or see the Web site, www.runzheimer.com.

Relocation Guidelines

We're assuming that if you're reading this section, that you're either thinking about moving to Washington or are deep into the process. You may have already arrived. The following tips are intended to help you with this transition:

• Keep the family involved in all discussions: Although the biggest decisions already have been made, it is imperative that even the youngest family members continue to feel like they are part of the relocating process, that they have a say as a newcomer.

• Sever the moving ties—unpack: It sounds so simple, but you'd be amazed how many people are still living out of boxes six months, sometimes even a year, after their move. Stories abound of young Capitol Hill staffers who come to Washington, work for two years, and leave without ever unpacking all their belongings. The quicker the boxes are emptied, the sooner your new place actually feels like home.

• Move into the culture: Don't drop long-held interests or traditions just because you've moved. If the kids were in Cub Scouts in St. Louis, get them in Cub Scouts here. If you were a member of a garden club in Boston, join one here. If you were into white-water rafting in Colorado, investigate the opportunities in these parts. At the same time, explore the myriad new possibilities unique to the Washington area.

• Get out and see the city and the region: It's somewhat natural to hibernate after a move, given all the unpacking and home maintenance logistics that loom. Try to budget time, even if it's just for an hour or two on weekends, to play tourist. You'll find that this will do wonders for reducing stress and, at the same time, will likely inspire a sense of pride in your new hometown.

• Drop the guilt trip about uprooting the kids: Although relocating can be traumatic for youngsters and teens, they're much more malleable than we may think. If you haven't made your final decision about when to move, don't feel that you must smooth the way for the kids with a summer transition. It used to be that parents were advised to wait and move during the summer, so the kids wouldn't have to be uprooted during the school year. Now, conventional wisdom has it that it's better for kids to move during the school year, even if it's just a few weeks before the summer break. They'll have a chance to get acclimated to their school and make friends before summer vacation.

• Stock up on regional and local maps: Coming to grips with Metro Washington's patchwork of roads and highways can be as trying as advanced calculus. Maps are required reading here and the best in the land can be had through the Alexandria Drafting Company (ADC) of Alexandria, Virginia. You'll see their maps in virtually all the area's bookshops, as well as in most grocery and convenience stores. For more information, call ADC at (703) 750-0510 or visit the Web site: www.adcmap.com.

• Make trial runs to places of work, school, etc.: A little planning here will greatly improve your mental health. Make the trial commutes during normal rush hours or the approximate times you'll be going to these places. Experiment with different routes and always have a contingency plan. We can't stress enough the importance of following this step.

• Subscribe immediately to a community newspaper and the *Washington Post* and/or the *Washington Times,* the region's two largest daily newspapers. We may be biased here, but there's still no better information access to Metro Washington than through the printed word. Tapping into the Fourth Estate is really the first step in becoming part of the community.

• Get involved with state societies, alumni groups, or embassy cultural programs. Homesickness is a natural consequence of relocation. Fortunately, the Washington area has a plethora of remedies. Virtually every state has a state society—a social and networking group—based in Washington. Chances are your alma mater also has an alumni chapter in Washington. If they don't, you may consider organizing one. Most embassies offer some type of cultural programming, whether it's through open houses, lecture series, or social clubs, for international newcomers. (See related information in the International Washington chapter.)

Child Care

As we have mentioned at least a couple of times by now, Metro Washington is a wonderful place to live and—as many people happily discover—raise children. Few places can match the abundance of stimulating cultural, educational, historical, and recreational outlets for youngsters to pursue. Here's a brief look at child care, an important consideration in an area where many household budgets may only be fulfilled with two incomes.

First, here are a few words about what to expect from this chapter. Like some of the other subjects we've covered, child care is one that could easily be the sole focus of an entire book. Because Washington-area residents can choose from literally thousands of child-care options, to present a complete rundown with descriptions, services, and other information is simply not possible here. Instead, we've tried to provide a primer on the subject, combining sound advice for choosing child-care facilities with a listing of agencies, nonprofit organizations, and referral agencies. The experts there can answer specific questions and help parents make decisions.

Few quality-of-life issues have become as important to families in recent years as the availability of top-notch child care, something that experts agree is crucial to a child's well-being and healthy development. As with any large expenditure, especially one involving a family member, parents should carefully weigh the various options and talk with relatives, friends, neighbors, and co-workers who have experience in this area.

Whether you're in search of a chain-affiliated commercial day-care center, a private in-home operation, a program associated with a school or religious institution, or something tailored to the special needs of groups such as the physically challenged, the learning disabled, and the non-English-speaking, you're sure to find it in the Washington area. A scan through the Yellow Pages, a community directory, or a listing provided by a human services agency will quickly confirm the wealth of choices available.

The High Cost of Care

Just as housing, groceries and other necessities tend to cost more in Metro Washington than in many parts of the nation, the same holds true for child care. Indeed, it can be one of the biggest financial issues for parents with moderate incomes, particularly if they don't have in-home offices, the luxury of subsidized day-care centers at work, or nearby relatives who can help out.

Typically, according to the Fairfax County Office for Children, full-time child care for infants and toddlers costs from $125 to $245 weekly in a private home, and $165 to $225 weekly at a child-care center. Preschool-age child care ranges from $100 to $155 weekly in a private home, and $110 to $175 weekly at a center. Before- and after-school care for school-age children costs $60 to $80 a week, or $3.00 to $5.00 an hour in a private home, $60 to $80 or $3.00 to $5.00 an hour at a center. Your best bet is to sign up as early as possible. Before- and after-school programs in particular often start taking first-come, first-serve applications in early spring before the next school year. The Fairfax Office notes that it has been giving out these cost estimates for several years, so the actual costs could be higher.

A growing segment of the child-care sector in Metro Washington involves in-home operations, often classified by licensing agencies as family day-care homes. Their popularity is a reflection not only of the region's number one national ranking in the number of working women, but also of the high cost of living here. Many people opt to set up child-care operations in their homes, providing a much-needed source of income without having to commute to faraway offices. Like other child-care facilities, private homes must be licensed, insured, inspected, and otherwise held to certain standards for safety, health, and sanitation. Also, those caring for more than five children (although the number may vary slightly in different jurisdictions) must obtain special permits and licenses from local and state authorities.

Parents who wish to examine licensing standards may request comprehensive booklets published by the area's licensing agencies: the D.C. Department of Consumer and Regulatory Affairs in Washington, the Virginia Department of Social Services in Virginia, or the Maryland Department of Human Resources in Maryland. (State guidelines are available through local government offices listed later in this chapter.) Regulations vary slightly among the three jurisdictions, but to receive licenses child-care centers and homes generally must meet requirements adhering to staff-to-children ratios (as small as one caregiver to four children younger than age 2 in centers, and one caregiver to two children in family day-care settings), providing developmentally appropriate activities, following safety precautions with furnishings and equipment, administering authorized health procedures, keeping records for each child, and maintaining a sanitary, smoke-free, drug-free environment.

Finding the Right Option

Remember that just because a child-care facility is licensed after meeting the minimum requirements, it doesn't necessarily guarantee your child a stimulating, high-quality educational experience. When considering a facility, observe the staff, the other children, and the indoor and outdoor spaces. Ask about the daily routine, nutrition, exercise, learning activities and materials, fees and payment schedules, child/staff ratio, extent of parental involvement, and other factors that are important to you.

Other types of child care include day-care centers, where group care is provided for children typically of ages six weeks to five years. These centers are open for full days all year, and some provide transportation. Nursery schools and preschools offer group care for the preschool-age child but may not be open full days or all year. Extended day-care programs, meanwhile, offer supervised settings for school-age children when school is not in session. Besides providing before- and after-school care, the programs—much to the delight of parents—often cover snow days and holidays, and some have full-day summer programs.

Nannies—private, full-time, and sometimes live-in—offer another option, although it is more expensive. Local child-care agencies often have lists of individual nannies or nanny services, or at least can put you in touch with sources that do. Weekly salaries for full-time nannies range from $250 to $600, with live-out nannies earning about $50 a week more than live-in nannies. If choosing a nanny through a placement agency, parents can expect to pay a registration/application fee of $75 or more and, on hiring, a placement fee of $1,500 or more.

Parents seeking a nanny should pay attention to the type of screening—such as criminal, background, and Social Security checks—required by an agency. Consider the person's experience, age, whether he or she smokes, whether the nanny has a valid driver's license, and whether he or she can speak English. Families planning to hire a live-in nanny should be prepared to provide a private room and bath, preferably on a separate level; a private phone line; and use of a car.

The au pair (French for "as an equal") program is perhaps the most unusual and interesting child-care option, and one that probably will continue to increase in popularity as the global society becomes further pronounced. It's little wonder that au pairs are popular in Metro Washington, with the region's strong multiethnic character and well-traveled populace. Au pair is an international youth exchange program organized to create cross-cultural understanding and cooperation between American families and Western European young adults. Sanctioned by the United States Information Agency (USIA), the program provides a great opportunity for young people from overseas to learn about American culture and family life while living in the United States, and it also serves as a wonderful learning experience for the hosts. The program typically involves au pairs between the ages of 18 and 25 who come to the United States for a year and care for the host family's children. Reciprocal programs allow American youths to perform these services in Europe.

Although most au pair experiences are positive for both young people and host families, it's not something for a family to enter into lightly. Veteran host families, as well as the organizations listed later in this chapter, can help steer prospective hosts in the right direction. Besides what can be a rewarding, memorable, cross-cultural experience, the au pair program can also mean cost savings for a family, compared with other types of in-home child care. Stipends average about $160 per week for 45 hours of child care, but bear in mind that host families must also be prepared to pay $200 or more for the application, $500 for tuition, and $3,000 to $4,000 for program fees that cover airfare, insurance, and child safety instruction.

All of these choices may seem mindboggling, but the following resources can help you narrow down your options and zero in on the best situation for your family.

Local Government-Based Child-Care Resources

For listings of the child-care centers in your area, tips on what to look for, guidelines, requirements, financial assistance, and other information on any facet of child care, contact the appropriate agencies in your jurisdiction.

Washington, D.C.

Department of Health—Licensing, Regulation, and Administration
825 N. Capitol St. NE, 2nd Floor
Washington, DC
(202) 442–5929

This department licenses and monitors child development facilities, home and center-based day care, and foster homes.

Office of Early Childhood Development
717 14th St. NW, Ste. 730
Washington, DC
(202) 727–1839, (202) 310–2020 (recording)
www.dhs.washington.dc.us/prog_cit_service

This office of the Department of Human Services provides financial assistance for day care for children ages 6 weeks to 14 years and for disabled children to age 15. The recorded message is available 24 hours

Insiders' Tip

The Parent Warmline is a free phone service for parents who need help dealing with their children. Anyone can call (301) 942-5374 with concerns about child development and behavior and other family issues. Trained volunteers provide empathy and support, information, practical advice, and referrals to community resources. A "service of first resort," the Parent Warmline seeks to provide the help that parents need when they need it—before problems become overwhelming.

a day, providing information about day-care provider training opportunities and education programs geared to parents.

Washington Child Development Council
2121 Decatur Pl. NW
Washington, DC
(202) 387–0002
Contact the council for referrals and other child-care resources.

Northern Virginia

City of Alexandria
Child Care Information Services
2525 Mt. Vernon Ave.
Alexandria, VA
(703) 838–0750
This service of the Office for Early Childhood Development in the city's Department of Human Services registers and trains child-care providers and provides lists of licensed centers, nurseries and preschools, in-home day care, before- and after-school programs, and summer camps.

Arlington County
Child and Family Services
1801 N. George Mason Dr.
Arlington, VA
(703) 228–5101
The county's child-care office licenses family day care, preschools, and centers and offers free referral lists.

Public Schools Extended Day Program
2801 Clarendon Blvd., Ste. 312
Arlington, VA
(703) 228–6069
Contact this division for details about the supervised before- and after-school recreational program offered in elementary and middle schools.

Fairfax County
Department of Family Services Office for Children
12011 Government Center Pkwy.
Fairfax, VA
(703) 324–8100
www.co.fairfax.va.us/childcare
This early childhood education agency

Good day-care centers provide opportunities for creative expression.

includes the following programs, each of which has its own phone number: You can also search for child care online

Child and Adult Care Food Program
8th Fl.
(703) 324–8019
This program provides nutrition education and food cost assistance for child-care providers.

Child Care Assistance Program
8th Fl.
(703) 449–8484
This office subsidizes day-care costs for low- and moderate-income families and offers parent education classes.

Child Care Resource System
9th Fl.
(703) 449–9555
Parents can contact this office for lists of child-care providers throughout the county.

Child Care Training Programs
8th Fl.
(703) 324–8043
Child-care providers can contact this office to enroll in training courses.

Employer Child Care Council
9th Fl.
(703) 324–8075
This office promotes on-the-job child care and early education.

Head Start Programs
9th Fl.
(703) 324–8290
This national program offers early childhood and parent education classes to low-income families.

Permits and Regulation
8th Fl.
(703) 324–8000
This division inspects and issues permits for family child-care homes.

School-Age Child Care Program
9th Fl.
(703) 449–8989

SACC provides before- and after-school and summer programs at county elementary schools.

City of Fairfax
Human Services Coordinator
10455 Armstrong St.
Fairfax, VA
(703) 385–7894
This office provides a list of licensed child care providers within the city.

City of Falls Church
Housing and Human Services
300 Park Ave.
Falls Church, VA
(703) 248–5005
This office provides a directory of day-care homes, preschools, and child-care centers and also provides one-on-one guidance to both parents and caregivers.

Office of Community Education—Extended Day Care Office
7124 Leesburg Pike
Falls Church, VA
(703) 248–5683
Contact this office for information about the before- and after-school child-care program.

Loudoun County
Department of Social Services
102 Heritage Way NE
Leesburg, VA
(703) 777–0353
This department provides a list of day-care providers, both facilities and individuals.

Prince William County
Department of Social Services/Child Care Options
15941 Cardinal Dr.
Woodbridge, VA
(703) 792–4300
www.pwcgov.org/DSS/childcare_home.htm
The office handles research and referrals of licensed day-care providers. It also provides certification and training and operates the USDA food program.

Suburban Maryland

Montgomery County

The Arc of Montgomery County
Family, Infant and Child-Care Center
1600 Nebel St.
Rockville, MD
(301) 279–2165
www.arcmontmd.org

This specialized center offers care for children between the ages of six weeks and five years who have chronic medical conditions.

Children's Resource Center
332 W. Edmonston Dr., Rm. D4
Rockville, MD
(301) 279–1260

This building houses a variety of child-care oriented programs, including the following:

Locate Childcare
(301) 279–1773

This division of the Department of Health and Human Services offers the county's only approved child-care referral for licensed providers. It also trains prospective child-care providers.
Montgomery County Child Care
Administration
51 Monroe St., Ste. 200
Rockville, MD
(240) 314–1400

This division of the Department of Human Resources licenses and monitors child-care providers in Montgomery County.

Montgomery County Infant and Toddler
Program
401 Fleet St., Lower Level
Rockville, MD
(301) 279–1250

Parents with developmentally delayed young children can find services through this collaborative program of the Department of Health and Human Services and public schools. Special education and speech and language therapy are among the types of services available to county residents. Your tax dollars at work!

Parenting Resource Center
332 W. Edmonston Dr.
Rockville, MD
(301) 279–8497

The Parenting Resource Center is sponsored by Montgomery County Public Schools. It provides resources to parents and caregivers and it offers parenting and other types of enrichment classes at three different locations.

Wintergreen Child Development Center
Rm. B-1
332 W. Edmonston Dr.
Rockville, MD
(301) 424–7522

Part of the Rockville Day Care Association, this nonprofit center offers a year-round program to more than 100 children.

Prince George's County

Child Resource Center, Locate Child Care
9475 Lottsford Rd., Ste. 202
Largo, MD
(301) 772–8400

As part of the Prince George's Child Resource Center, which offers child-care information and training to parents and providers, Locate Child Care provides referrals to licensed child-care programs in the county. Information is free by phone, or $10 by mail, to cover shipping costs. The office is open 9:30 A.M. to 3:30 P.M. Monday through Friday. A computerized, 24-hour referral service, (900) 773–2273, costs $2.00 per minute. Call (301) 772–8420 for information about upcoming parent and provider training opportunities.

Helpful Organizations

Metropolitan Washington Council of Governments (COG)
777 N. Capitol St. NE, Ste. 300
Washington, DC
(202) 962–3200
www.mwcog.org

COG, as it's often called, is an excellent source for child-care information and virtually anything else you can think of in

Playtime outside, weather permitting, is part of the daily routine at most day-care centers.

which local governments play some sort of role. COG provides such resources as reports on the status of child care, guidelines for seeking quality child care, and scholarship coordination for child-care providers. As a vast information clearinghouse, COG also refers residents to other organizations, many of which are headquartered in Metro Washington.

National Association for the Education of Young Children (NAEYC)
1509 16th St. NW
Washington, DC
(202) 232–8777, (800) 424–2460
www.naeyc.org

Founded in 1926, NAEYC is the country's largest professional organization focused on promoting quality education for children ages eight and younger. Membership includes more than 400 local, state, and regional affiliated organizations. Among many other services, the association offers educational literature and videos and a national voluntary accreditation program for early childhood centers.

National Black Child Development Institute
1101 15th St. NW, Ste. 600
Washington, DC
(202) 833–2200
www.nbcdi.org

This nonprofit organization, founded in 1970, strives to improve the quality of life for African American children. It provides child-care resources to parents and professionals and offers leadership training in child care and education.

Parent Encouragement Program (PEP)
10100 Connecticut Ave.
Kensington, MD
(301) 929–8824
www.parentencouragement.org

PEP is a community-based program that offers in-depth classes and workshops for parents and professionals who want to deal more effectively with children. Its mission is the development of stronger, more encouraging families through step-by-step education, skill training, and support. Students rave about the classes, which are taught by parents who've gone through years of intensive PEP training.

Nannies

These agencies place part-time, full-time, live-in, and live-out nannies throughout the Washington metropolitan area. Unless otherwise indicated, they also provide short-term and, with at least four hours notice, emergency or sitter referrals. For long-term placement, try to call at least a month in advance.

A Choice Nanny
5110 Ridgefield Rd., Ste. 403
Bethesda, MD
(301) 652–2229
www.achoicenanny.com/bethesda

This highly rated agency interviews all candidates in person and offers basic training to nannies. It has a full range of services, including weekend and evening babysitters, temporary nannies, and after-school "tutorcare" nannies who also do chores.

Mothers' Aides Inc.
5618 Ox Rd.
Fairfax Station, VA
(703) 250–0700, (800) 526–2669
www.mothersaides.com

Founded in 1979, this agency is a member of NAEYC, an organization described in the Helpful Organizations section. It provides permanent, temporary, and on-call nannies.

Nannies, Inc.
3031 Borge St., Ste. 107
Oakton, VA
(301) 718–0100 (Bethesda)
(703) 255–5312 (Oakton)
www.nanniesinc.net

Washington Families newspaper voted this 12-year-old agency, founded by a single dad, the Best Nanny Service in the Washington metropolitan area. The agency places only long-term, full-service nannies.

Potomac Nannies, Ltd.
7315 Wisconsin Ave., Ste. 1300-W
Bethesda, MD
(301) 986–0048

This agency, which opened in 1985, places both live-in and live-out nannies.

TeacherCare
1701 E. Woodland Rd., #700
Schaumburg, IL 60173
(888) TEACH–07
(703) 204–0511
www.teachercare.com

All nannies in this program are educated in early childhood education, Montessori, gifted, special needs, psychology or related specialties. TeacherCare recently opened an office in Arlington, but most communication goes through its national headquarters in Illinois.

TLC Nannies
1000 Hertford St.
Herndon, VA
(703) 736–0594, (703) 838–8444

Tami L. Cox, a former nanny, provides customized nanny searches for individual families, who pay a consultation fee and expenses for such services as newspaper advertising, phone screening, and interviewing.

White House Nannies
7200 Wisconsin Ave.
Bethesda, MD
(301) 654–1242 (for permanent)
(301) 652–8088 (for temporary)
www.whitehousenannies.com

This 18-year-old agency began when the owner experienced frustration during her own nanny search.

Au Pairs

For more information about au pairs, contact one of the following organizations, which are sanctioned by the United States Information Agency (USIA) to recruit European participants and unite them with American families.

Au Pair in America, 102 Greenwich Ave., Greenwich, CT 06830; (203) 869-9090, (800) 928-7247

AuPairCare, 1 Post St., 7th Fl., San Francisco, CA 94104; (415) 434-8788, (800) 428-7247, www.aupaircare.com

Au Pair Programme U.S.A., 6965 Union Park Center, Ste. 100, Salt Lake City, UT 84047; (800) 574-8889

EF Au Pair, EF Center Boston, 1 Education St., Cambridge, MA 02141; (800) 333-6056, www.efaupair.org

EurAupair, 250 North Pacific Coast Hwy., Laguna Beach, CA 92651; (800) 618-2002, www.euraupair.com

AuPair U.S.A. InterExchange, 161 6th Ave., 13th Fl., New York, NY 10013; (212) 924-0446, (800) 287-2477, www.interexchange.com

Healthcare

The adult population of the Washington metropolitan area is healthier than the nation as a whole, according to a 2001 study by the Metropolitan Washington Council of Governments. For 19 of 27 health indicators, the Washington region is doing as well or better than the national average. And for coronary heart disease deaths and mammography rates, this region already more than meets national targets for 2010. On some measures, however, the region appears less healthy than the nation. These include AIDS, sexually transmitted infections, binge drinking, firearm-related deaths, and low-birth weight babies.

So it's good to know that anyone seeking medical care in the Metro Washington area can take comfort in knowing help is literally right around the corner. In D.C. proper, you can't travel more than a few blocks without encountering a hospital, medical clinic, or a building full of doctors' offices.

The National Capital area is home to some of the world's finest medical researchers and healthcare professionals, and four area hospitals are consistently ranked among the 100 best in America by U.S. News and World Report. Three of the four are Georgetown University Medical Center, Fairfax Hospital and Children's National Medical Center. The one with the most stellar reputation, however, is Johns Hopkins University Hospital, about an hour away in Baltimore, Maryland. Though it may be a little farther, if you're struck with a serious illness, it's worth the drive. In many specialties, Hopkins is ranked number one by *U.S. News Surveys* and is invariably in the top five.

Looking beyond Metro Washington and Maryland for a moment, there are two other acclaimed medical institutions: the University of Virginia Medical Center in Charlottesville and the Medical College of Virginia in Richmond.

This chapter, however, sticks closer to home and offers an overview of approximately 50 major hospitals and other medical facilities in Metro Washington, including the teaching and research hospitals affiliated with university medical schools that play a vital role in the training of future doctors, nurses, and other healthcare professionals. We've also included some mental health facilities and touched on the popular walk-in medical centers where minor illnesses and injuries can be quickly treated (see the Emergency Numbers listed toward the end of this chapter). One caveat: By the time you read this, some of the names may have changed because takeovers by large managed-care organizations are ongoing.

We have intentionally omitted a list of hospices, because physicians or hospitals generally refer patients after initial medical treatment. There are, however, more than a dozen in the Washington metro area, and they are easily found in the Yellow Pages or through physician referrals. Also, an excellent clearinghouse for information on hospices and their services is the National Hospice Organization, 1901 North Moore Street, Arlington, Virginia, (703) 243–5900. Don't forget that all local governments offer community health clinics and other local treatment facilities, included in the government listings in the phone book.

Finding the Right Doctor: Physician Referrals

Although finding a hospital may be easy, the same doesn't always apply to finding the right doctor. So before delving too deeply into the hospital world, we've compiled a listing of some free dental and physician referral services—some of which are affiliated with area hospitals and some of which are financed by subscribing doctors. Aside from those listed here, almost every hospital we've named in this chapter has a referral service listed in the phone book along with the hospital's other departments. In most cases the referral services can provide access to hundreds of medical professionals in a wide range of fields and specialties. Caution: Because these services are often financed by those who stand to benefit, you may wish to check with the licensing board for credentials.

In Maryland, the state licensing board is at 4201 Patterson Avenue, Baltimore, MD 21215; (410) 764–4777, www.md.doc. board.org. In Washington, D.C., write to 614 H Street NW, Room 108, Washington, DC 20001; (202) 442–9200, www.dchealth. gov; and in Virginia, 6606 West Broad St., 4th floor, Richmond, VA 23230; (804) 662–9900, www.dht.state.va.us.

To get started here is a short list of some of the area's most popular referral services. It is by no means comprehensive, but it touches on most counties in Metro Washington:

Prologue, (800) DOCTORS
Inova HealthSource, (703) 204–3366, www.nova.org
Montgomery General Hospital Physician Referral Service, (888) 376–8881
Physician Match, (301) 896–3939

State hospital associations—smaller versions of the American Hospital Association—can be a valuable resource for information on medical facilities in Maryland, Virginia, and Washington, D.C. Just contact the public relations office at the appropriate organization: Maryland Hospital Association, 6820 Deerpath Road, Elkridge, MD 21075, (410) 379–6200. www.mdhospitals.org; Virginia Hospital and Healthcare Association, P.O. Box 31394, Richmond, VA 23294, (804) 747–8600, www.vhha.com; District of Columbia Hospital Association,1250 Eye Street NW, Suite 700, Washington, DC 20005, (202) 682–1581, www.dcha.org.

Most hospitals featured in this chapter offer community outreach health and education programs (CPR, smoking cessation, weight reduction, family planning and child birth, stress management, etc.), as well as speakers bureaus, outpatient testing, surgery and treatment programs, and other services beyond the usual realm of a hospital's everyday role. Many services are free, but call the individual facilities to find out more.

With one exception, we have not included any of the military or veterans hospitals because they don't serve the general public. If you are a newcomer seeking information on veteran's hospitals, contact the Veterans' Affairs Medical Center at (202) 745–8000.

Hospitals

Washington, D.C.

Children's National Medical Center
111 Michigan Ave. NW
Washington, DC
(202) 884–5000
www.cnmc.org

When children are seriously ill or hurt, this is one of the top places they can go for treatment—and the patients aren't from just Metro Washington. Children's National Medical Center, often referred to as Children's Hospital, is recognized as one of the preeminent medical-care providers to infants, children, and youths in the entire mid-Atlantic region. Some 75 percent of pediatricians in Metro Washington have trained here.

No one enjoys being hospitalized, particularly kids. Children's recognizes the trauma of hospitalization for children; since 1910 there has been a "rooming in" program for parents. Founded in 1870—although the present 272-bed facility opened in 1977—Children's is a private, nonprofit hospital with two comprehensive-care branch clinics in Washington, D.C. and several clinics in Maryland and Virginia.

Emergency trauma care is perhaps Children's best-known service, but the hospital's expertise extends well into other areas, including cardiology, sports medicine, genetics, plastic and reconstructive surgery, infectious diseases, neonatology, psychiatry, and physical therapy. Naturally, Children's is very active in the research field, with special emphasis on AIDS, sickle cell anemia, and autism.

The George Washington University Medical Center
901 23rd St. NW
Washington, DC
(202) 994–1000
www.gwumc.edu/

One of the area's most comprehensive healthcare and education centers, the 501-bed George Washington University Medical Center was founded in 1824 at the former Washington Infirmary on 16th Street NW. It moved to its present facility in Foggy Bottom in 1947. Private and nonprofit, it is composed of three entities: the University Hospital; Medical Faculty Associates, a full-time physician group practice; and the School of Public Health and Health Services.

A major teaching and research facility, "GW" is involved in research projects costing in the tens of millions annually (see the Education chapter also). The Medical Center has three research institutes: the Institute for Biomedical Sciences, the Institute for Clinical Research and Clinical Trials, and the Institute for Health Policy and Human Values. As could be expected from such a comprehensive healthcare facility, a broad range of services is offered, including women's health, alternative medicine, OB-GYN, orthopedics, infertility treatment, surgery, psychiatric services, internal medicine, sports medicine, speech pathology, and audiology. In addition the hospital is a level 1 trauma center with a busy 24-hour emergency room.

Perhaps its most visible claim to fame is as the hospital to which President Reagan was transported when he was shot by John Hinckley. As you know, the president was successfully treated and went on to serve another term, a testament to the fine care he received from GW physicians.

Georgetown University Hospital
3800 Reservoir Rd. NW
Washington, DC
(202) 784–3000
www.georgetown.edu/gumc

Probably the city's most prestigious teaching hospital, Georgetown University Hospital was founded in 1898 and went on to break new ground by offering such conveniences as a special entrance for horse-drawn ambulances—modern indeed for its time. Today's 535-bed facility, which opened in 1948, is located in tony upper Northwest on a residential street lined with gracious mansions and diplomatic residences. The hospital, like its namesake university (see the Education chapter), is highly regarded internationally, and a top-flight team of doctors, nurses, and other personnel have access to the most advanced technology in every clinical discipline.

The hospital has distinguished itself as a medical research hub and is known as an ultramodern teaching facility. Pioneering efforts at Georgetown led to later successes with heart-valve implants, while work today continues in disciplines such as cancer research, magnetic resonance imaging (MRI), and specialized perinatal and neonatal care. The Lombardi Cancer Center, founded in 1970, is one of only 50 comprehensive cancer centers in the U.S. that receive such a designation from the National Cancer Institute. The full range of services at the Medical Center includes OB-GYN, pediatrics, neurology, orthopedics, emergency medicine, internal medicine, and radiology.

Greater Southeast Community Hospital
1310 Southern Ave. SE
Washington, DC
(202) 574–6000

Greater Southeast Community Hospital, founded in 1966, is a 450-bed facility that serves over 400,000 city residents annually. It's the largest and most comprehen-

Georgetown University Hospital is a nonprofit, acute-care teaching and research facility and home to renowned Lombardi Cancer Center. PHOTO: COURTESY OF GEORGETOWN UNIVERSITY HOSPITAL

sive hospital of its kind in the immediate area. After D.C. General Hospital closed in 2001, GSCH took on the public hospital's former patients, particularly those needing emergency services.

GSCH offers a fairly broad range of surgical and medical services, including OB-GYN, pediatrics, neurology, orthopedics, emergency and internal medicine, radiology, family practice, ophthalmology, adult psychiatry, cancer screening, a diabetes management unit, geriatric assessment, oncology, neonatal intensive care, pathology, renal dialysis, and cardiology.

The Hospital for Sick Children
1731 Bunker Hill Rd. NE
Washington, DC
(202) 832–4400
www.hfscsite.org

The Hospital for Sick Children is another of the city's smaller (131 beds) healthcare

centers with a unique role: that of a pediatric "transitional care" facility—the only one of its kind in Metro Washington— that serves as a link between hospital and home. Here, the young patients are treated for respiratory and chronic illnesses and a host of other disabilities.

Founded in 1883 as a "fresh air" summer home, the present facility opened in 1968. Services focus on a wide range of therapies, including physical, occupational, recreational, nutritional, respiratory, speech, and language.

Howard University Hospital
2041 Georgia Ave. NW
Washington, DC
(202) 865–6100
www.huhosp.org

The second oldest of Washington D.C.'s three major university-based teaching and research medical centers, 550-bed Howard

University Hospital has come a long way since its founding in 1863 as Freedman's Hospital, a name that in itself speaks of history. The federal government created Freedman's as an emergency facility to treat the thousands of sick, destitute former slaves who poured into Washington after gaining their freedom. The Howard University Hospital of today opened in 1975 and remains synonymous with African American advancement (some of the nation's top black medical professionals, beginning with Dr. Charles Drew, a pioneer in blood plasma preservation, have been trained here). The school itself, meanwhile, ranks as one of the nation's leading, historically African American universities (see the Education chapter).

Howard is the third-largest private hospital and one of the busiest hospitals in Metro Washington, with annual inpatient admissions of around 13,000 and emergency room visits topping 53,000. Special services for the community include screening and counseling for sickle cell anemia, cancer screening, drug and alcohol addiction treatment, and renal dialysis.

Underscoring its role as a major healthcare provider, the hospital's vast range of services includes OB-GYN; pediatrics; neurology; orthopedics; internal medicine; radiology; family practice; ophthalmology; oncology; dentistry; dermatology; plastic and reconstructive surgery; neurosurgery; radiotherapy; psychiatric services for children, adolescents and adults; physical and occupational therapy; sports medicine; and areas dealing with infectious disease.

National Rehabilitation Hospital
102 Irving St. NW
Washington, DC
(202) 877–1000
www.nrhrehab.org

National Rehabilitation Hospital is a godsend for those severely disabled through accident or illness. It is the first and only freestanding facility in Metro Washington dedicated solely to thorough medical rehabilitation, with the aim of helping patients on to active and satisfying lives. The 160-bed hospital offers a host of inpatient and outpatient medical rehabilitation services, including driver evaluation and training, social work, neuropsychology, nutrition, physical therapy, speech and language pathology, and therapeutic recreation.

The hospital is particularly designed for those who are physically disabled by spinal cord and brain injuries, stroke, arthritis, postpolio syndrome, amputation, and other orthopedic and neurological conditions; a 40-bed unit is reserved solely for brain-injury patients. Besides its role as a rehabilitation center, NRH serves as a strong advocacy voice for the disabled.

Providence Hospital
1150 Varnum St. NE
Washington, DC
(202) 269–7000
wwwprovhosp.org

Providence is yet another District hospital with intriguing Civil War roots. Established in 1861 by four Catholic nuns in a renovated mansion, its original role was to care for the civilian population as the fighting between North and South raged. As luck would have it, Providence was the city's only medical facility not taken over by the military during the war. It is the only private hospital in Washington that has remained in continuous operation since.

Established at its present site in 1954, today's 382-bed Providence Hospital specializes in obstetrics and women's healthcare, geriatrics, and a full range of acute and emergency services. It also has a 240-bed nursing and rehabilitation center. Other programs include orthopedics, internal medicine, family practice, ophthalmology, infertility treatment, cardiology, psychiatric services for adults, substance abuse diagnosis, and physical and occupational therapy.

Sibley Memorial Hospital
5255 Loughboro Rd. NW
Washington, DC
(202) 537–4000
www.sibley.org

Sibley is yet another example of a truly "community" hospital, occupying a wooded parcel on a quiet residential street in upper Northwest. The 328-bed facility is also another example of a District medical center with a nineteenth-century heritage; it was founded in 1890 as a nurse-training school for deaconesses and missionaries. The hospital itself came later and was named in honor of William J. Sibley, an early supporter of the school's work, who donated $10,000 for the construction of the medical center in memory of his wife. The current building and site, however, date only to 1961. An extensive renovation and modernization program was completed in 1990.

Sibley has made its mark primarily as a surgical center, both inpatient and out. Specialties include eye and plastic surgeries, a wide range of programs for the elderly, and a sleep disorders center. Services include emergency medicine, family practice, internal medicine, neurology, OB-GYN, oncology, occupational and physical therapy, ophthalmology, orthopedics, radiology, and psychiatry for adults. It also has a residential Alzheimer's unit and an assisted living residence. Unlike the teaching hospitals or publicly founded ones, Sibley is noted for more personalized attention to patients—maybe the word should be *pampering*. So if you're having elective surgery, you might want to treat yourself to one of the private hotel-like "suites" that Sibley offers. After all, what better time to coddle yourself than when you're in the hospital?

The Washington Hospital Center
110 Irving St. NW
Washington, DC
(202) 877–7000
www.whcenter.org
Medlantic Healthcare Group and Helix Health merged in 1998 to form MedStar Health, one of the largest not-for-profit health systems in the East. The flagship hospital in the system, Washington Hospital Center, is the largest private teaching hospital in Washington, D.C. and a hub for research and education. Founded in 1958, the 900-bed facility has developed into one of Metro Washington's top medical centers with special emphasis on emergency shock-trauma care for the critically ill and injured, many of whom arrive via MedSTAR, the acclaimed air ambulance service. It serves more than 200,000 patients annually.

Washington Hospital Center's expansive list of facilities and services includes a comprehensive burn center and cardiology unit, organ transplantation, high-risk maternal fetal care, cancer and eye disorders, neurology, OB-GYN, orthopedics, radiology, oral surgery, neurosurgery, and treatment for diabetes, cancer, and eye disorders.

Northern Virginia

City of Alexandria
The Inova Alexandria Hospital
4320 Seminary Rd.
Alexandria, VA
(703) 504–3000
www.inova.com
The Inova Alexandria Hospital is the primary provider of medical services for city residents. It's also a primary provider of jobs, ranking as Alexandria's largest private employer with 1,600 workers and more than 700 physicians. Established in 1872, the hospital occupied five sites before the present 339-bed, nonprofit facility opened in 1962.

The hospital has one of the top cardiac surgery units in the area with advanced

> ## Insiders' Tip
> Most community hospitals in the metro area offer deluxe hotel-style wings suitable for those having elective surgery, or who simply wish for added comfort and better cuisine. Count on spending an extra $150 to $250 per day.

cardiac care, including preventative medicine, chest pain emergency service, and cardiopulmonary rehabilitation. Emergency medicine is also a specialty, and for good reason: Alexandria was the first hospital in the nation to staff its emergency department with full-time emergency physicians, a standard practice today at most major medical facilities. For minor emergencies when a private physician isn't available, the hospital offers an Express Care Center in the hospital's emergency department. There, you might be seen by a nurse or a nurse practitioner, although physicians are also on staff.

Cancer treatment is also a specialty at Alexandria Hospital, which houses the Northern Virginia Cancer Center. Other services include a birthing center, a neonatal intensive care unit, dialysis, a blood donor center, respiratory therapy, and a same-day surgery center for outpatients.

Inova Mount Vernon Hospital
2501 Parkers La.
Alexandria, VA
(703) 664–7000
www.inova.com

Alexandria's other major medical facility, Mount Vernon Hospital is a 232-bed nonprofit community hospital that opened in 1976. Like Inova Alexandria, it's a member of the Inova Health System, a nonprofit, community-based organization that also includes Inova Fair Oaks and Inova Fairfax hospitals (see subsequent entries). The system also offers home healthcare, long-term care, and behavioral services.

Located near its historic namesake, the hospital provides a full range of medical and surgical services, primarily to residents of Alexandria and southeastern Fairfax County. Services include 24-hour emergency medicine, a psychiatric unit for adolescents and adults, and a range of programs relating to cardiology, cancer, physical medicine, and rehabilitation. Its 350 physicians represent a wide spectrum of the healthcare field. Diagnostic services offered include magnetic resonance imaging, digital angiography, ultrasound, echocardiogram, cardiac catheterization,

stress tests, and mammography.

Perhaps Mount Vernon's broadest special service is the Inova Rehabilitation Center where patients receive comprehensive care and therapy for stroke, orthopedic injuries, head and spinal cord injuries, amputation, multiple sclerosis, arthritis, workplace injuries, and other neuromuscular disorders. The center includes an inpatient acute-care unit. The Inova Joint Replacement Center received a Mercury Award for its top-rate program from the American Health Network.

Arlington County

Northern Virginia Community Hospital
601 S. Carlin Springs Rd.
Arlington, VA
(703) 671–1200
www.nvchospital.com

Arlington's third major medical facility used to be known as the Northern Virginia Doctors Hospital and later Vencor Hospital, and many still refer to it as such. The Northern Virginia Community Hospital is a 164-bed medical/surgical and psychiatric facility that opened in 1961. The hospital offers a full range of psychiatric services, surgical services including ambulatory minimally invasive surgery, and a full range of medical specialties: gynecology, urology, neurosurgery, orthopedics, gastroenterology and endoscopy, neurology, and infectious diseases.

There's also an on-campus MRI center, computerized tomography, 24-hour emergency care, cardiac catheterization, nu-clear medicine, and an accredited diagnostic clinical lab service.

Virginia Hospital Center, Arlington
1701 N. George Mason Dr.
Arlington, VA
(703) 558–5000
www.virginiahospitalcenter.net

Arlington County's largest and most comprehensive healthcare facility is Virginia Hospital Center, a 334-bed, nonprofit teaching hospital affiliated with Georgetown University's School of Medicine and several nursing schools. Open since 1944, it's well-known locally not only for fine medical and surgical services

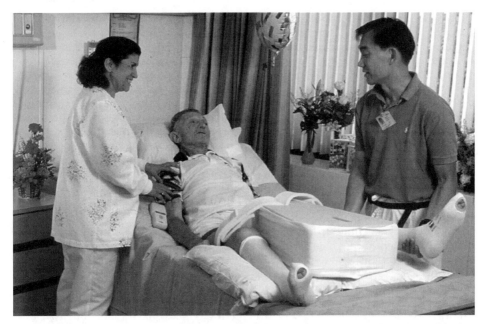

Inova Health System is known for its orthopedics and rehabilitation services as well as advanced cardiac care. PHOTO: ADAM B. AUEL, COURTESY OF INOVA HEALTH SYSTEM

but also as the hospital of the Washington Redskins, because the team's medical staff has privileges here.

With more than 700 physicians, Arlington Hospital offers a wide range of services including a 24-hour emergency department, treatment for adult alcoholism and other drug addictions, OB-GYN, high-risk nursery, open-heart surgery, outpatient clinics, physical medicine and rehabilitation, psychiatric treatment, and numerous diagnostic and therapeutic services, such as nuclear medicine, radiation therapy, and respiratory therapy. A $150 million expansion project will double the size of the emergency room and convert all semiprivate rooms to private rooms.

Fairfax County

Columbia-Dominion Hospital
2960 Sleepy Hollow Rd.
Falls Church, VA
(703) 538-2872
www.dominionhospital.com

Columbia-Dominion, owned by the Columbia Healthcare giant, is one of Northern Virginia's leading mental-health care centers for children, adolescents, and adults. "First Step," a free, confidential mental-health information, assessment, and referral service, offers assistance in various crisis situations, including suicide attempts and threats, substance abuse and other addictive illnesses, eating disorders, serious and prolonged depression, acute stress reactions, uncontrollable fears, behavioral problems in children and adolescents, sexual abuse, childhood trauma, and sleep disorders.

Columbia-Fairfax Surgical Center
10730 Main St.
Fairfax City, VA
(703) 691–0670

For outpatient surgical services without having to go to an actual hospital, many people opt for a facility such as Columbia-Fairfax Surgical Center, part of a national network. Offering what it calls "efficient, personal care in a pleasant atmosphere," the center charges a single fee that covers basic medical history, equipment and most supplies, routine drugs and anesthetics, recovery room services, and operating room time. Be aware, though, that the price does not include the professional services of the surgeon or assistants, the anesthesiologist, radiologist, pathologist, physician consultants, and pharmacist.

Inova Fair Oaks Hospital
3600 Joseph Siewick Dr.
Fairfax, VA
(703) 391–3600
www.inova.com

Inova Fair Oaks Hospital was one of two hospitals built in Fairfax County in the 1980s—in this case, 1987. The other was Reston Hospital Center (see subsequent entry). Its newness is underscored in such design features as bed-mounted telephones and nurse call buttons, wall-to-wall carpeting in patients' rooms, private televisions with in-room movies, solariums, gourmet meals, and rooms with deluxe amenities. The 151-bed, 950-employee facility is part of the Inova Health System that includes Alexandria, Mount Vernon, and Fairfax Hospitals. A western Fairfax location—just off U.S. 50 at I–66—makes Fair Oaks Hospital convenient to many county residents beyond its core service area of Chantilly, Reston, and Fairfax.

More than 900 physicians covering dozens of specialties have privileges at Fair Oaks, which can handle emergency, medical, surgical, critical-care, cardiac, orthopedic, obstetric, and pediatric patients. The 24-hour emergency department offers a helipad located just outside the doors. Two additions focus on the care and treatment of young patients: a maternal and infant health center (which opened in 1988), emphasizing a family-centered approach

to the birth process, and a children's unit (1990) specially equipped for infants and children through age 18. In-house pediatricians are available 24 hours a day.

Inova Fair Oaks also offers comprehensive sleep evaluations for patients suffering from sleep apnea, insomnia, chronic fatigue, and other problems related to sleep disorders.

Inova Fairfax Hospital
3300 Gallows Rd.
Fairfax, VA
(703) 698–1110
www.inova.com

This 656-bed, nonprofit regional medical center, the flagship hospital of the Inova Health System, is Northern Virginia's only level I emergency and trauma center, meaning it can handle the most critical illnesses and accidents. Fairfax has Northern Virginia's only pediatric intensive-care unit with 24-hour care. Helicopters are a familiar sight here.

Opened in 1961, Fairfax Hospital has seen tremendous growth over the years during its emergence as one of Metro Washington's premier medical facilities. In fact a major construction project now underway will add 177 beds and a new heart center by 2004. It's home to the nationally recognized Inova Heart Center where the region's first heart transplant was performed in 1986. The hospital was also the site of the area's first lung transplant (1991) and first heart-kidney combination transplant (1992). An amazingly busy obstetrics wing (actually its own building) has earned Fairfax its local nickname, "The Baby Factory." A total of 10,468 babies entered the world here in 2000, a figure that's the fourth highest in the nation. Indeed, babies are a specialty at Fairfax; there's even a unit for high-risk pregnancies, along with a neonatal intensive-care unit. The hospital offers the full range of other medical-surgical services and state-of-the-art technology, but it's also a major teaching hospital, affiliated with Georgetown and George Washington medical schools, the Medical College of Virginia, and nursing schools at George Mason and Marymount Universities and Northern Virginia Community College.

Insiders' Tip

Teaching hospitals may offer cutting-edge technology, but care will often be less personal than at community hospitals. If your procedure is simple, consider the latter.

Inova Fairfax Hospital for Children
3300 Gallows Rd.
Fairfax, VA
(703) 204–6777
www.inova.com

Inova Fairfax Hospital for Children is a comprehensive, highly specialized facility with more than 400 doctors, dedicated to caring for children through a full spectrum of pediatric services. The hospital provides everything from simple allergy relief to complex cardiac surgery. As a member of the national Children's Oncology Group, the hospital adheres to state-of-the-art protocols developed to treat childhood cancers. Its helicopter and ground transports, staffed by pediatric and neonatal nurse specialists, are designed especially for critically ill or injured children and infants.

Reston Hospital Center
1850 Town Center Pkwy.
Reston, VA
(703) 689–9000
www.restonhospital.com

With the opening of Reston Hospital Center in 1986, many residents of western Fairfax County, particularly those in Reston, Herndon, Great Falls, and parts of greater Vienna, realized the luxury of not having to travel across the county to Fairfax Hospital for comprehensive medical care. Residents of booming Eastern Loudoun County also visit this facility. To meet the growing area's needs, an expansion project will add 60 beds, and all of the hospital's rooms will be private. Its services are numerous and include most surgical and medical procedures as well as a 24-hour emergency room. Of particular note is its maternity center, pediatric center, and a new radiation oncology program. Now patients can receive complete cancer care, including surgery, chemotherapy, and radiation at Reston Hospital Center.

The same-day surgery department has seen significant growth in recent years, reflecting a national trend toward outpatient services. Reston Hospital Center is the "official" hospital of Washington Dulles International Airport due to its proximity, easy access (just a couple of minutes off the Dulles Toll Road and parallel Airport Access Road), and wide range of services.

Loudoun County

Loudoun Hospital Center
44045 Riverside Pkwy.
Leesburg, VA
(703) 858–6000
www.loudounhospital.org

The county's primary medical facility is the 80-bed Loudoun Hospital Center. Founded in 1912 as a six-room rural hospital, LHC has had five names through the years and today is the flagship facility of the nonprofit Loudoun Healthcare Inc., a growing network of affiliated services located throughout the county. LHC offers most major medical and surgical services, including 24-hour emergency medicine. Special features include an intensive care unit; an outpatient surgery department; comprehensive diagnostic imaging services; a birthing inn; a behavioral services unit; physical, occupational, and speech therapy; a pain management center; and business health management services. Its cardiopulmonary health center was one of Northern Virginia's first.

The hospital extends its community-outreach efforts to a new level with Lifeline, an electronic alert system that gives elderly residents or the severely disabled a direct connection to assistance (and no doubt provides family and friends with peace of mind).

Affiliated services include the Countryside Ambulatory Surgery Center (703–444–6060), in Sterling; the Loudoun Cancer Care Center (703–444–4460), also in the Countryside community, offering chemotherapy and radiation therapy; the NOVA Urgent Care Center, (703–430–4343), a walk-in facility in Sterling for minor emergencies; the Loudoun Healthcare Urgent Care Center in Western Loudoun (540–338–3360); and the Sterling-Dulles Imaging & MRI Center (703–444–5800), for the diagnosis and treatment of a wide variety of disorders and diseases.

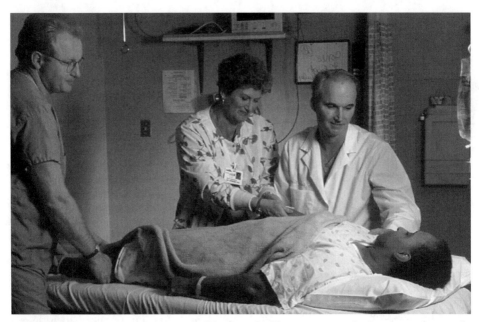

The Washington metro area boasts some of the finest healthcare services to be found anywhere in the United States. PHOTO: ADAM B. AUEL, COURTESY OF INOVA HEALTH SYSTEM

Prince William County

Mary Washington Hospital
1001 Sam Perry Blvd.
Fredericksburg, VA
(540) 899–1100
www.medicorp.org/marywashington
hospital.asp

Although located just outside the primary focus area of this book, Mary Washington Hospital merits inclusion for its size, services, branch facilities, and accessibility to many residents of Metro Washington, particularly those in parts of southeastern Prince William County. The 318-bed hospital is part of the regional MediCorp Health System. It offers private rooms, intensive care units (including neonatal ICU), neurosurgery, open-heart surgery, and a 24-hour emergency department. The hospital also offers special birthing suites for labor, delivery, and recovery for new mothers and their babies.

Affiliated facilities include Snowden at Fredericksburg, a psychiatric and addiction treatment center for adolescents and adults; the Family Health Center at North Stafford, a freestanding outpatient facility; Carriage Hill Nursing Home and Mary Washington

Health Center, providers of professional long-term care; Chancellor's Village of Fredericksburg, a retirement community; and Commonwealth Assisted Living Center, a modestly priced home for adults.

Potomac Hospital
2300 Opitz Blvd.
Woodbridge, VA
(703) 670–1313
www.potomachospital.com

Potomac Hospital, established in 1972 with 29 beds, has grown into a 153-bed comprehensive healthcare facility with more than 900 staff members. The hospital features a fully equipped pediatric unit, maternity unit, and neonatology program; 24-hour emergency medicine, magnetic-resonance imaging, and radiation therapy; and cardiac catheterization and angiography. The hospital offers services in the areas of allergy and immunology, dermatology, family practice, internal medicine, neurology, OB-GYN, pediatrics, psychiatry, radiation oncology, general surgery, neurosurgery, ophthalmology, oral surgery, orthopedics, plastic surgery, thoracic and vascular surgery, urology, anesthesiology, pathology, physical medicine rehabilitation, and radiology and nuclear medicine.

Prince William Hospital
8700 Sudley Rd.
Manassas, VA
(703) 369–8000
www.pwhs.org

The county's largest medical facility is 170-bed Prince William Hospital, a private, nonprofit community facility established in 1964. The hospital features comprehensive medical and surgical services and includes a critical-care unit, inpatient and outpatient surgery, oncology, pediatrics, a 24-hour emergency department, a helipad, OB-GYN, cardiology, nuclear medicine, radiology and other diagnostic services, dialysis treatment, and physical, speech, and occupational therapies.

Suburban Maryland

Anne Arundel County

Anne Arundel Medical Center
2001 Medical Pkwy.
Annapolis, MD
(410) 267–1000
www.aa-healthsystem.org

Established as Annapolis Emergency Hospital in 1902, AAMC has evolved into a regional medical center serving a population area of 650,000. The center went through a major revamping in 2001, including the addition of its $65 million acute care pavilion, serving critically ill patients. The medical center also includes a women's and children's center with the state's fourth-highest birth rate, an outpatient surgery center averaging 600 procedures a month, a radiation oncology center, a diabetes center, and a breast care center. The hospital has 244 beds, and the medical center's staff numbers more than 2,000.

North Arundel Hospital
301 Hospital Dr.
Glen Burnie, MD
(410) 787–4000
www.northarundel.org

This 320-bed nonprofit hospital focuses on short-term acute care and features a 24-hour emergency room with an immediate-care center for minor injuries and illnesses, and a center for severe trauma and injuries. The hospital offers numerous outpatient support programs and services at various locations.

Major extensions of North Arundel Hospital include the Life Center, 200 Hospital Drive, Glen Burnie, (410) 768–6644, featuring a variety of wellness programs, and the Mammography Center, 301 Hospital Drive, Glen Burnie, (410) 787–4642, featuring excellent diagnostic equipment.

Montgomery County

Holy Cross Hospital of Silver Spring
1500 Forest Glen Rd.
Silver Spring, MD
(301) 754–8800
www.holycrosshealth.com

One of Montgomery County's primary medical facilities, Holy Cross is a 442-bed nonprofit hospital founded in 1963 by Catholic nuns. Not only is this the largest acute-care facility in the county, it is also the only teaching hospital and boasts the largest medical staff in Montgomery with some 1,400 physicians enjoying privileges—a good thing, because the hospital's chief service area of southern Montgomery County and northern and western Prince George's County is home to some 600,000 residents.

Holy Cross Hospital is a recognized teaching center through affiliations with George Washington University's graduate medical education programs in obstetrics, gynecology, medicine, and surgery. The hospital works with GW and Children's National Medical Center in sponsoring a pediatric teaching program. Specialties include critical-care services, emergency medicine, OB-GYN, home care/hospice, pediatrics, psychiatry, and a range of surgical procedures. An expansion program slated for completion in 2004 will add more private rooms, a new neonatal intensive care unit and a larger ER.

Montgomery General Hospital
18101 Prince Philip Dr.
Olney, MD
(301) 774–8882
www.montgomerygeneral.com

Founded in 1920, this 244-bed nonprofit community hospital is in the northern

Montgomery County community of Olney, but it serves many residents of Howard and Prince George's Counties as well. Montgomery General has a full range of inpatient and outpatient medical and surgical services and programs, including obstetrics, pediatrics, 24-hour emergency and cardiac care, and cancer care. The hospital offers psychiatric and addiction treatment along with the latest medical imaging and diagnostic services, health education, and screening programs. Some 550 physicians are on staff.

The National Institutes of Health
9000 Rockville Pk.
Bethesda, MD
(301) 496–4000
www.nih.gov

Along with the Centers for Disease Control (CDC) in Atlanta, the National Institutes of Health is probably the best known and most widely recognized of the medical field's distinguished "alphabet" agencies. Still, there's more to NIH than most people probably realize. Internationally renowned for its work, NIH is one of the largest biomedical research centers in the world and the principal medical research arm of the U.S. Department of Health and Human Services. Some 75 buildings, including the 500-bed hospital and lab complex known as the Warren Grant Magnuson Clinical Center, are scattered about the 300-acre Bethesda campus just 12 miles from downtown Washington. NIH even has its own Metro stop. However, as mentioned in this chapter's introduction, not just anyone can obtain care at this hospital. You have to be referred by a physician, and even then you must qualify for a clinical trial that the center is funding.

Seeing the facility today, you'll be surprised to learn that NIH started out as a one-room hygiene lab in 1887. It now consists of 27 separate research institutes, centers, and divisions. Special components include the National Library of Medicine (the world's largest reference center devoted to a single subject), more than 1,400 labs with some of the best science equipment ever developed, and the Fogarty International Center, which houses foreign scholars-in-residence.

NIH focuses much of its efforts on combating the major life threatening and crippling diseases prevalent in the United States today. These diseases include heart disease, cancer, arthritis, Alzheimer's, diabetes, AIDS, neurological diseases, vision and mental disorders, infectious diseases, and dental diseases. Other work involves studying the human development and aging processes and exploring the relationship between the environment and human health.

A few numbers underscore the remarkable impact that such efforts have had on the nation's health. Mortality from heart disease—the nation's No. 1 killer—dropped 39 percent between 1972 and 1990, while death rates from stroke decreased about 58 percent during the same period; meanwhile, improved treatment methods have increased the five-year survival rate for cancer patients to 52 percent. Advancements don't come cheaply, though. The NIH's annual budget has gone from $300 in 1887 to some $20 billion today.

National Naval Medical Center
8901 Wisconsin Ave.
Bethesda, MD
(301) 295–4611
www.nnmc.med.navy.mil

Another of Bethesda's healthcare icons, the National Naval Medical Center provides care and treatment to active-duty military personnel and is not open to the general public. It does warrant a mention because this is where the president usually goes for annual physicals, routine examinations, and surgery. Not surprisingly, this hospital offers all medical and surgical services and the latest in equipment and technology.

The hospital was founded in 1802 but has only been at the present location since 1942. The site was personally selected by President Franklin Roosevelt, who actually sketched the design and grounds plans that the architect used as a guide. The National Naval Medical Center is among the 10 largest medical facilities in the nation and ranks as perhaps the best military hospital. More than 14,500 patients are admitted annually, while its clinic sees a whopping 520,000.

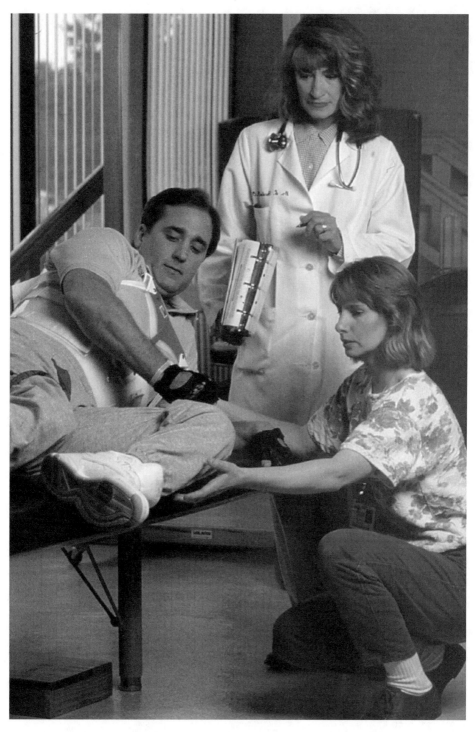

The rehabilitative services available in the Washington, D.C. area are in demand from residents and patients traveling from other states. PHOTO: ADAM B. AUEL, COURTESY OF INOVA HEALTH SYSTEM

Shady Grove Adventist Hospital
9901 Medical Center Dr.
Rockville, MD
(301) 279–6000
www.adventisthealthcare.com

This full-service hospital serves a huge swath of Montgomery County, seeing 60,000 patients in its ER annually. Open only since 1979, the 253-bed hospital delivers the second-highest number of babies in the state each year. A full range of other inpatient and outpatient medical and surgical services are also offered including a level III neonatal intensive care unit and a coronary-care unit.

Suburban Hospital
8600 Old Georgetown Rd.
Bethesda, MD
(301) 896–3100
home.suburbanhospital.org

Another of Montgomery County's comprehensive community hospitals, 397-bed, nonprofit Suburban Hospital opened in 1943 but has seen some dramatic changes. An extensive renovation completed during the 1980s included the addition of a luxury wing, the emergency and shock/trauma center, a pharmacy, a cafeteria and restaurant, and an addiction treatment center. Two additions completed in the '90s house radiology facilities, a medical library, the main entrance and admitting area, a 260-seat auditorium for medical and community education, and an elevated helipad.

The more than 900 physicians on staff at Suburban are trained in programs and services as diverse as orthopedics, cardiology, oncology (Suburban was the county's first comprehensive community cancer center and has a comprehensive breast cancer center as well), mental health, dermatology, gastroenterology, infectious diseases, and microvascular and thoracic surgery.

Washington Adventist Hospital
7600 Carroll Ave.
Takoma Park, MD
(301) 891–7600
www.adventisthealthcare.com

Located in what is nearly a trijurisdictional city—Takoma Park is actually in Montgomery County but is very near the Prince George's and District borders—this 300-bed, acute-care, church-affiliated facility has been in operation since 1907. Offering the most complete cardiology services in the county, Washington Adventist has been nationally recognized for innovative treatments in heart catheterization. The hospital's open-heart surgery center performs over 800 such procedures annually.

Other services include inpatient and outpatient surgery, maternity, radiation oncology, emergency medicine, rehabilitation medicine and pulmonary medicine. Mental health services are available on an inpatient or outpatient basis and include substance abuse programs.

Prince George's County

Doctors Community Hospital
8118 Good Luck Rd.
Lanham, MD
(301) 552–8118
www.princegeorges.com/health/dch.htm

Doctors Community Hospital serves a large portion of central Prince George's County, offering all major medical and surgical services except psychiatry and obstetrics. Open since 1975, the 250-bed adult, acute-care hospital underwent a major change in 1990, going from a national, chain-owned facility to a nonprofit community hospital.

This hospital is renowned for its comprehensive emergency department, which sees some 30,000 patients a year and is the only unit in the county certified to handle victims of hazardous-materials incidents. The hospital also specializes in general and same-day surgery, ophthalmology, cardiology, and physical and occupational therapy and offers complete radiological and laboratory diagnostic services. The Home Care Program is available to many patients upon discharge, helping them adapt to being back home and recuperating successfully.

Laurel Regional Hospital
7300 Van Dusen Rd.
Laurel, MD
(301) 725-4300
www.openseason.com/dhs/laurel.html

Laurel Regional Hospital (formerly Greater Laurel Beltsville Hospital) is a private, nonprofit, 185-bed facility located in the heart of the Baltimore-Washington corridor, close to the Washington, D.C. line, the Capital Beltway, and the Baltimore-Washington Parkway. Open since 1978, the hospital offers the full spectrum of medical, surgical and testing services, a 24-hour emergency room that sees some 34,000 patients annually, intensive care and coronary-care units, substance-abuse treatment programs, a maternal and child-health unit, a mental-health unit, and a comprehensive rehabilitation program. Because it is so conveniently located, the hospital is able to serve residents of Prince George's, Montgomery, Anne Arundel and Howard Counties.

Prince George's Hospital Center
3001 Hospital Dr.
Cheverly, MD
(301) 618-2000
www.openseason.dhs.pghc.html

Prince George's Hospital Center, with 450 beds, is the country's largest medical facility—and one of its most comprehensive. Private and nonprofit, PGHC is recognized nationwide for its outstanding 24-hour emergency care and is the designated regional trauma-care center for all of southern Maryland. Its level 1 shock-trauma unit boasts a 97 percent save rate for patients, one of the highest in the nation. PGHC also specializes in cardiac care and is the only hospital in the county with an open-heart surgery program. For minor emergencies and nonacute injuries and illnesses, the hospital offers an Express Care Center.

A wide range of obstetric services enables the hospital to handle high-risk pregnancies and difficult deliveries and to care for premature babies. A specialized unit called The Birthplace allows labor, delivery, and recovery to take place in one area. For outpatient services the hospital offers a newly redesigned short-stay center. Other services at PGHC include family practice, gastroenterology, neurology, orofacial plastic surgery, podiatry, psychiatry, sports medicine, and urology. A recently built ambulatory surgical wing features 10 operating rooms.

Southern Maryland Hospital Center
7503 Surratts Rd.
Clinton, MD
(301) 868-8000
www.southernmarylandhospital.com

"Southern Maryland" is certainly not a misnomer for this full-service, 358-bed facility that serves more than 500,000 residents in parts of Prince George's, Charles, Calvert and St. Mary's Counties—a big chunk of southern Maryland indeed, yet the hospital is located just 5 miles outside the Capital Beltway.

Open since 1977, Southern Maryland Hospital Center staffs over 400 physicians representing a wide range of fields including allergy and immunology, cardiology, dental surgery, dermatology, endocrinology, family practice, gastroenterology, oncology, neurosurgery, pathology, OB-GYN, pediatrics and pediatric cardiology, podiatry, psychiatry, pulmonary medicine, radiology, thoracic and vascular surgery, urology, plastic surgery, and emergency medicine.

Psychiatric Hospitals

Washington's psychiatric facilities have none of the celebrity cachet of places like the Betty Ford Clinic. They are serious facilities for the seriously ill, and those

> **Insiders' Tip**
> Each year, *Washingtonian* magazine publishes a rating of area doctors according to specialty. It's a good reference that is freely available in local libraries.

famous figures who have problems usually opt to go to places outside Metro Washington for treatment.

In the Metro area facilities range from those treating substance addiction to those housing the criminally insane. No matter what the case, rarely does one become a patient in such an institution without a referral by a mental-health care provider—or a judge. The list below is meant to serve as an overview of Metro area psychiatric facilities, not a guide from which to choose, as that is a decision best left to the patient (if possible), the mental-health care provider, and the family. As in the case of other long-term care facilities, a personal visit before checking in is a must except in emergency situations. You'll note that our list is in alphabetical order, not subdivided by regions. The reason is simple: If you need a psychiatric facility, you will likely base your decision on what kind of care the hospital offers rather than where it is.

Graydon Manor
801 Children's Center Rd. SW
Leesburg, VA
(703) 478-8767, (703) 777-3485
www.graydonmanor.org/

Parents of children with psychiatric and other mental difficulties worked together to found Graydon Manor in 1957. A private, 61-bed, nonprofit residential treatment center, Graydon Manor treats children and adolescents (boys ages 7 to 17, girls 12 to 17) diagnosed with severe emotional or psychiatric disorders. Although it does not treat those whose primary diagnoses are substance abuse, it does serve adolescents with secondary diagnoses of chemical dependency. Lengths of stay on the 100-plus-acre campus range from six to eight months, depending on need.

Also known as the National Children's Rehabilitation Center, Graydon offers outpatient services for adults and families in the community. It operates a therapeutic day school in Sterling for students in grades 1 through 12 who are learning disabled or emotionally disturbed. Its on-site school at Graydon Manor is accredited by the Virginia and Maryland departments of education.

Piedmont Behavioral Center
42009 Victory La.
Leesburg, VA
(703) 777-0800

Piedmont Behavioral Center, formerly known as Springwood Psychiatric Institute, offers comprehensive mental health treatment for adults, adolescents, and children on either an inpatient or outpatient basis. The hospital specializes in the treatment of depression, substance abuse, codependency, suicidal tendencies, school failure, domestic problems, and stress and anxiety. Special services include 24-hour admissions, free evaluations, and extensive aftercare programs for patients and their families.

The Psychiatric Institute of Washington, D.C.
4228 Wisconsin Ave. NW
Washington, DC
(202) 885-5600
www.psychinstitute.com

The first private psychiatric hospital in Washington, D.C., the 201-bed Psychiatric Institute of Washington was founded in 1967 and moved to its present location in 1973. The facility treats children, adolescents, and adults suffering from emotional and addictive illnesses and even offers an intensive care unit for especially serious cases. The hospital is acknowledged by the nation's psychiatric community as an education and professional development center for mental-health specialists.

Saint Elizabeth's Hospital
2700 Martin Luther King Jr. Ave. SE
Washington, DC
(202) 562-4000

For nearly 150 years, "Saint E's" has been perhaps the best known of the District's mental-health facilities. Its reputation may have something to do with criminally insane patients, such as would-be presidential assassin John Hinckley, who at this writing remains in residence. Still in the same place since its founding in 1855, the massive (1,500-bed) hospital actually sits on the grounds of D.C. General Hospital, but you wouldn't know it just by comparing addresses.

Formerly run by the federal government, Saint Elizabeth's is operated by the city under the purview of the Department of Human Services. Psychiatric services for children, adolescents, and adults are offered in the form of acute care, long-term care, nursing care, and residential care. The hospital also deals in forensic medicine. Services are being expanded for children and youth, in-home clients, and multicultural and immigrant populations.

Saint Luke Institute
8901 New Hampshire Ave.
Silver Spring, MD
(301) 445-7970
www.sli.org

This 35-bed, nonprofit psychiatric facility was founded by a minister/doctor and serves priests and other religious men and women active in church ministry. Initially treating only chemical dependency, St. Luke has broadened its focus to include mood disorders, compulsive eating or compulsive sexual behaviors, and reactive or chronic depression. The major areas of service are in evaluation, inpatient treatment, aftercare, residential living, outpatient therapy, and outreach.

Nursing Homes

Nursing homes here vary widely in terms of atmosphere and services offered. A look in the Metro Washington phone book will lead you to two pages of listings, and, indeed, you'll see many in your travels throughout the area—they are springing up everywhere to keep up with the graying of America. Some homes are actually luxury high-rises managed by hotel companies like Hyatt and Marriott, providing many of the same amenities. Others have the flavor of retirement communities in the degree of independence and the number of activities that patients enjoy. Some even look like summer resorts, complete with lush landscaping, wraparound verandas, and cheerful color schemes.

A nursing home is ultimately a place for long-term care and choosing one is a highly individual decision. Prospective patients—or their families—must base their decisions on the degree of attention they need, amenities and specialized medical care offered, location, and atmosphere. Choosing a nursing home requires careful investigation, personal visits, and, as in the case of hospices, physician referral. Two services in Metro Washington provide information and referrals expressly for nursing homes—they are a starting point, but ultimately the decision is too important to leave to a third party. For more information, contact the American Healthcare Association, 1201 L Street NW, Washington, DC 20005, (202) 842-4444, www.ahca.org; or Elder's Residential Facility, 10406 Thrift Road, Clinton, MD 20735, (301) 868-8843.

Alternative Healthcare

Washington is a conventional, conservative town of blue pinstriped suits, pumps and pearls. People try to fit in rather than stand out, and their approach to medical care reflects this. Unlike Los Angeles and Santa Fe, you generally won't find the locals comparing the latest medical trends, or even such commonplace alternative practitioners as herbalists, nutritionists, or chiropractors.

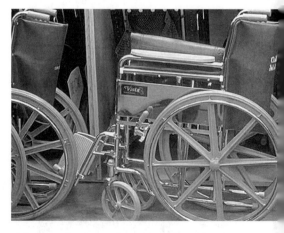

Ask your hotel concierge to make advance arrangements for special medical needs when traveling in the Washington, D.C. area.

Washington's upwardly mobile prefer to expend energy on their careers. Meals are an excuse for networking, and workaholics live on hors d'oeuvres, fast food, and liquor. Working out? Massages? Healthy cooking? Who has the time? To illustrate this, a recent nationwide survey ranked D.C. as number 1 in couch potatoes—people who exercise rarely and eat all the wrong foods.

Washington is of course much too cosmopolitan and diverse to have completely avoided trends in alternative, holistic medicine and nutrition. People who admit to seeing a chiropractor may say it with a sheepish smile, but there are four pages of chiropractic listings in the D.C. Yellow Pages, so someone must be using them.

Delve a little further into people's backgrounds and they may even admit to popping daily multiple vitamins, though independent health food stores in Metro Washington—the few that exist—are mostly dusty little nooks with the hushed, abandoned atmospheres of the library on Tuesday morning. On the other hand, every Washington-area mall has a GNC vitamin store, and gourmet groceries specializing in organic fare are cropping up all over. To top it off, the world-famous National Institutes of Health, a U.S. government agency, has established a specific office to investigate the value of vitamins, nutrition, biofeedback, acupuncture, and more.

So where to go if you want to try something more holistic than a shot or a prescription? For vitamins and herbs, the aforementioned groceries and GNC stores are numerous and well stocked, or you can search the phone book for independent health food stores. Massage therapists, unless you are working with a doctor-referred physical therapist, are most often found in Washington beauty salons and day spas, as they are still largely considered a frivolity—to be indulged in on rare occasions—rather than a necessity. If you're looking in the phone book, search under beauty salons rather than massage (unless you're really looking for a so-called escort service).

There are quite a few acupuncturists in Washington, but your first selection criterion should be that they use disposable needles. Most do. Second, a look in the Yellow Pages will reveal that some acupuncturists are actually board-certified medical doctors as well, and you may feel safer there. Finally, acupuncturists are licensed, so ensure that your practitioner's credentials are in order with the state licensing boards listed at the beginning of this chapter. If you choose carefully and get the proper clearances, you may even find that your treatments are covered by medical insurance. Indeed, acupuncture is a practice that the American Medical Association and many of its mainstream member physicians acknowledge as useful, so don't be embarrassed to ask your doctor, counselor, or physical therapist for a referral.

Many nutritionists and holistic practitioners now work on medical teams as adjunct therapy advisers, so check with your doctor about that too; and, don't forget that the Washington area is the home base for several organizations that can serve as useful resources for those seeking alternative medical care:

• American College of Preventive Medicine, 1660 L Street NW, (202) 466-2044, www.acpm.org

• American Osteopathic Association, 1090 Vermont Avenue NW, (202) 414-0140, www.aoa-net.org

• International Massage Association, P.O. Drawer 421, Warrenton, VA 20188, www.imagroup.com

• National Center for Complementary and Alternative Medicine, Clearinghouse, P.O. Box 7923, Gaithersburg, MD 20898, (301) 402-2466 and (888) 644-6226, www.nccam.nig.gov.

Walk-in Clinics

If you have a medical problem that is urgent, though not life threatening, a walk-in medical clinic may be a good bet. Most walk-in clinics are found in Virginia-area shopping centers and other high-traffic areas. There is one clinic in the Maryland section of Metro Washington, and, as of this writing, there is no such chain in Washington proper. Area

Emergency Numbers

In most areas of the country, people have been trained to call 911 in the event of a dire emergency, and the Washington Metro area is no exception. Still, other types of health emergencies may require more specific help. Here's a list of numbers for specific mental and physical health crises. (You may want to post a copy near your telephone, in case of emergency.)

Ambulance, Fire Department, Police, 911
AIDS Counseling and Information Hotline, (800) 590–2437
Alcoholics Anonymous Area Headquarters, (202) 966–9115
Battered Women's Shelter Hotline, (202) 529–5991
Crisis and Family Stress Line, (202) 223–2255
Domestic Violence Hotline, (202) 347–2777
Gay and Lesbian Help Line, (202) 939–7873
Metro Area Poison Center, (202) 625–3333
Narcotics Anonymous Hotline, (202) 399–5316
National Organization for Victim Assistance, (202) 232–6682
Rape Crisis Hotline, (202) 333–7273

For general mental-health crises, including suicide counseling, there are hotlines in Washington, D.C., (202) 223–2255; Virginia, (703) 527–4077; and Maryland, (301) 738–2255.

hospitals, however—D.C. included—have jumped on the bandwagon and, to compete with the freestanding facilities, have in many cases opened their own walk-in centers right in their emergency rooms.

This chapter's section on hospitals makes mention of walk-in centers where they existed at press time, but please remember that these minor-care emergency rooms are a growing trend, and more are opening every day. Free standing walk-in clinics are typically open seven days a week and into the evening, though hours vary from location to location. Call first to ensure that the office you want to visit is open.

No appointments are necessary, but waits can be long, as in hospital emergency rooms. With a small staff of doctors and nurses, the centers can perform some lab tests, blood work, sports physicals, and other services not requiring the traditional hospital's resources or facilities; however, if you suspect a serious illness, it's probably best to go to a hospital.

Northern Virginia

Inova Urgent Medical Care Locations
6201 Centreville Rd.
Centreville VA
(703) 830–5600
100 Maple Ave. E.
Vienna, VA
(703) 938–5300
www.nova.org

The Inova healthcare system includes several respected hospitals in Virginia, including Fairfax Hospital, so if it turns out you need more critical care, you'll be sent on quickly, perhaps by ambulance.

Inova Emergency Care Locations
Inova Emergency Care of Fairfax
4315 Chain Bridge Rd.
Fairfax City, VA
(703) 591–9322
Inova Emergency Care of Reston/Herndon
11901 Baron Cameron Ave.
Reston, VA
(703) 471–0175

Inova HealthPlex Franconia/Springield
6355 Walker La.
Alexandria, VA
(703) 204–3366

These are fully equipped hospital emergency rooms without the hospital. What these convenient and very efficient 24-hour facilities offer is a level of care somewhere between the walk-in shopping center facilities and regular hospitals. Part of the Inova Health System, these outlets also perform on-site lab and X-ray work and will arrange to transport you to a hospital if necessary.

Suburban Maryland

Inova Secure Care Center
803 Russell Ave.
Gaithersburg, MD
(301) 869–0700

Inova Secure Care Center, like its counterpart operation in Northern Virginia, known as Urgent Medical Care, is a convenient, cost-effective alternative to the hospital, best for treatment of minor illnesses and injuries. The center is staffed by a small team of doctors and nurses and is open seven days a week. Hours are 8:00 A.M. to 8:00 P.M. weekdays and 10:00 A.M. to 6:00 P.M. on the weekend and on holidays. It can also perform a limited amount of lab work and diagnostic tests, physical examinations, and other services.

Nighttime Pediatrics
12220 Rockville Pike
Rockville, MD
(301) 881–5000
www.nighttimepediatrics.com

Here's a place to take your child when she develops an ear infection on a Sunday or comes down with a 104-degree fever at bedtime. Although affiliated with Suburban Hospital, Nighttime Pediatrics is located in a strip mall several miles away. The center is staffed by pediatricians and pediatric nurses, with an on-site laboratory, pharmacy, and radiological services. It's open Monday through Friday from 5:00 P.M. to midnight and on weekends and holidays from noon to midnight.

Education

The Metro Washington area owes much of its well-respected business, political development, and economic development to a single driving force: education.

People here wax proud when they speak of our outstanding educational infrastructure, and with good reason: Few metro areas can hold a candle to our high-quality and diverse public and private schools, not to mention the concentration of internationally renowned colleges, universities, and research institutions.

This chapter highlights the educational opportunities found throughout the area, beginning with the public school systems and a selection of private institutions. The final section briefly describes the area's major colleges and universities, nearly all of which offer programs for working adults.

Public Schools

The common theme here, especially in the suburbs, is intense parental interest in quality public education. Whether they're tutoring beginning readers, assisting in computer labs, or working at PTA fundraisers, parent volunteers are helping schools create new and better programs for students. At the same time teachers and administrators are implementing strategies to improve reading skills and test scores. Maryland third, fifth, and eighth graders must participate in the Maryland School Performance Assessment Program (MSPAP), while Virginia third, fifth, and eighth graders and high school students must pass a comprehensive Standards of Learning (SOL) exam. The state and local jurisdictions continue to fine-tune the test-taking and evaluation guidelines.

Washington, D.C.

District of Columbia Public Schools
825 N. Capitol St. NE
Washington, DC
(202) 442–5635
www.k12.dc.us/dcps/home.html

Like many of America's inner-city public school systems suffering from budget cutbacks, violence, and chronic absenteeism, the District's has suffered through tough times of late. Numerous schools fell into disrepair, and, academically, 2000 SAT scores, averaging 822, remain the weakest in the metropolitan area. Under Superintendent Paul L. Vance, and with guidance from a Congressional subcommittee, D.C. schools continue their upward climb, implementing new language arts content and performance standards, reading and math initiatives, and more detailed report cards. Each student must complete 100 hours of community service in order to graduate.

D.C. public schools include 104 elementaries, 11 middle schools, and 17 high schools. Among the system's bright spots are its citywide magnet schools, which have always held their ground for students with special skills or artistic talents. The Ellington School of the Arts, named for esteemed native son Duke Ellington, has some of the finest dance, theater, and music departments in the metro area. Senior High Academies let students specialize in such areas as culinary arts, international studies, teaching, and travel and tourism. Eligible high school students can take advanced placement courses.

D.C. schools enroll 68,449 students. Testaments to the city's international character, students represent more than 130 nations and speak at least 90 languages. Bilingual programs in Spanish

This small (about 11,000 students) school system boasts a large emphasis on computers in education: The $3.5 million, five-year Technology Initiative works toward implementing such goals as having a multimedia computer workstation in each classroom, school-wide Internet access, laptops available for student loan, video production facilities, and faculty training. The program, funded through the school budget and private partnerships, brings five schools online annually.

The district includes 13 elementary schools, 2 middle schools, 1 ninth-grade school, and 1 senior high school. Special programs include all-day kindergarten, a gifted and talented curriculum, instruction for homebound students, and comprehensive special education services for handicapped students ages 2 to 21. The diverse student population includes children from 86 countries speaking 65 different languages. More than 1,000 students receive English as a Second Language education, and pupils in grades one through eight may participate in a Spanish immersion program. Volunteer tutoring services are available during and after school.

The city's lone high school, T. C. Williams, offers advanced placement and honors courses, a vocational education program with postsecondary degree credit, an award-winning JROTC program, and 17 varsity sports programs for boys and girls. In 2001, T. C. students averaged 963 on the SAT, compared with the national average of 1,020. Seven students in 2001 were National Merit Scholarship semifinalists. About 84 percent of Alexandria's graduates continue to some form of higher education.

Average class sizes are 20 in elementary grades, 21 in middle school and 23 in secondary grades. Alexandria's per-pupil expenditure of $11,158 is among the highest in Metro Washington. Teachers, 68 percent of whom have advanced degrees, receive starting salaries of $33,000 and average salaries of $49,875.

The system's Adult and Community Education Office provides adult basic education classes along with job skills and training, GED and high school diploma programs and special interest classes. A

and Chinese have earned the District kudos from educators around the country. Smaller groups of international students are taught English by itinerant teams of language teachers. There's even a school that teaches foreign adults English and prepares them for U.S. citizenship.

Like everything else in Washington, D.C., the public schools are constantly under the national microscope, especially in terms of funding and performance. All education programs, after being approved by an elected school board and the city government, must pass the financial scrutiny of Congress and the White House. Needless to say, not all plans win approval. Budgets and, unfortunately, politics often get in the way of much-needed resources. Student/teacher ratios average about 23 to 1.

Problems aside, the D.C. school system has the unlimited enviable educational resources of Washington in its backyard.

Northern Virginia

Alexandria Public Schools
2000 N. Beauregard St.
Alexandria, VA
(703) 824-6600
www.acps.k12.va.us

nine-member school board meets the first and third Thursdays of the month.

Arlington County Public Schools
1426 N. Quincy St.
Arlington, VA
(703) 228-7660
www.arlington.k12.va.us

This innovative public school system ranked number 1 in the 1997 Children's Environmental Index survey published by Zero Population Growth, which also named Arlington County the 11th most kid-friendly place in the country. Arlingtonians care deeply about education: 52 percent of residents age 25 and older are college graduates, and 24 percent have graduate or professional degrees.

Diversity defines Arlington County Public Schools, where 19,000 students hail from around the world and speak more than 30 languages, from Spanish and Vietnamese to Arabic and Farsi. Although the county is Virginia's smallest geographically, it boasts the 12th largest of the state's 136 school divisions. With 30 schools and several special programs, the district caters to all segments of its varied student population. Parents may choose to send their children to a neighborhood school or to an "alternative" school offering a unique learning environment. Some examples include the Claremont Early Childhood Center for grades kindergarten through second grade; Drew Model School, the county's only public Montessori program for ages six to nine; Science Focus School, at which kindergartners through fifth graders incorporate science into all areas of learning; Kenmore Middle School, where arts and communications technology take center stage; and H-B Woodlawn Secondary Program, in which sixth through twelfth graders control much of their educational experience.

Other special programs include instruction for gifted students, English for speakers of other languages/high-intensity language training, extended day care, outreach for teenage parents, a Spanish partial-immersion program at all grade levels, high school advanced placement and International Baccalaureate courses, summer school, special educa-

tion, and athletics and other extracurricular activities. Technology proves a high priority: All schools have Internet access, and the district boasts three "electronic classrooms." Kindergartners attend school all day.

The county's comprehensive Adult Education Program offers high school equivalency studies, senior citizens' activities, and an array of multicultural programs.

Arlington spends nearly $11,000 per pupil, and the average class size is 21 students. The investment is paying off: 88 percent of Arlington high school graduates go on to college. The average 2001 SAT score was 1,041, higher than both the state (1,011) and national averages. The five-member school board meets two Thursdays a month, and meetings are shown live on Cable TV Arlington Channel 30.

Fairfax County Public Schools
10700 Page Ave.
Fairfax, VA
(703) 246-2502
www.fcps.k12.va.us

Fairfax County Public Schools, with more than 165,000 students and more than 18,000 teachers, is the 12th-largest school district in the United States and the largest in Virginia. Growing every year, the district now boasts 132 elementary schools, 21 middle schools, 3 secondary (grades 7–12) schools, 21 high schools, 26 special-services centers, and 35 alternative schools. The county's more than 1,400 school buses handle 105,000 students every day, making the fleet one of the nation's largest.

These tremendous numbers do not equate to mediocrity or impersonalization in the classroom. More than 52 percent of the state's National Merit Scholarship Exam semifinalists come from Fairfax County Public Schools. Students averaged 1,116 on the 2001 SAT, one of the highest average scores in the region.

The system, with a per-pupil cost of more than $8,938, features countywide programs for students who are gifted and talented, for students with learning disabilities, and for international students who speak English as a second language.

Young students at this Fairfax County School use the latest technology. PHOTO: COURTESY OF FAIRFAX COUNTY ECONOMIC DEVELOPMENT AUTHORITY

Several elementary and middle schools provide partial-immersion programs in French, German, Japanese, and Spanish. Two elementary magnet schools feature arts and sciences curricula, and more than 50 elementaries are designated Model Technology Schools.

At the high-school level, about 92 percent of graduates go on to some form of higher education. The county's prized magnet school in Alexandria, Thomas Jefferson High School for Science and Technology, consistently boasts the country's largest concentration of National Merit Scholars (151 semifinalists in 2001). Admission is competitive and open to ninth and tenth graders in the county and other participating Northern Virginia school districts. Eight schools offer the academically demanding International Baccalaureate Program, which includes college-level courses. Extracurricular high school activities include award-winning

music programs and interscholastic team sports for boys and girls.

Vocational programs feature studies in business education, home economics, industrial arts, and horticulture. On-site technical studies programs take place at a shopping mall, airport, hotel, construction site, and car dealership. More than 100 elementary schools offer extended day care through the Fairfax County Office for Children. Fees are based on a sliding scale. A Head Start early childhood program is available for eligible three- to five-year-olds. The school system also sponsors adult education, alternative high school programs, a school-to-work transition academy, and a variety of enrichment classes for children and adults.

Administratively, the district is divided into eight clusters, each of which is represented by a director and an office staff. A 12-member elected school board holds meetings the second and fourth Thursdays at 7:30 P.M., broadcast live on Cable Channel 21. Parental involvement in the schools is high, with an average of more than 50,000 logging more than 1 million hours of service during a school year. Parents, teachers, administrators, and students regularly voice their opinions at school board meetings and have great influence over budgets, curriculum, and the establishment of new facilities and programs.

The system in 1998 hired a new superintendent, Daniel A. Domenech, an advocate of such issues as smaller class sizes and such experimental ventures as year-round school, which has been successfully implemented at eight schools.

The county also contains two separate municipal school districts: one serving the city of Fairfax and one serving Falls Church. Fairfax city's system, City Hall, 10455 Armstrong Street, Fairfax, Virginia, (703) 385-7855, www.ci.fairfax.va.us/school/school.asp, includes two elementaries, one middle school, and one high school. The system operates under a partnership with the county and has its own superintendent and school board. Falls Church City Public Schools, 803 West Broad Street, Falls Church, Virginia, (703) 248-5600, www.fccps.k12.va.us, enroll close to 1,500 students in its system, widely considered one of the best in the region. The district includes only four schools: Mt. Daniel for kindergarten through first grade, Thomas Jefferson for second through fifth grades, George Mason Middle School for sixth through eighth grades, and George Mason Junior-Senior High School for ninth through twelfth grades. Highlights include the International Baccalaureate Program, special education instruction, gifted and talented services, ESL courses, extended day care, and through the Office of Community Education and the Recreation and Parks Department, adult education and enrichment classes.

Loudoun County Public Schools
102 North St. NW
Leesburg, VA
(703) 771–6427
www.loudoun.k12.va.us

The rapidly growing, 34,000-student Loudoun County public school system is among the best in exurban Metro Washington. The average elementary class size is 22 students, and the per-pupil expenditure is approximately $7,669. The system has 51 schools, including three new buildings that opened for the 2001–02 school year. A technology center serves vocational and adult education students and an alternative education program helps middle school and high school students who have trouble fitting into traditional programs.

Courses are available for gifted and special education students, and several advanced placement courses are available at the high school level. Each school offers computer education, emphasizing state-of-the-art technology, and has Internet access. The 1.28 percent dropout rate is among the lowest in the state and the nation, and 87 percent of county graduates continue their formal education. SAT scores, consistent over the past two years, averaged 1,034 in 2001. Monthly meetings of the nine-member school board, held the second and fourth Tuesdays of most months, are shown live on Cablevision of Loudoun's Channel 59.

Prince William County Public Schools
14800 Joplin Rd.
Manassas, VA
(703) 791–7200
www.pucs.edu

The tremendous—and often overwhelming—growth that transformed Prince William over the past 15 or so years never shortchanged the county's public school system, now the fourth largest in the state. If anything, it improved it. Eighty-seven percent of the county's high school graduates go on to college, and the average SAT score keeps rising, with 2001's at 1,011. Educational staff, half of whom hold advanced degrees, have earned numerous awards in recent years, including, in 2001, the Milken Educator Award and Virginia Outstanding Career and Technical Educator of the Year. *Time* magazine recognized Stonewall Jackson High School as High School of the Year. In 1998 the school division earned a Medallion of Excellence from the U.S. Senate, honoring the schools' productivity and quality. The district maintains several health- and education-related partnerships, and continues to upgrade its school-wide computer technology.

In all, more than 57,800 students attend 72 public schools, where the per-pupil cost is $7,318. Prince William's curriculum earmarks specific learning objectives by grade level for each subject. The schools also offer extensive programs for gifted students in all grades, and rigorous advanced placement and International Baccalaureate courses for high school students. Other special programs target pupils with disabilities, students who want to pursue vocational studies, those who speak English as a second language, and adults interested in continuing education. Several elementary schools offer before- and after-school care.

Public school policy is set by the county school board of eight members elected to four-year terms. Widely attended public meetings of the school board take place the first, second, and fourth Wednesdays of each month.

Both independent cities within the county—Manassas City Public Schools,

9000 Tudor Lane, Manassas, Virginia, (703) 257–8800 and Manassas Park City Schools, One Park Center Court, Suite A, Manassas, Virginia, (703) 335–8850—have their own school systems. Academically, they tend to mirror the county.

Suburban Maryland

Montgomery County Public Schools
850 Hungerford Dr.
Rockville, MD
(301) 279–3391
www.mcps.k12.md.us

Arguably the best public school system in Metro Washington, Montgomery County boasts a 2001 average SAT score of 1,092, the highest in the state. The school system also boasts the highest MSPAP results. About 56 percent of high school students take honors courses, and 82 percent of county graduates go on to higher education. Schools, staff, and students frequently receive honors at national, state and local levels.

Like Fairfax, Montgomery has a gigantic system. More than 36,000 students attend 185 public schools, including 23 senior high schools, 35 middle schools, and 125 elementary schools, along with centers specializing in magnet programs, gifted and talented instruction, technology and research, visual arts, and foreign language immersion. The diverse student body includes 16,000 international pupils, who hail from more than 150 countries.

The county also offers some all-day kindergarten, extended elementary pro-grams, ESOL, instruction for disabled students, adult education, and on-the-job training in business and industry. The schools' Global Access initiative is integrating up-to-the-minute technology into classrooms. The per-pupil cost is approximately $8,688.

A seven-member elected school board, which sets the district's policies, recently hired Jerry D. Weast as superintendent. Volunteers also play a big part in the system, with some 55,000 logging 4 million hours of service annually.

Prince George's County Public Schools
Sasscer Administration Bldg.,
14201 School La.
Upper Marlboro, MD
(301) 952–6001
www.pgcps.pg.k12.md.us

Approximately 133,600 students attend Prince George's 188 schools, making the school system the 19th largest in the country. Per-pupil expenditure for fiscal year 2001 was $6,087, and the average teacher salary was $44,428.50.

SAT scores are among the region's lowest, averaging 886 in 2001. Graduation requirements for high school students emphasize math and social studies over electives. The University High School magnet program offers rigorous, college-prep courses like the International Baccalaureate Program. The Visual and Performing Arts High School houses a TV and recording studio, 1,000-seat auditorium, and dance studio. Through a special partnership, some dancers appear at the Kennedy Center for the Performing Arts. The county has innovative, comprehensive reading initiatives, ESL instruction, classes for gifted students, a K–12 French Immersion Program, schools for the learning and physically disabled, evening schools for adults, and even an educational project geared toward the needs of Native American children.

The nine-member elected school board meets two Thursdays a month. The school system hired a new superintendent, Iris T. Metts, in 1999.

Insiders' Tip

Watch teams from local high schools compete for scholarships on *It's Academic,* a Giant food-sponsored program that airs on NBC-TV, channel 4, on Saturday mornings.

Private Schools

Private schools in the region range from traditional liberal arts institutions to alternative programs for gifted or learning-disabled students. Of course, the benefits of such highly personalized and specialized study come with a price tag. Generally speaking, tuition fees here can range from $5,400 to $15,500 at day schools, and from $20,450 to $26,000 or more at boarding schools. A good clearinghouse for additional information on private schools in the area, the association can be reached at Post Office Box 9956, Washington, DC, 20016, (202) 625-9223, www.aisgw.org.

Washington, D.C.

Archbishop Carroll High School
4300 Harewood Rd. NE
Washington, DC
(202) 529-0900
www.ee.cua.edu/~carroll/index.htm
On a small campus near Catholic University, Archbishop Carroll is one of the city's leading Catholic high schools. The coed school, founded in 1951, has an enrollment of more than 700 students in grades 9 through 12 and is known for its rigorous academic standards, dedicated faculty, and strong athletic and activities programs. Its state-of-the-art computer lab includes Internet access. All students must participate in service projects, such as volunteering at a local soup kitchen. Ninety-eight percent of the school's graduates go on to Catholic, Georgetown, the University of Virginia, the University of Maryland, and other nationally competitive colleges.

Capitol Hill Day School
210 S. Carolina Ave. SE
Washington, DC
(202) 547-2244
www.chds.org
Founded in 1969, this independent, coed school for 225 children in prekindergarten through eighth grade offers an integrated curriculum with a hands-on emphasis. Students study such specialty subjects as Spanish, French, art, and music. The school encourages both self-reliance and care for others.

Georgetown Visitation Preparatory School
1524 35th St. NW
Washington, DC
(202) 337-3350
www.ee.cua.edu/~georgvis
Visitation has been grooming young women for higher education since 1799. About 430 students in grades 9 through 12 attend the prestigious day school, which is affiliated with the Roman Catholic Church and located on a 27-acre campus next door to Georgetown University. The school boasts honors and advanced placement courses in English, foreign language, history, mathematics, and science. A bridge program with the neighboring university enables some seniors to take college-level courses. The school's athletic program features a variety of team sports, and students can choose from more than 30 cocurricular activities, featuring such subjects as computers, Great Books, music, and Christian service. Visitation grads go on to a wide variety of colleges, including some of the top schools on the East Coast.

Gonzaga College High School
19 I St. NW
Washington, DC
(202) 336-7100
www.gonzaga.org
Founded in 1821, this Jesuit-sponsored boys' academy is one of the city's oldest schools. About 870 students in ninth through twelfth grade attend the day school, which offers a college preparatory curriculum, including advanced placement courses. Ninety-nine percent of the school's seniors go on to college. Gonzaga also is known for its sports program. The Gonzaga Eagles football team finished the 2001 season with a 9–2 record. The campus, situated in the heart of the city, proves easily accessible by bus and Metrorail.

The Lab School of Washington
4759 Reservoir Rd. NW
Washington, DC
(202) 965–6600
www.labschool.org

The Lab School is designed for intelligent students with learning disabilities, who benefit from the school's average class size of six students. Situated in a quiet residential area of upper Georgetown, the 35-year-old, coed day school boasts more than 100 teachers for its 310 students in grades kindergarten through 12. The school twice received the U.S. Department of Education's National Blue Ribbon School of Excellence designation. The ungraded elementary curriculum equally emphasizes academic skills and a variety of arts. Students study history by participating in Academic Clubs with themes such as Knights and Ladies and Industrialists. They also have the opportunity to dig for and study ancient artifacts buried on the school grounds. Grades 7 through 12 follow a more traditional college preparatory curriculum, supplemented by arts and humanities classes in junior high. High school students apprentice off campus in such places as museums and radio stations and perform community outreach like giving birthday parties at a homeless shelter. More than 90 percent of the school's graduating seniors go on to college.

Competitive team sports include basketball, soccer, and softball. An $8.7 million theater/art complex opened in 1999. The Lab School also offers career and college counseling, tutoring, clinical services, and night classes for adults with learning disabilities.

Nannie Helen Burroughs School Inc.
601 50th St. NE
Washington, DC
(202) 398–5266
www.nhburroughs.com

This private, coed Christian school, affiliated with the Progressive National Baptist Convention, enrolls approximately 200 students in grades prekindergarten through sixth. Burroughs founded the school in 1909 with a "three B's" philosophy: bath, Bible, and broom—signifying clean body, mind, and environment. Among the curriculum's prominent features are cultural enrichment, hands-on math and science, formal Bible instruction, values education, Spanish, and computer literacy. The students take many field trips. Pupils can participate in both before- and after-school care.

Sheridan School
4400 36th St. NW
Washington, DC
(202) 362–7900
www.sheridanschool.org

Founded in 1927, this small, coed elementary school (kindergarten through eighth grade) follows traditional liberal arts instruction in a familylike, values-oriented atmosphere. The 215 students, divided into one class per grade in kindergarten through fourth, learn through a "central subject" approach, in which a single topic such as anthropology is used to integrate the curriculum. Two teachers instruct each class. Program highlights include the annual science fair, visits to the school's 130-acre Mountain Campus next to Shenandoah National Park, a French trip for seventh and eighth graders, and an extended-day program loaded with extracurricular activities. The Sheridan campus is in North Cleveland Park, a residential neighborhood not far from the Tenleytown Metro station.

Sidwell Friends School
3825 Wisconsin Ave. NW
Washington, DC
(202) 537–8100
www.sidwell.edu

Sidwell Friends, affiliated with the Society of Friends, was founded in 1883 and has since become one of the preeminent college-prep schools in D.C. The coed day school enrolls more than 1,070 students on its two campuses, a Bethesda location for prekindergarten through fourth graders, and a District site for grades 5 through 12. The school follows a demanding liberal arts curriculum, including required studies in fine arts, foreign languages, math, and science. Extracurricular activities, such as interscholastic sports, also play an important role in student life. Personalized community service programs are required of all graduates. First Daughter Chelsea Clinton graduated from Sidwell Friends in 1997.

St. Anselm's Abbey School
4501 South Dakota Ave. NE
Washington, DC
(202) 269–2350
www.saintanselms.org/school

Part of the sprawling academic complex that radiates from Catholic University, St. Anselm's is a college-prep school for sixth-through twelfth-grade boys of all faiths. About 245 students attend the school, founded in 1942 and operated by the Benedictine monks of St. Anselm's Abbey. The small average student/teacher ratio of 8 to 1 pays off: A 10-year average 65 percent of the school's graduates receives National Merit recognition, and the 10-year average SAT score is 1,280. One hundred percent of graduates go on to attend four-year colleges. The curriculum includes challenging programs in music, drama, visual arts, publications, and athletics. The Brookland/CUA Metro is nearby.

St. John's College High School
2607 Military Rd. NW
Washington, DC
(202) 363–2316
stjohns-chs.org

Run by the De La Salle Christian Brothers, the religious order which founded the school in 1851, St. John's enrolls 1,070 students. The Catholic, coed college-prep high school is known for balancing academics with comprehensive extracurricular activities, such as an Army JROTC program and competitive league team sports. St. John's takes pride in its computer center, and the school boasts a new gym and a renovated arts center. The 27-acre campus borders scenic Rock Creek Park.

St. Patrick's Episcopal Day School
4700 Whitehaven Pkwy. NW
Washington, DC
(202) 342–2805
www.stpatricks.Washington.dc.us

This Episcopal day school, founded in 1956, touts traditional elementary school programs in the arts, music, and science, along with reinforcement of spiritual values. With nearly 460 students in nursery school through eighth grade, the school is the city's largest independent elementary. The average class size is 17, and the school boasts a 1-to-6 teacher/student ratio. Special features include three science labs, three music rooms, three computer labs, three libraries, a video technology center, art center, and several outdoor playing areas. The school is near Georgetown, between Foxhall Road and MacArthur Boulevard.

Washington International School
Grades 6–12
3100 Macomb St. NW
Washington, DC
(202) 243–1800
Grades pre-kindergarten–5
1690 36th St. NW
Washington, DC
(202) 243–1700
www.wis.edu

It's only fitting that an international city claims a bold international college-prep school. The coed academy enrolls more than 800 students, from prekindergarten through 12th grade, and promotes diversity. The students and their families represent more than 90 countries. A globalized curriculum, including bilingual studies, is the bread and butter of this independent day school. Nearly all eleventh- and twelfth-grade students follow the challenging International Baccalaureate curriculum, and most graduates continue their education. A new arts and athletics center on the upper campus opened in September 2000.

Northern Virginia

Burgundy Farm Country Day School
3700 Burgundy Rd.
Alexandria, VA
(703) 960–3431
www.burgundyfarm.org

Burgundy Farm, founded in 1946 and situated on a 25-acre rural campus, offers an interdisciplinary approach to its 250 coed students in prekindergarten through eighth grade. Two instructors teach all classes, with strong emphasis on the liberal arts. Parents are actively involved as volunteers. Extended-day programs feature a variety of enrichment activities. The school sponsors a summer day camp and a residential camp at its Burgundy Center for Wildlife Studies in the Appalachians in West Virginia.

The Congressional Schools of Virginia
3229 Sleepy Hollow Rd.
Falls Church, VA
(703) 533–9711
www.congressionalschools.org

These coeducational schools—which enroll 60 infants and toddlers, 120 preschoolers and kindergartners, and around 300 students from first through eighth grades—promote traditional education and values. The curriculum emphasizes language arts and accelerated math, and also includes hands-on learning in recently upgraded computer and science labs. The student/teacher ratio ranges from 16 to 2 in preschool to 18 to 1 in middle school. Graduates usually continue their education at the area's most prestigious college prep schools. Physical education, art, and music round out the curriculum, with many activities both during and after school taking place in a fairly new gym and auditorium. Founded in 1939, the schools are nestled on a 40-acre campus that features nature trails, playgrounds, swimming pools, and an outdoor education ropes course. During the summer, the campus hosts day camps for children, ages 3 to 14.

Episcopal High School in Virginia
1200 N. Quaker La.
Alexandria, VA
(703) 933–3000
www.episcopalhighschool.org/

One of Virginia's most celebrated prep schools, Episcopal is small, personal, and highly demanding of its 410 students. Founded in 1839 and mere minutes from the Nation's Capital, this coed boarding school for ninth through twelfth graders follows a tradition-rich Honor System that has created an environment of openness among students and teachers. Students follow a challenging liberal arts–based curriculum rich with advanced placement courses. Technology plays a big role, through such features as two computer labs, dormitories wired for Internet access, and a requirement that all ninth and tenth graders have their own laptops. The school takes advantage of the myriad resources of the neighboring District through field trips and internships at political and cultural institutions. Many students also spend time studying abroad. The school boasts numerous athletic facilities, including a 2,800-seat stadium, seven playing fields, and a six-lane, 400-meter outdoor track. Spirituality plays an important role in campus life, with students regularly attending chapel and volunteering for community service. The 130-acre, wooded campus resembles a small college, complete with historic buildings.

Fairfax Christian School
1624 Hunter Mill Rd.
Vienna, VA
(703) 759–5100
www.fairfaxchristenschool.webatonce.com

This coed school for kindergartners through twelfth graders, founded in 1961, stresses a traditional liberal arts curriculum in a nondenominational Christian setting. Enrollment numbers around 300 students. Most four-year-olds in the school's kindergarten learn how to read using a phonetic approach. The school offers extended care and provides transportation for most Northern Virginia students. The 30-acre, rural campus is conveniently situated between Vienna and Reston, close to the Dulles Toll Road.

Flint Hill School
East Campus, 10409 Academic Dr.
West Campus, 3320 Jermantown Rd.
Oakton, VA
(703) 584–2300
www.flinthill.org

Flint Hill is a nondenominational, coed college prep school of about 840 students. The school boasts a new campus for the upper grades. It is known for its lofty academic and competitive athletic programs. The student/faculty ratio is 17 to 1. Founded in 1956, the school also stresses community service: Graduation requirements include 60 hours of service to be completed by the end of the first senior semester. Pupils can take a variety of honors and advanced placement courses, and all seniors design and complete three-week independent study projects. (Senior projects in recent years have included such eclectic themes as living at a Buddhist monastery, working at a hospital in Uruguay, and designing costumes and sets for The Shakespeare Theatre.) The campuses are a stone's throw from I–66, in the upper-middle-class residential community of Oakton.

Foxcroft School
Foxcroft Rd., off U.S. 50
Middleburg, VA
(540) 687–5555, (800) 858–2364
www.foxcroft.org

Founded in 1914, this small, residential prep school strives to foster self-esteem and strong moral character in ninth-through twelfth-grade girls. Around 180 students attend Foxcroft, nationally recognized for its academic and athletic programs. About half the senior class receives merit scholarships. The student/faculty ratio is 6 to 1. Educational highlights include an interim term, featuring nontraditional course offerings, guest lecturers, and field trips; three-week, career-oriented senior projects; a fellowship program that brings to the school such notable visitors as Maya Angelou and Richard Leakey; an ESL program for international students; and an annual poetry festival. The beautiful 500-acre campus is slightly more than an hour away from Washington, in the heart of Virginia's Hunt Country; consequently, riding is a popular extracurricular activity here.

Gesher Jewish Day School of Northern Virginia
8900 Little River Pk.
Fairfax, VA
(703) 978–9789

3939 Prince William Dr.
Fairfax, VA
(703) 323–7274
www.gesher-jds.org

The only Northern Virginia Jewish day school for kindergarten through middle school, Gesher is conveniently situated in the bustling Jewish Community Center of Northern Virginia. Founded in 1982 by several community families, the school combines Jewish studies and general studies for its 200 students. The student/faculty ratio is 8 to 1. Curriculum highlights include all-day kindergarten, gifted instruction, accelerated reading, Hebrew study, computers, a science lab, and art studio. The school also uses the community center's full-size gymnasium, indoor swimming pool, and performing arts auditorium, and students can participate in the center's extended-day program. Bus service is available.

Green Hedges School
415 Windover Ave. NW
Vienna, VA
(703) 938–8323
www.greenhedges.org

Founded in 1942, this coed, nonsectarian school emphasizes a classical education for its 190 students in preschool through eighth grade. The student/teacher ratio is 7 to 1. Children ages three to six attend a Montessori Early School, where French is introduced. Phonics-based reading and a hands-on science lab highlight the curriculum for first through fifth grades. Middle-school students complete Algebra I by eighth grade, participate in an environmental observation project via the internet, perform community service, and take field trips. All fifth- through eighth-grade students study Latin and Spanish or French. The school is in residential, centrally located Vienna. Green Hedges places a major emphasis on fine arts and promotes a relaxed, happy atmosphere for the socially and culturally diverse student body.

The Langley School
1411 Balls Hill Rd.
McLean, VA
(703) 356–1920
www.langley.edu.net

The state's largest independent elementary, this coed day school for preschool through eighth-grade students prides itself on its personalized and accelerated instruction. The student/teacher ratio is 9 to 1. A 27,000-square-foot middle school building features a greenhouse, and every classroom has 18 computer terminals. The school offers all-day kindergarten, a structured extended-day program, and summer school and day camps. Founded in 1942, Langley is set on a 10-acre campus in one of Northern Virginia's most exclusive neighborhoods.

Loudoun Country Day School
237 Fairview St. NW
Leesburg, VA
(703) 777–3841
www.lcds.org

The mission of Loudoun Country Day is advanced instruction, including accelerated programs in foreign languages and the arts for more than 200 students in prekindergarten through eighth grade. The student/teacher ratio is 8 to 1. Sports also play a major role at the school, located in quaint, historic Leesburg, the county seat.

The Madeira School
8328 Georgetown Pike
McLean, VA
(703) 556–8200
www.madeira.org

Founded in 1906, Madeira offers its 300-plus young women, grades 9 through 12, a challenging academic environment that includes advanced placement courses. The average student/faculty ratio is 6 to 1, and the average class size is 10 to 12. The school's unique, Wednesday Co-Curriculum is a required full-day program that fosters independence and leadership skills through such activities as public speaking, outdoor education, community service, and Congressional and career-oriented internships. The boarding/day school's lovely 376-acre campus, one of the largest in Metro Washington, overlooks the Potomac River and houses such facilities as a 32,000-square-foot sports center, a riding ring and stables, and an indoor, competition-size swimming pool. The school is set in McLean, close to most points in the metro area.

Nysmith School for the Gifted
13625 EDS Dr.
Herndon, VA
(703) 713–3332
www.nysmith.com

As the name implies, accelerated academics are the rule here. Nysmith's more than 600 students, preschool to eighth grade, receive daily instruction in such subjects as computers, French, hands-on science and individualized math. Student/teacher ratios range from 7 to 1 for preschoolers to 9 to 1 for grade-school children. Students frequently go on field trips around the Washington area and to such places as Colonial Williamsburg and the United Nations. Extended-day and summer programs are available, as is van transportation. The school is in the northwest Fairfax County community of Herndon, convenient to the Dulles Toll Road and Washington Dulles International Airport.

The Potomac School
1301 Potomac School Rd.
McLean, VA
(703) 356–4101
www.potomacschool.org

This prestigious, independent, coed day school places a premium on competitive academics and extensive community service. Its 875 pupils, prekindergarten through twelfth grade, benefit from a student/teacher ratio of about 9 to 1 and average class size of 16. The school takes pride in its interscholastic sports, and its teams include some of the area's top athletes. Founded in Washington in 1904, the school moved in 1951 to its current location, an 82-acre campus in a residential section of McLean. Bus transportation is available.

St. Stephen's & St. Agnes School
Grades JK–8
400 Fontaine St.
Alexandria, VA
(703) 212–2736
Grades 6–8
4401 W. Braddock Rd.
Alexandria, VA
(703) 212–2741
www.ccacad.org
Grades 9–12
1000 St. Stephen's Rd.
Alexandria, VA
(703) 751–2700
www.sssas.pvt.k12.va.us

The emphasis behind this coed, 1,151-student Episcopal day school is balancing challenging academics with community service and other types of extracurricular activities. Courses in religion are required, as are 40 hours of community service and adherence to an honor code. Middle school students take single-gender math and science courses. Some students participate in foreign or specialized summer study programs. All graduates continue their studies in college. Interscholastic sports are a vital part of campus life. The school became established in 1991 through a merger of St. Stephen's, founded in 1944, and St. Agnes, founded in 1924. After-school and extended-day programs are available. The 15-acre lower school, 7-acre middle school, and 35-acre upper school campuses are minutes apart and easily reached via U.S. 395.

Suburban Maryland

The Bullis School
10601 Falls Rd.
Potomac, MD
(301) 299–8500
www.bullis.org

Students are immersed in a range of academic and extracurricular programs at Bullis, founded in 1930. The 600-student coed school, with students in grades 3 through 12, boasts a curriculum that includes traditional subjects and a heavy emphasis on the fine and performing arts, as well as many advanced placement courses. The average student/teacher ratio is 15-to-1. The school also takes pride in its extensive athletic program, in which a large percentage of the student body becomes involved. The Marriott Family Library, which includes a technology center, opened in October 1998. The Bullis Athletic Center houses a 1,000-seat gym, while the school's 2,000-seat stadium holds a football field and eight-lane track. The 80-acre, pastoral campus is nestled in the midst of Potomac, an attractive, wealthy community a short drive from Washington.

Capitol Christian Academy
610 Largo Rd.
Upper Marlboro, MD
(301) 336–2200
www.ccacad.org

Capitol Christian Academy, founded in 1961, offers both traditional and alternative academic programs for coed grades kindergarten through 12. Sponsored by Capitol Baptist Church, the school boasts an enrollment of 465 students. Of special note here are the intimate tutoring and counseling programs for special-needs children.

Charles E. Smith Jewish Day School
1901 E. Jefferson St.
Rockville, MD
(301) 881–1400
11710 Hunters La.
Rockville, MD
(301) 881–1404
www.cesjds.org

With 1,415 students in kindergarten through 12th grade and both lower- and upper-school campuses, Charles E. Smith is the largest Jewish community day school in the country. This coed, Conservative school, founded in 1966, blends a liberal arts curriculum with traditional

Jewish studies programs. The campuses are conveniently situated in downtown Rockville, near the Montgomery County administrative complex.

DeMatha Catholic High School
4313 Madison St.
Hyattsville, MD
(301) 864–3666
www.dematha.org

One of the region's true academic and athletic powerhouses, DeMatha is recognized by the U.S. Department of Education as an "Exemplary Private School." The all-male prep school, with 900 students in grades 9 through 12, is in Hyattsville, convenient to the District and most points in Suburban Maryland.

Georgetown Preparatory School
10900 Rockville Pike
Rockville, MD
(301) 493–5000
www.gprep.org

Founded in 1789 by the Jesuits, Georgetown Prep is one of the metro area's oldest private schools and is the country's oldest Jesuit school. The 435 ninth- through twelfth-grade students who attend the all-male boarding school follow a curriculum steeped in academic and religious tradition. Honors and advanced placement courses are plentiful. Seniors are required to perform 40 hours of community service and participate in an ethics class. The 90-acre, collegelike campus is just a mile from the Capital Beltway.

Holton-Arms School
7303 River Rd.
Bethesda, MD
(301) 365–5300
www.holton-arms.edu

The 101-year-old Holton-Arms is an all-girls college prep school that has a long-held reputation for its excellent liberal arts instruction. Subjects like computer science and African American history add a contemporary edge to the traditional curriculum. The Bethesda-based day school, with 645 students in grades 3 through 12, excels in athletics, fine and performing arts, and other extracurricu-

lar programs. Along with their traditional academic requirements for graduation, students must complete 50 hours of community service and pass a swimming competency test. Seniors participate in off-site senior projects and independent study options. After-school programs are available for all ages. The school holds a coed summer camp for ages 3 through 13 at its 58-acre wooded campus.

Landon School
6101 Wilson La.
Bethesda, MD
(301) 320–3200
www.landon.net

An independent, nonsectarian college prep school for boys, Landon is structured around rigorous academics and a variety of out-of-classroom opportunities in music, drama, and art. Founded in 1929, the day school has more than 600 students in grades 3 through 12. The average class size is 15. The rigorous curriculum includes many advanced placement courses. Volunteer work and community service are valued traditions here, as is an honor code among middle- and upper-school students. Off-campus learning opportunities include a semester spent on a working farm in Vermont and a summer language program in Spain and several French-speaking nations. The lush 72-acre campus is in Bethesda, not far from the National Institutes of Health.

Riverdale Baptist School
1133 Largo Rd.
Upper Marlboro, MD
(301) 249–7000
www.rbschool.org

Riverdale Baptist, with more than 700 students in preschool through 12th grade, is one of Maryland's largest Christian schools. An outreach of Riverdale Baptist Church, the coed school offers academic and extracurricular programs that revolve around the Bible and fundamentalist Christian beliefs. Honors and advanced placement courses are available for academically qualified high school students. The school's athletics department boasts 14 competitive varsity teams, including a

Louis J. Boland Hall was the first building at Georgetown Preparatory School's Rockville location.

PHOTO: COURTESY OF GEORGETOWN PREPARATORY SCHOOL

highly ranked boys baseball team and girls basketball program. A newly refurbished gymnasium offers seating for 700. The band, chorus, and yearbook also garner honors on a regular basis. Riverdale offers extended-day care options and bus transportation for county students.

Colleges and Universities

Metro Washington colleges and universities attract students and faculty from all 50 states and more than 125 countries. A dozen of the region's leading schools are linked by the Consortium of Universities (202-331-8080, www.consortium.org), a network that allows for extensive cross-study programs and sharing of resources such as libraries and faculty. Consortium members include the University of the District of Columbia and the University of Maryland, College Park; American, Catholic, Gallaudet, George Mason, George Washington, Georgetown, Howard, Marymount, and Southeastern Universities; and Trinity College. Of course, many residents of Northern Virginia and suburban Maryland choose to attend schools in their states, but outside the metro area. The State Council of Higher Education for Virginia, 9th Floor, 101 N. 14th Street, Richmond, Virginia 23219, (804) 225-2137, www.schev.edu, offers pamphlets with general information about the state's public and private colleges and universities. Virginia boasts 15 state-supported, four-year colleges and universities, including the highly respected College of William & Mary (757-221-4000), in Williamsburg; James Madison University (540-568-6211), in Harrisonburg; and University of Virginia (804-924-0311), in Charlottesville. Interested in Maryland schools? Obtain a copy of the Student Guide to Higher Education in Maryland through the Maryland Higher Education Commission, 16 Francis Street, Annapolis, Maryland 21401-1781, (410) 260-4500, www.mhec.state.md.us. The guide describes more than 50 colleges and universities in the state, including such popular, nearby choices as Hood College (800-922-1599), in Frederick; Mount Saint Mary's College and Seminary (301-

447-5802), in Emmitsburg; and St. John's College (410-263-2371), in Annapolis. The booklet also includes information about all five U.S military academies, including the United States Naval Academy (410-293-1000), in Annapolis, and private career schools offering training in fields from allied health to truck driving.

Washington, D.C.

American University
4400 Massachusetts Ave. NW
Washington, DC
(202) 885-6000
www.american.edu

"AU," as it's commonly known in these parts, attracts many who aspire to be diplomats and journalists. The independent, coed school, chartered in 1893 by an Act of Congress, offers competitive programs in arts and sciences, business administration, communications, international service, and public affairs. The independent, coed university features extensive study-abroad programs in Europe and Latin America. The campus also makes good use of its city as a learning lab: AU interns in the Washington Semester Program are almost as ubiquitous to D.C. as lawyers and lobbyists. The school takes pride in its university and law libraries, which contain hundreds of thousands of volumes and up-to-date technical support.

Student life is surprisingly close knit, with nearly 3,500 of the close to 11,000 students living on or very near the 84-acre campus, which is in a beautiful residential section of Northwest. Graduate students make up nearly a third of the enrollment, and various programs are available for working professionals. The university's athletic programs are gaining popularity, spurred by the fairly new on-campus gymnasium. Students also can choose from more than 110 co-curricular activities, 11 fraternities, and 12 sororities.

The Catholic University of America
620 Michigan Ave. NE
Washington, DC
(202) 319-5000
www.cua.edu

The Catholic Church's national university, founded in 1887, draws strength from the diversity of its students, who hail from all 50 states and 106 countries. Programs are offered through the schools of religious studies, philosophy, law, arts and sciences, engineering, social service, nursing, music, library and information science, and architecture and planning, and include 59 doctoral, 97 master's and 92 bachelor's programs. The university's 3,040 graduate students outnumber the 2,557 undergrads. The school's drama department is considered one of the nation's best, having produced the likes of Susan Sarandon, Jon Voight, and other stage and screen stars.

Housing on the 145-acre campus, adjacent to the stunning Basilica of the National Shrine of the Immaculate Conception, is guaranteed for freshmen and sophomores. Day care and kindergarten are available for young children of students and staff. Working adults can enroll in a bachelor of arts program through the Metropolitan College. Call (202) 319-5256 for more information. Many students commute to the Northeast campus from the suburbs and other parts of the District. Catholic's highly acclaimed library contains more than 1.43 million volumes and is often frequented by students from other schools in the metro area. The Center for Planning and Information Technology offers a sophisticated array of computer equipment for use by students and faculty.

Corcoran College of Art and Design
17th St. and New York Ave. NW
Washington, DC
(202) 639-1800
www.corcoran.org
The city's sole professional college of art and design, founded in 1890, offers fully accredited undergraduate programs for visual artists, photographers, and designers. Approximately 325 full-time students receive lots of personal attention: The student/faculty ratio is less than 7 to 1. More than 3,000 people annually register for the Division of Continuing Education's Open Program, filled with all kinds of nifty classes for children and adults. The school is affiliated with the venerable Corcoran Gallery of Art, near the White House and the National Mall.

Thousands of metro area residents take advantage of the Corcoran College of Art's classes, many of which are held in their main building, pictured here. PHOTO: COURTESY OF CORCORAN COLLEGE OF ART AND DESIGN

Gallaudet University
800 Florida Ave. NE
Washington, DC
(202) 651–5000
www.gallaudet.edu

Gallaudet, which grew from a small school founded in 1856, is the nation's only university dedicated exclusively to hearing-impaired students. The private liberal arts college, awards bachelor's and master's degrees in more than 50 areas, such as business, biology, communications, the arts, computer science, education, engineering, and environmental design.

The 2,000-strong student body is active in campus and community life. Fraternities and sororities, student societies and intercollegiate athletics are all vital components of the college. Gallaudet also operates model elementary, secondary, and college prep schools for hearing-impaired students. The Visitors Center conducts, by reservation, tours of the school.

The George Washington University
2121 I St. NW
Washington, DC
(202) 994–6040
www.gwu.edu

George Washington is a private, independent institution with more than 9,500 undergraduates, and approximately 11,000 graduate students. Students hail from all 50 states and more than 130 countries. Graduate programs for working professionals prove a growing commodity at GW. Bachelor degree sequences, meanwhile, span the liberal arts and technical spectrum, with international affairs, psychology, political science, business administration, finance, and electrical engineering also proving popular. The international MBA program is one of the best anywhere, and the university's highly acclaimed medical center bolsters the health professions school. The school offers 80 doctoral and 180 master's degree programs.

Washington's biggest school of higher education, GW started in 1821 via an act of Congress. Despite an urban setting, in the oddly named Foggy Bottom, the 43-acre campus maintains a distinctive collegiate atmosphere. Fraternities and sororities prove popular here, as do the more than 200 active student organizations, ranging from international and political societies to literary and theater groups. GW athletics are a growing attraction, especially the men's and women's basketball teams. Freshmen are guaranteed on-campus housing, which also is available to upperclass students who prefer to live here. Many students choose to commute.

The school recently added a 26-acre Mount Vernon campus, formerly Mount Vernon College, at 2100 Foxhall Road NW, Washington, D.C. It specializes in programs for women and is situated in the prestigious Foxhall neighborhood just 3 miles from the main campus. GW also has a Virginia campus (see the listing later in this chapter).

Georgetown University
37th and O Sts. NW
Washington, DC
(202) 687–4328
www.georgetown.edu

Georgetown is undoubtedly one of Washington's—and one of the nation's—most visible and highly regarded universities. The 213-year-old school, the oldest Catholic college in America, has outstanding programs in the arts and sciences, business, engineering, the health professions, and foreign service. The enrollment of nearly 12,700 is almost evenly split between undergrads and graduate students, who are drawn to Georgetown's fine law, business, and medical schools, the last of which includes a teaching hospital. The university also has one the area's most comprehensive continuing education programs, including dozens of interesting noncredit courses open to all adults.

Some may argue that the university's raison d'être is its government department, which each year pumps out scores of budding lawmakers, policy analysts, advisors, researchers, and diplomats. (The alumni list includes former president Bill Clinton.) And when it comes to sports, men's basketball is among the country's finest, producing such stars as former coach John Thompson, Patrick Ewing, and Alonso Mourning.

Students come here from all 50 states and 84 countries, giving the beautiful 104-acre campus an unmistakably cosmopolitan air. As you can imagine, campus life is rich and intense. Undergrads tend to be the fashion- and trendsetters for Washington's 20-something set. The school also promotes spirituality and community service.

Howard University
2400 6th St. NW
Washington, DC
(202) 806–6100
www.howard.edu

Howard is the nation's largest predominantly African American university—and one of the most respected. The school's list of distinguished alumni includes Thurgood Marshall, Andrew Young, Douglas Wilder, Jessye Norman, Roberta Flack, and Vernon Jordan, to name a few. Twelve schools and colleges, supported by 26 research centers, institutes, and special programs, accommodate around 11,000 students. Medicine, law, and engineering are among the top draws. Founded in 1867, the school has grown to include numerous resources, such as a hospital, radio and television stations, and press specializing in African American–oriented topics. The school's athletic program includes acclaimed football and women's basketball teams among its 26 Division I sports.

Howard students (80 percent African American) come from nearly every state and more than 100 countries. More than a third live in student housing, while most of the rest live in the neighboring LeDroit Park section of Northwest D.C. The 89-acre campus is just a couple of miles north of the Capitol.

Southeastern University
501 I St. SW
Washington, DC
(202) 488–8162
www.seu.edu

Founded in 1879, this business school offers flexible class schedules as a convenience to its students, most of whom are working adults who take classes part-time. Programs of study include such

Insiders' Tip

Hoya, the name used for Georgetown University's bulldog mascot, comes from a Greek and Latin phrase, hoya saxa, which means something like "what rocks"! Nobody's quite sure whether the term refers to the school's stone walls or is a cheer for the school's Stonewalls baseball club.

fields as accounting, business management and marketing, and computer science. Close to two Metro stops, the school is convenient for commuters.

Strayer University
1025 15th St. NW
Washington, DC
(202) 408–2400, (888) 4–STRAYER
www.stayer.edu

Strayer is a private, independent business university with campuses in the District (including Takoma Park), Maryland (Germantown, Millersville, and Suitland), and Virginia (Alexandria, Arlington, Ashburn, Fredericksburg, Manassas, and Woodbridge). The commuter school, originating in 1892, offers associate, bachelor's and master's degree programs. Many of the more than 10,000 students are working adults, most of whom take classes in the evenings and on weekends. Classes now are offered on-line too.

Trinity College
125 Michigan Ave. NE
Washington, DC
(202) 884–9400, (800) 492–6882
www.trinitydc.edu

Founded in 1897 by the Sisters of Notre Dame, Trinity is one of the first Roman

Catholic women's colleges. The school boasts a personalized, liberal arts–oriented learning atmosphere and enrollment of around 1,300. Business admin- istration, political science, and information studies are the most popular degrees. Some of the school's graduate programs are coed. A large athletic center opened in 2002.

About 95 percent of Trinity's day stu-dents live on the 26-acre campus just across the street from the Basilica of the National Shrine of the Immaculate Con-ception. About 650 students take courses through the Weekend College, founded in 1984 to meet the needs of working women hoping to complete their bachelor's degrees.

University of the District of Columbia
4200 Connecticut Ave. NW
Washington, DC
(202) UDC–4888
www.udc.edu

UDC is the only publicly funded college in the District and therefore its mission is a bit different than that of its neighbors. Many of its 5,100-plus students enrolled in credit courses are D.C. high school graduates. UDC offers two-year, bache-lor's and master's degrees through its Col-lege of Arts and Sciences, College of Professional Studies, a graduate studies program, and the Division of Continuing Education.

This is exclusively a commuter school, having no on-campus housing. In addition, the university is spread across several loca-tions. Features include a media center, 1,000-seat auditorium, and athletics facility.

Northern Virginia

George Mason University
4400 University Dr.
Fairfax, VA
(703) 993–1000
www.gmu.edu

Fast-growing George Mason is now the second-largest university in the Com-monwealth. Since its founding in 1957, the college has undergone the transfor-mation from a fledgling regional institu-tion into a powerful national public

university. Mason draws on a diverse and impressive faculty, many of whom come from the public policy, business, and political ranks of Washington. Undergrad-uate programs include studies in the arts and sciences, education, information tech-nology, engineering, fine arts, business, and nursing. The graduate school accounts for about 30 percent of the stu-dent body and contains rapidly expanding programs in business and international studies, public policy, and biotechnology, among others.

The vast majority of Mason's more than 24,000 students attend classes on the expansive main campus just outside Fair-fax City. The compact Arlington campus houses the international commerce and policy program and the law school, which is housed in a new building. The school opened a campus in Prince William County in August of 1997.

Almost 85 percent of GMU students are commuters and nearly the same per-centage hail from Virginia. The school can, however, accommodate 3,000 people in university housing. Campus life is what you'd expect from a commuting school: sparse. However, the fine arts center and Patriot Center arena (see our Arts chapter for further details) bring a growing slate of nationally renowned entertainment to the campus. Completed in 1996, the George W. Johnson Center, with eight acres of floor space, houses restaurants and a food/study court in addition to a library and media center. The campus also boasts an aquatics and fitness center, featuring a 50-meter Olympic pool and whirlpool sauna. The school's sports program boasts 300 student athletes.

The George Washington University Virginia Campus
20101 Academic Way
Ashburn, VA
(703) 726–8200
www.gwu.edu

This satellite campus of GWU (see listing under Washington, D.C. in this chapter) is an innovative venture between industry and education. The school offers 17 mas-ter's and doctoral degree programs in areas such as engineering, business, infor-

A statue of George Mason stands before the Johnson Center at George Mason University in Fairfax, Virginia. PHOTO: TOM LEGRO, COURTESY OF GEORGE MASON UNIVERSITY

mation systems, and human resources. The center also conducts a number of nondegree professional development workshops. The National Crash Analysis Center, which crash tests automobiles, is one of several research facilities here. The school is located in the sprawling University Center, a corporate and research park that sits in the middle of eastern Loudoun County's rapidly growing Route 7 corridor, convenient to Washington Dulles International Airport.

Mary Washington College
1301 College Ave.
Fredericksburg, VA
(540) 654-1000
www.mwc.edu
Thanks to the Virginia Railway Express

and a large stock of affordable housing, Fredericksburg has become an exurb of Metro Washington. That being the case, we thought it only appropriate to include in this list the city's academic pride and joy: Mary Washington College. This publicly funded coed college is consistently rated among the nation's top regional liberal arts schools and one of the best buys in higher education. Undergrads number more than 3,000, and highly competitive admission standards will likely keep that figure stable in coming years. Students seem to migrate to the school's psychology, business, and English departments. Bachelor's and master's degree programs in liberal studies are offered to working professionals. MWC's lush, tree-lined 176-acre campus is a recruiting tool in itself.

Marymount University
2807 N. Glebe Rd.
Arlington, VA
(703) 522–5600
www.marymount.edu

Marymount began as a private Catholic college for women. In 1986 it went coed and today it continues to expand, with a branch campus in Loudoun County and school of business in a separate location in Arlington. The mission remains the same, though: to provide an intimate and accelerated atmosphere to grow and learn. The university offers undergraduate and graduate programs in such areas as nursing, business, education, human resource development, psychology, and liberal studies. Day and evening classes are available for working professionals. The school's enrollment of around 3,700 features almost equal distribution between undergraduate and graduate students.

Virginia Tech/University of Virginia Northern Virginia Center
7054 Haycock Rd.
Falls Church, VA
(703) 538–8324 (Virginia Tech)
(703) 536–1100 (UVA)
www.nvgc.vt.edu

This jointly run, 105,000-square-foot center in Falls Church links Northern Virginia with two of the Commonwealth's largest and arguably most influential universities. The main campus of the University of Virginia is in Charlottesville, in central Virginia, while Tech is in Blacksburg, in the southwestern part of the state.

> ## Insiders' Tip
> Area campuses offer great entertainment bargains for all ages. Call for information about film series, concerts, and art exhibitions.

The Northern Virginia center offers adult students an array of graduate and continuing education liberal arts and technical courses. Graduate degree programs are offered in such fields as urban planning, education and engineering. More than 1,500 students attend each school each semester.

Suburban Maryland

Bowie State University
14000 Jericho Park Rd.
Bowie, MD
(301) 860–4000
www.bowiestate.edu

Part of the University of Maryland system, Bowie State is a regional liberal arts institution that boasts strong undergraduate programs in business, education, and computer science. The majority of the circa-1865 school's 5,000-plus students are African Americans, but Bowie's enrollment is multicultural and international. About a third of all students are enrolled in the graduate school. The 312-acre campus includes such features as a learning-resource center, art gallery, radio and TV station, and the Adler-Dreikurs Institute of Human Relations. The school also boasts a strong athletic program, including the NCAA Division II Bulldogs. Close proximity to the MARC commuter rail makes the school easily accessible.

Capitol College
11301 Springfield Rd.
Laurel, MD
(301) 369–2800, (800) 950–1992
www.capitol-college.edu

This college opened in 1927 as a correspondence school called the Capitol Radio Engineering Institute. Today, the private college champions "teaching tomorrow's technology," and awards bachelor's and associate's degrees in communications and engineering, including programs in telecommunications management, computer engineering, optoelectronics, and engineering technology. The majority of students are professionals. The school takes pride in the fact that 95 percent of graduates receive job offers in their chosen fields within 90 days after graduation. Capitol is situated on a 52-acre campus in Laurel, a Prince George's County community between Washington and Baltimore.

Columbia Union College
7600 Flower Ave.
Takoma Park, MD
(301) 891–4080, (800) 835–4212
www.cuc.edu

Tiny Columbia Union (enrollment about 1,100) is a private liberal arts college founded in 1904 and affiliated with the Seventh-day Adventist Church. It's on a pretty, 19-acre campus in Takoma Park, a city known for its grass-roots activism and progressive politics. Business and nursing prove popular among the school's 36 baccalaureate degree majors. Students also can choose from 8 associate degrees and 27 minors. (There are no graduate programs.) Spiritual life and community service play active parts in extracurricular activities, which include several outreach projects. The school also takes pride in its music and sports programs. Most students commute to campus.

University of Maryland at College Park
U.S. 1
College Park, MD
(301) 405–1000
www.umcp.umd.edu

With more than 33,000 students in its 13 undergraduate and graduate schools, The University of Maryland may be large, but with its size comes almost unlimited opportunities for academic and social life. Three-quarters of the students here are undergraduates, and they flock to the university's strong programs in engineering, computer science, physics, education, and business management. Graduate programs in the physical sciences and engineering are bolstered by expanding research facilities on and off campus. *U.S. News and World Report* in 1999 listed the Robert H. Smith School of Business as 22nd in the nation. The National Research Council gives top-20 rankings to the school's programs in agricultural economics, art history, astronomy, busi-

ness, computer science, criminology, economics, education, engineering, journalism, mathematics, oceanography, physics, and others.

The University of Maryland's innovative University College was established in 1947 as one of the nation's pioneering adult education programs. Today, it is one of the metro area's most popular continuing-ed programs, offering bachelor's and master's degrees in business, biology, communications, the arts, engineering, and health professions, among others.

Campus life at Maryland tends to be pretty traditional. About 10 percent of the students are members of Greek societies, and those groups are joined by more than 400 social and professional clubs. Terrapins have always been bullish on their 24 Division I NCAA sports teams, particularly the men's basketball team, which has made numerous NCAA tournament appearances (see our Sports chapter).

Community Colleges
Northern Virginia

Northern Virginia Community College
4001 Wakefield Chapel Rd.
Annandale, VA
(703) 323–3101
www.nv.cc.va.us

Northern Virginia Community College, or "NOVA" in the local vernacular, awards two-year associate degrees in more than 130 occupational, technical, and college transfer programs. The 60,000-plus-student school, the largest college in Virginia and the second-largest multicampus community college in the country, has additional campuses in Alexandria, Loudoun County, Manassas, and Woodbridge. The Extended Learning Institute provides credit and noncredit courses for study at home. Continuing education programs abound on all five campuses and community facilities throughout Northern Virginia, with more than 200,000 students enrolled in noncredit courses.

Suburban Maryland

Maryland College of Art and Design
10500 Georgia Ave.
Silver Spring, MD
(301) 649–4454
www.mcadmd.org

This small school, with about 85 students, has a two-year professional program culminating in an Associate of Fine Art degree. Students concentrate in fine art studies or visual communication areas like graphic design. Class sizes are small, and students spend a lot of time doing studio work.

Montgomery College
51 Mannakee St.
Rockville, MD
(301) 279–5000
20200 Observation Dr.
Germantown, MD
(301) 353–7700
7600 Takoma Ave.
Takoma Park, MD
(301) 650–1300
www.mc.cc.md.us

This community college, with 22,000 credit students and 15,000 continuing education students per semester, is spread across three campuses in Maryland's largest county, and is the state's oldest and largest community college. The Rockville campus, by far the largest with nearly 14,000 students, offers numerous technical and liberal arts transfer programs. The Takoma Park campus specializes in health studies and professional programs. The Germantown campus offers specialized career programs plus the gamut of arts and science courses. In addition to regular, for-credit courses, noncredit programs are taught at campuses and community sites across the county. These popular classes, ranging from auto maintenance to canoeing, enroll more than 17,000 students a year.

Prince George's Community College
301 Largo Rd.
Largo, MD
(301) 336–6000
pgweb.pg.cc.md.us

Another one of Maryland's fine community colleges, Prince George's, founded in 1958, has an open admissions policy and a menu of more than 50 areas of study including accounting, health sciences, education, and law enforcement. Students, numbering more than 35,000, are as diverse as the curriculum, and class enrollment may include a mix of recent high school graduates, midcareer adults, and senior citizens. Summer programs, contract training arrangements, and extension and telecredit courses are all available here. More than half of all credit students transfer to four-year colleges and universities, with the University of Maryland among the top destinations.

Senior Scene

Area Agencies on Aging
Publications
Other Helpful Resources
Community and Senior
  Centers
Retirement Communities

Metro Washington doesn't exactly top the list of the country's most popular retirement destinations. Certainly it's no Boca Raton, Florida, or Phoenix, Arizona. Pervasive national lifestyle trends are working in favor of dynamic urban areas like ours, however. Urban retirement is gaining steam today as more seniors look to metropolitan areas for their healthcare, transportation, recreation, and education needs.

As America's nearly 80 million baby boomers age, they bring with them new expectations. More want to be near family and close to business and volunteer activities. Retiring to Florida's beaches or Arizona's deserts, while still a viable option, isn't for everyone in this new generation of seniors.

The implications of urban retirement are especially profound in the Nation's Capital, a region that's saturated with the types of diversions and opportunities so craved by active seniors. Whether you're just visiting or considering the area as a permanent home, you may be pleasantly surprised at the variety of resources for people ages 60 and older. Housing options include luxury apartments and lush campus developments, geared toward both independent residents and those requiring varied degrees of assistance. Hundreds of senior and community centers offer classes, exercise programs, and field trips, and numerous organizations and businesses feature volunteer and employment options. Meals on Wheels and Friendly Visitor programs provide nourishment and companionship to homebound seniors. Families facing difficult decisions regarding medical care, legal aid, and financial management can find assistance through local agencies.

In this chapter we offer an overview of helpful resources, as well as a sampling of retirement communities. See our Healthcare chapter for information about hospitals and urgent-care facilities, and for suggestions on finding nursing homes and hospice care.

Area Agencies on Aging

Are you trying to locate a senior center to meet your recreational needs? Confused about housing options? Looking for home healthcare? Help is close at hand, through the nearest Area Agency (or Office) on Aging. Mandated by the Older Americans Act of 1965, these offices oversee federally and locally funded grants for programs serving citizens ages 60 and older. The agencies either directly provide or put seniors in touch with such services as Meals on Wheels, senior centers, adult day care, home health visits, long-term care concerns, transportation, discounts, volunteer programs, job banks, emergency aid, financial planning, moving assistance and numerous other resources.

What follows is a list of Metro Washington's offices on aging and some of their programs.

Washington, D.C.

District of Columbia Office on Aging
One Judiciary Sq., 441 4th St. NW, Ste. 900 S.
Washington, DC
(202) 724–5622 (main office),
(202) 724–5626 (info and assistance)
www.dcoa.dc.gov

The office's Senior Service Network features 30 agencies that run more than 42 programs, a 262-bed nursing home, adult day care, and meal delivery. It also publishes a monthly newsletter, *Spotlight on Aging*. The office's six lead agencies listed below, coordinate many nutrition, social, and health programs, along with senior transportation for residents in the city's eight divisions, known as wards.

Barney Neighborhood House Senior Citizen Satellite Center
504 Kennedy St. NW
Washington, DC
(202) 939–9020
This agency serves elderly residents in Wards 1 and 4.

Friendship House Association, Senior Network
619 D St. SE
Washington, DC
(202) 675–9075
Friendship House serves residents of the Southwest section of Ward 2, and Ward 6, west of the Anacostia River.

Greater Southeast Community Center for the Aging/Comprehensive Senior Services—Project KEEN
4025 Minnesota Ave. NE
Washington, DC
(202) 279–5871
This agency serves residents of Ward 6, east of the Anacostia River, and Ward 7.

Greater Washington Urban League, Aging Division
2900 Newton St. NE, 1st Fl.
Washington, DC
(202) 529–8701
This agency serves residents of the downtown and Shaw neighborhoods of Ward 2 and all of Ward 5.

IONA Senior Services
4125 Albemarle St. NW
Washington, DC
(202) 966–1055
IONA serves residents of the Kalorama Heights section of Ward 1, the Foggy Bottom and Dupont Circle areas of Ward 2, and all of Ward 3.

Senior Citizens Counseling and Delivery Services Inc.
2401 Good Hope Rd. SE
Washington, DC
(202) 678–2800
This agency serves residents of Ward 8.

Northern Virginia

Alexandria Agency on Aging
2525 Mt. Vernon Ave., Unit 5
Alexandria, VA
(703) 838–0920
ci.alexandria.va.us/human_services/agnc_aging.html
Besides providing information and referrals, the agency operates a 10-bed assisted living facility and an adult day-care program, oversees two multiservice senior centers, and runs an in-home respite program for Alzheimer's patients and their families. It also offers job training and counseling for low-income seniors, operates a bus service, and publishes a quarterly newsletter. The city council-appointed, 21-member Commission on Aging studies and makes recommendations regarding issues and programs for the elderly.

Arlington Agency on Aging
3033 Wilson Blvd., Ste. 700-A
Arlington, VA
(703) 228–1700
www.co.arlington.va.us/dhs/aging
This information and referral agency also trains volunteers to provide more in-depth assistance to seniors. The agency offers details on such programs as Meals on Wheels, adult day healthcare, and housing concerns.

Fairfax County Area Agency on Aging
12011 Government Center Pkwy., Ste. 708
Fairfax, VA
(703) 324–5411, (703) 449–1186 TTY
www.co.fairfax.va.us/service/aaa/homepage.html
A division of the Department of Family Services, this agency serves elderly residents of Fairfax County and the cities of Fairfax and Falls Church. It offers such services as job training for people ages 55 and older, volunteer visits to and assistance for homebound elderly residents, Meals on Wheels, the Seniors in Action volunteer program, resources for finding home healthcare, and medical claims assistance. The agency also publishes a monthly newspaper, *The Golden Gazette*,

Metro Washington offers numerous attractions, indoors and out, that grandparents and grandchildren can enjoy together.

featuring senior center program schedules and articles about topics and local events of interest to seniors.

Loudoun County Area Agency on Aging
102 Heritage Way NE, Ste. 102
Leesburg, VA
(703) 777-0257
www.co.loudoun.va.us/prcs/aaa/index.htm

The agency's Elder Choices program provides information and referrals. Other services include a licensed respite center for Alzheimer's patients, home-delivered meals, four senior centers for ages 60 and older, a Retired Senior Volunteer Program for ages 55 and older, a discount program that includes some medical care, and a free taxi service to and from medical appointments. The Commission on Aging serves as a citizens advisory board to the agency and the county's board of supervisors.

Prince William Area Agency on Aging
7987 Ashton Ave., Ste. 231
Manassas, VA
(703) 792-6400
www.co.prince-william.va.us/aoa

Among the agency's services are home-delivered meals, two senior centers, two adult day-care centers, home-care assistance, chore and personal-care services for financially eligible seniors, and a popular tour bus program for day and overnight trips, including an annual "mystery trip." The agency serves Prince William County and the cities of Manassas and Manassas Park.

Virginia Department for the Aging
Preston Bldg., 1600 Forest Ave., Ste. 102
Richmond, VA
(800) 552-3402
www.aging.state.va.us

This agency directs state and federal funds to local programs. Call the toll-free number to voice concerns or receive information about local services, finances, scams, and long-term care or visit the Web site.

Suburban Maryland

Maryland Office on Aging
State Office Bldg., Rm. 1007
301 W. Preston St.
Baltimore, MD
(410) 767–1100
www.mdoa.state.md.us

This office oversees the network of 19 local agencies throughout the state. It offers a wealth of information in such areas as senior employment, grandparenting, local events, and wellness. It also includes a report card evaluating Maryland nursing homes.

Montgomery County Department of Health and Human Services Aging and Disability Services
401 Hungerford Dr., 3rd Fl.
Rockville, MD
(240) 777–3000
www.co.mo.md.us/hhs/ads

This agency offers information, assistance, assessments and referrals to elderly residents and their families. The Commission on Aging (240–777–1120), researches pertinent issues and offers recommendations to local government.

Insiders' Tip

Washington Metropolitan Area Transit Authority (METRO); (202-637-7000), offers priority seating for seniors and disabled passengers. Area residents and visitors ages 65 and older can buy discounted fare cards by showing a Metro ID card, available free at public libraries and Metro sales offices.

Prince George's County Department of Family Services
Aging Services Division
5012 Rhode Island Ave.
Hyattsville, MD
(301) 699–2696
www.co.pg.md.us/government/familyservices/Aging_Services/index.html

Besides offering an information and referral service, the agency provides such services as senior centers, a foster grandparents program, a Retired Senior Volunteer Program, and assistance with housing issues.

Publications

Guide to Retirement Living
9302 Lee Hwy., Ste. 750
Fairfax, VA
(703) 383–1111
www.retirement-living.com

This twice-yearly magazine features a comprehensive guide to senior housing options, lifestyle articles, and information about helpful organizations. Call for a free copy.

Senior Beacon Newspaper
3720 Farragut Ave.
Kensington, MD
(301) 949–9766
www.seniorbeacon.com

Published monthly, this Mature Media award-winning newspaper focuses on national and local news and feature stories for the over-50 crowd. The *Senior Beacon* covers health, finance, travel, arts, and volunteer topics. Each year, it publishes three special sections on senior housing options in the area. The paper also sponsors several annual expos and senior job fairs that include speakers and exhibitors on a range of topics of interest to seniors. Every other year, it publishes the *Montgomery County Seniors' Resource Guide,* a comprehensive, one hundred-plus page directory for local housing, healthcare, government, and services. Ads include discount offers for restaurants. The paper is available free of charge at libraries, places of worship, banks, drugstores, bookstores, and restaurants.

Washington, D.C.

AARP
601 E St. NW
Washington DC
(202) 434–2277
www.aarp.org

This national nonprofit, nonpartisan membership organization, headquartered in Washington, offers many benefits for people ages 50 and older, retired or not, which is why it changed its name from American Association of Retired Persons to just AARP. Members receive discounts on lodgings and car rentals and are eligible for insurance, prescription, and credit card programs. AARP's almost 4,000 local chapters provide tax and legal assistance, 55 Alive driving classes and social and volunteer opportunities. The $10-per-couple annual membership includes a subscription to *My Generation* or *Modern Maturity* magazines and the monthly AARP Bulletin, special rates for online services, and free publications on topics of interest to seniors.

The organization boasts more than 35 million members nationwide, more than 85,000 in Washington, D.C., and more than 790,000 in Virginia and 665,000 in Maryland. For local chapters call (202) 434–7701 in Washington, D.C, (410) 837–4300 in Maryland, and (703) 739–9220 in Virginia.

Family and Child Services of
Washington D.C. Inc.
929 L St. NW
Washington, DC
(202) 289–1510
www.familyandchildservices.org

This agency, founded in 1969, offers a variety of services, including a Retired and Senior Volunteer Program with more than 500 participants, respite opportunities for Alzheimer's patients families, help for homebound patients, and recreational and social activities. With the D.C. Office on Aging, Family and Child Services publishes the annual Goldmine Directory, a compact guide to area attractions and

Senior facilities often have spacious grounds or nearby parks where residents can take advantage of a beautiful spring day.

services, many of which offer 10 percent discounts to Washington seniors.

IONA Senior Services
Isabella Breckinridge Center
4125 Albemarle St. NW
Washington, DC
(202) 966–1055
www.iona.org

This 23-year-old nonprofit community organization, largely supported by local churches and synagogues and volunteers, offers a large network of programs for residents ages 60 and older. Some of IONA's many services include an information and assistance specialist (202–895–9448); Healthy Aging Programs such as IONAcise, trips, classes, and lunch clubs; a volunteer network featuring such activities as telephone calls and visits to homebound elderly, meal deliveries, help with medical claims, and cleanup; transportation; a long-term care ombudsman; an adult day-care program; and a resource guide jam-packed with information.

National Association of Retired Federal Employees (NARFE)
606 N. Washington St.
Alexandria, VA
(703) 838–7760
www.narfe.org

Founded in 1921 by 14 federal employees, this membership organization promotes legislation benefiting retired civil servants. NARFE boasts about a half-million members nationwide. Contact the headquarters for information about local chapters.

National Caucus and Center on Black Aged (NCBA)
1424 K St. NW, Ste. 500
Washington, DC
(202) 637–8400
www.ncba-blackaged.org

Health, housing, and other issues of concern to low-income and minority elderly receive this organization's focus. Membership is open to anyone. NCBA also offers a job training and location program (202–483–0220), for people ages 55 and older.

National Council on the Aging Inc. (NCOA)
409 3rd St. SW
Washington, DC
(202) 479–1200
www.ncoa.org

NCOA produces programs and publications that educate seniors and those who work with the aging on such topics as retirement planning, job training, and healthcare standards. Annual dues vary, but cost $50 for retirees.

Insiders' Tip

Call Eldercare Locator, (800) 677-1116, 9:00 A.M. to 8:00 P.M. eastern standard time, Monday through Friday, to find community services for seniors anywhere in the country.

Older Adult Service and Information System (OASIS)
Lord & Taylor, 2nd Fl., 5255 Western Ave. NW
Washington, DC
(202) 362–9600 ext. 562

This educational program for seniors ages 55 and older features classes, lectures, and discussions on topics related to health, fitness, the arts, history, travel, and other areas of interest. Hours are 10:00 A.M. to 3:00 P.M. Monday through Friday. Held at the Lord & Taylor department store in Friendship Heights, the program also is sponsored by the D.C. Office on Aging, IONA Senior Services, and Suburban Hospital. Most classes are inexpensive and a few are free, but registration requires a $10 semester fee. OASIS also has two Maryland locations. (See our Suburban Maryland listings.)

Northern Virginia

All the Right Moves
3284 Laneview Pl.
Herndon, VA
(703) 758–2577

Moving is stressful at any age, but the experience can prove extra unsettling for seniors preparing to relocate to a smaller home or retirement community. This company specializes in making the process go smoothly through such services as decluttering a household; holding moving or estate sales; locating real estate agents, moving services, and contractors; coordinating moving arrangements; designing floor plans; and unpacking and putting away items in your new home. The initial consultation is free.

Elder Crafters of Alexandria Inc.
405 Cameron St.
Alexandria, VA
(703) 683–4338
www.eldercrafters.com

You'll find such handcrafted goodies as quilts, cloth dolls, stuffed animals, carved wooden miniatures, woven baskets, pottery, and stitched, smocked, knitted, and crocheted babies' and children's outfits at this nonprofit consignment shop, just across the street from historic Gadsby's

Tavern in Old Town. It showcases an array of items created by area crafts persons ages 55 and older. Hours are 10:00 A.M. to 5:00 P.M. Tuesday through Saturday, and 1:00 to 5:00 P.M. Sunday; the shop is closed on Monday.

Retired and Senior Volunteer Program (RSVP)
418 S. Washington St.
Alexandria, VA
(703) 549–1607

If you're 55 or older and seeking an interesting volunteer opportunity, contact this organization for information about a variety of options in the Alexandria community.

The Seniors Coalition
9001 Braddock Rd., Ste. 200
Springfield, VA
(703) 239–1960
www.senior.org

This conservative lobbying organization, with 2.4 million members nationwide, focuses on such issues as Social Security, healthcare reform, and the Global Climate Treaty. Annual membership is $10 per person, $13 per couple, and includes a subscription to *The Seniors Coalition Advocate,* a quarterly magazine.

Suburban Maryland

Jewish Council for the Aging of Greater Washington
11820 Parklawn Dr., Ste. 200
Rockville, MD
(301) 255–4200
www.jcagw.org

This organization's Senior HelpLine, (301) 255–4200 in Washington and Maryland and (703) 425–0999 in Virginia, fields a wide array of inquiries regarding elderly concerns. The 25-year-old, non-profit organization offers several other programs, including transportation, adult day care, in-home help with chores and personal care, aerobics programs, computer training, employment services, and estate planning. All programs are open to people of all faiths.

Jewish Social Service Agency
6123 Montrose Rd.
Rockville, MD
(301) 881–3700
www.jssa.org

Kosher home-delivered meals, home health and hospice care, counseling, and long-term care planning are among the services this agency provides for elderly adults, their caregivers, and families of all faiths.

Older Adult Service and Information System (OASIS)
Hecht's, Prince George's Plaza
3500 East-West Hwy.
Hyattsville, MD
(301) 559–6575
Lord & Taylor
Lakeforest, 701 Russell Ave.
Gaithersburg, MD
(301) 947–0502, ext. 560

See the Washington, D.C. listing for information about this learning program.

Over-60 Counseling and Employment Service
4700 Norwood Dr.
Chevy Chase, MD
(301) 652–8072

The Montgomery County Federation of Women's Clubs, Inc., sponsors this employment counseling and referral service for seniors ages 55 and older.

Pam Newton & Company
10121 Donegal Ct.
Potomac, MD
(301) 765–9656

This interior design company specializes in working with seniors who are downsizing their residences. The firm helps clients choose furnishings to move and select colors and accessories for decorating their new home. The business also oversees the move, organizes household goods, and unpacks and puts away items in the new residence.

Senior's Interfaith Resource Center. Inc. (SIRC)
3950 Ferrara Dr.
Wheaton, MD
(301) 962–0820
This nonprofit, volunteer-run organization offers information and assistance to elderly residents of Bethesda, Chevy Chase, and Kensington. SIRC's Hands of Shared Time (HOST) program trains volunteers ages 15 and older willing to provide two hours of weekly service to frail or lonely seniors. Office hours are 9:00 A.M. to 3:00 P.M. Monday through Friday.

Community and Senior Centers

You'll find many senior centers by contacting the area agencies on aging listed earlier in this chapter. The following centers and recreation departments also offer numerous seniors' activities.

Washington, D.C.

Bodywise
University of the District of Columbia Institute of Gerontology
4340 Connecticut Ave. NW, 2nd fl.
Washington, DC
(202) 274–6697
This free exercise program for D.C. residents age 60 and older features water exercise, stretch, walk, movement, and chair exercise in eight locations around the city. Each participant must complete an application form and submit an annual signed medical release form.

District of Columbia Department of Parks and Recreation, Senior Services Division
1350 Pennsylvania Ave. NW
Washington, DC
(202) 576–8677
www.dpr.dc.gov

Contact the Senior Services Division at the above number to locate the nearest of the department's 16 locations, including 14 senior centers, most of which feature daily fitness classes, lunch programs, and special interest activities like creative design classes and drama from 10:30 A.M. to 7:00 P.M. on weekdays. The department also sponsors special activities throughout the year, such as a seasonal farm and garden project, daytrips, concerts, parties, and dances.

District Of Columbia Jewish Community Center
1529 16th St. NW.
Washington, DC
(202) 518–9400
www.dcjcc.org
The center sponsors the Behrend-Adas Senior Fellowship Program from 10:00 A.M. to 2:00 P.M. Monday through Friday at Adas Israel Congregation, 2850 Quebec Street NW. Open to every D.C. senior age 60 and older, the program features a hot kosher lunch ($2.00 donation suggested) along with exercise and nutrition classes, musical performances, bridge, special interest clubs, and at a nominal fee, bus outings. Call (202) 363-7530 to make reservations at least two days in advance. Senior programs, open to all faiths, also take place at the JCC. Senior memberships are $500 annually including non-peak fitness hours, $115 annually without fitness privileges. Nonmembers can attend most events for an additional fee. Seniors can earn a month's membership by volunteering 18 hours of time at the center.

YMCA of Metropolitan Washington
1112 16th St. NW, 7th fl.
Washington, DC
(800) 473–YMCA
www.ymcawashdc.org
Seven YMCA membership facilities in the District, Arlington, Alexandria, Bethesda, Montgomery Village, and Silver Spring offer reduced rates for seniors age 65 and older. Each location schedules a free senior swim session. Members also can choose from a variety of fitness classes.

Both full-privilege and program memberships are available; rates vary at each site.

Northern Virginia

Alexandria Department of Recreation, Parks and Cultural Activities
1108 Jefferson St.
Alexandria, VA
(703) 838–4831
www.ci.alexandria.va.us/rpca/rpca_seniors.html

Four centers serve Alexandria seniors: Nannie J. Lee Recreation Center, 1108 Jefferson Street, (703) 838–4845; Mt. Vernon Recreation Center, 2701 Commonwealth Avenue, (703) 838–4825; Charles Houston Senior Center, 901 Wythe Street, (703) 838–4832; and St. Martin de Porres Senior Center, 4650 Taney Avenue, (703) 751–2766. They all offer a mix of activities, including art, tai chi, bridge classes, walking clubs, wellness lectures, bingo, and trips. In addition, the de Porres Senior Center offers citizenship and English classes to Alexandria's growing Hispanic senior population.

Arlington County Department of Parks, Recreation and Community Resources
300 N. Park Dr.
Arlington, VA
(703) 228–4744
www.co.arlington.va.us/prcr/index.htm

Contact the Office of Senior Adult Programs for a newsletter describing activities at nine senior centers and several activity sites. Membership cards cost $5.00 annually for Arlington residents, $10.00 for nonresidents. Health and fitness classes feature several types of dance, strength training, tai chi, aqua exercise, for arthritis, chair exercise, and more. Other popular programs include walking clubs, a bowling league, performing arts groups, arts and crafts classes, film screenings, special interest clubs featuring such topics as genealogy and books, and cards and games, including duplicate bridge. The travel program features numerous trips each month.

City of Fairfax Senior Center
3730 Old Lee Hwy., Rm. 3
Fairfax, VA
(703) 359–2487
www.ci.fairfax.va.us/parks/senior.html

Residents ages 55 and older can visit weekdays and Saturdays for drop-in and scheduled activities, such as lectures, arts and crafts classes, games, and trips.

Fairfax County Community and Recreation Services
12011 Government Center Pkwy., Ste. 1050
Fairfax, VA
(703) 324–5532
www.co.fairfax.va.us/rec/Senior_Ctr/Senior_Main_Pg.htm

The department's 13 senior centers, most of which are open 9:00 A.M. to 4:00 P.M. Monday through Friday, offer classes, games, discussion groups, outings, and fellowship. Call a day in advance to reserve a hot lunch. Four other sites offer adult meals. Call for locations. Some cen-

Nearby Chesapeake Bay attracts sailors of all ages.

ters feature choral, drama, and tap-dancing performing groups. Fairfax County and City seniors age 55 and older pay half the registration fee for recreation classes, held at senior centers and schools throughout the county.

Fairfax County Park Authority
12055 Government Center Pkwy., Ste. 927
Fairfax, VA
(703) 246–5700
www.co.fairfax.va.us/parks/parks.htm
The park authority's eight full-service recreation centers offer several exercise classes for seniors ages 60 and older. Call for the latest *Parktakes* magazine, which lists detailed information about classes and events. Residents of Fairfax County and the city of Fairfax age 60 and older can register for most events and classes at half off the regular cost.

Falls Church Recreation and Parks
223 Little Falls St.
Falls Church, VA
(703) 248–5077
www.ci.falls-church.va.us/services/park/index.html
Seniors' activities take place at the community center at the address listed and at the adjacent Falls Church Senior Center, 401 West Great Falls Street, (703) 248–5020, and Winter Hill Senior Center, 330-B South Virginia Avenue, (703) 237–4750. Popular programs include fitness classes like line dancing, aerobics, chair exercise, and P.A.C.E.; weekly conversation groups in Italian, Spanish, French, German, and Russian; games such as bridge and mah-jongg; twice-monthly duckpin bowling; Thursday walking trips; and movies on the second and fourth Friday. Special entertainment takes place once a month at the community center. Daytrips include recreational outings and grocery shopping.

Herndon Parks and Recreation
814 Ferndale Ave.
Herndon, VA
(703) 435–6868
www.herndonweb.com/rec/hcchours.htm
Senior programming highlights include art classes, movies, and fitness programs such as indoor walking in the gym, with mileage rewards for those seniors who pile up the most distance.

Ida Lee Recreation Center
50 Ida Lee Dr. NW
Leesburg, VA
(703) 777–1262
www.parksandrec.leesburgva.org/
This facility of the Leesburg's Department of Parks and Recreation offers several fitness classes at half price to seniors ages 60 and older.

Jewish Community Center of Northern Virginia
8900 Little River Tnpk.
Fairfax, VA
(703) 323–0880
www.jccnv.org
Ongoing clubs, requiring an annual $40 Senior Associate fee, meet weekly on Mondays or Thursdays for lectures and seminars on Judaic issues and other topics. Other programs of interest to seniors include bridge, canasta, mah-jongg, chess, discussion groups, Yiddish conversation hours, aquatic exercise classes, and events for singles ages 55 and older. Full senior membership, including use of fitness facilities, is $165 per single, $295 per couple. To join the Senior Club for classes only is $54. Activities are open to all faiths, and most are available to members and nonmembers.

Loudoun County Department of Parks, Recreation, and Community Services
1 Harrison St. SE
Leesburg, VA
(703) 777–0343
www.loudoun.gov/prcs/home.htm
The department's 10 community centers offer a variety of fitness programs and leisure classes for seniors. Contact the Loudoun County Department of Parks and Recreation office for a schedule.

Prince William County Park Authority
14420 Bristow Rd.
Manassas, VA
(703) 792–7060
www.pwcparks.org

Two Prince William County Park Authority facilities offer aqua exercise programs for seniors and reduced admission and membership fees for people ages 60 and older: Chinn Aquatics and Fitness Center, 13025 Chinn Park Drive, Prince William, Virginia, (703) 791-2338; and Dale City Recreation Center, 14300 Minnieville Road, Dale City, Virginia, (703) 670-7112.

Town of Vienna Parks and Recreation
Vienna Community Center
120 Cherry St. SE
Vienna, VA
(703) 255-6360
www.ci.vienna.va.us/town_Departments/
Parks_and_Rec.htm

The center hosts numerous senior activities, including pickleball, bocce ball, mahjongg, fitness classes, blood-pressure checks, craft instruction, travel lectures, financial classes, and meetings of clubs such as AARP and NARFE.

Suburban Maryland

Bethesda Senior Source
4805 Edgemoor La.
Bethesda, MD
(301) 951-1990
www.holycross.org

This health and wellness center, a partnership between Holy Cross Hospital and Montgomery County Government features tai chi, stretching, aerobics, and other exercise classes, as well as films, crafts, lectures, and very popular computer courses for seniors age 50 and older. A $30 annual membership entitles people to reduced fees for classes.

Greenbelt Recreation Department
Greenbelt Community Center
25 Crescent Rd.
Greenbelt, MD
(301) 397-2208
www.ci.greenbelt.md.us

A senior game room and lounge are open during regular hours. Other seniors' activities include hot lunches on weekdays, available by reservation at least a day in advance; a weekly Golden Age Club; monthly movies; craft and continuing education classes, and a weekly intergenerational program with nursery school and kindergarten students. Call for the latest program guide.

Jewish Community Center of Greater Washington
6125 Montrose Rd.
Rockville, MD
(301) 881-0100, ext. 3751
www.jccgw.org

The Senior Adult Division offers activities and hot kosher lunches Tuesdays, Thursdays, and Fridays. Among senior-oriented programs are seminars, craft lessons, a chess club, cards and games, Yiddish, a choral group, a quarterly magazine, Elderhostel classes, trips, water aerobics, and arthritis exercise. Special Sunday for Seniors features a performance or lecture and social time at 1:00 P.M. the first Sunday of the month. Activities are open to all faiths, and most are open to nonmembers for a small fee. Membership for seniors age 65 and older is $350 per single or $550 per couple for full rights, including sports and fitness. A social membership is $125.

Laurel Department of Parks And Recreation
Laurel Municipal Center,
8103 Sandy Spring Rd.
Laurel, MD
(301) 725-7800
www.laurel.md-us/srserv.htm

Senior programming and meetings of senior-oriented organizations like AARP and the Retired Senior Volunteer Program take place at the Phelps Senior Citizens Center, 701 Montgomery Street, (301) 776-6168. Other sites around the city also host classes, workshops, exercise programs, and daytrips for seniors.

Maryland-National Capital Park and Planning Commission
Prince George's County Park and Recreation Administration Bldg.
6600 Kenilworth Ave.
Riverdale, MD
(301) 699-2407
www.mncppc.org

For information about seniors' activities at the county's 40 community centers, contact the above number or these area administrative offices: Central at (301) 249-9220, Northern at (301) 445-4500, and Southern at (301) 292-9006.

Montgomery County Department of Recreation
12210 Bushey Dr.
Silver Spring, MD
(301) 468–4540
www.co.mo.md.us/rec/home/html

Seniors' activities take place at three senior centers and 13 community recreation centers. Especially popular are the 1:00 P.M. programs at Holiday Park Multiservice Senior Center, 3950 Ferrara Drive, Wheaton, (301) 468-4448, featuring such activities as tea dances, concerts, travel lectures, and bingo. Other center offerings include hula and folk dance classes, photography, duplicate bridge, ceramics, painting, woodshop, and several exercise choices. The county's Senior Travel program features a variety of day- and overnight trips, while Senior Outdoor Adventures in Recreation (SOAR) offer trips involving a lot of walking and exercise.

The four other senior county-supported senior centers are: Damascus Senior Center, 9701 Main Street, Damascus, (301) 253-1801; Gaithersburg Upcounty Senior Center, 80A Bureau Drive, Gaithersburg, (301) 258-6380; Long Branch Senior Center, 8700 Piney Branch Road, Silver Spring, (301) 431-5708; and Margaret Schweinhaut Senior Center,1000 Forest Glen Road, Silver Spring, (301) 681-1255.

Rockville Senior Center
1150 Carnation Dr.
Rockville, MD
(301) 309–3025
www.ci.rockville.md.us/seniorctr.htm

Serving city residents 60 and over, this center in a former elementary school offers such programming as low-impact aerobic exercise classes, a fitness room, a computer lab, and bridge. The Carnation Players write and perform two skits a year. Special social activities include the Carnation Supper Club, featuring dinner and

entertainment on Tuesday nights; the annual May Gala dinner dance; and a prom with high school students. The center also sponsors about 40 daytrips, four to five overnighters, and a cruise each year through the Trips and Tours program. Registration is by lottery. Center membership is $15 annually for city residents, $75 for nonresidents, $38 for a nonresident spouse.

Takoma Park Recreation Department
7500 Maple Ave.
Takoma Park, MD
(301) 270–4048
www.cityoftakomapark.org

Bingo games for ages 55 and older take place regularly, along with daytrips. The Takoma Park Community Center, 7315 New Hampshire Avenue, holds seniors' arts and crafts programs.

Retirement Communities

These independent living sites include 24-hour security and safety features such as medical alert systems. Some also offer assisted living options for residents who require some degree of medical or personal care.

Washington, D.C.

Friendship Terrace
4201 Butterworth Pl. NW
Washington, DC
(202) 244–7400
www.esm.org/ft.htm

Convenient to IONA Senior Services, this apartment complex includes a daily meal, health and fitness programs, and cultural and religious activities in the $698 monthly rent. Features include a library, garden, sundecks, laundry, and hair salon. Residents may have pets.

Methodist Home of the District of Columbia
4901 Connecticut Ave. NW
Washington, DC
(202) 966–7623

This nonsectarian apartment community offers independent and assisted living options, with sizes ranging from efficiency to four-bedroom. Rent starts at $2,650 and includes such amenities as three daily meals, housekeeping service, activities, transportation, a hair salon, library, and chapel.

Northern Virginia

Caton Merchant House
9201 Portner Ave.
Manassas, VA
(703) 335–8401

Affiliated with Prince William Hospital and Annaburg Manor Nursing Home, this facility offers four levels of care, from independent to intensive assisted living. Residents can choose from three floor plans among the site's 77 apartments. On-site amenities include laundry and hairstyling facilities, a library, and activity and lounge areas. A certified recreation therapist leads optional educational and social programs. Nursing care is available 24 hours a day, and residents receive three meals daily. The facility does not require an admission fee. Single-occupancy monthly costs range from $1,495 for a studio to $2,095 for a one-bedroom apartment; double occupancy costs an additional $500. Care fees range from no extra charge for independent living to $900 per month for intensive assisted living.

First Centrum Senior Communities
Forest Glen at Sully Station
14401 Woodmere Ct.
Centreville, VA
(703) 802–9501
River Run at Prince William Commons
13910 Hedgewood Dr.
Woodbridge, VA
(703) 878–4618
Manchester Lakes
7131 Silver Lake Blvd.
Alexandria, VA
(703) 921–5500
www.affordableseniorapts.com

These one- and two-bedroom apartments for active seniors range from $695 to $870 and feature such amenities as optional meal programs, hair salons, libraries, lounges, and activities. Both communities are located in bustling suburbs with lots of shopping and community services. First Centrum also has apartments in Maryland (See Suburban Maryland.)

Greenspring Village
7440 Spring Village Dr.
Springfield, VA
(800) 788–0811
www.sclrc.com

This Senior Campus Living property features both independent and assisted living options, as well as nursing care. The complex targets active retirees with such activities as health and wellness programs, classes, cultural events, special interest clubs, and gardening. On-site services include banking and beauty shops. Refundable apartment entrance deposits begin at $111,000. Residents have easy access to both I–95 and public transportation. Senior Campus Living also built Riderwood Village, a similar housing complex in Silver Spring, Maryland, that opened in 2000 (See Suburban Maryland).

The Jefferson
900 N. Taylor St.
Arlington, VA
(703) 351–0011
www.Marriott.com/senior/independent/thejefferson.asp

Just a block's walk from the Ballston Common Metro station and shopping mall, this Marriott condominium complex offers such services as daily meals, a weekly linen and housekeeping service, a hair salon, and activities planned by a full-time coordinator. Residents can take advantage of a creative arts center, library, game room, exercise room, heated pool and

> ## Insiders' Tip
> Before dining out, call ahead to find out if the restaurant offers early-bird or other specials for seniors.

Jacuzzi, lounge area, and private dining room for parties. Choose from 10 floor plans, subject to availability, for one- and two-bedroom residences, with purchase prices starting at $160,000. Monthly service fees start at $1,407, and condo fees start at $95. The complex also offers assisted living and Alzheimer's care, and an on-site home health agency and nursing care.

Retirement Unlimited Inc.
2917 Penn Forest Blvd., Ste. 110
Roanoke, VA
(540) 774-4433

This company owns and operates two retirement communities for adults age 62 and older in Northern Virginia: Heatherwood, 9642 Burke Lake Road, Burke, (703) 425-1698, and Paul Spring, 7116 Fort Hunt Road, Alexandria, (703) 768-0234. Monthly rates include one daily meal, weekly housekeeping, a linen service, special activities, a wellness program, and scheduled transportation to medical appointments and shopping. Rates, per single occupant, range from $1,930 for a studio to $3,323 for a two-bedroom apartment at Paul Spring; $2,090 to $3,045 at Heatherwood. Residents do not have to pay an entrance fee. Additional options include more comprehensive meal plans and assisted living care. The Retirement Unlimited sites also offer such amenities as walking trails, individual gardening sites, picnic areas, hair salons, chapels, and private dining rooms.

Sommerset Retirement Community
22355 Providence Village Dr.
Sterling, VA
(703) 450-6411

Set in eastern Loudoun County, about 45 minutes from D.C., this rental community includes in its monthly rental fees a daily meal, weekly housekeeping and linen services, and scheduled transportation. Residents have access to hairstyling, a community store, a dining area, lounge areas featuring a fireplace and solarium, an arts and crafts studio, games and billiards, programs, and free laundries. Monthly rent ranges from $1,950 for a one-bedroom apartment to $2,350 for a

two-bedroom with two baths. Double occupancy adds $475 per month.

The Virginian
9229 Arlington Blvd.
Fairfax, VA
(703) 385-0555
www.thevirginian.org

This apartment complex, set on 32 landscaped acres, includes such services as two daily meals and housekeeping twice a month and such special features as a wellness center, chapel, library, arts and crafts and woodworking areas, hair salon, convenience store, and hospitality suites. Rent runs from $2,420 for a one-bedroom apartment to $3,630 for a two-bedroom, two-bath design, single occupancy. The Virginian also offers assisted living options, including a newly built Alzheimer's care facility.

Suburban Maryland

Charter House
1316 Fenwick La.
Silver Spring, MD
(301) 495-1600

Convenient to Metro and numerous stores and restaurants, this apartment building for independent seniors also offers assisted living options. Residents do not have to pay an entrance fee. The monthly fee ranges from $1,715 for a studio to $3,355 for a two-bedroom, two-bath apartment. The rental fee includes daily continental breakfast and one additional meal, Sunday brunch, weekly housekeeping and scheduled transportation, wellness and social programs, arts and game rooms, a library, and an activity center. A hair salon and garage parking also highlight the facilities.

Classic Residence by Hyatt
8100 Connecticut Ave.
Chevy Chase, MD
(301) 907-8895
www.hyattclassic.com

Daily breakfast and dinner, weekly housekeeping and linen services, scheduled transportation and utilities are included in the monthly rent, ranging from $2,350 for a one-bedroom model to $4,330 for an apartment with two bedrooms and two baths. Pets are permitted. Residents of the posh rental complex, which is right next door to a country club golf course, have access to a fitness center, indoor swimming pool, wellness center, hair salon, planned activities, transportation and on-site home health care and physical therapy.

Collington Episcopal Life Care Community Inc.
10450 Lottsford Rd.
Mitchellville, MD
(301) 925–9610
www.collington.com

This 128-acre campus community in Prince George's County features garden apartments and cottages for independent seniors, as well as assisted living options and nursing care. Highlights include private balconies and patios, weekly linen service, housekeeping every two weeks, and washers and dryers in the cottages. The Community Center houses a convenience store, hair salon, bank, an interfaith chapel, library, creative art room, woodworking shop, exercise facilities, and a heated pool and Jacuzzi. Residents have access to recreational programs and scheduled transportation. Entrance fees range from $71,950 to more than $592,000. Monthly fees, including three daily meals, range from around $1,829 to $3,659. Construction of 24 new cottages and 50 new apartments was completed in the fall 2002.

First Centrum Senior Communities
Bay Forest
930 Bay Forest Ct.
Annapolis, MD
(410) 295–7557
Glen Forest
7975 Robert Crayon Hwy.
Glen Brunei, MD
(410) 969–2000

See Northern Virginia listing for description.

Leisure World of Maryland
3701 Rossmoor Blvd.
Silver Spring, MD
(301) 598–1000, (800) 398–0085
www.idigroup.com/Maryland.html

Insiders' Tip
Looking for a rewarding volunteer opportunity? Your neighborhood elementary school welcomes older adults who can help students practice reading, assist teachers with projects, and share talents with classes.

Geared toward active adults ages 50 and older, this huge IDI Group Companies retirement community—founded in 1966 by Ross Cortese—houses more than 7,000 residents in 19 condominiums and two cooperatives on a 620-acre site. The latest development, Turnberry Courts, includes three low-rise condominium buildings next to an 18-hole golf course. Prices start in the $160,000s, with monthly amenities fees averaging less than $400. The recreation-oriented Leisure World community includes two clubhouses with features like dining, bowling, swimming, tennis, fitness rooms, spas, and chapels. Residents can choose from more than 80 clubs and numerous activities. Nearby Leisureworld Plaza offers a supermarket, restaurants, specialty shops, services, and medical offices. If you'd prefer to live on the other side of the Potomac, check out the sister community, Leisure World of Virginia, 19400 Leisure Boulevard, Leesburg, Virginia, (703) 581–1711, where condominiums start in the $140,000s.

Maplewood Park Place
9707 Old Georgetown Rd.
Bethesda, MD
(301) 564–5102

Managed by Marriott, a corporation known for its posh hotels, this cooperative in bustling Bethesda takes pride in its many features designed to make senior living worry free. Homes cost $245,000 to $510,000. A monthly fee of $1,662 for a one-bedroom, one-bath model to $3,402 for a two-bedroom with a den pays for taxes, utilities, and such services as 27 dining-room meals, weekly linens and housekeeping, a heated pool and Jacuzzi, a fitness center, activities, a library and other club rooms, and scheduled transportation. Residents have access to a hair salon, bank and general store. Pets are permitted. Maplewood also offers assisted-living and nursing care as needed.

Riderwood Village
3112 Gracefield Rd.
Silver Spring, MD
(301) 572–1300
www.ericksonretirement.com.

Riderwood Village opened in 2000 and offers independent living, assisted living and nursing care. The 500 apartments range from efficiencies to two bedroom/two bath plus sunroom. Entrance fees for independent living range from $75,000 to $362,000, with monthly charges running from $1,000 to $1,600. Residents enjoy a fitness center, arts and crafts and woodworking rooms, an indoor pool, and hot tub. Other amenities include a bank, hair salon, on-site convenience store, and a medical center with a doctor who practices only at Riderwood Village, transportation, and 24-hour security.

Worship

While Washington's unseemly and—sometimes inter-twined—political facets receive endless public scrutiny, the city's intense spiritual side often maintains a low profile. Nevertheless, behind the city's power struggles and political machinations, a religious current runs deep here.

Virtually every denomination under the sun worships in Metro Washington. A quick scan through the Yellow Pages reveals everything from the mainstream to the obscure to the fringe: African Methodist Episcopal, Armenian Apostolic, Baptist, Catholic, Charismatic, Christian Science, Christian (Disciples of Christ), Episcopal, Foursquare Gospel, Jewish, Lutheran, Metaphysical, Moravian, Swedenborgian, and Unitarian, to name but a few.

The Washington area's international character also is reflected in the way its citizenry worships. Throughout the region you'll find Korean Baptist and Greek Orthodox churches; Islamic mosques; Buddhist, Hindu, and Sikh temples, including, in Lanham, Maryland, Sri Siva Vishnu Temple, one of North America's largest Hindu temples; and less-formal congregations representing religious practices from every corner of the globe.

WASPs—British Anglicans, to be exact—founded Metro Washington, and the Protestant influence still dominates, especially in Northern Virginia. Newcomers should be aware of some interesting dynamics, however. Maryland, a state founded as a haven for persecuted Catholics, continues to boast a strong Catholic heritage. (The first Catholic chapel founded by English settlers sprouted in nearby St. Mary's County in 1635.) Washington, D.C. and suburban Maryland boast the nation's fourth-largest concentration of African American Roman Catholics, numbering 80,000 out of half a million members of the denomination. Another 220,000 are Hispanics. In addition Jewish families traditionally have migrated to the Maryland suburbs. These factors partly explain why Maryland and Washington historically have been more ethnically diverse than Virginia, but all that is changing as immigrant enclaves alter the face of even the most homogenous sections of the metro area. Drive through Annandale, Virginia, for example, and you'll likely see many traditional churches bearing signs in Asian characters. Korean, Vietnamese, Indian, and Hispanic settlers all have established their own religious communities in the area. The Jewish community is now a significant presence in Northern Virginia as well, particularly in Fairfax County, home of the busy Jewish Community Center of Northern Virginia and the ultra-Orthodox Chabad Lubavitch organization.

In this brief chapter, we'll introduce you to some of Metro Washington's most colorful and historical houses of worship. We won't recommend or list churches and temples to attend. We'll leave that to clergy and the Yellow Pages. At the end of the chapter, however, we list phone numbers of several religious umbrella groups and associations that might help you get started in finding a specific church, meeting house, temple or synagogue that suits you.

Washington's Spiritual Legacy

Washington, D.C.'s most prominent spiritual icon is also one of the city's newest churches, only recently completed—after 83 years in the making! Construction of the awe-inspiring **Washington National Cathedral**, at Wisconsin and Massachusetts avenues NW (202–537–5596), began in 1907 with the laying of the first cornerstone. It wasn't completed until 1990. The cathedral, said to be the sixth largest in the world, is widely revered as "the last of the great cathedrals," a church built in the Old World fashion—stone by stone. Worship services, concerts, and recitals have been conducted here since Theodore Roosevelt's presidency.

The fourteenth-century Gothic-style structure sits atop Mount Saint Alban, the highest point in the District of Columbia. Despite its recent vintage, the cathedral's soaring towers and huge stained-glass rosettes lend it the same grandeur—and the same graceful patina—as its centuries-old counterparts in Europe. The cathe-

Washington National Cathedral tours describe the Gothic structure's stained-glass windows and gargoyles.

dral's commanding perch above Washington's skyline not only affords great views from its ornate bell towers, but also makes the massive structure a distinct presence, viewable for miles even beyond the city. On a clear day, one can discern the 200-yard-long cathedral from as far away as Fort Washington, Maryland, some 15 miles to the south.

Although officially known as the Cathedral Church of St. Peter and St. Paul, affiliated with the Episcopal Church, the National Cathedral truly serves as an interdenominational place of worship, hosting an array of Protestant, Catholic, and Jewish services. Tours take place several times daily, focusing on such highlights as the building's diverse gargoyles and grotesques, more than 200 stained-glass windows, some 1,500 needlepoint pieces, and interments of such well-known Americans as President Woodrow Wilson, Admiral George Dewey, Helen Keller, and her teacher, Anne Sullivan Macy. (For tour and event information, see the Attractions and Kidstuff chapters. For more information on the cathedral, see the Web site at www.cathedral.org.)

With its vibrantly decorated blue dome, lofty bell tower, and ornately carved, arching entryway, the **Basilica of the National Shrine of the Immaculate Conception** takes your breath away even before you enter the Byzantine-Romanesque stone structure, at 400 Michigan Avenue NE, (202) 526-8300. The largest Roman Catholic Church in the Western Hemisphere, the shrine sits adjacent to Catholic University, a fascinating destination itself. The National Shrine's bell tower, reminiscent of St. Mark's in Venice, contains a 56-bell carillon that chimes concerts on Sundays. Guided tours, available daily, feature the church's amazing artwork, including many elaborate mosaics and more than 50 decorated chapels dedicated to Mary, the mother of Jesus. (For tour and concert information, see the Attractions chapter; to see the basilica's Web site, go to www.national-shrine.com.)

The **New York Avenue Presbyterian Church**, at 1313 New York Avenue NW, (202) 393-3700, is not as well known as the previously mentioned churches, but it's every bit as rooted in Washington history. The Scottish stonemasons who built the White House organized the church in 1803. In contrast, the building itself is of modern vintage, completed in 1951. It contains 19 stained-glass windows, more contemporary than traditional in design. Both Abraham Lincoln and John Quincy Adams were members of the congregation. Visitors can thrill to the sight of Lincoln's original manuscript proposing the abolition of slavery, as well as other historical artifacts described during docent-led tours that begin at the Lincoln pew after Sunday worship services. Visit the Web site at www.nyapc.org.

At one time or another it seems that just about every church in Washington has been honored by the presence of an important politician, statesman, or celebrity. Teddy Roosevelt was a regular at **Grace Reformed Church**, at 1405 15th Street NW, (202) 387-3131, at which he laid the foundation stone in 1903. On Sunday mornings he walked from the White House so quickly his bodyguards couldn't keep up with him, and the single time he was late, he apologized to the head usher and promised never to be tardy again. Roosevelt's wife and family often attended services at **St. John's Episcopal Church**, right across the street from the White House at Lafayette Square, at 16th and H Streets NW, (202) 347-8766. Known as the "Church of the Presidents," because every president since Madison has at some time attended services there, St. John's is where President George H. W. Bush regularly worshiped. Benjamin Latrobe, the architect who restored the Capitol and White House after fire damage during the War of 1812, designed the building. St. John's houses an extensive collection of Roosevelt memorabilia and to this day remains the church most visited by presidents. Visit the Web site at www.us.net/edow/1/stjls.

President Lyndon B. Johnson attended the neoclassical **National City Christian Church** at Thomas Circle, Massachusetts Avenue and 14th Street NW, (202) 232-0323, designed by John Russell Pope, also responsible for the National Gallery of Art and the Jefferson Memorial. Tours take place after Sunday worship services. For more information, go to the Web site: www.natcitychristian.org. **National Presbyterian Church And Center**, 4101 Nebraska Avenue NW, (202) 537-0800, houses the Chapel of the Presidents, a tribute to President Dwight D. Eisenhower, who was baptized at the church's previous location and laid the cornerstone for its current site in 1967. Guided tours following Sunday worship services also include the contemporary Gothic sanctuary's 42 windows, depicting such themes as the Confessions of Faith. The Web site is www.natpresch.org.

President John F. Kennedy attended services at **St. Matthew's Cathedral** (Catholic), downtown at 1725 Rhode Island Avenue NW, (202) 347-3215, also the familiar site of the president's funeral mass. This Renaissance-style structure also has an exotic hint of Asia, thanks to the altar and baptismal font, gifts from India. Guided tours take place from 2:00 to 4:30 P.M. Sundays. Find more information at www.stmatthewscathedral.org. Herbert Hoover, a devout Quaker, worshiped at the quaint stone **Friends Meeting House**, 2111 Florida Avenue NW, (202) 483-3310, www.quaker.org.

Striking Gothic architecture and a rich history give the **Metropolitan African Methodist Episcopal Church**, 1518 M Street NW, (202) 331-1426, its distinctive nickname, "The National Cathedral of African Methodism." The church traces its roots to Israel Bethel, a congregation formed in 1821 by African Americans who had become unhappy with segregated seating arrangements at Ebenezer Meth-odist Episcopal Church. One of the early congregations, at 17th and M Streets, served as a stop on the Underground Railroad. Visitors can sit in pews dedicated to famous people associated with Metropolitan, including abolitionist Frederick Douglass, who often attended services; poet Paul Laurence Dunbar, a frequent guest speaker; and historian Charles H. Wesley, who once directed the church choir. Douglass's funeral took place at the church in 1895.

President Grant attended the dedication in 1876 of **Adas Israel**, the first synagogue built in Washington. The building nearly fell victim to the wrecking ball before being moved to its present location at Third and G Streets NW, now the **Lillian and Albert Small Jewish Museum**, (202) 789-0900, where the sanctuary is restored to its original appearance. The Conservative congregation now worships in a synagogue at 2850 Quebec Street NW, (202) 362-4433, where you'll also find the city's first Holocaust Memorial, featuring a sculptured tribute and Holocaust artifacts. The Web site is at www.adasisrael.org.

Another Jewish landmark, the **District of Columbia Jewish Community Center** at 16th and Q Streets, is an 83-year-old limestone structure built in the classical style. A local Jewish group in 1990 purchased the building from longtime owner University of the District of Columbia and returned it to its original use. (See the Parks and Rrecreation Chapter for more information.)

The oldest church in Washington is **St. Paul's** (Episcopal), established in 1712. It's in the middle of Rock Creek Cemetery, at Rock Creek Road and Webster Street NW, (202) 726-2080. (Despite the street and cemetery name, the church sits several blocks from Rock Creek Park.) On the grounds you'll see one of the most artful and poignant sculptures in Washington: Augustus Saint-Gaudens' bronze statue of a young woman. Henry Adams commissioned the memorial in 1890 in honor of his wife, who had committed suicide. Noted critic Alexander Wolcot called it "the most beautiful thing ever fashioned by the hand of a man on this continent."

The greatest concentration of houses of worship in Washington can be found along 16th Street (a.k.a. the "Street of Churches") in Northwest—one of the city's widest, most stately north-south boulevards. Among the eye-catchers here is **First Baptist Church**, at 16th and O Streets, (202) 387-2206, built in 1955 in a pseudo-Gothic style. Presidents Harry Truman and Jimmy Carter, while in office, frequented First Baptist. Stained-glass window tours follow Sunday worship services. Visit the Web site at www.first-baptistdc.org.

At the southeast corner of 16th and Corcoran Streets is the **Church of the Holy City** (National Swedenborgian Church), an 1896 English-Country, Gothic-influenced building distinguished by a tower, fanciful gargoyles, and numerous stained-glass windows, including one by Tiffany and another by the Lamb studios. For more information, call (202) 426-6734 or go to www.forministry.com/church/church.asp?siteId=20009COTHC.

The **Scottish Rite Temple**, at 1733 16th St., designed by John Russell Pope. largely resembles the Mausoleum of Halicarnassus in Greece. The temple serves as the headquarters of the Supreme Council of the Southern Jurisdiction of the Thirty-Third Degree of the Ancient and Accepted Scottish Rite of Freemasonry.

Also not to be overlooked on 16th Street at Harvard Street is **All Souls Unitarian Church**, (202) 332-5266. The church, whose parishioners include some of the leading African American power-brokers in Washington, was built in 1924 as a reproduction of London's St. Martin's-in-the-Fields. Visit its Web site at www.all-souls.org.

Nearby, at 16th Street and Columbia Road, stands the **Unification Church of Washington** (202-332-5343), a denomination started by the eccentric South Korean Rev. Sun Myung Moon, who also founded the *Washington Times* newspaper (see our Media chapter). Up until 1975, however, the church housed the Mormon Washington Chapel, designed in the 1930s by Don Carlos Young, the grandson of Brigham Young.

One of the most intriguing facades in Washington is that of the **Islamic Center of Washington, D.C.**, 2551 Massachusetts Avenue NW. Located in the thick of Embassy Row, the long white building and its 160-foot-high minaret are the religious and cultural focal points of the Washington area's Islamic community. With its elaborate arches, mysterious courtyard, and decorative tile work, the structure looks as though it belongs in a Middle Eastern oasis. Outside, worshipers—many clad in the traditional snowy white garments—can be seen leaving and entering the building. Inside are a library and a changing exhibit on Islamic culture and religion. Visitors are welcome, but proper attire is the rule here—arms and legs (and, yes, women's heads) must be covered.

Virginia's Colonial Churches

Across the river in Northern Virginia, one can peek into the world of colonial worship at **Christ Church** and the **Old Presbyterian Meeting House** in Old Town Alexandria. Built in 1773 by city founder John Carlyle, Christ Church was the regular place of worship for George Washington and, later, Robert E. Lee. Signature-engraved plaques mark Washington's pew, and across the aisle, the pew rented by Lee, who was 46 years old when confirmed at the church in 1853.

The English country-style church sits in the center of Old Town, at 118 North Washington Street (also known as the George Washington Memorial Parkway), (703) 549-1450. The courtyard's centuries-old poplar and oak trees provide natural shelter for the graves of several Confederate soldiers who died in Alexandria hospitals. Just about every president has attended services at this historic Episcopal church. (See Attractions for tour information.) Visit the Web site at www.historicchristchurch.org.

Alexandria's Scottish forefathers also built the **Old Presbyterian Meeting House** at 316 South Royal Street, (703) 549-6670. George Washington's funeral services, originally scheduled for Christ Church, were held here because icy roads made the trip to the center of town impossible. Buried in the cemetery behind the meeting house is the Unknown Soldier of the American Revolution. The Web site is www.opmh.org.

In nearby Lorton, Washington, George Mason and George William Fairfax were among the prominent people who attended the Georgian-style **Pohick Church**, listed on the National Register of Historic Sites. Visitors' tours follow Sunday services. The church is at 9301 Rich-

Christ Church in Old Town Alexandria was the regular place of worship for George Washington and Robert E. Lee. PHOTO: COURTESY OF VIRGINIA TOURISM CORPORATION

mond Highway, Lorton, (703) 339-6572, www.pohick.org.

The **Falls Church** (Episcopal), 115 East Fairfax Street, Falls Church, (703) 532-7600, dates to 1734. George Washington was a vestryman here. Read more about the church and its history at www.thefallschurch.org.

Latter-day Saints and a Literary Landmark

Suburban Maryland has its share of spiritual landmarks, but none is more imposing than the **Washington Temple of the Church of Latter-day Saints**, which towers above the Capital Beltway in Montgomery County like a vision of Dorothy's Emerald City. The $15 million white marble temple, complete with gold spires, is a sight to behold, especially when dramatically lit after dark. The outside is all that most people will ever see of this imposing structure because it's off-limits to non-Mormons (although public tours were given for a short time after construction was completed). However, during the winter holiday season, everyone is invited to the temple's Festival of Lights, a not-to-be-missed spectacle. (See the Close-up in this chapter.) In addition, the visitor center features tours, films and literature.

Literary buffs may want to venture up to Rockville, the Montgomery County seat about 30 minutes from downtown Washington, to view the grave sites of F. Scott Fitzgerald and his wife, Zelda, at the cemetery at **St. Mary's Catholic Church**, at Viers Mill Road and Rockville Pike, (301) 424-5550. Their remains were moved here in 1975 from their original graves in Rockville Cemetery. Visit the Web site at www.stmarysrockville.org.

We have not yet even begun to scratch the surface of Metro Washington's fascinating spiritual landmarks. Should you venture into the Washington exurbs, you'll find additional interesting religious sites, but we'll save that for another chapter (see Daytrips).

Worship Resources

Interdenominational

Council of Churches of Greater Washington
5 Thomas Circle, NW
Washington, DC
(202) 722–9240
Approximately 400 Protestant churches of about 17 denominations belong to this organization, which sponsors such unifying events as joint worship services.

Interfaith Conference of Metropolitan Washington
1419 V St. NW, Washington, D.C.
(202) 234–6300
www.interfaith-metrodc.org/ifc.htm
The unique alliance of eight faiths—Baha'i, Hindu-Jain, Islamic, Jewish, Latter-day Saints, Protestant, Roman Catholic, and Sikh—sponsors a fall concert, winter Martin Luther King Jr. prayer day, spring public dialogue led by youth, and summer pilgrimage to places of worship. Call for a schedule of events.

Protestant

African Methodist Episcopal/
Second Episcopal District Headquarters
1134 11th St. NW
Washington, DC
(202) 842–3788
Bishop Vinton R. Anderson's office oversees more than 360 congregations in Baltimore, Washington, D.C., Northern Virginia, and North Carolina.

Insiders' Tip
George Washington purchased pew number 60 at Christ Church in Alexandria, Virginia, for 36 pounds and 10 shillings when the church opened in 1773.

An Enlightening Experience

A dazzling holiday spectacle little known to Washington visitors is the Festival of Lights, held each Christmas season at the Washington Temple of the Church of Jesus Christ of Latter-day Saints. This seasonal extravaganza of lights, music, and theater is sure to appeal to anyone, regardless of religious affiliation.

The Mormon Temple, as it's commonly known in the metro area, is just a 30-minute drive from downtown Washington—an Oz-like beacon high above the Capital Beltway in Kensington, Maryland. From early December until early January, the temple displays 300,000 multicolored lights topped off by the illuminated spires of the temple itself. So laborious is the illumination that stringing and testing must begin in September of each year to ensure completion in time for the holidays.

Besides the lights, visitors can enjoy the traditional life-size nativity, which features a live Mary and Joseph. The narration of the Biblical Christmas story takes place each evening (check at the on-site visitor center for the time and exact location).

Inside the visitor center, you'll discover a display of tall Christmas trees decorated in scriptural themes and adorned with thousands of ornamental lights and ornaments such as international and handmade dolls.

Artists from Europe, South America, Africa, and Asia contribute to an international collection of nativity sets, also on display in the visitor center. The sets, or crèches, reflect a colorful blend of the traditional nativity scene and the cultural perspective of each artist.

The Festival of Lights is featured at the Washington Mormon Temple visitor center of the Church of Jesus Christ of Latter-day Saints. PHOTO: DAVID HOFELING, HOFELING & ASSOCIATES PHOTOGRAPHY

In addition to the displays, nightly concerts feature choirs and instrumental groups from schools and area churches of many denominations. On Christmas Day a local theater group presents a special family show. The center's five theaters screen Christmas and holiday films such as Mr. Krueger's Christmas, starring Jimmy Stewart, as well as some Spanish presentations.

All events are open to the public. Lights come on at dusk each evening. The center is at 9900 Stoneybrook Drive, Kensington, Maryland. For directions and visitor center hours, call (301) 587–0144 or visit the Web site at www.washingtonlds.org.

Baltimore Yearly Meeting of the Religious Society of Friends (Quakers)
17100 Quaker La.
Sandy Spring, MD
(301) 774–7663, (800) 962–4766
www.bym-rsf.org

Based in the Washington area's largest traditional Quaker community, this office can locate area meeting houses.

Christian Church-Capital Area (Disciples of Christ)
8901 Connecticut Ave.
Chevy Chase, MD
(301) 654–7794
www.ccca.chevy-chase.md.us

This regional office oversees about 50 congregations in the Washington area, Delaware, and West Virginia.

Church of the Brethren, Mid-Atlantic District
10378 Baltimore National Pk.
Ellicott City, MD
(410) 465–8777
mad.cob.home.mindspring.com

Sixty-three congregations in the Washington area, Pennsylvania, Delaware, and West Virginia fall under the jurisdiction of this regional office.

D.C. Baptist Convention
1628 16th St. NW
Washington, DC
(202) 265–1526
www.dcbaptist.org

This organization coordinates more than

125 Southern, American, and Progressive congregations in Washington, D.C., Northern Virginia, and Suburban Maryland.

Episcopal Diocese of Washington
Episcopal Church House,
Washington National Cathedral grounds,
Mount Saint Alban, Wisconsin and
Massachusetts Aves. NW
Washington, DC
(202) 537–6555
www.us.net/edow

The office oversees more than 90 Episcopalian churches in Washington, D.C., Southern Maryland, and Montgomery County.

Metropolitan Washington, D.C. Synod of the Evangelical Lutheran Church of America
1030 15th St. NW, Ste. 1010
Washington, DC
(202) 408–8110
www.metrodcelca.org

Seventy-eight congregations in Washington, D.C., Maryland, and Northern Virginia fall under the office's jurisdiction.

National Capital Presbytery
4915 45th St. NW
Washington, DC
(202) 244–4760
www.natinalcapitalpresbytery.org

The regional office oversees 114 congregations of the Presbyterian church (U.S.A.) in the Washington area.

Southeastern District Lutheran Church, Missouri Synod
6315 Grovedale Dr.
Alexandria, VA
(703) 971–9371
www.sc.lcms.org

The district oversees 206 congregations in the D.C. area, Maryland, Virginia, Delaware, North and South Carolina, and Pennsylvania.

United Church of Christ, Central Atlantic Conference, Potomac Association
916 S. Rolling Rd.
Baltimore, MD
(410) 788–4190, (800) 441–1965
www.cacucc.org

The conference's Potomac Association includes more than 30 congregations in the Washington vicinity.

United Methodist General Board of Church and Society
100 Maryland Ave. NE
Washington, DC
(202) 488–5600
www.umc-gbcs.org

This board deals with United Methodist Ministry programs.

Roman Catholic

Archdiocese of Washington
5001 Eastern Ave.
Hyattsville, MD
(301) 853–4500
www.adw.org

This governing body oversees more than 140 parishes in the capital and in several Maryland counties.

Arlington Diocese
200 N. Glebe Rd., Ste. 914
Arlington, VA
(703) 841–2500

The diocese's new bishop, the Most Rev. Paul S. Loverde, oversees 63 parishes in 21 counties and seven independent cities in Virginia.

Jewish

Jewish Information and Referral Service of Greater Washington
6101 Montrose Rd.
Rockville, MD
(301) 770–4848
www.jirs.org

Part of the Jewish Federation of Greater Washington, this office helps people find synagogues and other Jewish organizations in the Washington area.

Media

It's been said that information is a fundamental component of power. If so, residents of Metro Washington could be considered some of the most powerful people in the world. Indeed, many are just that, with number 1 on the list living at 1600 Pennsylvania Avenue NW.

This chapter isn't about the political players, however, but rather the awesome presence of the information players. There are few places beyond Washington where the incoming and outgoing stream of information—specifically the written and spoken products of the print and electronic media—is as intense. There are also few places beyond Washington where citizens have as much interaction with and exposure to the conveyors of that information: literally thousands of reporters, editors, correspondents, broadcasters, freelance writers, and others of the same ilk from around the globe who practice their trade here.

Washington has the highest concentration of journalists anywhere in the world, a staggering testament to the sphere of influence of the so-called fourth estate, the term used to denote the public press (traditionally, the first three estates, each with its own influence in government, are nobility, clergy and townspeople). It's also a downright scary thought to many people (at least until they count the lawyers!) that there are all those nosy journalists running around. It's to be expected, however, Washington plays the dual role of capital of the nation and capital of the free world.

When Local Means National

Living in Metro Washington, you soon get used to much of the "local" news also being national and international. Call it a blessing or a curse—it's reality. It's what happens when reporters have beats that include not only city hall, the county courthouse, and the school board, but also the White House, Capitol Hill, the Supreme Court, the Pentagon, and other focal points of the federal establishment.

Beyond the newspapers, magazines, radio and TV stations, and other media based in Metro Washington, nearly all major (and some minor) news outlets in the world have a presence here, whether they're full-blown bureaus with dozens of staffers and a complement of high-tech machinery or lone correspondents holding court at the National Press Building with little more than desk, telephone, and laptop computer.

Metro Washington is home to such media giants as The Washington Post Company, publisher of one of the world's most influential newspapers; Gannett Co. Inc., proud parent of "The Nation's Newspaper," *USA TODAY,* and a large stable of other print and broadcast properties; America Online, the popular computer network, with more than 17 million subscribers nationwide; United Press International, a Pulitzer-Prize winning news service; and the National Geographic Society, an American publishing institution that produces not only great magazines, but also maps, globes, books, and TV specials. Numerous trade associations based here also represent the press in one form or another.

The winds of change are forever blowing in our fair city, and even prominent media are not immune to their gusts. Some longtime residents still mourn the loss of the popular afternoon daily, the *Washington Star.* The *Washington Times* has strived mightily since 1982 to fill the void, but it just hasn't been the same. The *Washington Post* has long been, and remains, the undisputed king of the local media hill. Local magazines that stopped their presses for good over the past few years include *Regardie's,* which profiled Washington's power hitters; *Dossier,* which chronicled the significant society and party circuit in the Nation's Capital; *Museum & Arts Washington,* an outstanding monthly that focused on the city's impressive arts and cultural scene; and *New Dominion,* a Northern Virginia lifestyle/business magazine. But Washingtonians also have witnessed the birth of new publications, such as *Washington Flyer,* the nation's first in-airport magazine and an official product of the Metropolitan Washington Airports Authority, launched at Ronald Reagan National and Washington Dulles International Airports; and, in the fall of 1997, *Capital Style,* devoted to "the art of political living."

It's All Within Your Reach

Whether scanning the radio or TV dial, or flipping through a newspaper or magazine, you quickly realize Washington media are diverse to say the least. The region's global influence is evident in the availability of foreign and domestic publications at neighborhood convenience stores, bookshops, libraries, and sidewalk newsstands. News junkies, students, academicians, and homesick transplants will be relieved to know they can find numerous foreign and domestic reads at such publication sources as Newsroom, 1753 Connecticut Avenue NW, (202) 332–1489, which carries scholarly journals and bilingual directories, and many large chain bookstores in the metropolitan area.

Several major newspapers based elsewhere, such as the *New York Times* and the *Wall Street Journal,* offer same-day delivery to certain areas of Metro Washington. Virginians wanting to keep close tabs on events in their state capital can pick up a current copy of the *Richmond Times-Dispatch*—one of the South's oldest and most respected newspapers—at some area newsstands; the paper also maintains a Washington bureau. Maryland residents keep up with statewide news by reading the *Baltimore Sun* and the *Capital,* a daily out of Annapolis.

As with other topics covered in this book, this chapter is intended as an overview, not an encyclopedic compilation. We've avoided, for the most part, mentioning any personalities and other details that could become outdated quickly. Although we've tried to be as current as possible, bear in mind that publication titles, radio and TV formats, and the ownership of such entities can and do change with little warning.

Newspapers

Although TV and radio have come a long way since their inception in delivering the news with unprecedented speed and, in the case of television, amazing visual impact, the newspaper still provides expansive coverage and an overriding sense of permanence.

Dailies

The Journal Newspapers
6408 Edsall Rd.
Alexandria, VA
(703) 846–8000
www.jrnl.com

The *Journal* publishes separate editions Monday through Friday in six area jurisdictions: the city of Alexandria plus the counties of Arlington, Fairfax, Prince William, Montgomery and Prince George's. It also produces four Sunday editions. Circulation is 126,649 Mondays through Thursdays; 178,743 on Fridays, and 386,000 on Sundays.

Suburbanites now depend on the *Journal* for in-depth coverage of their communities beyond what the *Washington Post* and the *Washington Times* provide. It takes a full-time presence to maintain the suburban readership, and the *Journal* certainly has that.

The chain does a respectable job of covering its own turf, particularly in the areas of news, sports, and features, and it has been known to scoop its two major competitors in bread-and-butter categories such as local government, crime, and the courts.

The Washington Post
1150 15th St. NW
Washington, DC
(202) 334–6000
www.washingtonpost.com

Scan virtually any list of the most influential newspapers in the nation, even the world, and the *Washington Post* is sure to be there with domestic powerhouses such as the *New York Times*, the *Wall Street Journal* and the *Los Angeles Times*. It boasts an average daily circulation of 759,864 and 1,026,227 on Sundays.

Like many publications, the *Post* is making high-tech changes: In a gradual makeover that began in 1997 with new printing presses, the paper is changing its appearance, with the most notable difference being color photos throughout the paper. The paper is also accessible online with current editions and recent articles. Another resource is Post-Haste, a free information service accessible by touch-tone telephone, (202) 334–9000. Its aggressive on-line counterpart constantly introduces new services from comprehensive restaurant reviews to neighborhood overviews.

No matter what you think of its liberal bent, you'll find the *Post* to be a top-notch major newspaper, with its wealth of resources, its worldwide presence and an immense staff replete with Pulitzer Prize-winning reporters, editors, photographers and even a cartoonist (the inimitable "Herblock," who died in 2001). After all, this is the paper that broke the Watergate scandal, propelling two formerly obscure reporters, Bob Woodward and Carl Bernstein, to international notoriety and forever changing investigative journalism.

Living in Metro Washington and reading the *Post* day in and day out, you come to expect what readers of many other papers do not: in-depth analysis and commentary, from both sides of the political fence, on a broad range of topics; reprints of the entire text of presidential speeches and news conferences; a Sunday magazine; stories and photos from the farthest reaches of the world provided by *Post* staffers, not wire services; heavy coverage of national and international news to complement local happenings; in-depth special series; and stimulating editorial and op-ed pages. The paper also boasts lively lifestyle pages; weekly food, health, business, and community sections; and Friday's tabloid, *Weekend,* a comprehensive guide to upcoming events. Because of its heavy national and international news bent, local news has sometimes taken the backseat. But recently beefed-up zoned weekly sections have helped remedy that. Still, it's easy to get spoiled; just a few days out of town can cause acute information withdrawal.

The Washington Times
3600 New York Ave. NE
Washington, DC
(202) 636–3000
www.washtimes.com

If nothing else, the *Washington Times* gives conservatives a loud, colorful voice. Plucky and aggressive, the *Times* (which also publishes a weekly news magazine, *Insight*) has only been a seven-day-a-week paper since 1991, but you wouldn't know it from the way it challenges the *Post* everywhere in its marketing strategies and daily news coverage.

The *Times* distinguishes itself not only with its strong right-wing tilt, but by its ownership: the Rev. Sun Myung Moon's Unification Church. Controversy and circulation figures aside, the *Times* has come a long way in little more than a decade in making Washington a two-newspaper town again and in convincing people to give them a try. With their own wealth of talented staffers, many of them former *Star* employees, the *Times* has earned praise for its visual appeal, outstanding sports and business sections, hard-hitting investigative instincts, and for hustle, gumption, and chutzpah in the face of a David and Goliath sort of rivalry with the *Post*.

The *Times* publishes its weekend section on Thursdays as a service to those who like to have Saturday and Sunday planned by the time Friday rolls around—a novel idea indeed. The *Times*, like the *Post*, can be perused online.

virtually every enclave in Washington, D.C., Northern Virginia, and Suburban Maryland having some sort of newspaper to call its own.

Many publications are free and distributed either by mail or to the doorstep based on ZIP code.

Washington, D.C.

The Current Newspapers
5125 MacArthur Blvd. NW, Ste. 18
Washington, DC
(202) 244–7223

The *Northwest Current* and *Georgetown Current* newspapers print news and features in neighborhoods from Chevy Chase to Foggy Bottom. The free papers are distributed every Wednesday via bulk drop and home delivery. A yearly subscription for home delivery is $52.

The Georgetowner Newspaper
1054 Potomac St. NW
Washington, DC
(202) 338–4833
www.georgetowner.com

This free paper, founded in 1954, is devoted exclusively to Georgetown, featuring community news and features, historical lore, book reviews, and an events calender. Published every other week, it's circulated throughout Georgetown and surrounding areas.

Hill Rag
224 7th St. SE
Washington, DC
(202) 543–8300
www.hillrag.com

This monthly magazine-style newspaper, founded in 1976, features neighborhood news, film and book reviews, and editorials geared toward readers who live or work on Capitol Hill. Distributed the first weekend of each month, the free paper is widely available at restaurants, bars, and in news boxes.

Washington City Paper
2390 Champlain St. NW
Washington, DC
(202) 332–2100
www.washingtoncitypaper.com

As long as the money doesn't run out, the *Times* will continue to be the proverbial fly in the *Post*'s ointment and the darling of the conservative establishment. The battle is good old-fashioned newspaper competition at its finest.

USA Today
1000 Wilson Blvd.
Arlington, VA
(703) 276–3400
www.usatoday.com

With its extensive use of color and digest-style news coverage, "The Nation's Newspaper" originated the look that's become the trend in print journalism. The locally headquartered paper, which published its first edition in 1982, is sold Monday through Friday in newsboxes almost everywhere. It boasts an average circulation of 2.2 million readers. *USA Today* is also online.

Community Newspapers

Residents of Metro Washington have dozens of community news outlets. The weekly chains in particular are vast, with

This hip weekly attracts predominantly young, single professionals, who are drawn to its extensive coverage of culture, the arts, music, and nightlife. It gives a comprehensive rundown of upcoming events, covers controversial and newsworthy issues through in-depth features, and runs personal ads like you don't usually see in mainstream publications. This free tabloid is published on Thursdays and is typically available at book and music stores in the metropolitan area.

The Washington Sun Newspaper
830 Kennedy St. NW
Washington, DC
(202) 882–1021

This weekly targets the entire Metro Washington area, with a mixture of local and world news and information about community events. Published on Thursdays and distributed throughout the area, it costs 25 cents per issue, or $50 for a yearly subscription.

Northern Virginia

Connection Publishing Inc.
7913 Westpark Dr.
McLean, VA
(703) 821–5050

The area's largest local newspaper publisher has numerous weeklies throughout Northern Virginia. The *Alexandria Gazette Packet* features news of the city of Alexandria, while the county's southern end receives coverage in the *Mount Vernon Gazette*. The bustling western Fairfax communities of Centreville and Chantilly receive coverage in *Centre View*. The Connection weekly tabloids cover news and features in Arlington, Burke, Fairfax, Fairfax Station, Springfield, Reston, Herndon, McLean, Great Falls, Loudoun, and Vienna/Oakton.

Falls Church News-Press
929 W. Broad St.
Falls Church, VA
(703) 532–3267
www.fcnp.com

The city's free "Independent, Locally Owned Newspaper of Record" is published every Thursday and distributed throughout the city and neighboring areas. It is accessible online.

The Metro Herald
901 N. Washington St., Ste. 603
Alexandria, VA
(703) 548–8891
www.metroherald.com

This weekly, published on Fridays, actually covers the entire Metro Washington area through regional news, commentary, business and sports updates, events listings, and lifestyle and entertainment features. A single copy costs 75 cents, and a subscription is $75 annually.

Old Town Crier
112 S. Patrick St.
Alexandria, VA
(703) 836–0132
www.oldtowncrier

Another Alexandria-based periodical, this one prints lifestyle features, entertainment and restaurant news, business briefs, and events listings, "From the Bay to the Blue Ridge." This monthly paper is available at the Alexandria Visitors and Convention Bureau and local businesses in Alexandria, Fairfax, Fredericksburg, and the Blue Ridge area of Virginia; Annapolis, Maryland; and Georgetown in Washington, D.C. The company launched the monthly Georgetown Crier in 1999. Both publications are also online.

SunGazette
2710-C Prosperity Ave.
Fairfax, VA
(703) 204–2800
www.sun-weekly.com

The Sun Gazette chain consists of three weekly newspapers: the *Sun Gazette* (serving McLean, Vienna, Oakton and Great Falls), the *Arlington Sun Gazette,* and the *Fairfax/Fairfax Station Sun Gazette.*

Times Community Newspapers
1760 Reston Pkwy., Ste. 411
Reston, VA
(703) 437–5400
www.timespapers.com

ARCOM Publishing owns this massive, ever-growing newspaper group, featuring

14 community weekly newspapers, including the flagship *Loudoun Times Mirror* in Leesburg. Other links in this vast chain include the *Eastern Loudoun Times* and the Times Community newspapers in the Fairfax County communities of Burke, Centreville, Chantilly, Fairfax, Fairfax Station, Great Falls, Herndon, McLean, Reston, Springfield, and Vienna. A bit more removed from the Metro Washington area are the *Fauquier Times Democrat,* the *Clarke Courier* and *Rappahannock News* (which also has a Web site).

Suburban Maryland

Almanac Newspapers
10220 River Rd.
Potomac, MD
(301) 983–3350
Owned by Connection Publishing, Inc., a major force in Northern Virginia community news, the Almanac carries local news about Bethesda and Chevy Chase and the Potomac vicinity. The paper has earned numerous awards from the Maryland Delaware D.C. Press Association. Distribution is free, and it arrives by bulk drop.

Bowie-Blade News
Crofton News Crier
6000 Laurel-Bowie Rd., Ste. 101
Bowie, MD
(301) 262–3700
www.capitalonline.com

Insiders' Tip

Check *Washingtonian* magazine and the weekend sections of the *Washington Post* and the *Washington Times* for helpful guides to local dining, shopping, nightlife, and assorted recreational diversions.

Owned by Capital Gazette Communications Inc., which also publishes the *Capital* daily newspaper in Annapolis and *Maryland Gazette,* a weekly in Glen Burnie, these suburban weeklies carry news and features from their respective communities. Published on Thursdays, they're available at newsstands and by carrier delivery ($1.47 for four weeks) or subscription by mail ($13 for six months).

The Enquirer-Gazette
14760 Main St.
Upper Marlboro, MD
(301) 627–2833
This weekly covering Prince George's County and parts of nearby Charles, St. Mary's, and Calvert Counties was founded in 1851. Distributed on Thursdays by mail and at local newsstands, it costs 25 cents a copy. The parent company, Chesapeake Publishing, also owns weeklies in the three nearby counties previously mentioned.

Gazette Newspapers
1200 Quince Orchard Blvd.
Gaithersburg, MD
(301) 948–3120
www.gazette.net
They seem to be everywhere: The Gazette Newspapers publish news and features in the communities of Aspen Hill, Bethesda, Burtonsville, Chevy Chase, Damascus, Frederick, Gaithersburg, Germantown, Kensington, Mt. Airy, Olney, Poolesville, Potomac, Prince George's County, Rockville, Silver Spring, Takoma Park, and Wheaton. The papers are published Wednesdays and distributed free to homeowners. The company also publishes the monthly *Montgomery Business Gazette* and *Tech Gazette.* You can find Gazette newspapers online.

Montgomery County Sentinel
615 S. Frederick Ave.
Gaithersburg, MD
(301) 838–0788
www.thesentinel.com
Covering community news, the *Sentinel* is the county's oldest weekly newspaper. It's published on Thursdays.

Prince George's Sentinel
9458 Lanham-Severn Rd.
Seabrook, MD
(301) 306–9500
www.thesentinel.com

This weekly features community news about Prince George's County. This one's also published on Thursdays.

African-American Newspapers

The African Shopper
P.O. Box 2540
Washington, DC 20003
(202) 882–8840

This free monthly newspaper includes international news briefs, columns on business and legal issues, a guide to African currency, and assorted features. It's available locally and nationally at libraries, the African embassies, universities, and various stores.

Capital Spotlight Newspaper
National Press Bldg.
529 14th St. NW, Ste. 202
Washington, DC
(202) 745–7858

This free weekly, founded in 1953, focuses on noncontroversial, inspirational news and features geared toward the local African American community. The paper is distributed on Thursdays in bulk drops at apartment buildings, churches, and schools throughout the metropolitan area.

The Prince George's Post
15207 Marlboro Pk.
Upper Marlboro, MD
(301) 627–0900
www.pgpost.com

Founded in 1932, this weekly newspaper serves the African American community in Prince George's County. Distributed on Thursdays, free copies are available at county libraries, but most papers are circulated through subscriptions which cost $15 annually, and are half-price for senior citizens and students.

Washington Afro-American Newspaper
1612 14th St. NW
Washington, DC
(202) 332–0080
www.afroam.org

Founded in 1892, the *Washington Afro-American* is one of the oldest newspapers in the city. It's published every Thursday and contains news and features aimed at Metro Washington's black community. It is widely distributed and costs 50 cents per issue, or $27.48 for a yearly subscription. This paper is also online.

The Washington Informer Newspaper
3117 Martin Luther King Jr. Ave. SE
Washington, DC
(202) 561–4100

This weekly newspaper, founded 36 years ago, features positive news aimed at the metro area's African American residents. Active in the community, the paper sponsors the annual citywide spelling bee. It's available for 25 cents per copy, or $20 for a one-year subscription.

Business and Real Estate

Montgomery Business Gazette
1200 Quince Orchard Blvd.
Gaithersburg, MD
(301) 670–2690
www.gazette.net/business

Published weekly by the Gazette newspaper chain, this aggressive publication aims to be a must-read for Montgomery County's business community. The monthly *Tech Gazette* (www.gazette.net /tech) is just as sophisticated, providing wide-ranging coverage of Maryland's fast-growing high-tech industry.

Mortgage Banking
1125 15th St. NW
Washington, DC
(202) 861–1930
www.mbaa.org

Published monthly by the Mortgage Bankers Association of America, covering the field of real-estate finance, this magazine features topical articles and provides regular departments focusing on areas like training, technology, breaking news, and noteworthy people in the field. A subscription costs $40 annually.

The Northern Virginia Association of Realtors Update
8411 Arlington Blvd.
Fairfax, VA
(703) 207–3206
www.nvar.com

Geared toward real estate agents in Northern Virginia, this magazine contains news briefs, awards announcements, selling tips, market trends, and a calendar of upcoming training sessions. It's published eight times a year.

Washington Business Journal
1555 Wilson Blvd., Ste. 400
Arlington, VA
(703) 875–2200
washingtonbcentral.com/washington

Published on Fridays, this weekly examines the local business scene with news and features and regular columns on subjects like advertising and marketing, banking and finance, healthcare, international business, real estate and tourism, and hospitality. It costs $2.00 per copy.

Foreign

Asian Fortune
P.O. Box 230879
Centreville, VA 20120
(703) 968–0202
www.asianfortune.com

Written in English, this monthly newspaper adheres to the motto "Where East Meets West," targeting Asian Americans throughout the Metro Washington area. It is free and can be found at libraries, bookstores, Asian markets, and restaurants. It's also available by subscription for $15.

El Tiempo Latino
1916 Wilson Blvd., Ste. 204
Arlington, VA
(703) 527–7860
www.eltiempolatino.com

This weekly for Hispanic residents in the Washington-Baltimore area covers local and international news, entertainment, sports, and features. Published on Friday, it's free at libraries, universities, restaurants, and ethnic businesses. A yearly subscription is $40.

Washington Journal
23–03 45th Rd., Ste. 401
Long Island City, NY
(718) 349–0500
www.washingtonjournal.com

The city's oldest newspaper, established in 1859, publishes local and international news in German. This weekly comes out on Friday and is available by subscription for $40 a year.

Lifestyles

Pathways Magazine
4931 St. Elmo Ave.
Bethesda, MD
(301) 656–3127
www.pathwaysmag.com

Published quarterly, this unique journal focuses on New Age topics such as metaphysical sciences, holistic health, vegetarian cuisine, and spiritual awareness. Besides in-depth features on subjects like herbal health and becoming your own guru, the magazine features an exhaustive listing of resources and lots of intriguing advertising. It's circulated via direct mail ($10 for a two-year subscription) and is free of charge at libraries and local businesses. It is accessible online.

The Washington Blade
1408 U St. NW, 2nd Fl.
Washington, DC
(202) 797–7000
www.washingtonblade.com

This free weekly for the gay and lesbian community offers comprehensive coverage of hard news and features, as well as entertainment reviews, commentaries, events calendars, and a large classified and personal ads section. The paper, now in its third decade, is distributed widely at bookstores, libraries, and businesses throughout the metropolitan area. Check it out online.

Washington Woman
6002 Gloster Rd.
Bethesda, MD
(301) 229–0247
www.washingtonwoman.com

This free newspaper covers a variety of topics generally aimed at women in the 35- to 55-year-old age bracket. Regular features focus on unique events and businesses, arts programs, places to go with friends, and expert advice on topics such as fitness and home decorating. An extensive regional calendar lists scores of upcoming lectures, concerts, shows and other activities. Published monthly the paper is widely distributed at area libraries, bookstores, medical centers, and supermarkets.

Your Health Magazine
9706 Pennsylvania Ave.
Upper Marlboro, MD
(301) 805–6805
www.themedicalnews.com

In *Your Health Magazine*, health professionals write about current health news, covering everything from coping with slipped discs to controlling weight through hypnosis. This is a free monthly, published by Hunter Management Consultants, Inc. Regionalized editions are distributed locally throughout Montgomery, Prince George's, and Anne Arundel Counties.

Political

The Hill
733 15th St. NW, Ste. 1140
Washington, DC
(202) 628–8500
www.hillnews.com

Specializing in behind-the-scenes coverage of Congress, it's distributed free to congressional offices and is available at newsstands for $2.50 per issue or by annual subscription for $100. It is available online.

Legal Times
1730 M St. NW
Washington, DC
(202) 457–0686
www.americanlawyer.com

This weekly paper focuses on "Law and Lobbying in the Nation's Capital" and its target readership naturally consists of lawyers, lobbyists, the Supreme Court, and members of Congress. A single copy, available at newsstands, is $6.50.

The New Republic
1220 19th St. NW, Ste. 600
Washington, DC
(202) 331–7494
www.thenewrepublic.com

Founded in 1914, the New Republic is one of the most highly respected periodicals of its type. It features an impressive array of political commentary, poetry, art news, and reviews of films and books. It's available for $3.50 an issue, and $60 for a yearly subscription.

Roll Call
50 F St. NW
Washington, DC
(202) 824–6800
www.rollcall.com

This biweekly (published Mondays and Thursdays), founded in 1955, covers Capitol Hill in depth and is distributed to all House and Senate offices. A subscription costs $280 annually.

The Stars and Stripes
P.O. Box 187
Thurmont, MD 21788
(301) 271–1145 (business)
P.O. Box 1803
Washington, D.C. 20013
(202) 543–4740
www.thestarsandstripes.com

This nationally circulated newspaper, available by subscription for $19 annually, focuses on veterans affairs. The first issue appeared in 1861, during the Civil War. Published by the National Tribune Corporation since 1886, it comes out every other week and sometimes features themed issues on special events like monument dedications in Washington.

Washington Monthly
1611 Connecticut Ave. NW
Washington, D.C.
(202) 462–0128
www.washingtonmonthly.com

Featuring commentary on current affairs, this magazine presents a monthly award honoring media stories "that demonstrate a commitment to the public interest" by chronicling such issues as successful or failing government programs. An issue costs $4.50.

National Membership Magazines

Air and Space Magazine
901 D St. SW, 10th fl.
Washington, D.C.
(202) 275-1230
www.airspacemag.com

Produced by the Smithsonian Institution's National Air and Space Museum, this magazine is just the ticket for flight enthusiasts. Published six times a year, *Air and Space* features news about upcoming special exhibits, a calendar of museum events, and assorted features on both historical and current topics, with many photographic illustrations. An Air and Space membership, which includes the subscription, costs $20 annually. (See the Attractions and Kidstuff chapters for museum information.)

Civilization
666 Pennsylvania Ave. SE, Ste. 303
Washington, D.C.
(202) 707-4032
www.civmag.com

The magazine of the Library of Congress contains eclectic features, tidbits on popular culture and puzzles, and a calendar of events and exhibits coming up at the library. It's published bimonthly and is included in a $20, one-year Associate membership. A single copy is $4.50.

National Geographic Magazine
1145 17th St. NW.
Washington, D.C.
(202) 857-7000
www.nationalgeographic.com

With its incredible accounts and photography of people and places all over the world, not to mention those great maps,

National Geographic is one of the country's oldest and most treasured periodicals. Published by the National Geographic Society, which was founded in 1888, the magazine is included in a 12-month society membership for $34. The society also publishes magazines for children, books, and maps. (See the Attractions and Kidstuff chapters for more about things to see and do at the headquarters.)

Smithsonian Magazine
900 Jefferson Dr. SW
Washington, D.C.
(202) 786-2900
www.smithsonianmag.si.edu

For Smithsonian Institution members, reading this magazine is like making an armchair visit to the museums. Each monthly issue contains a variety of features, vivid photographs, intriguing profiles of Smithsonian exhibits, and listings of upcoming events. (See The Arts, Attractions, and Kidstuff chapters for museum information.) The subscription cost is $48 yearly.

Regional Publications

Washington Flyer Magazine
1707 L St. NW, Ste. 700
Washington, D.C.
(202) 331-9393
www.fly2dc.com

This glossy bimonthly owned by the Metropolitan Washington Airport Authority covers a range of business and travel topics pertinent to air travelers—locals and visitors alike. With complimentary distribution at Ronald Reagan National and Washington Dulles International Airports, the magazine occupies a unique market niche with impressive demographics and a high pass-along rate.

Washington Jewish Week
12300 Twinbrook Pkwy., Ste. 250
Rockville, MD
(301) 230-2222
www.washingtonjewishweek.com

Washington Jewish Week, founded in 1965, is chock-full of local, national, and international news and features aimed at Metro

Washington's ever-growing Jewish community. Published on Thursdays, each issue features an extensive calendar of events scheduled by area synagogues, Jewish community centers, museums, and organizations and regular departments devoted to sports, seniors, singles, food, travel, real estate, and social announcements. In July the paper publishes the *Guide to Jewish Life in Washington,* a comprehensive source of more than 200 pages. Other special editions focus on such topics as weddings, bar and bat mitzvahs, and party planning. The paper costs $1.00 per copy or $36.00 per yearly subscription.

Washingtonian
1828 L St. NW
Washington, DC
(202) 331–0715
www.washingtonian.com

The area's true city magazine—although its readership is predominantly suburban—is a slick, thick monthly known for its "best of" lists, dining/shopping guides, maps of stars' homes, interesting features and personality profiles, and the occasional hard-hitting investigative piece. High paid-circulation numbers, a well-heeled readership, and a large staff have helped *Washingtonian* maintain its enviable position in the local magazine market. A one-year subscription is $24.

Radio

Turn on your car radio and push the "scan" button. In a matter of seconds you will lock on a station. Push it again and again and you'll get the same result. Metro Washington is by no means New York or Los Angeles in terms of market size or listening choices, but it does offer more than 50 AM and FM stations with a wide range of formats.

Here's a look around the dial:

Adult Contemporary/Soft Adult Contemporary Stations
WASH 97.1 FM
WRQX 107.3 FM

Classical Stations
WETA 90.9 FM (also information/National Public Radio)
WGMS 103.5 FM

Country Stations
WFRE 99.1 FM
WMZQ 98.7 FM

Jazz Stations
WJZW 105.9 FM
WPFW 89.3 FM (also Pacifica radio)

News/Talk/Sports/Information Stations
WAMU 88.5 FM (National Public Radio; also, folk and bluegrass music)
WCSP 90.1 FM (C-SPAN)
WJFK 106.7 FM
WMAL 630 AM
WMET 1100 AM (business)
WTNT 570 AM (all talk)
WTOP 1500 AM and 107.7 FM
WWDC 1260 AM (business)
WWRC 980 AM
WXTR 820 AM

Oldies Stations
WARW 94.7 FM (classic rock)
WBIG 100.3 FM

Religious/Inspirational/Gospel Stations
WABS 780 am
WAVA 105.1 FM
WCTN 950 am
WFAX 1220 AM
WGTS 91.9 FM
WPGC 1580 am
WYCB 1340 AM

Rock Stations
WHFS 99.1 FM (modern/alternative)
WMUC 88.1 FM (progressive)
WWDC 101.1 FM

Soul/Talk Stations
WOL 1450 AM

Top 40/Contemporary Hits Stations
WIHT 99.5
WWVZ 103.9 FM
WWZZ 104.1 FM

Urban Adult Contemporary Stations
WHUR 96.3 FM
WKYS 93.9 FM
WPGC 95.5 FM

Foreign Language/Ethnic Stations
WDCT 1310 AM (Korean)
WILC 900 AM (Spanish)
WKDL 1050 AM (Spanish)
WKDM 1600 AM (Spanish)
WKDV 1460 AM (Asian)
WMDO 1540 AM (Latin music/news)
WPLC 94.3 FM (Spanish)
WUST 1120 AM (multicultural)
WZHF 1390 AM (Chinese)

Television

As you'd expect in this high-profile city, news coverage is a big deal at the major networks' local affiliates. The stations are highly competitive, whether trying to be first to break a story or attempting to put together the most comprehensive "team coverage" of an event. You'll find newscasts first thing in the morning, at noon, late afternoon, and twice in the evening—and around-the-clock on cable's News Channel 8.

Insiders' Tip
Tune in to the *D.C. Politics Hour* with *Mark Plotkin* for a lively, radio call-in show that covers the latest scandals and issues facing our nation's capital. It's broadcast on WAMU (88.5 FM) every Friday from noon to 1:00 P.M. and repeated from 8:00 to 9:00 P.M. on Friday evenings.

Virtually anything a television viewer wants is available in Metro Washington. Along with all the major networks, numerous independent stations, and literally hundreds of cable channels are at your fingertips.

Local TV Stations
Following are Washington's major local TV stations and their network affiliates:
WRC Channel 4 (NBC)
WTTG Channel 5 (Fox)
WJLA Channel 7 (ABC)
WUSA Channel 9 (CBS)
WDCA Channel 20 (UPN)
WMPT Channel 22 (PBS)
WETA Channel 26 (PBS)
WHMM Channel 32 (PBS)
WBDC Channel 50 (WB)

Others:
WNVT Channel 53 (PBS)
WNVC Channel 56 (PBS)

Baltimore and Hagerstown TV
These stations are available to many residents of Metro Washington:
WMAR Channel 2 (ABC)
WBAL Channel 11 (NBC)
WJZ Channel 13 (CBS)
WHAG Channel 25 (NBC)
WBFF Channel 45 (Fox)
WNUV Channel 54 (UPN)
WMPB Channel 67 (PBS)
WJAL Channel 68 (WB)

Cable TV

Most Metro Washington residents are now able to get cable TV, although pockets remain where service has yet to be provided and may never be for various reasons. Surprisingly, the District is a fledgling cable community, with the first cable franchise having been awarded only in the late 1980s. Comcast is the Washington area's largest provider of cable services, but its prices and offerings differ depending on which jurisdiction you live in. Cox Communications is the rare exception, serving Fairfax County's more than 250,000 cable subscribers.

Cable offerings for local residents run the gamut, from local public access channels that offer community and civic information to the major players such as premium movie channels (HBO, Showtime, Disney, etc.), the locally owned Black Entertainment Television (BET), CNN, Discovery, MTV, ESPN, TNT, USA Network, and Chicago and New York "super stations." Let's not forget C-SPAN (Cable-Satellite Public Affairs Network) and C-SPAN II, which offer live coverage of the U.S. House of Representatives and U.S. Senate, respectively, and related political programming; for some strange reason these channels seem especially popular around here.

The following companies provide cable TV service to residents of Metro Washington.

Washington, D.C.

Comcast
900 Michigan Ave. NE
Washington, DC
(202) 832–2001
www.comcast.com

This company offers more than 104 channels to homes throughout the city. Its expanded basic package with 65 channels costs approximately $39.

Northern Virginia

Adelphia Communications
21545 Ridgetop Cir.
Sterling, VA
(703) 430–8200

Providing service throughout Loudoun County, Adelphia offers 55 channels to its more than 40,000 subscribers. While the most basic service costs $18 monthly, 60 plus channels costs $40.

Comcast
2707 Wilson Blvd.
Arlington, VA
(703) 841–7700

With 75 channels available to Arlington County residents, this company offers basic options ranging from approximately $38. Digital cable with 150 channels is $52.95.

> ## Insiders' Tip
> Check out your cable TV's public access station for an eclectic array of programming produced by and starring local citizens.

Comcast
617A S. Pickett St.
Alexandria, VA
(703) 823–3000

Subscribers set 75 chennels for $39. Digital cable is available for $52.95 for 150 channels.

Comcast
4391 Dale Blvd.
Woodbridge, VA
(703) 730–2225

This cable company serves most of Prince William County, as well as Fort Belvoir, Reston, and Manassas. One of the pricier cable jurisdictions, residents pay $48.38 for 69 channels or pay $59.95 or $72.55 for a package of more than 100 digital channels.

Cox Communications
14650 Old Lee Rd., Chantilly, Va.
(703) 378–8422

The company has the capacity for 100 channels, and basic full service starts at approximately $40. Digital cable is still being phased in across the county, with completion expected at the end of 2002. Digital rates vary depending on package selected, from $67.19 to $92.19 a month.

Westgate Cable Company
8019 Ashland Ave., Apt. 4
Manassas, VA
(703) 369–6213

Residents of Westgate apartments and town houses receive their cable service through this company. HBO and 63 channels are included in the rent.

Suburban Maryland

Comcast
20 W. Gude Dr.
Rockville, MD
(301) 424-4400

Serving all of Montgomery County, this cable service offers up to 70 channels, with services ranging from the most basic at $15 to $43.80P for analog cable and $65.95 for 170 digital channels.

Comcast
9609 Annapolis Rd.
Lanham, MD
(301) 731-4260

This Prince George's County cable service offers 60 channels in its preferred package, which costs approximately $40 for analog; $63.95 for digital in areas of the county where it is available.

Index

psychiatric hospitals, 425–27
Psychiatric Institute of Washington, D.C.,
 The, 426
public schools
 Northern Virginia, 432–36
 Suburban Maryland, 436
 Washington, D.C., 431–32
Public Schools Extended Day Program, 404
Puppet Co. Playhouse, The, 306

Q

Quality Hotel Courthouse Plaza, 80–81
Quality Inn Iwo Jima, 81
Quantico Orienteering Club, 350

R

radio stations, 491–92
Radisson Barcelo Hotel, 70
Rainforest Cafe, 292
Ramada Inn New Carrollton, 78
Ramsay House Visitors Center, 232
Raspberry Falls Golf & Hunt Club, 346
real estate and neighborhoods
 current market conditions, 385–86
 ethnic neighborhoods, 55
 Northern Virginia neighborhoods and
  homes, 389–95
 property taxes, 397
 real estate companies, 397–99
 relocation guidelines/information sources,
  399–400
 Suburban Maryland neighborhoods and
  homes, 395–97
 Washington, D.C. neighborhoods and
  homes, 386–89
recreation. See specific activity
Red, Hot & Blue, 113–14, 127
Red Cross Waterfront Festival, 193
Red Fox Inn, The, 373
Red Fox Inn and Tavern, The, 363
Red Roof Inn Downtown D.C., 79
Red Roof Inn Gaithersburg, 81–82
Red Sage, 104–5
Red Sea, 97–98
Rehoboth Beach, Delaware, 381
Reiter's Scientific & Professional Books, 167
RE/MAX Central, 398–99
Renaissance Mayflower, 70
Renaissance Washington, D.C. Hotel, 70–71
Renwick Gallery, 219, 275
Reprint Bookshop, 167
Restaurant Nora, 94
restaurants
 African, 97–98
 American/continental, 90–97, 108–15, 125–27

Asian, 98–101, 115–18, 127–31
children-friendly, 290–93
French, 101–3, 118–19, 131–32
German, 103
Hispanic/Caribbean/Tex-Mex, 103–5,
 119–21, 135
Italian, 105–7, 121–23, 132–34
Middle Eastern/Mediterranean/Indian/
 Afghan, 107–8, 123–25, 134–35
Northern Virginia, 108–25, 291–92
Suburban Maryland, 125–35, 292–93
Washington, D.C., 90–108, 291
Reston Community Center, 355
Reston Hospital Center, 419
Reston Ice Skating Pavilion, 348
Reston National Golf Course, 346–47
Reston Storefront Museum & Shop, 302
Reston Town Center, 156
Retired and Senior Volunteer Program
 (RSVP), 461
retirement and senior services
 agencies/offices on aging, 455–58
 community and senior centers, 462–66
 publications, 458
 resources, 459–62
 retirement communities, 466–70
Retirement Unlimited Inc., 468
Reynolds of Derwood Bed and Breakfast,
 The, 87–88
RFK Stadium, 265
Richmond, Virginia, 362
Ride-On, 31
Riderwood Village, 470
Rio Grande Cafe, 120, 135
Ritz-Carlton, Pentagon City, 77
Ritz-Carlton Tysons Corner, 74
Riverdale Baptist School, 444, 446
River Farm, 310
River Inn, The, 61
Road Runners Club of America, 350
Robert E. Lee's Birthday Celebration, 181
Robert M. Watkins Regional Park, 311, 339
Robert Morris Inn, The, 376
Roche Salon, 176
Rock Creek Park, 307–8, 331–32
Rock Creek Park Day, 197
Rock Creek Park Forts, The, 244–45
Rock Creek Park Golf Course, 346
Rock Creek Regional Park, 339
Rocket Grill, 148
Rock Sports Bar and Restaurant, The,
 141–42
Rockville Senior Center, 466
Roll Call, 489
Romano's Macaroni Grill, 293

About the Authors

Mary Jane Solomon

A native of Dayton, Ohio, Mary Jane Hook Solomon left the Buckeye State for the Old Dominion 18 years ago. She is well acquainted with Metro Washington, having lived in Washington, D.C., Rosslyn, Old Town Alexandria, Leesburg, and Reston before settling with her family in Annandale, Virginia, five years ago.

As a lifestyle editor and feature writer at the *Alexandria Gazette* and the *Loudoun Times-Mirror*, Mary Jane received nine Virginia Press Association awards, including a first-place honor for an article about the effects of Alzheimer's disease on families. She also served as the *Times-Mirror*'s deputy editor, helping the paper earn the National Newspaper Association's top award for general excellence.

After a job producing special sections and the company newsletter for Arundel Communications Inc., Mary Jane decided to freelance so she could stay home with her then-infant daughter. Her articles appear regularly in the *Washington Post*'s "Weekend" section and in *Virginia Parent News*, where she also works on the editorial staff. She also has written for such publications as *Where Washington Magazine*, *Sesame Street Parents*, *The Journal* and *Fast Forward*.

Mary Jane and her husband, Steve, live with daughters Rachel and Anna and cat Macaroon in the heart of Fairfax County. She enjoys exploring area attractions with her family, playing in the Mothers of Basketball league at the Jewish Community Center of Northern Virginia, and volunteering at her daughters' schools.

Barbara Ruben

Barbara Ruben has lived in the Washington area for nearly 20 years, since graduating from Miami University in Oxford, Ohio, and taking an internship with National Geographic. She has served as editor of a national environmental magazine and an international health magazine, and has written freelance articles for numerous publications, including the *Washington Post*, *Interactive Week*, and *Physician's Financial News*.

Barbara is currently managing editor of the *Senior Beacon*, a newspaper that reaches more than 200,000 Washington-area senior citizens, where she has won first-place awards for feature and news writing from the North American Mature Press Association and the Mature Market Resource Center. She is also a freelance reporter for the *Washington Post* and regularly writes about local restaurants, real estate, schools and senior citizens.

Barbara lives in Kensington, Maryland, with her daughter, Sarah.